T0368370

Lecture Notes in Computer Science   15567

The series Lecture Notes in Computer Science (LNCS), including its subseries Lecture Notes in Artificial Intelligence (LNAI) and Lecture Notes in Bioinformatics (LNBI), has established itself as a medium for the publication of new developments in computer science and information technology research, teaching, and education.

LNCS enjoys close cooperation with the computer science R & D community, the series counts many renowned academics among its volume editors and paper authors, and collaborates with prestigious societies. Its mission is to serve this international community by providing an invaluable service, mainly focused on the publication of conference and workshop proceedings and postproceedings. LNCS commenced publication in 1973.

Cecilia Testart · Roland van Rijswijk-Deij ·
Burkhard Stiller
Editors

Passive and Active Measurement

26th International Conference, PAM 2025
Virtual Event, March 10–12, 2025
Proceedings

 Springer

Editors
Cecilia Testart
Georgia Institute of Technology
Atlanta, GA, USA

Roland van Rijswijk-Deij
University of Twente
Enschede, The Netherlands

Burkhard Stiller🆔
University of Zürich
Zürich, Switzerland

ISSN 0302-9743   ISSN 1611-3349 (electronic)
Lecture Notes in Computer Science
ISBN 978-3-031-85959-5   ISBN 978-3-031-85960-1 (eBook)
https://doi.org/10.1007/978-3-031-85960-1

Preface

It is with great pleasure that we present you the proceedings of the 26th annual Passive and Active Measurement Conference, PAM 2025! The program featured an excellent set of papers that span the breadth of network measurement research and contribute to advancing our understanding — amongst others — of the core of the Internet, access networks, network security and network performance. This year the conference took place from March 10-12, 2025, virtually hosted by the Universidad de San Andrés, Victoria, Provincia de Buenos Aires, Argentina. Hosting PAM as a virtual conference is a tradition we proudly continued, as it lowers the barrier for participation and reduces the impact of long-distance travel on the environment.

For this year's edition, we received 67 submissions, of which — after verification by the chairs — 59 were admissible for review. The papers that entered review came from 75 different institutions in 19 countries on 5 continents. After 4 double-blind reviews per paper, the program committee selected 13 long and 7 short papers for publication. Of these 20 papers, 15 received shepherding from our experts in the program committee to ensure we had a set of high-quality final papers. The 20 selected papers cover diverse topics, which were presented in 8 sessions covering everything from 5G to IPv6 and from Web to Fraud.

Our program committee consisted of a diverse group of 55 subject matter experts covering all topics in network measurement research. We had a mix of junior and senior reviewers from 23 countries on 4 continents. We are also proud of the gender diversity in our TPC, with 36% female members. To ensure we had enough fresh insights in the TPC, we also invited people to self-nominate and accepted 13 self-nominations (~25% of the TPC). We had an especially tight review schedule this year due to new deadlines as a result of changes in submission options for other measurement conferences. We are extremely grateful to our TPC members for delivering high-quality reviews on time, ensuring we had all our decisions in by the deadline. We would like to extend a special token of gratitude to our shepherds. Similarly, we thank all authors for having all final versions complete and fully submitted by our camera-ready deadline!

We thank our hosting organization, the Universidad de San Andrés in Argentina, for ensuring we have a wonderful website and for helping us run the conference. We also thank the PAM steering committee for the trust they put in us and for their guidance. Finally, we want to give a big shout-out to all authors that submitted work to PAM, whether accepted or not, and hope that you will consider submitting to PAM again next year!

March 2025

Cecilia Testart
Roland van Rijswijk-Deij
Mariano Beiró

Organization

General Chair

Mariano Beiró   Universidad de San Andrés, Argentina

Technical Program Committee Co-chairs

Cecilia Testart   Georgia Institute of Technology, USA
Roland van Rijswijk-Deij   University of Twente, The Netherlands

Publications Chair

Burkhard Stiller   University of Zürich, Switzerland

PAM Steering Committee

Marinho P. Barcellos   University of Waikato, New Zealand
Fabian E. Bustamante   Northwestern University, USA
Michalis Faloutsos   University of California, Riverside, USA
Anja Feldmann   MPI Informatik, Germany
Oliver Hohlfeld   University of Kassel, Germany
Jelena Mirkovic   University of Southern California, USA
Giovane Moura   SIDN Labs and TU Delft, The Netherlands
Cristel Pelsser   Université catholique de Louvain, Belgium
Steve Uhlig   Queen Mary University of London, UK

Technical Program Committee

Abhishta   University of Twente, The Netherlands
Alessandro Finamore   Huawei Technologies, France
Alexander Gamero-Garrido   University of California Davis, USA
Anna Brunström   Karlstad University, Sweden
Anna Sperotto   University of Twente, The Netherlands
Anne Josiane Kouam   TU Berlin, Germany

Aristide Tanyi-Jong Akem	IMDEA Networks, Spain
Ben Du	University of California San Diego, USA
Carlos Hernandez Gañan	TU Delft and ICANN, The Netherlands
Casey Deccio	Brigham Young University, USA
Daphné Tuncer	École des Ponts ParisTech, France
Diana Andreaa Popescu	University of Cambridge, UK
Eman Ramadan	University of Minnesota, USA
Esteban Carisimo	Northwestern University, USA
Ha Dao	Max Planck Institute for Informatics, Germany
Hannaneh B. Pasandi	University of California Berkeley, USA
Haoyu Wang	Huazhong University of Science & Technology, China
Idilio Drago	University of Turin, Italy
Ioana Lividariu	SimulaMet, Norway
Johan Mazel	ANSSI, France
Kévin Vermeulen	CNRS, France
Lars Prehn	Google, Germany
Marcel Flores	Netflix, USA
Matthew Luckie	CAIDA/University of California San Diego, USA
Mirja Kühlewind	Ericsson, Germany
Moritz Müller	SIDN Labs and University of Twente, The Netherlands
Nguyen Phong	Hoang University of British Columbia, Canada
Olaf Maennel	University of Adelaide, Australia
Oliver Gasser	IPinfo, Germany
Orlando Eduardo Martinez Durive	IMDEA Networks, Spain
Pawel Foremski	IITiS PAN and DomainTools, Poland
Philipp Richter	Akamai, USA
Polly Huang	National Taiwan University, Taiwan
Ramin Sadre	Université catholique de Louvain, Belgium
Ricky Mok	CAIDA/University of California San Diego, USA
Robert Beverly	San Diego State University, USA
Romain Fontugne	IIJ Research Laboratory, Japan
Sarah Wasserman	Vade Secure, France
Shuai Hao	Old Dominion University, USA
Simone Ferlin	Red Hat and Karlstad University, Sweden
Solang Rito Lima	University of Minho, Portugal
Soudeh Ghorbani	Johns Hopkins University, USA
Stephen McQuistin	University of St. Andrews, UK
Taejoong "Tijay" Chung	Virginia Tech, USA
Tanya Shreedhar	TU Delft, The Netherlands
Thomas Krenc	CAIDA/University of California San Diego, USA

Contents

5G

IPv6

The Razor's Edge: IPv6 Extension Headers Survivability

Justin Iurman[iD] and Benoit Donnet[(✉)][iD]

Montefiore Institute, Université de Liège, Liège, Belgium
{justin.iurman,benoit.donnet}@uliege.be

Abstract. While IPv6 was standardized in the 90's, only the last decade has seen a growth in its global adoption. In addition to dealing with IPv4 addresses exhaustion, IPv6 comes with a mechanism, called IPv6 Extension Header (IPv6 EH), allowing the protocol to be more flexible and extensible. In this paper, we investigate how IPv6 EHs are processed in the network. In particular, we focus on the survivability of IPv6 EHs, i.e., the fact that an IPv6 EH traverses the Internet and arrives unmodified at the destination. We first design experiments in a controlled environment, testing different IPv6 EHs and sizes on different routers from various vendors. Then, we confront our observations with several measurement campaigns between vantage points hosted by different Cloud Providers (CPs) around the world, and we compare them to the responses received from a survey of operators. Our results show that the survivability of IPv6 EHs is quite limited (around 50%) and is a consequence of operators' policies, with some Autonomous Systems being responsible for most of the IPv6 EHs drops. Measurement tool and data collected are provided to the research community.

1 Introduction

During the last decade, IPv6 has been more and more adopted [23]. If IPv6 allows for dealing with IPv4 address exhaustion [26], it also comes with a mechanism, called IPv6 *Extension Header* (IPv6 EH) [6,13], that leads to more flexibility and innovation. Examples of such innovations based on IPv6 EHs are Segment Routing with IPv6 as forwarding plane [17,18] and In-Situ Operations, Administration, and Maintenance (IOAM) [5] for in-band telemetry. The purpose of IPv6 EHs is to extend IPv6 without any modification to the core protocol. IPv6 EHs form a chain, using the IPv6 *Next Header* field, and are placed between the IPv6 header and the upper-layer protocol header. While new IPv6 EHs might be defined in the future, the current list mainly includes the `Hop-by-Hop Options` Header, the `Destination Options` Header, the `Routing` Header, the `Fragment` Header, the `Encapsulating Security Payload`, and the `Authentication` Header [6,13]. Up to now, few efforts have been made in assessing how operators process IPv6 EHs, e.g. [6,14,21,24,35,47], focusing mainly on a subset of IPv6 EHs or relying on limited measurements campaign.

C. Testart et al. (Eds.): PAM 2025, LNCS 15567, pp. 3–29, 2025.
https://doi.org/10.1007/978-3-031-85960-1_1

In this paper, we provide a comprehensive view of how IPv6 EHs are processed in the network. In particular, we are interested in IPv6 EHs *survivability*, i.e., the capacity of IPv6 EHs to traverse the Internet and arrive unmodified at the destination. This is important as we expect a complete survivability for some IPv6 EHs, such as the `Destination Options` Header or `Fragment` Header, but not necessarily for some others that are more designed for limited domain use cases (e.g., the `Hop-by-Hop Options` Header or `Routing` Header). Also, a too low level of survivability may damage the IPv6 extensibility and, consequently, innovation, leading to an ossification of IPv6. More precisely, this paper makes the following contributions:

- We develop an eBPF [45] program called eBPF **I**Pv6 Extension **H**eaders Injection (FISHNET) to easily inject IPv6 EHs, whatever the type and size, in network traffic.
- We build a controlled environment to perform measurements with FISHNET spanning all specified IPv6 EHs, with different parameters such as the IPv6 EH type and size, and so for routers from various vendors. We show that all IPv6 EHs have a perfect survivability rate with default configuration on routers, which tends to suggest that potential drops of packets with IPv6 EHs is mainly caused by operators' policies.
- Next, in order to determine whether our lab observations are applied in the real world, we deploy FISHNET in different Cloud Providers (CPs) scattered around the world and perform measurements in full mesh. Our results show that, on the contrary to controlled environment experiments, IPv6 EHs survivability is quite limited (around 50% on average). We also show that IPv6 EHs drop is caused by some ASes, generally quite close to the packet source. We also compare those observations with the results from a survey of operators.
- Measurement software (i.e., FISHNET) and collected data are provided to the research community.

The remainder of this paper is organized as follows: Sect. 2 provides the required background for this paper; Sect. 3 describes FISHNET, the tool we implemented to inject IPv6 EHs in network traffic; Sect. 4 investigates IPv6 EHs survivability in a controlled environment; Sect. 5 introduces our Internet measurement methodology; Sect. 6 discusses our Internet measurement results; Sect. 7 positions this paper with respect to the state of the art; finally, Sect. 8 concludes this paper by summarizing its main achievements.

2   Background

The purpose of IPv6 EHs is to extend IPv6 without any modification to the core protocol. The IPv6 `Next Header` field specifies which upper-layer protocol comes after the IPv6 header. All IPv6 EHs share a common field in their respective headers, namely a `Next Header` field, whose name and purpose are identical to the one in the IPv6 header. This design allows for a chaining mechanism. Figure 1

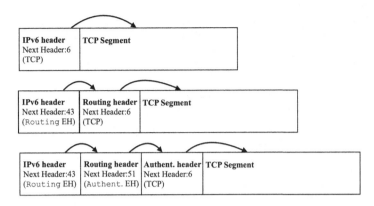

Fig. 1. Example of chain of pointers formed by the `Next Header` field in IPv6.

illustrates how it works with three examples: the first one represents a TCP segment, the second one represents a `Routing` Header followed by a TCP segment, and the third one represents a `Routing` Header followed by an `Authentication` Header followed by a TCP segment.

The Internet Assigned Number Authority (IANA) currently defines the following IPv6 EHs [29]: the `Hop-by-Hop Options` Header, the `Destination Options` Header, the `Routing` Header, the `Fragment` Header, the `Encapsulating Security Payload`, the `Authentication` Header, the `Mobility` Header, the `Host Identity Protocol` Header, and the `Shim6 Protocol` Header. The `Hop-by-Hop Options` Header is used to carry optional information, also called *Options*, that may be examined and processed by every node along a packet's delivery path, while the `Destination Options` Header is used to carry optional information to be examined only by the packet's destination. An example of `Hop-by-Hop Options` Header or `Destination Options` Header usage is In-Situ Operations, Administration, and Maintenance (IOAM) [5]. With IOAM, telemetry data is carried within packets rather than being sent through packets specifically dedicated to that. The IOAM traffic is thus embedded in data traffic, but not part of the packet payload. The `Routing` Header is used by an IPv6 source to list one or more intermediate nodes to go through on the way to a packet's destination (i.e., to steer a packet), and has several types defined: Source route (type 0) and Nimrod (type 1) [7] which are both deprecated, Mobility support (type 2) [32], RPL (type 3) [25], and Segment Routing (type 4) [17]. The `Fragment` Header is used by an IPv6 source to send a packet larger than it would fit in the path MTU to its destination. It works like IPv4 fragmentation except that only the packet source can fragment the packet. The `Authentication` Header (sender authentication, data integrity) [33] and `Encapsulating Security Payload` (sender authentication, data integrity, confidentiality) [34] are both part of the IPsec protocol suite. The `Mobility` Header is used to allow devices to move from one network to another while maintaining a permanent IPv6 address. The `Host Identity Protocol` Header is used to separate the end-point identifier and loca-

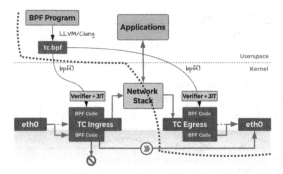

Fig. 2. Overview of how Tc works with eBPF [46].

tor roles of IPv6 addresses [39]. The `Shim6 Protocol` Header is used to determine valid locator pairs that could be used when an outage is detected [41].

3   FishNet

This section describes and evaluates eBPF IPv6 Extension Headers Injection (FishNet), our tool for easily injecting IPv6 EHs in network traffic. The reason for using eBPF is twofold: (*i*) a fast implementation compared to the modification of existing probing solutions; and (*ii*) it injects IPv6 EHs in "real" traffic, not only the one from probing tools, which is really interesting as it allows for some corner cases to be tested, e.g., one may inject IPv6 EHs after the `TCP` 3-way handshake to check whether stateful filters influence the IPv6 EHs processing.

3.1   Overview

In order to inject one or multiple IPv6 EHs in outgoing traffic using eBPF, FishNet must be attached to an interface. More specifically, one needs to add a `clsact qdisc` [37] to an interface, which is like a scheduler holding only classifiers and that works both on ingress and egress. Then, FishNet must be attached to an egress filter on that interface, with a specific section to be run. Both commands use Tc [44], a traffic control tool as part of the `iproute2` [30] solution. Finally, the user program is used to configure the IPv6 EHs injection. Figure 2 provides a high-level picture of how it works. What was previously described is represented on the right side of the dashed blue line.

Overall, FishNet is completely agnostic of whether one or more IPv6 EHs are injected, or their order. The only thing that it knows is that it has to inject a buffer of bytes. Therefore, the overhead only depends on the number of bytes to inject (see Sect. 3.2 for performance evaluation). Indeed, the buffer construction is delegated to the user program which is responsible for configuring what will be injected (one or more IPv6 EHs, their order, etc.). Very briefly, IPv6 EHs can be injected with constraints on respective sizes, and in any order. If the chosen order does not respect RFC8200 [13], an error is returned as a security, although the user could force such a behavior with a special flag.

3.2   Evaluation

To evaluate FISHNET, we rely on TREX [8], an open source, low cost, stateful and stateless traffic generator fueled by DPDK. It has multiple advantages, such as the ability to generate Layer3–7 traffic and multiple streams, as well as the ability to easily craft your own packets with the underlying Scapy [43] layer. TREX can scale up to 200Gbps with only one server.

The testbed is straightforward: one machine for TREX, and another one for the *Device Under Test* (DUT). Both are equipped with an *Intel XL710 2×40GB QSFP+* NIC, each connected port to port in order to close the loop (i.e., TREX client and server run on the same machine). This kind of topology provides an easy way to isolate a specific function on the DUT and evaluate it, i.e., the egress injection of IPv6 EHs with FISHNET. The DUT has an *Intel Xeon cpu e5-2630 v3 at 2.40 GHz*, with 8 Cores, 16 Threads, and has a 16GB RAM. It runs a kernel version $6.9.0 - rc6+$ (net-next) and FISHNET was compiled with clang version 14.0.6. Equivalent iproute2 version has been compiled with libbpf 1.4.0. During measurements, the DUT is configured to maximize its performance (e.g., CPU in performance mode, network settings). It is also configured to only use one queue for all traffic received, therefore only one core being responsible for that queue. Doing so allows us to see the impact on a single core, which is better to compare performance on a common basis. The MTU is set to $2,148$ so that the maximum size injected (i.e., $2,048$ bytes) would not make packet sizes to exceed it. Overall, each experiment (i.e., measurement) lasts 30 s and is run 20 times. We determine 95% confidence intervals for the mean based on the Student t distribution (they are too tight to be visible in the subsequent plots).

As explained in Sect. 3.1, i.e., FISHNET is completely agnostic of the content of the buffer, only the number of bytes to be injected may have an impact on performance, whatever the combination of IPv6 EHs. Since most of these IPv6 EHs are limited to a maximum of $2,048$ bytes (except for the Encapsulating Security Payload), we evaluate the impact of an injection from 0 to $2,048$ bytes, although, less likely, a combination of IPv6 EHs could result in a much bigger buffer.

Figure 3a shows the impact of different injection sizes on throughput. The forwarding baseline is, in our case, approximately $1,195,000$ packets per second (pps) on a single core (roughly 14.34 Gbps with $1,500$-byte packets). One can directly observe a loss of 19% (i.e., approximately $225,000$ pps) when injecting the minimum size of 8 bytes, which then remains stable up to 128 bytes. The fact that such a loss occurs immediately will be discussed below based on Fig. 3b. When injecting 256 bytes or more, the loss rate bumps to 58%. This huge drop is due to a lack of space in the sk_buff headroom, where the headers of a packet are located, which involves implicit reallocation by the kernel to make the headroom larger. Depending on the architecture and the NIC driver, the headroom space may vary. In our case, i.e., ×86_64 architecture and *i40e* driver, the headroom

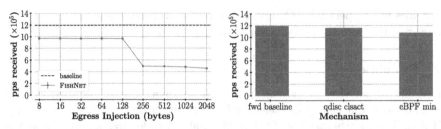

(a) IPv6 EHs injection with FISHNET and its impact on throughput.

(b) Impact on throughput between adding a `clsact qdisc` [37] and running a minimal version of a Tc/eBPF program on egress.

Fig. 3. FISHNET performance evaluation.

has an initial size of 256 bytes. If we remove 14 bytes for the Ethernet header (in our case), plus 2 bytes to align the IPv6 header, plus 40 bytes for the IPv6 header, we are left with 200 bytes available in the headroom. This means that as soon as we inject 201 bytes or more, the drop will happen, which is indeed between 128 and 256 in Fig. 3a.

Figure 3b shows the impact on throughput when only a `clsact qdisc` is added and it is compared to when a minimal[1] eBPF kernel program is running. One can see that only adding the `qdisc` gives a 3% loss already, while running a minimal eBPF kernel program gives an additional 7% loss, which makes it a total of 10% loss. Despite being out of scope of this paper, it would be interesting to investigate if improvements can be made on that part. In fine, the real loss rate of FISHNET is 9%, in addition to the initial and unavoidable 10% loss.

Another interesting observation is that some network drivers (tested with *e1000e* and *vmxnet3*) have issues with TX checksum offloading when there is an IPv6 EH or more in a packet, with or without FISHNET. Indeed, the checksum calculated in Layer-4 is incorrect, even if adding one or more IPv6 EHs should have no impact since it does not modify the pseudo-header (except when there is a `Routing` Header, where the destination in the pseudo-header is the last segment). As a result, packets may disappear along the path, which could wrongly suggest a Layer-2 problem and is therefore hard to debug. Despite being out of scope of this paper, it should also be investigated to help NIC vendors address this issue. Note that we have also started fixing some bugs related to checksums with IPv6 EHs in the Linux kernel.

Finally, it is worth mentioning this section evaluates the worst case, i.e., line rate traffic on a single core. Overall, it is highly unlikely we would need FISHNET to inject IPv6 EHs at line rate on a single core. For example, in Sect. 4 to Sect. 6, FISHNET is used to carefully inject IPv6 EHs in `traceroute` traffic such that we avoid losing packets or hitting rate limits. However, independently of FISHNET and its usage, people may want to inject IPv6 EHs in line-rate traffic. The initial cost shown in Fig. 3b could prevent them from following that path.

---

[1] Minimal means the section handler directly returns `TC_ACT_OK`.

Table 1. List of tested routers in our controlled environment.

	Vendor	Model	Version
R1	Cisco	ASR1001-X (ASIC based)	IOS XE 03.16.05.S
R2			IOS XE 17.06.04
R3		ASR9904 (NPU based)	IOS XR 7.9.21
R4	Huawei	AR617VW-LTE4EA	V300R019C10
R5	Juniper	vMX	Junos OS 20.2R1.10
R6	Linux	–	Kernel 6.11
R7	Nokia	7750 SR-7	20.10

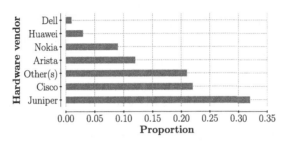

Fig. 4. Distribution of hardware vendors in our survey of operators.

4   IPv6 EHs Processing in a Controlled Environment

This section investigates the capacity of IPv6 EHs to traverse a single router and arrive unmodified at the destination, in a controlled environment. We first describe our infrastructure (Sect. 4.1) and, next, discuss our results (Sect. 4.2).

4.1   Infrastructure Setup

Our controlled environment is made of two devices, i.e., the sender and the receiver, and a physical router (i.e., the DUT, a real hardware) in between them. We evaluate seven different routers (DUTs) separately, each of them running a default configuration. Those routers are listed in Table 1 and were deliberately chosen based on the responses received from our survey of operators.[2] Fig. 4 shows the various hardware deployed by operators, according to our survey. Both Juniper and Cisco routers seem to share the biggest part of the market [1,2,38], followed by Linux or FreeBSD (with BIRD or FRRouting running on top – "Other(s)" category in Fig. 4), followed by Arista, Nokia, Huawei, and Dell. Note that Mikrotik and Ubiquity also appeared in the "Other(s)" category in Fig. 4. Unfortunately, we were unable to get routers from all vendors. But we still managed to get routers from those that are highly represented. As for the Juniper

---

[2] The survey was sent on both RIPE and NANOG mailing-lists on September 4th 2024. At the time of writing this paper, we received 50 responses.

router, its results may not be entirely accurate, since we had to test a virtual image of the MX series with Containerlab [10] instead of physical hardware. Overall, routers from different vendors are expected to share the same kind of behavior with a default configuration, which therefore gives a trend and a big picture of what should be observed in the wild. Therefore, we assume our infrastructure being as representative as possible.

The sender relies on FISHNET (see Sect. 3) to inject IPv6 EHs in its egress traffic. The sender generates TCP and UDP traffic with Netcat [40], and ICMPv6 traffic with ping6 [36]. Traffic is collected on the sender and the receiver with tcpdump.

Table 2 shows all experiments (IPv6 EH types and sizes) performed on the routers. All existing IPv6 EHs are tested, except the Routing Header type 1 (Nimrod) as we were not able to find its Routing Header format in the RFCs, probably because it is too old and deprecated. Routing Header type 55 is included for testing a routing header with an undefined type and see how the routers behave. Each IPv6 EH with a specific size is tested three times: with TCP, UDP, and ICMPv6. The MTU is increased to 8, 192 on both links to support large IPv6 EH sizes (e.g., 2, 048 bytes or more).

4.2 Results

This section presents results based on experiments performed in our controlled environment. What is observed here might not necessarily reflect the reality in the Internet, although representative enough to provide a trend. That is why we will perform measurements in the wild in Sect. 5 and Sect. 6. Table 2 shows successful experiments (with a ✓) for each router. With a default configuration running on the routers, every single IPv6 EH is successfully forwarded, whatever its size or the Layer-4 in packets. Some combinations of two or three IPv6 EHs were also tested and were successful for all routers as well (e.g., a Hop-by-Hop Options Header followed by a Destination Options Header, up to $2 \times 2,048$ bytes in total), despite not being in Table 2 for readability reasons. Such results tend to suggest that there is no hardware limit by default on those routers. For example, Ouellette [42] reports a router running a default configuration with hardware limit (i.e., with a limited parsing buffer size for the headers), which seems to drop a packet as soon as the total size of IPv6 EHs reaches something between 160 and 192 bytes. This kind of limit exists in old routers, where the parsing buffer size is quite small (usually 256 bytes max, sometimes even smaller, e.g., 64 or 128 bytes, for older routers [9]). Also, an interesting observation that is worth mentioning is about a specific test where a Hop-by-Hop Options Header is not in first position (e.g., a Destination Options Header followed by a Hop-by-Hop Options Header). Some routers would drop the packet, while some would not. It is due to the fact that RFC8200 [13] (Sect. 4.1) does not use normative language to enforce those requirements. As a consequence, dropping the packet or not in such a situation are both valid. However, the best approach here is probably to not drop the packet, i.e., be liberal on what is received and conservative on what is sent out. This, for interoperability reasons and to avoid

Table 2. IPv6 EHs survivability in the controlled lab, for each tested router. Each IPv6 EH is tested with different sizes when it makes sense. All tests are performed three times: one with UDP, one with TCP, and one with ICMPv6. Each ✓ corresponds to a successful test, i.e., when it successfully goes through the router.

IPv6 EHs	Routers						
	R1	R2	R3	R4	R5	R6	R7
Hop-by-Hop Options Header (8, 16, 32, 64, 128, 256, 512, 1024, 2048)	✓	✓	✓	✓	✓	✓	✓
Destination Options Header (8, 16, 32, 64, 128, 256, 512, 1024, 2048)	✓	✓	✓	✓	✓	✓	✓
Fragment Header *atomic* (Fixed size: 8)	✓	✓	✓	✓	✓	✓	✓
Fragment Header *non-atomic* (Fixed size: 8)	✓	✓	✓	✓	✓	✓	✓
Routing Header *Type 0* (24, 72, 136, 264, 520, 1032, 2040)	✓	✓	✓	✓	✓	✓	✓
Routing Header *Type 2* (Fixed size: 24)	✓	✓	✓	✓	✓	✓	✓
Routing Header *Type 3* (24, 72, 136, 264, 520, 1032, 2040)	✓	✓	✓	✓	✓	✓	✓
Routing Header *Type 4* (24, 72, 136, 264, 520, 1032, 2040)	✓	✓	✓	✓	✓	✓	✓
Routing Header *Unknown Type 55* (24, 72, 136, 264, 520, 1032, 2040)	✓	✓	✓	✓	✓	✓	✓
Authentication Header (16, 32, 64, 128, 256, 512, 1024)	✓	✓	✓	✓	✓	✓	✓
Encapsulating Security Payload (16, 32, 64, 128, 256, 512, 1024, 2048)	✓	✓	✓	✓	✓	✓	✓
Mobility Header *Type 0, no option* (Fixed size: 8)	✓	✓	✓	✓	✓	✓	✓
Host Identity Protocol Header *Type 1* (Fixed size: 48)	✓	✓	✓	✓	✓	✓	✓
Shim6 Protocol Header (Fixed size: 8)	✓	✓	✓	✓	✓	✓	✓

any protocol ossification. After all, operators tend to dislike when a router drops packets that do not break normative rules.

Routers usually need to parse past the IPv6 header because of lookups. Indeed, they also need Layer-4 for, e.g., ports. When there is one or more IPv6 EHs after the IPv6 header, the upper-layer protocol header is pushed further in

Table 3. IPv6 EH types and sizes tested during a measurement campaign. Each × corresponds to an experiment, for a total of 38 experiments.

IPv6 EH		IPv6 EH Size (Bytes)														
Name	Type	∅	8	16	24	32	40	48	56	64	128	256	512	680	1,024	1368
Destination Options Header			×	×	×	×	×	×	×	×	×	×	×	×		
Hop-by-Hop Options Header			×										×	×		
Fragment Header	atomic	×														
	non-atomic	×														
Routing Header	2	×														
	0				×									×		×
	3				×									×		×
	4				×									×		×
	55				×									×		×
Authentication Header				×								×	×			
Encapsulating Security Payload				×								×	×			
Mobility Header	0	×														
Host Identity Protocol Header	1	×														
Shim6 Protocol Header		×														

the packet, and old routers may not have a parsing buffer large enough for the headers. As a result, such routers would drop the packet. As a comparison, we run the same experiments in Table 2 again but, this time, a simple filter on TCP (destination port 22) is added to routers configuration. This is to make sure a lookup is performed by routers. The results are exactly the same as with default configuration on routers. This tends to suggest that routers with default configuration are not responsible for dropping a packet with IPv6 EHs, except for old routers that may have hardware limitation. Should we observe drops in the wild, the main reason would therefore likely be policies applied by operators. The TX checksum offloading issue described at the end of Sect. 3.2 may also affect IPv6 EHs survivability, since this feature is often enabled by default.

The question of whether routers apply different treatment to packets when there is an IPv6 EH must be answered. In our case, some routers punt a packet to the slow path every time a Hop-by-Hop Options Header is present. For other IPv6 EHs, a packet stays on the fast path (when it applies). This observation can be useful, especially for the Hop-by-Hop Options Header. Indeed, since such a packet goes through the slow path, a router under heavy load (quite frequent for some routers in the Internet) may drop it. In that case, IPv6 EHs are not really the direct cause but the consequence is the same, i.e., the packet is dropped.

5   Internet Measurement Methodology and Data Collection

In this paper, we want to provide a comprehensive view on how IPv6 EHs are processed in the network. To double-check observations made in a controlled environment (see Sect. 4), we conduct multiple *experiments*, each one being a five-step process run by a vantage point (VP) towards others VPs in our measurement infrastructure:

Step$_1$: 20 pings towards the destination VP;
Step$_2$: 1 vanilla Paris `traceroute` [4] towards the destination VP;
Step$_3$: 5 Paris `traceroutes` with a given IPv6 EH towards the destination VP.
    An IPv6 EH is injected in Paris `traceroute` using FISHNET (see Sect. 3);
Step$_4$: 1 vanilla Paris `traceroute` towards the destination VP;
Step$_5$: 20 pings towards the destination VP.

Step$_3$ is the core of an experiment and aims at testing the survivability of a given IPv6 EH through five consecutive Paris `traceroutes` between two VPs. To limit the risk of a path from being changed between consecutive traces (e.g., load balancing), all Paris `traceroute` identifiers are kept identical between traces of all experiments. Pings and classic Paris `traceroutes` before and after Step$_3$ are there for reachability reasons, i.e., to check whether the experiment destination is reachable, and for comparison, i.e., to detect whether the path or the RTT changes compared to traffic with IPv6 EHs. Any experiment is thus made of seven Paris `traceroutes` and 40 pings. We run each experiment around a particular upper-layer protocol, i.e., TCP, UDP, and ICMPv6 (leading thus to 21 Paris `traceroutes` per IPv6 EH). The objective here is to see whether the upper-layer protocol has an impact on IPv6 EHs processing. Finally, data is collected at each VP through `tcpdump`.

To obtain a comprehensive view of IPv6 EHs survivability, we conduct several *measurement campaigns*. We define a measurement campaign as a set of experiments, run in full mesh between VPs, considering all possible IPv6 EHs and possibly varying the IPv6 EH size and type when it makes sense. Table 3 lists all considered IPv6 EHs, with their varying parameters. Note that the size ∅ means that the corresponding IPv6 EH has a fixed and predefined size. Combining all parameters (i.e., those with ×) leads to 38 different experiments. This means that, for a pair of VPs in one direction, a measurement campaign corresponds to 798 Paris `traceroutes` (21 traces multiplied by 38 experiments). Table 3 also has all IPv6 EHs tested in Table 2, with some strategic choices on sizes. One reason is simply to reduce the measurements execution time (e.g., min, mid and max values for a `Routing` Header instead of all sizes, fewer sizes tested for a `Hop-by-Hop Options` Header since it has been reported a low survivability for small ones – see Sect. 7 –, etc.), while another reason is to not exceed the MTU (e.g., sizes of 1,500 bytes and more).

To run our measurement campaigns, we build a full mesh infrastructure around Cloud Providers (CPs). The reason for this approach is twofold: (*i*) we wanted full control on destinations in order to capture the received traffic and make sure they are configured to process all IPv6 EHs correctly, which is not possible with Internet data measurement systems such as RIPE Atlas; and (*ii*) we were interested in the core/edge point of view, without end-users. Table 4 gives the list of considered CPs and the exact location of the virtual machines (VMs) running our experiments. We made efforts in spreading our experiments

Table 4. Measurement infrastructure running our experiments. 23 Cloud Providers (CPs) are considered for full mesh experiments, leading to 506 pairs combinations, for a total of 403,788 traces per experiment (798 traces × 506 VPs pairs). The "Label" column is used to easily identify each VM in this paper.

Cloud Provider	ASN	VM Location	Label
Google Cloud	396982	Belgium	BEL
Huawei Cloud	136907	Ireland (Dublin)	DUB
AlphaVPS	203380	Bulgaria (Sofia)	SOF
Vultr	20473	South Korea (Seoul)	SEO
Linode	63949	USA (Dallas)	DAL
Alibaba Cloud	37963	China (Beijing)	BEI
MPVS.net	202448	Cyprus	CYP
Contabo	141995	Japan (Tokyo)	TOK
BlackHOST	174	Austria (Vienna)	VIE
Veesp	43317	Russia (Saint Petersburg)	RUS
Hostiko	203394	Ukraine (Kyiv)	UKR
HostZealot	57814	Georgia (Tbilisi)	TBI
DigitalOcean	14061	Australia (Sydney)	SYD
OVHCloud	16276	Singapore	SGP
Misaka Network	35487	Nigeria (Lagos)	NIG
Microsoft Azure	8075	India (Pune)	IND
EdgeUno	7195	Guatemala (Guatemala City)	GUA
Atlantic.NET	6364	USA (New York City)	NYC
ZappieHost	61138	Chile (Valdivia)	CHI
Heficed	61317	Brazil (Sao Paulo)	BRA
Amazon AWS	16509	South Africa (Cape Town)	AFR
Mythic Beast	44684	UK (Cambridge)	CAM
	60011	USA (Fremont, CA)	FMT

over distinct CPs to avoid the particular case of inter data-center traffic, with VMs scattered around the world. The majority of the VMs are located in Europe (39.1%), followed by Asia (21.7%). 13% of VMs are located in North America, the same proportion in South/Latin America. Finally, we were able to deploy a few VMs in Africa (8.7%) and Oceania (4.3%).

We run five measurement campaigns (called *Runs* in the following) over two weeks. Each Run roughly lasts 40 hours. This allows us to finally collect 2,018,940 traces (5 × 403,788 traces per measurement campaign). Figure 6 depicts an UpSet plot [11] illustrating the unique IPv6 addresses we collected during $Step_2$, $Step_3$, and $Step_4$ of each Run and how they intersect. It is another representation for a Venn diagram with a large number of sets (i.e., more than three sets). The figure is made up of three parts: the matrix (bottom right)

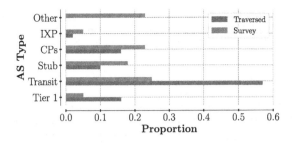

Fig. 5. Category of ASes traversed by our measurements (total is 64) and survey respondents. Important note: there is no intersection between the list of traversed ASes and the list of ASes that responded to the survey.

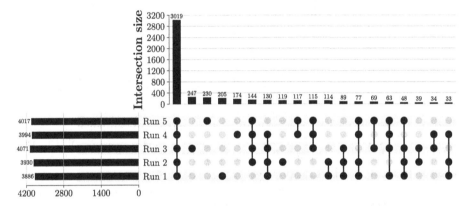

Fig. 6. UpSet plot – IPv6 addresses collected during $Step_2$, $Step_3$, and $Step_4$ of each Run, and the intersection between Runs.

shows the number of different IPv6 addresses collected in Runs. A dot in the matrix means that at least one IPv6 address has been collected during that Run (e.g., the dot, second column, third row, indicates that some IPv6 addresses were collected during Run 3). If there are multiple black dots on a column, it corresponds to IPv6 addresses collected during multiple Runs (e.g., the first column refers to IPv6 addresses seen in every Run). The histogram on the bottom left is the size of each matrix row, while the histogram on top right gives the number of IPv6 addresses in the corresponding column of the matrix (if we focus on the dot, second column, third row, 4,071 IPv6 addresses were collected during Run 3 – left histogram – with, in particular, 247 of them uniquely observed during Run 3 – top histogram). It is worth mentioning that, for readability reasons, intersection sizes lower than 30 are not shown on Fig. 6. Run 3 is the one in which we collected most IPv6 addresses (4,071) while the minimum was in Run 1 (3,886). Most of IPv6 addresses (3,019) were observed during every Run. Those addresses are mapped to 64 ASes (consistent over the five Runs – relying on ipwhois, for lookups against RIR's databases), most of them (56.25%) being Transit ASes, and 15.62% of them being Tier1 ASes (see Fig. 5).

6   Survivability in the Wild

This section describes our results for IPv6 EHs survivability in the wild, i.e., as we measure it in the Internet. As discussed in Sect. 5, survivability is assessed through Paris `traceroute` measurements (Step₃).

In Sect. 6.1, we provide a general overview of IPv6 EHs survivability, while Sect. 6.2 shows results on a per IPv6 EH basis. Then, Sect. 6.3 discusses where the drop of packets with IPv6 EHs occurs in the network. Finally, Sect. 6.4 and Sect. 6.5 respectively discuss the impact of IPv6 EHs on path lengths (i.e., number of hops), and on the round-trip time.

6.1   General Overview

Figure 7 provides a high level overview of IPv6 EHs survivability between CPs. In particular, it shows the proportion of survivability, whatever the IPv6 EH considered, between the full mesh of CPs. Tick labels used in Fig. 7 refer to labels in Table 4. IPv6 EHs survivability is summarized per upper-layer protocol, i.e., `ICMPv6` (Fig. 7a), `UDP` (Fig. 7b), and `TCP` (Fig. 7c). A value of 0 in the heatmap colorbar means that, somewhere on the path between two CPs, the packet with an IPv6 EH is dropped every time. Said otherwise, it never reaches the destination. On the contrary, a value of 1 means that the packet with an IPv6 EH is never dropped and always reaches the destination.

We see that IPv6 EHs with `ICMPv6` offers the best survivability (average of 50.4%), while `TCP` and `UDP` offer roughly the same survivability rate (average of 49.67% and 49.9% respectively). The lowest survivability, whatever the upper-layer protocol, is between SGP and IND (in that direction), i.e., 38.59% for `ICMPv6`, 36.84% for `UDP`, and 35.43% for `TCP`. On the contrary, the highest survivability depends on the upper-layer protocol: between UKR and NYC (in both directions – 52.63%) for `ICMPv6`, NYC to FMT (50.99%) for `UDP`, and UKR to CYP (51.01%) for `TCP`.

To summarize, half of the Paris `traceroutes` containing an IPv6 EH are dropped along the path. This result is inconsistent[3] with our results in the controlled environment (see Sect. 4), where we observed a perfect survivability rate with default configuration on routers. In the next section, we investigate drops on a per IPv6 EH basis and we try to understand who is responsible for the drop of IPv6 EHs.

---

[3] An effort was made to identify [1] vendors for each encountered router. However, only 85 were identified, which only represents 2% of the total. The distribution is as follows: Juniper (57), Cisco (16), Huawei (12).

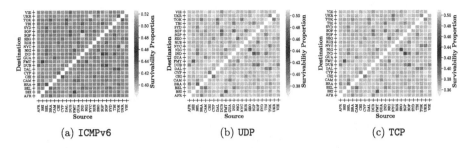

(a) ICMPv6   (b) UDP   (c) TCP

Fig. 7. High level overview of IPv6 EHs survivability between CPs, according to a specific upper-layer protocol. Results have been merged between the five Runs.

6.2 IPv6 EHs Survivability

Figure 8 shows the survivability rate on a per IPv6 EH basis. For each plot, the results have been merged over the five Runs. It is worth mentioning that the observed survivability rates are consistent over all traces, i.e., if the drop of a packet with an IPv6 EH is observed in one trace during Step$_3$, then it is also observed in the four other traces. However, in a very limited number of cases (between 0.02% and 0.05%), we detected inconsistent experiments in which a packet with an IPv6 EH was dropped in a few traces, and reached the destination in others. Some incomplete vanilla traces (Step$_2$ and Step$_4$) were also detected: between 1.05% and 1.32% of two incomplete vanilla traces, and between 0.49% and 0.61% of only one (out of two) complete vanilla trace. More generally, we can say that the above does not affect our results and we believe such situations are most probably due to temporary failures.

Figure 8a shows the survivability of the Routing Header according to its type (first value in the X-Axis couple) and its size (second value in the X-Axis couple – ∅ for type 2 as it has a fixed and predefined size). It is worth mentioning that a Routing Header mechanism is to be deployed only in limited domains, for security reasons, thus we might see a low survivability. In Fig. 8a, we see that the Routing Header survivability is dependent on its size, but not necessarily on its type. In particular, the best survivability (up to 0.7) is obtained with a 24-byte Routing Header (i.e., the smallest size), while considering larger ones leads to a low survivability (< 0.1). There is no real difference between upper-layer protocols, except for a small Routing Header where UDP provides a slightly better survivability. The fact that Type 0 suffers from more drops is not surprising since it is deprecated. Types 2 (Mobility support), 3 (RPL), 4 (Segment Routing), and 55 (undefined Routing Header type) receive the same treatment, except maybe for Segment Routing that suffers from a few more drops, which could be explained by the fact that it is more deployed and is treated more aggressively for security reasons. One can conclude that the Routing Header hits operators' policies, which is especially true for small sizes. Those policies are applied on Layer-3 and are therefore completely independent of the upper-layer protocol. As for a larger Routing Header, one cannot say for sure by looking at Fig. 8a

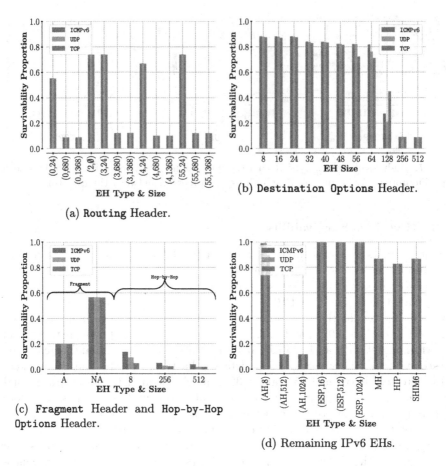

(a) **Routing** Header.

(b) **Destination Options** Header.

(c) **Fragment** Header and **Hop-by-Hop Options** Header.

(d) Remaining IPv6 EHs.

Fig. 8. Survivability on a per IPv6 EH basis. Results have been merged over the five Runs.

alone. At first glance, it is most likely due to operators' policies as well, but there seems to be a pattern that may suggest hardware limits. Indeed, it is not impossible that some traversed ASes still have old routers deployed. However, large **Encapsulating Security Payload** sizes (see Fig. 8d) have a perfect survivability (compared to larger **Authentication** Header sizes). This hint is a clear indication that the main cause is therefore operators' policies. Overall, having a low **Routing** Header survivability in the wild is not a problem, since the **Routing** Header should be deployed in limited domains. The only condition for operators is to ensure that their hardware supports **Routing** Header deployment.

Figure 8b focuses on the survivability of the **Destination Options** Header, according to its size. We expect packets with a **Destination Options** Header to have a high survivability, due to its nature (i.e., processed only by the destination). In Fig. 8b, we see that the **Destination Options** Header is slightly reliable until 64 bytes (above 0.7). On the contrary, for larger sizes, the survivability strongly drops below 0.2, except for TCP with a 128-byte size that offers a survivability of 0.45. Again, in the fashion of the Routing Header, there is no strong difference according to the upper-layer protocol for a small Destination Options Header, but ICMPv6 performs slightly better than UDP and TCP. For sizes 56 and 64, TCP performs worse than UDP, but tends to decrease more slowly than ICMPv6 and UDP until 128 bytes. Such a difference between upper-layer protocols rules out hardware limits as a cause. Instead, it is a clear indication that operators' policies are the main reason, again. The difference with TCP was investigated since middleboxes were suspected to apply different treatment, but only a few MSS modifications were found and were not problematic. Overall, one may try to rely on the Destination Options Header over the global Internet, but one must pay attention to its size.

Figure 8c shows the survivability of both a Fragment Header and a Hop-by-Hop Options Header. We focus first on the Fragment Header as an Atomic fragment ("A" on Fig. 8c – a packet that contains a Fragment Header without being actually fragmented into multiple pieces, i.e., the fragment offset is 0 and the M (more) bit is also 0) and as a Non-Atomic fragment ("NA" on Fig. 8c). We expect a low survivability for Atomic fragments [22], but a high survivability for Non-Atomic fragments. In fact, none of them are reliable, although Non-Atomic fragments survive more easily. Atomic fragments are more frequently dropped either for security reasons [19], or because stateful middleboxes drop them assuming they are unexpected whenever no previous related fragment has been seen. Considering the small size of a Fragment Header (i.e., 8 bytes), hardware limit is ruled out and the main cause is therefore operators' policies. Overall, one could hardly rely on the Fragment Header, as already observed by Jaeggli et al. [31]. Some actors seem to rely on a fixed and conservative MTU value rather than fragmentation. Note that the Fragment Header might be allowed for some specific services such as large DNS requests [27]. Due to its small size, we can say that a Fragment Header definitely hits policies on transit, which is bad for IPv6 fragmentation in general. Second, Fig. 8c shows the survivability of the Hop-by-Hop Options Header (processed by all devices along the path), according to its size. The observed Hop-by-Hop Options Header survivability is quite low (< 0.1), which makes it totally unreliable, even with the smallest 8-byte size. Therefore, the main reason is definitely operators' policies. Indeed, the Hop-by-Hop Options Header is heavily dropped by operators for security and performance reasons, whatever the size and due to the lack of use cases outside of limited domains. It is not necessarily due to the fact that it goes to the slow path under heavy load, considering the low survivability rate of even a small 8-byte Hop-by-Hop Options Header.

Figure 8d shows the survivability of other IPv6 EHs. We first notice that there is no difference between upper-layer protocols. Also, both an 8-byte Authentication Header and Encapsulating Security Payload (whatever the size) offer nearly perfect survivability, which is good news for IPsec and proves that having a strong use case helps a lot. This is also another good example of how encryption can help bypass filters. However, unsurprisingly since

Encapsulating Security Payload is generally preferred and more used for security reasons, larger Authentication Header sizes have very low survivability, which is a consequence of operators' policies. Finally, Mobility Header, Host Identity Protocol Header, and Shim6 Protocol Header offer quite good survivability, without any distinction between upper-layer protocols, even though Mobility Header and Host Identity Protocol Header are not standardized with an upper-layer protocol yet. Considering their respective small sizes (i.e., 8, 48, and 8 bytes), this suggests that they hit operators' policies as well.

In summary, size matters when it comes to IPv6 EHs [20]. Note that IPv6 EHs modified on transit were also considered. However, 100% of the IPv6 EHs received were unmodified. Now, let us compare these observations with the responses received to our survey. First, 81.8% of operators declare they do not explicitly filter IPv6 EHs, while the other 18.2% declare they do. This is not representative of what we observed, probably because none of the respondent ASes were traversed during our measurements, and because it only represents a small set of operators. However, this could highlight some cases where old routers or bugs are the main cause of IPv6 EHs drops. A good illustration is the following comment from an operator: *" While we don't intentionally filter Extension Headers, we don't intentionally use them either and have never done any testing to confirm they are functional on our network"*. Also, those who explicitly filter IPv6 EHs mainly do it on the type (100%), while filters on the size (12.5%) and data (12.5%) seem less frequent. It is not representative of what we observed either, as only the size seems to matter. Again, this can be explained by the fact that the respondent ASes only represent a small set of operators. But it could also highlight that hardware limits (i.e., old routers) may still be more present than one thinks, in addition to operators' policies. Finally, 72.7% of respondents declare they apply a filter on Layer-3 (e.g., next header, source or destination address), while 61.4% declare they apply a filter on Layer-4 (e.g., ports). While it was proved in Sect. 4 that it does not cause issues for IPv6 EHs, trying to filter on the IPv6 "Next Header" field versus the *protocol* (i.e., Layer-4 "proto", the upper-layer protocol after the IPv6 EHs chain) is not the same. Indeed, should an operator intentionally use (or not) the former and only accept, e.g., TCP, UDP, and ICMPv6, any IPv6 EH would therefore not be allowed. After all, it is up to operators to decide what they accept or not. IPv6 EHs are controversial and some operators would strictly forbid them, as illustrated by the following comments received to our survey: "death to extension headers", as well as "Extension Headers were a trash idea and need to be eradicated". Some others are more flexible and listen to *i.e.*tf discussions, as illustrated by the following comment: "We are following the current tests and waiting for BCP in relation to EH processing". This one shows that good RFCs and BCPs can influence operators' decisions on IPv6 EHs. To conclude, some IPv6 EHs need incentives to be widely adopted, which is not the case right now.

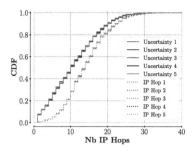

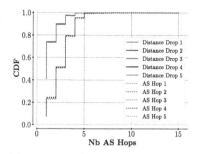

(a) Uncertainty zone size distribution, with respect to traceroute length.

(b) Distance (in terms of AS hop) distribution of IPv6 EHs drop, with respect to traceroute AS path length.

Fig. 9. IPv6 EHs drop attribution.

6.3 Ipehs Drop Attribution

This section tries to assign the IPv6 EHs drops to an AS. The problem is not trivial due to classic traceroute issues, e.g., incomplete traces. Indeed, some hops along the path may not respond to probes during a given traceroute but may respond to subsequent ones. This behavior is usually due to rate limiting [3] or ICMPv6 "Time Exceeded" being lost in its way back to the source. Note that some hops never respond, probably because they are configured to not do so. We also have observed traces with load balancing effects or path modifications (roughly, 8–9% of the cases, on average, for Step₃ for all experiments in a Run), despite our efforts to rely on Paris traceroute to maintain flows. This is discussed in Sect. 6.4 and Sect. 6.5.

To deal with traceroute issues, we introduce the notion of *uncertainty zone*, i.e., a set of potentially guilty hops, starting from the IP hop after the last replying one, and ending at the penultimate IP hop (i.e., the one before the destination). From that, we derive the uncertainty zone size as the number of IP hops between those two points. Note that the destination is not part of the guilty possibilities because we have access to it and we made sure all IPv6 EHs were accepted. Obviously, the earlier a drop in a trace, the bigger the uncertainty zone, and the more difficult it will be to assign the drop responsibility to an AS. Said otherwise, the uncertainty zone size spans between 1 (the best case, as the uncertainty zone has the smallest size) and the entire path length (the worst case). Figure 9a compares the uncertainty zone size distribution and the path length distribution (in terms of IP hops). In particular, curves labeled "IP Hop n" refer to the path length distribution of Run n, while "Uncertainty n" is the uncertainty zone size distribution for Run n. We first notice that most of the paths are between 5 and 25 hops long. It is not surprising to have longer paths (25+ hops) due to how CPs are spread all over the world. Some anomalies were also detected, i.e., traces with a loop, which explains some extreme hop counts (e.g., 35+). Over the five Runs, we have between 15% and 17% of *successful* vanilla traces (i.e., $Step_2$ and $Step_4$) with a loop, and between 8% and 9% of *successful* IPv6 EHs traces with a loop (i.e., $Step_3$). More importantly, we notice that most of the uncertainty zone sizes are between 2 and 20, which confirms that many traces have an uncertainty zone so large that it complicates the AS responsibility attribution.

In order to determine the AS responsible for a drop, we chose to follow this simple assumption: *an AS will generally apply ingress filtering on IPv6 EHs* [20]. This assumption and trend has been confirmed by contacting different operators. Of all the operators who responded to our survey, 62.5% declare they filter IPv6 EHs on the edges (on ingress), while 37.5% declare they filter IPv6 EHs everywhere. Note that some ASes may do it on egress as well, like some CPs that prohibit sending IPv6 EHs out. Based on the aforementioned rule and the fact that we reduce the probability of having errors by doing five IPv6 EH Paris `traceroutes` ($Step_3$) for a single experiment, we implemented the following algorithm: (*i*) we find the ASN for each hop in a trace and rebuild the AS path; (*ii*) we take the last responding AS in the AS path of each IPv6 EH trace; (*iii*) we keep the furthest AS based on the AS path from vanilla traces; (*iv*) we declare the next AS guilty, or the current one if it is the destination one. Figure 9b compares the distance (in terms of AS hops) distribution of ASes responsible for dropping (curves labeled "Distance Drop *n*", where *n* refers to Run *n*) and the AS path length of the full trace (labeled "AS Hop *n*"). We first notice that most of the paths are between 1 and 5 ASes long. More importantly, we notice that, based on our algorithm, most of the drops seem to occur early in the path, i.e., within 1–3 ASes. It is worth mentioning that the IPv6 EH drop attribution algorithm was applied to 96.9% of all incomplete IPv6 EHs experiments (consistent over the five Runs). The other 3.1% represents incomplete experiments where the algorithm could not find a satisfactory solution. As a result, the drop percentage of IPv6 EHs per AS type is consistent over the five Runs as well and is as follows: Transit (46.95%), CP (36.03%), Tier1 (13.68%), Stub (3.31%), and IXP (0.03%).

Overall, IPv6 EHs seem to have more difficulty passing through Transit and CP ASes. It is not surprising for CP ASes, i.e., an IPv6 EH is likely to hit strict policies, or a bug due to infrastructure complexity, both leading to packet drops. On the other hand, and according to their role, Transit ASes could do a better job and relax their policies regarding IPv6 EHs, or upgrade their hardware in case of limitation. Also, based on the algorithm naivety and the proximity between CP and Transit ASes in collected traces, it is possible that a part of guilty Transit ASes might be attributed to CP ASes instead. Others do a decent job, even though Tier1 ASes could do better. A good balance must be found between avoiding the ossification of the IPv6 protocol and security (i.e., filtering IPv6 EHs). It probably starts with educating people on this topic, so that operators can better evaluate the pros and cons of their policies. Depending on where someone operates, a small decision can have big consequences.

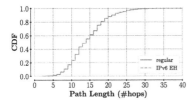

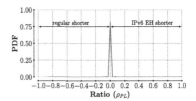

(a) Cumulative distribution of path length (#hops) over the five Runs for both Paris **traceroute** and IPv6 EHs.

(b) Path length ratio (See Formula 1) between Paris **traceroute** and IPv6 EHs.

Fig. 10. Path length comparison between Paris **traceroute** and IPv6 EHs (data from $Step_2$, $Step_3$, and $Step_4$).

6.4 IPv6 EHs Path Length

As mentioned previously, we have observed traces with load balancing effects or path modifications (roughly 8–9% of the cases, on average), despite relying on Paris **traceroute** to maintain flows. Therefore, we want to understand if IPv6 EHs have an impact on the path length (i.e., number of hops). For each experiment, we compare the two vanilla traces with the five IPv6 EH traces. Only complete traces with no loop are kept, the others are ignored. Figure 10a shows that most of complete traces are approximately between 10 and 20 hops long. There is no difference between the path length of a vanilla trace and the path length of an IPv6 EH trace, for a same experiment. It means that despite load balancers and path modifications, the number of hops remains consistent.

To better observe potential differences in path lengths between vanilla and IPv6 EH traces, we compute a path length ratio as follow:

$$\rho_{PL} = \frac{\#Hops_{IPv6EH} - \#Hops_{regular}}{\#Hops_{regular}}. \tag{1}$$

ρ_{PL} has values in $[-1, 1]$, where negative values mean that vanilla traces are shorter than IPv6. Positive values, on the contrary, mean that IPv6 EH traces are shorter. Obviously, a null value means that both traces have the same number of hops. Figure 10b plots ρ_{PL} for the five Runs merged. It shows that the ρ_{PL} distribution is quite symmetric and centered on 0, which confirms that both traces have generally the same length. Overall, IPv6 EHs do not have an impact on path length (i.e., IPv6 EHs do not arbitrarily expand or shorten paths).

6.5 IPv6 EHs Round-Trip Time

This section aims at understanding if IPv6 EHs have an impact on the round-trip time (RTT). For each experiment, we compare the two vanilla traces with the five IPv6 EH traces. Only complete vanilla traces with no loop are kept, as well as any IPv6 EH traces with no loop, while the others are ignored. Figure 11a shows

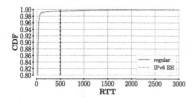

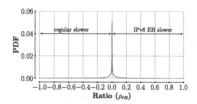

(a) Cumulative distribution of RTTs over the five Runs for both Paris traceroute and IPv6 EHs.

(b) RTT ratio (ρ_{RTT} – See Formula 2) between Paris traceroute and IPv6 EHs.

Fig. 11. Round-trip time comparison between Paris traceroute and IPv6 EHs (data from Step1, Step3, and Step5).

that most of the RTTs are approximately between 0 and 150 milliseconds. There is no difference between the RTTs of a vanilla trace and the RTTs of an IPv6 EH trace, for a same experiment. It means that routers do not spend additional time to process IPv6 EHs, even those in the slow path (e.g., the Hop-by-Hop Options Header), which would tend to suggest that most routers ignore (i.e., do not process) IPv6 EHs.

In the fashion of path length, for better understanding the RTT potential differences between vanilla and IPv6 EH traces, we compute an RTT ratio as follow:

$$\rho_{RTT} = \frac{RTT_{IPv6EH} - RTT_{regular}}{RTT_{regular}}. \tag{2}$$

ρ_{RTT} has values in $[-1, 1]$, where negative values mean that vanilla traces are slower than IPv6. Positive values, on the contrary, mean that IPv6 EH traces are slower. Obviously, a null value means that both traces follow roughly the same RTT. Figure 11b plots ρ_{RTT} for the five Runs merge. In the fashion of ρ_{PL}, the distribution is symmetrical and centered on 0. Overall, for our datasets, IPv6 EHs do not have an impact on RTT.

7   Related Work

RFC7045 [6] provides guidelines on how IPv6 EHs should be transmitted, also with a focus on middleboxes influence on the traffic.

The seminal work by Gontt et al. [21] observes how an 8-byte Hop-by-Hop Options Header, an 8-byte Destination Options Header, and a Fragment Header survive over the Internet, which comes from the *i.e.tf* and dates back in 2015. Gontt et al. perform traceroute measurements towards servers belonging to the Alexa top 1M domains and find that such IPv6 EHs are often dropped in transit networks. Since then, efforts have been made to measure the adoption of emerging standards around IPv6 EHs and the way they are processed within the network, as listed below.

Hendrikx et al. [24] state that dropping all traffic containing any IPv6 EH is the de facto rule applied by operators, for security reasons. To support their claim, they perform limited measurement campaign on a national research network (CSNET) and a campus network (UTNET). In the same spirit, Padurean et al. [47] run large-scale `traceroute` measurements to find the presence of Segment Routing [17,18] with IPv6 as forwarding plane. They reported no presence of such a deployment, probably due to IPv6 EHs filtering.

Elkins et al. [15] have proposed a methodology for isolating the reasons and network devices responsible for IPv6 EHs drops. In particular, they discuss a situation in which a tested server is behind a Content Delivery Network (CDN). However, they do not perform any measurements. Elkins et al. [14] also focus on the Performance and Diagnostic (PDM) `Destination Options` Header Option [16]. Such an IPv6 EH option provides sequence numbers and timing information as a basis for measurement. They do not report any drop when measurements are performed between hosting services while they observe some drops when measurements are sent towards Alexa top 1M domains.

Huston and Damas [28] report an improvement, over the years, in processing the IPv6 `Fragment` Header. They also notice that `Destination Options` Header and `Hop-by-Hop Options` Header IPv6 EHs are generally not supported on public Internet infrastructure.

Custura et al. [12] present an extensive measurement campaign with a focus on access and server edge networks, and provide results indicating the traversal across Internet paths of packets that include either a `Hop-by-Hop Options` Header or a `Destination Options` Header. Their results indicate that successful reception across an IPv6 path can currently depend on the type of included IPv6 EHs, its size, and on the transport protocol used.

JAMES [35,49] tests a large set of IPv6 EHs in full mesh through multiple vantage points, with some of them located in distinct Autonomous Systems. By definition, both source and destination of measurements are controlled. Among others, JAMES reports that path traversal diminishes as the size of IPv6 EHs increases.

Finally, Ouelette [42] tested the forwarding of the `Hop-by-Hop Options` Header and `Destination Options` Header on six different routers. Ouelette noticed that one router failed in forwarding packets in certain scenarios (i.e., packets with IPv6 EHs of 256 and 512 bytes), which is likely due to hardware limitation.

This paper goes further by testing all IPv6 EHs currently defined, i.e., the `Hop-by-Hop Options` Header, the `Destination Options` Header, the `Fragment` Header, the `Routing` Header, the `Authentication` Header, the `Encapsulating Security Payload`, the `Mobility` Header, the `Host Identity Protocol` Header, and the `Shim6 Protocol` Header. Each of them is tested with different sizes when it applies. All vantage points are unique, i.e., hosted by different Cloud Providers and running in distinct locations, therefore evaluating the edge and core of the Internet. This paper also provides observations in a controlled environment, comparing the behavior of routers from different vendors when processing IPv6 EHs, and investigates additional features such as RTTs and path lengths.

8   Conclusion

This paper offers an extensive vision of IPv6 EHs survivability, i.e., the capacity of an IPv6 packet carrying an Extension Header to traverse the Internet and arrive unmodified at its destination. To study this survivability, we first setup a controlled environment, tested multiple scenarios with default router configuration, and injected IPv6 EHs traffic with a specially crafted eBPF program, FISH-NET. We showed that, in such a context, the IPv6 EHs survivability is perfect. To confront those results with real world, we also performed measurements in the wild, relying on FISHNET, in a full mesh of Cloud Providers virtual machines. On the contrary to controlled environment, our results show that IPv6 EHs survivability is quite limited (around 50% on average) in the wild. Depending on the type of IPv6 EH, survivability might be a good point (e.g., Destination Options Header), while it is not expected for others (e.g., Routing Header). We also showed that IPv6 EHs drops are caused by some ASes, generally quite close to the packet source, due to policies. In terms of path lengths and round-trip time, we did not observe any particular differences between regular IPv6 and IPv6 EHs traffic. Measurement software and collected data are provided to the research community.

Acknowledgments. This work has been supported by the CyberExcellence project, funded by the Walloon Region, under number 2110186.

Ethical Considerations. For our Internet measurement campaigns, we implemented RFC9511 [48] for attribution of Internet probes. In particular, we implemented both in-band and out-of-band recommendations, except for TCP probes where only out-of-band was used to avoid potential packet drops due to the presence of data with a TCP SYN. For in-band, an email address was added to the data payload. For out-of-band, a web server (both HTTP/HTTPS) was running, with the main page being an alias of /.well-known/probing.txt. That text file described the on-going measurement campaign. Until now, it is important to note that no one has contacted us.

Source Code. The source code of FISHNET is available at https://github.com/iurmanj/ebpf-ipv6-exthdr-injection. The dataset with all our measurements is available at https://shorturl.at/MHwKQ.

References

1. Albakour, T., Gasser, O., Beverly, R., Smaragdakis, G.: Third time's not a charm: exploiting SNMPv3 for router fingerprinting. In: Proceedings of the ACM Internet Measurement Conference (IMC), November 2021
2. Albakour, T., Gasser, O., Beverly, R., Smaragdakis, G.: Illuminating router vendor diversity within providers and along network paths geolocation. In: Proceedings of the ACM Internet Measurement Conference (IMC), October 2023
3. Alvarez, P., Oprea, F., Rula, J.: Rate-limiting of IPv6 traceroute is widespread: measurements and mitigations, July 2017. https://shorturl.at/RyY4l. Accessed 22 May 2024

4. Augustin, B., et al.: Avoiding traceroute anomalies with Paris traceroute. In: Proceedings of the ACM Internet Measurement Conference (IMC), October 2006
5. Brockners, F., Bhandari, S., Mizrahi, T.: Data fileds for in-situ operations, administration, and maitenance(IOAM). RFC 9197, Internet Engineering Task Force, May 2022
6. Carpenter, B., Jiang, S.: Transmission and processing of IPv6 extension headers. RFC 7045, Internet Engineering Task Force, December 2013
7. Castineyra, I., Chiappa, N., Steenstrup, M.: The Nimrod routing architecture. RFC 1992, Internet Engineering Task Force, August 1996
8. Cisco: TRex: Realistic traffic generator. https://trex-tgn.cisco.com. Accessed 7 June 2024
9. Cisco: IPv6 extension headers review and considerations, October 2006. https://www.cisco.com/en/US/technologies/tk648/tk872/technologies_white_paper0900aecd8054d37d.html. Accessed 4 May 2024
10. Containerlab: Containerlab. https://containerlab.dev/. Accessed 7 Oct 2024
11. Conway, J.R., Lex, A., Gehlenborg, N.: UpSetR: an R package for the visualization of intersecting sets and their properties. Bioinformatics **33**(18) (2017)
12. Custura, A., Secchi, R., Boswell, E., Fairhurst, G.: Is it possible to extend IPv6? Comput. Commun. **214**, 90–99 (2024)
13. Deering, S., Hinden, R.: Internet protocol, version 6 (IPv6) specification. RFC 8200, Internet Engineering Task Force, July 2017
14. Elkins, N., Ackermann, M., Deshpande, A.: IPv6 extension headers (performance and diagnostic metics (PDM) destination option) testing across the Internet, July 2022. https://shorturl.at/GrC2a. Accessed 19 Apr 2024
15. Elkins, N., Ackermann, M., Dhody, D.: Deep dive into IPv6 extension header testing. Internet Draft (Work in Progress) draft-elkins-v6ops-eh-deepdive-fw-01, Internet Engineering Task Force, October 2022
16. Elkins, N., Hamilton, R., Ackermann, M.: IPv6 performance and diagnostic metrics (PDM) destination option. RFC 8250, Internet Engineering Task Force, September 2017
17. Filsfils, C., Dukes, D., Previdi, S., Leddy, J., Matsushima, S., Voyer, D.: IPv6 segment routing header (SRH). RFC 8754, Internet Engineering Task Force, March 2020
18. Filsfils, C., Previdi, S., Grinsberg, L., Decraene, B., Likowski, S., Shakir, R.: Segment routing architecture. RFC 8402, Internet Engineering Task Force, July 2018
19. Gont, F.: Processing of IPv6 atomic fragments. RFC 6946, Internet Engineering Task Force, May 2013
20. Gont, F., Hilliard, N., Doering, G., Kumari, W., Huston, G., Liu, W.: Operational implications of IPv6 packets with extension headers. RFC 9098, Internet Engineering Task Force, September 2021
21. Gont, F., Linkova, J., Chown, T., Liu, W.: Observations on the dropping of packets with ipv6 extension headers in the real world. RFC 7872, Internet Engineering Task Force, June 2016
22. Gont, F., Liu, W., Anderson, T.: Generation of IPv6 Atomic Fragments Considered Harmful. RFC 8021, Internet Engineering Task Force, January 2017
23. Google: IPv6 statistics (2008–2024). https://www.google.com/intl/en/ipv6/statistics.html. Accessed 21 May 2024
24. Hendrikx, L., Velan, P., Schmidts, R., De Boer, P.T., Pras, A.: Threats and surprises behind IPv6 extension headers. In: Proceedings of the IFIP Network Traffic Measurement and Analysis (TMA), June 2017

25. Hui, J., Vasseur, J.P., Culler, D., Manral, V.: An IPv6 routing header for source routes with the routing protocol for low-power and lossy networks (RPL). RFC 6554, Internet Engineering Task Force, March 2012
26. Huston, G.: IPv4 address report (2013–2024). https://ipv4.potaroo.net. Accessed 20 May 2024
27. Huston, G.: Dealing with IPv6 fragmentation in the DNS, August 2017. https://blog.apnic.net/2017/08/22/dealing-ipv6-fragmentation-dns/. Accessed 25 Apr 2024
28. Huston, G., Damas, J.: IPv6 fragmentation and EH behaviours, March 2022. https://www.potaroo.net/presentations/2022-03-20-iepg-v6frag.pdf. Accessed 17 Apr 2024
29. IANA – Internet Assigned Numbers Authority: Internet protocol version 6 (IPv6) parameters - IPv6 extension header types. Technical report, Internet Assigned Numbers Authority (2024)
30. iproute2: Introduction to iproute2. https://tldp.org/HOWTO/Adv-Routing-HOWTO/lartc.iproute2.html
31. Jaeggli, J., Colitti, L., Kumari, W., Vyncke, E., Kaeo, M., Taylor, T.: Why operators filter framgents and what it implies. Internet Draft (Work in Progress) draft-taylor-v6ops-fragdrop-02, Internet Engineering Task Force, December 2013
32. Johnson, D., Perkins, C., Arkko, J.: Mobility support in IPv6. RFC 3775, Internet Engineering Task Force, June 2004
33. Kent, S.: IP authentication header. RFC 4302, Internet Engineering Task Force, December 2005
34. Kent, S., Atkinson, R.: IP encapsulating security payload (ESP). RFC 2406, Internet Engineering Task Force, November 1998
35. Léas, R., Iurman, J., Vyncke, E., Donnet, B.: Measuring IPv6 extension headers survivability with james. In: Proceedings of the ACM Internet Measurement Conference (IMC), Poster Session, October 2022
36. Linux: ping6(8) - Linux man page. https://linux.die.net/man/8/ping6. Accessed 21 May 2024
37. LWN.net: net, sched: add clsact qdisc, January 2016. https://lwn.net/Articles/671458/. Accessed 1 June 2024
38. Marechal, E., Donnet, B.: Network fingerprinting: routers under attack. In: Proceedings of the International Workshop on Traffic Measurements for Cybersecurity (WTMC), September 2020
39. Moskowitz, R., Nikander, P., Jokela, P., Henderson, T.: Host identity protocol. RFC 5201, Internet Engineering Task Force, April 2008
40. Netcat project: The GNU Netcat project. https://netcat.sourceforge.net. Accessed 21 May 2024
41. Nordmark, E., Bagnulo, M.: Shim6: Level 3 multihoming shim protocol for IPv6. RFC 55533201, Internet Engineering Task Force, June 2009
42. Ouellette, K.: IPv6 Hop-by-hop and Destination Options Forwarding in Routers. Internet Draft (Work in Progress) draft-ouellette-v6ops-eh-router-forwarding-00, Internet Engineering Task Force, March 2024
43. Scapy Community: Scapy. https://scapy.net. Accessed 7 May 2024
44. tc: tc(8) – linux manual page. https://man7.org/linux/man-pages/man8/tc.8.html
45. The Linux Foundation: eBPF, October 2021. https://ebpf.io
46. Tuxology: An entertaining eBPF XDP adventure, May 2017. https://suchakra.files.wordpress.com/2017/05/cls-xdp1.png?w=696. Accessed 7 May 2024

47. Padurean, V.-A., Gasser, O., Bush, R., Feldmann, A.: SRv6: is there anybordy out there? In: Proceedings of the International Workshop on Traffic Measurements for Cybersecurity (WTMC), June 2022
48. Vyncke, E., Donnet, B., Iurman, J.: Attribution of Internet Probes. RFC 9511, Internet Engineering Task Force, November 2023
49. Vyncke, E., Léas, R., Iurman, J.: Just another measurement of extension header survivability (JAMES). Internet Draft (Work in Progress) draft-vyncke-v6ops-james-02, Internet Engineering Task Force, July 2022

A Closer Look at IPv6 IP-ID Behavior in the Wild

Fengyuan Huang, Yifan Yang, Zhenzhong Yang, Bingnan Hou[✉],
and Yingwen Chen, and Zhiping Cai[✉]

National University of Defense Technology, Changsha 410073, China
{huangfengyuan,yangyifanyyf,zzy.nudt,houbingnan19,ywch,zpcai}@nudt.edu.cn

Abstract. The IP Identification (IP-ID) field, which provides fragmentation and reassembly support for the network layer, is included in an extension header in IPv6, unlike in IPv4, where it is a fixed field. By sending packets such as ICMPv6 Too Big, it is possible to induce fragmented responses and thereby retrieve IP-IDs from remote IPv6 hosts. In this study, we propose a framework for active probing to obtain the IP-ID sequences of IPv6 targets. By probing over 20 million IPv6 addresses, we found that IPv6 hosts can be induced to fragment primarily depending on their device type and security policy. Furthermore, we built a classifier with an accuracy of 98.4% to distinguish different IP-ID behaviors. We discovered that 46.1% of addresses still use predictable IP-IDs, which can be susceptible to various network attacks, such as IP spoofing and session hijacking.

1 Introduction

The IPv6 fragmentation identifier (IP-ID) is a 32-bit field in the IPv6 header. Along with the offset field, it uniquely identifies fragmented datagrams, which are reassembled at the destination to preserve the integrity of the transmitted data [13,27]. Specification documents, such as RFCs [3,4,13,27,33], do not explicitly define the method for generating IP-IDs. They only require that different triplets (i.e., source address, destination address, and protocol) must contain at least one non-repeating IP-ID value within the maximum datagram lifetime. This has led to different methods of IP-ID generation across various operating systems.

Predictable IP-IDs can easily leak device privacy and have been widely studied and exploited for tasks such as port scanning [24], alias resolution [5,6,20,22,31], DNS cache poisoning attacks [18,37], and more, posing a significant threat to the security of network devices. Salutari et al. [28] conducted a study on IP-ID behavior in IPv4 networks and found that only 2% of detected IPv4 addresses used Random IP-IDs, which are considered more secure according to RFC6274 [17]. Studies [6,7,21,22] on IPv6 IP-IDs have primarily focused on alias resolution and outage detection in routers, which do not provide a broader perspective on IPv6 IP-ID behaviors in the wild.

C. Testart et al. (Eds.): PAM 2025, LNCS 15567, pp. 30–43, 2025.
https://doi.org/10.1007/978-3-031-85960-1_2

Motivated by the goal of understanding IPv6 IP-ID behavior, we propose an efficient probing framework to collect IPv6 IP-ID sequences from various hosts. By probing a large-scale and diverse set of IPv6 addresses across the Internet, we find that the rate of fragmentation is highly correlated with device type and network/AS. Furthermore, we develop an accurate classifier to distinguish between IP-ID behaviors, revealing that 7.5% and 38.6% of IPv6 addresses use Global and Local IP-IDs, respectively. We also investigate IP-ID behavior across different countries and operating systems. We summarize our major contributions as follows:

– We propose an efficient framework for collecting IPv6 IP-ID sequences, which utilizes two different vantage points to send nearly back-to-back probes. This approach also distributes the probes across different networks to reduce the impact of ICMP rate-limiting on the measurements.
– We build a classifier to distinguish between different IP-ID behaviors, such as Global and Local, achieving a high accuracy of 98.4%.
– We probed over 20 million IPv6 addresses in the wild and classified them into four types based on the features of their IP-ID sequences, providing a global overview of IP-ID adoption. We have made our entire dataset and results available to the scientific community at https://github.com/Huangfengyuan/IP-ID.

2   Background and Related Work

Background. IPv6 networks allow end nodes to fragment datagrams while prohibiting fragmentation by intermediate routing devices. Unlike in IPv4, the IP-ID does not appear as a fixed field; instead, it is placed in the extension header in IPv6 and is only used when an IPv6 source sends a packet larger than the path MTU to its destination [13].

When a router determines that the outgoing link cannot handle the size of the packet to be forwarded, it discards the packet and sends an ICMPv6 "Packet Too Big" error message to the source address, specifying the MTU size of the outgoing link. Upon receiving this error message, the source updates its MTU. If the original packet was a TCP probe, the source adjusts the MSS, resizes the data segments accordingly, and retransmits the data. However, if the probe originates from an upper-layer protocol without a retransmission mechanism (such as UDP or ICMPv6), the packet is ignored, and subsequent packets larger than the MTU will be fragmented. This process repeats until a packet is successfully delivered to its destination, with the source's Path MTU reflecting the smallest MTU along the entire path.

IP-ID Behavior. The behavior of IPv4 IP-ID has been widely studied. RFC4413 [34] categorizes IPv4 IP-ID generation types into three categories: Sequential Jump, Random, and Sequential (most literature also uses Global, Random, and Local/Per-Destination as substitutes). Salutari et al. [28] conducted probing on 16 million IPv4 addresses from a publicly available address hitlist, covering all /24 IPv4 prefixes. They classified the IP-ID counter into five types based on the IP-ID sequence of the returned packets: Constant, Global, Local, Random, and Odd. The Odd type, i.e., anomalies in IP-ID values, can be caused by various factors. For example, while most routers transmit ID values in big-endian order, some use little-endian order [20]. The proportions of these five types were 34%, 18%, 39%, 2%, and 7%, respectively. This indicates that the safest Random type is still not widely used in IPv4. Beverly [7] proposed the Too Big Trick (TBT) to induce the fragmentation of IPv6 addresses and probed over 20,000 IPv6 router addresses. The results showed that about 40% of the responding addresses were of the Random type, suggesting significant differences in the usage and distribution of IP-ID between IPv4 and IPv6.

IP-ID Abusing. Predictable IP-ID (referring to Global and Local IP-ID types) has been widely abused for various tasks. Attackers can infer the communication status of a target host with other hosts by calculating the differences in the Global IP-IDs. By observing the growth of the zombie host's IP-ID, the attacker can determine whether the target host is sending response packets to the zombie host, thereby assessing whether the target host's port is open, which helps conceal the attacker's actions. Global IP-ID has also been utilized for tasks such as traffic measurement [10], alias resolution [5,6,20,22,30,31], counting hosts behind NAT [23], SAV detection [29], and fragmentation attacks, in which the attacker sends DNS fragment packets with the same IP-ID as that in the victim's buffer. This can poison the victim's DNS records when these fragment packets are reassembled and recorded [18,30].

Zhang et al. [36] utilized the mechanism of hash collisions to find addresses that use the same counter as the victim. It can be calculated that if an attacker has ten thousand IPv4 addresses, the probability that at least one address collides with any target address is 99.24%. Subsequently, many works have employed this collision mechanism, such as Alexander et al. [2], who inferred whether a TCP connection exists between two hosts by analyzing the IP-ID information in the returned RST packets; and Feng et al. [15], who used collision addresses to infer the sequence number and acknowledgment number currently used by the target address's TCP connection, thereby hijacking that connection. In 2021, Eric [14] modified the number of counters, changing it from 2048 to an adjustable amount based on available memory. With 4 GB of memory, the number of counters increased to 65,536, significantly reducing the associated risks.

3   Methodology

3.1   Fragmentation Inducing

IPv6 IP-ID is placed in the fragment header, which is an extension header. To induce the target hosts to fragment and generate IP-ID, Beverly et al. [7] proposed the Too Big Trick (TBT), which involves three steps: (1) the prober sends a 1300B ICMPv6 Echo Request message and receives a response; (2) the prober sends an ICMPv6 Too Big message, setting the MTU to 1280, and includes the response from the first step without exceeding the MTU; (3) the prober sends a 1300B ICMPv6 Echo Request message again to obtain the fragmented response containing the IP-ID. TBT has proven to be an effective method for triggering IPv6 fragmentation [12]; therefore, our probing framework leverages TBT to induce fragmentation.

Algorithm 1. Probing Process

Input: A batch of IPv6 target addresses T; IP-ID sequence length N; Prober A; Prober B

1: $r = \text{len}(T)$
2: $c = 4 + N + r - 1$
3: **for** i in range c **do**
4:     **for** j in range r **do**
5:         **if** $(i + j) \mod 2 = 0$ **then**
6:             $source = A$
7:         **else**
8:             $source = B$
9:         **end if**
10:         **if** $0 \leq i - j \leq 1$ **then**
11:             Send_Request(src=$source$,dst=T_j,seq=0)
12:         **else if** $1 < i - j \leq 3$ **then**
13:             Send_Too_Big(src=$source$,dst=T_j,mtu=1280)
14:         **else if** $3 < i - j \leq 4 + N - 1$ **then**
15:             Send_Request(src=$source$,dst=T_j,seq=$i - j - 3$)
16:         **end if**
17:     **end for**
18: **end for**

3.2 Probing Process

To obtain the IP-ID sequence of the target addresses and differentiate between various IP-ID behaviors, we employ two probers, as a single prober cannot distinguish between Global and Local IP-ID behaviors. Following the TBT process, for each target address, prober A and prober B each send an ICMPv6 Echo Request with a Sequence Number of 0 in the ICMPv6 Echo probe. Next, an ICMPv6 'Too Big' message is sent to induce fragmentation. Subsequently, A and B alternately send $N/2$ ICMPv6 Echo Requests with increasing sequence numbers to the target, where N is the desired length of the IP-ID sequence. The IP-ID sequences obtained by probers A and B will be $S_A = [x_1, x_3, \ldots, x_{N-1}]$ and $S_B = [x_2, x_4, \ldots, x_N]$, respectively.

We designed a lightweight and efficient probing framework to sequentially send probes to the target, as outlined in Algorithm 1. Let T represent a batch of IPv6 target addresses and N denote the length of the IP-ID sequence. We traverse T a total of $4 + N + len(T) - 1$ times, where the first 4 probes are the two trigger fragments sent by prober A and prober B, respectively. For the i-th traversal, probes are sent to target T_j where $0 \le i - j \le 4 + N - 1$. This approach distributes probes across different addresses, reducing the likelihood of being filtered due to ICMPv6 rate limiting [11]. In our real-world experiments, the probing process is conducted exclusively on host A due to the difficulties in precisely synchronizing the sending processes of different hosts. As a result, A spoofs the address of B.

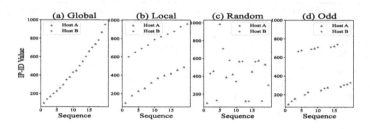

Fig. 1. IPv6 IP-ID Behavior Example

3.3 IP-ID Classifying

In this work, we classify the IP-ID behavior types of IPv6 devices into four categories, as shown in Fig. 1. This figure represents possible IP-ID sequence examples obtained when host A and B alternately probe the target address. We can observe that different IP-ID behaviors exhibit distinct characteristics, which are:

- **Global:** The device maintains the same counter for all incoming packets, with the counter increasing for each packet received. As a result, the IP-ID sequence values of hosts A and B increase alternately, appearing as a monotonically increasing sequence overall.
- **Local:** The device maintains per-destination counters, meaning different flows use different counters. Each time a packet arrives, the corresponding counter increases. Consequently, the IP-ID sequence values of host A and host B increase independently and are unrelated to each other.
- **Random:** The device uses a pseudorandom number generator to produce IP-ID values, resulting in an unpredictable IP-ID sequence, which is considered the most secure option.
- **Odd:** This behavior is rare and not systematically documented in the literature. Figure 1(d) illustrates one such case: the device maintains different counters for different flows across various time periods, resulting in an increasing trend over time.

After obtaining the IP-ID sequences S_A, S_B, and their combination $S_T = [x_1, x_2, \ldots, x_{(N-1)}, x_N]$, we analyze the features of these sequences to classify different IP-ID behaviors. We employ Classification and Regression Trees (CART) to build a decision tree, where each node is evaluated based on different features. Our selected features include:

- **Permutation Entropy** H: The entropy of the random variable that samples occurrences of permutation patterns from time series, given a fixed window length, making it a function of the distribution of permutation patterns.
- **First-order Moments** E: Referred to as the mean (arithmetic mean or expected value), representing the central tendency of the data. For the sequence $S = [x_1, x_2, \ldots, x_{(N-1)}, x_N]$, the formula is $E = \frac{1}{n} \sum_{i=1}^{n} x_i$.
- **Second-order Moments** σ: Related to the variance and standard deviation of the data, measuring the squared deviations of data points from the mean. For the sequence $S = [x_1, x_2, \ldots, x_{(N-1)}, x_N]$, the formula is $\sigma = \frac{1}{n} \sum_{i=1}^{n} x_i^2$.

We use these three features for the sequences S_T, S_T', S_A, and S_A', where S_T' and S_A' represent the differences between adjacent elements in S_T and S_A.

4   Experimental Setup

4.1   Datasets

The scanning work [8,19,35] and topology study of IPv6 can provide us with a large and diverse range of IPv6 target addresses, we choose to utilize three public IPv6 datasets:

- Gasser et al.'s IPv6 Hitlists [16,32,38] provide a vast collection of IPv6 addresses gathered through various active and passive methods. We downloaded the hitlists containing 20.5 million addresses on July 5, 2024.
- The RIPE Atlas traceroutes dataset [25] allows us to extract addresses while ignoring source and destination addresses, ensuring that only router addresses remain. From the snapshot of traceroute data on June 18, 2024, we extracted 533.8K router addresses.
- The IPv6 DNS Names Dataset [9] includes DNS PTR lookup records for IPv6 addresses. We extracted the successfully queried addresses for all records in June 2024, yielding 1.3 million IPv6 addresses.

4.2   Decision Tree Building

We manually selected 3,000 IP-ID sequences from the fully responsive results in the datasets (i.e., IPv6 Hitlists, RIPE, and IPv6 DNS datasets) and labeled them accordingly. Of these labeled sequences, 70% were designated as the training set, while the remaining 30% were used as the validation set. After training, we tested the performance of our classifier on the validation set. The confusion matrix is shown in Fig. 2. The classifier demonstrates high accuracy, achieving 99.9% true positives in the Global class, 97.5% in the Local class, and 98.1% in the Random class, with an overall validation set accuracy of 98.4%. The lowest performance is seen in the Odd class, which has a true positive rate of 73.8%. This lower classification performance for the Odd type is attributed to its diverse behaviors and a small sample size. The macro average precision, recall, and F1 scores for the model, which are 81.5%, 92.4%, and 84.3%, respectively.

We also analyze the feature importance of the classifier. The features $H(S_T)$, $H(S_A)$, $E(S_T)$, $\sigma(S_T')$, and $\sigma(S_A')$ are relatively significant, with their respective relative importance values being 54.4%, 33.7%, 2.9%, 2.9%, and 2.4%. To investigate the impact of N on classifier performance, where N denotes the length of the IP-ID sequence, we sample N' terms from the labeled sequence for training and validation for every $N' \leq N$. We start with $N' = 8$ and increment up to the maximum $N' = 30$. Figure 3 shows that the accuracy is 91.7% when $N' = 8$ and increases to 98.4% when $N' = 30$.

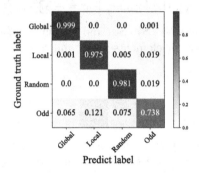

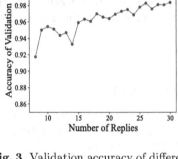

Fig. 2. Confusion matrix of validation result

Fig. 3. Validation accuracy of different reply number

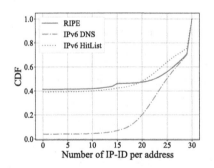

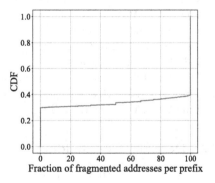

Fig. 4. Distribution of number of IP-ID per address for IPv6 Hitlists, RIPE and IPv6 DNS Names datasets

Fig. 5. Distribution of fraction of fragmented addresses per prefix for IPv6 Hitlists

4.3   Ethical Considerations

During the scanning process, we aimed to minimize potential harm to the target networks and hosts by sending only 34 probes (i.e., $N = 30$) to each IPv6 address, using a randomized scanning strategy. We imposed strict limits on the probing rate of 10Kpps, adhering to the guidelines set forth by [26]. Throughout our active experiments, we did not receive any complaints or opt-out requests.

5 Results

5.1 Responsiveness

We ran our probing framework with a batch size of 20 ($T = 20$) and set the number of probes to 30 ($N = 30$). Excluding addresses with no replies, we obtained 16.9M, 307.3K, and 1.0M addresses with valid IP-ID sequences from the three datasets. Figure 4 illustrates the detailed distribution of IP-ID values per target address. The success rate of fragmentation (with at least one IP-ID in the sequence) is 58.2% in the RIPE dataset, compared to 98.0% in the IPv6 DNS Names Dataset and 60.7% in the IPv6 Hitlists, indicating that routers are less likely to fragment IPv6 packets than servers.

We explore the relationship between fragmentation rates and networks by grouping addresses with the same /48 prefix and calculating the fraction of fragmented addresses for each prefix in the IPv6 Hitlists dataset. The distribution is shown in Fig. 5. Among the 747.5K /48 prefixes, 30.0% have no fragmented addresses, while 60.3% consist entirely of fragmented addresses. We hypothesize that whether an ICMPv6 'Too Big' message triggers fragmentation primarily depends on the configuration and security policies of the network or AS.

5.2 Comparison with Other Method

To evaluate the effectiveness of the proposed probing framework, we sampled 20 million addresses from our datasets and compared it with the probing strategy described in [28], which sends a stream of probes, one address at a time. The fragmentation rates of the two methods are nearly identical; however, the proposed approach achieves a 4.3% higher IP-ID response rate for addresses that received 30 replies. This indicates that the proposed method can reduce packet loss by lowering the impact of ICMP rate limiting, thereby obtaining more IP-IDs per address, which in turn makes the subsequent classification more accurate.

Table 1. Classification Result of different datasets

Datasets	IPs	Global	Local	Random	Odd
IPv6 Hitlists	9179.6K	7.8%	42.5%	48.3%	1.3%
RIPE	163.7K	26.4%	24.1%	47.1%	2.4%
IPv6 DNS Names Dataset	890.6K	0.8%	1.2%	96.0%	2.0%
Total	10233.9K	7.5%	38.6%	52.4%	1.4%

5.3   IP-ID Classification

For the IP-ID sequences in the three datasets, we selected those with a response rate exceeding 60%, specifically sequences containing more than 18 IP-ID values. We then applied the trained classifier to these sequences. Table 1 presents the number of IPs from each dataset and their classification results.

We observe that most addresses in the IPv6 DNS Names Dataset use Random IP-ID. This dataset contains a large number of server addresses, and we speculate that servers are more likely to adopt the more secure Random IP-ID type. Additionally, 26.4% of addresses in the RIPE dataset use Global IP-ID, indicating that routers are more inclined to use simple and predictable IP-IDs, which poses a significant privacy risk. Turning to the IPv6 Hitlists, which contains a broader range of addresses, 48.3% of addresses use Random IP-ID, significantly higher than the 2% observed in an IPv4 IP-ID study [28]. These findings suggest that IPv6 places greater emphasis on protecting IP-ID privacy. We combined three datasets and found that 46.1% of addresses (7.5% Global and 38.6% Local) still use predictable IP-IDs, which can be susceptible to various network attacks, such as IP spoofing and session hijacking.

Table 2. Predictable IP-ID rate in different country addresses

Country	France	Germany	America	China	Brazil	Japan	Netherlands	Britain
Percentage	6.5%	9.1%	22.0%	25.4%	40.0%	72.0%	15.0%	15.6%

5.4   Geo-Location

We investigate the geo-location distribution of different IP-ID behaviors using the MaxMind GeoLite2 database [1]. Table 2 presents the top eight countries with the highest number of validly classified IP-IDs and their corresponding predictable IP-ID ratios. Notably, some countries exhibit a lower proportion of predictable IP-ID usage, with France recording the lowest at only 6.5%. In contrast, Japan has the highest proportion of IPv6 addresses using Global or Local IP-IDs, reaching an impressive 72.0%.

We analyzed the country with the highest predictable IP-ID ratio, Japan. The total number of addresses is 633,388, with 83,978 global and 371,866 local addresses, resulting in a 72.0% predictable ratio. The predictable IP-ID addresses are associated with 255 ASes, while the other IP-ID types are associated with 353 ASes, with 222 ASes common to both. Based on this, we are inclined to believe that the differences in IP-ID behavior within each AS are influenced by the device vendors' choices. Additionally, please note that this conclusion reflects the regional imbalance of predictable IP-ID based on measurements from our vantage points and the IPv6 addresses collected from the three datasets.

Table 3. IP-IDs in different operating system

OS	IP-IDs
Linux 4.15.0	Random
Linux 6.5.0	Random
Windows 11 64bit	Local, incremental by 2
Windows 10 64bit	Local, incremental by 2
Windows Server 2022	Local, incremental by 2
OpenBSD 7.2	Random
FreeBSD 13.1	Random
NetBSD 9.3	Random
Solaris 11.4	Global, incremental by 1

6 Discussion

6.1 Different OS IP-ID Behavior

We obtained the IP-ID types of several popular operating system versions by reviewing their source code or actively probing them while building them in a virtual machine, as presented in Table 3. It can be observed that most operating systems, except for the Windows family and Solaris, employ secure random IP-IDs. From these findings, we can see that differing operating systems and versions may contribute to the varying usage of IP-IDs, which could be one reason for the differences observed among countries.

6.2 Comparison Between IPv4 and IPv6

We also attempted to replicate the IPv4 IP-ID measurement experiments from [28] to analyze how IPv4 IP-ID behavior has evolved in recent years and to compare it with IPv6 IP-ID behavior. However, in our testbed setup, the two probers were located within the same private network. Due to NAT, both probers shared the same public IPv4 source address for their packets. Consequently, we were unable to reliably distinguish between the Global and Local types in IPv4 networks and therefore combined them into a single type, referred to as the Predictable type.

Using ZMap, we scanned the IPv4 /24 networks and obtained one active address per /24, resulting in a total of 1.8 million addresses. After probing and classifying the IP-IDs, we observed the following distribution: Predictable (i.e., Global and Local combined) at 83.0%, Constant at 14.3%, Random at 1.1%, and Odd at 1.5%. The proportion of Predictable types has significantly increased compared to the 2018 IPv4 IP-ID study [28], which reported 57% Predictable types (18% Global and 39% Local). In contrast, the Random and Odd types remain rare, indicating that IPv4 networks have not improved in enhancing IP-ID side-channel privacy in recent years.

We also found that there has been a significant improvement in the Random type for IPv6 IP-ID. We speculate that there are two reasons why IPv4 devices use fewer Random IP-IDs: 1) The Constant IP-ID in IPv4 can provide protection by filling the IP-ID field with a constant when the packet is not fragmented, making it simpler than other methods. However, we believe the Constant IP-ID is unreliable compared to the Random IP-ID when packets need to be fragmented. 2) Performance considerations: Since the IPv4 IP-ID field requires a unique value for each packet, using a pseudorandom number generator to assign these values during high traffic loads can increase computational overhead, potentially leading to performance degradation.

6.3   Urge for Random IP-ID

In IPv6, intermediate routers do not allow packet fragmentation, making it less common compared to IPv4. Probing results indicate that 64.8% of global IP-ID addresses have an average IP-ID value of less than 10,000, suggesting these devices rarely send fragmented packets. This observation aligns with findings reported in [22], which noted that most IP-ID values in responses were small, despite the 32-bit ID space, and that these routers did not generate many fragmented packets. From a usage perspective, most applications do not rely on fragmentation and can avoid it by adjusting the TCP Maximum Segment Size (MSS). Therefore, from both performance and security standpoints, using Random IP-IDs in IPv6 networks offers distinct advantages over other methods. Random IP-IDs can significantly reduce the likelihood of IP-ID prediction, thereby enhancing the security of IPv6 devices.

6.4   Limitations

The results of this study are influenced by several factors, which we address as limitations: **1) Address Coverage of the Public Address Dataset**: The dataset can not cover all IPv6 addresses. This incomplete coverage could lead to misidentification or gaps in detecting active addresses. **2) Accuracy of the Geolocation Database**: The geolocation database used to map IP addresses may have varying accuracy. Inaccuracies in mapping addresses could affect the geographic distribution analysis. **3) Accuracy of the Classification Model**: The classification model's accuracy depends on the quality of training data and its ability to generalize. Misclassifications, such as false positives or false negatives, may occur, impacting the results. **4) Geographical Distribution of Probers**: The location of probers affects the coverage and potential biases in the collected active address data.

7   Conclusion

In this work, we propose an efficient framework for collecting IPv6 IP-ID sequences and develop an accurate classifier to distinguish between different

IP-ID behaviors. This is the first systematic study of the prevalence of various IP-ID behaviors in the IPv6 Internet. By probing over 20 million IPv6 addresses, we find that 62.7% of addresses return fragmented packets, and the rate of fragmentation is highly correlated with device type and network/AS. After classifying over 10 million IP-ID sequences, we discover that 46.1% of addresses still use predictable IP-IDs, highlighting a potential security risk. Additionally, IP-ID behaviors vary among different devices; for routers, 26.4% of addresses use Global IP-IDs. Further analysis of IP-ID distribution indicates that differing operating system usage patterns and version update habits may contribute to the variability of IP-ID usage among IPv6 devices across different countries.

Acknowledgments. We thank the anonymous reviewers for their thoughtful feedback and extend our gratitude to our shepherd, Dr. Oliver Gasser, for his guidance in improving the presentation of this paper. This work is supported by the National Natural Science Foundation of China (62472434), the China Postdoctoral Science Foundation (2023TQ0089), and the Science and Technology Innovation Program of Hunan Province (2022RC3061, 2023RC3027). Fengyuan Huang and Yifan Yang contributed equally to this work.

References

1. Maxmind geolite2 free geolocation data (2024). https://dev.maxmind.com/geoip/geolite2-free-geolocation-data
2. Alexander, G., Espinoza, A.M., Crandall, J.R.: Detecting TCP/IP connections via IPID hash collisions. Proc. Priv. Enhancing Technol. (2019)
3. Almquist, P.: RFC1349: type of service in the internet protocol suite (1992)
4. Baker, F., Black, D.L., Nichols, K., Blake, S.L.: RFC 2474: definition of the differentiated services field (DS field) in the IPv4 and IPv6 headers (1998)
5. Bender, A., Sherwood, R., Spring, N.: Fixing ally's growing pains with velocity modeling. In: Proceedings of the ACM Internet measurement Conference (IMC), pp. 337–342 (2008)
6. Beverly, R., Brinkmeyer, W., Luckie, M., Rohrer, J.P.: IPv6 alias resolution via induced fragmentation. In: Proceedings of the Passive and Active Network Measurement (PAM), pp. 155–165 (2013)
7. Beverly, R., Luckie, M., Mosley, L., Claffy, K.: Measuring and characterizing IPv6 router availability. In: Proceedings of the Passive and Active Network Measurement (PAM), pp. 123–135 (2015)
8. Cai, Z., Hou, B., Su, J., Wu, K., Xiong, Y.: 6hit: a reinforcement learning-based approach to target generation for internet-wide ipv6 scanning. In: 40th IEEE Conference on Computer Communications (IEEE INFOCOM) (2021)
9. CAIDA: The IPv6 DNS names dataset (2024). https://www.caida.org/catalog/datasets/ipv6_dnsnames_dataset/
10. Chen, W., et al.: Exploiting the IPID field to infer network path and end-system characteristics. In: Proceedings of the Passive and Active Network Measurement (PAM), pp. 108–120 (2005)
11. Conta, A., Deering, S.: RFC 4443: Internet control message protocol (ICMPv6) for the internet protocol version 6 (IPv6) specification (2006)

12. Custura, A., Fairhurst, G., Learmonth, I.R.: Exploring usable path MTU in the internet. In: Proceedings of the IEEE Network Traffic Measurement and Analysis Conference (TMA) (2018)
13. Deering, S., Hinden, R.: RFC 8200: Internet protocol, version 6 (IPv6) specification (2017)
14. Dumazet, E.: Use bigger hash table for IP ID generation (2021). https://git.kernel.org/pub/scm/linux/kernel/git/stable/linux.git/commit/id=aa6dd211e4b1dde9d5dc25d699d35f789ae7eeba
15. Feng, X., Fu, C., Li, Q., Sun, K., Xu, K.: Off-path TCP exploits of the mixed IPID assignment. In: Proceedings of the ACM SIGSAC Conference on Computer and Communications Security (CCS), pp. 1323–1335 (2020)
16. Gasser, O., et al.: Clusters in the expanse: understanding and unbiasing IPv6 hitlists. In: Proceedings of the ACM Internet Measurement Conference (IMC), pp. 364–378 (2018)
17. Goni, F.: RFC 6274: security assessment of the internet protocol version 4, Internet eng (2011)
18. Herzberg, A., Shulman, H.: Vulnerable delegation of DNS resolution. In: Proceedings of the European Symposium on Research in Computer Security, pp. 219–236 (2013)
19. Hou, B., Cai, Z., Wu, K., Yang, T., Zhou, T.: 6scan: a high-efficiency dynamic internet-wide IPv6 scanner with regional encoding. IEEE/ACM Trans. Netw. 1–16 (2023)
20. Keys, K., Hyun, Y., Luckie, M., Claffy, K.: Internet-scale IPv4 alias resolution with MIDAR. IEEE/ACM Trans. Netw. **21**(2), 383–399 (2013)
21. Luckie, M., Beverly, R.: The impact of router outages on the as-level Internet. In: Proceedings of the ACM Special Interest Group on Data Communication (SIG-COMM), pp. 488–501 (2017)
22. Luckie, M., Beverly, R., Brinkmeyer, W., Claffy, K.: Speedtrap: Internet-scale IPv6 alias resolution. In: Proceedings of the Passive and Active Network Measurement (PAM), pp. 119–126 (2013)
23. Mongkolluksamee, S., Fukuda, K., Pongpaibool, P.: Counting natted hosts by observing TCP/IP field behaviors. In: Proceedings of the IEEE International Conference on Communications (ICC), pp. 1265–1270. IEEE (2012)
24. Morbitzer, M.: TCP idle scans in IPv6. Master's thesis, Radboud University Nijmegen (2013)
25. NCC, R.: Ripe atlas (2024). https://atlas.ripe.net/
26. Partridge, C., Allman, M.: Ethical considerations in network measurement papers. Commun. ACM **59**(10), 58–64 (2016)
27. Postel, J.: RFC0791: Internet protocol (1981)
28. Salutari, F., Cicalese, D., Rossi, D.J.: A closer look at IP-ID behavior in the wild. In: Proceedings of the Passive and Active Network Measurement (PAM), pp. 243–254 (2018)
29. Schulmann, H., Zhao, S.: Insights into sav implementations in the Internet. In: Proceedings of the Passive and Active Network Measurement (PAM), pp. 69–87 (2024)
30. Song, G., et al.: DET: enabling efficient probing of IPv6 active addresses. IEEE/ACM Trans. Netw. **30**(4), 1629–1643 (2022)
31. Spring, N., Mahajan, R., Wetherall, D.: Measuring ISP topologies with rocketfuel. ACM SIGCOMM Comput. Commun. Rev. **32**(4), 133–145 (2002)

32. Steger, L., Kuang, L., Zirngibl, J., Carle, G., Gasser, O.: Target acquired? Evaluating target generation algorithms for IPv6. In: Proceedings of the IEEE Network Traffic Measurement and Analysis Conference (TMA), pp. 1–10 (2023)
33. Touch, J.: RFC 6864: updated specification of the IPv4 id field (2013)
34. West, M., McCann, S.: RFC 4413: TCP/IP field behavior (2006)
35. Yang, T., Cai, Z., Hou, B., Zhou, T.: 6forest: an ensemble learning-based approach to target generation for Internet-wide IPv6 scanning. In: 41st IEEE Conference on Computer Communications (IEEE INFOCOM) (2022)
36. Zhang, X., Knockel, J., Crandall, J.R.: Onis: inferring TCP/IP-based trust relationships completely off-path. In: Proceedings of the IEEE Conference on Computer Communications (INFOCOM), pp. 2069–2077 (2018)
37. Zheng, X., et al.: Poison over troubled forwarders: a cache poisoning attack targeting {DNS} forwarding devices. In: Proceedings of the USENIX Security Symposium (USENIX Security), pp. 577–593 (2020)
38. Zirngibl, J., Steger, L., Sattler, P., Gasser, O., Carle, G.: Rusty clusters? Dusting an IPv6 research foundation. In: Proceedings of the ACM Internet Measurement Conference (IMC), pp. 395–409 (2022)

Understanding IPv6 Aliases and Detection Methods

Mert Erdemir$^{(\boxtimes)}$, Frank Li, and Paul Pearce

Georgia Institute of Technology, Atlanta, GA, USA
{merterdemir,frankli,pearce}@gatech.edu

Abstract. Recent advancements in IPv6 address discovery methods provide new capabilities for Internet measurements. However, these measurement techniques are encountering a significant challenge unique to IPv6: large IPv6 prefixes that appear responsive on all addresses. The sheer sizes of these so-called IPv6 aliases preclude each responsive address as representing distinct devices; thus, these prefixes can confound measurements of IPv6 hosts. Although prior work proposed initial methods for identifying aliased regions, there has been limited characterization of IPv6 aliases and investigation into the resulting impact on the alias detection methods. In this work, we explore IPv6 aliasing in-depth, characterizing the properties of IPv6 aliases and exploring improvements to alias detection. We first analyze the state-of-the-art public IPv6 alias dataset, evaluating the accuracy and consistency of the alias resolutions. We uncover substantial misclassifications, motivating our development of a distinct high-confidence dataset of IPv6 aliases that enables us to correctly identify the distribution of aliased prefix sizes, detect real-world inconsistencies, and characterize the effects of different alias detection parameters. In addition, we show how small differences in the alias detection methods significantly impact address discovery (i.e., target generation algorithms). Our findings lay the foundation for how alias detection can be performed more effectively and accurately in the future.

1   Introduction

IPv6 adoption continues to grow, with more than 45% of Google's users connecting over IPv6 [33]. As the protocol landscape shifts, it is imperative that our measurement tools and methods adapt to the changing environment. Such adaption is challenging, though, as the nature of IPv6 combined with the vast address space size requires fundamentally different understanding and methods.

To perform Internet measurements, researchers must first identify active IPv6 hosts. Existing efforts have either harvested IPv6 addresses from Internet datasets (*e.g.* DNS), or developed generative approaches that predict which addresses are likely to be active. However, these approaches have encountered a problem unique to the vast size of the IPv6 address space: the existence of large prefixes that appear responsive on all addresses. These so-called *IPv6 aliases* (sometimes referred to as pseudo-dense regions) are too large to plausibly contain

C. Testart et al. (Eds.): PAM 2025, LNCS 15567, pp. 44–73, 2025.
https://doi.org/10.1007/978-3-031-85960-1_3

distinct hosts on each address. Although the aliasing is being utilized for various reasons, including, but not limited to, running multiple services on a single server, DDoS protection, load balancing, SYN proxies, or honeypots [23,29,48,62], it has confounded existing address discovery methods, driving them to produce numerous addresses within these regions that do not yield distinct hosts to fruitfully analyze. As we will show, **without accurately identifying and handling these aliased regions, Internet measurement results can become heavily skewed and paint an incorrect view of the IPv6 Internet.**

Despite the frequency with which prior IPv6 measurements have encountered aliased regions [7,17,36,37,44,46,51,54,64–66,76,77], there has been limited investigation into the characteristics of IPv6 aliases and the resulting impact on detection methods. Existing efforts have applied ad-hoc approaches for identifying and filtering aliased regions from their measurements, such as assuming the common prefix size of aliased subnets, probing randomly selected addresses within a prefix, and inferring aliasing if probed addresses are uniformly responsive [29,36,37,44,51,77,79]. These ad-hoc approaches have been used to produce the primary public dataset of detected aliased and non-aliased regions [29,30,79]. However, to date, we still lack a comprehensive evaluation of real-world alias properties, such as true alias sizes, and the influence of fundamental probing parameters within aliased subnets, such as probing frequency, the number of probes to use, or how many responsive probed addresses are needed (*i.e.* threshold).

In this work, we seek to understand the underlying properties of IPv6 aliases and how these characteristics inform alias detection methods. We begin by analyzing the accuracy of the state-of-the-art public dataset on aliased and non-aliased regions, exploring the extent to which the dataset correctly identifies aliases and their sizes. We identify substantial inaccuracies, that 85.3% of previously-identified aliased regions are mis-sized, reflecting both our current lack of deep understanding of IPv6 aliased regions and the ad-hoc detection methods applied. Motivated by our findings, we develop a high-confidence dataset of aliased Internet regions, which we then use to evaluate the true properties of IPv6 aliases and the impact of alias detection method parameters. Our analysis highlights and informs important design decisions with alias detection. In addition, we summarize the ethical considerations of our work in Appendix B.

Leveraging these insights, in a bulk dealiasing scenario, we find improved alias detection method parameters can reduce missed aliases (false negatives) up to 76.2%. When pairing this improvement with IPv6 Target Generation Algorithms (TGAs), we can reduce aliases in generated active targets by 80x, even when two dealiasing methodologies only differ slightly in detected aliases. We thus provide recommendations to enable more accurate and reliable alias detection methods in the future. Ultimately, our contributions include:

- Analyzing and characterizing the state-of-the-art public dataset of known aliased and dealiased IPv6 subnets, finding that 85.3% of aliases are mis-sized, and that more than 50% of aliased prefixes are less-specific than a /64 prefix granularity.

- Creating and characterizing a high-confidence dataset (HCD) of aliased prefixes for further research into IPv6 aliases.
- Showing that 98.7% of the aliased and 99.9% of the non-aliased subnets in the HCD remain the same for a long period (*i.e.* 3 months).
- Evaluating the selection of alias detection method parameters on our HCD, finding that improved parameters can reduce false negatives by 76.2%.
- Showing that requiring complete responsiveness to label a subnet as aliased leads to poor alias detection accuracy, which can be significantly improved by setting different threshold values.
- Showing that even a small number of aliases significantly impact TGAs, and deploying our recommended alias detection configuration can reduce aliases in generated active addresses by as much as 80x.
- Providing specific recommendations for future alias detection studies.

2   Background and Related Work

We begin with an overview of IPv6 and its aliasing phenomena, and prior work on detecting IPv6 aliases.

Background on IPv6 and Aliases. IPv6 addresses consist of 128 bits represented with 32 hexadecimal digits, each comprising 4 bits. These hexadecimal digits are referred to as *nybbles*. Due to the vast address space available in IPv6 (340 trillion trillion trillion addresses), address assignments to end sites are generous. RFCs on IPv6 allocation strategies suggest that allocation of the address spaces to networks should consider either /48 or /64 prefix sizes [13,56,59,60].

Given the abundance of addresses, a variety of novel address assignments have been utilized [73]. Perhaps the most prevalent and well-described addressing phenomena in IPv6 is *aliasing*. IPv6 aliasing occurs when large regions of contiguous IP address space are *fully responsive* to probes [29]. These regions, each of which may be larger than the entire IPv4 address space, are prohibitively large to reflect actual unique hosts. Instead, network devices or end hosts are configured to be responsive across entire ranges of addresses, presenting the appearance of full responsiveness.

This phenomenon can confound measurement as the basic act of counting hosts becomes challenging, leading to biased and incorrect results. In the context of generative IPv6 scanning [16,18,44,51,66,74,77], these regions present a fundamental challenge as, without intervention, algorithms will discover aliased regions as rich in active addresses. As a result, this reinforces further generation of addresses within the same regions, yielding millions of results which are, in actuality, non-distinct devices. Thus, developing methods to effectively identify aliases during IPv6 measurements is critical.

2.1   Related Work

We distinguish related work across three dimensions: IPv6 scanning, IPv6 address discovery, and IPv6 aliasing.

IPv6 Scanning. The introduction of fast Internet-wide scanning tools such as ZMap [22] enabled researchers to scan the entire IPv4 address space in a matter of hours. Unfortunately, given the exhaustive nature of these tools, they cannot be used to actively explore the IPv6 space. This gap gave rise to a series of methods aimed at producing generative IPv6 scanning tools. These Target Generation Algorithms (TGAs) input lists of known addresses and generate new addresses to explore [18,27,36,37,42,44,51,65,66,70,74,77]. A core challenge across all these works is aliasing, as it results in these tools over-generating addresses within aliased regions rather than in more meaningful networks to explore.

IPv6 Address Discovery. Besides TGAs, an alternative approach to IPv6 address discovery is collecting known IPv6 addresses from various sources. So-called *hitlists* [7,29,38,61,65,79] can be produced via both passive and active data sources [7,10,20,25,26,30,31,68,70]. Today, Gasser et al.'s *IPv6Hitlist* provides the largest public dataset of IPv6 addresses continuously sourced from various resources [2,3,9,21,45,47,52,57,67,71,78], and also resolves the aliased and non-aliased prefixes of those addresses [29,63,79]. The IPv6Hitlist is the primary dataset used for alias resolution by numerous studies [7,36,39,44,65, 66,74,77,79]. In this work, we analyze this dataset in depth.

Aliasing and Alias Detection in IPv6. The problem of IPv6 aliasing is well-documented. Proposed alias detection methods have focused on fingerprinting the routers [6,46,50], probing techniques [49], unused addresses [54], protocol-specific features [6,72], delay sequences [69], analyzing application layer headers [1] and a combination of previously proposed methods [43]. However, recent developments in large-scale IPv6 scanning have created an increased demand for faster and less resource-intensive, probabilistic alias detection methodologies [17,37,38,44,51,65,66,74], which we focus on in this paper.

At the core of existing probabilistic methods is the assumption that within a large non-aliased prefix, the likelihood of an address being responsive, if selected uniformly at random, is exceedingly low. However, when exploiting this assumption, existing approaches make ad-hoc decisions on the prefix sizes to evaluate and the scan parameters. For example, Murdock et al. [51] only resolved aliases at the /96 and /112 prefix granularities, generating three random addresses for each prefix and sending 3 TCP SYN probes on port 80 to each address, classifying aliasing only when all addresses are responsive. Meanwhile, Gasser et al. [29,79] used a different alias detection method when resolving aliases for the IPv6Hitlist. For an evaluated prefix (*e.g.* dead:beef::/32), they generate 16 random addresses that cover all subprefixes in the next nybble (*e.g.* dead:beef:[0-f]000::/36) and send 3 probe packets on ICMPv6 and TCP/80 to each address. Prefixes where all addresses are responsive are considered aliased. We should note that we deploy this alias detection method on ICMPv6 for all the experiments in the paper since it ensures that the probes are evenly balanced across all next nybble sub-prefixes while still probing randomly selected targets. For prefixes more specific than a /64 (up to a /124), the IPv6Hitlist performs alias resolution only if 100 addresses are observed within that prefix. For /64 prefixes, a single observed address triggers alias detection. Prefixes less specific than /64 are only considered if they are BGP announced. Due to these method decisions, aliases identified by these works are skewed towards specific prefix ranges, such as /64 s or /96 s.

Later, the IPv6Hitlist investigated aliased prefixes using detailed fingerprinting [29,79]. However, the analyses did not evaluate the effectiveness or the accuracy of the initial aliased detection method (and its parameters). Therefore, our work seeks to address this gap by incrementally characterizing IPv6 aliases in the wild, and identifying parameters for efficient, accurate alias identification.

3   Evaluating Public IPv6 Alias Data

Existing IPv6 alias datasets have largely originated as a by-product of active scanning [30,44,66] and attempts to generate hitlists [7,29,65,79]. As such, the methods used to identify aliases are ad-hoc and varied. For example, prior work focused on exploring aliases at specific granularities, such as /64 [79] and /96 [51] prefixes, rather than attempting to determine the actual aliased prefix size. Furthermore, the mechanism commonly used for alias detection—probing randomly selected addresses within a prefix and testing for complete responsiveness— has not been incrementally evaluated. Incorrectly classifying aliasing status and size can confound IPv6 measurement, leading to biased results.

In this section, we seek to understand the correctness of the canonical existing IPv6 alias dataset, the IPv6Hitlist's Aliased Prefixes list [29,63]. We focus our efforts on understanding three aspects of the dataset: 1) prefix sizing (Sect. 3.1), 2) dataset inconsistencies (Sect. 3.2), and 3) the impact of scanning parameters (Sect. 3.3). We note that our exploration here is not a critique of the IPv6Hitlist, but rather an attempt to understand how commonly-used method parameters affect the correctness of alias detection.

We collected the Gasser et al. hitlist data on November 25, 2023, consisting of 61K non-overlapping aliased prefixes ranging in size from /28 s to /120 s. It also contained 90.7M non-aliased prefixes ranging from /16 s to /120 s.

3.1   Understanding and Evaluating Sizing

In this section, we will assess if the assumptions made by prior work reflect aliasing on the Internet, by both verifying the provided granularities and performing inconsistency checks on the datasets. We first examine how existing alias detection methods lead to incorrect sizing broadly; then, we build an understanding of what these results suggest in terms of the aliasing population.

Scanning Setup. We conducted all the experiments on a machine equipped with a 24-core AMD EPYC 7402P processor, Intel X550T 10GbE ethernet converged network adapter, and 256 GB RAM. We have a dedicated 1Gbit path to our local router (Juniper Networks MX304), with no stateful devices or filtering upstream, and the router's upstream is multiple 40Gbps links. We have conducted significant scanning activity on this network at significantly higher speeds than this study and observed no loss.

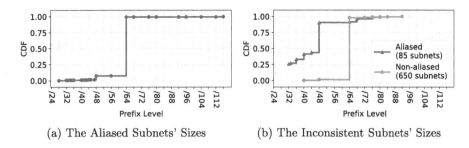

Fig. 1. The prefix size distribution of (a) the aliased prefix sizes in the non-overlapping IPv6Hitlist's Aliased Prefixes dataset and (b) the inconsistent regions for both aliased and non-aliased regions in the IPv6Hitlist Datasets.

IPv6Hitlist Prefix Size Distribution. Figure,1a shows the distribution of prefix sizes in the IPv6Hitlist's Aliased Prefixes list. We should note that we do not consider more specific prefixes than /116 in our analysis since at /120 or more specific levels, the subnet space is small enough (256 addresses or less) where distinguishing aliased prefixes from dense but non-aliased subnets is probabilistically challenging unless scanning the entire region, which becomes unpractical in large scale settings. The dataset is dominated by /64 prefixes comprising 92% of all identified aliased prefixes. This distribution is unsurprising, as it stems from the methodology of Gasser et al. [29], whereby alias detection is triggered starting from /64 prefixes unless there are less specific BGP-announced prefixes. In other words, the IPv6Hitlist method does not proactively search for less specific aliased prefixes than /64. Even though these subnets are indeed fully responsive at a /64 granularity, it remains unclear if they are *actually* aliased at a /64 prefix; they could be aliased at less specific prefix levels.

Inaccurate Alias Sizes. To understand if the existing alias detection effort adequately identified alias sizes, we conduct an experiment where we identify the true alias prefix size of aliased /64 subnets in the IPv6Hitlist dataset.

Since /64s dominate the dataset and are handled uniquely as the initial prefix size to trigger dealiasing, we begin by randomly sampling 1000 /64 aliased subnets. Although the 1000 sample size might sound small, it corresponds to almost 2% of the aliased /64s and covers all the ASes in the dataset. Thus, we argue that it is sufficient to demonstrate the alias prefix size inaccuracies due to methodological choices. For each /64 subnet, we expand the prefix into the set of all possible less-specific prefixes at nybble intervals [29,79], starting from /24s to /60s. For /64s that share common prefixes, we de-duplicate generated prefixes. We utilize the same alias detection methodology used by the IPv6Hitlist, as explained in Sect. 2.1.

We probe each of these addresses on ICMPv6 [66] using a purpose-built tool, shuffling the order of all addresses and prefixes probed. We send three back-to-back ICMPv6 Echo requests to each target address, and count a target responsive if *any* probe packet results in a response, in an effort to account for packet loss. To address rate-limiting, we scan at an overall rate of 100 packets per second (pps), a rate three orders of magnitude lower than the default rate of ZMap [22]. To label a prefix as aliased, we require all 16 IPs to be responsive, aligning with prior methods [29,79].

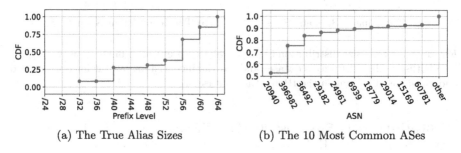

(a) The True Alias Sizes   (b) The 10 Most Common ASes

Fig. 2. (a) Distribution of the true alias sizes for the randomly sampled 1000 /64 s from the IPv6Hitlist. (b) The ten most frequent ASes of the mis-sized subnets in the sampled aliased /64 s. The y-axis is truncated at 0.5. Sampling is performed randomly, and the sample size is set to 2% of the aliased /64 s.

Results. Figure 2a shows the results of our experiment. In total, 849 of the tested /64 s were fully responsive to all tested IPs. We exclude four active but non-aliased, and 147 /64 s which were fully unresponsive at the time of scanning; we speculate such subnets are now offline due to IPv6 address churn. We find that broadly, most /64 s are misclassified; only 14.7% of purported /64 aliases are actually aliased at that granularity. Instead, the actual granularities of these aliased prefixes vary, with /56 s and /40 s being the most common, comprising 29.7% and 19.4% of our sampled aliased /64 s, respectively.

Table 1 shows the overall breakdown of the population of less-specific prefixes. We did not find any aliased /24 and /28 prefixes. Almost 82% and 72% of these subnets were fully unresponsive (*i.e.* inactive), respectively. Merging all true-sized aliased prefixes across all tested granularities resulted in 557 non-overlapping aliased subnets, in which /56 and /60 were the most common granularities, comprising 31.8% and 23.3% of the merged aliased prefixes.

AS Distribution. To further characterize the mis-sized aliased prefixes, we now examine their AS distribution. To map the prefixes to ASes, we use the December 31, 2023 snapshot of RIPE RIS collector rcc00 [53], which contains BGP routing data. Then, by using CAIDA's Inferred AS to Organization Mapping Dataset from December 31, 2023, we mapped ASes to organizations [11]. Figure 2b shows the ten most common ASes out of 45 distinct ASes. Nearly 85% of mis-sized aliased prefixes belong to three ASes, which comprise two logical ASes. Akamai (AS20940) accounts for 52.8% of incorrectly-sized subnets, and 31.1% belong to Google (22.8% in AS396982 and 8.3% in AS36492). The remaining subnets correspond to 35 other ASes shown as *other* in the figure.

Overall, these results show that the vast majority of active /64s believed to be aliased at a /64 granularity are actually aliased at less specific sizes, indicating a need for improved alias detection methods. Section 5 explores this question from the first principles across our high-confidence dataset.

3.2 Dataset Inconsistencies

The dynamic nature of alias detection can lead to different datasets disagreeing about whether a specific prefix is aliased or not. An inconsistency arises when a non-aliased region, such as a /96, appears to be present within a less-specific aliased region, such as a /32. This would be an unexpected behavior from an aliased region since such regions are anticipated to be fully responsive for *any* sub-prefix or address within them [29]. While this phenomenon has been observed [29] and discussed as SYN proxy behaviors [23], packet loss, or rate limiting, these inconsistencies have yet to be studied specifically.

Figure 1b explores inconsistencies in the IPv6Hitlist Aliased Prefixes dataset. We find that there are 85 aliased subnets, containing 650 non-aliased subnets at more specific granularities, indicating an inconsistency in alias labeling. We find most inconsistencies occur within /48 and /32 aliased subnets, and 96.8% of the inconsistent non-aliased subnets are /64s. We note that the IPv6Hitlist's focus on /64s means that it is unlikely to contain aliased /64s with more-specific non-aliased subnets. These inconsistencies point directly to areas of exploration to understand methodology concerns. Of particular note is the notion that packet loss may generate these inconsistencies, which we explore further in Sect. 5.

3.3 Scanning Parameters

Since alias detection requires active scanning, understanding the effects of varying scanning parameters is critical to performing alias detection accurately. We examine three key parameters: 1) the number of probe packets to send per target, which can be thought of as retries for a given address, 2) how fast to scan overall, which influences the rate at which prefixes are probed, and 3) the order in which subnets are scanned (*e.g.* subnet-by-subnet vs generating all addresses to probe across all subnets, and then shuffling). We note that while some of these metrics may seem trivial, *e.g.* clearly, it is preferable to shuffle scanning across subnets, these restrictions become more challenging in the context of large-scale IPv6 Internet scanning. When conducting such scans, a natural formulation is to set an overall scanner rate-limit, and, when encountering an unknown prefix, to immediately evaluate that prefix directly [66,74]. Thus, understanding the precise effects of each of these scanning parameters influences the broad design of IPv6 scanning tools, in addition to alias detection methods.

Experiments. We begin to explore the effects of these parameters on the IPv6Hitlist Aliased Prefixes with coarse-grained experiments here, and we

Table 1. Breakdown of the true alias sizes for a random sample of 1000 /64s ($\sim$ 2%) from the IPv6Hitlist Aliased Prefixes dataset. We show the population of common, inactive and aliased subnets within [/24, /64] range, and the prefix size distribution of resulting aliased subnets.

Prefix Size	/24	/28	/32	/36	/40	/44	/48	/52	/56	/60	/64
Count	87	91	126	231	306	377	475	518	786	935	1000
Inactive		81.6%	71.4%	69.1%	72.3%	73.9%	69.8%	57.3%	29.0%	17.7%	14.2%	14.7%
Aliased	0	0	30.2%	26.4%	22.9%	18.6%	21.3%	33.4%	58.3%	71.6%	84.9%
% in Merged Aliases	0%	0	6.8%	0.2%	0.2%	0	5.2%	10.1%	31.8%	23.3%	22.4%

explore them in more depth based on our high-confidence data in Sect. 5. We experiment on the same set of randomly selected /64s used earlier. We perform a set of experiments across three dimensions: 1) scan rate, testing 100pps and 1000pps, noting again that these scan rates are orders of magnitude below those of traditional scanning tools [22, 28], 2) the number of probes sent per address, testing both a single probe versus three probes per address, and 3) packet order, trying both subnet-by-subnet or sequential, probing versus shuffling addresses to probe across the entire run. We argue that randomizing addresses across all runs is not feasible in large-scale IPv6 scanning. However, here, we focus on dealiasing as a separate process, rather than dealiasing during scanning.

In total, our evaluation comprises eight individual experiments. All addresses are scanned on ICMPv6, using the same alias detection method as the prior experiments. In order to classify a subnet as aliased, we require all 16 addresses to be responsive, based on the IPv6Hitlist method [29].

Table 2. Population of the misclassified subnets in the IPv6Hitlist scan parameter experiments. Misclassified subnets have at least one inactive IP address on ICMPv6.

Experiments	Misclassified (100pps)	Misclassified (1000pps)
1 probe, Randomized	0.5%	0.5%
1 probe, Non-randomized	1.6%	1.1%
3 probes, Randomized	0.2%	0.2%
3 probes, Non-randomized	1.1%	1.0%

Results. Figure 3 shows the percentage of subnets with active probed addresses as per the address scan order for all eight experiments. All experiments resulted in high response rates for active subnets, with none exhibiting lower than 98.5% responsiveness. Despite these high response rates, it should be noted that given that existing methods require *complete* responsiveness, all subnets that did not

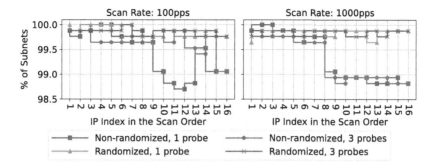

Fig. 3. Results of combining varying scanning parameters (*i.e.* the scan rate, the number of probes, the scan order) to measure their effects on the IP responsiveness in randomly sampled /64 aliased subnets over time. The y-axis is truncated to 98.5%.

yield 100% responsiveness (recall, these are aliased regions) result in incorrect classification as non-aliased. Table 2 shows how many subnets per experiment had at least one non-responsive address, which would result in a misclassification as non-aliased. We find the number of misclassified subnets would range from 0.1% to 1.6% of subnets across the eight experiments. As in Sect. 3.1, we excluded 151 inactive subnets from our analysis. We also note that although some of these misclassifications might stem from not performing TCP/80 probing, we aim to reveal the parameter effects in a simplified experimental setting.

Effects of Shuffling. Broadly, shuffling address probing across the entire experiment yields 54.5% and 68.7% fewer mislabeled subnets compared to the sequential probing, for 1000pps and 100pps, respectively.

Effects of Number of Probe Packets. Switching from 1 to 3 probe packets reduces the mislabeling by 60% when combined with shuffling, providing the best accuracy. Thus, we utilize a tweaked version of sending three probe packets during our high-confidence dataset (HCD) construction for the best accuracy.

Effects of Scan Rate. A slower scanning rate does not always yield better accuracy, especially when the addresses across all subnets are shuffled. During sequential probing experiments, we observe a 9.1% decrease in mislabeled subnets when we send three probe packets; one probe packet experiments result in a 31.2% decrease in mislabeled subnets, both when switching to 1000 pps rate from 100 pps rate. Manual investigation of the misclassified subnets in the slower scan rate experiments shows that the small differences mainly stem from the highly lossy networks, as also reported by Gasser et al. [29]. Thus, for larger experiment population sizes, utilizing faster rates with randomization can be more practical, as it maintains suitable accuracy. As a result, we use population-dependent scan rates in our HCD construction.

Effects of Probe Order. Address probe order matters, as the first address probed in a subnet is almost 85% less likely to be misidentified as unresponsive compared to the last address without randomization, especially at the faster scan rates. These initial results show that combining different parameters (*i.e.* randomization and more probe packets) is crucial for better dealiasing accuracy, and point to the need for careful alias detection design and parameter selection.

4 Creating and Characterizing A High-Confidence Dataset

We now seek to understand the actual characteristics of IPv6 aliases in the wild, through creating a high-confidence dataset (HCD) of aliased subnets. This dataset affords the analysis of the *true* prevalence, size, composition, and distribution of aliases, which informs IPv6 measurements. Furthermore, we explore how different alias detection parameters influence alias classification (Sect. 5).

4.1 Data Collection

We begin by collecting domain names from the following sources utilized by prior work [7,29,79] (using snapshots between November and December 2023): all X.509 certificates found in Censys [21], the CAIDA DNS dataset [12], the Rapid7 Forward DNS dataset [58], and a collection of top lists [15,47,55,71,75]. For each of these data sources, we resolve all domains using ZDNS [41] against Google's public DNS resolver [32], querying for AAAA records. We then add to this dataset all IPv6 addresses from the IPv6Hitlist [29,63], CAIDA's Scamper [45], AddrMiner [65], and RIPE Atlas [14].

In total, we collect 284.5M unique IPv6 addresses. Given IPv6 churn [19,24], we then check if the collected addresses are still active via ICMPv6 scans [27] at the time of our dataset construction, which reduces our dataset to 98.5M responsive addresses. As building the HCD is a slow and resource-intensive task, and IPv6 aliases are dynamic over time [29], we construct the HCD off of a large random sample of all addresses (which is still representative of the full dataset).

We initially sampled 5M IPv6 addresses at random, but later identified that 78.4% of the sampled addresses belong to AS16509 (Amazon). We removed these addresses to avoid biasing our measurements towards the behavior of this one AS, as well as to avoid potentially heavily scanning a single AS. After filtering all Amazon IPs, no AS comprises the majority of our sampled dataset; thus, our final sample consists of 1.1M IPv6 addresses. The 3 most common ASes for the sampled addresses are AS47583 (Hostinger), AS12322 (Free SAS), and AS51468 (One.com), comprising 16.3%, 15.1%, and 7.9% of the sampled IPs, respectively.

Across these addresses, we calculate all distinct prefixes at the nybble granularity (every 4 bits), from /24s to /116s[1] (we do not explore beyond /116s, as

---

[1] During construction, our HCD could encounter NAT64 /96 transition prefixes. We do not expect such prefixes to have a significant impact on our results, given: 1) Hsu et al. showed that there are very few publicly available NAT64 gateways [40], 2) such regions would either relay ICMP messages to the IPv4 Internet, thus having such prefixes take on sparsity [5] of the underlying IPv4 Internet, or would respond uniformly, thus being classified as either aliased or not aliased.

explained in Sect. 3.1). Our sampled addresses reside in a total of 11.9M unique subnets, of which prefix size breakdown is shown in Table 3.

Table 3. The number of unique subnets per prefix granularity in our HCD, calculated by computing common prefixes of the 1.1M input IPs, totaling up to 11,948,007 subnets.

Prefix	Count	Prefix	Count	Prefix	Count	Prefix	Count	Prefix	Count
/24	4,261	/44	71,569	/64	597,036	/84	680,126	/104	850,860
/28	8,898	/48	116,228	/68	613,360	/88	744,454	/108	872,025
/32	15,086	/52	224,387	/72	618,125	/92	819,839	/112	894,190
/36	27,209	/56	397,690	/76	620,390	/96	835,112	/116	914,821
/40	45,213	/60	507,335	/80	628,475	/100	841,318		

4.2 Method

To label all 11.9M subnets for the HCD, we run a three-round classification process. In the first two rounds, we probe and label subnets in ascending prefix size order, starting from /24s up to /116s (incrementing at the nybble granularity). The last round evaluates only non-aliased subnets that appear to cause aliasing inconsistencies (as defined in Sect. 3.2) based on the prior two rounds.

To mitigate the effects of rate-limiting, in all rounds, we follow a modified version of the dealiasing approach described in Sect. 3. Although rate-limiting is not an IPv6-specific problem, Vermeulen et al. showed that the rate-limiting in IPv6 is commonly triggered at scan rates even slower than 2Kpps, hinting at a high chance of subnet mislabeling when fast but practical scan rates are deployed [34,72]. Thus, specifically, for each prefix level, we pre-generate and randomly order all target addresses to probe, to avoid contiguous scanning of each subnet. We then round-robin probe all addresses across three iterations, thus avoiding back-to-back repeat probing of an address. Furthermore, we rate limit our probing of regions that we already identified as aliased (given that we evaluate from less specific to more specific prefixes). For example, if evaluating /48s, we rate limit probing of any /48, that is within a /32 previously resolved as aliased, by the number of probes we send to this /32. We further explore the impact of these probing parameters on alias detection in Sects. 5.2 and 5.1.

We choose different scanning rates across prefix levels and rounds, depending on the number of addresses to probe. When there are fewer addresses, we scan slower to avoid rate limiting. Meanwhile, when there are more addresses, we can scan at a faster rate as the random shuffling of addresses more widely distributes the probing across subnets (and we still employ per-subnet rate limiting). Furthermore, by using multiple rounds, we can account for ambiguous classifications (where only a subset of the 16 probed addresses within a subnet are responsive) in one round, potentially due to some rate limiting or packet loss, by re-evaluating during a subsequent round.

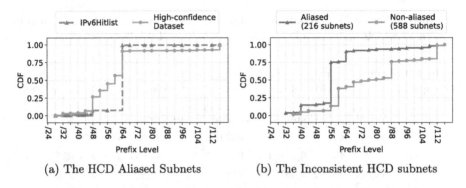

(a) The HCD Aliased Subnets   (b) The Inconsistent HCD subnets

Fig. 4. The prefix size distribution of (a) the non-overlapping HCD aliased subnets and the IPv6Hitlist, and (b) the non-overlapping inconsistent subnets in the HCD.

Concretely, in the first round, if there are $\leq 250K$ addresses for a prefix level, we scan at 100 pps with a 10 pps/subnet rate limit. If the address pool is in the range of $(250K, 1M]$ addresses, we scan at 1K pps with a 100 pps/subnet cap. For larger address pools, we scan at 10K pps (the default ZMap scan rate [22, 28]) while keeping a 100 pps/subnet cap. For the second round, we reduce the scan rates further, such that the subnet rate limit is always 10 pps/subnet, and when the address pool exceeds $250K$ addresses, we scan at 1K pps (instead of 10K pps). In the final round (which only evaluates non-aliased subnets exhibiting aliasing inconsistencies), we scan at only 10 pps, with a 1 pps/subnet cap.

For each round, we generate a new set of addresses per subnet (recall, we generate one address for all 16 sub-prefixes of the subnet). However, we classify based on merging across rounds, such that if each of the 16 sub-prefixes of the subnet is responsive in any round, we consider that sub-prefix as active for the sake of alias classification. We then classify a subnet as aliased if all 16 sub-prefixes are active (across any round). Finally, we merge aliased subnets within larger aliased subnets (e.g., an aliased /48 within an aliased /32) but preserve inconsistencies. Across the three rounds, we construct an HCD with 8,402 unique aliased subnets. In total, we classified 30% of all 11.9M subnets as aliased. We further perform a longitudinal analysis to understand aliasing behavior changes over time in Sect. 4.4, and utilize TLS fingerprinting to confirm identical behaviors of the aliased subnets' sub-prefixes in Sect. 4.5.

4.3   Prefix Level Distribution

Figure 4a shows the prefix size distribution of the 8,402 merged aliased subnets in our HCD. The figure also shows the prefix size distribution from the IPv6Hitlist Aliases dataset we presented in Fig. 1b as a blue dashed line.

The comparison paints a stark contrast. We find that 52.7% of the aliased subnets are less specific than /64, which accounts for 36.2% of the aliases. This contrasts with the prior work showing that aliases are significantly dominated by /64s, comprising 92% of aliases from the IPv6Hitlist Aliased Prefixes.

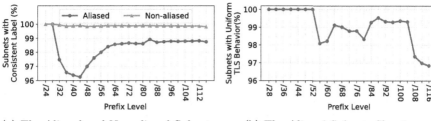

(a) The Aliased and Non-aliased Subnets
Maintaining their Label for 3 Months

(b) The Aliased Subnets Showing
Uniform Behavior for TLS

Fig. 5. The population of (a) both the aliased and non-aliased subnets that have been classified the same over three months (see Sect. 4.4), (b) the aliased subnets showing a uniform behavior for ZGrab2 port 443 TLS scans for all of their 16 sub-prefixes (see Sect. 4.5). Note that the y-axis is truncated at 96%.

In addition, although /64 is the most common prefix size, our dataset shows that /48 s account for a significant 18.5% of the population followed by /60 s comprising 10.6% of the aliased prefixes. Moreover, as the datasets portray a different picture of IPv6 Aliasing, we further explore their similarities and differences in the labels they provide for the HCD input sample of 1.1M addresses in Appendix A. Even though the comparison shows that the labels across the two datasets are highly consistent (95.9%), the prefix sizes of the detected aliases for the identically labeled addresses are not. Table 5 shows that 4.4% of the aliased addresses are mapped to a more-specific granularity by the IPv6Hitlist, supporting the inaccurate alias size results in Sect. 3.1. We further investigate the impact of these small differences on the TGA generation in Sect. 5.5. These explorations further our motivation for improved alias detection methods beyond existing constructions, especially to account for dynamic prefix sizes.

4.4 Longitudinal Label Analysis

In order to understand whether the subnets remain aliased or not over time, we repeated HCD construction a total of 3 times, one month apart, totaling coverage of 3 months (*i.e.* 2024-04-25, 2024-05-30, and 2024-07-16).

Our analysis showed that 98.7% of the aliased subnets reported in Sect. 4.2 remained aliased in all construction instances. In contrast, only 0.1% of the non-aliased subnets changed their label to aliased in at least one of the later two HCD constructions. Moreover, we find that only 792 aliased (0.02%) and 606 non-aliased (0.01%) subnets exhibit a flip-flop behavior in their labels (*e.g.* having the opposite label only for the second iteration). The majority of this label-changing behavior happens in /116 granularity, accounting for 19.2% and 20.1% of the aliased and non-aliased flip-flop subnets, respectively.

Figure 5a shows the prefix-size breakdown of the subnets that stayed as aliased or non-aliased across three constructions. Although the non-aliased subnets remain the same across all prefix sizes compared to the aliased subnets, we suspect this behavior originates from the majority of the non-aliased subnets being fully inactive. For the aliased subnets, the less-specific prefix sizes (except /28 s), especially in the [/32, /44] range, show slightly more variation across time compared to more-specific prefix sizes (although the vast majority of aliased subnets remain aliased over time). This variation in the [/32, /44] range mainly stems from significantly smaller subnet population sizes in the HCD, where a small number of non-uniform behavior instances appear as a larger portion among the tested subnets compared to other prefix sizes. Moreover, even though a tiny portion of the label changes happen in non-aliased to aliased direction (*i.e.* missing new aliases), suggesting that frequent HCD reconstruction might not be necessary, we further show how these small differences negatively impact the IPv6 address discovery in Sect. 5.5.

4.5   Label Validation with TLS Fingerprinting

Although the HCD construction utilizes a modified version of aliased detection deployed in prior work, we aim to gain more confidence in our HCD labels by investigating whether the aliases are indeed subnets behaving uniformly across IPs within it by fingerprinting application layer information. While doing so, we expect to see identical behaviors from the sub-prefixes of an aliased subnet, especially when probed for host-specific information, such as a TLS certificate.

We start our experiment by randomly sampling 1% of the aliased subnets that maintained the aliased label across three constructions, as reported in Sect. 4.4. Then, we pre-generate one address per 16 sub-prefixes for all sampled subnets. For each active address on port 443, we utilize ZGrab2 [21] to establish a TLS connection, if possible, and collect the TLS handshake logs. With this methodology, we aim to reveal the similarities in the sub-prefix behaviors for a subnet for a different protocol than ICMPv6. We categorize the behaviors as uniform and non-uniform. A subnet shows a uniform behavior if all the sub-prefixes: 1) share the same TLS certificate, 2) return an identical error (such as refusing the connection or canceling the request), or 3) are inactive on port 443. A non-uniform behavior arises when the responses of the sub-prefixes vary.

Figure 5b shows the prefix-size breakdown of what population of the aliased subnets showing uniform behavior. The aliased subnets commonly exhibit a uniform behavior across all prefix sizes, none comprising less than 96.8%. The results also indicate that groups of adjacent prefix sizes exhibit similar behaviors. For example, large regions such as prefixes from /28 s to /52 s unanimously show uniform behavior to TLS scans. Moreover, subnets within the prefix-size ranges of [/56, /80], [/84, /104], and [/108, /116] have similar non-uniform behavior populations. We argue that the high number of uniform TLS-scan behavior among all aliased subnets enhances confidence in the HCD.

Limitations. Since we consider some weak cases of uniform behavior (*e.g.* inactiveness), and only consider port 443, this validation alone does not robustly show that all these tested addresses are indeed single devices, or behave exactly the same; thus, it can possibly result in false positives. We suspect this approach might be more successful in detecting these behaviors in CDNs than routers, resulting in an analysis of a limited population. Although confidence in our labels can be further improved by deploying other fingerprinting techniques [35,72], we would like to emphasize that our main goal is to perform a rough demonstration of uniformity to give us more confidence in data quality.

4.6   Inconsistencies

Similarly to Sect. 3, we also explore inconsistencies in our HCD. After the second round of the HCD construction, we found 5,041 (588 non-overlapping) non-aliased subnets under 2,923 (216 non-overlapping) less-specific (*i.e.* larger) aliased subnets. Figure 4b shows the prefix distribution of the non-overlapping inconsistent subnets. Aliased subnets exhibiting inconsistencies are dominated by /56 s and /64 s, comprising 57.4% and 14.4% of the subnets, respectively. Moreover, 24.7% of the non-aliased subnets that cause inconsistencies appear at the /60 granularity, 23% are /80 s, and 19% are /112 s. We observe that 50.1% of the inconsistent non-aliased prefixes belong to AS47583, Hostinger. Similarly, 23.5% of the aliased subnets belong to the same AS, and 28.5% originate from 2 logical ASes (AS49392 and AS51659) of an organization, LLC Baxet.

We found that 2.2% of these non-aliased subnets causing inconsistencies were indeed aliased, causing label changes in the HCD. In addition, 83.1% of these subnets were actually inactive, while their parent prefixes were active and aliased. Manual investigation indicates that the majority of these inconsistencies are legitimate inactive prefixes within larger aliased prefixes, but some exhibit stochastic inactive behavior explained in Sect. 5.1.

Although this experiment validates that aliasing inconsistencies exist in the wild and are not simply due to packet loss or network effects, further analysis of why this phenomenon happens in practice is left for future studies. We strongly encourage researchers to account for inconsistencies when performing measurements.

4.7   ASes with Aliases

Next, we characterize the aliased prefixes in our dataset by analyzing their ASes. We apply the same method as Sect. 3.1, mapping aliased subnets to ASNs using routing data, and then identifying each AS's organization by using the same datasets in Sect. 3.1. Figure 6b shows the distribution of the aliased subnets across ASes, depicting the 10 most common ASes. We see that 51.3% of the aliased subnets belong to only 3 ASes out of 312 total distinct ASes. Akamai (AS20940) accounts for 28.1% of these subnets; each Google (AS36492) and Hostinger (AS47583) account for 11.6%.

Figure 6a approaches this analysis from a different angle to understand how diverse the alias sizing is within these ASes. When we grouped the aliased prefixes by ASes, we observed that the ASes contain aliased subnets of varying (up to 12) prefix sizes. Most ASes (70.2%) had aliased subnets of a size, and 16.7% had aliased prefixes of 2 different sizes.

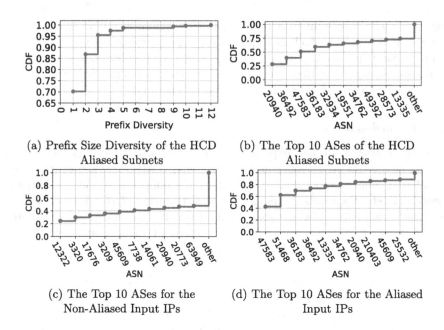

(a) Prefix Size Diversity of the HCD Aliased Subnets

(b) The Top 10 ASes of the HCD Aliased Subnets

(c) The Top 10 ASes for the Non-Aliased Input IPs

(d) The Top 10 ASes for the Aliased Input IPs

Fig. 6. Figure (a) shows the prefix size diversity within the ASes of the HCD Aliased Subnets, with the y-axis truncated at 0.65. The 10 most common ASes are shown for: (b) the HCD aliased subnets, (c) the non-aliased, and (d) the aliased input IPs.

We further classify the aliasing status of 1.1M input addresses, finding that 37.8% are in the aliased subnets. Figure 6c and Fig. 6d show the top 10 most common ASes for the non-aliased and aliased addresses, respectively. We see that 69.9% of the aliased addresses belong to 3 ASes: 42.7%, 19.8%, and 7.4% in Hostinger (AS47583), One.com (AS51486), and Akamai (AS36183), respectively. For non-aliased addresses, 24.2% were in Free SAS (AS12322), 5.7% in Deutsche Telekom (AS3320), and 3.1% in SoftBank Corp (AS17676).

5   Exploring Alias Detection Methods: HCD Experiments

In Sect. 4, we fully characterized our HCD and the aliased prefixes identified. We now investigate the effects of varying alias detection method parameters, leveraging our HCD to evaluate detection correctness. Since the alias detection methods entail active probing of addresses, the probing parameters can impact alias detection accuracy. Especially, because misinterpretation of prefixes negatively affects the aliased subnets more than non-aliased subnets, finding the right parameters and their values play a crucial role in IPv6 Aliasing studies. For example, if a non-aliased subnet gets labeled as non-aliased due to rate limiting or packet loss, the classification would still hold; however, for the aliased subnets, this would result in a misclassification, negatively impacting measurements.

Therefore, this section aims to understand what parameter values result in the most accurate and efficient large-scale bulk alias detection (*i.e.* performing alias detection on a given set of subnets at once). By building upon the lessons learned at each step, we produce guidance on how best to perform alias detection.

For all the experiments, we utilize the method of sending 16 probes proposed in the IPv6Hitlist [29] since it ensures the randomly generated targets are evenly distributed across all next nybble subprefix values. We think that this method takes the fragmented prefixes into account better compared to the method proposed by Murdock et al. [51]. For example, in a scenario where a non-aliased subnet neighbors only one aliased subnet in its next bit value, the random address generation without considering sub-prefixes could just sample from this fully active neighboring subnet, resulting in a misclassification despite the subnet actually being non-aliased.

We start by evaluating the rate at which we should probe the subnets, (Sect. 5.1). Then, we assess whether performing repeated probing improves the detection of aliased regions (Sect. 5.2). Next, Sect. 5.3 investigates whether probing new targets versus the same targets when performing repetitions improves classification accuracy. We then put these parameters together and compare alias detection results when using our recommended parameters against a measurement conducted using a diametric configuration in Sect. 5.4. Finally, in Sect. 5.5, we show the practical impact of improved alias resolution by evaluating how small differences in the alias detection methodologies can propagate to larger problems in IPv6 scanning outcomes.

Subnets with Stochastic Network Behavior. During our initial explorations, we observed high loss in some inconsistent aliased regions. A longitudinal activeness analysis at varying prefix granularities showed a stochastic behavior as these subnets change active status without a pattern. Also, collecting traceroutes during this dynamic behavior led to the same route. We think that these networks (*e.g.* AS49392) might be behind a DDoS protection or a proxy service since most packets are being dropped at the same last hop without a specific pattern. Although why we observe such behavior is unclear, it shows that alias detection is a highly time-sensitive task [29]. Thus, we filter these subnets from our aliased subnets list for the rest of the paper, resulting in 8,360 aliased prefixes. In addition, we exclude the aliased subnets that are no longer active during any of the experiments due to the churn in aliased networks.

5.1   Subnet Probing Rates

One of the most challenging problems in IPv6 alias detection is accounting for rate limiting [72]. Probing a network too fast could trigger rate limiting or cause packet loss (*e.g.* overprobing a middlebox on the path more than it can process), resulting in false negatives, which can significantly impact the IPv6 scanning measurements. Thus, in this section, we aim to evaluate the impact of probe rate on aliased subnets to find out what rates one can avoid rate limiting.

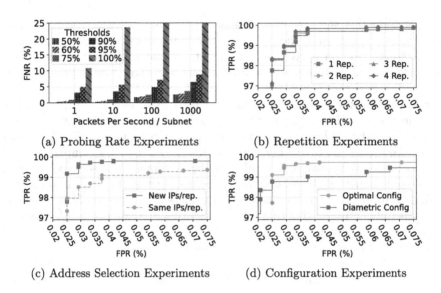

(a) Probing Rate Experiments   (b) Repetition Experiments

(c) Address Selection Experiments   (d) Configuration Experiments

Fig. 7. ROC Curves of False and True Positive rates, for 8,360 aliased and 24K non-aliased subnets (1K per prefix size, selected at random), (a) aliased subnet probing rate (with the y-axis truncated at 25%), (b) the repetition, (c) the address selection, and (d) the HCD optimal configuration vs a diagonal configuration experiments, with the y-axis (x-axis) truncated at 97%([0.02, 0.075]%).

We perform four experiments on the HCD aliased prefixes. For the experiments, we utilize the rate-limited subnet probing approach from Sect. 4.2 with 1 pps/subnet, 10 pps/subnet, 100 pps/subnet, and 1000 pps/subnet. We probe all the aliased subnets for a minute at each given rate, and continuously analyze their network behaviors. This methodology also enables us to determine when the rate limit is triggered in a wide range of 1–60K probes per minute.

Figure 7a shows the false negative rates at different threshold values for all four experiments. The threshold value determines the least number of responsive addresses required to label a subnet as aliased throughout an entire one-minute run (*e.g.* the threshold value of 100% represents full responsiveness). By analyzing different threshold values, we aim to understand if requiring complete responsiveness is accurate enough for aliased subnet classification.

Complete Responsiveness. Albeit commonly deployed in prior work [29,51, 66], requiring complete responsiveness to label a subnet as aliased compared to when the threshold is set to 95% results in 2.2x higher FNR for 1 pps/subnet, and roughly 4.3x higher for all other scan rates. These initial results indicate that even only considering the scan-rate parameter, finding an optimal threshold value is as crucial as finding parameter values for higher accuracy.

Scan Rates. Scan rates faster than 10 pps/subnet lead to significantly higher FNR for all the threshold values. For example, although 1 pps/subnet and 10 pps/subnet have a 0.29% FNR at a 50% threshold setting, both 100 pps/subnet and 1000 pps/subnet result in 5.9x and 8.75x higher FNR, respectively. Even though 1 pps/subnet outperforms all other experiments, especially for threshold configurations set ≤75%, utilizing 10 pps/subnet is more practical due to not only providing a similar FNR but also running 10x faster.

Conclusion. We argue that running at 10 pps/subnet rate provides the most optimal settings, especially when a stochastic network behavior is present. The results hint that choosing a threshold value around 75% rather than 100% reduces the FNs by more than 95%.

5.2   Repetition

In this experiment, we aim to explore whether repeated experiments improve aliased subnet labeling accuracy due to sending multiple probes accounting for the packet loss. We perform our evaluation over 8,360 HCD aliased subnets, and 1,000 non-aliased subnets selected at random per prefix level size between /24 and /116 at 4-bit intervals (*i.e.* 24,000 non-aliased prefixes in total). Testing non-aliased prefixes is crucial since small but densely active non-aliased regions might introduce false positives in repeated scans. Our non-aliased samples follow a similar AS distribution of the non-aliased input IPs (see Fig. 6c).

Next, we utilize the same rate-limited subnet probing strategy from Sect. 4.2 at 10 pps/subnet rate. However, this time, we repeat the same experiment 10 times, shuffling the scan order of the addresses each time. We label an address as active at repetition R_x if it responds to at least one of the probes within $R_{\leq x}$ repetitions. Also, the threshold values represent the number of required responsive addresses per subnet across repetitions.

Figure 7b is a ROC curve showing how the true positive rates (TPR) and false positive rates (FPR) for varying repetition values (plotted as curves) at different alias labeling threshold values (plotted as data points on the curves). For clarity, we truncate the y-axis to show TPR above 97%, and the x-axis to show FPR above 0.025% and below 0.07%. We only show the first four repetitions since further repetitions do not result in increased TPR, but FPR.

Different Threshold Values. When no repetition is performed, both the threshold values of 9 and 10 result in the same 0.375% FPR, with the TPR of 99.69% and 99.62%, respectively. Although the TPR can be improved by setting lower threshold values, it also results in significantly higher FPR (*e.g.* 1.6x higher at threshold 8). When the threshold value is set to 9, performing 2–5 repetitions does not increase either TPR or FPR, converging them at 99.88% and 0.0375, respectively. The TPR improvements over more repetitions beyond 5 are minimal, rendering these parameter values more costly than more accurate.

However, after nine repetitions, we observe a 12% increase in FPR, remaining the same thereafter. Although there are only a few FPs present in the results, we manually investigate each prefix. 85.7% of the prefixes map to two ASes, AS209737 and AS61317. We observe the same stochastic behavior mentioned earlier on 57.2% of the prefixes. The rest shows fully responsive behavior two weeks after the HCD construction, which we attribute to the dynamic nature of the aliases and the IPv6 churn.

Conclusion. We find that when repeating experiments, setting a lower threshold value results in significant improvements compared to complete responsiveness. Thus, performing two repetitions, while setting the alias labeling threshold to 9 gives the optimal results, while considering the probing cost. This is because performing more repetitions with smaller threshold values is more likely to increase the FPR, and provide smaller TPR gains, which do not compensate for the number of probes needed to be sent, and the longer experiment times.

5.3   Address Selection During Repetition

Here, we explore one final alias detection method parameter related to address selection during scan repetition. Previously, we re-scanned the same set of addresses across each scan repetition. However, upon each repetition, one could potentially probe a new set of randomly selected addresses per subnet. This approach largely precludes re-scanning the same addresses to confirm responsiveness (especially when prior probes are incorrectly inferred as inactive), but allows subsequent repetitions to evaluate the responsiveness of different addresses within subnets. Nevertheless, this might result in more FPs, especially at more specific granularities such as /116, due to increasing the likelihood of finding more active addresses in really dense regions.

To evaluate the impact of this parameter, we conduct the same experiment as in Sect. 5.2, and test with the same addresses versus new addresses for all subnets per scan repetition. During labeling, we check the activeness of the sub-prefixes, rather than individual addresses. We consider a sub-prefix active if at least one of the addresses under it is responsive across all repetitions. Figure 7c is a ROC curve showing the TPR and FPR under both address selection methods when the experiments were repeated two times. We do not present the results for one repetition as it is the first step, and only show the cumulative result at the end of the second repetition. We should also note that the same addresses curve represents the same 2 repetitions curve in Fig. 7b. Due to running experiments at different times, and filtering out separate sets of inactive subnets for both parameter experiments, the orange line is shifted to the bottom by less than 0.5% in Fig. 7c. The shift might sound significant at our TPR scales, but we find it expected since the new addresses approach is more likely to find active regions compared to the same addresses approach as explained above.

Comparison. We observe that the new addresses curve always stays above the same addresses curve, improving the TPR by 76.9% compared to using the same addresses, at the previously recommended threshold value of 9, when experiments are repeated two times. However, the new approach results in a higher FPR, 0.042%, whereas the same addresses approach has a 0.0375% FPR. Performing more repetitions with the new approach introduces two new FPs at the /116 granularity. This shows that for small but dense, non-aliased regions, generating new addresses per repetition is more likely to label them as aliased.

Interestingly, the same FPR can be achieved with the new addresses approach by setting the threshold value to 10, increasing the TPR with a 79.6% overall improvement.

Conclusion. We argue that generating new addresses per repetition significantly increases the TPR as its curve always stays above the same addresses approach. Although the previously suggested threshold value, 9, results in a 99.79% TPR, setting the threshold to 10 not only decreases FPR to 0.038% but also provides nearly the same TPR (*i.e.* 99.78%). Therefore, we recommend using the new addresses approach with the new adjusted threshold value of 10.

5.4   Optimal Alias Detection Parameters

Based on the presented experiments, we conclude that the optimal alias detection parameters are:

- Rate limiting individual subnets at 10 pps/subnet
- Performing two scan repetitions
- Setting alias labeling threshold to 10
- Generating new random addresses per subnet for each scan repetition

To demonstrate that our recommended dealiasing parameters result in significant improvements to the dealiasing accuracy, we experiment with our recommended configurations versus a diametric configuration: dealiasing without scan repetition in shuffled address scan order, sending 1 probe packet per address at 10 pps (chosen to minimize the potential impact of packet loss and rate limit).

Figure 7d is a ROC curve showing the TPR and FPR under both configurations. We observe that with two repetitions, our optimized configuration curve stays above the diametric configuration curve for all the threshold values. However, for thresholds 11–16, the FPR of the diametric configuration stays behind the optimal values, due to performing two repetitions and subnet-based rate-limiting. Noting the significant impact of TPR in IPv6 studies, we argue that this difference is affordable, considering that the optimal configuration reduces the misclassified aliases by 73.3% at the complete responsiveness threshold. For the recommended threshold value of 10 active subprefixes, the HCD configurations improve the accuracy by 76.2%. In addition, at this threshold, the diametric and the HCD configurations show different FPRs of 0.025% and 0.042%, respectively.

Therefore, we find that performing dealiasing based on the traditional experiment configurations at slow scan rates does not always yield better accuracy, while carefully selecting dealiasing parameters and considering different labeling threshold values result in a substantial increase in the dealiasing performance.

5.5   Impact of Aliasing Accuracy on TGAs

Modern IPv6 host discovery uses TGA models to generate *potentially* active targets. How a TGA generates these targets highly depends on what seed input data is provided to the model. To prevent generation within aliased regions, seed addresses are typically dealiased before being inputted to TGAs, which creates a direct dependency between dealiasing method parameters and generated targets. Therefore, in this section, we aim to show how small amounts of misclassified addresses (*i.e.* 3.8% as shown in Appendix A) can heavily impact the TGAs, causing them to find a significant number (in some cases the majority) of the active addresses from the aliased regions.

In other words, we evaluate the effects of different IPv6 dealiasing method parameters on IPv6 host discovery by experimenting with state-of-the-art TGAs that are actively being used by the IPv6Hitlist to generate the Hitlist targets, and to trigger alias detection on the prefixes that are shared across multiple active targets [79]. Applying different seed dealiasing methods, we generate addresses with these models, and explore how many are aliased (labeled by the HCD). The models we deploy are: 1) IPv6Hitlist's version of 6Tree [44], 2) 6Graph [77], and 3) 6VecLM [18].

We start with filtering 0.3% of the 1.1M addresses, which we used in constructing the HCD, that cannot be labeled by the IPv6Hitlist dataset. Then, we use the remaining addresses to produce two dealiased datasets: 1) Non-aliased addresses as labeled by the IPv6Hitlist, 2) Non-aliased addresses as labeled by the HCD. Both datasets share at least 95.7% of their addresses. Finally, we ran each TGA model two times, each time inputting only one of the dealiased datasets. We follow the prior work's address generation approach, keeping all the parameters at their default values [79], and set the generation budget to 100M for both 6Graph and 6Tree.

Table 4 shows the number of generated and aliased addresses, the number of identical addresses generated for both the HCD and Hitlist dealiased inputs, and the HCD coverage for each model. We note that the number of generated addresses and the analyses exclude the seed input addresses of each dataset to quantify a model's actual generative performance. We observe that 9.8M, 21.6M, and 3.1K addresses that 6Tree, 6Graph, and 6VecLM generated are shared among the two dealiased datasets, respectively.

For all generated addresses, we perform an offline alias classification by using the HCD. Since the HCD coverage is limited with its input set, the majority of candidates cannot be mapped to a region in the HCD. However, we argue that the unlabeled addresses have a negligible impact on our overall analysis. First, considering that the HCD is constructed from randomly chosen addresses, we expect it to generalize to other addresses. Second, for all model-dataset pairs except the 6Graph-Hitlist pair, the number of HCD-covered addresses is larger than the experiment hit rates, indicating that the HCD coverage would be sufficient to characterize most active addresses. Thus, we limit our analysis to the candidate addresses that can be HCD-labeled.

Although the two dealiased datasets are slightly different, the models generated significantly more aliased targets when using the IPv6Hitlist, resulting in 83x and 19x more targets in responsive aliased regions for 6Graph and 6VecLM, respectively. Also, 6Tree using the HCD only produced 18 active aliased targets

Table 4. The number of the generated addresses for each model-dataset pair in the TGA experiments, the HCD coverage, the generated aliased address population, and the aliased active targets population. §: The number of generated addresses excludes the seed addresses. †: 45 targets are produced. ‡: 18 responsive targets are present.

Model	# of Genenerated Targets§			Targets Present in the HCD		% of Aliased in Generated		% of Aliased Hits in All Hits	
	HCD	Hitlist	Common	HCD	Hitlist	HCD	Hitlist	HCD	Hitlist
6Graph [77]	99.6M	99.6M	21.6M	11.2%	16.9%	0.1%	6.2%	**0.87%**	72.61%
6Tree [44]	819.9M	285.4M	9.8M	1.0%	3.0%	0%†	0.2%	**0.0%**‡	32.57%
6VecLM [18]	53.5K	57.3K	3.1K	31.5%	40.2%	0.4%	6.8%	**2.13%**	40.89%

under a single subnet, whereas using the IPv6Hitlist generated 32.6% of active targets within aliases. Although the proportion of aliased targets to all generated addresses may seem small, these aliased addresses actually *do* have a drastic impact on IPv6 host discovery. As shown in Table 4, **between 32.6–72.6% of the active addresses found by the models are in aliased regions, when using the IPv6Hitlist for dealiasing seeds. In comparison, when dealiasing with the HCD, only 0.9–2.13% of active addresses are in aliases.** Thus, even a few inaccuracies in input dealiasing heavily impact the IPv6 host discovery process, motivating the need for accurate dealiasing methods.

6 Conclusion

IPv6 aliasing is a common yet challenging problem that confounds IPv6 Internet scanning and measurements. In this work, we found that existing methods detected aliases at largely incorrect granularities, and these inaccuracies are distributed across ASes. We uncovered that almost 53% of aliases exist at less specific levels than /64, unlike previously observed /64 dominance. Further, we confirmed that alias inconsistencies exist in practice, where aliased prefixes contain non-aliased subprefixes. These findings demonstrate the care with which IPv6 aliases must be handled.

To aid future measurements, we identified parameter recommendations for the alias method used in prior work (random probing of the 16 sub-prefixes of a subnet): probing subnets at 10 pps/subnet, repeat probing addresses twice while generating new addresses for each repetition, and using a 62.5% threshold for labeling a subnet as aliased. Compared to a diametric configuration, we showed that this configuration reduced missed aliases by 76.2%.

We also evaluated the impact of alias classification accuracy on TGAs, observing that even a few misclassified aliases in TGA input seeds can cause some TGAs to generate a majority (over 70%) of active addresses within aliases, compared to less than 1% of generated active addresses within aliases when the input aliases are correctly labeled. This stark result illustrates the importance of accurate alias detection.

Future work can expand upon our initial exploration of dealiasing parameters for different use cases, such as performing real-time alias detection. As online TGA models, like 6Sense, have been shown to be more effective, the need for an efficient and accurate real-time alias detection is growing [74]. Real-time alias detection requires novel aliasing strategies and parameters to be explored, like the optimal number of addresses to probe per subnet, and whether different configurations should be applied per prefix size and AS. These new methods can also be used to explore the services distinctively run by the aliased subnets. Ultimately, this study serves to lay the foundation for further improvements in IPv6 alias detection, in support of broader IPv6 measurements.

A   Overlap with the IPv6Hitlist

In order to understand the similarities and differences between the labels provided by the HCD and the IPv6Hitlist, we compare our HCD labeling of the input sample of 1.1M addresses to that from using the IPv6Hitlist Aliased Prefixes dataset. Even though 0.3% of the addresses were not in the IPv6Hitlist dataset, precluding comparison, roughly 95.9% of the addresses are labeled identically in both datasets, and 3.8% had conflicting labels in the IPv6Hitlist dataset. These contradictory labels consist of 1% of the non-aliased IPs, and 2.8% of the aliased IPs in the HCD. We further explore how this minor misidentification results in TGAs generating significantly more aliased addresses in Sect. 5.5.

Table 5. Comparison of aliased or non-aliased prefix sizes for IPs with identical aliasing labels in both the HCD and the IPv6Hitlist. †: The IPv6Hitlist dataset mapped two non-aliased IPs to a more specific subnet.

	HCD Match Less Spec.	HCD Match Same	HCD Match More Spec.
Hit. & HCD Aliased	4.4%	95.5%	0.1%
Hit. & HCD Non-Aliased	0.0%†	17.9%	82.1%

Although the alias labeling across the two datasets is highly consistent, the size of detected aliases is not, as shown in Table 5. We see that both datasets have the same prefix size for 79.4% of aliased addresses and 16.7% of non-aliased addresses. Interestingly, 4.4% of the aliased addresses are mapped to a less-specific prefix granularity in our HCD, indicating that the aliased subnet is a larger region than inferred by the IPv6Hitlist dataset; also, accounting for 98% of the size mismatches for the aliased addresses. Moreover, 83.2% of the non-aliased addresses are mapped to a more specific prefix size in our HCD (*i.e.* /116), hinting that future online alias detection methodologies might benefit from starting to explore from more specific prefix sizes to label the addresses in non-aliased regions, resulting in more efficient measurements. However, we should note that one exception for such methodology is the inconsistent regions, which we explored as a phenomenon in Sect. 4.6.

B   Ethical Considerations

Due to the nature of our measurement work, we strongly recognize the importance of ethics in scanning studies. We uphold the ethical standards previously established in Belmont [8] and Menlo [4] reports. Probing of aliased subnets was done following the best practices of our community [22]. Namely, our scanning was conducted via a university network that had PTR records indicating the research nature of the machines. Each machine hosted an opt-out webpage. However, we have not received any requests to opt out during our study. Scans were randomized where appropriate, and all except full-Internet scans were rate-limited at no faster than 1K pps/subnet with a 10K pps cap. In addition, all data used in this study is from publicly available sources. No human subjects were involved in this research.

References

1. Albakour, T., Gasser, O., Smaragdakis, G.: Pushing alias resolution to the limit. In: ACM Internet Measurement Conference (IMC) (2023)
2. Alexa: Alexa top 1 million (2021). http://s3.amazonaws.com/alexa-static/top-1m.csv.zip. Accessed 2021
3. Ark: Ark IPv6 Topology Dataset (2024). https://catalog.caida.org/dataset/ipv6_allpref_topology
4. Bailey, M., Dittrich, D., Kenneally, E., Maughan, D.: The Menlo report. IEEE Secur. & Privacy (2012)
5. Bano, S., et al.: Scanning the Internet for liveness. In: ACM SIGCOMM (2018)
6. Beverly, R., Brinkmeyer, W., Luckie, M., Rohrer, J.P.: IPv6 alias resolution via induced fragmentation. In: Passive and Active Measurement (PAM). Springer, Cham (2013)
7. Beverly, R., Durairajan, R., Plonka, D., Rohrer, J.P.: In the IP of the beholder: strategies for active IPv6 topology discovery. In: ACM Internet Measurement Conference (IMC) (2018)
8. The National Commission for the Protection of Human Subjects of Biomedical and Behavioral Research: The Belmont report - ethical principles and guidelines for the protection of human subjects of research (1979). https://www.hhs.gov/ohrp/regulations-and-policy/belmont-report/read-the-belmont-report/index.html
9. Bloomquist, Z.: TLDR 2 - a continuously updated historical TLD records archive (2024). https://github.com/flotwig/TLDR-2

10. Borgolte, K., Hao, S., Fiebig, T., Vigna, G.: Enumerating active IPv6 hosts for large-scale security scans via DNSSEC-signed reverse zones. In: IEEE Symposium on Security and Privacy (S&P). IEEE (2018)
11. CAIDA: Inferred as to organization mapping dataset (2024). https://www.caida.org/catalog/datasets/as-organizations/
12. CAIDA: The IPv6 DNS names dataset (2024). https://www.caida.org/catalog/datasets/ipv6_dnsnames_dataset/
13. Centre, R.N.C.: IPv6 address allocation and assignment policy (2020). https://www.ripe.net/publications/docs/ripe-738
14. Centre, R.N.C.: Ripe atlas (2024). https://www.ripe.net/analyse/raw-data-sets
15. Cloudflare: Cloudflare radar (2024). https://radar.cloudflare.com/domains
16. Cui, T., Gou, G., Xiong, G.: 6GCVAE: gated convolutional variational autoencoder for IPv6 target generation. In: Lauw, H.W., Wong, R.C.-W., Ntoulas, A., Lim, E.-P., Ng, S.-K., Pan, S.J. (eds.) PAKDD 2020. LNCS (LNAI), vol. 12084, pp. 609–622. Springer, Cham (2020). https://doi.org/10.1007/978-3-030-47426-3_47
17. Cui, T., Gou, G., Xiong, G., Liu, C., Fu, P., Li, Z.: 6GAN: IPv6 multi-pattern target generation via generative adversarial nets with reinforcement learning. In: IEEE Conference on Computer Communications (INFOCOM). IEEE (2021)
18. Cui, T., Xiong, G., Gou, G., Shi, J., Xia, W.: 6vecLM: language modeling in vector space for IPv6 target generation. In: ECML PKDD 2020. Springer, Cham (2021)
19. Dhamdhere, A., Luckie, M., Huffaker, B., Claffy, K., Elmokashfi, A., Aben, E.: Measuring the deployment of IPv6: topology, routing and performance. In: ACM Internet Measurement Conference (IMC) (2012)
20. van Dijk, P.: Finding v6 hosts by efficiently mapping IP6.arpa (2012). https://7bits.nl/blog/posts/finding-v6-hosts-by-efficiently-mapping-ip6-arpa
21. Durumeric, Z., Adrian, D., Mirian, A., Bailey, M., Halderman, J.A.: A search engine backed by Internet-wide scanning. In: ACM SIGSAC Conference on Computer and Communications Security (CCS) (2015)
22. Durumeric, Z., Wustrow, E., Halderman, J.A.: ZMap: fast Internet-wide scanning and its security applications. In: USENIX Security Symposium (2013)
23. Eddy, W.: TCP SYN Flooding Attacks and Common Mitigations. RFC 4987 (2007). https://www.rfc-editor.org/info/rfc4987
24. Elmokashfi, A., Dhamdhere, A.: Revisiting BGP churn growth. ACM SIGCOMM (2014)
25. Fiebig, T., Borgolte, K., Hao, S., Kruegel, C., Vigna, G.: Something from nothing (there): collecting global ipv6 datasets from DNS. In: Passive and Active Measurement (PAM). Springer, Cham (2017)
26. Fiebig, T., Borgolte, K., Hao, S., Kruegel, C., Vigna, G., Feldmann, A.: In rDNS we trust: revisiting a common data-source's reliability. In: Passive and Active Measurement (PAM). Springer, Cham (2018)
27. Foremski, P., Plonka, D., Berger, A.: Entropy/IP: uncovering structure in IPv6 addresses. In: ACM Internet Measurement Conference (IMC) (2016)
28. Gasser, O.: ZMapv6: Internet scanner with ipv6 capabilities (2024). https://github.com/tumi8/zmap
29. Gasser, O., et al.: Clusters in the expanse: understanding and unbiasing ipv6 hitlists. In: ACM Internet Measurement Conference (IMC) (2018)
30. Gasser, O., Scheitle, Q., Gebhard, S., Carle, G.: Scanning the IPv6 Internet: towards a comprehensive hitlist. In: International Workshop on Traffic Monitoring and Analysis (TMA) (2016)
31. Gont, F., Chown, T.: Network Reconnaissance in IPv6 Networks. RFC 7707 (2016). https://www.rfc-editor.org/info/rfc7707

32. Google: Google public DNS (2024). https://dns.google/
33. Google: IPv6 statistics (2024). https://www.google.com/intl/en/ipv6/statistics.html
34. Guo, H., Heidemann, J.: Detecting ICMP rate limiting in the Internet. In: Passive and Active Measurement (PAM). Springer, Cham (2018)
35. Holzbauer, F., Maier, M., Ullrich, J.: Destination reachable: what ICMPv6 error messages reveal about their sources. In: ACM Internet Measurement Conference (IMC) (2024)
36. Hou, B., Cai, Z., Wu, K., Su, J., Xiong, Y.: 6Hit: a reinforcement learning-based approach to target generation for Internet-wide IPv6 scanning. In: IEEE Conference on Computer Communications (INFOCOM). IEEE (2021)
37. Hou, B., Cai, Z., Wu, K., Yang, T., Zhou, T.: 6scan: a high-efficiency dynamic Internet-wide IPv6 scanner with regional encoding. IEEE/ACM Trans. Netw. (2023)
38. Hou, B., Cai, Z., Wu, K., Yang, T., Zhou, T.: Search in the expanse: towards active and global IPv6 hitlists. In: IEEE Conference on Computer Communications (INFOCOM) (2023)
39. Hsu, A., Li, F., Pearce, P.: Fiat lux: illuminating IPv6 apportionment with different datasets. In: ACM on Measurement and Analysis of Computing Systems (POMACS) (2023)
40. Hsu, A., Li, F., Pearce, P., Gasser, O.: A first look at nat64 deployment in-the-wild. In: Passive and Active Network Measurement (PAM) (2024)
41. Izhikevich, L., et al.: ZDNS: a fast DNS toolkit for Internet measurement. In: ACM Internet Measurement Conference (IMC) (2022)
42. Li, X., Liu, B., Zheng, X., Duan, H., Li, Q., Huang, Y.: Fast IPv6 network periphery discovery and security implications. In: IEEE/IFIP Dependable Systems and Networks (DSN) (2021)
43. Liu, M., et al.: FBAR: an effective method for resolving large-scale IPv6 aliases. Int. J. Commun. Syst. **36**(18) (2023)
44. Liu, Z., Xiong, Y., Liu, X., Xie, W., Zhu, P.: 6Tree: efficient dynamic discovery of active addresses in the IPv6 address space. Comput. Netw. (2019)
45. Luckie, M.: Scamper: a scalable and extensible packet prober for active measurement of the Internet. In: ACM SIGCOMM Internet Measurement Conference (IMC) (2010)
46. Luckie, M., Beverly, R., Brinkmeyer, W., Claffy, K.: Speedtrap: Internet-scale IPv6 alias resolution. In: ACM Internet Measurement Conference (IMC) (2013)
47. Majestic: Majestic million (2024). https://majestic.com/reports/majestic-million
48. Majkowski, M.: Abusing Linux's firewall: the hack that allowed us to build Spectrum (2018). https://blog.cloudflare.com/how-we-built-spectrum/
49. Marchetta, P., Persico, V., Pescapé, A.: Pythia: yet another active probing technique for alias resolution. In: ACM Conference on Emerging Networking Experiments and Technologies (CoNEXT) (2013)
50. Marder, A.: Apple: alias pruning by path length estimation. In: Passive and Active Measurement (PAM). Springer, Cham (2020)
51. Murdock, A., Li, F., Bramsen, P., Durumeric, Z., Paxson, V.: 6Gen - target generation for Internet-wide IPv6 scanning. In: ACM Internet Measurement Conference (IMC) (2017)
52. NCC, R.: IPmap (2024). https://ipmap.ripe.net/
53. NCC, R.: Routing information service (RIS) (2024). https://www.ripe.net/analyse/internet-measurements/routing-information-service-ris/

54. Padmanabhan, R., Li, Z., Levin, D., Spring, N.: UAV6: alias resolution in IPv6 using unused addresses. In: Passive and Active Measurement (PAM). Springer, Cham (2015)
55. Pochat, V.L., Van Goethem, T., Tajalizadehkhoob, S., Korczyński, M., Joosen, W.: Tranco: a research-oriented top sites ranking hardened against manipulation. In: Network and Distributed System Security Symposium (NDSS) (2018)
56. Popoviciu, C., Hahn, C., Bonness, O., de Velde, G.V., Chown, T.: IPv6 Unicast Address Assignment Considerations. RFC 5375 (2008). https://www.rfc-editor.org/info/rfc5375
57. Rapid7: Project sonar (2013). https://www.rapid7.com/research/project-sonar/
58. Rapid7: Rapid7 forward DNS (2023). https://opendata.rapid7.com/sonar.fdns_v2/
59. RIPE: Best current operational practice for operators: Ipv6 prefix assignment for end-users - persistent vs non-persistent, and what size to choose (2023). https://www.ripe.net/publications/docs/ripe-690
60. Roberts, R., Huston, G., Narten, D.T.: IPv6 Address Assignment to End Sites. RFC 6177 (2011). https://www.rfc-editor.org/info/rfc6177
61. Rye, E., Levin, D.: IPv6 hitlists at scale: be careful what you wish for. In: ACM SIGCOMM (2023)
62. Schindler, S., Schnor, B., Kiertscher, S., Scheffler, T., Zack, E.: Honeydv6: a low-interaction IPv6 honeypot. In: International Conference on Security and Cryptography (SECRYPT) (2013)
63. Service, I.H.: Understanding and unbiasing IPv6 hitlists (2024). https://ipv6hitlist.github.io/
64. Song, G., et al.: Towards the construction of global IPv6 hitlist and efficient probing of IPv6 address space. In: IEEE/ACM International Symposium on Quality of Service (IWQoS). IEEE (2020)
65. Song, G., et al.: AddrMiner: a comprehensive global active IPv6 address discovery system. In: USENIX Annual Technical Conference (USENIX ATC) (2022)
66. Song, G., et al.: DET: enabling efficient probing of IPv6 active addresses. IEEE/ACM Trans. Netw. (2022)
67. Spamhaus: The spamhaus project (2024). https://www.spamhaus.org
68. Strowes, S.D.: Bootstrapping active IPv6 measurement with IPv4 and public DNS. arXiv preprint arXiv:1710.08536 (2017)
69. Tao, Y., Hu, G., Hou, B., Cai, Z., Xia, J., Fong, C.C.: An alias resolution method based on delay sequence analysis. Comput. Mater. Continua **63**(3) (2020)
70. Ullrich, J., Kieseberg, P., Krombholz, K., Weippl, E.: On Reconnaissance with IPv6: a pattern-based scanning approach. In: International Conference on Availability, Reliability and Security. IEEE (2015)
71. Cisco umbrella popularity list (2024). http://s3-us-west-1.amazonaws.com/umbrella-static/index.html
72. Vermeulen, K., et al.: Alias resolution based on ICMP rate limiting. In: Passive and Active Measurement (PAM). Springer, Cham (2020)
73. Vyncke, E.: IPv6 over Social Networks. RFC 5514 (2009). https://www.rfc-editor.org/info/rfc5514
74. Williams, G., et al.: 6sense: Internet-wide ipv6 scanning and its security applications. In: USENIX Security Symposium (USENIX Security) (2024)
75. Xie, Q., et al.: Building an open, robust, and stable Voting-Based domain top list. In: USENIX Security Symposium (USENIX Security). USENIX Association (2022)

76. Yang, T., Cai, Z., Hou, B., Zhou, T.: 6forest: an ensemble learning-based app-roach to target generation for internet-wide ipv6 scanning. In: IEEE Conference on Computer Communications (INFOCOMM) (2022)
77. Yang, T., Hou, B., Cai, Z., Wu, K., Zhou, T., Wang, C.: 6graph: a graph-theoretic approach to address pattern mining for internet-wide ipv6 scanning. Comput. Netw. (2022)
78. Yeow, A.: Bitnodes API (2024). https://bitnodes.io/api/
79. Zirngibl, J., Steger, L., Sattler, P., Gasser, O., Carle, G.: Rusty clusters? Dusting an IPv6 research foundation. In: ACM Internet Measurement Conference (IMC) (2022)

Measurement Platforms

Marionette Measurement: Measurement Support Under the PacketLab Model

Tzu-Bin Yan[1]([✉])(iD), Zesen Zhang[2](iD), Bradley Huffaker[2,3](iD), Ricky Mok[2,3](iD),
kc claffy[2,3](iD), and Kirill Levchenko[1](iD)

[1] UIUC, Urbana, IL 61801, USA
{tbyan2,klevchen}@illinois.edu
[2] UC San Diego, La Jolla, CA 92093, USA
zez003@eng.ucsd.edu
[3] CAIDA, La Jolla, CA 92093, USA
{bradley,cskpmok,kc}@caida.org

Abstract. The PacketLab Internet measurement framework is designed
to facilitate vantage point (VP) sharing for active Internet measurements.
The core idea behind PacketLab is to have experimenters instruct remote
VPs to perform a series of monitored low-level network operations to conduct measurements, which would reduce costs and security concerns of
VP sharing. Despite these benefits, PacketLab users have to update their
existing tools to adapt to the new *measurement model*, where available
VP capabilities and the method of access differ from traditional models
such as shell access to VPs. This change in the measurement model introduces limitations in measurement feasibility that merit deeper analysis.
We undertook this analysis, based on a survey of recent Internet measurement studies, followed by a result accuracy evaluation of PacketLab
implementations of selected representative measurements. Our results
showed the PacketLab measurement model allows the implementation
of a major portion (40 out of 54 studies, 74%) of distributed active
measurements in relevant studies in our survey. Further evaluation also
showed that the PacketLab model not only accurately supports a diverse
set of measurements ranging from latency, throughput, network path, to
other non-timing data categories, but also measurement requiring precise spatial and temporal coordination. To assist with porting non-timing
data measurements to PacketLab, we also introduce a new porting tool,
`pktwrap`, which allows existing measurement executables to communicate
over PacketLab without modification.

Keywords: Internet Measurement · Vantage Point Sharing ·
PacketLab

1 Introduction

A large class of Internet measurements depends on having multiple vantage
points (VPs) in the network. In some cases, the location of VPs is an essential

C. Testart et al. (Eds.): PAM 2025, LNCS 15567, pp. 77–105, 2025.
https://doi.org/10.1007/978-3-031-85960-1_4

element of the study (e.g. censorship), while others only require a geographically diverse set of locations (e.g. anycast). To gain access to desired VPs, researchers have deployed hardware—ranging from dongles to rack servers—at locations of interest to their study. The high cost of establishing and operating such infrastructure suggests amortizing this cost by *sharing VP access* across experiments and research groups.

Despite benefits, VP sharing is not without challenges. In the past, VP sharing has faced several key issues: compatibility, incentives, and trust [26]. The varying and often incompatible architectures of VPs have required experimenters to repeatedly port measurements to access appropriate VPs. Additionally, many sharing approaches necessitate VP operator assistance, such as deploying and vetting new measurements, which discourages operators from supporting more measurements due to limited resources. Lastly, VP operators who allow general use of their VPs (e.g. shell access) need to trust experimenters to behave responsibly, leading to access being granted only to a select group of trusted personnel. These challenges have thus hindered widespread, high measurement flexibility VP sharing in practice.

In an IMC '17 short paper, Levchenko *et al.* [26] proposed PacketLab, a novel Internet measurement framework. PacketLab presents a new direction in VP design for sharing—relocating almost all measurement (control) logic away from the VP and instead providing experimenters with an interface to the VP network access. Under PacketLab, experimenters use their own machines as *experiment controllers* that communicate with *measurement endpoints*, where the endpoint functions similarly to a VPN server by forwarding traffic (Fig. 1). This VPN-like sharing approach contrasts with existing approaches, where most measurement logic resides on VPs, keeping PacketLab endpoints lightweight and simple. Levchenko *et al.* argued that this simplicity allows VP operators to more easily contribute PacketLab VPs. Such an interface approach also enables operators to support new measurements without incurring extra costs beyond maintaining the existing static interface.

In addition to exporting a lightweight interface, PacketLab offers flexible access control mechanisms to address VP operator security concerns. These mechanisms allow operators to define endpoint usage policies as monitors and ensure compliance by monitoring controller actions. By reducing the cost of adoption, maintenance, and security for VP operators, PacketLab aims to make VP sharing more accessible, which would, in turn, lower the measurement porting costs for experimenters due to the increasing availability of PacketLab endpoints and the interface approach allowing easy porting across endpoints. Finally, to enhance measurement flexibility, PacketLab endpoints support scheduling packets for future transmission and send back timestamps for all sent and received packets. These features enable many kinds of timing-based network measurements that would otherwise be impossible to do accurately using a VPN server.

Central to the PacketLab framework is the novel *measurement model* that it introduces. By measurement model, we mean the set of VP capabilities for performing Internet measurements and the method to access the capabilities, which characterizes the way of performing Internet measurements under vari-

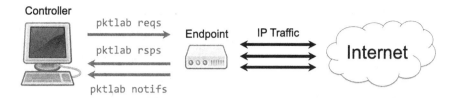

Fig. 1. Controller-endpoint interacton under the PacketLab model.

ous setups. The *PacketLab measurement model* exports remote VP capabilities through a set of requests resembling BSD socket operations along with notifications to provide endpoint operation information across the network (Sect. 2.1). This model differs from the traditional *native model* where experimenters have access to VP hardware capabilities (e.g. via shell) to implement and conduct measurements directly on the VP.

In our view, the PacketLab proposal presumes what we call the *PacketLab assumption*:

◆ **PacketLab Assumption.** The PacketLab measurement model can support a significant fraction of—perhaps even most—distributed active measurements of interest to the Internet measurement community.

where we define *supporting a measurement under a measurement model* to be:

◆ **Model Measurement Support.** It is possible to develop an implementation of the measurement under the model (using the model-exported VP capabilities via the model-specified method of access) s.t. the implementation produces accurate measurement results.

Such an assumption is core to the applicability of the PacketLab framework, as despite the advantage of facilitating VP sharing, a substantially restricted measurement model supporting few measurements of interest benefits little. The assumption stands unsubstantiated in the original proposal, which is concerning as under the PacketLab model there is an inevitable delay between when the experimenter sees traffic and when the VP sees traffic, potentially preventing sufficiently timely reactions by the experimenter. In addition, the set of exported capabilities in the PacketLab model is a strict subset of those in the native model, indicating potential missing capabilities for some measurements. Without further analyses, it remains uncertain the extent to which these two limitations would affect measurement support, and in turn, whether the PacketLab assumption holds true.

The aim of this work is a first attempt to answer the research question of whether the PacketLab assumption is valid. We took an analytical and empirical approach in our investigation. We surveyed 284 measurement studies published in recent top networking and measurement conferences—SIGCOMM, IMC, PAM, CoNEXT, and TMA—to identify distributed active measurements relevant to the Internet measurement community. Our survey identified 54 studies that conducted distributed active measurements. As an initial assessment, we examined the methodology for each study to determine whether their distributed active measurements could, in principle, be *implemented* under the PacketLab model based on criteria derived from the two inherent limitations of the model. We determined that such measurements in 40 of the 54 studies (74%) could be implemented under the model.

We then implemented selected measurements under the PacketLab model using the published framework implementation [60,64]. We directly ported most measurements to PacketLab, while for the web content retrieval measurement, we developed a new general-purpose tool for porting non-timing data measurements: pktwrap. pktwrap enables existing measurement executables to communicate over PacketLab endpoints without modification. Using pktwrap, we were able to port with minimal effort the web content retrieval measurement by leveraging curl's logic to perform HTTP and TLS operations, which demonstrates pktwrap's potential to facilitate HTTP(S) and other non-timing data measurements over PacketLab.

We then performed result accuracy evaluation using the measurement implementations. As our experiments were directly conducted on the Internet, where measurement ground truth is unavailable, we define accuracy based on the results of a native implementation of the same measurement. The intuition is that because the native-implementation approach is the traditional and common way to collect measurement data, so long as the PacketLab implementation yields results close to the native implementation, the PacketLab implementation provides sufficiently accurate data.

Overall, we found that our PacketLab implementations yielded accurate results in most cases for four measurements: traceroute, TCP pipe saturation, web content retrieval, and MIDAR (Monotonic ID-based Alias Resolution [20]).[1] We found results from our PacketLab implementations were less than 5.8% off in mean for throughput and hop round-trip time, and had Jaccard indices no less than 0.92 for network path, HTTPS response bodies, and IP address alias pairs (MIDAR) when comparing with results given by native implementations of the same measurement. Such accuracy results combined with our survey outcome serve as strong evidence supporting the PacketLab assumption.

2 Background

PacketLab is an Internet measurement framework proposed to facilitate Internet measurement VP sharing. An implementation of the framework is available [60, 64]. Here, we summarize elements relevant to the current work, as well as the

---

[1] We also evaluated a fifth measurement, the send gap microbenchmark, to test the model's ability to achieve arbitrary packet spacing, though we omit the details here due to space constraints. In summary, our PacketLab implementation matched the performance of the native implementation down to 7.3 μs packet spacing. We invite interested readers to request further details from the authors.

benefits PacketLab brings to VP sharing compared to existing approaches to motivate this study. We refer readers to the original proposal and project website [26, 60] for further details.

2.1 The PacketLab Framework and Model

The core idea behind PacketLab is to move almost all measurement logic for a distributed active measurement from the endpoint that sends packets to a separate host operated by the experimenter, turning the endpoint into something like an enhanced VPN server. To perform a measurement in PacketLab, an experiment controller that implements the measurement logic sends a measurement endpoint requests to open a socket, send packets, and so on, where the endpoint serves the requests (Fig. 1). The set of requests mostly mimics the BSD socket API, with one notable difference: the send request (nsend) takes in a schedule-send time parameter where the controller can request the send to happen at some later specific time. An endpoint may also send asynchronous notifications to the controller.[2] These are used to deliver received network data as well as timestamps for network data receive time and queued data send time to the controller. These asynchronous notifications can be buffered at the endpoint up to available memory, configurable via separate requests. Table 1 lists the core set of network requests and notifications defined in the PacketLab framework. These requests and available information propagated from the endpoint back to the controller characterize the VP capabilities available to perform measurements, which combined with their over-the-network method of access defines the PacketLab measurement model.

2.2 PacketLab Advantages over Other Sharing Approaches

A main advantage of PacketLab over existing VP sharing approaches, as highlighted in the original proposal, is its low adoption cost on existing VPs, achieved by maintaining a simple and lightweight endpoint design.

Another main advantage PacketLab offers over existing approaches is its ability to reduce VP operator costs during operation, particularly in supporting new measurements at low cost and preventing abuse, while at the same time maintaining some level of measurement flexibility for experimenters. A key way PacketLab achieves this cost reduction is by minimizing operator involvement in the sharing process. Many existing measurement platforms, such as CAIDA Ark [3], M-Lab [30], FCC MBA [15], BISmark [59], and Dasu [52], require VP operator to vet and/or deploy any custom measurements, which limits the support for additional measurements due to budget constraints. In contrast, supporting new measurements within PacketLab does not require operator involvement, as experimenters rely on the same VP interface for any new measurement, with existing endpoint usage policies still enforced.

---

[2] Asynchronous notification is a modification to the framework, which supersedes npoll requests in the original proposal.

Table 1. Excerpt of defined controller-endpoint messages in the PacketLab framework

---

`nopen(sktid,prfram,proto,rbufsz,locaddr,...)`

Open a socket on the endpoint with the given protocol family (IPv4 or IPv6) and protocol (UDP, TCP, or raw IP).

`nsend(sktid,prfram,proto,sndtime,tag,...,data)`

Schedule data to be sent at some specified time (0 sends immediately). Result (including actual endpoint send time) is returned in `ntag` notifications containing the same `tag` identifier.

`ncap(sktid,prfam,proto,endtime,recvfilter)`

Capture packets from a raw IP socket until some specified time. The `recvfilter` parameter is a BPF program that defines which packets to receive.

`nclose(sktid)`

Close a socket on the endpoint.

`ndata(sktid,prfram,proto,rcvtime,...,data)`

Asynchronous notification sent by endpoint (to controller) with received data and timestamp.

`ntag(sktid,tag,time,...)`

Asynchronous notification sent by endpoint with send timestamp (see `nsend`).

Alternatively, measurement platforms like the PlanetLab testbed [55] and EdgeNet [5], which provided shell access to VPs, also reduced VP operator involvement by granting experimenters significant freedom. However, these platforms rely heavily on trust that experimenters will comply with the acceptable use policies [13] or simply behave responsibly. Scriptroute [56] similarly minimized operator involvement by allowing unvetted measurement script execution on VPs. They also supported limited VP security policy specifications, such as rate limiting and packet field checks, to address security concerns. In comparison, PacketLab enables operators to actively prevent abuse by supporting endpoint monitors that could enforce more complex, stateful endpoint usage policies.

Another common approach to reducing VP operator costs is to limit VPs to a static set of vetted, rate-limited measurements, as seen in platforms like RIPE Atlas [49], perfSONAR [16], and others [22,39]. This approach minimizes both operator involvement and security concerns, and has led to widespread adoption in some cases [42,50]. Nevertheless, it comes at the cost of low measurement flexibility. PacketLab offers greater flexibility by allowing experimenters to create arbitrary measurements using PacketLab requests. However, the extent of PacketLab's capability to support measurements relevant to the Internet measurement community has not been explored in prior work, which we address in this study.

3   Methodology

The PacketLab assumption is that the PacketLab model can effectively support the deployment of a significant fraction of distributed active measurements. A natural way to validate this assumption would be to implement such measurements and evaluate the implementations' ability to yield accurate measurement results in experiments. Accordingly, our method has two phases: (1) a survey to identify prevalent measurements and (2) an implementation evaluation of selected measurements either commonly used in the surveyed studies or of special characteristics.

3.1   Internet Measurement Literature Survey

Our first phase requires identifying the set of measurements to use to test the PacketLab assumption. The difficulty we face is the sheer number and diversity of distributed active measurements performed throughout the years by the Internet measurement community; there are simply too many measurements for us to evaluate given limited resources and time. We addressed this problem by focusing on measurements that are more relevant to the community, which we argue are measurements more frequently performed in recent measurement studies. Accordingly, we surveyed recent editions of top networking and measurement conferences—SIGCOMM, IMC, PAM, CoNEXT, and TMA. We employed a twofold strategy to enhance the diversity of measurement studies: breadth, by covering the most recent editions of the top conferences to capture diversity across venues, and depth, by examining editions of SIGCOMM and IMC since 2020 to identify long-standing measurement trends over time.

During our survey, we first manually identified studies that conducted one or more distributed active measurement experiments, which we define as:

◆ A data collection process involving orchestration of one or more active measurements at one or more VPs, and where the collected data are VP location sensitive.

These studies would benefit the most from easier access to distributed VPs, which is the primary motivation for PacketLab. We determined data *location sensitivity* by applying one of the following two criteria:

◆ The study stated, explicitly or implicitly (by using multiple distributed VPs), that the data collected differ or could differ based on VP locations.
◆ The experiment contained an Internet-wide HTTP/HTTPS/SSH service scan, which Wan *et al.* [63] found varies based on VP locations.

For studies that performed distributed active measurement experiments, we further manually examined the measurements in the experiments as an initial assessment to determine if they are *implementable* under PacketLab by requiring both criteria:

♦ **IMPL1.** The measurement does not require timely reactions (less than one controller-endpoint RTT reaction time) to endpoint events (e.g., data reception).

♦ **IMPL2.** The measurement does not require VP capabilities not exported by the PacketLab model (Sect. 2.1).

We then categorized the measurements in the experiments based on measured metric type and selected representative measurements covering all major categories for evaluation: *traceroute* (measuring hop RTT and network path), *TCP pipe saturation* (measuring TCP throughput), and *web content retrieval* (measuring HTTPS response). We also included another measurement based on the special characteristic of requiring VP coordination: *MIDAR* [20] (measuring IP address alias pairs). Section 4 summarizes our survey results regarding the prevalence of distributed active measurements, study measurement implementability, observed major measurement categories, and representative measurement selection.

Cross-Validation. Our study labeling process was initially performed by the first author only. To reduce human bias, we had a separate author independently verify these results using the same criteria. The two authors agreed on the 54 distributed active measurement experiment studies but had four disagreements on implementability labeling. To be conservative, our implementability result in Sect. 4 is an intersection of results by both authors, where we only report a study as implementable when both authors reported it implementable.

3.2   Result Accuracy Evaluation

After selecting the representative measurements, the next step was to evaluate result accuracy of the chosen measurements. To ensure a realistic testing environment, we performed our experiments directly over the Internet using globally distributed VPs. Such a setup meant that we could not obtain the underlying measurement ground truth. We overcame this issue by performing *native implementation result comparison*: we compared the results of a native implementation and a PacketLab implementation of the same measurement. A close match between the two would suggest that the PacketLab implementation produces results *congruent* with its native counterpart, which is the traditional and common way to collect measurement data. We used the following *congruence criteria* to determine if the implementation results were sufficiently close.

Numerical Results. For traceroute hop RTT and TCP throughput, we devised two congruence criteria. Denoting the sample mean of the PacketLab-implementation data to be $\bar{x}_{PL}$, and the sample mean of the native-implementation data to be $\bar{x}_{NT}$, our two criteria are as follows:

♦ **C1.** Over all samples, $|1 - \frac{\bar{x}_{PL}}{\bar{x}_{NT}}| \leq c$ where $c \geq 0$ is some small constant specifying the allowed error margin between implementations based on criteria in past works.

◆ **C2.** Over all samples, we cannot find statistical significance for a two-sample Kolmogorov-Smirnov (KS) test with significance level $\alpha = 0.05$ between the PacketLab and native results.

Our C1 criterion captures the common approach in measurement studies that tolerates result deviation below a small threshold across methods for practical purposes. For latency measurements, Chhabra *et al.* [8] validated their DoH latency measurement method by comparing the median of their VPN-based method results with results collected by directly performing DoH resolution at the VP. They reported that their method result medians were off by no more than 10 ms for all test cases, based on which they claimed high consistency and, thus, validity. Translating their reported absolute errors to relative errors, in the worst case their medians were off by approximately 10.6% from direct measurements. We therefore used *10%* as the c for latency measurements. For throughput measurements, MacMillan *et al.* [28] showed that major speedtest implementations—Ookla [38] and M-Lab NDT7 [31]—gave increasingly deviating throughput results when increasing client-server RTT. Such findings combined with the accepted approach of combining throughput results for different speedtest implementations [33] suggest that the community is willing to tolerate the degree of throughput deviation caused by varying speedtest implementations. Accordingly, we used the reported relative error—*6%*[3]—by MacMillan *et al.* for the 100 ms RTT test case as the c for throughout measurements. We chose to use the reported relative error for the 100 ms RTT case as throughput results in Mok *et al.* [33] commonly had corresponding RTTs around 100 ms.

Our C2 criterion checks the similarity between two result distributions by checking if we could find any distinctive difference under one hundred samples. This criterion captures an arguably stronger idea of result congruence, requiring the whole distribution to appear close. We highlight that by no means do we intend to claim that the two distributions are the same if they satisfy C2, as the lack of statistical significance may be simply due to insufficient sample size.

Non-numerical Results. For traceroute hop addresses, HTTPS responses, and MIDAR alias pairs collected in our evaluation experiment, which are non-numerical measurement data, our congruence criterion is based on the well-known set similarity metric—Jaccard index[4]:

◆ **C3.** Over all samples, $j \geq 0.9$, where j is the Jaccard index for the two measurement result sets by the two implementations.

Ideally, we would select a Jaccard index threshold based on relevant criteria in prior work similar to C1, but we were unable to find such information. Therefore, we chose to use 0.9 as the threshold, as we believe a ≥ 0.9 Jaccard index is high enough for the two result sets to be considered congruent. To illustrate the strictness of C3, consider two traceroute results from the same source to the same destination. Suppose both identified 15 network hops, with the hop

---

[3] From MacMillan *et al.* Fig. 2b.

[4] Also known as intersection over union or IoU.

addresses only differing for one intermediate hop. Despite this minor difference, the Jaccard index for these two results would be only 0.875^5, already violating the C3 criterion.

Section 5 summarizes our experiment outcome.

4   Survey of Measurement Studies

We surveyed measurement studies presented at top networking and measurement conferences, including SIGCOMM (2020–2024), IMC (2020-2023), PAM (2024), CoNEXT (2023), and TMA (2024).[6] Due to space restrictions, we summarize our findings in the following text and omit the full list of identified distributed active measurement experiment studies and per-study labeling results. We invite interested readers to request the full list and labeling results from the authors. Starting with 284 papers, we identified 54 papers, about 1 in 5, that performed one or more distributed active measurement experiments. Further examining the 54 studies, we found 14 (26%) contained experiments that could not be implemented under PacketLab, mainly due to their need for non-exported VP computation capabilities (violating criterion IMPL2). In particular, many studies measured client-side computation performance such as browser page load time [19,21,23] and video conferencing performance [7,62]. Some studies also performed measurements requiring other non-exported capabilities such as access to physical layer information (mobile signal strength [35]) and OS congestion control algorithm modification [19]. A few studies were unimplementable because the measurements required timely endpoint event reaction (violating criterion IMPL1) for QUIC congestion control [21] and SSH honeypot interactive behavior [34].

For the 54 identified distributed active measurement experiment papers, we further categorized the measurements into four main categories: *latency, throughput, network path,* and *other non-timing data.*

Latency Measurement. Latency measurements capture time intervals between events, including query latency and network hop round-trip time. 19 of the 54 (35%) studies we surveyed included latency measurement, e.g., DNS query latency [8,21], hop latency [11,12,19,24,62] and ping latency [7,11,12,24,32,51,54]. Studies of web performance [19,21,23,32,61] frequently used browser native mechanisms or browser extensions to collect latency metrics such as page transit time, page load time, speed index, and first contentful print. Such browser-originated metrics usually also factor in VP local computational power due to the inclusion of delays in browser parsing and rendering web content.

Throughput Measurement. Throughput measurements capture the amount of data transferred in a unit of time. Nine of the 54 (17%) papers estimated

---

[5] 14 shared hops out of 16 distinct observed hops, computed using the same approach in Sect. 5.3.

[6] For SIGCOMM and CoNEXT, we only looked at the 21+7 works in the measurement/telemetry sessions for relevance.

throughput from VPs using two main methods: TCP pipe saturation [19,32, 33,35,62] and packet trace collection and inference [7]. TCP pipe saturation measurements were either performed using the HTTP protocol against public speedtest services such as LibreSpeed, Ookla Speedtest, Netflix Fast.com, M-Lab NDT, and Comcast Xfinity Speed Test [19,32,33,62] or via iPerf [19,35].

Network Path Measurement. Twelve of the 54 (22%) studies measured the network path taken by traffic, all using traceroute. Five of them also used the hop RTT of the traceroute output; as such, we also consider them to include latency measurement.

Other Non-timing Data Measurement. Most (38 of the 54, 70%) of the studies collected and analyzed non-path non-timing data retrieved over the network, such as DNS resource records [18,21,43,44] and web content [14,23,27,45,63].

Based on the observed measurement prevalence, we chose the *traceroute*, *TCP pipe saturation*, and *web content retrieval* measurements for further evaluation. Other than being popular methods used in a major portion of studies (traceroute: 12/54, 22%; TCP pipe saturation: 6/54, 11%; web content retrieval: 11/54, 20%), these three measurements cover all four of our measurement categories. Regarding measurement with special characteristics, we picked another extra measurement for evaluation: *MIDAR* [20], which requires VP coordination to spread probing load for improving efficiency and to perform synchronized VP actions for accurate data collection.

5   Implementation Evaluation

We performed implementation evaluation on the selected measurements. As described in Sect. 3.2, our analysis adopted criteria C1∼3 depending on the data characteristics. This section we describe our evaluation setup, including PacketLab and native implementation details, and result comparison findings.

5.1   Vantage Points

We deployed 6 VPs for our experiments, aiming to maximize geographic and network diversity. One VP was a local residential fiber connection in the same metro area as UIUC. The provider advertised the connection as 250 Mbps in both directions. The hardware machine was an Intel NUC7i7BNH, 2 cores (4 threads) at 3.5 GHz, 32 GB RAM, with a 1 Gb Ethernet interface, running Ubuntu 22.04 with Linux kernel 5.15.0. Five VPs were `t2-medium` AWS VM instances (2 vCPUs, 4 GB RAM, network performance class "Low to Moderate") running Ubuntu 22.04 with Linux kernel 6.2.0, located in the following data centers: `us-west-2` (Oregon), `ap-northeast-1` (Tokyo), `ca-central-1` (Montréal), `eu-central-1` (Frankfurt), and `sa-east-1` (São Paulo). We deployed the PacketLab endpoint daemon in the published framework implementation on these VPs to run our PacketLab implementations of the measurements. For native implementations, we ran them as a native OS process directly on the VPs.

5.2   TCP Pipe Saturation

Our first experiment tested model support for the throughput measurement, TCP pipe saturation, used by 6 of the 54 identified studies in our survey.

Overview. We conducted a TCP throughput measurement experiment between each of the 6 VPs and a test server located at UIUC. We transferred a 25 MiB payload of random bytes over a TCP connection from the VP to the test server (upload) and from the test server to the VP (download). We ignored the first 1 MiB of data to mitigate TCP slow start effects and measured the time to transfer the remaining 24 MiB. We implemented the measurement natively using the VP OS interface and in PacketLab using the published framework implementation. We ran the native and PacketLab implementations back-to-back in alternating order 100 times each, which we repeated for all VPs. This process yielded four sets of 100 TCP throughput results per VP (upload/PacketLab, upload/native, download/PacketLab, and download/native). We applied the C1∼2 criteria to evaluate the congruence between the two upload sets and the two download sets.

Native Implementation. Our native implementation consists of two programs: a client and a server, both written in C. The client program runs on the VPs and opens a TCP connection to the server. The server program runs on the test server and sends or receives 25 MiB random bytes as requested by the client, and reports upload statistics to the client. The receiver records the first timestamp t_0 and byte count b after receiving 1 MiB, and the second timestamp t_1 once it receives all 25 MiB. The throughput is then calculated, in bits per second, as $8 \times (25 \times 2^{20} - b)/(t_1 - t_0)$.

PacketLab Implementation. Our PacketLab implementation works with the native implementation server program by performing actions similar to the native implementation client program through the PacketLab endpoint. For the download measurement, the experiment controller disables **ndata** events (causing the endpoint to buffer all received data; see Table 1 for event description), schedules the endpoint to send a request to the server to request 25 MiB of data, and waits 10 s for the download to finish. The 10-second delay avoids link contention between download traffic to the VP and **ndata** messages from the VP to the controller. After waiting 10 s, the controller re-enables **ndata** events and receives the data from the endpoint. The received **ndata** events contain the data the endpoint received and a timestamp taken by the endpoint when **recv()** returned, signifying the receive time for the data. The controller uses these timestamps to calculate the download throughput after the first 1 MiB of data, in the same way as the native implementation.

To measure the upload throughput, the controller disables **ntag** (Table 1) events to avoid link contention between **ntag** messages and upload traffic. It then queues 25 MiB of data to be sent 10 s from the current time using **nsend** messages. Similar to **ndata**, the 10-second delay avoids link contention between

Table 2. Throughput and RTT measured using native and PacketLab implementations of the TCP pipe saturation (throughput) and traceroute (RTT) measurements. The *VP* column shows the vantage point/endpoint. The remainder of the table shows three columns: download throughput (*DL Tput*), upload throughput (*UL Tput*), and *RTT*. The *NT* subcolumn shows the sample mean measured using the native implementation. The *PL err.* subcolumn shows the difference between the PacketLab and the native sample mean in absolute and relative terms. The *C1* subcolumn shows the C1 criterion (relative difference between the PacketLab and native sample mean $\leq 6\%$ for throughput and $\leq 10\%$ for RTT) satisfaction for the case, where a $\bullet$ indicates satisfaction and a $\circ$ otherwise. For all measurements $n = 100$. **We found that the throughput and RTT results given by both implementations of the TCP pipe saturation and traceroute measurements are similar for all VP cases, satisfying congruence criterion C1.**

VP	DL Tput (Mibps)			UL Tput (Mibps)			RTT (ms)		
	NT	*PL err.*	*C1*	*NT*	*PL err.*	*C1*	*NT*	*PL err.*	*C1*
Local res. fiber	203.0	+1.0 (+0.5%)	$\bullet$	237.6	−0.9 (−0.4%)	$\bullet$	17.3	−0.9 (−5.4%)	$\bullet$
AWS Frankfurt	35.3	−0.8 (−2.3%)	$\bullet$	74.1	−2.8 (−3.8%)	$\bullet$	108.1	−0.1 (−0.1%)	$\bullet$
AWS São Paulo	32.0	−0.3 (−0.9%)	$\bullet$	77.2	−4.4 (−5.7%)	$\bullet$	138.8	−0.0 (−0.0%)	$\bullet$
AWS Montréal	75.4	−1.1 (−1.4%)	$\bullet$	187.5	+0.4 (+0.2%)	$\bullet$	25.9	−0.0 (−0.1%)	$\bullet$
AWS Tokyo	31.0	−0.5 (−1.6%)	$\bullet$	68.5	−3.5 (−5.1%)	$\bullet$	167.1	−0.0 (−0.0%)	$\bullet$
AWS Oregon	64.7	+2.7 (+4.2%)	$\bullet$	109.6	+1.2 (+1.1%)	$\bullet$	59.5	−0.0 (−0.1%)	$\bullet$

the `nsend` messages and upload traffic. When the upload finishes, the test server sends the measured values b, t_0, and t_1 to the endpoint, and the endpoint forwards them to the controller for calculation.

Throughput Results. The throughput results given by both implementations were similar for all VPs (**Column *DL Tput* and *UL Tput*** in Table 2 and Fig. 2), satisfying congruence criteria C1 and C2. For C1, the relative errors between the PacketLab and native result sample means were always no larger than 5.8%, which falls below the C1 c for throughput (6%). For C2, the KS tests did not reveal significant differences between the two distributions (see Appendix A for test details), which is consistent with the similarity of the CDF curves per VP in Fig. 2. Based on the satisfaction of the C1 and C2 criteria, we consider the results given by the two implementations to be congruent with each other.

Takeaway. With our congruence results, we consider the PacketLab model to support the TCP pipe saturation measurement, and potentially other throughput measurements as well.

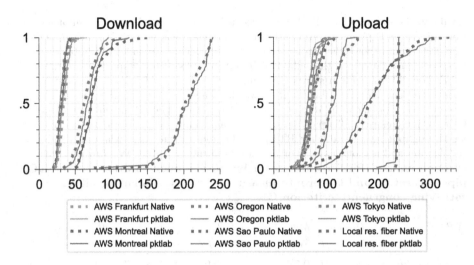

Fig. 2. Empirical CDFs of VP - test server TCP throughput (in Mibps) measured using native and PacketLab implementations of the TCP pipe saturation measurement. **We found that the throughput results given by both implementations have high distribution similarity for all VP upload and download cases, satisfying congruence criterion C2** (see Appendix A for C2 KS test details).

5.3   Traceroute

Our second experiment tested model support for the common hop latency and network path measurement, traceroute, used in 12 of the 54 distributed active measurement studies in our survey.

Overview. We conducted a traceroute measurement experiment from our 6 VPs to a test server at UIUC. We followed the well-known traceroute algorithm—sending TTL-limited UDP probes from the VP to the test server and receiving ICMP error responses for the probes, where we limited ourselves to one UDP probe per hop. We implemented the PacketLab version using the published framework implementation, while for the native implementation, we employed the popular version by Butskoy [1] for Linux. To minimize routing variation caused by packet content, we ensured that the probes of both implementations were as similar as possible, including the UDP ports and the packet payload. We could not craft the probes to be exactly the same. Notably, the kernel fills the packets' IP ID field (and consequently IP header checksum) with random numbers based on the kernel internal state for Butskoy's implementation, whereas in PacketLab the experiment controller decides the field. Similar to the TCP pipe saturation experiment, this experiment ran the two implementations back-to-back in alternating order for 100 times each on all VPs. The outcome of the experiment was two sets of traceroute data per VP. We compared the network path part of the measurement data with the C3 criterion and the hop RTT part of the measurement data with the C1 and C2 criteria.

Native Implementation. We used Butskoy's traceroute [1] (version 2.1.2) based on its wide availability in major Linux distributions. Butskoy's traceroute by default sends UDP probes with their destination ports starting from 33434 (incremented per probe sent) and source port selected by the kernel at random (`bind(0)`) per probe. To maximize the similarity between implementations, we used the `--sport` option to set the source port to 20556. We reduced the per-hop probe count from the default three to one (with `-q 1`), increased the maximum hop count from 30 to 64 (with `-m 64`), and disabled reverse DNS lookup (with `-n`). We left the remaining options to their default values. For each probe, Butskoy's traceroute obtains the send timestamp by calling `gettimeofday()` *immediately before* the probe `send()` call, while the kernel supplies the ICMP response receive timestamp via an accompanying `SO_TIMESTAMP` control message. The implementation then takes the difference between the send and receive timestamps as the hop RTT.

PacketLab Implementation. We implemented the traceroute algorithm under PacketLab by iteratively probing and receiving ICMP responses per hop. To transmit a probe, the experiment controller schedules one TTL-limited UDP probe to be sent immediately (with the `nsend` message) through an endpoint raw IP socket. We used a raw IP socket rather than a UDP socket on the endpoint for probing, as the PacketLab framework only supports TTL customization for raw IP sockets. We designed the probe to be as close as possible to Butskoy's implementation, where for IP ID we attempted to mimic the kernel's behavior by picking a value uniformly at random within the possible field range. To collect ICMP responses, the controller issues an `ncap` (Table 1) request with no end time to capture ICMP TTL exceeded and destination unreachable packets at the endpoint, which the endpoint then sends back to the controller via `ndata` notifications. For hop RTT, the controller gets probe send timestamps from the endpoint `ntag` notifications, which the endpoint daemon records *after* the `sendto()` call with `clock_gettime`. The ICMP response receive timestamp is available in the `ndata` message. For comparable accuracy with the native implementation, we also modified the endpoint daemon to use kernel receive timestamps (`SO_TIMESTAMPNS`) for this experiment. The controller then calculates the difference between the send and receive timestamps as the hop RTT.

Hop RTT Results. For our hop RTT results, we focused on the VP - test server (i.e. traceroute target) RTT as the representative set of hop RTT data for checking result accuracy, as such data are available for all VPs. Our hop RTT results are summarized in **column *RTT* in** Table 2 and Fig. 3. We found that our hop RTT results satisfied C1 of the congruence criteria, where the relative errors between the sample means were always smaller than 5.5% (recall C1 c for latency measurements is 10%). Notably, our results were in most cases off by no more than 0.2% of the native sample mean. However, our hop RTT results violated C2 for AWS Montréal, Tokyo, and Oregon (see Appendix A), meaning that hop RTT distributions were quite different between the two implementa-

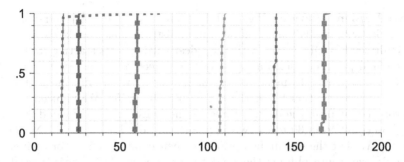

Fig. 3. Empirical CDFs of VP - test server RTT (in ms) measured using native and PacketLab implementations of the traceroute measurement. See Fig. 2 for plot legend. VP cases where we obtained KS test significance for the C2 criterion are highlighted to have thicker curves (see Appendix A for C2 KS test details). **We found that the RTT results fail to achieve high distribution similarity (violating congruence criterion C2) for AWS Montréal, Tokyo, and Oregon, despite seemingly close CDFs for all VP cases. We believe this phenomenon is due to the small variance in RTT distributions for most VPs, which allows small distribution deviation to be sufficient for KS test significance.**

tions. We believe the reason for the violation was due to the rather small variance in hop RTT results (less than 1 ms standard deviation for most VPs except local residential fiber), implying that even small deviation in result distribution could be sufficient for KS test significance. The small-variance phenomenon could also be observed via the hop RTT empirical CDFs in Fig. 3. We believe the root cause of the small deviation was the difference in send timestamp collection between the implementations: in Butskoy's traceroute, the send timestamp is collected *before* the probe `send` call, while in the PacketLab endpoint implementation, the send timestamp is collected *after* the `sendto` call. Nevertheless, with our hop RTT results satisfying C1, we consider the PacketLab and native implementation results congruent for practical purposes.

Network Path Results. For network path results, we chose to perform an aggregation over all runs per implementation and VP due to potential route variation over time [46]. We performed our aggregation by first taking a traceroute run outcome, which consists of a list of (hop count, hop address, hop RTT) tuples, and extracting all unique (hop count, hop address) tuples within that outcome. We then combined all unique (hop count, hop address) tuples from all 100 runs of an implementation on a VP into a set. By performing the (hop count, hop address)-tuple extraction and aggregation per implementation and VP, we had at the end two (hop count, hop address)-tuple sets per VP, one for each implementation. Our Jaccard index computations were then based on the two (hop count, hop address)-tuple sets per VP.

Overall, we found that our two implementations obtained highly similar network path results. For AWS VPs, our calculated Jaccard index was all 1, indicating an exact match of two sets. Although we did not have an exact match for the local residential fiber VP (the native implementation saw one extra unique address for hop 5, suspected due to infrequent route variations), the Jaccard index for the VP was still 0.93 (> 0.9), satisfying C3 and indicating that the network path results from both implementations were congruent.

Takeaway. Based on our congruent results for both hop RTT and network path, we consider the PacketLab model to support the traceroute measurement and potentially also other latency measurements for practical purposes.

5.4   Web Content Retrieval

Our third experiment tested model support for the common non-timing data measurement, web content retrieval, used in 11 of the 54 distributed active measurement studies in our survey.

Overview. We conducted a web content retrieval measurement experiment from our Tokyo and Oregon AWS VPs as well as the local residential fiber VP. We did not use all AWS VPs due to losing access to some (funding issues). Our experiment involved querying the default webpage for the top 1K websites on the Tranco list [25], generated on August 5, 2024.[7] During our experiment, we used the same measurement executable to collect data directly at the VP (native implementation) and indirectly at the controller server via the Packet-Lab endpoint by running the executable with our new non-timing data measurement porting tool `pktwrap` (PacketLab implementation). For these 1K websites, we intentionally queried the HTTPS default port (443) instead of HTTP (80), because HTTPS querying is a more complex test case involving TLS's multiround interactions. This approach allows us to stress test `pktwrap` in terms of complex interaction support, which would provide more evidence on the general applicability of the `pktwrap` tool to other non-timing data measurements. The experiment produced two sets of HTTPS response data per VP. We then compared the HTTPS response bodies for each website, excluding the HTTPS response headers to avoid skewing the results with session-specific values (e.g., `Date` and cookies). In cases where one or both implementations failed to retrieve the HTTPS response, we considered it a match only if both implementations failed. Finally, we calculated the Jaccard index based on the comparison between the two data sets to apply the C3 criterion.

Native Implementation. We used `curl` [10] (ver 8.7.1) for our native implementation. We primarily used the default options, except for the `-i` option, which instructs `curl` to include the HTTPS response headers in its output.

---

[7] Available at https://tranco-list.eu/list/7X79X.

PacketLab Implementation. For our PacketLab implementation, we developed a new general-purpose tool called `pktwrap` to port non-timing data measurements. `pktwrap` enables repurposing existing measurement executables as PacketLab controllers *without requiring modification or recompilation*. It does so by intercepting executable socket function calls and bridging them through the PacketLab endpoint—a process we term as "wrapping" the measurement executable. Specifically, `pktwrap` incorporates a libc shim that intercepts function calls such as `bind`, `connect`, and `send`-variants, and translates them into PacketLab requests (e.g., `nopen` and `nsend`; see Table 1 for request description) that perform similar, if not equivalent, actions on the endpoint. In addition, as certain functions require information from PacketLab asynchronous notifications (e.g., `recv`-variants need data from `ndata` messages), `pktwrap` further incorporates a background communication manager. This manager runs on a dedicated thread to process and buffer notifications, which the libc shim then retrieves to fulfill wrapped executable operations.

We prototyped `pktwrap` on Linux using the published framework implementation, and used it to wrap `curl` to query the HTTPS web server through the VP PacketLab endpoint, using the same executable options and arguments. This approach significantly accelerated our evaluation process by reusing `curl`'s logic for TLS and HTTP.

Web Content Results. We computed the Jaccard index for the two data sets by first constructing a (web domain, HTTPS response body)-tuple for each response in each data set, and then aggregating the tuples for each set. In cases of query failure, we stored a special identifier as the HTTPS response body that will only match with itself. This process produced two sets of (web domain, HTTPS response body)-tuples per VP, which we used to compute the Jaccard index by checking whether the tuples matched exactly (byte-by-byte for non-failure HTTPS response bodies) between the two sets. Our initial results gave relatively low Jaccard indices: 0.84 for both Oregon and Tokyo and 0.85 for local residential fiber, which is below our C3 criterion threshold of 0.9.

Upon further investigation, we discovered that many differing websites embedded session-specific values in their response bodies, despite being otherwise identical. To prevent these websites from skewing our results, we collected another set of HTTPS responses for the 1K websites per VP using only the native implementation. We then compared this with our previous native implementation responses to identify outlier websites that gave differing bodies across native implementation queries. After removing these outlier websites (84 for Oregon, 83 for Tokyo, and 79 for local residential fiber) from our Jaccard index computation, we found significantly improved results: 0.99 for Oregon and local residential fiber, and 0.98 for Tokyo, all above the 0.9 threshold. This agreement indicates that our results satisfy the C3 criterion, demonstrating that the web content retrieval results from both the native implementation (non-wrapped `curl`) and the PacketLab implementation (`pktwrap`-wrapped `curl`) were congruent.

Takeaway. Based on our congruence results, we consider the PacketLab model to support the web content retrieval measurement, and potentially also other non-timing data measurements.

When conducting the experiment on the local residential fiber VP, we also tested the PacketLab endpoint monitor mechanism, which we found could be leveraged to restrict controller access to selected website servers. Due to space limitations, we refer readers to Appendix B for further testing details.

5.5   MIDAR

Our final evaluated measurement was MIDAR for router alias resolution [20]. Our goal is to test the ability of PacketLab to support complex measurements where the experiment controller must coordinate actions from many global VPs.

Overview. MIDAR (Monotonic ID-based Alias Resolution) constructs a router-level Internet topology by inferring which IP (v4) addresses in observed traceroutes belong to the same physical router, i.e. are *IP address aliases*. The outcome of MIDAR is a set of IP address alias pairs. For the native implementation results, we directly used the alias data from CAIDA's Macroscopic Internet Topology Data Kit [4] collected in late February 2023 (labeled 2023-03 on the website) using a native implementation of MIDAR on 55 CAIDA Ark [3] nodes. We implemented MIDAR in PacketLab and ran the implementation in May 2023 using 25 of the 55 Ark nodes along with 30 `t2-medium` AWS instances spread across all available regions as PacketLab endpoints to match the VP count in the native MIDAR run. We did not use all 55 original Ark nodes due to software incompatibilities and node instabilities. We applied the C3 criterion to evaluate congruence between the two alias pair sets.

Vantage Point Coordination. The MIDAR measurement uses a phased sequence of coordinated sub-measurements (estimation, discovery, elimination, and corroboration) from many VPs to many IP addresses (theoretically, all reachable ones) to infer whether interfaces belong to the same router. Specifically, the IP header ID field of responses from interfaces allows the inference of whether different addresses belong to the same router. We refer the readers to the original MIDAR study [20] for further details of the method, while we highlight here parts of the measurement that require VP coordination. With a large number of IP targets (2.6 million initially), all four of MIDAR's phases split the probing load across all VPs for efficiency, which requires coordination among VPs on which set of targets to run per VP. In addition, the MIDAR discovery phase in particular adds an extra requirement among VPs where the probe transmission needs to be synchronized regardless of potential VP clock skew.

PacketLab Implementation. Each MIDAR phase has two parts: probing and analysis. In the native implementation, each Ark node probes a target list, performs initial analysis on probing results, and sends back the initial analysis outcome to a central machine for final analysis. The central machine then generates the target list for the next phase based on the final analysis outcome. For our PacketLab implementation, we ported the probing component to PacketLab using the published framework implementation and reused the analysis components of the native MIDAR implementation. The PacketLab centralized controller design made it easy to divide probing load among VPs. To synchronize the sending of probes, we implemented the NTP protocol in PacketLab to estimate clock skew between VPs and the controller server, which we then used to schedule simultaneous probe transmissions.

Alias Pair Results. Overall, we found a low Jaccard index (0.64) between CAIDA's native MIDAR alias pair results (1.99M pairs) and our PacketLab MIDAR implementation results (2.03M pairs). The native MIDAR campaign discovered around 426K unique alias pairs not present in the PacketLab campaign, while the PacketLab campaign found about 465K unique alias pairs not present in the native campaign. Further examination revealed that these extreme disparities derived from slight differences in large alias sets, i.e., when one more IP appears in an alias set of a campaign but not the other, which we believe was caused by potential churn in responsive IP addresses during the two-month period along with differences in the VPs used for the two campaigns. For instance, PacketLab (but not native) MIDAR concluded that IP 38.23.192.18 belonged to the same router as 896 other addresses. This IP increased PacketLab MIDAR's final alias pair count by 896 (recall MIDAR produces alias *pairs* as the final outcome). When we removed outlier IPs that only appeared in one campaign but not the other (a total of 108K IPs, where both campaigns gave around 1.58M pairs post-removal), the Jaccard index between native and PacketLab MIDAR increased to 0.98 (> 0.9), satisfying the C3 criterion and suggesting that the results of both implementations are congruent.

Takeaway. This general agreement on a global alias resolution measurement campaign suggests the PacketLab model would successfully manage the complex MIDAR measurement process, and in turn potentially support other measurements requiring VP coordination.

6 Discussion

6.1 Model Limitations

In our survey (Sect. 4), we identified two classes of distributed active measurements that pose a challenge for the PacketLab model: those that include host computation (e.g., browser load times) and those that require a timely response (e.g., congestion control). Here we discuss these measurements in more detail.

Host Computation. Eight of the surveyed studies measured some element of end-host behavior. For example, Netravali *et al.* [23] experimentally evaluated JavaScript dead code elimination on web pages served to mobile clients. The authors measured page load time, which included both a network and browser component, requiring direct browser execution on the VP. The PacketLab model does not export such arbitrary computation capability of the endpoint, so such a measurement is not possible directly.

One alternative is to run the computation on the controller and forward traffic through the endpoint, treating the endpoint as a VPN server. The nature of the PacketLab model meant that the measured delay could then include the path from the controller to the endpoint, increasing the network overhead of the measurement. It may be possible to use the send and receive timestamps supported by the PacketLab model to compensate for the controller-endpoint portion of the network overhead. However, such trickery introduces inaccuracies in the results due to differences in computational power between the VP and the controller.

Timely Response. Another class of measurements where the PacketLab model stumbles are those that require a timely response. Congestion control is a notable example: the sending side of a TCP session will adjust its sending rate in response to observed real-time responses from the receiver. The PacketLab model does support native TCP sockets provided by the VP operating system, where the kernel would assist in real-time responses via the kernel network stack. Consequently, certain TCP measurements, such as throughput, are still doable via the model as demonstrated in Sect. 5.2. However, implementing custom congestion control support appears out of the question for the PacketLab model. This includes measuring QUIC performance [21] or evaluating different congestion control algorithms [19]. To support user-space congestion control and other measurements where measured behavior is sensitive to response timing, the endpoint needs to allow running measurement logic on the VP. The PacketLab model does not export such logic-running capability of the VP, indicating such measurements are not possible under the current model.

Endpoint Measurement Logic Execution. The identified limitations shed light on a framework improvement: adding native measurement logic execution support to the endpoint. This improvement would allow the framework to accommodate measurements requiring timely responsiveness that were not possible before and allow an arguably better estimation of endpoint host computation power. However, this improvement raises concerns about increasing the complexity of PacketLab endpoints, which could elevate adoption costs for endpoint operators, as well as the risk of abuse by malicious experimenters. Further research is thus needed to develop a lightweight and secure method for executing measurement logic on the endpoint.

6.2   Performance

When evaluating the traceroute measurement, we modified the endpoint daemon to use kernel receive timestamps (SO_TIMESTAMPNS) to achieve accuracy comparable to Butskoy's traceroute. While this suggests that the published framework still has room for performance improvements, it also presents opportunities for experimenters to enhance measurement accuracy. By improving a shared endpoint implementation, PacketLab experimenters can directly benefit from these upgrades without needing to engineer native implementations incorporating mechanisms behind the improvement. For example, incorporating kernel timestamp support into the endpoint daemon implementation could allow more accurate timestamps for PacketLab measurements compared to the common recv() followed by gettimeofday() approach in naive measurement implementations. This would save other researchers the effort to learn esoteric system call parameters necessary for accurate network measurements.

6.3   Congruence Criteria

For implementation evaluation, we picked several result congruence criteria to represent potential experimenter standards on data similarity: sufficiently close for practical purposes based on past study criteria (C1), having high distribution similarity (C2), and subjective judgments as Internet measurement researchers (C3). Our criteria do not cover all cases, where an experimenter could have tighter or different requirements. In this manner, one could interpret our experiment results as evidence of potentially achievable result accuracy under the PacketLab model. Experimenters could use this information to decide whether or not to conduct their measurement over PacketLab, where it would be debatable if there is a stricter accuracy requirement than found in our results.

6.4   PacketLab Usage Insights

We summarize some of our insights when working with PacketLab during our evaluation experiments to assist future experimenters in their adoption efforts.

Control Traffic Interference. Our TCP pipe saturation PacketLab implementation temporarily disabled notifications during endpoint data download and upload, and scheduled endpoint upload to happen further in the future to prevent link contention between PacketLab control traffic and measurement traffic from distorting the measurement results. We performed this adjustment because we expected high measurement and control traffic for this measurement and our VPs had only a single Internet-accessible network interface, shared for both measurement and control purposes. Experimenters should be wary of similar link contention problems when designing their measurements, especially for heavy traffic ones, and employ workarounds such as suppressing endpoint notification and scheduling transmissions to avoid undesirable PacketLab control traffic interference on measurement outcome.

Clock Desynchronization. PacketLab notification timestamps and `nsend` schedule send times are based on the endpoint clock rather than the controller clock. For most of our evaluation, our VPs and controller server periodically synchronized with external NTP servers, keeping clock skew minimal (within a few milliseconds). This setup allowed us to schedule future sends easily using the controller clock by specifying a large schedule delay. As VPs in real-world scenarios may have significant clock skew due to lack of or delayed clock synchronization, experimenters should consider this possibility when designing measurements. This is particularly important when scheduling future sends, as an unhandled significant clock skew can result in undesirable delayed or premature transmissions. Experimenters could leverage PacketLab endpoints' exported clock value to estimate clock skew with NTP and adjust the scheduling delay.

6.5 `pktwrap` Limitation

A limitation of `pktwrap` in its current form is that it does not preserve timing data fidelity, as `pktwrap` currently does not manipulate timing information observed by the executable. This limitation is similar to the distortion observed in timing data measurements performed over a VPN. Given the prevalence of timing data measurements in our survey, this limitation suggests an avenue for further research: enhancing `pktwrap` to maintain timing data fidelity. One potential approach is to implement a form of *timing information forgery* within `pktwrap`, where the forged timing information, while not accurate itself, would enable accurate estimation of measurement data by preserving network event delays as observed at the endpoint. We leave this as a direction for future work.

6.6 Adoption Cost Evaluation

In this work, we investigated the PacketLab model's measurement support capability in an effort to understand the impact of PacketLab's design choice on measurement logic relocation. We found mostly positive results. A separate issue we did not address in this work is the proposal-claimed low adoption cost of PacketLab for VPs due to its supposed simplicity and lightweightness. Incorporation with existing measurement platforms may be more involved than simply running the reference endpoint daemon on the VP due to different platform operational models. In addition, the hardware resource requirements for running PacketLab endpoints also need further investigation to see if machines with limited hardware capabilities could function as endpoints. We leave this adoption cost evaluation as future work.

7 Related Work

There have been a number of attempts to organize a list of comprehensive network monitoring tools, most notably the now defunct "Internet tools taxonomy" page by CAIDA [2] and the currently active "Network Monitoring Tools" page by Stanford SLAC [57]. The CAIDA list organized tools based on intent and was used by Scriptroute [56] to understand the need for existing measurements and demonstrate approach capability. The Stanford list contains a diverse range of (over 700) network monitoring tools organized into specific categories such as commercial/public domain, wireless, web etc., and serves as a reference for network administrators. For this study, we surveyed recent network measurement studies to understand the needs of the network measurement community and evaluated the PacketLab model in accordance with the identified needs.

Measurement platform studies often present case studies of selected measurements for evaluation [9,22,52,56,59] to demonstrate efficacy and familiarize readers with the system. The original PacketLab proposal [26] followed a similar strategy by giving examples of both bandwidth measurement and traceroute and only provided on-paper arguments on model limitations without any empirical evidence on impact. Our study extends this previous work by evaluating measurement support of the PacketLab measurement model through a survey of PacketLab-relevant distributed active measurement studies and performing result accuracy experiments on selected representative measurements.

For space reasons, we also discuss some further related work in Appendix C.

8   Conclusion

The goal of this work was a first attempt to validate the *PacketLab assumption* of the original PacketLab proposal, namely that the PacketLab measurement model can effectively support the deployment of a significant fraction of distributed active measurements. To validate this assumption, we surveyed recent measurement studies published at SIGCOMM, IMC, PAM, CoNEXT, and TMA that included relevant distributed active measurement experiments and assessed whether they could be implemented under the PacketLab model. We found that a majority (74%) of distributed active measurement studies could be implemented under PacketLab. Furthermore, for selected prevalent measurements and measurement of special characteristics, we found that we were able to implement measurements yielding congruent results for practical purposes under the PacketLab model using the published framework implementation, and in some cases even achieve congruent results with high distribution similarity. Based on our survey analysis and implementation evaluation, we believe that the PacketLab assumption holds despite the simplified VP design, making it a strong candidate for VP sharing within the Internet measurement community. Our new `pktwrap` measurement porting tool could also potentially assist Internet measurement experimenters in porting non-timing data measurements to the framework at minimal cost.

Acknowledgments. AWS results presented in this paper were obtained using Cloud-Bank [37], which is supported by the National Science Foundation (NSF) under award #1925001. The PacketLab project was supported by NSF award #1764055/1903612 and a gift from Comcast. We would like to thank our shepherd Dr. Alessandro Finamore and anonymous reviewers for their valuable feedbacks.

Ethical Considerations. This work does not raise any ethical issues.

A   Throughput and RTT KS Test Results

Table 3. Throughput and RTT KS test results between measurement results of native and PacketLab implementations of the TCP pipe saturation and traceroute measurements. Similar to Table 2, each row is divided into three columns, with each column showing the KS test results for download throughput, upload throughput, and RTT per VP. The *KS D* and *p* subcolumns show the KS test statistic and p-value, while the *C2* subcolumn shows C2 criterion satisfaction for the case. **We found that throughput result distributions were close between implementations, satisfying congruence criterion C2, while RTT result distributions already differ for AWS Montréal, Tokyo, and Oregon, violating C2.**

VP	DL Tput (Mibps)			UL Tput (Mibps)			RTT (ms)		
	KS D	p	C2	KS D	p	C2	KS D	p	C2
Local res. fiber	0.090	0.815	●	0.130	0.368	●	0.160	0.155	●
AWS Frankfurt	0.134	0.300	●	0.187	0.052	●	0.080	0.908	●
AWS São Paulo	0.114	0.498	●	0.177	0.080	●	0.170	0.111	●
AWS Montréal	0.060	0.988	●	0.103	0.628	●	0.220	0.016	○
AWS Tokyo	0.106	0.578	●	0.144	0.229	●	0.470	0.000	○
AWS Oregon	0.163	0.122	●	0.119	0.437	●	0.270	0.001	○

B   Testing the PacketLab Endpoint Monitor Mechanism

When conducting the experiment on the local residential fiber VP, we also tested the PacketLab endpoint monitor mechanism to restrict access to selected website servers. This test was motivated by similar applied policies in real-world VP sharing scenarios, such as RIPE Atlas's HTTP measurement target restriction toward RIPE Atlas anchors [47]. Given the legal and security concerns surrounding arbitrary HTTP queries [48], we expect PacketLab endpoint operators to enforce similar restrictions in practice. It is therefore valuable to investigate the feasibility of using endpoint monitors to implement these website server access policies.

The PacketLab framework provides access control mechanisms—the PacketLab public key system (PPKS) and WebAssembly-based monitors—to allow operators to define and enforce endpoint usage policies. To enforce a policy, an operator first procures or implements a monitor program that statefully audits PacketLab message exchanges between the controller and the endpoint based on the policy. The operator then compiles the program into a monitor binary and signs a PacketLab *experiment privilege certificate*, embedding the binary's hash, for some requesting experimenter. The certificate and monitor binary are then provided to the experimenter. At experiment time, the experimenter instructs the controller to supply the certificate and binary to the endpoint during measurement session setup, which the endpoint then verifies and applies the monitor throughout the measurement process to enforce the policy.

Our testing involved generating an experiment privilege certificate containing the hash of a custom monitor binary that only allowed TCP communication with the top 1K website IPs. The monitor enforced this policy by checking and permitting only TCP connection `nopen` requests targeting these specific IP addresses (embedded within the monitor) and allowing `nsend` requests and `ndata` notifications only for TCP communication. We used the certificate to access the local residential fiber endpoint for collecting the PacketLab implementation HTTPS response data for the top 1K websites, as well as another 100 websites ranked 1001 to 1100 to verify monitor efficacy. When collecting data, we used the `--resolve` option to force curl to query the specific web server IP addresses permitted by the monitor, which we also specify when collecting native implementation data.

In our blocking test, we found that the endpoint monitor successfully blocked attempts to access all websites ranked 1001 to 1100 while still allowing queries to the top 1K websites via the permitted addresses. This suggests that PacketLab endpoint operators can employ monitors to implement access control policies for regulating website server access similar to RIPE Atlas's policy on HTTP measurement targets and potentially other similar access control policies, which highlights PacketLab's capability to mitigate security concerns through its access control designs.

C   Further Related Work

In addition to measurement platforms mentioned in Sect. 2, there also exist(ed) other platforms that focus on collecting and sharing insightful data, including ICLab [36], GFWatch [17], Censored Planet [58], PingER [29], Censys [6], Shodan [53], OpenINTEL [40], and DScope [41]. In essence, these platforms are large-scale measurement experiments that could serve as evaluation targets for PacketLab. For this work, we instead opted to perform the evaluation based on recent measurement studies with the aim of evaluating the PacketLab model via prevalent measurements.

References

1. Butskoy, D.: Traceroute for Linux (2024). https://traceroute.sourceforge.net/
2. CAIDA: Internet Tools Taxonomy (2004). https://web.archive.org/web/20210422112114/https://www.caida.org/tools/taxonomy/
3. CAIDA: Ark (2024). https://catalog.caida.org/software/archipelago
4. CAIDA: ITDK: Internet Topology Data Kit (2024). https://catalog.caida.org/dataset/ark_itdk
5. Cappos, J., Hemmings, M., McGeer, R., Rafetseder, A., Ricart, G.: EdgeNet: a global cloud that spreads by local action. In: IEEE/ACM SEC 2018 (2018)

6. Censys: Censys Search (2024). https://search.censys.io/
7. Chang, H., Varvello, M., Hao, F., Mukherjee, S.: Can you see me now? A measurement study of zoom, webex, and meet. In: Proceedings of ACM IMC 2021 (2021)
8. Chhabra, R., Murley, P., Kumar, D., Bailey, M., Wang, G.: Measuring DNS-over-HTTPS performance around the world. In: Proceedings of ACM IMC 2021 (2021)
9. Claffy, K., Hyun, Y., Keys, K., Fomenkov, M., Krioukov, D.: Internet mapping: from art to science. In: IEEE CATCH 2009 (2009)
10. curl: curl (2024). https://curl.se/
11. Dang, T.K., Mohan, N., Corneo, L., Zavodovski, A., Ott, J., Kangasharju, J.: Cloudy with a chance of short RTTs: analyzing cloud connectivity in the Internet. In: Proceedings of ACM IMC 2021 (2021)
12. Darwich, O., Rimlinger, H., Dreyfus, M., Gouel, M., Vermeulen, K.: Replication: towards a publicly available internet scale IP geolocation dataset. In: Proceedings of ACM IMC 2023 (2023)
13. EdgeNet: Acceptable Use Policy | EdgeNet (2020). https://www.edge-net.org/OMTpages/usage-policy.html
14. Elmenhorst, K., Schütz, B., Aschenbruck, N., Basso, S.: Web censorship measurements of HTTP/3 over QUIC. In: Proceedings of ACM IMC 2021 (2021)
15. FCC: Measuring Broadband America | Federal Communications Commission (2024). https://www.fcc.gov/general/measuring-broadband-america
16. Hanemann, A., et al.: PerfSONAR: a service oriented architecture for multi-domain network monitoring. In: Proceedings of ICSOC 2005 (2005)
17. Hoang, N.P., et al.: How great is the great firewall? Measuring China's DNS censorship. In: USENIX Security 2021 (2021)
18. Hsu, A., Li, F., Pearce, P., Gasser, O.: A first look at NAT64 deployment in-the-wild. In: Proceedings of PAM 2024, Part I. Springer, Cham (2024)
19. Kassem, M.M., Raman, A., Perino, D., Sastry, N.: A browser-side view of starlink connectivity. In: Proceedings of ACM IMC 2022 (2022)
20. Keys, K., Hyun, Y., Luckie, M., Claffy, K.: Internet-scale IPv4 alias resolution with MIDAR. IEEE/ACM Trans. Netw. **21**(2) (2013)
21. Kosek, M., Schumann, L., Marx, R., Doan, T.V., Bajpai, V.: DNS privacy with speed? Evaluating DNS over QUIC and its impact on web performance. In: Proceedings of ACM IMC 2022 (2022)
22. Kreibich, C., Weaver, N., Nechaev, B., Paxson, V.: Netalyzr: illuminating the edge network. In: Proceedings of ACM IMC 2010 (2010)
23. Kupoluyi, J., et al.: Muzeel: assessing the impact of JavaScript dead code elimination on mobile web performance. In: Proceedings of ACM IMC 2022 (2022)
24. Laniewski, D., Lanfer, E., Meijerink, B., van Rijswijk-Deij, R., Aschenbruck, N.: WetLinks: a large-scale longitudinal starlink dataset with contiguous weather data. In: Proceedings of TMA 2024 (2024)
25. Le Pochat, V., Van Goethem, T., Tajalizadehkhoob, S., Korczyński, M., Joosen, W.: Tranco: a research-oriented top sites ranking hardened against manipulation. In: Proceedings of NDSS 2019 (2019)
26. Levchenko, K., Dhamdhere, A., Huffaker, B., Claffy, K., Allman, M., Paxson, V.: Packetlab: a universal measurement endpoint interface. In: Proceedings of ACM IMC 2017 (2017)
27. Liu, S., Bischof, Z.S., Madan, I., Chan, P.K., Bustamante, F.E.: Out of sight, not out of mind: a user-view on the criticality of the submarine cable network. In: Proceedings of ACM IMC 2020 (2020)

28. MacMillan, K., Mangla, T., Saxon, J., Marwell, N.P., Feamster, N.: A comparative analysis of ookla speedtest and measurement labs network diagnostic test (NDT7). Proc. ACM Meas. Anal. Comput. Syst. **7**(1) (2023)

29. Matthews, W., Cottrell, L.: The PingER project: active Internet performance monitoring for the HENP community. IEEE Commun. Mag. **38**(5) (2000)

30. Measurement Lab: Home - M-Lab (2024). https://www.measurementlab.net/

31. Measurement Lab: NDT (Network Diagnostic Tool) - Tests (2024). https://www.measurementlab.net/tests/ndt/

32. Michel, F., Trevisan, M., Giordano, D., Bonaventure, O.: A first look at starlink performance. In: Proceedings of ACM IMC 2022 (2022)

33. Mok, R.K.P., Zou, H., Yang, R., Koch, T., Katz-Bassett, E., Claffy, K.C.: Measuring the network performance of google cloud platform. In: Proceedings of ACM IMC 2021 (2021)

34. Munteanu, C., Saidi, S.J., Gasser, O., Smaragdakis, G., Feldmann, A.: Fifteen months in the life of a honeyfarm. In: Proceedings of ACM IMC 2023 (2023)

35. Narayanan, A., et al.: Lumos5G: mapping and predicting commercial MmWave 5G throughput. In: Proceedings of ACM IMC 2020 (2020)

36. Niaki, A.A., et al.: ICLab: a global, longitudinal internet censorship measurement platform. In: IEEE S&P 2020 (2020)

37. Norman, M., et al.: CloudBank: managed services to simplify cloud access for computer science research and education. In: Proceedings of ACM PEARC 2021 (2021)

38. Ookla: Speedtest by Ookla - The Global Broadband Speed Test (2024). https://www.speedtest.net/

39. OONI: Open Observatory of Network Interference (2024). https://ooni.org/

40. OpenINTEL: OpenINTEL: Active DNS Measurement Project (2024). https://openintel.nl/

41. Pauley, E., Barford, P., McDaniel, P.: DScope: a cloud-native internet telescope. In: USENIX Security 2023 (2023)

42. perfSONAR: View panel - perfSONAR Public - Dashboards - Grafana (2024). https://stats.perfsonar.net/goto/Ia2l8mzNR?orgId=2

43. Randall, A., et al.: Home is where the hijacking is: understanding DNS interception by residential routers. In: Proceedings of ACM IMC 2021 (2021)

44. Randall, A., et al.: Trufflehunter: cache snooping rare domains at large public DNS resolvers. In: Proceedings of ACM IMC 2020 (2020)

45. Rasaii, A., Gosain, D., Gasser, O.: Thou shalt not reject: analyzing accept-or-pay cookie banners on the web. In: Proceedings of ACM IMC 2023 (2023)

46. Reda, W., et al.: Path persistence in the cloud: a study of the effects of inter-region traffic engineering in a large cloud provider's network. SIGCOMM Comput. Commun. Rev. (2020)

47. RIPE NCC: HTTP Measurements with RIPE Atlas | RIPE Labs (2015). https://labs.ripe.net/author/kistel/http-measurements-with-ripe-atlas/

48. RIPE NCC: Ethics of RIPE Atlas Measurements | RIPE Labs (2016). https://labs.ripe.net/author/kistel/ethics-of-ripe-atlas-measurements/

49. RIPE NCC: RIPE Atlas (2024). https://atlas.ripe.net/

50. RIPE NCC: RIPE Atlas - Coverage (2024). https://atlas.ripe.net/coverage/

51. Rizvi, A.S.M., Huang, T., Esrefoglu, R., Heidemann, J.: Anycast polarization in the wild. In: Proceedings of PAM 2024. Springer, Cham (2024)

52. Sánchez, M.A., et al.: Dasu: pushing experiments to the Internet's edge. In: Proceedings of NSDI 2013 (2013)

53. Shodan: Shodan Search Engine (2024). https://www.shodan.io/
54. Sommese, R., et al.: MAnycast2: using anycast to measure anycast. In: Proceedings of ACM IMC 2020 (2020)
55. Spring, N., Peterson, L., Bavier, A., Pai, V.: Using planetlab for network research: myths, realities, and best practices. SIGOPS Oper. Syst. Rev. (2006)
56. Spring, N., Wetherall, D., Anderson, T.: Scriptroute: a public internet measurement facility. In: Proceedings of USITS 2003 (2003)
57. Stanford SLAC: Network Monitoring Tools (2023). https://www.slac.stanford.edu/xorg/nmtf/nmtf-tools.html
58. Sundara Raman, R., Shenoy, P., Kohls, K., Ensafi, R.: Censored planet: an internet-wide, longitudinal censorship observatory. In: Proceedings of CCS 2020 (2020)
59. Sundaresan, S., Burnett, S., Feamster, N., de Donato, W.: BISmark: a testbed for deploying measurements and applications in broadband access networks. In: Proceedings of USENIX ATC 2014 (2014)
60. The PacketLab Team: Home | PacketLab (2024). https://packetlab.github.io/
61. Umayya, Z., Malik, D., Gosain, D., Kumar Sharma, P.: PTPerf: on the performance evaluation of tor pluggable transports. In: Proceedings of ACM IMC 2023 (2023)
62. Varvello, M., Chang, H., Zaki, Y.: Performance characterization of videoconferencing in the wild. In: Proceedings of ACM IMC 2022 (2022)
63. Wan, G., et al.: On the origin of scanning: the impact of location on internet-wide scans. In: Proceedings of ACM IMC 2020 (2020)
64. Yan, T.B., et al.: PacketLab: tools alpha release and demo. In: Proceedings of ACM IMC 2022 (2022)

A Tree in a Tree: Measuring Biases of Partial DNS Tree Exploration

Florian Steurer[1,2(✉)] [ID], Anja Feldmann[1] [ID], and Tobias Fiebig[1] [ID]

[1] Max Planck Institute for Informatics, Saarbruecken, Germany
{fsteurer,anja,tfiebig}@mpi-inf.mpg.de
[2] Saarland University, Saarbruecken, Germany

Abstract. The Domain Name System (DNS) is a cornerstone of the Internet. As such, it is often the subject or the means of network measurement studies. Over the past decades, the Internet measurement community gathered many lessons-learned and captured them in widely available measurement toolchains such as ZDNS and OpenINTEL as well as many papers. However, for feasibility, these tools often restrict DNS tree exploration, use caching, and other intricate methods for reducing query load. This potentially hides many corner cases and unforeseen problems.

In this paper, we present a system capable of exploring the full DNS tree. We gather 87 TB of DNS data covering 812M domains with over 85B queries over 40 days. Using this data, we replicate four earlier studies that used feasibility and time-optimized DNS datasets. Our results demonstrate the need for care in selecting which limitations regarding the perspective on DNS can be accepted for a given research question and which may alter findings and conclusions.

1 Introduction

The Domain Name System (DNS) was introduced in the late 1980s to replace the host file [35] for mapping names to numbers. Today, it has become one of the cornerstones of the Internet. DNS is continuously evolving. It has seen a multitude of additions, e.g., to enhance its security [5], or to facilitate additional use-cases [37,69,71]. This resulted in almost 300 RFCs related to DNS [64], making it a canonical example of a complex protocol. Not surprisingly, this complexity facilitates misconfigurations and corner cases. Hereby, part of the complexity arises from the fact that DNS is a hierarchical distributed database, a tree, where different name servers (NSs) are responsible for different branches.

In the past, DNS has been involved in many network studies, either as *subject* or as *means*, i.e., for studying other aspects of the Internet with help of the DNS. Studies about DNS include those on authoritative DNS (e.g., [11,55]), recursive DNS (e.g., [12,31,38]), and those on DNS features (e.g., [13,43]). Studies leveraging DNS data include questions regarding cloud deployments [28], IPv6 scans [8,26], or email [16,47,48]. Yet, DNS is a notoriously difficult protocol to measure efficiently and without (accidentally) causing harm [25] due to its sheer size, complexity, and abundance of corner cases.

© The Author(s) 2025
C. Testart et al. (Eds.): PAM 2025, LNCS 15567, pp. 106–136, 2025.
https://doi.org/10.1007/978-3-031-85960-1_5

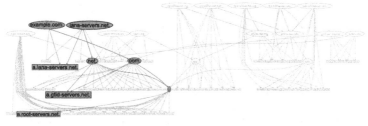

(a) Full DNS resolution graph for **A example.com**.

(b) Minimal set of queries for resolving **A example.com**.

Fig. 1. DNS tree for querying **A example.com**., including all zones (round) and NSs (square) that *may* be involved in a resolution (Fig. (a)). The minimal set of queries, five, for the best case is shown in Fig. (b). It assumes that glue for resolving **example.com** can be trusted. The corresponding zones and authoritative servers of Fig. 1a are highlighted in red. ZDNS would explore a sub-tree close to this subset, while our system explores *all* possible paths (gray). (Color figure online)

Past efforts have led to methodological insights and measurement toolchains for conducting DNS studies. Among the lessons learned are that DNS replies may depend on the probe's vantage point [68] and that caching can reduce scan duration as well as measurement overhead/impact [41]. Hereby, ZDNS [41]–a tool for performing active DNS queries—has made large-scale DNS measurements feasible. ZDNS leverages adaptive caching, external DNS-resolution services, and–by default[1]–opportunistic traversal of the DNS tree, i.e., not all possible paths in the DNS tree are evaluated (see also Sect. 3.4). OpenINTEL [68] uses Unbound for DNS resolution, which will terminate name resolution when an answer is found without exploring additional paths, i.e., also performs opportunistic traversal. This is in line with OpenINTEL's objective of creating a historical dataset by *daily* querying as many records as possible.

To visualize how these optimizations inflict on the gathered data's completeness, Fig. 1 shows the minimally necessary DNS queries to resolve the **A** record for **example.com** as seen by optimized measurements in comparison to the full tree that *may* be involved in DNS resolution for that name. While the optimizations of ZDNS and, to a degree, OpenINTEL reduce overhead and runtime, they miss major parts of the DNS tree and may hide corner cases or inconsistencies, potentially biasing results.

The biases induced by such partial tree exploration *may* be reasonable tradeoffs in comparison to an overall better runtime of measurements. Still, biases and

---

[1] Even though an iterative and 'all-nameservers' mode is available, its implementation is incomplete, see Sect. 3.4.

trade-offs have not been systematically explored. Thus, in this paper, we answer: **What is the impact of partial tree exploration on DNS measurements?**

To capture the extent of the existing limitations, we start by discussing the methodological impact of exploring subsets of the DNS tree. Next, we discuss how to realize a DNS measurement system, YoDNS, that can potentially capture the full DNS tree. Among the important differences is that YoDNS gathers responses from all authoritative NSs of a DNS zone and chases all emerging paths even if they are inconsistent with prior responses. We use YoDNS to gather an extensive dataset using over 812M input names from various public and non-public sources, sending 85B queries over 40 days. Finally, we utilize the collected data to assess the impact of partial DNS tree exploration on four earlier studies, reproducing their results and quantifying biases induced by opportunistic DNS traversal. Our results show that some research questions, e.g., inconsistency between NSs, are prone to biases of limited tree exploration, while others are not.

Contributions: *All* active DNS measurement studies need to accept limitations in DNS tree exploration to remain feasible. A common limitation is opportunistic traversal, where only a subset of possible DNS resolution paths is explored. However, the impact of this choice has not been systematically assessed. We address this crucial methodological gap with our contributions:

- We present and publish YoDNS, an open-source framework for exhaustive DNS-tree exploration and measurements.
- We collect and share a large DNS dataset, containing full resolutions for over 812M names, spanning over 85B queries and 87 TB of compressed DNS data, enabling researchers to reproduce further studies based on our data.
- We evaluate the impact of limiting DNS tree exploration in four earlier studies and derive recommendations to balance exploration vs. efficiency for a given research question in order to not impact results, or–at least–to make the impact quantifiable.

2   Reliably Measuring DNS: A Primer

In this section, we first revisit how DNS in general and DNS resolution specifically, work. Subsequently, we review techniques for accelerating DNS resolution often used during DNS measurements and their impact on the results.

2.1   DNS Resolution Revisited

DNS was first introduced in RFC1032-RFC1035 [51,53,54,76]. RFC8499 [36] gives a contemporary overview of DNS terminology and developments since then.

DNS Abstraction and Terminology: DNS is a tree, where each node ('label') is connected via dots as delimiters ('.') to the root. The root is an empty label behind a single dot '.', and a path in the DNS tree from a leaf to the root is a

'Fully Qualified Domain Name' (FQDN). 'Zones' are sub-trees, often operated by a different authority than their parents. Such 'delegations' take place at vertices referred to as 'zone cuts'. Nodes in the DNS tree can have values ('Resource Records', or 'RR') of a type ('RRtype') assigned to them, whereby multiple RRs of the same type form an 'RRset'.

DNS Implementation: Each zone, including the root, is hosted by at least one (ideally multiple [22]) 'name server' (NS) providing authoritative answers for the zone. These are 'authoritative NSs'. To delegate a zone, a parent contains an NS RRset for the child's name, listing the FQDNs of authoritative NS for the child zone. For authoritative NSs whose names are in or below the child, the parent zones' operator must add additional 'glue records', which explicitly list the NS' IP address(es). The child zone should contain corresponding RRsets.

DNS Resolution: DNS queries resolve a FQDN to an RRset given an RRType. To reply to a query, a *recursive* resolver needs to traverse the DNS tree to find the authoritative NS for a name's zone. A recursive resolver first checks the FQDN with the root servers or the label closest to the root, if QNAME minimization [10] is used. Since the root servers are typically not authoritative for the requested name, they respond with a referral, i.e., the NS records plus potential glue records of the NS authoritative below the next zone-cut in the FQDN. Next, the resolver repeats this process with one of the new NSs until an NS returns an authoritative answer instead of a referral.

2.2 DNS Measurement Trade-Offs

DNS measurements can be active or passive [68]. Passive measurements, e.g., rely on traces captured at authoritative NSs or DNS resolvers. Thus, they only capture those parts of the DNS tree that the NS is responsible for or that the resolver queries to answer user queries. In contrast, active DNS measurements, the focus of this paper, explore the DNS tree in a structured manner. Still, traversing the full DNS tree without any optimizations is practically impossible due to the size of the tree and abundance of parameters. Below, we summarize possible optimizations. See also Table 2 for how related-work handles these limitations.

Limiting Exploration Depth: Here, the measurement considers only zones higher up in the tree, e.g., by including only second level domains in the target list or stopping resolution at a certain depth. This may bias results towards zones which are likely to receive more scrutiny from delegating authorities.

Limiting Exploration Width: By limiting the number of input zones, or not chasing all out-of-zone records, one may bias the results towards specific TLDs, DNS operators, or popular sites. Similarly, one may restrict the number of followed paths, e.g., by considering only one resolution path (just like a resolver) rather than all possible paths, potentially hiding inconsistencies.

Vantage Point Selection: DNS responses differ by vantage point, e.g., due to load balancing [78] or anycast [1].

Caching: Using caches of previous DNS responses speeds up DNS lookups [29]. However, it can hide short-lived effects and inconsistencies between NSs. For example, when records are cached based solely on the tuple (`RRName`, `Type`, `Class`), as done by some resolvers, inconsistencies become invisible.

Using External Recursive Resolvers: Using professionally operated, well-provisioned resolvers, e.g., Google or PCH, can speed up resolution but hides many details, such as caching strategy, needed to analyze results. Moreover, anycasted resolvers may respond from different nodes having different (cache) states.

Dynamic Resources: DNS trees of arbitrary depth [26], e.g., via `LUA` records [65], and responses that are unique *per request* need to be pruned carefully.

Transport Protocol: DNS supports UDP/TCP and requires handling ICMP/ICMPv6. Missing any of these may lead to biases in observed NS reachability or loss of responses due to packet fragmentation [57].

Internet Protocol: Not considering IPv6 reduces measurement overhead, but may bias results with respect to IPv6-only and dual-stack resolvability.

Relying on RFC Compliance: Presuming RFC compliance can lead to unexplored parts of the DNS tree when encountering corner cases. For example, `CNAME`s should not be used in certain RRs (e.g. NS records [23]) or responses should be consistent, regardless of whether a FQDN or minimized query name is asked. However, Internet reality does not adhere to this. Thus, relying on RFCs compliance may limit the ability to study the effect of such misconfigurations.

2.3   Impact of Challenges on Query Load

DNS resolution in practice, i.e., using the optimizations above, requires significantly fewer queries than a full exploration of the tree, see Fig. 1. But how many more queries are actually necessary? We can calculate a lower bound on the number of queries for the full resolution of `example.com` as follows:

- For all zones, ask all authoritative NSs for the zones' `NS` records.
- For all zones, ask all of its parents' authoritative NSs for referrals to the zone.
- For all NS names, ask all NSs authoritative for them for the `A`/ `AAAA` records.

For example, the zone `icann-servers.net` has four authoritative NSs. Thus, we need to ask for `NS icann-servers.net` four times. We need to ask for a referral to `icann-servers.net` at all 13 nameservers of the `net`-zone. Finally, there are three NSs names in the zone, namely {`a,b,c`}.`icann-servers.net`. Asking the four authoritative NSs for the three `A` records requires 12 queries. Thus summing the queries for each zone from Fig. 1, leaves us with 637 queries, over 100 times more than the minimal resolution shown in Fig. 1.

We see, that full tree exploration entails more than simply identifying the answer to a specific query. However, certain measurements (IPv4 vs. IPv6, TCP

Table 1. Minimal queries needed for resolving `example.com` for selected measurement parameters, when only retrieving `NS`, `A`, `AAAA` records for all discovered names and involved zones, all using QNAME minimization. It is clear, that a truly exhaustive exploration of the parameter space is infeasible for a large number of domains. Note that the resolution paths for `example.com` are full dual-stack, i.e., IPv4 and IPv6 resolution require the same number of queries.

Exploration	#VPs	RR types	Transp.	#IPv4 Q.	#IPv6 Q.	$\sum$
Minimal	1	NS, A	UDP	5	-	5
Full	1	NS, A	UDP	637	-	637
Full	1	NS, AAAA	UDP	-	637	637
Full	1	NS, A, AAAA	UDP	980	980	1,960
Full	1	NS, A, AAAA	UDP+TCP	1,960	1,960	3,920
Full	10	NS, A, AAAA	UDP+TCP	19,600	19,600	39,200

and UDP, etc.) effectively double the number of queries again, see Table 1. Requesting DNSSEC or using small EDNS0 buffer sizes may cause truncated responses, so to accurately capture UDP-only behavior, queries have to be sent with/without DNSSEC requested, yet again doubling the number of queries. Adding more RRtypes adds queries linear to the number of discovered names and servers, similar to adding more vantage points.

This combinatorial explosion of queries inevitably forces measurements to accept *some* trade-offs. However, these trade-offs need to be chosen carefully and w.r.t. the research question. This work, for example, limits itself to using QNAME minimization, relies on a single vantage point and uses TCP only as a fallback mechanism. We discuss these limitations in detail in Sect. 3.

3   Related Work

Here, we discuss related work using a selection of publications representing the state of the art. We cluster them into three categories: *(i)* Work performing measurements *of* the DNS, *(ii)* Work performing measurements *with* the DNS, i.e., work where DNS is the *means* rather than the main subject being studied, *(iii)* Work describing DNS measurement methods and frameworks. Passive DNS measurements, e.g., work using traces collected at resolvers or NSs, are out of scope. We map challenges from Sect. 2 to related work in Table 2.

3.1   Measurements of DNS

With DNS being over 30 years old, there has been an abundance of DNS-related work. Initially, this work was industry-focused, e.g., Thompson et al. [81] noted the volume of DNS traffic on the Internet in a broader passive study. Darst & Ramanathan [17] discussed active DNS measurements to assess network performance in 1999, Huitema & Weerahandi [38] discussed the impact of DNS on active measurements in 2000. Last, in 2002 Liston et al. [49] conducted one of the first studies focusing on measuring DNS itself. Moreover, a study using data from 2003 by Pappas et al. [63] connects earlier work on DNS measurements to current times, measuring DNS misconfigurations and their impact on the DNS. Since 2002, there has been an explosion in DNS measurement work.

Focussing on transitive DNS dependencies, Ramasubramanian & Sirer [66] show that the number of NSs that *may* be involved in DNS resolution can be surprisingly large (>400). Further formalizing the dependency graph model, Deccio et al. [19] find that transitive dependencies can lead to additional lookups and false redundancy.

Other notable examples of DNS measurements include Nosyk et al. [62], who used RFC8914 [44] extended DNS errors for DNS measurements, Streibelt et al. [79], who measured IPv6 support in the DNS, and Fukuda et al. [30], who characterized DNS query response sizes. Similarly, Yajima et al. [89] measured the adoption of DNS security measures.

Akiwate et al. [3] measured 'Lame Delegations', taking a more general, yet IPv4-centric, approach to DNS. Furthermore, work by Rijswijk-Deij et al. [67] from 2014 assessed the potential of DNSSEC for DDoS attacks.

3.2 Measurements Using DNS

DNS is not a purpose unto itself but enables other services and applications. Hence, in addition to measurements *of* DNS, researchers regularly leverage active DNS measurements to infer information about other protocols and services.

For example, Gojmerac et al. [33] used active DNS measurements to assess the deployment state of email security mechanics. This research track is continuing, with recent work investigating specific–often new–email security mechanics like DMARC [6], SPF [16], and TLSA/DANE [47,48].

Zirngibl et al. [91] used active measurements to study domain parking, finding that artifacts produced by it are often overlooked in measurement studies. Other use-cases for active DNS measurements are identifying IPv6 hosts [9,26,27], re-assessing and probing targets [8] or asset discovery [28,85].

3.3 DNS Measurement Frameworks

DNS measurement frameworks only became prevalent in the recent past. Early DNS measurements often used commodity utilities such as dig [50] which was possible as they were often only used for scanning top lists, e.g., the now discontinued Alexa list. However, with larger and more abundant domain sources, such as ICANN CZDS [39] (≈220M names) and Certificate Transparency (CT) logs (≈589M in our dataset), DNS measurement frameworks became necessary.

The first example of an elaborate DNS measurement framework is Open-INTEL [68], which has performed daily measurements of the DNS since 2015, claiming coverage of around 60% of the DNS. Due to the availability of the gathered historical data, OpenINTEL is also frequently used in other studies (e.g. [72,73,75,82–84,91]). Subsequently, in 2023, ZDNS was published as open-source software, providing a framework that allows researchers to perform their own active DNS measurement studies [41]. Both frameworks focus on resolvability, i.e., the red part of Fig. 1a, rather than extensive exploration of the DNS tree. Furthermore, MassDNS [7], a high performance stub resolver, can query resolvers at scale. However, it does not support internal recursion, and thus, cannot easily be used for studies that rely on the resolution path. Both Streibelt et al. [79] and Naab et al. [59] report to have implemented their own frameworks and utilized them to measure 476k and 1M domains (note that our target list contains 812M). However, the tool of Streibelt et al. lacks scalability for Internet-scale studies (running 4 days for 476k zones [79]) and the tool of Naab et al. is not fully feature-ready, e.g. is missing features related to CNAME handling. As of Oct. 2024, neither tool is publicly available.

Finally, there is DNSViz [18], which was created for troubleshooting (DNSSEC-related) misconfigurations and is a well-known resource for DNS operators. DNSViz is able to query records from all NSs of a zone (and its parents) and, necessarily, resolves all *direct* dependencies of a zone. Contrary to YoDNS, transitive dependencies are learned through normal resolution. Given that DNSViz is not primarily designed for large scale measurement, features such as rate-limiting or a storage-efficient output format are also not natively integrated in the tool. However, it does provide similar (though not the same) functionality to YoDNS, albeit for a different use-case.

> **Example Packet Traces:** To further highlight the practical differences between YoDNS, OpenINTEL, DNSViz, ZDNS v1.0.0, and ZDNS v1.1.0, we included packet captures for a resolution of example.com with these tools in our published dataset [77].

When it comes to existing DNS measurement frameworks, the natural choice for a study like ours would have been OpenINTEL. However, OpenINTEL's focus is the efficient resolution of as many *different* names and RRsets as possible during a day to collect a historical dataset. For that, it leverages commodity Unbound resolvers. It does not attempt to find *all possible* resolution paths for a single name or RRset, making it not suitable for our objective.

With Streibelt et al. [79] and Naab et al. [59] not yet having published their frameworks, this only leaves ZDNS as a viable option. However, when evaluating ZDNS, we noted that the implementation of iterative resolution across all NSs is incomplete[2] and uses cached responses from one NS to synthesize responses for *other* NSs of the same zone. Furthermore, ZDNS does not use QNAME minimization, preventing the evaluation of zone-cuts. When evaluating ZDNS against common misconfigurations like parent-child NS mismatches[3], and RFC violations like the use of CNAMEs in NS records, it did not provide reliable results. Finally, ZDNS does not track ICMP responses and lacks methods for effective rate-limiting when running in iterative mode due to its parallelization approach which relies on a large number of parallel sockets instead of asynchronous I/O.

---

[2] https://github.com/zmap/zdns/issues/362.
[3] https://github.com/zmap/zdns/issues/352.

As addressing these challenges in ZDNS would require significant architectural changes, we decided to use a clean-slate approach, see Sect. 4.

3.4 Reflections on Related Work

Earlier studies made methodological choices around the challenges we summarize in Sect. 2, see Table 2. Oftentimes, this includes relying on opportunistic DNS resolution, i.e. following a single resolution path instead of exploring all possible paths. In this section, we argue why this might influence results and how an open measurement framework for full DNS tree traversal can be helpful. However, we do *not* argue that all these studies should have used full tree traversal, rather that a systematic quantification of these biases is necessary.

Studies using OpenINTEL rely on opportunistic resolution. While this allows to take a longitudinal perspective, problematic resolution paths and NS inconsistencies may remain undiscovered and can bias results.

For example, van der Toorn et al. [84] identified private keys in TXT records as a security concern. However, exposing a private key has security implications, regardless of whether it was exposed via all or only a single authoritative NS. Yet, the latter is easily missed by opportunistic traversal. Similar considerations apply to issues such as very large response sizes that allow for DDoS amplification [75] or stale glue records that might redirect clients to malicious IP addresses [72].

For a study of delegation inconsistency by Sommese et al. [73] using OpenINTEL, we explore the effects of such partial tree exploration in Sect. 6. We find that inconsistencies can amplify, especially for domains below second level.

A study from Akiwate et al. [3], investigating unresponsive NSs, limits probing to five authoritative NSs per domain, thus providing a lower bound on the actual unresponsiveness. Furthermore, they do not consider IPv6.

Studies that focus on public resolvers, such as that by Nosyk et al. [62], exploring extended DNS error codes [44] in resolver responses, might have used an exhaustive measurement framework to obtain ground-truth for certain misconfigurations and to verify results obtained from public resolvers even further.

In a recent study, Zhang et al. [90] measure the dependencies involved in DNS resolution using ZDNS [41], focusing on the implications for security and robustness, yet, they limit tree exploration by focussing on IPv4 and UDP. We discuss some of their findings in detail in Sect. 6.

Overall, we note that many prior studies are susceptible to biases introduced from partial tree exploration and NS inconsistencies. A flexible DNS measurement framework for full tree exploration would have allowed for better quantification of measurement errors, e.g., through supplemental measurements.

Table 2. Overview of related active DNS studies

	Pappas et al. [63] (2009)	Rijswijk-Deij et al. [67] (2014)	Gojmerac et al. [33] (2015)	OpenIntel & rel. [68]a (2016)	Fiebig et al. [27] (2017)	Scheitle et al. [70]b (2018)	Moura et al. [56]	Akiwate et al. [3]. (2019)	Yajima et al. [89] (2020)	Fukuda et al. [30] (2021)	Zirngibl et al. [91]b	Izhikevich et al. [41] (2022)	Streibelt et al. [79] (2023)	Naab et al. [59]	Ashiq et al. [6]	Nosyk et al. [62]d (2024)	Zhang et al. [90]	This Paper
Full Tree Depth																		
Below SLD	✔	✗	✗	~	-	✔	~	✗	✗	✗	-	✔	✗	✗	✔	✔	~	✔
No Pruning	?	-	?	?	✗	?	?	?	?	?	?	?	✔	✗	?	?	?	✔
Full Tree Width																		
All NS	✔	✔	✗	✗	✗	✔	?	~	✔	✗	✗	~	✔	✔	?	-	✔	✔
Targets	✗	~	✗	~ᶜ	✔	✔	✗	✔	✗	✗	~	✔	✗	✗	✗	✔	~	✔
Res. Strategy																		
Contr. Recursion	✔	✔	?	✔	✔	?	-	✔	?	✗	?	✔	✔	✔	?	-	✔	✔
QMIN	-	✗	?	✗	?	?	?	?	?	?	?	✗	✔	✔	?	-	✗	✔
Traditional	✔	✔	?	✔	✔	?	?	?	?	?	?	✔	✗	✗	?	-	✔	✗
Multi-Vantage Pts.	?	✗	?	~	✗	✔	✗	✗	?	✔	✗	✗	✗	?	?	✔	?	✗
No Over-Caching	✔	✔	?	✔	?	✔	✔	?	?	?	✔	✔	✔	?	-	✔	?	✔
Parallelization	?	✔	✔	✔	~	✔	?	?	?	?	✔	✔	✔	?	?	✔	✔	✔
Enum. Dynamic R.	?	-	?	✗	✗	?	?	?	?	?	?	?	?	?	?	-	?	✔
CNAME Misconf.	?	~	?	✔	?	✗	?	?	?	?	?	✔	✗	?	-	✗	?	✔
TCP/ICMP	?	✗	?	?	?	?	?	✔	?	?	✗	?	~	~	?	?	✗	~
IPv6	?	✔	?	✔	✔	✔	?	✗	✗	✗	✔	✗ᵉ	✔	✔	?	?	✗	✔

Legend: ✔: Addressed   ~: Part. addr.   ✗: Not addr.   -: Not rel.   ?: No inform.

a Used in various studies, e.g.: [72, 73, 75, 82–84, 91]
b Also uses OpenIntel data.
c Claims ≈60% coverage, input is zonefiles/toplists/rDNS.
d Resolver study: some fields are not applicable.
e IPv6-support added after the paper was presented.

Fig. 2. YoDNS architecture.

4   YoDNS Design

Here, we present the architecture of YoDNS. It allows for more extensive exploration of the DNS tree than previous tools, and therefore, to better quantify effects induced by partial tree exploration.

YoDNS is configurable regarding DNS exploration depth and width, caching strategy, and rate limits. It remains robust to RFC incompliance and misconfigurations – following an 'accept liberal, send conservative' approach – and ensuring that all failures are recorded. Furthermore, our system supports standard quality-of-life features including monitoring integration and restart capabilities.

4.1 Architecture

To enable scale-out, YoDNS consists of multiple independent components, i.e., we decided *against* a monolithic architecture. See Fig. 2 for an overview.

Overview We implement YoDNS in Go. Go's concurrency model maps independent units of work to separate virtual threads called Go-routines and communication is handled by passing messages via channels, allowing to easily scale components horizontally with more workers.

To execute a measurement, a `target list` with domain names to be scanned and a `configuration` specifying how to scan are supplied to the system. The `target list` is processed by the `resolver` which creates several independent, parallel `resolution jobs` based on the specification.

A `resolution job` entails resolving one or multiple names sharing a path towards the root. Jobs use asynchronous I/O to handle DNS requests and mitigate wait times from, e.g., transport delays. Jobs are parameterized with a `resolution strategy`, defaulting to QNAME minimization [10].

Queries are processed by the `RequestWorker`, which is responsible for cache-lookup, enqueueing wire queries, and retrying failed queries. Responses are stored in the infrastructure cache. Additionally, an `ICMP worker` (not shown) updates the cache when receiving ICMP `unreachable` messages.

Upon receiving DNS answers, the `resolution job` uses callbacks to the selected `resolution strategy`. During processing of the answer, the resolution strategy updates the `domain model` and enqueues new requests as necessary. The `domain model` also provides callback capabilities enabling us to 'go back in time' and enqueue more requests, e.g. when new NSs/IPs are discovered.

Queries are forwarded to the DNS client, which is based on Miekg DNS [32] but offers additional features including asynchronous I/O, rate limiting, UDP port reuse, and TCP connection reuse.

Termination is ensured by using a `been-there-map` to prevent duplicate queries from being asked (per NS address). Whenever a resolution job finishes, the results are written to offset-encoded protobuf messages and compressed. In addition, YoDNS provides JSON output for debugging purposes.

Extensibility and Versatility. The configuration is used to adjust YoDNS's base properties, including which queries to ask, rate limits, backoff-strategy and various other settings. Changes to the resolution strategy, e.g., not minimizing QNAMEs or not iterating over all NSs, are possible through a plugin interface. Modules allow intercepting the program flow whenever NSs, IPs, or zones are modified or responses are received. Data adapters can adjust data persistence, e.g., to use a database instead of files. This allows researchers to adapt YoDNS to their demands without having to reimplement a full DNS resolver.

Caching and Ordering. The order of the target list greatly impacts performance and cacheability. If domain names which share a common suffix are scanned in temporal proximity on the same machine, more queries can be answered from the local cache. However, when too many related names are grouped together, this creates activity hotspots, putting strain on authoritative NSs.

To strike a balance between cacheability and randomization, we first group our input targets by their first non-public suffix, as determined using Mozillas Public Suffix list [58]. For our input (see Sect. 6), 99.71% of these groups have 20 or less domains, whereas the remaining 0.29% contain 27.78% of all domains–potentially causing activity hotspots for shared nameservers. Thus, we order domains in these groups by number of common labels, split them into subgroups of 20 and distribute them randomly within the target list. In test runs, this strategy resulted in a 280% speedup and reduced the actual queries by 50% compared to a randomized target list.

Given this pre-processing, YoDNS can use standard DNS caching, i.e., limiting the cache time to the TTL set by the authoritative servers, while being able to scale-out the measurements to multiple machines with dedicated caches.

To limit memory used by the cache, YoDNS supports a least-recently-used eviction policy. Lastly, while QNAME minimization may require more queries [88], it boosts cacheability, as more queries are common between FQDNs.

Performance. To fully take advantage of parallelism we cannot afford to halt resolutions while waiting for a response, especially, given the per-IP rate limits, see Sect. 4.1. Instead, YoDNS advances resolution as far as possible and handles delayed responses and new resolution paths asynchronously. We use asynchronous UDP port reuse so each socket can have multiple outstanding queries, limiting each socket to 2^{16} active queries per remote IP (size of the ID field). However, to account for misconfigured servers responding from a different IP than the one queried, YoDNS does not reuse ID field values for outstanding queries for a cool-down period of 5 s. Under the rate limits of our measurement, our scans need less than 100 UDP ports per machine. YoDNS also pools TCP connections, supporting connection-reuse [20], and keep-alive [10], increasing performance and reducing the number of connections to remote servers [20].

Restart-Capabilities. We combine target list state-keeping and the use of atomic groups to allow for graceful restarts. Even facing a sudden power loss, YoDNS can restart in-flight groups without having to re-resolve completed groups.

Rate Limiting. While ethical measurements entail questions unique to each individual study, it is imperative that a general instrument supports measurement best practices necessary for ethical measurements, e.g., rate limiting of requests, opt-out [42], as well as curbing bandwidth requirements [46]. To realize rate limiting, YoDNS implements both, a query-per-second and a queries-in-flight limit per DNS server IP per measurement instance.

Both are needed. The first one limits how many queries have to be handled by well-provisioned servers. The latter limits how many queries have to be handled by low-resource or busy servers. Using only an in-flight limit may impose an undue burden on well-provisioned servers. For example, servers able to handle a single query in less than 10ms would receive up to 5,000 queries per second despite using a modest queries-in-flight limit of 50. Still, the in-flight limit avoids overloading slow servers that cannot keep up with the query-per-second rate.

In addition, YoDNS uses a time-slotted N-strike rule. If it receives no reply N times in a row the server is marked unreachable for 5 min. The same applies upon receiving an ICMP(v6) unreachable message. For opt-out, YoDNS implements a block list for IPs, NSs (by name), or queries for specific names.

RFC-Compliant but Resilient to Incompliance. To account for remote servers deviating from DNS best practices, YoDNS is resilient to various non-standard behaviors. Specifically, it gracefully re-attempts resolution when the remote closes TCP connections when pipelining is attempted. Similarly, YoDNS accepts CNAMEs at apex and NS records pointing at CNAMEs interpreting them based on the likely, yet non-standard, intention, as well as multiple CNAMEs at the same name. Finally, it allows for out-of-zone glue and responses with invalid or incomplete flags, e.g., lacking the AA bit. Moreover, YoDNS always *records* such incompliance.

Monitoring. For monitoring, YoDNS can be instrumented with a Prometheus [80] metrics endpoint. This allows for easy integration with off-the-shelf visualization and alerting solutions such as Grafana [34]. Current metrics include resolved domains per second, number of TCP connections, query response codes, rate limiting statistics, cache size, queries in-flight, RTTs, memory, and CPU usage.

5 Data Collection and Dataset

Here, we discuss the dataset we collected using YoDNS. For applicable ethical considerations, please see Appendix A.

5.1 Domain Name Input Datasets

As active DNS measurements need a list of target domains, we utilize the superset of all lists commonly used in the literature for YoDNS, Table 3. The corresponding lists have been retrieved on 5th December 2023. (1) ct: Names from unexpired certificates from Certificate Transparency logs: Argon, Xenon, Oak, Sectico Sabre, CloudFlare Nimbus, DigiCert Nessie, DigiCert Yeti, and TrustAsia. (2) `zf`: Zone files from ICANN's Centralized Zone Data Service (CZDS) [39] and available TLDs (.se, .nu, .ee, .ch, and .li). (3) `opendata`: Names from the open-data efforts of AFNIC [2] and SK-NIC [60]. (4) `tranco` [45], `majestic` [52], `radar` [15], `umbrella` [14]: Names from the corresponding domain top-list.

In total, we find almost 813M different names, of which 319M names are second level domains (SLD) and 494M are below. Of the 319M SLDs, 280M resolve in our scan[4], indicating a coverage of ~78% of an estimated 360M total registrations for 2023 [21].

589M names are unique to CT logs, including 104M AWS-related domains and domains from many ccTLDs [74] not available via ICANN CZDS.

From zone files we gather another 217M (113M unique) names, including 23K names below the second level from the `.name` TLD (such as `john.doe.name`). The open data efforts contribute roughly 4.6M domains (2.5M unique).

By including names from the popular top list (Radar [15], Umbrella [14], Majestic [52], Tranco [45]) we add more than 4M domains. Yet, only the Cisco Umbrella list adds a notable set of new names. Among the top-level domains com with ≈56% is by far the largest contributor. It is followed by net (41M), org (23M), de (18M), io (13M), uk (12M) and ru (10M). Finally, we see that most names under a TLD are obtained through a single source only, for example, 377M out of 455M domains in `.com` are unique to a source.

5.2 YoDNS Configuration

Even though technically engineering-focused, documenting the exact configuration and design parameters for YoDNS is essential for reproducibility, and to avoid the presence of implicit limitations. Hence, we document our exact settings during data collection and applicable considerations here.

DNS tree Exploration Strategy: YoDNS is configured to query all encountered NSs, i.e., those listed in a parent zone as well as those in a zone apex (root level of that domain) and to follow `CNAME`s up to a depth of 64. It uses all discovered IPv4 and IPv6 addresses (encountered either as Glue or as authoritative response). This would cause significant load on the NSs for root and top-level zones, e.g., com with its 13 authoritative NSs would receive almost 12B queries for the second-level domains of our input set. Thus, similar to Naab et al. [59], YoDNS only queries one of the authoritative NSs (selected at random) for root, root-servers.net, com, net, and org. Hereby, it includes the IPv4 as well as the IPv6 addresses of the chosen NSs. We assess the impact of this choice on the completeness of our results in Sect. 6.5.

Queried Records: YoDNS uses QNAME minimization by default and, thus, issues queries for all full and partial names of the target list as well as dependencies encountered during resolution. For names from the target list, YoDNS

---

[4] Please note that these 319M SLDs include a full year of CT logs, i.e., also a high number of SLDs that have been unregistered in the meantime.

Table 3. Target list composition. #Domains for $\text{Sum}_{bySource}$ includes duplicates.

		#Domains	#Unique to source	#Below SLD
By Source	ct	696,487,135	589,186,623	492,898,606
	zf	217,438,044	112,862,815	23,341
	opendata	4,626,781	2,489,116	72
	tranco	1,000,000	18,203	0
	majestic	1,000,000	45,760	921
	radar	1,000,488	18,169	345
	umbrella	1,000,000	602,276	790,167
$\text{Sum}_{bySource}$		922,552,448	705,222,962	493,509,151
By TLD	com	454,938,301	377,277,850	276,016,574
	net	41,284,999	36,081,396	26,418,624
	org	22,798,581	17,671,810	11,033,936
	de	17,569,119	17,522,361	10,866,642
	io	12,770,554	12,750,067	11,456,784
	uk	11,503,887	11,468,806	7,062,585
	ru	9,767,399	9,694,778	7,323,877
	rest	242,113,140	222,755,894	143,330,129
Sum_{byTLD}		812,745,980	705,222,962	493,509,151

queries for `A`, `AAAA`, and `TXT` records of all of its private suffix parents as well as `www.` of the first private parent. At zone cuts, `YoDNS` queries for `DS`, `DNSKEY`, `CDS`, `CDNSKEY`, `CAA`, `TXT`, `MX`, `SOA`, plus the `TXT` records for the name `_dmarc.` in that zone. Also, every NS is asked for version.bind.

If the referral is bogus, i.e. the referred-to-zone is not the queried name or a parent thereof, we ask for the `SOA`, `NS`, `A`, `AAAA`, `TXT`, `SOA`, `DNSKEY`, `DS`, `MX` of the bogus name, but do not chase this path further. If a parent NS does not serve required glue, `YoDNS` asks it for the `A` and `AAAA` of the child NS directly.

Query Parameters: `YoDNS` announces a EDNS0 buffer size of 1232 and requests DNSSEC records (`DO=1`) in initial queries, but disables EDNS0 if the server responds with FormErr (`RCode=1`) or truncation (`TC=1`) even though TCP was used. Queries are retried up to 6 times with increasing back-offs and TCP being used at least once. The DNSSEC chain is not evaluated during the scan, but can be reconstructed from the results.

5.3 Measurement Platform

We ran the data collection from 4 virtual machines within a dedicated IPv4/IPv6 network segment. Each machine has 16 cores, 128 GB of RAM, and a 10 GBit/s network connection. Memory use averaged around 30 GB per machine. CPU use averaged 13 fully utilized cores. Bandwidth utilization averaged around 15 MBit/s outbound (60MBit/s inbound), following our rate limits, see Sect. 4.1.

5.4   Scanning and Dataset

The data collection lasted for 40 days from 7th Dec 2023 09:13 UTC to 16th Jan 2024 11:40 2023. During the measurements, multiple events briefly impacted network connectivity. First, from 8th Jan 2024 15:30 UTC to 16:05 UTC and from 9th Jan 2024 17:50 UTC to 18:05 UTC one of the upstreams encountered connectivity problems due to anomalies in their peering relationships. Next, from 11th Jan 2024 18:10 UTC to 21:55 UTC one of the upstreams was impacted by a denial-of-service attack, which reduced throughput and caused timeouts. Finally, from 15th Jan 2024 00:06 UTC to 00:20 UTC and from 15th Jan 2024 03:00 UTC to 07:00 UTC, another one of the upstreams encountered a denial-of-service attack. All in-flight domains were remeasured after these events.

Our final dataset consists of 85B individual queries collected during these 40 days. Its compressed size on-disk is 87 TB and spans over 812M input names.

5.5   Notable Events

During dataset collection, we encountered multiple domains with unexpected behavior which may have impacted YoDNS if we had sized it smaller. The first group of domains have an unusual parent-child inconsistency. While the parent lists four authoritative NSs, the zone apex contains 300 authoritative NSs with glue for IPv4 and IPv6. The latter implies sending queries to these 600 addresses (for 300 names and 5 record types). This leads to notable spikes in memory usage. Just the raw message bytes already need 18 GB of memory. Another domain created an infinite, non-repeating chain of zone delegations. Here, YoDNS chases this sub-tree up to the maximum allowed length of 255 labels or until a 3M query limit per target list domain is reached. Finally, 3,384 domains in the Tranco top million list (3 in the top 10K) are linked to the socks5systemz malware. While this did not impact the measurement itself, we were contacted by the National CSIRT regarding a possible infection of the vantage point.

6   Evaluation

In this section, we evaluate the impact of limiting DNS tree exploration in various ways by revisiting four prior studies using our dataset. As the raw datasets from prior work are not available, we focus on comparing the published results and inferred metrics. The four studies we selected for our comparison are:

- **Delegation Inconsistency (OpenINTEL)** by Sommese et al. [73], as they only query a single NS per zone, thus limiting the explored DNS tree width.
- **A-Record Inconsistency (ZDNS)** by Izhikevich et al. [41], as the study identifies significant differences to prior work and requires querying all NSs.
- **Dependency Complexity (ZDNS)** by Zhang et al. [90], as the study depends on full dependency resolution but limits exploration to IPv4 and UDP.

– **DNS IPv6 Resolvability** by Streibelt et al. [79], as they run comparable active measurements, but limit their (active) tree exploration to 1M domains. Most of their analysis is based on a passive approach which does not provide full visibility into the DNS tree.

6.1 Delegation Inconsistency

Study Description: To delegate a zone, two conditions must be met: (i) the parent zone must serve NS records for the child, and, (ii) the child must authoritatively serve the same NS records from the zone apex. A delegation inconsistency is, when different record sets are served from zone apex and parent NSs. This may result in unresponsiveness, longer resolution times or security risks [3].

Sommese et al. [73] study the prevalence of delegation inconsistencies below three large TLDs, finding up to 8.2% of inconsistent delegations below `net`.

The study acknowledges that inconsistencies in authoritative NSs can impact the observed delegation inconsistency when only a single NS is queried. Moreover, inconsistencies between parent NSs can affect results, too.

Original Dataset: The original study uses OpenINTEL [68]. Since OpenINTEL only queries a single authoritative NS for the parent and the child zone, it is susceptible to biases induced by partial tree exploration. Thus, the study offers a lower bound on the actual prevalence of delegation inconsistency.

Reproduction Setup: We reproduce the original study with our dataset, recall Sect. 5, which considers all possible resolution paths. Furthermore, our dataset covers roughly 3 times more domains than used in the original study, and features domains below the second level. Note, that our data is from late 2023/early 2024, while the original data is from 2020.

Result Comparison: Table 4 summarizes the results. To quantify biases that may occur due to partial tree exploration, we simulate three perspectives using our comprehensive data: A 'best case', where we always select the consistent resolution path (if such a path exists), a 'worst case' where we always select the path with inconsistency, and a 'randomized' one, simulating the behavior of a normal DNS resolver—similar to the OpenINTEL approach.

Like Sommese et al., we categorize domains as unresponsive, if no authoritative answer can be obtained from the nameservers of the delegated zone. We classify retrieved NS sets as either consistent ($P{=}C$) or inconsistent ($P{\neq}C$). Here, P denotes the set of NS records served from a NS of the parent zone and C denotes the NS records served from a child NS. Assessing the set intersections of '$P{\neq}C$' we find the majority of inconsistent NS sets to be disjoint, with around 1.61% of all zones having an NS set at the child that is a superset of the one from the parent. 0.73% have a parent set that is a superset of the child's NS set. Our results roughly match those of Sommese et al. for `.com`, `.org`, and `.net`. As expected, the random strategy is between best- and worst-case.

Looking beyond `.com`, `.org`, and `.net`, we find inconsistencies between two NSs of the same level (serving the parent or the child) differ considerably based

Table 4. Delegation Inconsistency. C denotes the set of all NS records served from the zone apex, whereas P is the NS records as served by the zones' parents.

			Unresp.	$P = C$	$P \neq C$	Disjoint	$P \supset C$	$P \subset C$	Rest	C-C incon	P-P incon
.com	156M	Best	10.38	83.67	5.95	3.72	0.41	1.60	0.22		
		Wst.	10.43	80.44	9.14	6.44	0.69	1.72	0.28	1.04	-
		Rnd.	9.35	82.61	8.04	5.52	0.58	1.69	0.25		
	142M	[73]	14.0	78.0	8.0	4.64	0.48	2.47	0.41	-	-
.org	11M	Best	8.97	85.23	5.80	3.50	0.38	1.63	0.29		
		Wst.	9.70	83.42	6.88	4.16	0.59	1.74	0.39	0.30	-
		Rnd.	8.96	84.61	6.43	3.89	0.50	1.70	0.34		
	10M	[73]	9.5	82.9	7.6	4.20	0.64	2.37	0.39	-[a]	-
.net	13M	Best	11.84	82.46	5.52	3.18	0.38	1.73	0.22		
		Wst.	11.93	80.09	7.97	5.10	0.68	1.89	0.30	0.74	-
		Rnd.	11.09	81.79	7.11	4.40	0.60	1.84	0.27		
	13M	[73]	12.6	79.2	8.2	4.18	0.75	2.82	0.45	-	-
.top	3M	Best	16.76	76.17	7.06	3.38	0.13	3.54	0.01		
		Wst.	15.89	70.74	13.37	9.27	0.35	3.66	0.09	0.35	0.55
		Rnd.	13.95	74.75	11.27	7.32	0.30	3.63	0.05		
<SLD	37M	Best	2.03	97.68	0.28	0.18	0.01	0.09	0.00		
		Wst.	10.23	87.29	2.47	1.84	0.28	0.21	0.15	5.99[b]	7.67
		Rnd.	6.17	92.58	1.24	0.84	0.16	0.16	0.09		
All	316M	Best	8.14	86.75	5.11	3.05	0.38	1.49	0.18		
		Wst.	9.72	82.76	7.52	4.91	0.73	1.61	0.27	1.70	0.96
		Rnd.	8.13	85.24	6.63	4.23	0.60	1.57	0.23		

[a] Though not directly C-C inconsistency, [73] report ~2% of P-C inconsistent cases in .org, *also* have C-C inconsistency on a sample of 10k domains.
[b] While a higher C-C than P-C inconsistency may seem odd, it is an artifact of DNS and *only* visible when doing a full tree traversal, see Appendix B.

on the type of zone investigated. For zones below second level, we find far fewer inconsistencies between parent and child 2.47%, likely because parent and child are often operated by the same organization. However, the inconsistency among children and parents is larger (5.99% for $C-C$ and 7.67% for $P-P$). Due to this, a single delegation path may see *up to 9 times fewer inconsistent NS sets* than our approach (0.28% in the best-case vs 2.47% in the worst-case). Similarly, we find more inconsistencies for some TLDs, e.g., .top shows a $P-C$ inconsistency of 13.37%, of which 52% are due to a recurring combination of two DNS hosters.

Conclusion: We can reproduce the results of Sommese et al., especially given their goal of providing a lower bound for the number of inconsistent delegations.

However, due to our extensive exploration of the DNS tree and larger input set, we find zones below second level and TLDs exhibiting different behaviors. Especially below second level, $C-C$ and $P-P$ inconsistencies, which are not captured by OpenINTEL, have comparable impact to $P-C$ inconsistencies. Hence, we argue that measurements of domains below second level, should consider full tree exploration to avoid biases induced by NS inconsistencies.

6.2 A-Record Inconsistency

Study Description: For a given RRset, all authoritative NS should always return the entire set of resource records [23], and be in sync, i.e., provide the same data [87]. Returning inconsistent records can lead to seemingly random problems that only affect a subset of clients. For example, out-of-sync A/AAAA records may direct traffic to unresponsive or, in the worst case, malicious IPs [8].

Izhikevich et al. [41] studied A record inconsistency as a case study for ZDNS. The study focusses on IPv4 only. By comparing our results, we can also compare the different DNS exploration strategies of ZDNS and YoDNS.

Original Dataset: The dataset used by Izhikevich et al. was gathered using ZDNS with names from CT logs. It used an input set of 234M FQDNs in 93M base domains. ZDNS successfully resolves 70% of these names. The paper notes a 99.99% consistency for authoritative A RRsets over its input dataset.

Reproduction Setup: We mirror Izhikevich et al.'s analysis on our data and the Tranco subset, i.e., comparing the returned A record sets from all authoritative NSs of a name, extending the analysis to AAAA records. In total, we evaluate 1072M names, including names from our target list and resolved dependencies.

We present a Sankey plot of the following parameters in Fig. 3:

- **Has A/AAAA:** domains with an A/AAAA record.
- **A/AAAA-Inc:** with a mismatch for A/AAAA between NSs.
- **Level:** Level 2 for PSL private suffixes, Level 3 below.

Result Comparison: We find significantly higher inconsistencies for A and AAAA records than previous work. Recall that they found 99.99% consistency. For the Tranco list, 89.6% have an A record and 13.2% have an A record inconsistency across NSs. Notably, most of these records *do* also have an AAAA record, which *also* shows inconsistency across different NSs.

Looking at all names, we find 49.2% have an A record and 3.8% have an A record inconsistency across NSs. Again, we find a notable stream of A record inconsistencies for names that also have an AAAA record inconsistency. Due to our target list, a large number of third-level domains (dark yellow flow) lack A and AAAA records. This is due to the AWS domains (14.9% of all names) in our target list, which often have no associated records.

Next, we determine the DNS hosters for names with inconsistent A records. For this, we inspect the name of the authoritative NSs which might result in Akamai being underrepresented as they often use in-domain NS. Figure 4 shows that a large portion of domains with inconsistency is hosted by Cloudflare, likely due to CloudFlare's dynamic IP assignment at query time [24]. In this case however, adverse effects are unlikely as services are reachable on all served IPs.

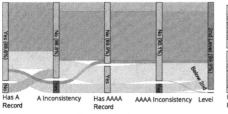

(a) Tranco Top 1M.

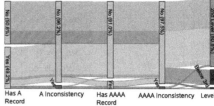

(b) All names incl. dependencies (1072M).

Fig. 3. Inconsistencies in A and AAAA records. Each flow (by color) corresponds to a unique combination of parameters. Its height corresponds to its share of unique domains. For example, the large light-blue flow in Fig. 3a contains domain which have an A Record, show no inconsistency, and are lacking an AAAA record. Flows which exhibit A/AAAA record inconsistency are colored red and flows which have no A record are colored yellow. (Color figure online)

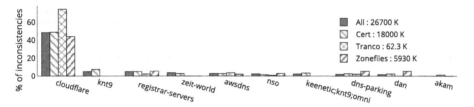

Fig. 4. Hosters of domains with inconsistent A records.

Conclusion: In conclusion, we find notably more A record inconsistencies between NSs than the 0.01% reported by Izhikevich et al. when using ZDNS [41]. With a restricted dataset, which closely matches the one used by Izhikevich et al.–including only records served from IPv4 addresses and names from CT logs– we find that 50.2% have an A record, of which 5.15% have inconsistent A records. Given our observations for CloudFlare, it is unlikely that a difference in the used domain samples cause this disparity. A review of the source code of ZDNS indicates that over-caching in `all-nameserver` mode, i.e., reuse of prior responses from *other* authoritative NS, may be responsible. The resulting limited tree exploration, may have introduced a bias towards consistency.

In summary, we are unable to reproduce the results of Izhikevich et al. [41]. Their conclusion that A record inconsistencies are rare due to the ongoing centralization of the Internet cannot be supported by our dataset.

6.3 Dependency Complexity

Study Description: In order to resolve a zone, resolvers need to resolve the zones' parent zones as well as the zones of their nameservers.

However, a large number of transitive dependencies can negatively affect resolution times, make zones appear more redundant than they actually are [19], or even pose security risks, as compromised domains can affect the resolution of

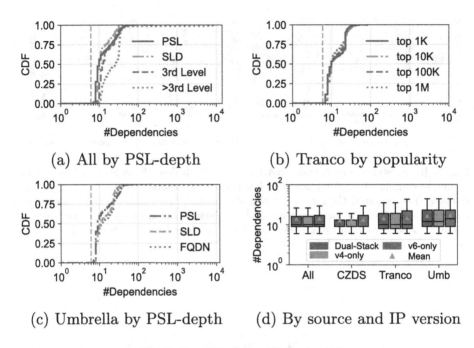

(a) All by PSL-depth (b) Tranco by popularity

(c) Umbrella by PSL-depth (d) By source and IP version

Fig. 5. Zone Resolution Dependencies

dependent domains [66,86]. A recent study by Zhang et al. [90] measures effects of dependencies on robustness and security of DNS resolution for 217M domains.

Original Dataset: The dataset from Zhang et al. [90] consists of zones obtained via ICANN CZDS and the Tranco and Umbrella top lists. The measurement is conducted using ZDNS on 8 distributed vantage points. For their study, Zhang et al. implemented a custom caching strategy for ZDNS, ensuring requests are cached per NS IP. However, they conduct their study using IPv4 and UDP only.

Reproduction Setup: Our dataset contains full-dependency resolutions for each encountered domain, enabling us to quantify the number of dependencies. In addition to the original study, our measurement features IPv6 and a TCP fallback mechanism. Furthermore, our target list contains a considerable number of additional domains from certificate transparency logs and open data efforts.

Like Zhang et al., we define the set of dependencies of a zone as all zones that are encountered during the resolution. This transitively includes the zone itself, its parents, and the zones of its nameservers.

Result Comparison: We present the number of zone dependencies as CDFs in Fig. 5. Contrary to Zhang et al., we consider `root-servers.net` to be a dependency of the root zone, which is why we observe a minimum of 6 dependencies (`root`, `root-servers.net`, `gtld-servers.net`, `nstld.com`, `net` and `com`) for all zones. This minimum is marked by the vertical line. The first notable increase in zones is at 7 dependencies for in-domain hosted SLD zones.

Like Zhang et al., we find that popular Tranco zones exhibit slightly more dependencies. For Umbrella, we find only slightly more dependencies when looking at the fully qualified domain names as compared to the SLDs in the list. However, we observe a long tail of zones with over 9,000 dependencies. Upon closer inspection, this tail is caused by related domains (sharing the same SLD), generating endless delegation chains. However, these domains were not present in the version of Umbrella used by Zhang et al. (25th of April, 2024). In total, we find 150K out of 316M (0.05%) zones with more than 100 dependencies. Again, all of these appear misconfigured to automatically generate delegations.

To quantify biases induced by scanning via IPv4 only, we consider the dependencies of *resolvable* zones in Fig. 5d. IPv4-only and dual-stack resolution show almost identical numbers of (resolvable) dependencies. For IPv6-only, we see slightly more dependencies, indicating that those zones that *are* IPv6-only resolvable, have slightly more dependencies than those that are not. However, less zones overall are IPv6-only resolvable, see Sect. 6.4.

Conclusion: Our results match those of Zhang et al. qualitatively, although we count more dependencies due to different handling of the `root-servers.net` dependency. Additionally, dependencies in the original study may be missed due to the lack of TCP support. However, we show that the number of zone dependencies is only marginally biased by the lack of IPv6 in the measurement.

6.4   DNS IPv6 Resolvability

Study Description: The complexity of DNS results in a plethora of potential misconfigurations that can impair resolvability and redundancy of a zone. In case of IPv6, this is especially difficult, as redundancy and fallback mechanisms can make zones *appear* to be resolving even though misconfigurations do not allow resolution in an IPv6-only scenario. This was first studied by Streibelt et al. [79], using passively collected traces and a small scale active measurement.

In their study, Streibelt et al. find that 55.1% of zones are IPv6 resolvable as of August 2022 and that IPv6 adoption steadily increased since 2015. Furthermore, they note that zones deeper in the DNS tree are less likely to be IPv6 resolvable and that individual operators can have significant impact on global IPv6 resolvability if they host a large number of zones. They find that IPv6 resolution problems are often due to NSs in the parent zone not resolving, i.e., because the parent zone or the zone of the NSs does not resolve via IPv6.

Using our active approach, we can re-evaluate and extend their study by providing reasons for unresolvability from the perspective of a resolver.

Original Dataset: The original study relies on passively collected traces that are collected on globally distributed DNS resolvers. The dataset contains only the recorded and aggregated cache misses of the resolvers. Naturally, this might limit visibility of the DNS tree, as records that are never requested cannot appear. The passive approach is verified using a small scale active measurement.

Reproduction Setup: Given that the work by Streibelt et al. is based on passive DNS data, we leverage data from all zones we measured in our study.

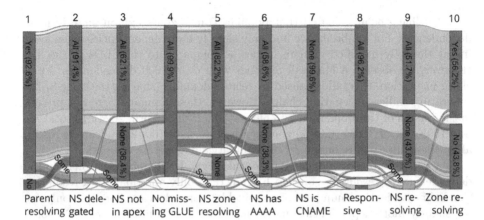

Fig. 6. IPv6-resolvability problems (316M zones). Each flow (by color) corresponds to a unique value combination of parameters. Its height corresponds to its share of unique domains. IPv6-only-resolving domains are colored in shades of blue, while non-IPv6-resolving domains are colored in shades of red. At each column, blue indicates that all NSs of that domain are ok and red (yellow) indicates that all (some) NSs exhibit a specific problem. (Color figure online)

However, we extend the categories of unresolvability reasons. The results are shown as Sankey plot, in Fig. 6.

Specifically, we say a zone is resolvable (column 10 in Fig. 6) if its parent zone is resolvable (column 1) and if at least one of its NSs is resolvable (col. 9) and authoritatively responds (col. 8), i.e., has none of these issues:

- **Missing Delegation (col. 2):** If an NS is not in the delegation for the zone, i.e., only returned from the apex, the NS cannot be used to resolve the zone.
- **NS record not in zone (col. 3):** If an NS is delegated but not returned from the zone apex. Some resolvers require this to harden glue, e.g. Unbound [61].
- **No AAAA glue (col. 4):** As with IPv4, in-domain NSs need glue [4].
- **Unresolvable NS zone (col. 5):** If an out-of-domain NS's name is in an unresolvable zone the NS cannot be used.
- **No AAAA records for NS (col. 6):** An NS needs a resolvable authoritative AAAA record, as some resolvers are hardening glue, e.g., Unbound [61].
- **NS CNAME (col. 7):** RFC2181 [23] prohibits CNAMEs as NS names. Thus, resolvers often do not support this [40].

Result Comparison: Overall, we find 56.2% of 316M zones are IPv6-only resolvable, which is well-aligned with the 55.1% from Streibelt et al. [79]. 8.6% of zones have non-delegated NSs, i.e., NSs not listed in the parent, which only prevents resolution in 0.16% of cases, e.g., when the NSs only listed in the child are IPv6 resolvable, while the ones in the parent are not. Only a fraction of 0.005% of zones is unresolvable due to missing glue. However, like Streibelt et al., we find non-resolving NS zones to be a major problem for resolvability, with

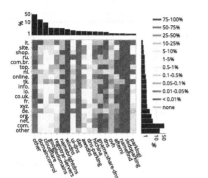
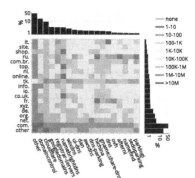

(a) IPv6-resolvability per PSL / provider   (b) Total zones per PSL / provider

Fig. 7. Connection between public suffixes, DNS hosters, and IPv6-resolvability.

16% of zones being unresolvable and 1.8% of zones being partially affected by this. Furthermore, CNAMEs in NS records are not frequent, with only 0.01% of domains being unresolvable (0.4% affected) due to CNAMEs being entered as NS names. Finally, 2.7/1.2% of domains are unresolvable/affected because the listed NSs are not (authoritatively) replying. In summary, we find 51.7% of domains have only correctly configured NSs, whereas 4.8% have some NSs with problems.

Next, we revisit the correlation between public suffixes, DNS hosters, and IPv6 resolvability. Figure 7 shows heatmaps of (a) percentage not IPv6-resolving zones (b) the number of zones for the top 18 public suffixes vs. the top 18 largest hosters. Note, we may again underestimate Akamai-hosted domains. The impact of individual hosters on IPv6 resolvability is clearly visible in Fig. 7a, with, e.g., WixDNS (wix.com, a SaaS web hoster) being completely IPv6 unresolvable. Interestingly, for DomainControl (GoDaddy), IPv6 resolvability is overall good, except for some European zones, most notably .fr and .it, where essentially all zones are not IPv6-resolvable. Investigating further, we find that GoDaddy uses different NSs for these two TLDs, and, while they added IPv6 glue for most of their authoritative servers in the past, this was not done for these NSs, leaving these zones still not IPv6 resolvable. Similarly, we see the positive impact of CloudFlare on IPv6 resolvability, hosting a major portion of domains.

Conclusion: Overall, we can reproduce the results of Streibelt et al., while we also find additional corner cases missed by their analysis. The relatively small number of zones with unresponsive NSs (3.8%) indicates that–especially for long-term perspectives–the use of passive DNS data is a viable option for IPv6 resolvability assessments, despite not having full tree visibility. However, such studies should reconstruct the resolution path, to distinguish failing IPv6 resolution due to parent zones and zones hosting out-of-zone NS, not IPv6 resolving. Overall, active measurements allow a more fine-grained classification of the reasons for lacking IPv6 resolution, see Fig. 6. Finally, we recommend contacting major hosters contributing large portions of non-IPv6 resolving zones directly to rectify these. We reached out to GoDaddy, but a conclusive reply is still pending.

6.5 Result Sensitivity

To reduce the load on Internet core infrastructure, we configured YoDNS to only query a single authoritative NS via IPv4 and IPv6 for the root, root-servers.net, com, net, and org zones, assuming consistency between NSs.

To estimate the impact of this choice on our results, we conduct a measurement on a random sample of 1M zones from com, net, and org each on March, 27th 2024, querying all the NSs of these zones.

We observe no cases where the authoritative nameservers of trusted zones disagree. To further ensure no results have been influenced, we run all our analyses twice. For the first run, we analyze the data considering all the responses from the TLD NSs. For the second run, we only consider the responses of a single TLD NS, emulating the behavior of our large-scale measurement. For the delegation inconsistency analysis that involves random sampling, results deviate only by 0.02%. For all other analyses, the results remain unchanged.

Conclusion: We cannot discard the possibility that the resolution of individual domains would have differed, had we queried all NSs of our five trusted zones. However, an analysis of 3M domains shows no such incident. We conclude that not querying all NSs for selected zones had no notable influence on our results.

7 Concluding Discussion

In this paper, we present YoDNS, a DNS measurement framework for full zone exploration. We employ this framework to replicate four studies, finding that incomplete explorations of the DNS tree can impact results.

For a study on delegation inconsistencies, by Sommese et al. [73], we show that the inconsistency measured by full exploration can be up to 9 times higher than with opportunistic traversal for domains below second level (0.28% in the best-case vs. 2.47% in the worst-case). Similarly, for a study on IPv6-readiness by Streibelt et al. [79], our approach provides richer data and improves classification compared to their passive measurements. It is on par with their active measurements, yet using a significantly larger sample.

However, for both studies, our results also highlight the trade-offs, and–most importantly–that the selected data sources of these two studies *are* reasonable choices for their research questions. Even though our results indicate the need for full tree traversal for zones *below* second level, for Sommese et al.'s selection of second level zones, a full-tree traversal only marginally improves accuracy. Similarly, passive data enabled Streibelt et al. to take an eight-year perspective, which is impossible with full-tree data. Even though having limited visibility into the tree, their numbers are well-aligned with ours.

For other studies, our full tree exploration shows differences in results. For a study Zhang et al. [90], we find more dependencies. However, we also show, that the number of zone dependencies is only marginally influenced by the lack of IPv6. We cannot reproduce a study of A record inconsistencies by Izhikevich et al. [41], finding over two orders of magnitude more inconsistencies.

Recommendations: Our evaluation shows that the DNS tree is not homogeneous, while DNS is notoriously complex. Subsets, e.g., specific TLDs, limited zone depth, or resolution path exploration may hide or amplify effects, making measurements challenging. Hence, we have the following recommendations:

- **Consider full-tree traversal for zones below second level:** We have seen that inconsistencies can have severe effects deeper in the tree. Therefore, we argue that measurements of zones below second level, should strongly consider full tree exploration to avoid or quantify the induced uncertainty.
- **Find qualitative explanations and cross-check results:** In our evaluation, studies that cross-checked results with supplemental measurements have shown to be less prone to biases of partial tree exploration. When identifying differences from prior work, it is important to find qualitative explanations and verify conclusions, for example, by using longitudinal data and/or identifying potential root causes.
- **Accept and Document Limitations:** Given the complexity of the DNS, it is infeasible for a single study to cover all (possible) aspects of DNS that *may* influence results. For example, full tree traversal uses significant time and resources, while mitigating some, but not all, limitations. Hence, researchers should carefully assess if their research question is amendable to optimizations (see Sect. 2) and transparently document these optimizations.

Limitations: While exploring the full DNS tree, the YoDNS configuration used in our measurements only uses (a) TCP fallbacks instead of always forcing TCP *and* UDP queries, (b) one vantage point, (c) QNAME minimization, and (d) naturally does not know *all* possible zones. We decided to accept these limitations since the gathered dataset is sufficient to reach our objective of evaluating whether incomplete DNS tree exploration can bias results. However, YoDNS could easily be run from multiple vantage points given available measurement systems.

Artifact Availability: Our measurement instrument is available at https://github.com/DNS-MSMT-INET/yodns. The collected data [77] is available at https://doi.org/10.17617/3.UBPZXP.

A   Ethical Considerations

Before starting our measurement, we considered ethical implications, following our institution's guidelines and the Menlo Report [42]. Given that we collect generally public data, and analyze only technical aspects, we consider rate-limiting and reducing harm towards other networks as the main ethical objective.

As our measurements may exceed the query load of normal DNS resolution, we took precautions not to concentrate load on individual authoritative

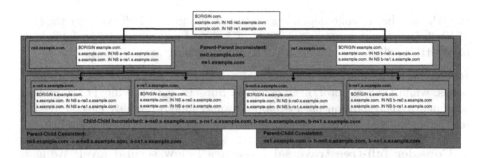

Fig. 8. Example of a zone with two auth. NSs serving different NS sets, leading to parent-parent and child-child mismatches. The latter only become visible when all parts of the DNS tree are resolved, i.e., all four children are detected.

nameservers, i.e., by limiting query rates and queries in-flight, reusing TCP connections, not sending malformed DNS packets, and not querying unresponsive servers, see Sect. 4.1. We seed our measurements from public sources or receive them under an agreement that allows their use for measurements (zone files).

We ensure that our measurements can be attributed to us by (a) hosting a Web page with a project description and contact details on all scan machines; (b) using informative reverse DNS entries; (c) dedicating a network segment to the scans, with associated WHOIS information describing the project and contact details; (d) YoDNS enables opt-out; yet we received no requests for this.

In addition, we submit our study design to our institution's ethical review board, which attested no concerns in response to our application No. 23-09-2.

B   Hidden Child-Child Inconsistency

Seemingly, the number of child-child inconsistencies in Table 4 is "inconsistent" with the number of worst-case parent-child inconsistencies. Intuitively, one would assume that the number of child-child inconsistencies should always be *lesser or equal* to the number of parent-child inconsistencies. However, we find that some child-child inconsistencies cannot be detected by following a resolution path, if, at the same time, a parent-parent inconsistency exists, see Fig. 8.

Here, we have two authoritative NS for a parent zone, ns0.example.com and ns1.example.com, delegating s.example.com. We have a parent-parent inconsistency since they both return different NS sets. Here, ns0.example.com could return an NS set for s.example.com, containing a-ns0.s.example.com and a--ns1.s.example.com, along with valid glue for both. At the same time, ns1.example.com could return an NS set for s.example.com, containing b-ns0 and b-ns1.s.example.com, again, along with glue for both.

If we now query the NS set for s.example.com on a-ns0 and a-ns1.s.example.com, we receive two consistent NS sets containing only a-ns0 and a--ns1.s.example.com. Similarly, if we query b-ns0 and b-ns1.s.example.com, we would receive an NS set containing only b-ns0 and b-ns1.s.example.com.

However, when we evaluate the *complete* zone tree, there is not only an obvious inconsistency between the parents but also between the NSs authoritative for `s.example.com`, the child. All *four* children are inconsistent.

However, our three synthesized perspectives follow a DNS resolution path: If we traverse the tree, regardless of whether we do it randomly (rnd.), or in an attempt to minimize (resp. maximize) paths with parent-child mismatches, there is no path down the tree that lets us receive the parent NS set from `ns0.example.com` while also receiving responses from `b-ns0` or `b-ns1`. We can only evaluate the NS sets from `a-ns0` and `a-ns1`, that are consistent to each other.

Hence, numbers in Table 4 may *look* odd but are correct, as *no* standard DNS resolution strategy for zones would identify inconsistent parents returning internally-consistent NS sets. Only exploring the full DNS tree will find such cases, which are especially prevalent in $>2^{nd}$ level zones.

References

1. Abley, J., et al.: Operation of anycast services. RFC 4786 (2006)
2. afnic, Données partagées : l'open-data du .fr (2023). https://www.afnic.fr/produits-services/services-associes/donnees-partagees/
3. Akiwate, G., et al.: Unresolved issues: prevalence, persistence, and perils of lame delegations. In: IMC (2020)
4. Andrews, M., et al.: DNS glue requirements in referral responses. RFC 9471 (2023)
5. Arends, R., et al.: DNS security introduction and requirements. RFC 4033 (2005)
6. Ashiq, M.I., et al.: You've got report: measurement and security implications of DMARC reporting. In: USENIXSEC (2023)
7. Blechschmidt, B.: MassDNS (2024). http://github.com/blechschmidt/massdns
8. Borgolte, K., et al.: Cloud strife: mitigating the security risks of domain-validated certificates. In: ANRW (2018)
9. Borgolte, K., et al.: Enumerating active IPv6 hosts for large-scale security scans via DNSSEC-signed reverse zones. In: SP (2018)
10. Bortzmeyer, S.: DNS query name minimisation to improve privacy. RFC 7816 (2016)
11. Brownlee, N., et al.: DNS measurements at a Root server. In: GLOBECOM (2001)
12. Callejo, P., et al.: Measuring the global recursive dns infrastructure: a view from the edge. IEEE Access (2019)
13. Chung, T., et al.: Understanding the role of registrars in DNSSEC deployment. In: IMC (2017)
14. Cisco, Umbrella List (2023). https://s3-us-west-1.amazonaws.com/umbrellastatic/index.html
15. CloudFlare, Cloudflare Radar List (2023). https://radar.cloudflare.com/
16. Czybik, S., et al.: Lazy gatekeepers: a large-scale study on SPF configuration in the wild. In: IMC (2023)
17. Darst, C., et al.: Measurement and management of internet services. In: IM (1999)
18. Deccio, C.: DNSViz (2012). https://dnsviz.net/
19. Deccio, C., et al.: Measuring availability in the domain name system. In: INFOCOM (2010)
20. Dickinson, J., et al.: DNS transport over TCP - implementation requirements. RFC 7766 (2016)

21. DNIB Quarterly Report Q4 2023. https://dnib.com/articles/the-domainname-industry-brief-q4-2023
22. Durand, A., et al.: DNS IPv6 transport operational guidelines. RFC 3901 (2004)
23. Elz, R., et al.: Clarifications to the DNS specification. RFC 2181 (1997)
24. Fayed, M., et al.: The ties that un-bind: decoupling IP from web services and sockets for robust addressing agility at CDN-scale. In: SIGCOMM (2021)
25. Fiebig, T.: Crisis, ethics, reliability & a measurement network. In: ANRW (2023)
26. Fiebig, T., et al.: Something from nothing (there): collecting global ipv6 datasets from DNS. In: PAM (2017)
27. Fiebig, T., et al.: In rDNS we trust: revisiting a common data-source's reliability. In: PAM (2018)
28. Fiebig, T., et al.: Heads in the clouds? Measuring universities' migration to public clouds: implications for privacy & academic freedom. In: PETS (2023)
29. Fujiwara, K., et al.: Aggressive use of DNSSEC-validated cache. RFC 8198 (2017)
30. Fukuda, K., et al.: Characterizing DNS query response sizes through active and passive measurements. In: NOMS (2022)
31. Gao, H., et al.: Reexamining DNS from a global recursive resolver perspective. TON (2014)
32. Gieben, M.: MiekgDNS git (2023). https://github.com/miekg/dns
33. Gojmerac, I., et al.: Large-scale active measurements of DNS entries related to E-mail system security. In: ICC (2015)
34. Grafana Labs, Grafana (2024). https://grafana.com/
35. Harrenstien, K., et al.: DoD internet host table specification. RFC 952 (1985)
36. Hoffman, P., et al.: DNS terminology. RFC 8499 (2019)
37. Hoffman, P., et al.: The DNS-based authentication of named entities (DANE) transport layer security (TLS) protocol: TLSA. RFC 6698 (2012)
38. Huitema, C., et al.: Internet measurements: the rising tide and the DNS Snag. In: ITC Specialist Seminar on Internet Traffic Measurement and Modelling (2000)
39. ICANN, ICANN CZDS (2023). https://czds.icann.org/home
40. Internet Systems Consortium, Can an NS record refer to a CNAME?. https://kb.isc.org/docs/aa-00203
41. Izhikevich, L., et al.: ZDNS: a fast DNS toolkit for internet measurement. In: IMC (2022)
42. Kenneally, E., et al.: The Menlo report: ethical principles guiding information and communication technology research. SSRN Electron. J. (2012)
43. Kosek, M., et al.: Measuring DNS over TCP in the era of increasing DNS response sizes: a view from the edge. ACM SIGCOMM Comput. Commun. Rev. (2022)
44. Kumari, W., et al.: Extended DNS errors. RFC 8914 (2020)
45. Le Pochat, V., et al.: Tranco list (2023). https://tranco-list.eu/
46. Learmonth, I.R., et al.: RFC guidelines for performing safe measurement on the internet. Technical report (2023). https://datatracker.ietf.org/doc/draft-irtfpearg-safe-internet-measurement
47. Lee, H., et al.: A longitudinal and comprehensive study of the DANE ecosystem in email. In: USENIXSEC (2020)
48. Lee, H., et al.: Under the hood of DANE mismanagement in SMTP. In: USENIXSEC (2022)
49. Liston, R., et al.: Diversity in DNS performance measures. In: SIGCOMM Workshop on Internet Measurement (2002)
50. Liu, C., et al.: DNS and Bind. O'Reilly Media, Inc. (2006)
51. Lottor, M.: Domain administrators operations guide. RFC 1033 (1987)

52. Majestic, Majestic List (2023). https://majestic.com/reports/majestic-million
53. Mockapetris, P.: Domain names - implementation and specification. RFC 1035 (1983)
54. Mockapetris, P.: Domain names: concepts and facilities. RFC 1034 (1987)
55. Moura, G.C.M., et al.: Anycast vs. DDoS: evaluating the November 2015 root DNS event. In: IMC (2016)
56. Moura, G.C.M., et al.: Cache me if you can: effects of DNS time-to-live. In: IMC (2019)
57. Moura, G.C.M., et al.: Fragmentation, truncation, and timeouts: are large DNS messages falling to bits? In: PAM (2021)
58. Mozilla Foundation, Public Suffix List (2022). https://publicsuffix.org/
59. Naab, J., et al.: Gotta query 'em all, again! Repeatable name resolution with full dependency provenance. In: ANRW (2023)
60. sk-nic, sk-nic OpenData (2023). https://sk-nic.sk/subory/domains.txt
61. NLnet Labs, Unbound (2023). https://unbound.docs.nlnetlabs.nl
62. Nosyk, Y., et al.: Extended DNS errors: unlocking the full potential of DNS troubleshooting. In: IMC (2023)
63. Pappas, V., et al.: Impact of configuration errors on DNS robustness. In: SIGCOMM (2004)
64. PowerDNS, DNS Camel (2024). https://powerdns.org/dns-camel/
65. PowerDNS B.V., Lua Records (2024). https://doc.powerdns.com/authoritative/lua-records/
66. Ramasubramanian, V., et al.: Perils of transitive trust in the domain name system. In: IMC (2005)
67. van Rijswijk-Deij, R., et al.: DNSSEC and its potential for DDoS attacks. In: IMC (2014)
68. van Rijswijk-Deij, R., et al.: A high-performance, scalable infrastructure for large-scale active DNS measurements. JSAC (2016)
69. Rosenbaum, R.: Using the domain name system to store arbitrary string attributes. RFC 1464 (1993)
70. Scheitle, Q., et al.: A first look at certification authority authorization (CAA). CCR (2018)
71. Schlyter, J., et al.: Using DNS to securely publish secure shell (SSH) key fingerprints. RFC 4255 (2006)
72. Sommese, R., et al.: The forgotten side of DNS: orphan and abandoned records. In: EuroS&P Workshop (2020)
73. Sommese, R., et al.: When parents and children disagree: diving into DNS delegation inconsistency. In: PAM (2020)
74. Sommese, R., et al.: This is a local domain: on amassing country-code top-level domains from public data (2023)
75. Sperotto, A., et al.: TIDE: threat identification using active DNS measurements. In: SIGCOMM Posters and Demos (2017)
76. Stahl, M.: Domain administrators guide. RFC 1032 (1987)
77. Steurer, F., et al.: A tree in a tree: measuring biases of partial DNS tree exploration, version 1.0 (2024). https://doi.org/10.17617/3.UBPZXP
78. Streibelt, F., et al.: Exploring EDNS-client-subnet adopters in your free time. In: IMC (2013)
79. Streibelt, F., et al.: How ready is DNS for an IPv6-only world? In: PAM (2023)
80. The Linux Foundation, Prometheus - Monitoring system & time series database (2024). https://prometheus.io/

81. Thompson, K., et al.: Wide-area Internet traffic patterns and characteristics. IEEE Netw. (1997)

82. van der Toorn, O., et al.: Melting the snow: using active DNS measurements to detect snowshoe spam domains. In: NOMS (2018)

83. van der Toorn, O., et al.: Saving Brian's privacy: the perils of privacy exposure through reverse DNS. In: IMC (2022)

84. der Toorn, O.V., et al.: TXTing 101: finding security issues in the long tail of DNS TXT records. In: EuroS&PW (2020)

85. Vermeer, M., et al.: SoK: a framework for asset discovery: systematizing advances in network measurements for protecting organizations. In: EuroS&P (2021)

86. Vissers, T., et al.: The wolf of name street: hijacking domains through their name-servers. In: SIGSAC (2017)

87. Vixie, P.: A mechanism for prompt notification of zone changes (DNS NOTIFY). RFC (1996)

88. de Vries, W.B., et al.: A first look at QNAME minimization in the domain name system. In: PAM (2019)

89. Yajima, M., et al.: Measuring adoption of DNS security mechanisms with cross-sectional approach. In: GLOBECOM (2021)

90. Zhang, S., et al.: Robust or risky: measurement and analysis of domain resolution dependency. INFOCOM (2024)

91. Zirngibl, J., et al.: Domain parking: largely present, rarely considered! In: TMA (2022)

An Integrated Active Measurement Programming Environment

Matthew Luckie[1(✉)], Shivani Hariprasad[1(✉)], Raffaele Sommese[2(✉)],
Brendon Jones[1(✉)], Ken Keys[1(✉)], Ricky Mok[1(✉)], and K. Claffy[1(✉)]

[1] CAIDA, UC San Diego, San Diego, USA
{mjl,shari,brendonj,kkeys,cskpmok,kc}@caida.org
[2] University of Twente, Enschede, The Netherlands
r.sommese@utwente.nl

Abstract. Active Internet measurement is not a zero-risk activity, and
access to Internet measurement vantage points typically requires navigating trust relationships among actors involved in deploying, operating,
and using the infrastructure. Operators of vantage points (VPs) must
balance VP capability against who gets access: the more capable a vantage point, the riskier it is to allow access. We propose an integrated
active measurement programming environment that: (1) allows a platform operator to specify the measurements that a user can run, which
allows the platform operator to communicate to the VP's host what their
vantage point will do, and (2) provides users with reference implementations of measurement functions that act as building blocks to more complex measurements. We first review active measurement infrastructures
and how technical and usability goals have evolved over the years. We
prototype and deploy an integrated active measurement programming
environment on an existing measurement infrastructure, and illustrate
its potential with several case studies.

1 Introduction

Network operators and researchers often require the ability to conduct active
measurements of networks from a specific location in order to understand some
property of the network. However, access to vantage points requires navigating
trust relationships among three types of actors involved in deploying, operating,
and using the infrastructure: (1) the hosting site that deploys a vantage point
(VP) in their network, (2) the platform operator that maintains the VPs in the
field, and (3) the researchers that use the platform. The hosting site incurs risk
in hosting a VP, and has to trust that the platform operator will use the VP
in ways that do not harm the hosting network. The platform operator incurs
significant risk when they allow researcher access to the platform. These trust
requirements inhibit deployment of active measurement infrastructure, impeding
progress in the field of Internet measurement.

Figure 1 illustrates a spectrum of access models for active measurement
infrastructure, ordered from least to most restrictive. The least restrictive solutions grant researcher access directly to the VP, either bare-metal, or within a

C. Testart et al. (Eds.): PAM 2025, LNCS 15567, pp. 137–152, 2025.
https://doi.org/10.1007/978-3-031-85960-1_6

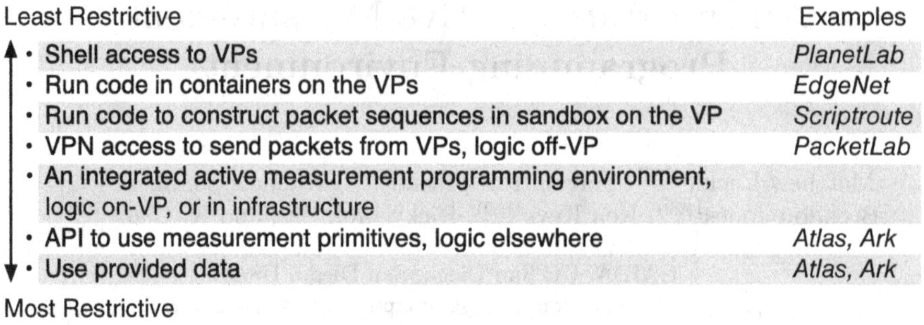

Least Restrictive	Examples
• Shell access to VPs	*PlanetLab*
• Run code in containers on the VPs	*EdgeNet*
• Run code to construct packet sequences in sandbox on the VP	*Scriptroute*
• VPN access to send packets from VPs, logic off-VP	*PacketLab*
• An integrated active measurement programming environment, logic on-VP, or in infrastructure	
• API to use measurement primitives, logic elsewhere	*Atlas, Ark*
• Use provided data	*Atlas, Ark*
Most Restrictive	

Fig. 1. Spectrum of active measurement infrastructures.

container. The platform operator can restrict access with process and capability limits, but has little other control over what the researcher does, and thus assumes significant risk. A step removed from this is VPN-like access: the VP acts as a simple packet forwarder, allowing a researcher to use the node without providing shell access. These solutions allow researchers to craft specific packet sequences that allow for inference based on how the receiver reacts.

More restrictive solutions do not allow access to the VPs, or do not allow researchers to construct their own packet sequences. The most restrictive solutions provide raw data, which relies on the platform operator knowing the needs of the measurement community *a priori*, or provide access to a restricted set of tests via an API. The utility of the platform hinges on the usefulness of the data, the provided tests, and responsiveness of the API.

This paper proposes, implements, and deploys a solution that lies in the middle of the spectrum. Our contribution is to provide a Python-based integrated active measurement programming environment that exposes both a set of distributed VPs, and a set of useful measurement primitives from which to build sophisticated measurement tools. The key benefits to *researchers* are that (1) the environment can provide reference implementations of measurement primitives that are difficult to implement correctly, making the environment useful especially for novice programmers, (2) the environment allows researchers to focus on the logic that ties a series of measurements together in an experiment, and (3) the logic is close to the VP, reducing experiment latency.

The key benefit to a *site host* is that the environment makes it difficult for a researcher to cause harm, intentionally or not, as researchers are restricted to the available measurements. The environment allows the *platform operator* to describe to the hosting site how researchers can use their VPs. However, researchers rely on the environment maintainers and platform operators to expose useful measurement primitives and to keep the environment current with modern systems and evolving Internet protocols.

After a review of related measurement platforms, we articulate our design goals, describe our architecture and implementation, and demonstrate its potential using several case studies.

2 Researcher-Oriented Client-Side Measurement Platforms

Several early (now defunct) active measurement platforms such as Skitter [12], Surveyor [14], AMP [22], NIMI [25,26], and DIMES [31] provided (primarily simple traceroute topology) data for use by the research community. We do not discuss M-Lab because it provides server-side facilities for client-server active measurements [10], or NLNOG RING because the infrastructure requires a user be an operator at an AS with a participating VP [24].

PlanetLab: In 2002, Peterson *et al.* began deploying PlanetLab, a platform for deploying and managing distributed network services [27]. PlanetLab operators distributed *customized* Linux-based hardware systems to research and education organizations. The customizations included (1) virtual *slices* isolated from other slices running on the same system, (2) the ability to use socket APIs that typically required root privileges, and (3) management software. The measurement community made extensive use of PlanetLab. At its peak, PlanetLab had systems in ≈700 organizations. PlanetLab shut down in 2020.

Scriptroute: Released in 2003, Scriptroute [32] provided (1) a set of distributed VPs, and (2) a sandboxed scripting environment so that unvetted users could use them. An application programmer wrote Ruby scripts that embedded logic for sending packets and processing received packets. Users found VPs with DNS queries, and uploaded scripts to VPs of interest via an HTTP API, requiring that each VP have a publicly reachable IP address. Each VP's Scriptroute instance protected the hosting site from accidental or malicious transgressions by running user scripts in distinct sandboxes that limited the resources and system capabilities available to each script, enforced policy around the types and frequency of packets that each script could send, and matched probes with responses so that each script could only observe responses to packets it sent.

Ark: In 2007, CAIDA began operating the Ark infrastructure to perform comprehensive global topology mapping as well as support third-party experiments on the platform. As of October 2024, the infrastructure consists of ≈170 VPs distributed in 57 countries across 133 ASes. The infrastructure consists of x86 rackmount systems, Raspberry Pis (versions 2–4), as well as VMs and containers. To coordinate measurements between VPs, CAIDA implemented (in Ruby) a distributed tuple-space named Marinda. CAIDA made extensive use of Marinda for its own global measurements and research, but no external researcher published a paper where they had used Marinda to coordinate measurements. Researchers could deploy vetted measurement software on the nodes, but deployment was cumbersome because Ark had a mix of operating systems, both vendors and vintages, and a mix of CPU architectures.

RIPE Atlas: operated by RIPE NCC since 2010, Atlas is currently the largest deployed operational active measurement infrastructure, with 12,111 VPs in 3,649 IPv4 (1,844 IPv6) ASes as of October 2024, representing 4–5% of routed ASes [30]. Atlas consists of different types of VPs. The majority (7,697) are small single-board computers with limited CPU, storage, and memory. Atlas also consists of more-powerful *anchors* (794), as well as software VPs (3,620) using the same software as deployed on the single-board computers. Factors in Atlas' success include (1) the VPs were cheap to produce, (2) RIPE restricts the types of measurements conducted on the VPs to mitigate risk to site hosts, (3) these primitives provide useful building blocks, (4) RIPE incentivizes VP deployment by providing credits to site hosts that enables site hosts to conduct measurements from other Atlas VPs, and (5) RIPE subsidizes Atlas through RIR fees. Atlas exposes simple measurement primitives through their web-based API that allows users to conduct ping, traceroute, and selected DNS and NTP queries. Users schedule measurements through the API, and then fetch the results when they become available. To accomplish a complex measurement, the user must parse the raw data, and then issue new requests through the API. It is challenging to deploy reactive measurements, as it "generally takes a few minutes to get the result of a measurement" [8] and most VPs send 4–12 packets per second [8].

PacketLab: Proposed in 2017, PacketLab [17] provides a packet-oriented interface for sending and receiving packets via a distributed set of VPs, similar in goal to Scriptroute. PacketLab's architecture includes (1) a controller that provides centralized access to a set of VPs, (2) packet-sending policy enforced through BPF filters, and (3) authentication of measurements through cryptographic certificates. In recent years, the PacketLab authors reported prototype deployment on EdgeNet [33, 34] and implementations of ping, traceroute, DNS lookups, and HTTP requests. A PacketLab implementation of a protocol that uses TLS (such as HTTPS) would be complex, requiring the implementer to marshal packets through a TLS library off the VP.

EdgeNet: In 2017, researchers at Sorbonne began building a software-only platform for deploying distributed network services, motivated by the observation that maintaining and debugging hardware required six full-time people at PlanetLab [6]. Site hosts contribute *software* (VM) nodes to EdgeNet. EdgeNet operators seek to manage the nodes with off-the-shelf software, such as Kubernetes, rather than customize the operating system. Researchers use these software nodes by publishing Docker containers that EdgeNet can deploy on the nodes [7]. As of 2024, EdgeNet consists of ≈ 50 nodes.

FLOTO and PINOT: Both PINOT [4] and FLOTO [15] are recent (2022) infrastructures consisting of densely deployed Raspberry Pi 4 VPs in select locations. As of October 2024, PINOT is mostly deployed in Santa Barbara, while FLOTO is mostly deployed in Illinois. Following EdgeNet's lead, both are managed with existing solutions – FLOTO uses openBalena and Kubernetes, while PINOT uses SaltStack. Both FLOTO and PINOT invite researchers to deploy containers built for the ARM architecture on their nodes.

3   Platform Goals and Design Decisions

Goal: Easy to Use: To make the environment easy to use, we provide Python interfaces to measurement capabilities present on a collection of remote vantage points, and thoroughly document our interfaces [20]. The environment executes the measurements on the VPs, and provides the results as objects. We chose to provide Python interfaces as Python is extensively used in the measurement community, both in academia and industry, with a large set of modules available for re-use.

Goal: Performant: The delay between measurement and result should be small, so that researchers can build complex reactive measurements. We built our environment with an event-driven API, where results return to the researcher's code as they arrive, with simple method calls. Further, we provide centralized access to the VP controller interface, where code runs as close as possible to the VP controller to further minimize delay.

Goal: Site-Host Transparent: The environment should allow platform operators to accurately describe the types of measurements the VPs will do. We chose to build our enviroment with measurement primitives, rather than provide a packet sending interface, so that we can precisely describe the type of traffic that the site host should expect to see, and communicate risks around each of the available measurement primitives.

Goal: Interoperable and Extensible: Using off-the-shelf and easily deployable components will maximize avenues of future deployment. We used components available in scamper [18] to provide measurement capabilities on VPs, and to support centrally scheduling and receiving of measurements on VPs (Sect. 4). Importantly, scamper is interoperable, as it builds and runs on a diverse set of operating systems and architectures, has few (all optional) external dependencies, can run inside containers, and is available in packaged form. Crucially, scamper is extensible, and provides interfaces to add measurement primitives.

Value of Our Approach: In 2023, Fiebig described four requirements for producing robust and effective measurement artifacts [11]. Our proposal shares Fiebig's aspirations for a community measurement infrastructure that improves reliability and accessibility of active measurement capability. Compared to prior work (Sect. 2), our approach provides programmatic interfaces to coordinate the use of measurement primitives across a distributed collection of VPs. These interfaces allow researchers to focus on collecting and analyzing data, which we believe will increase accessibility of active measurement capability. Researchers do not have to build containers in order to use VPs, or reimplement measurement techniques using packet-sending interfaces. Our approach allows for performant researcher access to VPs through a centralized controller, while being transparent with site-hosts about what types of measurements their VPs will do.

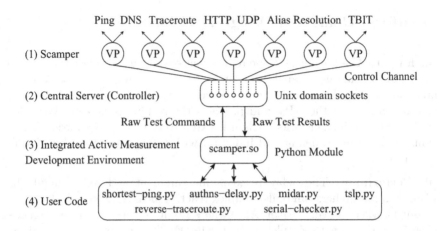

Fig. 2. System Architecture. Scamper processes on VPs connect to a central controller. Scripts access measurement primitives on VPs using an integrated active measurement development environment deployed on, or next to, the controller.

4   Architecture

Our system consists of three components: (1) reference implementations of active measurement primitives deployed on VPs around the world, (2) a controller that interfaces with VPs, making them available for use from a central location, and (3) an environment for scheduling, interpreting, and storing measurements. Figure 2 illustrates our high-level architecture.

For the first component, we deploy scamper to provide implementations of our measurement primitives. Scamper, written in C, contains implementations of traceroute and ping for simple IP topology and delay measurements, DNS lookups for resolving names, HTTP(S) to interact with webservers, UDP probes to interact with query-response services such as NTP and SNMP, alias resolution methods for identifying which IP addresses belong to the same router, packet capture to selectively record specific packets, and TBIT [23] for inferring properties of a remote TCP stack.

Scamper's remote controller terminates connections from these VPs on the central server. Each VP is represented by a Unix domain socket in the file system. To overcome the complexity of scamper's existing APIs, we built a Python module that abstracts this complexity. We implemented this module using Cython [28], which provides a simple way to write Python bindings for C libraries, allowing us to provide native Pythonic interfaces for scamper's active measurement capabilities. The binding is implemented in ≈11K lines of Cython.

Our module exposes two broad collections of classes. The first collection consists of interfaces for interacting with vantage points, which minimize the complexity of managing tasks distributed across a collection of VPs. The second collection consists of interfaces for interacting with measurement results, which normalize the methods and attributes across different measurement types, as

Coordination Classes		Primitives	Result Classes
ScamperCtrl	coordinate measurements across VPs	do_ping()	ScamperPing
add_*()	add VPs	do_trace()	ScamperTrace
do_*()	execute measurement (ping, http, dns, etc)	do_dns()	ScamperHost
instances()	list of connected VPs	do_http()	ScamperHttp
responses()	return data for all outstanding tasks	do_udpprobe()	ScamperUdpprobe
poll()	return first item of data	do_tracelb()	ScamperTracelb
		do_sniff()	ScamperSniff
ScamperInst	represent and store properties of VP	do_tbit()	ScamperTbit
done()	signal no more measurements to come	do_ally()	ScamperDealias
		do_mercator()	ScamperDealias
ScamperTask	an in–progress measurement	do_prefixscan()	ScamperDealias
halt()	cancel in–progress measurement	do_radargun()	ScamperDealias
		do_midarest()	ScamperDealias
ScamperInstError	a Python exception reporting error from VP	do_midardisc()	ScamperDealias
inst	which ScamperInst reported the error		
ScamperFile	a file containing measurement data		
read() write()	read and write measurement data		

Fig. 3. VP coordination classes (left), primitives (middle), and result classes (right) in our integrated active measurement development environment.

the interfaces presented by scamper's underlying primitives were inconsistently named or presented [13].

Coordination Classes: Figure 3 identifies the core classes and methods for managing and executing measurements across VPs. The most important class is the *ScamperCtrl* class, through which scripts schedule measurements, find VPs, and obtain measurement results. We illustrate these methods with examples in Sect. 5. Briefly, the *add* methods allow a script to add VPs to an experiment. Because selecting an initial set of VPs is a common workflow, the *ScamperCtrl* constructor allows specification of VPs when creating a *ScamperCtrl* object.

The *do* methods allow a script to instruct a VP to use one of its measurement primitives (middle-column of Fig. 3). The *do* methods allow measurements to execute synchronously, where the *do* method blocks until it returns the completed measurement, or asynchronously, where the method returns a *ScamperTask* object representing the issued measurement, with control immediately returning to the script. A script would use a synchronous call when a measurement must complete before the script will issue additional measurements, and would use an asynchronous call when it wanted to issue further measurements or do some other computation. These *do* methods present a consistent API over the inconsistent API provided by scamper. The parameters to each method have the same name when they mean the same thing, and the parameters have consistent units. For example, all time-related parameters use Python's *timedelta* or a *float* representing the number of seconds. The *instances* method lists the available VPs, with each VP represented in the environment with a *ScamperInst* object.

Finally, the *responses* method returns measurement results, as they arrive, for all scheduled measurements, while the *poll* method allows a script to obtain just the next available result, waiting for up to the specified length of time. This provides researchers with multiple possible workflows, each of which is applicable in different scenarios. A script can use (1) synchronous measurement via *do* when a measurement must complete before the script will issue additional measurements, (2) blocking asynchronous measurements via *do* and *responses* when the script needs to issue multiple parallel measurements, and then collect all responses before reacting to the results of the measurement, or (3) non-blocking asynchronous measurements via *do* and *poll* when they have a large number of measurements to stream in parallel across one or more VPs. We decided to centralize as much of the coordination on the *ScamperCtrl* object as possible, including issuing measurements, as otherwise scripts would issue measurements via *ScamperInst* and collect them via *ScamperCtrl*, which we judged to be an unusual, inelegant, workflow.

Scripts can indicate that they have no further work for a given VP by calling the *done* method on a *ScamperInst* object. Similarly, scripts can indicate that they no longer need a given measurement to complete by calling the *halt* method on a *ScamperTask* object. If any VP encounters an error while executing a measurement, the environment will raise a *ScamperInstError* exception, allowing the script to identify the specific instance that raised the exception, and a text string explaining the exception condition. Finally, the *ScamperFile* class allows scripts to work with scamper's native binary output format. To support the common workflow of writing measurement output to a file, a script can provide a *ScamperFile* object to the *ScamperCtrl* constructor, which will automatically record all measurements to that file.

Measurement Result Classes: The middle and right columns of Fig. 3 list the available measurement primitives and measurement result classes. For each measurement result, we added Pythonic interfaces to the data. We represent time using Python's *datetime* and *timedelta* classes, provide iterators and generators for convenience, normalize the names of fields across result classes, and provide convenient methods to minimize the amount of code and increase clarity. For example, our environment provides a *min_rtt* attribute for *ScamperPing* that internally iterates through the responses the script receives to obtain the minimum RTT observed so that the script's author does not have to embed that code themselves. Similarly, our environment provides an *ans_addrs* method for *ScamperHost* that internally iterates through the DNS resource records in the answer section of the response, collecting only IPv4 and/or IPv6 addresses in the answer. This method saves the script's author from writing code to interpret each resource record's class and type.

5   Illustrative Examples

We detail three examples that illustrate the capabilities described in Sect. 4, and demonstrate the elegance and succinctness of code that uses the environment. We then summarize several other experiments the environment has supported.

```
import sys
from scamper import ScamperCtrl

if len(sys.argv) != 3:
  print("usage: shortest–ping.py $dir $ip")
  sys.exit(-1)

ctrl = ScamperCtrl(remote_dir=sys.argv[1])
for inst in ctrl.instances():
  ctrl.do_ping(sys.argv[2], inst=inst)

min_rtt = min_vp = None
for res in ctrl.responses():
  if res.min_rtt is None: continue
  if min_rtt is None or min_rtt > res.min_rtt:
    min_rtt, min_vp = res.min_rtt, res.inst

print("%s %.1f ms" % (min_vp.name,
      min_rtt.total_seconds() * 1000))
```

(a) Shortest Ping

(b) Authoritative Nameserver Delay →

```
import sys
from scamper import ScamperCtrl

if len(sys.argv) != 3:
  print("usage: authns–delay.py $inst $zone")
  sys.exit(-1)

inst, zone = sys.argv[1:]
ctrl = ScamperCtrl(remote=inst)
res = ctrl.do_dns(zone, qtype="NS", sync=True)
for ns in res.ans_nses():
  ctrl.do_dns(ns, qtype="A")
  ctrl.do_dns(ns, qtype="AAAA")

addrs = {}
for res in ctrl.responses():
  for addr in res.ans_addrs():
    addrs[addr] = res.qname
for addr in addrs.keys():
  ctrl.do_ping(addr)

for res in ctrl.responses():
  if res.min_rtt is not None:
    print(f"{res.dst} {addrs[res.dst]}",
          f"{res.min_rtt.total_seconds() * 1000")
  else:
    print(f"{res.dst} {addrs[res.dst]} none")
```

Fig. 4. Illustrative examples: finding the VP closest to an IP address (left) and measuring the delay from a VP to a zone's authoritative nameservers (right).

Asynchronous Case, Shortest Ping: Figure 4(a) contains a complete script that finds the VP with the shortest delay to a given IP address, rendering that VP a proxy for the approximate geolocation of that IP address. First, the script instantiates a *ScamperCtrl* object with a directory of Unix domain sockets, each of which represents a remote VP. Then, the script issues a ping measurement using each instance held in the *ScamperCtrl* object. These measurements run on the VPs asynchronously in parallel. The script collects measurement replies using the *responses* method on *ScamperCtrl*, finally exiting when there are no measurements outstanding. The script tracks the minimum RTT observed across all VPs, printing the name of the VP that provided the minimum RTT. Figure 4(a) is a complete script in 19 lines of code, with 4 blank for readability, and 3 reporting the correct usage of the script. The script completes in ≈ 5 s on Ark (Sect. 2): 4 s for 4 echo requests from each VP, plus time sending measurement commands and receiving responses from VPs.

Synchronous Case, Nameserver Delay: Figure 4(b) illustrates the synchronous approach with a script that determines the RTT to nameservers authoritative for a given zone. The first measurement – to determine the names of those nameservers – must complete before subsequent measurements can proceed. Therefore, the first DNS query in Fig. 4(b) uses *sync=True* so that the measurement completes synchronously. Note, the script could have issued the measurement asynchronously and collected the result using *responses* or *poll* (§4), but that would have been inelegant, and would have required writing more code. The remaining steps in Fig. 4(b), which determine the IP addresses of those nameservers, and then obtain the RTTs to them, complete asynchronously. This is a complete 27-line script, with 4 blank lines, lines, 3 usage lines, and one wrapped line to fit within a single column. The script completes in $\approx 7\,s - 4\,s$ for 4 echo requests, 1–2 seconds for the DNS queries, plus time sending measurement commands and receiving responses.

```
if len(sys.argv) != 2:
  print("usage: fast.py $dir")
  sys.exit(-1)

url = "https://api.fast.com/netflix/speedtest/v2?"
date = datetime.now().strftime(
      "%Y-%m-%d_%H:%M:%S")
filename = f"fast.{date}.warts.gz"
ctrl = ScamperCtrl(remote_dir=sys.argv[1],
      outfile=ScamperFile(filename, "w"))

# query for api.fast.com IP address from each VP
http_addrs = {}
for inst in ctrl.instances():
  ctrl.do_dns(urlparse(url).hostname, inst=inst)
for obj in ctrl.responses(timeout=5):
  addrs = obj.ans_addrs()
  if len(addrs) > 0:
    http_addrs[obj.inst] = addrs[0]

# HTTP query for server names from each VP
dns_hosts = {}
for inst, ip in http_addrs.items():
  ctrl.do_http(ip, url, inst=inst)

for obj in ctrl.responses(timeout=25):
  if not isinstance(obj, ScamperHttp): continue
  json_data = json.loads(obj.response.decode())
  tgts = json_data.get("targets", [])
  tgturls = [tgt["url"] for tgt in tgts]
  dns_hosts[obj.inst] = [urlparse(tgt).hostname
                         for tgt in tgturls]

# query for speedtest server IPs from each VP
server_ips = {}
for inst, hosts in dns_hosts.items():
  for host in hosts:
    ctrl.do_dns(host, inst=inst)
for obj in ctrl.responses(timeout=5):
  if isinstance(obj, ScamperHost):
    server_ips[obj.inst] = obj.ans_addrs()

# collect topology to each IP with TCP traceroute
for inst, ips in server_ips.items():
  for ip in ips:
    ctrl.do_trace(ip, wait_timeout=1, dport=443,
                  method="tcp", inst=inst)
for obj in ctrl.responses(timeout=25): pass
```

Fig. 5. Collecting data on topological deployment of fast.com speed test servers with VP-specific DNS lookups, HTTP queries, and TCP traceroutes.

Characterizing Netflix CDN Infrastructure: Characterizing CDNs requires geographically distributed VPs to discover and probe cache servers from different locations [1,9]. Our example collects the IP topology towards Netflix's CDN infrastructure of Open Connect Appliances (OCAs) [5], through Netflix's fast.com speed test service. Netflix directs clients (usually a web browser) to a nearby OCA, from which the client would then transfer large objects in order to measure speed. The speedtest servers returned by Netflix depend on the VP. From each VP, (1) we need DNS lookups to know the IP address of the fast.com web-based API that returns speedtest servers for each VP, in case the address returned depends on the resolver used by the VP, (2) we need HTTP capability to fetch JSON from the fast.com RESTful API via HTTP that contains URLs, one for each speedtest server recommended by Netflix for the VP to test against, (3) we need DNS lookups to know the IP addresses of these servers, and (4) we need traceroute and ping to determine basic topological and performance properties. Our environment provides all of these primitives, and our example (Fig. 5) closely follows these steps, collecting measurements from all available VPs in parallel. The script runs in $\approx 60\,s$ on Ark – up to $25\,s$ each for the traceroutes and HTTP queries, plus two rounds of DNS queries. Appendix A describes this example in further detail.

Complex Measurements: We reproduced a portion of Truffehunter [29], which infers the popularity of rare domains through queries to large public recursive resolvers operated by Google, OpenDNS, Quad9, and Cloudflare (see [21]). We have also reproduced two macroscopic studies of the Internet's router infrastructure – the first used SNMPv3 queries to identify router vendors and aliases [3], and the second used those vendors to train a fingerprint classifier to infer vendors for other routers that did not return an SNMPv3 response [2]. Finally, we added primitives to support MIDAR [16], which uses a set of VPs to probe router interfaces with the goal of finding which interface IP addresses belong to the same router (are aliases) – those where response IPID values appear to be derived from a central counter. Intuitively, MIDAR solves this problem at Internet scale by providing a distributed set of VPs with a set of probe definitions (ICMP, UDP, TCP, IP addresses) and a sliding-window schedule that specifies when these probes should enter the network, so that two candidate aliases have a high chance of receiving probes that allow this single central counter property to be observed. We replaced 2554 lines of opaque Ruby code with a 902 line Python script that clearly conveys the organizational requirement involved in the measurements. Appendix B describes this example in further detail.

These experiments are difficult to support on existing measurement platforms (Sect. 2), as they require distributed, coordinated probing facilities that allow for fine-grained control of measurements. We found these examples straightforward to implement. We did not have to write code to execute directly on VPs, copy results off the VPs, or coordinate VPs, and the remainder of the scripts used environment features that made our measurement intentions clear.

6   Discussion and Future Work

We have designed and built a programming environment to accelerate innovation in scientific Internet measurement. Our priorities were to lower the threshold for implementing complex measurement experiments, in a performant environment, while also allowing platform operators to accurately describe the types of measurements the VPs will do to site hosts.

One gratifying outcome of our Python-based platform architecture is its use in a Python-based Jupyter Notebook environment. Rather than edit scripts in a text editor, one student developed solutions in a Jupyter Notebook environment, with which they were familiar. They reported that this approach significantly lowered the learning curve required to conduct their active measurements.

We designed our environment to operate on, or adjacent to, a central controller that interfaces with VPs distributed around the world. The logic for measurement primitives (e.g., traceroute, HTTP, etc.) executes on the VPs, while the logic that uses the results executes on or adjacent to the central controller. For experiments where delay between the controller and VP is problematic, we are currently exploring deployment architectures, such as sandboxed containers, that would enable researchers to safely deploy scripts onto the VPs, without requiring a platform operator to manage shell accounts for platform users.

We have publicly released our implementation [19] and documentation [20], so that the Internet measurement and operations communities can extend it, and benefit from our work. We plan to support its use on CAIDA's Archipelego (Ark) infrastructure, and seek to spur discussion with other active measurement infrastructures as to how they can safely modernize their capabilities. We believe that thinking about distributed measurement through the lens of required measurement primitives, rather than ad-hoc collections of software to collect measurement data, is a useful exercise, as implementing primitives lowers the barrier to other researchers continuing the work and increases incentives to repeat measurements. Our ultimate vision for this work is a world where researchers can ask, and answer, grand questions about the global Internet in near-real-time.

Acknowledgments. This work started with a suggestion from Bill Herrin during a CAIDA AIMS workshop that a Domain Specific Language (DSL) could accelerate discovery with active measurement. Alexander Marder suggested that we start with Python bindings for scamper. We thank the anonymous reviewers for their comments. This research was supported by National Science Foundation (NSF) grants OAC-2131987, CNS-2120399, CNS-2323219, and CNS-2212241.

A   Measuring CDN Catchment and Routing

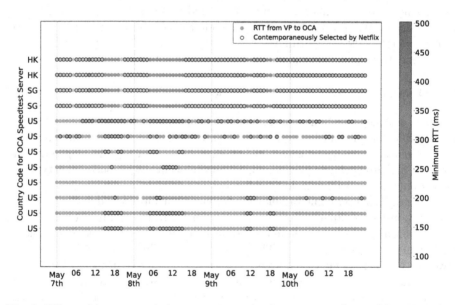

Fig. 6. Effect of latency variation on server selection strategy during May 2024, for a VP located in Thimphu, Bhutan. The X-axis shows the VP's local time. Each row shows a unique /24, annotated with the country using Netflix-assigned hostnames.

This measurement consists of two scripts. The first collects details of the fast.com servers returned to each VP, and is shown in Fig. 5. This script runs hourly out of cron, and stores the results in scamper's archival format for subsequent analysis. The second script, which we elide, processes the archived data returned from the first script to extract the speedtest servers that Netflix had returned over time for each VP, building history of possible speedtest servers for each VP. The script measures latency, with ping, between the VPs and the set of OCAs (one randomly selected per /24) for each VP, to characterize the condition of the path between the VPs and the proximate OCAs.

With the data that we collected beginning April 11th 2024, we were able to observe some interesting patterns, one of which we highlight here as an illustrative example. We observed how traffic load appeared to influence which OCA servers Netflix would return to the VP. Figure 6 shows RTT values to speedtest servers returned to a VP located in Bhutan during four days in May 2024. Those servers contemporaneously selected by Netflix are noted with black circles. Netflix generally returned servers in Hong King and Singapore, and those had the lowest observed latency of ≈100 ms. However, those servers occasionally had significant latency spikes to ≈500 ms. During those latency spikes, Netflix directed the Bhutan VP to servers in the U.S., which had a latency of ≈250 ms.

B   Router Alias Inference and Fingerprinting

Table 1. Properties of ITDKs collected before (2023-02) and after (2024-02) we developed our solution.

	2023-02	2024-02
Input		
IPv4 addresses probed	2.64M	3.58M
Traceroute data window	2 weeks	3 weeks
Ark VPs w/ traceroute data	93	142
Number of countries	37	52
Alias Resolution		
Ark VPs used for MIDAR	55	101
Ark VPs used for iffinder	46	101
Ark VPs used for SNMP	–	7
MIDAR + iffinder Graph		
Nodes with at least two IPs	75,660	107,976
Addresses in nodes with at least two IPs	284,479	425,964
SNMP Graph		
Nodes with at least two IPs	–	48,899
Addresses in nodes with at least two IPs	–	208,313
MIDAR + iffinder + SNMP Graph		
Nodes with at least two IPs	–	125,370
Addresses in nodes with at least two IPs	–	516,867

These measurements, briefly described in Sect. 5, consisted of multiple related scripts that we integrated into an automated workflow for building the 2024-02 ITDK. Table 1 provides statistics illustrating the growth of the ITDK between February 2023 and February 2024, driven by the expansion of Ark VPs. Overall, we increased the number of Ark VPs providing topology data from 93 to 142, the number of addresses probed from 2.64M to 3.58M, doubled the number of VPs that we use for alias resolution probing, and found aliases for 50% more addresses in 2024-02 than we did for 2023-02. These 3.58M addresses were observed in the middle of a traceroute path, and are most likely router interface addresses. We use the term "node" to distinguish between our router inferences, and the actual routers themselves. By definition, all routers have at least two IP addresses. Our "nodes with at least two IPs" are the subset of routers we were able to observe with that property.

For 2024-02, we also evaluated the gains provided by SNMPv3 probing, following the work by Albakour et al. published in 2021 that showed many routers return a unique SNMP Engine ID in response to a SNMPv3 request [3]. The basic idea is that different IP addresses returning the same Engine ID, number of boot counts, and inferred boot time in response to SNMPv3 queries are likely aliases. Of the 3.58M addresses we probed, 669K returned an SNMPv3 response. We inferred that IP addresses belonged to the same router when they return the same SNMP Engine ID, the size of the engine ID was at least 4 bytes, the number of engine boots was the same, and the router uptime was the same; we did not use the other filters in Sect. 4.4 of the IMC paper [3]. This inferred 48,899 nodes with at least two IPs, many of which were shared with existing nodes found with MIDAR + iffinder. In total, when we combined MIDAR, iffinder, and SNMP probing, we obtained a graph with 125,370 nodes with at least two IPs, covering 516,867 addresses.

Finally, we also implemented the methodology published in 2023 by Albakour et al. that described a way to infer router vendors [2]. An SNMPv3 response embeds a vendor identifier in the SNMP Engine ID. The basic idea is that the subset of routers that return an SNMPv3 response allow us to learn fingerprint rules for other routers that do not respond to SNMPv3 probes, but will send responses to TCP, UDP, and ICMP probes. For the 2024-02 ITDK, we sent TCP, UDP, and ICMP probes to the 3.58M router interface addresses, using the probing strategy described in [2], implemented in 170 lines of code. We inferred 96 rules to infer vendors from TCP, UDP, and ICMP response patterns, implemented in 483 lines of code (which also includes logic to infer router aliases from the same SNMP responses). Our inference script followed the same approach as in [2] except that it also considered byte-swapped IPID values for TCP responses. When we used these rules to map response patterns to vendors, we inferred vendors for 248K router interface addresses, in addition to the 669K SNMPv3-responsive addresses that directly returned a vendor identifier.

References

1. Adhikari, V.K., et al.: Measurement study of Netflix, Hulu, and a tale of three CDNs. IEEE/ACM Trans. Netw. **23**(6), 1984–1997 (2014)
2. Albakour, T., Gasser, O., Beverly, R., Smaragdakis, G.: Illuminating router vendor diversity within providers and along network paths. In: IMC, pp. 89–103 (2023)
3. Albakour, T., Gasser, O., Beverly, R., Smaragdakis, G.: Third time's not a charm: exploiting SNMPv3 for router fingerprinting. In: IMC, pp. 150–164 (2021)
4. Beltiukov, R., Chandrasekaran, S., Gupta, A., Willinger, W.: PINOT: programmable infrastructure for networking. In: ANRW, pp. 51–53 (2023)
5. Böttger, T., Cuadrado, F., Tyson, G., Castro, I., Uhlig, S.: Open connect everywhere: a glimpse at the Internet ecosystem through the lens of the Netflix CDN. ACM SIGCOMM Comput. Commun. Rev. **48**(1), 28–34 (2018)
6. Cappos, J., Hemmings, M., McGeer, R., Rafetseder, A., Ricart, G.: EdgeNet: a global cloud that spreads by local action. In: SEC, pp. 359–360 (2018)
7. Şenel, B.C., Mouchet, M., Cappos, J., Fourmaux, O., Friedman, T., McGeer, R.: EdgeNet: a multi-tenant and multi-provider edge cloud. In: EdgeSys, pp. 49–54 (2021)
8. Darwich, O., Rimlinger, H., Dreyfus, M., Gouel, M., Vermeulen, K.: Replication: towards a publicly available internet scale IP geolocation dataset. In: IMC, pp. 1–15 (2023)
9. Doan, T.V., Bajpai, V., Crawford, S.: A longitudinal view of Netflix: content delivery over IPv6 and content cache deployments. In: IEEE INFOCOM (2020). https://doi.org/10.1109/infocom41043.2020.9155367
10. Dovrolis, C., Gummadi, K., Kuzmanovic, A., Meinrath, S.D.: Measurement lab: overview and an invitation to the research community. Comput. Commun. Rev. **40**(3), 53–56 (2010)
11. Fiebig, T.: Crisis, ethics, reliability & a measurement. Network: reflections on active network measurements in academia. In: ANRW, pp. 44–50 (2023)
12. Huffaker, B., Plummer, D., Moore, D., k claffy: Topology discovery by active probing. In: SAINT,Nara City, Japan, pp. 90–96 (2002)
13. Jonglez, B.: drakkar-lig scamper-pywarts (2021). https://github.com/drakkar-lig/scamper-pywarts
14. Kalidindi, S., Zekauskas, M.J.: Surveyor: an infrastructure for internet performance measurements. In: INET, San Jose, CA (1999)
15. Keahey, K., et al.: Discovery testbed: an observational instrument for broadband research. In: eScience (2023)
16. Keys, K., Hyun, Y., Luckie, M., Claffy, K.: internet-scale IPv4 alias resolution with MIDAR. IEEE Trans. Netw. **21**(2), 383–399 (2013)
17. Levchenko, K., Dhamdhere, A., Huffaker, B., Claffy, K., Allman, M., Paxson, V.: PacketLab: a universal measurement endpoint interface. In: IMC, pp. 254–260 (2017)
18. Luckie, M.: Scamper: a scalable and extensible packet prober for active measurement of the Internet. In: IMC, pp. 239–245 (2010)
19. Luckie, M.: Scamper (2024). https://www.caida.org/catalog/software/scamper/
20. Luckie, M.: Scamper Python module documentation (2024). https://www.caida.org/catalog/software/scamper/python/
21. Luckie, M.: Understanding the deployment of public recursive resolvers (2024). https://blog.caida.org/best_available_data/2024/05/06/understanding-the-deployment-of-public-recursive-resolvers/

22. McGregor, T., Braun, H.W.: Balancing cost and utility in active monitoring: the AMP example. In: INET, Yokohama, Japan (2000)
23. Medina, A., Allman, M., Floyd, S.: Measuring the evolution of transport protocols in the Internet. Comput. Commun. Rev. **35**(2), 37–52 (2005)
24. NLNOG: Ring. https://ring.nlnog.net/
25. Paxson, V., Mahdavi, J., Adams, A., Mathis, M.: An architecture for large-scale Internet measurement. IEEE Commun. Mag. **36**(8), 48–54 (1998)
26. Paxson, V., Adams, A., Mathis, M.: Experiences with NIMI. In: PAM, Hamilton, New Zealand (2000)
27. Peterson, L., Bavier, A., Fiuczynski, M.E., Muir, S.: Experiences building Planet-Lab. In: OSDI, Seattle, WA, pp. 351–366 (2006)
28. Project, C.: Cython: C-extensions for Python (2024). https://cython.org/
29. Randall, A., et al.: Trufflehunter: cache snooping rare domains at large public DNS resolvers. In: IMC, pp. 50–64 (2020)
30. RIPE NCC: RIPE Atlas - coverage. https://atlas.ripe.net/coverage/
31. Shavitt, Y., Shir, E.: DIMES: let the Internet measure itself. Comput. Commun. Rev. **35**(5), 71–74 (2005)
32. Spring, N., Wetherall, D., Anderson, T.: ScriptRoute: a public internet measurement facility. In: USITS, Seattle, WA, pp. 225–238 (2003)
33. Yan, T.B., et al.: Poster: PacketLab - tools alpha release and demo. In: IMC, pp. 766–767 (Oct 2022)
34. Yan, T.B., Zhang, Z., Huffaker, B., Mok, R., Levchenko, K., Claffy, K.: Poster: empirically testing the PacketLab model. In: IMC, pp. 724–725 (2023)

Web/HTTP

HTTP Conformance vs. Middleboxes: Identifying Where the Rules Actually Break Down

Ilies Benhabbour[✉], Mahmoud Attia, and Marc Dacier

KAUST, Thuwal, Kingdom of Saudi Arabia
{ilies.benhabbour,mahmoud.attia,marc.dacier}@kaust.edu.sa

Abstract. HTTP is the foundational protocol of the World Wide Web, designed with a strict set of specifications that developers are expected to follow. However, real-world implementations often deviate from these standards. In this study, we not only confirm these inconsistencies but build on previous work [45] to reveal a deeper issue: the impact of network middleboxes. Using a novel framework, we demonstrate that HTTP server conformance cannot be accurately assessed in isolation, as middleboxes can alter requests and responses in transit. We conducted 47 conformance tests on 12 popular proxy implementations. Our results show that none of them are fully compliant with the relevant RFCs, and there is significant variation in their behaviors. This inconsistency stems from ambiguities in the RFCs, which fail to provide clear guidelines for these middleboxes. In some cases, the implementation choices made can lead to vulnerabilities.

Keywords: HTTP Conformance · Network Security · Network Middleboxes

1 Introduction

The Hypertext Transfer Protocol (HTTP) is the standard protocol that governs the World Wide Web. It is defined through Request for Comments (RFCs) published by the Internet Engineering Task Force (IETF). Over its 30-year evolution, HTTP has continuously adapted to introduce new features, improve performance, and enhance security.

Despite its ubiquity—with Cloudflare reporting an average of 50 million HTTP(S) requests per second in 2023 [6]—studies show that implementations often deviate from the official specifications [45]. While it is commonly assumed that these deviations occur at the endpoints, this is not always the case. Network elements, often referred to as middleboxes [10], can modify packets, potentially introducing non-conformance. For example, Edeline et al. [16] demonstrated in 2019 that more than one-third of network paths traverse at least one middlebox, while Hilal et al. [23] found in 2021–2022 that 10% of observed IPv4 traffic passed through middleboxes.

© The Author(s), under exclusive license to Springer Nature Switzerland AG 2025
C. Testart et al. (Eds.): PAM 2025, LNCS 15567, pp. 155–181, 2025.
https://doi.org/10.1007/978-3-031-85960-1_7

Rautenstrauch et al. [45] recently studied the conformance of the HTTP protocol implementation in 9 popular origin server implementation and close to 10000 popular webservers. Quoting the authors, their tests remain *"inherently incomplete"* as *"they cannot reliably attribute a violated rule to one specific entity in a complex HTTP processing chain, as any intermediaries might generate or modify the response"*.

In this paper, we aim to address the following question: Do network middleboxes affect the conformance of HTTP traffic? To investigate this, we measured 47 different test cases using the framework we propose and implement. This framework is designed to simplify the detection, fingerprinting, and conformance verification of network middleboxes.

Our key contributions are as follows:

- We present a new, user-friendly framework that is accessible, modifiable, and deployable by both users and network administrators.
- We not only find that all twelve tested application-layer network middleboxes (proxies) accept non-conforming HTTP requests or responses, violating the standard, but also demonstrate that ambiguities in the standard itself lead these middleboxes to modify packets in an attempt to make them conformant[1].
- In a real-world measurement campaign across multiple cloud providers, none of the 225 tested routes included a transparent application middlebox under the default server configurations, suggesting an absence of built-in security policies.

The paper is structured as follows. Section 2 provides the necessary background on the HTTP protocol and network middleboxes. Section 3 formalizes the objectives and scope of this study. Section 4 details the methodology employed to achieve our research goals. Section 5 describes the experimental setup used in our investigation. Section 6 outlines the ethical considerations relevant to this study. Section 7 presents the results of our experiments. Section 8 discusses the findings, and outlines future work. Section 9 concludes the paper, summarizing the key takeaways.

2   Background

This section focuses on HTTP conformance in the context of network middleboxes. To provide a common understanding, Subsect. 2.1 offers an overview of the evolution of the HTTP protocol. Subsection 2.2 describes the structure of HTTP/1.1, which is used throughout this paper. Subsection 2.3 covers related work on HTTP standard conformance. Finally, Subsect. 2.4 introduces network middleboxes and explains their relevance to HTTP.

---

[1] Although the intention is to achieve conformance, this behavior is itself non-conformant, as the RFCs state that non-conforming requests or responses should be rejected, not modified.

2.1   Evolution of the HTTP Protocol

HTTP is an essential component of today's Internet, initially developed to facilitate document transfer between web servers and clients. Created by Tim Berners-Lee and his team at CERN between 1989 and 1991, HTTP was designed to enable efficient information sharing. As web communication demands have evolved, so too have the versions of HTTP, each aiming to enhance performance and functionality.

The first version, HTTP/0.9, was a minimal protocol that supported only the GET method and specified the path to the requested resource. To address its limitations, HTTP/1.0 was introduced in November 1996 through RFC 1945 [42]. This version added status codes to indicate request success or failure and introduced the Content-Type header for transferring various document types beyond HTML. Subsequently, HTTP/1.1 was released in January 1997 in RFC 2068 [17], bringing significant advancements such as chunked transfer encoding, support for virtual hosting via the Host header, enhanced caching mechanisms, and pipelined data transfers.

HTTP/2, standardized in May 2015 through RFC 7540 [5], marked a major leap in web performance. Based on Google's SPDY protocol [51], which was deprecated in 2009, HTTP/2 introduced features such as binary framing, multiplexing, server push, and header compression. HTTP/3, defined in RFC 9114 [8], builds on the foundation of HTTP/2 but introduces multiplexing over QUIC, a transport protocol using multiple UDP streams. This approach enhances performance and reliability compared to previous versions.

2.2   HTTP Message Structure

Throughout the remainder of this paper, we refer to HTTP in the context of the HTTP/1.1 version[2]. HTTP is a protocol that defines a standardized communication language between a client and a server. As shown in Fig. 1, the HTTP protocol follows a request-response structure. The client initiates communication by sending a request to the server. This request consists of three main components: a request line, request headers, and an optional request body.

- The request line specifies:
  - The request method (e.g., GET, POST, HEAD)
  - The Uniform Resource Identifier (URI) of the requested resource
  - The HTTP protocol version
- The request headers contain key-value pairs that provide additional information required to process the request. For example, the Host header (the only mandatory one in HTTP/1.1) specifies which server should handle the request in scenarios where multiple servers share the same IP address. Other headers might convey information about accepted data formats, authorization credentials, content types, and more.

---

[2] Measurements related to HTTP/2 and HTTP/3 fall outside the scope of this paper and will be examined in future work.

After receiving the client's request, the server responds with an HTTP response. The response structure is similar to that of the request, comprising a status line, response headers, and an optional response body.

- The status line includes the HTTP protocol version, the status code (indicating the outcome of the request, such as 200 OK or 404 Not Found), and a status message.
- The response headers convey metadata about the response, such as when the content was last modified (using the Last-Modified header) or the type of content being returned (through the Content-Type header).
- The response body contains the requested data, if applicable (for instance, an HTML page or JSON data).

```
GET /index.html HTTP/1.1
Host: hello-world.com
Accept-Language: en-US,en;q=0.9
Accept-Encoding: gzip, deflate, br
User-Agent: Mozilla/5.0 (Windows NT 10.0; Win64; x64)
            AppleWebKit/537.36 (KHTML, like Gecko)
            Chrome/116.0.0.0 Safari/537.36
```

(a) HTTP Request

```
HTTP/1.1 200 OK
Date: Sun, 15 Sep 2024 12:34:56 GMT
Server: Apache/2.4.41 (Ubuntu)
Content-Length: 12
Content-Type: text/html; charset=UTF-8

Hello World!
```

(b) HTTP Response

Fig. 1. Structure of an HTTP request (top) and response (bottom). The request includes the request line, headers, and an optional request message body, while the response includes the status line, headers, and response message body

For the remainder of this paper, it is important to note that Carriage Return (CR) and Line Feed (LF), collectively known as CRLF, are used in the HTTP protocol to signify the end of a line. These sequences are essential for web servers and browsers to correctly parse HTTP requests and responses, including separating individual headers and distinguishing headers from the message body.

2.3   HTTP Conformance

RFCs define protocols and prescribe the rules that implementations should follow, using terms such as MUST, SHOULD or MAY. However, web server implementations frequently deviate from these standards. As early as 2001, Krishnamurthy et al. introduced PRO-COW [34] to examine `HTTP/1.1` compliance and found that many popular web servers failed to implement critical protocol specifications, such as new methods and persistent connections. In the same year, The Measurement Factory (TMF) released a project evaluating `HTTP` compliance in web intermediaries, discovering that Squid `HTTP` proxies did not meet the standard on numerous aspects [54]. In 2008, Adamczyk et al. investigated the compliance of `HTTP` among 176 popular websites, testing methods such as `OPTIONS`, `TRACE`, `GET`, conditional `GET`, `HEAD`, and `CONNECT` [2]. They found that both implementations and configurations were often faulty, revealing that while some implementations were correct, misconfigurations were prevalent. In 2024, Rautenstrauch et al. [45] demonstrated that these issues persist, presenting a study on `HTTP` rule violations across nine popular web server implementations and almost 10,000 websites. Their findings revealed that out of 106 rules examined, most systems violated at least one. In 2018, Nguyen et al. [41] introduce a testing tool comprising 397 test cases designed to evaluate the conformance of web caching servers to `RFC 7234` [18]. This tool was used in a follow-up study [40], where it was applied to seven widely-used caching servers, including Nginx, Apache, and Squid. The results revealed that these servers sometimes cached responses to requests containing `Authorization` headers, potentially exposing sensitive information—behavior explicitly prohibited by the RFC standard. Some tools may also target specific versions of `HTTP`, such as h2spec [27], which aims at verifying the compliance of `HTTP/2` implementations, including header compression (`HPACK`), with the standard.

2.4   Network Middleboxes

Network middleboxes, as defined in `RFC 3234` [10], are intermediate devices that disrupt the end-to-end principle defined by Saltzer et al. [49]. According to this principle, network functions are *"correctly implemented only with the knowledge and help of the application standing at the endpoints"*. The rise of network middleboxes has effectively shifted the Internet from an end-to-end paradigm to an end-to-middle-to-end model. This shift is well-documented in the literature [4, 13–15, 23–25, 43]. While middleboxes can enhance performance and security, their presence also introduces new attack surfaces.

For instance, `HTTP` Request Smuggling (HRS), first documented in 2005 [22], exploits interpretation mismatches between implementations of the same protocol standard by web proxy middleboxes and end servers. This vulnerability enables attackers to bypass access controls enforced by proxies, CDNs, and firewalls, allowing them to smuggle unauthorized requests. A decade later, Chen et al. [12] showcased an attack called "Host of Troubles". They revealed that ambiguities in how `Host` headers are implemented, especially when multiple `Host` headers appear in a request, can be exploited when the same `HTTP` request is handled sequentially by different implementations.

In 2019, James Kettle presented at a DEFCON conference that discrepancies between `Content-Length` and `Transfer-Encoding` `HTTP` headers could lead to web session hijacking and credential theft, earning him over $70,000 in bug bounty rewards. Follow up works, like T-Reqs [30], HDiff [50], HTTP Garden [31], and Gudifu [28] have leveraged differential fuzzing strategies to uncover other implementation gaps in HTTP protocols. Another way to carry out an HRS attack is via HTTP/2 to HTTP/1 downgrades, as demonstrated by Kettle [32]. While client-side support for HTTP/2 is rapidly increasing, server-side support lags behind, enabling new potential HTTP desynchronization attacks. In 2022, Jabiyev et al. [29] developed Frameshifter to analyze anomalies in HTTP/2 to HTTP/1.1 downgrades, identify their root causes, and explore potential attacks that could exploit these vulnerabilities.

Web Cache Deception (WCD) is another attack that targets interpretation mismatches between a frontend middlebox and a backend server. Originally introduced at Black Hat in 2017 [21], WCD exploits cache proxies to store sensitive data from victim users. WCD has gained attention with study [36] showing in 2020 that 295 sites among the Alexa Top 5K were leaking sensitive authentication and authorization tokens. A follow-up paper in 2022 [37] revealed that among the Alexa Top 10K, 1,188 websites were vulnerable.

All these attacks share a common characteristic: they operate in ways that deviate from the specifications outlined in the RFCs. This may involve altering requests and/or responses, and in some cases, generating erroneous responses on behalf of the server. Therefore, it is important to systematically measure the impact that middleboxes have on end-to-end communications. This paper presents a framework for such measurements, along with preliminary results from HTTP/1.1 conformance testing.

3   Scope

In their paper [45], Rautenstrauch et al. examine HTTP response conformance with respect to specifications and explore the associated security implications. Their approach enables testing of arbitrary websites but is constrained by the inability to pinpoint the origin of compliance issues, whether they originate from the end servers or any potential middleboxes in between. Additionally, their focus is mainly on the responses received to non-conforming requests, ignoring the issues associated to non-conforming responses.

We enhance the authors' framework by addressing these limitations. Specifically, we adapt their test cases for integration into our framework and introduce mechanisms to identify HTTP non-conformance originating from intermediate middleboxes. Specifically, we answer the following questions:

Q1: Do middleboxes accept non-conforming requests (with modifications or as-is) or reject them?
Q2: Do middleboxes accept non-conforming responses (with modifications or as-is) or reject them?

We use NoPASARAN [7] to evaluate the conformance of network middleboxes with the test suite from Rautenstrauch et al. in [45]. For **Q1**, we send non-conforming HTTP requests from the client to see if they are received in a conforming state by the server. For **Q2**, we investigate whether the middlebox corrects non-conforming responses sent by the server.

Rautenstrauch et al. [45] classified 106 test cases[3] into three categories: recommendations, requirements, and Augmented Backus–Naur Form (`ABNF`), a standardized grammar notation used to define syntax in specifications. In this paper, we extend their work, by focusing on the requirements category (`MUST` and `MUST NOT`) that is affected on the network path rather than at the edges.

We analyze a total of 47 requirement rules. We begin by reviewing the 106 test cases provided by Rautenstrauch et al., narrowing them down to 41 requirement rules. From these 41, we exclude 5 `HTTP/2` rules, resulting in 36 remaining rules. Additionally, we introduce 11 new requirement rules, which either have not been tested in prior studies—specifically regarding the impact of middleboxes on non-conforming responses sent directly by the server—or are derived from decomposing specific test cases into more fine-grained scenarios. For example, `Host` headers are semantically stronger than other headers, and duplicates may be treated differently depending on their context. This brings the total to 47 unique test cases. A more detailed description of the tests can be found in Appendix A.

4   Methodology

In this section, we provide a more detailed explanation of the framework we are using, which is based on `NoPASARAN` as introduced in [7], a distributed and collaborative framework. The original paper outlined the specifications, design, and implementation details of `NoPASARAN`, emphasizing how machines collaborate in pairs to test for network middlebox presence or check their compliance. Here, we not only refine and improve its design but also delve deeper into the distributed aspects of the framework. Subsection 4.1 provides a high-level overview of the framework. Subsection 4.2 details the role of each machine within the distributed system, while Subsect. 4.2 revises the terminology used for testing network middleboxes. Finally, Subsect. 4.3 demonstrates the framework's practical application through an illustrative example.

4.1   Framework Overview

The original paper presents three key concepts that `NoPASARAN` relies on to analyze the network path: nodes, channels, and tests. Some of these notions are redefined more precisely in Sect. 4.2.

Nodes: The framework introduces three types of nodes: masters, workers, and proxies. Masters are responsible for instructing workers to perform network tests between one another using specially crafted network packets. When workers are behind middleboxes that filter incoming non-established network connections,

---

[3] These test cases are accessible on their GitHub repository: https://github.com/cispa/http-conformance.

such as firewalls, the master assigns a proxy to the workers. This proxy serves as an anchor to enable communication between the workers.

Channels: NoPASARAN defines two types of channels: data channels and control channels. Workers establish data channels with each other or with another machine to conduct probes. The control channel, on the other hand, is a secure end-to-end communication channel used to synchronize the workers. This channel is also used to establish a baseline for comparing discrepancies between what is sent on the data channel and what is received, as well as differences in responses depending on the workers and a third-party machine.

Tests: To analyze the network communication path between workers, NoPASARAN leverages two main components: test cases and test campaigns. A test case is represented by a finite state machine and aims to be the simplest form to check a specific property (e.g., checking if the TCP sequence numbers between two workers are exactly the same). Workers perform a sequence of actions following this state machine representation, synchronized by control channels. A test campaign, in contrast, is a sequence of test cases that follow conditional logic.

For more detailed information, we refer the interested reader to the original paper [7].

4.2 Enhanced Framework Design

While the original paper establishes the foundational aspects of the framework, it mainly focuses on the concepts of channels and tests. This subsection delves deeper into refining these concepts and expanding on the node network topology and its orchestration mechanisms.

Network Topology and Coordination: In addition to the previously defined node terminology, we introduce the role of the coordinator. The coordinator functions as a pivotal interface between users seeking network path analysis and the network of nodes. It is responsible for updating users on the current network state through mechanisms such as a REST API and managing the registration of nodes.

Coordinator: The coordinator is a replicable entity designed to mediate interactions between users and the underlying NoPASARAN framework. Its responsibilities include node registration, monitoring the network's state, and advising master nodes on which worker nodes to engage for executing network tests.

Masters: Masters are specialized nodes designated to handle workload downloaded from the coordinator. They manage the execution of a test tree—a structured sequence of tests to be performed between workers. This enables efficient distribution of testing tasks and enhances the overall system's scalability.

Workers: Workers maintain their original role as defined in the original paper, with no changes in their operational mode. Their primary function remains to execute tests as directed by master nodes, ensuring that the testing process adheres to predefined protocols and requirements.

Proxies: In our initial work, we introduced the concept of nodes functioning as proxies. We now refine this approach by incorporating full-mesh VPN solutions, as outlined in [33]. Technologies such as Headscale [3], Netbird [39], and ZeroTier [26] leverage the Interactive Connectivity Establishment (ICE) framework [47] to facilitate communication between peers behind NAT middleboxes. This is achieved through the use of the STUN [48] protocol and its extension, TURN [46]. Our updated NoPASARAN design incorporates STUN and TURN servers to enhance proxy functionality, optimizing connectivity and communication across the network.

Revised Test Structure. This subsection revisits and clarifies the structure of tests within NoPASARAN, including test cases, test trees, and test tree campaigns.

Test: A test is defined as the execution of the same state machine representation by different workers, as in [7]. For example, a test might determine if cooperating workers' TCP sequence numbers are equivalent. Essentially, tests are conducted by the workers.

Tests Tree: A tests tree is a decision tree that combines different test results to gather more information about a specific attribute, such as the presence and type of a proxy. The processing of the tests trees is done by the masters. They use the decision tree structure to direct the workers' sequence of tests.

Tests Trees Campaign: A tests trees campaign represents the aggregation of different test trees following a specific logic to study and analyze more complex components. The goal is to obtain a comprehensive understanding of the state of a network communication path, such as determining the impact of a proxy on the network connection. This high-level aggregation is typically performed by the end user through the coordinator, using an interface such as an API.

4.3   Illustrative Scenario

Figure 2 presents a diagram illustrating how a user U can set up and add a node, in this case worker W_{N+1}, to the framework. The process begins with the user requesting a NoPASARAN administrator to create a node data structure in the system's database. The user then contacts the coordinator C to obtain a configuration file for setting up W_{N+1}. Using this configuration file, the NoPASARAN node implementation automatically contacts the coordinator, which responds with the credentials needed to authenticate the node within the network. These credentials include keys for integrating the node into the mesh network and

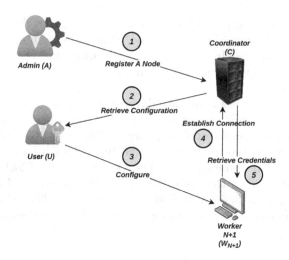

Fig. 2. Diagram illustrating the steps to set up and add a node to the NoPASARAN framework. In ①, a NoPASARAN administrator adds a node data structure to the system. In ②, an authorized user retrieves the configuration information for this node. In ③, the user configures the worker accordingly. On startup, illustrated in ④, the machine connects to the coordinator, which pushes credentials to authenticate the node in the network, as shown in ⑤.

certificates for communication with master nodes and control channels between workers.

After obtaining all its credentials, W_{N+1} remains connected to the coordinator, similar to the existing N workers and M masters. They all obtain an IP address using the VPN mesh network, in this case Netbird, and are able to communicate with each other regardless of any NAT devices in front of them. This is illustrated in Fig. 3.

In addition to adding a networked device to the system, user U can perform tests between available workers. This process is illustrated in Fig. 4. User U contacts coordinator C (e.g., using a REST API) to inquire about the operational status of workers and masters, as well as the available tests trees[4]. Coordinator C responds with the requested information, including the $N+1$ workers, M masters, and O tests trees. User U then selects the workers to study the middleboxes on a specific network path, in this case, workers W_i and W_j, master M_k, and test tree TT_l. Coordinator C takes care of informing M, who then independently directs W_i and W_j to conduct the tests specified in TT_l. Upon completion of these tests, M returns the results to C. Subsequently, C notifies user U of the obtained results.

---

[4] Our tests trees are open source and accessible at https://github.com/nopasaran-org/nopasaran-tests-trees.

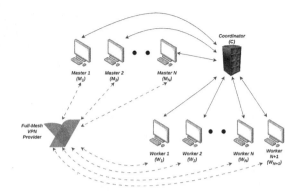

Fig. 3. Diagram of the network topology within the NoPASARAN framework. Workers maintain a persistent connection to the coordinator and use a full-mesh VPN for peer-to-peer communication.

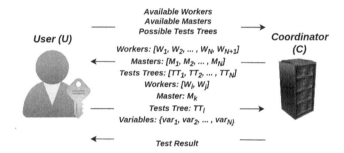

Fig. 4. Interaction between a user and the NoPASARAN framework. The user contacts the coordinator to request information about available workers, masters, and test trees that can be run. The coordinator responds with the current state of the system. Based on this information, the user selects a number of workers, a master, and the test tree to run with the appropriate variables.

5   Experimental Setup

We present here the results of our most recent tests campaign carried out between September 1st and September 25th of 2024. In the first phase of our experiments, we investigated the presence of proxies in the cloud and their behavior by leveraging 15 Virtual Private Servers (VPSs) as worker nodes. These VPSs were provided by various cloud providers to introduce diversity in the variables that may impact the number of middleboxes along the network path, such as the provider company and the location of the VPS instances. Additionally, two other instances within our local network were used: one acting as the master node and the other as a worker node. Finally, we rented a dedicated server from a bare-metal hosting provider to serve as the coordinator node. Thus, our framework consists of 1 coordinator, 1 master, and 16 workers. Only 15 workers are directly accessible from the Internet and can play the role of a server. The

16th, behind a firewall, can only be used as a client. This configuration enables the 16th worker to test 15 distinct paths on the Internet. In contrast, the other workers can collaboratively test 15×14 paths. Consequently, we achieve a total of 225 paths tested. Table 1 lists the IP addresses, providers (if VPS), locations, and whether the nodes are accessible from the Internet.

Table 1. Machines used for HTTP conformance checking. The column **DIA** indicates whether the machine is directly accessible from the Internet.

Node Number	Provider	Region	Public IP	DIA	Role
1	Worldstream	Netherlands	80.79.4.113	Yes	Coordinator
2–3	KAUST	Thuwal	109.171.133.89	No	Master
		Thuwal	109.171.167.3	No	Worker
4–7	AWS	Frankfurt	52.29.1.26	Yes	Worker
		Tokyo	52.192.75.255	Yes	Worker
		Montreal	3.99.151.247	Yes	Worker
		Mumbai	3.109.132.69	Yes	Worker
8–9	Azure	Switzerland	51.107.18.40	Yes	Worker
		Mexico Central	158.23.136.41	Yes	Worker
10–11	Digital Ocean	Sydney	170.64.148.202	Yes	Worker
		Singapore	174.138.30.249	Yes	Worker
12–13	Linode	Stockholm	172.232.140.126	Yes	Worker
		Milan	172.232.209.4	Yes	Worker
14–15	Fotbo	Netherlands	45.91.201.56	Yes	Worker
		Poland	185.253.7.182	Yes	Worker
16	vps-mart	Houston	108.181.201.176	Yes	Worker
17	Hivelocity	Los Angeles	107.155.87.38	Yes	Worker
18	Ultahost	Sao Paulo	140.99.164.81	Yes	Worker

In the second stage of our experiments, we investigate the conformance of 12 middlebox instances. Among these, 7 are proxy servers that can be downloaded and configured by network administrators[5]. The remaining 5 instances include an Azure Application Gateway and four CDN providers: Cloudflare, Imperva, Bunny, and Fastly. This selection was made to highlight the practical implications of conformance issues on non-configurable middleboxes. Table 2 summarizes this list of middlebox instances. We run the seven configurable proxies on two workers located within our local area network. In contrast, for testing the Azure

---

[5] The selection of proxies was based on popularity (e.g., GitHub stars). Their default configuration and version were chosen, assuming most users would stick with them or use the main proposed version.

Application Gateway and the four additional CDNs, we used the two VPSs provided by Linode, which were situated in Stockholm and Milan, and were running Ubuntu 22.

Table 2. List of the investigated middlebox instances.

Configurability	Name	Version
Configurable	Apache	2.4.41 (Aug 14, 2019)
	HAProxy	2.0.33 (Aug 19, 2023)
	Squid	4.10 (Feb, 03 2020)
	Lighttpd	1.4.55 (Jan 31, 2020)
	Mitmproxy	6.0.2 (Dec 15, 2020)
	Nginx	1.18.0 (Apr 21, 2020)
	Node	10.19.0 (Feb 06, 2020)
Non-Configurable	Azure Application Gateway Standard V2	×
	Cloudflare	×
	Imperva	×
	Bunny	×
	Fastly	×

6   Ethical Considerations

In our experiments, we conduct tests on seven of our own deployed proxies within an isolated environment. However, five other proxies are provided by cloud services or CDNs, which could impact their infrastructure. To minimize this risk, we limit the number of tests performed so that, on average, the total test duration does not exceed 20 min. Furthermore, we ensure that a test campaign is never run twice on the same proxy within a one-hour period.

Beyond reducing the frequency of our tests, we carefully select payloads to avoid any well-known attacks. For example, when testing the coexistence of the `Transfer-Encoding` and `Content-Length` headers in a single request, we specifically choose `Content-Length` values that prevent valid exploits, such as `HTTP` request smuggling. Additionally, none of our tests are performed on live web servers.

7   Evaluation

We present the results of our experiments as follows: Subsect. 7.1 discusses the default presence or absence of middleboxes in front of our worker nodes. Subsection 7.2 analyzes the global behavioral trends observed among the tested proxies. Finally, in Subsect. 7.3, we perform a detailed comparison of specific tests against the corresponding RFC specifications.

7.1   Assessing the Presence of HTTP Middleboxes in the Cloud

In the following paragraphs, we assess whether cloud providers, by default, instantiate any type of middlebox in front of their cloud instances. To investigate this, we repeated the 47 tests across our 16 workers, covering 225 different routes, using NoPASARAN to identify any discrepancies in the exchanged data.

Interestingly, across the 225 routes tested, we observed no discrepancies between what was sent and received by the workers. This suggests that no proxy is applied by default on these routes, even though HTTP without TLS enables on-path attackers to perform man-in-the-middle attacks. However, it is also possible that transparent proxies, capable of such attacks, may choose not to alter the forwarded application data. We further investigate the presence of transparent proxies at the transport level, we applied two techniques from the literature using NoPASARAN[6].

Out-of-Order Packet Detection: As described in [55], this technique leverages the fact that a proxy implementation may send packets in different orders, such as sending an acknowledgment back to the client before forwarding the initial SYN TCP packet to the end server. If a client receives a SYN-ACK while the server has not sent one, then it must have been generated by a middlebox present on the network path.

Sequence Numbers Mismatch: Vitale et al. [53] describe a method to detect sequence number mismatches between the client and the server. Generally, network middlebox implementations do not send the same TCP sequence numbers, making it possible to detect their presence through these discrepancies.

Similar to the application layer tests, we observed no discrepancies in the sequence numbers. These results further confirm the absence of proxies along the network path. Although testing 225 routes does not capture the behavior of all cloud providers, it offers a reasonable snapshot of typical traffic patterns. Our findings indicate that, by default, cloud servers do not have any proxy protection, which may differ from customer expectations regarding built-in security measures.

7.2   Global Results of Proxies HTTP Conformance

In the previous subsection, we demonstrated that there appears to be no application layer middlebox in front of our baseline workers. In this subsection, we present the results after adding ourselves different proxies. Figure 5 illustrates the vector representation of the behavior of twelve proxies when they receive non-RFC conforming messages (requests or responses)[7]. None of the tested proxies exhibited the expected behavior of rejecting all malformed packets. Instead,

---

[6] NoPASARAN leverages state machine representation to conduct tests as described in Sect. 4.1. A state machine representing the TCP three-way handshake performed between two workers can be found in Appendix B.

[7] We direct interested readers to Appendix C, where a visual summary of our comprehensive test results is presented.

the behavior of these proxies when handling HTTP traffic falls into one of three categories:

Unmodified (U): The proxy forwards the request or response to the intended recipient without making any changes.

Rejected (R): The proxy rejects the request or response, returning a 4XX or 5XX status code error to the client. If the response is non-conforming, the client may receive nothing.

Modified (M): The proxy modifies a non-conforming HTTP request or response, transforming it into a compliant one before forwarding it to the intended recipient.

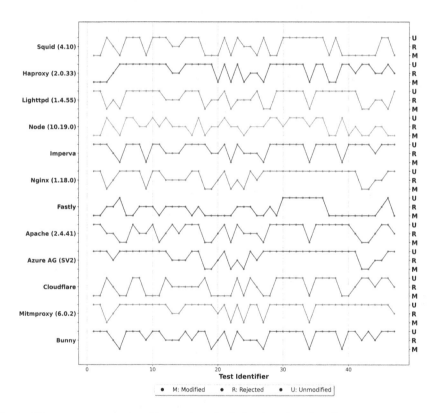

Fig. 5. Vector representation illustrating the behavior of twelve distinct proxies across forty-seven test cases. Vectors that are closely aligned indicate similar behaviors of the proxies concerning HTTP standard conformance.

Moreover, Fig. 5 highlights the variability in how different proxies handle non-conforming HTTP messages, indicating distinct behaviors. These variations are further illustrated in Fig. 6, where a Pearson correlation matrix is used to compute similarity scores between proxy pairs. For example, Nginx and the Azure

Application Gateway exhibit a high correlation, whereas Fastly and Mitmproxy show little to no correlation. This suggests the potential for fingerprinting intermediate proxies in transparent setups by leveraging HTTP conformance tests.

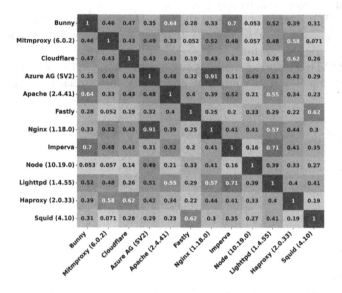

Fig. 6. Pearson correlation (symmetric) matrix illustrating the relationships among twelve different proxies based on their behaviors regarding non-conforming HTTP requests and responses. Higher correlation scores indicate stronger similarities in behavior between the proxies.

As of September 2024, 6Sense reports that Cloudflare dominates the CDN market with a 40.82% market share and nearly 1.8 million customers [1]. One might therefore expect Cloudflare to adhere strictly to RFC standards. However, Fig. 7 reveals otherwise, with only 10 non-conforming HTTP requests and responses being rejected. Rather than consistently modifying non-compliant HTTP messages, Cloudflare appears to decide on a case-by-case basis, modifying 17 and leaving 20 unaltered.

7.3   Comparison Between Implementation and Specification

In the previous subsection, it might appear that all implementations are flawed. However, in the following paragraphs, we demonstrate that this is not always the case by examining how the wording of RFCs affects implementations. We analyze instances where most implementations agree on specific behaviors, as well as cases where there is no clear consensus on handling non-conforming HTTP messages against the RFCs. Finally, we highlight the discrepancies in how non-conforming requests and responses are managed.

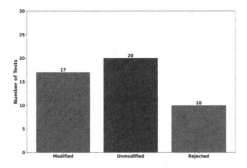

Fig. 7. Distribution of Cloudflare's proxy behavior in response to non-conforming HTTP requests and responses.

Out of our tests, 7 yielded unanimous results, with 5 of them consistently accepting and then retransmitting a non-conforming HTTP message. In the remaining 40 tests, we observed that the majority sometimes agreed on how to handle non-conforming data, resulting in some outliers exhibiting different behaviors. According to RFC 9110, *"the HEAD method is identical to GET except that the server MUST NOT send content in the response"*. In this instance, 11 of the tested proxies modified the non-conformant response by removing the content, Node rejects the response outright, responding with a 500 Internal Server Error. Similarly, RFC 9110 states that *"a server MUST NOT generate a Content-Range header field in the HTTP header section of a multiple part response"*. While 11 proxies left the non-conforming response unmodified, Node is again the only proxy to reject the response. This behavior suggests that Node interprets its role as a proxy in the same way it would follow RFC 9110 as a server. Supporting this observation, Node rejected the highest number of non-conforming HTTP messages—19 out of 47. Moreover, RFC 9110 specifies that for a HEAD response, a *"server MUST NOT send Content-Length in such a response unless its field value equals the decimal number of octets that would have been sent in the content of a response if the same request had used the GET method"*. 10 proxies left the non-conforming response unmodified. In contrast, Fastly was the only one to reject the response by not forwarding it, while Cloudflare was the only proxy to modify the response by removing the Content-Length header.

While some RFC rules are enforced uniformly, this is not always the case. RFC 9112 specifies that a *"server MUST reject, with a response status code of 400 (Bad Request), any received request message that contains whitespace between a header field name and colon. A proxy MUST remove any such whitespace from a response message before forwarding the message downstream"*. Note that the RFC mentions *"request"* when talking about the server, but *"response"* when mentioning the proxy, providing no guideline to the proxy when confronted with a non-conforming request. In our tests, we sent requests with a header containing a whitespace between the field name and colon. Out of the 12 proxies tested, 4 forwarded the request as is and 8 rejected it. RFC 9112 also mandates that a *"server MUST respond with a 400 (Bad Request) status code to any HTTP/1.1 request message [...] that contains more than one* `Host` *header field line"*, as this could be exploited for access control bypass via `HTTP` request smuggling. In our tests, we sent requests containing two `Host` headers—one with the IP address of the worker and the other with the value www.google.com. Out of the 12 proxies tested, half of them forwarded the request as is, while the other half rejected it. Since the standard does not explicitly define proxy behavior for such requests, proxies either act as a server and reject the request, or pass it to the server for processing. Another example highlighting this lack of completeness is where only senders are provided guidelines, excluding recipients. RFC 9112 states that *"A sender* `MUST NOT` *generate a bare* `CR` *(a* `CR` *character not immediately followed by* `LF` *) within any protocol elements other than the content"*. In cases where a server included a bare `CR` character in a header value, 3 proxies opted to modify the header. All 3 removed the `CR` character at the end and in the middle of the header value, except for Mitmproxy, which does not modify `CR` characters in the middle. In contrast, the other 8 proxies rejected the response outright.

The behavior of proxies can vary between requests and responses, even when following the same rule. According to `RFC 9112`, a *"recipient that receives whitespace between the start-line and the first header field* `MUST` *either reject the message as invalid or consume each whitespace-preceded line without further processing of it"*. To test this, we conducted separate experiments on requests and responses for each proxy, uncovering inconsistencies in their handling. Our findings revealed that while all proxies complied with this RFC, 8 of them demonstrated divergent behaviors: 5 rejected requests while sanitizing the payload in the response, whereas three rejected the responses while sanitizing the requests[8]. Similarly, *"sender* `MUST NOT` *generate multiple field lines with the same name in a message*, but it does not specify how the recipient should respond to such cases. In this instance, 5 proxies exhibited inconsistencies: 4 retained the payload in the responses as it was received while modifying it in the requests, while 1 proxy, Fastly, reversed this behavior. Finally, `RFC 9110` mandates that a *"recipient of* `CR`, `LF`, *or* `NUL` *within a field value* `MUST` *either reject the message or replace each of those characters with* `SP` *before further processing or forwarding of that message"*. In this case, we observed an even greater discrepancy: all twelve proxies rejected non-conforming requests, while the responses were either modified or left unchanged.

8   Discussion and Future Work

In the previous section, we addressed **Q1** and **Q2**, demonstrating that middleboxes can either modify, reject, or immediately accept non-conforming requests and responses, depending on the tests performed. In this section, we take a step back to discuss the implications of these findings and explore potential avenues for further research. Subsection 8.1 delves deeper into the results, while Subsect. 8.2 outlines directions for future work.

---

[8] In this context, sanitizing refers to either removing the entire header or removing the whitespace.

8.1   Discussion

Rautenstrauch et al. [45] argue that if either the end server or any intermediary element in the processing chain modifies or generates a response (or a request in general), the configuration of the entire chain should be considered non-conformant. Based on our findings, we consider that this stance is too radical when proxies are involved. There are two reasons for that: inadequate terminology and lack of completeness. We discuss these two points in detail below.

Inadequate Terminology: We argue that the use of certain keywords does not adequately reflect the importance of specific actions in request or response handling, leading to security risks. RFC 9112 [20] specifies that a *"server MAY reject a request that contains both `Content-Length` and `Transfer-Encoding` or process such a request in accordance with the `Transfer-Encoding` alone"*. The use of MAY in RFC 9112 follows the conventions established in RFC 2119 [9], and further clarified in RFC 8174 [35]. According to RFC 2119, MAY indicates that the action is truly optional. As a result, when a server receives a request, there is no clear directive on what action should be taken, since MAY leaves the decision open to interpretation. In this specific case, the authors write *" MAY reject [...] or process"*. Stricto sensu, any action other than rejecting or processing is still compliant with this wording. However, one could reasonably argue that the authors intended to convey *" MUST either reject [...] or process"*. As a matter of fact, this ambiguity has contributed to 28 CVEs related to HTTP request smuggling attacks involving the `Transfer-Encoding` header between 2019 and 2024 [38].

Lack of Completeness : While RFC 9111 [19] outlines the rules that a cache must follow to be compliant with HTTP, we argue that the IETF has not clearly defined the entire processing chain of HTTP communications. From reading RFC 9112, it appears that five roles exist within this processing chain: client, server, proxy, sender, and recipient. The first two roles represent endpoints, while the third refers to an intermediary. However, we contend that the RFC often lacks completeness when using the client, server, and proxy terminology. For instance, RFC 9112 specifies that a *"client MUST send a Host header field"* and that a *"server MUST respond with a 400 (Bad Request) status code to any HTTP/1.1 request message that lacks a `Host` header field"*. In this scenario, nothing is defined for the proxy that has to choose between several possible actions when it receives a request from a client that lacks a `Host` header field. The options include:

– Acting as a server and returning a 400 (Bad Request) status code.
– Allowing the request to proceed, leaving the end server to address the issue (typically by using the SNI in the case of TLS to direct the request to the appropriate server).
– Modifying the request to include a `Host` header, either by using the SNI (as in the previous case) or by inserting a default value.

We argue that RFC 9112 is incomplete, as a similar lack of completeness frequently arises throughout the standard.

8.2   Future Work

While HTTP conformance testing serves as proof of concept for the NoPASARAN framework, the following paragraphs provide guidance on how to build upon our work.

This paper excludes both HTTP/2 and HTTP/3, as standardized in RFC 9113 [52] and RFC 9114 [8], from its scope. However, these protocols are not free from vulnerabilities [11]. In late 2023, Cloudflare observed a record-breaking distributed denial-of-service (DDoS) attack that exploited HTTP/2's request cancellation feature [44]. HTTP downgrade attacks often exploit ambiguities in the RFCs [32]. While HTTP/3 appears to have avoided such issues thus far, this may not remain the case. Future work could extend this research to cover these protocols, using their respective RFCs as a basis, and incorporate recommendations and ABNF tests that our paper excluded from [45].

This study evaluates twelve application-layer middleboxes, including five from third-party providers that require minimal user configuration. We acknowledge that several factors may still influence our results: the proxies were tested under default configurations, and any modifications could yield different outcomes. Additionally, configurations from providers like Azure, Imperva, or Cloudflare may vary by geographic location, and discrepancies in proxy versions could also affect the results. This highlights the potential of our framework to further investigate these factors in the future.

We encourage interested researchers, network administrators, or even individual users to collaborate with us in deploying this framework within their own infrastructures[9].

9   Conclusion

The literature consistently highlights a gap between practical implementations and RFC standards. This paper addresses this issue by focusing on HTTP conformance, with a novel approach that includes network middleboxes, which were often overlooked in previous studies. Using 47 tests and a newly developed framework, we not only build on prior research but also show that the observed inconsistencies are not solely the result of poor implementation choices. Instead, they often arise from ambiguities in the interpretation of vague terminology and incomplete RFC specifications. Our findings suggest that more precise and explicit directives in RFC guidelines could significantly enhance conformance.

We invite interested readers to collaborate with us to further develop and expand our newly introduced middlebox framework. This could involve deploying it in a wider range of environments or adapting it for new test cases, thereby enriching its applicability and impact.

---

[9] NoPASARAN is open source and ready for deployment; any user can also create their own library of tests for any kind of protocol.

A   HTTP Tests List

(See Table 3).

Table 3. Summary of the total 47 `HTTP/1.1` tests used in our experiments, including the 36 tests extracted from [45].

Index	Description
1	Ensure `Max-Age` directive in requests uses token form without quotation marks
2	Ensure `Max-Age` directive in responses uses token form without quotation marks
3	Ensure `S-Maxage` directive in requests uses token form without quotation marks
4	Ensure `S-Maxage` directive in responses uses token form without quotation marks
5	Reject or replace CR, LF, or NUL characters in request field values
6	Reject or replace CR, LF, or NUL characters in response field values
7	Prevent duplicate fields in request headers
8	Prevent duplicate fields in response headers
9	Prohibit `Content-Length` header in 204 No Content responses
10	Prohibit `Content-Length` header in 1XX responses
11	Prohibit `Content-Length` header in 2XX responses to CONNECT requests
12	Ensure `Content-Length` in HEAD response matches potential GET response
13	Ensure `Content-Length` in 304 Not Modified response matches potential 200 OK response
14	Prohibit `Transfer-Encoding` header in 204 No Content responses
15	Prohibit `Transfer-Encoding` header in 1XX responses
16	Prohibit `Transfer-Encoding` header in 2XX responses to CONNECT requests
17	Do not send `Transfer-Encoding` header unless the request indicates HTTP/1.1 or later
18	Require `Date` header for 2XX status codes
19	Require `Date` header for 3XX status codes
20	Require `Date` header for 4XX status codes
21	Send `Upgrade` header field with 101 Switching Protocols response
22	Send `Upgrade` header field with 426 Upgrade Required response
23	Do not switch to a protocol not indicated by the client in the request's `Upgrade` header field
24	If a client sends both `Upgrade` and `Expect 100-continue`, a server MUST send a 100 Continue response first, then a 101 Switching Protocols response
25	Ensure STS directives appear only once in an STS header field
26	Include only one STS header field in the response
27	Do not include STS header field in HTTP responses over non-secure transport
28	Require `Max-Age` directive in STS header
29	Do not send content in response to HEAD requests
30	Do not include content after header section in 204 No Content responses
31	Do not include content in 205 Reset Content responses
32	Do not include content in 304 Not Modified responses
33	Prevent 206 Partial Content from being sent in response to POST requests
34	Prevent 304 Not Modified from being sent in response to POST requests
35	Prevent 416 Range Not Satisfiable from being sent in response to POST requests
36	Generate `Content-Range` header field for single-part 206 Partial Content responses
37	Do not generate `Content-Range` header field in HTTP header section of multiple-part 206 Partial Content responses
38	Generate required headers for 206 Partial Content responses
39	Generate required headers for 304 Not Modified responses
40	Include `WWW-Authenticate` header field in 401 Unauthorized responses
41	Include `Allow` header field in 405 Method Not Allowed responses
42	Include `Proxy-Authenticate` header field in 407 Proxy Authentication Required responses
43	Reply with 400 Bad Request to requests with invalid Host header
44	Reject requests with whitespace between the start-line and first header field
45	Reject responses with whitespace between the start-line and first header field
46	Reject requests with whitespace between header field name and colon
47	Do not generate bare CR within protocol elements other than content

B   State Machine Implementation: TCP 3-Way Handshake

(See Fig. 8).

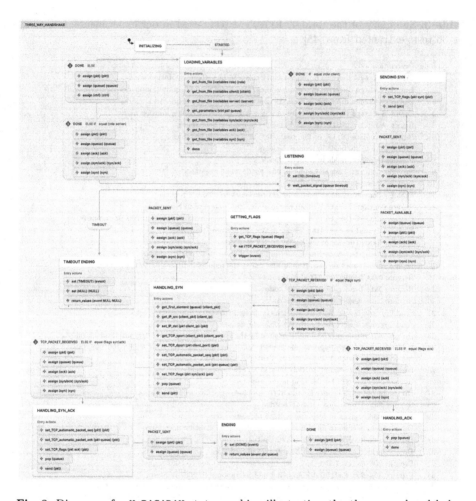

Fig. 8. Diagram of a NoPASARAN state machine illustrating the three-way handshake, used to send and receive specially-crafted TCP sequence numbers that are later compared in a separate state machine.

C Synthesis of Test Results

(See Fig. 9).

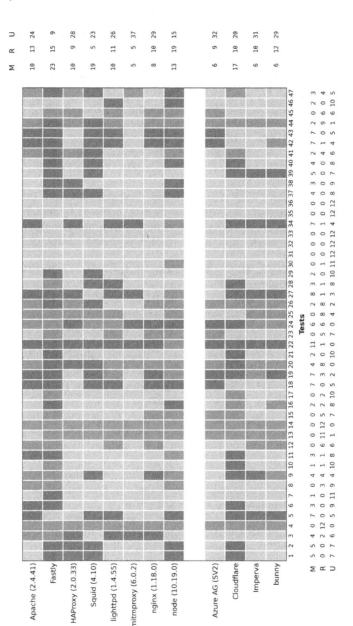

Fig. 9. Pictorial representation that showcases the behavior of the 12 proxies, illustrating the distribution of requests and responses that were Modified, Rejected, or left Unmodified.

References

1. 6sense: Content delivery network (CDN) (2024). https://6sense.com/tech/content-delivery-network-cdn. Accessed 26 Sept 2024
2. Adamczyk, P., Hafiz, M., Johnson, R.E.: Non-compliant and proud: a case study of http compliance (2008). https://www.ideals.illinois.edu/items/11454. Accessed 26 Sept 2024
3. Alonso, J.F., Dalby, K.: Github - juanfont/headscale: an open source, self-hosted implementation of the tailscale control server (2024). https://github.com/juanfont/headscale. Accessed 21 July 2024
4. Barik, R., Welzl, M., Elmokashfi, A.M., Gjessing, S., Islam, S.: fling: a flexible ping for middlebox measurements. In: 2017 29th International Teletraffic Congress (ITC 29), vol. 1, pp. 134–142. IEEE (2017)
5. Belshe, M., Peon, R., Thomson, M.: Hypertext transfer protocol version 2 (HTTP/2). RFC 7540 (2015). https://doi.org/10.17487/RFC7540, https://www.rfc-editor.org/info/rfc7540
6. Belson, D.: Cloudflare 2023 year in review—blog.cloudflare.com (2023). https://blog.cloudflare.com/radar-2023-year-in-review/. Accessed 14 Sept 2024
7. Benhabbour, I., Dacier, M.: Nopasaran: a novel platform for analysing semi-active elements in routes across a network. Appl. Cybersecuri. Internet Govern. 1(1), 1–25 (2022)
8. Bishop, M.: HTTP/3. RFC 9114 (2022). https://doi.org/10.17487/RFC9114, https://www.rfc-editor.org/info/rfc9114
9. Bradner, S.O.: Key words for use in RFCs to indicate requirement levels. RFC 2119 (1997). https://doi.org/10.17487/RFC2119, https://www.rfc-editor.org/info/rfc2119
10. Brim, S.W., Carpenter, B.E.: Middleboxes: taxonomy and issues. RFC 3234 (2002). https://doi.org/10.17487/RFC3234, https://www.rfc-editor.org/info/rfc3234
11. Chatzoglou, E., Kouliaridis, V., Kambourakis, G., Karopoulos, G., Gritzalis, S.: A hands-on gaze on HTTP/3 security through the lens of HTTP/2 and a public dataset. Comput. Secur. 125, 103051 (2023)
12. Chen, J., Jiang, J., Duan, H., Weaver, N., Wan, T., Paxson, V.: Host of troubles: multiple host ambiguities in http implementations. In: Proceedings of the 2016 ACM SIGSAC Conference on Computer and Communications Security, pp. 1516–1527 (2016)
13. Chung, T., Choffnes, D., Mislove, A.: Tunneling for transparency: a large-scale analysis of end-to-end violations in the internet. In: Proceedings of the 2016 Internet Measurement Conference, pp. 199–213 (2016)
14. Craven, R., Beverly, R., Allman, M.: A middlebox-cooperative TCP for a non end-to-end internet. ACM SIGCOMM Comput. Commun. Rev. 44(4), 151–162 (2014)
15. Detal, G., Hesmans, B., Bonaventure, O., Vanaubel, Y., Donnet, B.: Revealing middlebox interference with tracebox. In: Proceedings of the 2013 Conference on Internet Measurement Conference, pp. 1–8 (2013)
16. Edeline, K., Donnet, B.: A bottom-up investigation of the transport-layer ossification. In: 2019 Network Traffic Measurement and Analysis Conference (TMA), pp. 169–176. IEEE (2019)
17. Fielding, R.T., Nielsen, H., Mogul, J., Gettys, J., Berners-Lee, T.: Hypertext transfer protocol – HTTP/1.1. RFC 2068 (1997). https://doi.org/10.17487/RFC2068, https://www.rfc-editor.org/info/rfc2068

18. Fielding, R.T., Nottingham, M., Reschke, J.: Hypertext transfer protocol (HTTP/1.1): caching. RFC 7234 (2014). https://doi.org/10.17487/RFC7234, https://www.rfc-editor.org/info/rfc7234

19. Fielding, R.T., Nottingham, M., Reschke, J.: HTTP caching. RFC 9111 (2022). https://doi.org/10.17487/RFC9111, https://www.rfc-editor.org/info/rfc9111

20. Fielding, R.T., Nottingham, M., Reschke, J.: HTTP/1.1. RFC 9112 (2022). https://doi.org/10.17487/RFC9112, https://www.rfc-editor.org/info/rfc9112

21. Gil, O.: Web cache deception attack. Black Hat USA (2017). https://www.blackhat.com/docs/us-17/wednesday/us-17-Gil-Web-Cache-Deception-Attack-wp.pdf. Accessed 26 Sept 2024

22. Heled, R.: HTTP request smuggling (2005). https://www.cgisecurity.com/lib/HTTP-Request-Smuggling.pdf. Accessed 26 Sept 2024

23. Hilal, F., Gasser, O.: Yarrpbox: detecting middleboxes at internet-scale. Proc. ACM Netw. **1**(1), 1–23 (2023)

24. Honda, M., Nishida, Y., Raiciu, C., Greenhalgh, A., Handley, M., Tokuda, H.: Is it still possible to extend TCP? In: Proceedings of the 2011 ACM SIGCOMM Conference on Internet Measurement Conference, pp. 181–194 (2011)

25. Huang, S., Cuadrado, F., Uhlig, S.: Middleboxes in the internet: a HTTP perspective. In: 2017 Network Traffic Measurement and Analysis Conference (TMA), pp. 1–9. IEEE (2017)

26. Ierymenko, A., Henry, J.: Github - zerotier/zerotierone: a smart ethernet switch for earth (2024). https://github.com/zerotier/ZeroTierOne. Accessed 21 July 2024

27. Ishizawa, M.: GitHub - summerwind/h2spec: a conformance testing tool for HTTP/2 implementation—github.com (2020). https://github.com/summerwind/h2spec. Accessed 15 Sept 2024

28. Jabiyev, B., Gavazzi, A., Onarlioglu, K., Kirda, E.: Gudifu: guided differential fuzzing for http request parsing discrepancies. In: Proceedings of the 27th International Symposium on Research in Attacks, Intrusions and Defenses, RAID 2024, pp. 235–247. Association for Computing Machinery, New York (2024)

29. Jabiyev, B., Sprecher, S., Gavazzi, A., Innocenti, T., Onarlioglu, K., Kirda, E.: {FRAMESHIFTER}: security implications of {HTTP/2-to-HTTP/1} conversion anomalies. In: 31st USENIX Security Symposium (USENIX Security 2022), pp. 1061–1075 (2022)

30. Jabiyev, B., Sprecher, S., Onarlioglu, K., Kirda, E.: T-Reqs: HTTP request smuggling with differential fuzzing. In: Proceedings of the 2021 ACM SIGSAC Conference on Computer and Communications Security, pp. 1805–1820 (2021)

31. Kallus, B., Anantharaman, P., Locasto, M., Smith, S.W.: The HTTP garden: discovering parsing vulnerabilities in HTTP/1.1 implementations by differential fuzzing of request streams. arXiv preprint arXiv:2405.17737 (2024)

32. Kettle, J.: HTTP/2: the sequel is always worse—portswigger.net (2021). https://portswigger.net/research/http2. Accessed 25 July 2024

33. Kjorveziroski, V., Bernad, C., Gilly, K., Filiposka, S.: Full-mesh VPN performance evaluation for a secure edge-cloud continuum. Softw.: Pract. Exp. (2024)

34. Krishnamurthy, B., Arlitt, M.: {PRO-COW}: protocol compliance on the {Web–A} longitudinal study. In: 3rd USENIX Symposium on Internet Technologies and Systems (USITS 2001) (2001)

35. Leiba, B.: Ambiguity of uppercase vs lowercase in RFC 2119 key words. RFC 8174 (2017). https://doi.org/10.17487/RFC8174, https://www.rfc-editor.org/info/rfc8174

36. Mirheidari, S.A., Arshad, S., Onarlioglu, K., Crispo, B., Kirda, E., Robertson, W.: Cached and confused: web cache deception in the wild. In: 29th USENIX Security Symposium (USENIX Security 2020), pp. 665–682 (2020)

37. Mirheidari, S.A., Golinelli, M., Onarlioglu, K., Kirda, E., Crispo, B.: Web cache deception escalates! In: 31st USENIX Security Symposium (USENIX Security 2022), pp. 179–196 (2022)

38. MITRE Corporation: CVE search results. https://cve.mitre.org/cgi-bin/cvekey.cgi?keyword=smuggling. Accessed 25 Sept 2024

39. NetBird Team: Github - netbirdio/netbird: connect your devices into a secure wireguard®-based overlay network with SSO, MFA, and granular access controls (2024). https://github.com/netbirdio/netbird. Accessed 21 July 2024

40. Nguyen, H.V., Iacono, L.L., Federrath, H.: Mind the cache: large-scale explorative study of web caching. In: Proceedings of the 34th ACM/SIGAPP Symposium on Applied Computing, pp. 2497–2506 (2019)

41. Nguyen, H.V., Lo Iacono, L., Federrath, H.: Systematic analysis of web browser caches. In: Proceedings of the 2Nd International Conference on Web Studies, pp. 64–71 (2018)

42. Nielsen, H., Fielding, R.T., Berners-Lee, T.: Hypertext transfer protocol – HTTP/1.0. RFC 1945 (1996). https://doi.org/10.17487/RFC1945, https://www.rfc-editor.org/info/rfc1945

43. Pahdye, J., Floyd, S.: On inferring TCP behavior. ACM SIGCOMM Comput. Commun. Rev. **31**(4), 287–298 (2001)

44. Pardue, L., Desgats, J.: HTTP/2 rapid reset: deconstructing the record-breaking attack (2023). https://blog.cloudflare.com/technical-breakdown-http2-rapid-reset-ddos-attack/. Accessed 24 Sept 2024

45. Rautenstrauch, J., Stock, B.: Who's breaking the rules? Studying conformance to the http specifications and its security impact. In: Proceedings of the 19th ACM Asia Conference on Computer and Communications Security, pp. 843–855 (2024)

46. Reddy.K, T., Johnston, A., Matthews, P., Rosenberg, J.: Traversal using relays around NAT (TURN): relay extensions to session traversal utilities for NAT (STUN). RFC 8656 (2020). https://doi.org/10.17487/RFC8656, https://www.rfc-editor.org/info/rfc8656

47. Rosenberg, J.: Interactive connectivity establishment (ICE): a protocol for network address translator (NAT) traversal for offer/answer protocols. RFC 5245 (2010). https://doi.org/10.17487/RFC5245, https://www.rfc-editor.org/info/rfc5245

48. Rosenberg, J., Huitema, C., Mahy, R., Weinberger, J.: STUN - simple traversal of user datagram protocol (UDP) through network address translators (NATs). RFC 3489 (2003). https://doi.org/10.17487/RFC3489, https://www.rfc-editor.org/info/rfc3489

49. Saltzer, J.H., Reed, D.P., Clark, D.D.: End-to-end arguments in system design. ACM Trans. Comput. Syst. (TOCS) **2**(4), 277–288 (1984)

50. Shen, K., et al.: HDiff: a semi-automatic framework for discovering semantic gap attack in http implementations. In: 2022 52nd Annual IEEE/IFIP International Conference on Dependable Systems and Networks (DSN), pp. 1–13. IEEE (2022)

51. The Chromium Project: Spdy: An experimental protocol for a faster web. https://www.chromium.org/spdy/spdy-whitepaper/. Accessed 23 July 2024

52. Thomson, M., Benfield, C.: HTTP/2. RFC 9113 (2022). https://doi.org/10.17487/RFC9113, https://www.rfc-editor.org/info/rfc9113

53. Vitale, A., Dacier, M.: Inmap-t: leveraging TTCN-3 to test the security impact of intra network elements. J. Comput. Commun. **09**, 174–190 (2021)

54. World Wide Web Consortium (W3C): Factory: HTTP compliance and W3C QA (2001). https://www.w3.org/2001/01/qa-ws/pp/alex-rousskov-measfact. Accessed 24 July 2024

55. Zullo, R., Pescapé, A., Edeline, K., Donnet, B.: Hic sunt proxies: unveiling proxy phenomena in mobile networks. In: 2019 Network Traffic Measurement and Analysis Conference (TMA), pp. 227–232. IEEE (2019)

A First Look at Cookies Having Independent Partitioned State

Maximilian Zöllner[1]([✉]), Anja Feldmann[2], and Ha Dao[2]

[1] Universität des Saarlandes, Saarbrücken, Germany
`maximilian.zoellner@mailbox.org`
[2] Max Planck Institute for Informatics, Saarbrücken, Germany

Abstract. The introduction of Cookies Having Independent Partitioned State (CHIPS) marks a significant step toward balancing user privacy with essential web functionalities. CHIPS isolates data within specific contexts, preventing cross-site tracking while maintaining the functionality of websites. However, the adoption of CHIPS in real-world web usage remains largely unexplored. In this paper, we investigate the state of CHIPS deployment, providing an overview of how CHIPS has been integrated into web ecosystems since its introduction. Leveraging the HTTP Archive dataset, we first find that the adoption of partitioned cookies remains slow, with most domains still relying on non-partitioned cookies, though a slight increase in both types is observed starting in early 2024, coinciding with Google's phase-out of third-party cookies for 1% of users. This sudden onset of the third-party cookie phase-out has resulted in a haphazard way of adoption for some domains, which caused them to overlook important configuration requirements, resulting in improper settings due to limited awareness of the specific guidelines such as *SameSite=None* and *Secure*. In addition, we observe a positive signal for privacy as third-party trackers begin adopting partitioned cookies, with a noticeable increase starting in early 2024. However, as of September 2024, only a small number of trackers have fully transitioned to using partitioned cookies (up to 0.5% of tracking domains), while some continue to rely on both partitioned and non-partitioned cookies (up to 3.1% of tracking domains), highlighting that the shift is still in its early stages, especially for tracking domains. Finally, we observe stark asymmetry among the early adopter tracking domains: some have already added *some* partitioned cookies to all sites with a presence, while others, notably Google's *doubleclick.com* has only deployed partitioned cookies to around 5% of pages where it is present.

Keywords: CHIPS · partitioned state · CHIPS adoption · web tracking · tracker · privacy

1 Introduction

Targeted advertisement, the dominant business model of the modern Internet, is fundamentally at odds with privacy concerns of the users. Internet users often

C. Testart et al. (Eds.): PAM 2025, LNCS 15567, pp. 182–196, 2025.
https://doi.org/10.1007/978-3-031-85960-1_8

express fear and distrust regarding the potential loss of personal privacy in the online environment [21]. In response to these concerns, browser vendors have started implementing or planning various restrictions on third-party tracking technologies, such as third-party cookies, which are sent in requests to sites other than the top-level domain. These cookies enable cross-site tracking, allowing servers to track users' behavior across different websites. To counteract these privacy risks, browsers are now considering blocking third-party cookies and implementing technologies like Cookies Having Independent Partitioned State (CHIPS) [7]. CHIPS is an opt-in technology that isolates third-party cookies from different first-party contexts. In essence, CHIPS is a less drastic version of Firefox' Enhanced Tracking Protection strict mode [16], which imposes the CHIPS-behavior on all third-party cookies, which has led to broken webpages in the past. Still, Google has almost phased out third-party cookies in Chrome and Google does in fact have a track record of first introducing a new web technology where not using it conforms to the previous behaviour and then later setting a more aggressive standard. For example, there is the *SameSite* attribute, which governs whether a cookie may be attached to third-party requests. *SameSite=None*, the behaviour all browsers had before the introduction of the attribute, is no longer the standard in Chrome, instead defaulting to *SameSite=Lax* [17], which prevents the cookie from being attached to third-party requests. With that in mind, it is not unreasonable to expect further development against unrestricted third-party cookies, and, at least for Chrome, seeing CHIPS at the center of that. As CHIPS is rather new, there remains a significant gap in research regarding the real-world adoption and impact of partitioned cookies. Understanding how domains adopt CHIPS and the implications for both privacy and functionality remains critical in the current landscape.

In this paper, we uncover the state of deployment for CHIPS to provide a comprehensive overview of how CHIPS has been integrated into web ecosystems since its introduction. Our main findings can be summarized as follows:

- Using the HTTP Archive dataset, we track the longitudinal behavior of CHIPS adoption over time, from its start in May 2022 until September 2024 (Sect. 3). We highlight a slow adoption of partitioned cookies in both first-party and third-party contexts, with the majority of domains still relying on non-partitioned cookies. This indicates that the web ecosystem continues to depend heavily on non-partitioned cookies, with only a slight shift toward partitioned cookie usage emerging in 2024, though they remain in the early stages of deployment (Sect. 4.1.

- By evaluating the *misconfigured* partitioned cookie settings based on the CHIPS design principles, we find a significant number of *misconfigured* cookie headers among partitioned cookies, with misconfigurations being more common in first-party usage. These *misconfigurations* often involve missing key attributes such as *Secure* and *SameSite=None*, which are essential for partitioned cookies to function correctly in third-party contexts and provide their intended privacy benefits (Sect. 4.2).

- We find that whereas CHIPS were designed to enhance privacy by isolating cookies in specific partitions, adoption by third-party tracking domains has been slow, with most trackers continuing to rely on non-partitioned cookies. We observe a small, slowly increasing number of domains (2–3%) have started using partitioned cookies at the beginning of 2024 before the start of the third-party cookie phaseout by Google. The overwhelming majority of those domains are using non-partitioned cookies simultaneously. Interestingly, some early adopters, e.g., *doubleclick.net*, which belongs to Google, are still in the early phase of partitioned cookie adoption, as their cookies use both partitioned and non-partitioned types, and they are only using partitioned cookies on a small subset of pages (Sect. 4.3).

Finally, we address the implications of our analysis, outline the limitations, and discuss the ethical considerations of our study (Sect. 5).

2 Background and Related Work

2.1 Cross-Site Tracking and Cookie Mechanisms

Despite the growing commercialization of the Internet, paying for access was never seen as a dominant business model for large parts of the Internet. Instead, the usual method of monetization is advertisement, in many cases, targeted advertisement as targeted ads are commonly regarded as more valuable [4].

For targeted advertisement, user profiles must be built [3,6,19]. Traditionally, this is done using cookies, one of the first extensions to the formerly stateless HTTP protocol. Cookies can be set by a webserver using a *Set-Cookie* header and will be stored by the web browser, and be attached as a request header on subsequent requests to appropriate domains. Cookies have a variety of uses, such as session management or storing user preferences across multiple visits [5]. This already allows website operators to create usage profiles by storing a unique identifier in a cookie and then logging which parts of the website are accessed. While a static text webpage can be fetched with a single HTTP request, modern webpages make excessive use of embedded content, such as images, scripts, and videos. They can result in the total number of HTTP requests that constitute a site reaching triple digits. These embeds need not be hosted on the same domain as the main site, and those third-party embeds are indeed very common. In this ecosystem, website operators typically no longer manually insert advertisements into the site. Instead, they rely on third-party providers, whose embeds provide the advertisements. As advertising service providers are present on a multitude of content sites, they are in a position to correlate users if their embeds set cookies. A mere understanding of the embedding context on a select few sites can already be sufficient to construct interest profiles. If the tracker companies are in a direct relationship with the site visitor, e.g., because they also operate a social network where the user happens to be logged in, the profiles can become very detailed.

2.2 Cookies Having Independent Partitioned State (CHIPS)

CHIPS introduces a new attribute called *partitioned* into the *Set-Cookie* header. This attribute can be attached to embeds (that have the SameSite attribute set to None) and will instruct the browser to involve the embedding context in the decision of whether the cookie should be attached to a request. If the same embed is used on two different sites with the Partitioned attributes, the browser will assign different states to them. The embeds can still have state, but it will not be shared across sites. Figure 1 illustrates the difference between non-partitioned (*normal*) and partitioned third-party cookies. For non-partitioned cookies, the cookie jar is assigned by origin only, so an embed to the same origin (*tracker.net* in this example) will have access to the cookies irrespective of the embedding context. Partitioning changes this - now, for embeds, the cookie jar assignment uses both the embed origin as well as the embedding context as criteria. Since in this example, *site1.com* and *site2.com* are different embedding contexts, *tracker.net* will be assigned two different cookie jars.

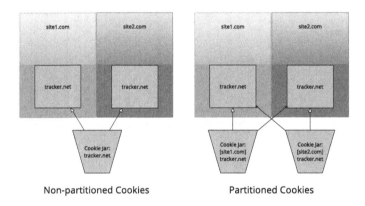

Fig. 1. Comparison of third-party cookies with and without partitioning.

3 Methodology

3.1 Data Collection

In order to analyze the adoption of CHIPS, we leveraged the publicly available crawling data from the HTTP Archive [1]. This dataset originates from visiting the home page of all origins included in the Chrome User Experience Report (CrUX), which lists websites frequently visited by Chrome users. CrUX includes a popularity ranking, so the crawl data in essence spans the most popular websites of that particular month. The data used in this study is based on desktop crawls, focusing on HTTP requests that include the *Set-Cookie* header. We collected data from January 2022, but we only retained data starting from May

2022, as this marks the first occurrence of the CHIPS attribute in our dataset. The data spans until September 2024, covering a period during which the adoption of CHIPS was observed across multiple domains. The dataset consists of 86,143,446 webpages from 18,130,717 unique eTLD+1 domains. All request and response headers, including those with the *set-cookie* header, were analyzed to track the implementation of CHIPS. The dataset overview is in Fig. 2. While both first-party and third-party requests increase over time, third-party requests consistently make up the majority of interactions, indicating the pervasive presence of third-party tracking and services on the web. This underscores the importance of analyzing third-party behavior, particularly in the context of cookie deployment and privacy-related developments like CHIPS.

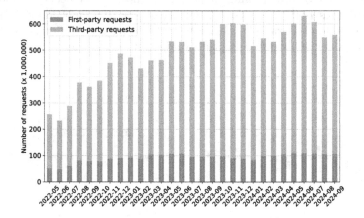

Fig. 2. Dataset overview.

3.2 Cookie Classification

To categorize cookies as first-party and third-party, we utilize the public suffix list [15] to determine the domains of the webpage and the cookies based on their `host` attribute. We then compare each cookie's domain to its webpage's domain (i.e., it's embedder). If they match, the cookie is classified as first-party; if not, it is deemed third-party. To identify third-party tracking cookies, following the approach from Ref. [12,18], we utilize the *justdomains* blocklist [13]. This list, updated in March 2024, comprises entries from various popular tracking blocklists, including *EasyList* [9], *EasyPrivacy* [10], *AdGuard* [2], and *adservers* [14] blocklists. These blocklists are designed to target advertising and tracking resources and are commonly used by browser extensions that aim to safeguard user privacy while browsing. If a cookie's domain matches any domain in the *justdomains* list, it is classified as a tracking cookie.

4 Results

4.1 Overview

We present the adoption of partitioned and non-partitioned cookies between May 2022 and September 2024 in Fig. 3. We show that first-party domains largely rely on non-partitioned cookies throughout this period, with minimal adoption of partitioned cookies. A slight increase in the use of both partitioned and non-partitioned cookies begins in early 2024. Similarly, third-party domains primarily use non-partitioned cookies, with only a small number of domains adopting both partitioned and non-partitioned cookies during the same period. Non-partitioned cookies are consistently more prevalent across both first-party and third-party domains throughout the observation period, indicating that partitioned cookies have not yet gained significant traction. The small increase in domains adopting both partitioned and non-partitioned cookies beginning in early 2024 coincides with Google's decision to phase out third-party cookies for 1% of users, suggesting an emerging trend toward partitioned cookie usage. However, this shift remains limited to a small fraction of domains.

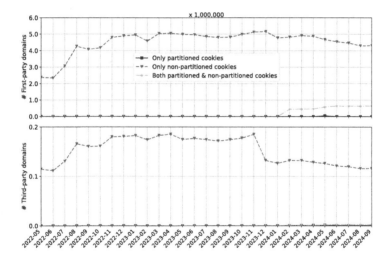

Fig. 3. Adoption of partitioned and non-partitioned cookies in first-party and third-party domains over time.

4.2 *Misconfigured* Partitioned Cookie Settings

According to the CHIPS design principles [7], user agents must reject any partitioned cookie that does not include the *Secure* attribute, ensuring that these cookies are only sent over secure channels. Additionally, user agents may only accept partitioned cookies if their *SameSite* attribute is set to *None*, allowing

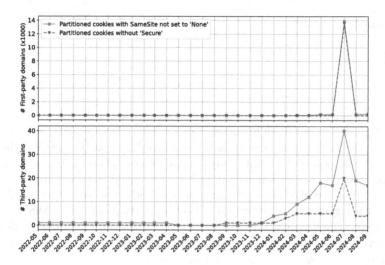

Fig. 4. *Misconfigured* partitioned cookie settings in first-party and third-party domains over time.

the cookie to function in a third-party context. A partitioned cookie without *SameSite=None* is effectively just a same-site cookie, meaning it cannot be sent across different sites. In this section, we analyze any *misconfiguration* of partitioned cookies across both first-party and third-party domains over time in Fig. 4. The most obvious feature of the data is an extreme spike in misconfigurations in July 2024. While the uptick is noticeable for third-party domains too, it is most pronounced for first-party domains. These misconfigured embeds were distributed across a large number of different domains. It may indicate a phase where a large number of domains attempted to adopt partitioned cookies quickly, possibly due to external pressures such as evolving privacy standards or the gradual phase-out of third-party cookies by major browsers like Google. In their haste, many domains may have overlooked key configuration requirements, leading to improper settings. July is the month Google canceled their plans of the third-party cookie phaseout, which may contribute to the rapid reduction in the month after. In addition, given that partitioned cookies are still in their early stages, many developers may not yet be fully aware of the specific requirements, e.g., *SameSite=None and Secure*, to ensure compliance with CHIPS guidelines.

4.3   Have Trackers Adopted CHIPS?

Since CHIPS is designed to enhance user privacy by isolating cookies within specific browser partitions and preventing cross-site tracking, here, we explore how third-party tracking domains have responded to this mechanism. We show the percentage distribution of third-party tracking domains based on their use of partitioned and non-partitioned tracking cookies over time in Fig. 5. The green area represents domains that use only non-partitioned tracking cookies, while the blue

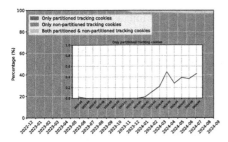

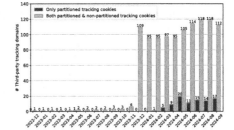

Fig. 5. Distribution of partitioned and non-partitioned tracking cookies.

Fig. 6. Number of trackers that set partitioned cookies.

(imperceptibly small) and orange areas represent those that use only partitioned tracking cookies and both partitioned and non-partitioned cookies, respectively. We first show that most tracking domains rely solely on non-partitioned cookies, with a small percentage adopting partitioned cookies or both types in early 2024. We observe that CHIPS adoption does not gain any traction until just before the start of the third-party cookie phaseout by Google. This indicates that in a vacuum most trackers are unwilling to use partitioned cookies. Most (around 80%) of the trackers that use partitioned cookies, also use non-partitioned ones. In this state, the privacy benefit of partitioned cookies is dubious, because the non-partitioned ones can be used to link cookies from different partitions. We also observe a slight drop in CHIPS-using domains in August and September 2024, suggesting that the end of the third-party cookie phaseout may have discouraged some trackers from continuing to use partitioned cookies. This shift indicates that, despite the earlier increase of CHIPS, the changing landscape around third-party cookies could be influencing their adoption.

We also show the absolute number of third-party tracking domains implementing partitioned, non-partitioned, or both types of tracking cookies in Fig. 6. We reveal a slow initial uptick of partitioned cookies, with only isolated occurrences in late 2022 and 2023. However, starting in late 2023, we observe a noticeable increase, particularly in domains using both partitioned and non-partitioned cookies (orange bars). This may be explained by the beginning of the trial run of the third-party cookie phaseout that was also starting in 2024. The number of tracking domains setting only partitioned cookies (blue bar) also shows a significant upward trend, indicating a growing shift in cookie deployment strategies. This number remains relatively small, however, especially if compared to the ones using both partitioned and non-partitioned cookies. This sharp rise post-December 2023 suggests that partitioned cookies have become an integral part of the tracking ecosystem, albeit still in the early stages of adoption. Towards the end of the dataset, there are around 100 different tracking domains using partitioned cookies (up to 3.1% of tracking domains) alongside non-partitioned ones and around 15 different ones using exclusively partitioned cookies (up to 0.5% of tracking domains). The third-party tracking domains that consistently deploy partitioned cookies are listed in Table 1 in the Appendix, categorized by the date of their first observed appearance. Some tracking domains have transitioned to only using partitioned cookies, likely influenced by evolving privacy standards and the phase-out of third-party cookies. These trackers do have an overall very small presence, however. Notably, *doubleclick.net*, which belongs to Google, is still in the early phase of partitioned cookie adoption, as its cookies use both partitioned and non-partitioned types.

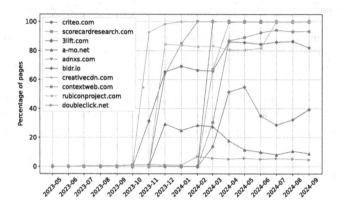

Fig. 7. CHIPS usage of top 10 CHIPS tracking domains (present in the highest amount of pages) as a percentage of all sites where they are present.

Finally, in Fig. 7 we show the development of the ten domains that have, over the entire dataset, most usages of partitioned cookies. In particular, we show how many different webpages they are present with partitioned cookies, as a percentage of the total number of different webpages on which they are present. We can see large differences in deployment strategy here. Firstly, all ten domains were deploying partitioned and non-partitioned tracking cookies over time. Some domains, namely *rubiconproject.com, creativecdn.com, scorecardresearch.com, 3lift.com* and *adnxs.com* are using partitioned cookies on almost all webpages. Others, like for example *doubleclick.net* which have a very high absolute number of CHIPS-usage, still only use partitioned cookies in about 5% of the pages where they are present (embedded in 37% of webpages as of September 2024).

5   Discussion

In this section, we discuss the implications of our findings on the adoption and effectiveness of CHIPS. We also address the limitations of our methodology and the ethical considerations of using publicly available data in our study.

5.1   Implications

Our findings provide important insights into the early-stage adoption of CHIPS and its implications for the broader web ecosystem. The slow uptake of partitioned cookies, despite their design to enhance privacy, suggests that the web continues to rely heavily on non-partitioned cookies, limiting the privacy benefits that CHIPS aims to deliver. As CHIPS adoption remains in its infancy, its long-term impact on cross-site tracking and user privacy is still unclear. The presence of misconfigured partitioned cookies, particularly among first-party domains, highlights the need for increased awareness and better implementation practices. Some domains have yet to fully comply with the CHIPS design principles, such as ensuring the *Secure* and *SameSite=None* attributes are correctly applied. This has practical implications for both developers and browser vendors, as improper configurations will cause breakage that might be conflated with a problem with CHIPS. Furthermore, while we observe a small but growing number of third-party trackers adopting partitioned cookies, the fact that most continue to use non-partitioned cookies raises concerns about the effectiveness of CHIPS in reducing cross-site tracking. The use of both partitioned and non-partitioned cookies suggests that the privacy advantages of CHIPS are not fully realized, as non-partitioned cookies can still facilitate tracking across domains and, consequently, link the partitioned cookies. Our research indicates that the biggest push for adoption coincided with the beginning of Chrome's third-party cookie phaseout, suggesting that trackers lack an intrinsic motivation to use partitioned cookies and only did so in the face of breakage. In addition, further research and industry guidance will be critical to ensure that privacy mechanisms like CHIPS are effectively implemented and used as intended. To speed up adoption, revisiting the policy to generally block unrestricted third-party cookies at a later date may be prudent. Since this change adversely affects the same industry, advertisement, Google is majorly engaged in, we acknowledge Google's difficult position in implementing this change.

5.2   Limitations

Firstly, our tracking cookie detection approach may be incomplete. We rely on *EasyList* [9], *EasyPrivacy* [10], *AdGuard* [2], and *adservers* [14] blocklists to detect tracking cookies and CHIPS adoption. These lists are widely recognized and used both by end-users and as ground-truth in academic studies [8,11,20]. While these blocklists provide strong coverage of well-known trackers, they may not comprehensively capture all third-party trackers or CHIPS adopters, potentially leading to underreporting in our analysis. Nevertheless, we believe that this limitation does not significantly impact our overall measurements and that the work still provides an in-depth view of the various aspects of online tracking, including CHIPS adoption. Secondly, while our detection methodology focuses on analyzing cookies through HTTP requests, it may overlook certain cookies set through alternative mechanisms. Cookies that are deployed via server-side operations or asynchronous JavaScript requests outside the browser's immediate view may not be captured in the HTTP Archive. As a result, this limitation could lead to underestimating the prevalence of CHIPS, particularly for domains using more sophisticated or indirect cookie-setting techniques. Despite this, we believe that the majority of tracking cookies, including those adopting CHIPS, are set through detectable client-side interactions, minimizing the overall impact of this limitation on our findings. Finally, user interaction with cookie consent banners can also affect the accuracy of our tracking cookie detection. Many websites set tracking cookies, including CHIPS, only after a user consents via cookie banners. Since the HTTP Archive does not simulate user interaction with these banners, cookies that are conditionally set after consent may not be captured in our analysis. This could lead to incomplete insights into CHIPS adoption, especially for websites that implement stricter privacy practices. Nonetheless, we believe our methodology still captures a significant portion of the cookie-setting behavior and provides meaningful insights into the broader trends of CHIPS adoption.

6   Conclusion

In this paper, we provided a comprehensive analysis of the adoption of CHIPS over time. By examining data collected from January 2022 to September 2024, we identified key trends in first-party and third-party domains, highlighting the shift in cookie-setting practices since May 2022 when the CHIPS attribute was first observed. We noted that significant adoption coincides with the start of Chrome's trial run of the third-party cookie phaseout, suggesting a causal connection here. In addition, the rate of the rollout has slowed down even before the third-party cookie phase-out was canceled. Finally, some select trackers opted for a comprehensive approach and partitioned all their cookies, but these represent a small overall share of the trackers. We observe a significant heterogeneity as to how different trackers approach partitioning their cookies, with some limiting CHIPS to a number of select pages and others using partitioned cookies on almost all the pages where they are present, albeit mostly alongside non-partitioned cookies. Our findings contribute to a deeper understanding of how CHIPS is being integrated into the ecosystem, offering valuable insights into its adoption and the evolving landscape of web tracking. As major browsers phase out third-party cookies, it is important to conduct further research and provide industry guidance to ensure that privacy mechanisms like CHIPS are properly implemented and used as designed. To encourage reproducibility, we release our analysis scripts at [22].

Ethical Consideration. Our work does not involve active measurements and relies entirely on data provided by third parties, specifically the HTTP Archive dataset. We do not process the data in a way that focuses on personally identifiable information (PII), and we only extract and aggregate data related to the technical functioning of the Internet. Therefore, we conclude that no specific ethical considerations apply to our measurements.

Appendix

Table 1 details third-party tracking domains that consistently deploy partitioned cookies, categorized by their first observed appearance. The domains are organized by month, to showcase the development of CHIPS-using domains over time. Domains highlighted in red represent those that exclusively rely on partitioned cookies, underscoring a specific subset of trackers that have committed to this cookie technology alone. Early adopters, such as *ladsp.com* in December 2022, *doubleclick.net* in May 2023, and *taboola.com* in September 2023, demonstrate the initial, slow uptake of partitioned cookies. Notably, *doubleclick.net*, which belongs to Google, is still in the early phase of partitioned cookie adoption, as its cookies use both partitioned and non-partitioned types. From early 2024, some domains—highlighted in red, such as *digitalthrottle.com* and *mmondi.com* in March, and *gayadnetwork.com* in April were observed setting only partitioned cookies. However, as of September, no other trackers continue this trend.

Table 1. List of tracking domains deploying partitioned cookies consistently over time. The red line represents domains that set only partitioned tracking cookies.

First appearance	Domains
2022-12	ladsp.com
2023-05	doubleclick.net
2023-09	taboola.com
2023-11	openx.net, creativecdn.com, criteo.com
2023-12	onetag-sys.com, casalemedia.com, omnitagjs.com, smaato.net, adnxs.com, media.net, minutemedia-prebid.com, technoratimedia.com, 33across.com, contextweb.com, a-mo.net, adroll.com, ingage.tech, cootlogix.com, the-ozone-project.com, blismedia.com, rubiconproject.com, pubnation.com, 4dex.io, richaudience.com, t13.io, serverbid.com, yellowblue.io, aniview.com, servenobid.com, intentiq.com, 1rx.io, mediavine.com, logly.co.jp, bidr.io, smilewanted.com, yieldmo.com, advertserve.com, bidswitch.net, lwadm.com, pubmatic.com, undertone.com, nexx360.io, adingo.jp, servebom.com, connatix.com, sharethrough.com, adsrvr.org, seedtag.com, dotomi.com, lijit.com, kargo.com, nextmillmedia.com, wknd.ai, mgid.com
2024-01	rlcdn.com, ew3.io, 3lift.com, dable.io
2024-02	livenza-il.com, bagly.co.il, leadlife.com, skcrtxr.com, mmstat.com, adtdp.com, 50bang.org, sonobi.com, userreport.com, tadpull.com, berp.com, im-apps.net, rpofsweden.se
2024-03	lead.im, scorecardresearch.com, digitalthrottle.com, cpxinteractive.com, mmondi.com, 0cf.io, googleadservices.com

(continued)

Table 1. (*continued*)

First appearance	Domains
2024-04	q1media.com, prnx.net, brealtime.com, playgirl.com, ymetrical.com, springserve.com, gayadnetwork.com
2024-05	kaizenplatform.net, coinminerz.com, shrinktheweb.com, sundaysky.com, indoleads.com, groundtruth.com, bridge.link, filetarget.com, liveintent.com, adzbazar.com, camghosts.com, scarlet-clicks.info, involve.asia, avantlink.com, shareasale.com, maropost.com, woomio.com, flashtalking.com, mediafuse.com, ninjacat.io, neobux.com, adsvert.com, gixmo.dk, webeyez.com, aerserv.com, wts.one, runetki.com, qashbits.com, demandbase.com, hotjar.com, profitshare.ro, clickguard.com, clickbank.com, revive-adserver.net, upsales.com, kms-tool.com, bright-sdk.com, avapartner.com, vfreecams.com, piano.io, diskaa.com, ongsono.com, danbo.org, bongacams7.com, roirocket.com, webstats1.com, commissionkings.ag, uii.io, joinads.me, xlivesex.com, permutive.com, moengage.com, nicequest.com, appnext.com, pushwoosh.com, smallseotools.com, comscore.com, inspectlet.com, chartbeat.com, acclienquan365.com, vietnamfb.com, rotate5url.com, optimizely.com, juicyads.com, iceprogs.ru, find-ip-address.org, getintopc.today, nakamasweb.com, blueconic.com, leadspace.com, fout.jp, zeotap.com, sleeknote.com, mediaz.vn, cameraprive.com, nicklienquan247.com, retentionscience.com, crazyegg.com, funnelytics.io, sitest.jp, jango.com, bidvertiser.com, supercounters.com, primeleech.com, pollster.pl, fullstory.com, clickcease.com, partnerstack.com, contactmonkey.com, ru.net, noibu.com, appsflyer.com, ardalio.com, wts2.one, brightedge.com, thecounter.com, madkudu.com, abtasty.com, dz4ad.com, mutinyhq.com, adcryp.to, ometria.com, ergadx.com, iplogger.org, getlasso.co, cision.com, ec-concier.com, vungle.com, ip-tracker.org, sheeme.com, sumome.com, feathr.co, sizmek.com, adespresso.com, adshnk.com, star-clicks.com, callrail.com, sendwebpush.com, snitcher.com, admitad.com
2024-06	kameleoon.com, admatic.com.tr, visitorqueue.com, bongacash.com
2024-07	youvisit.com, askfollow.us, synerise.com, cpx.to, ipnoid.com, tracemyip.org, zigzag.vn, ad.gt
2024-08	calltrackingmetrics.com, samuraiclick.com, exitbee.com, clickz.com, tctm.co, liadm.com, getstat.net, wowpornlist.xyz, ay.delivery, mixpanel.com
2024-09	adblock-pro.org, amp.vg, pornearn.com, baremetrics.com, authanalysis.com, icorp.ro, coinadster.com, agkn.com

References

1. The http archive tracks how the web is built (2016). https://httparchive.org/. Accessed 10 Sept 2024
2. AdGuard: Adguard tracking protection filter (2005). https://filters.adtidy.org/extension/chromium/filters/3.txt. Accessed 10 Sept 2024
3. Balebako, R., Leon, P., Shay, R., Ur, B., Wang, Y., Cranor, L.: Measuring the effectiveness of privacy tools for limiting behavioral advertising. In: Proceedings of W2SP - SP (2012)
4. Beales, H.: The value of behavioral targeting. Netw. Advertising Initiative 1(2010) (2010)
5. Bujlow, T., Carela-Español, V., Solé-Pareta, J., Barlet-Ros, P.: A survey on web tracking: mechanisms, implications, and defenses. Proc. IEEE 105(8), 1476–1510 (2017)
6. Carrascosa, J.M., Mikians, J., Cuevas, R., Erramilli, V., Laoutaris, N.: I always feel like somebody's watching me: measuring online behavioural advertising. In: Proceedings of ACM CoNEXT, pp. 1–13 (2015)
7. Cutler, D., Selya, A.: Chips (cookies having independent partitioned state) (2024). https://github.com/privacycg/CHIPS?tab=readme-ov-file. Accessed 06 Oct 2024
8. Dao, H.: Detection, characterization, and countermeasure of first-party cooperation-based third-party web tracking. Ph.D. thesis, The Graduate University for Advanced Studies (2022)
9. EasyList: Easylist (2005). https://easylist.to/easylist/easylist.txt. Accessed 10 Sept 2024
10. EasyPrivacy: Easyprivacy (2005). https://easylist.to/easylist/easyprivacy.txt. Accessed 10 Sept 2024
11. Englehardt, S., Han, J., Narayanan, A.: I never signed up for this! privacy implications of email tracking. Proc. PETs 2018(1), 109–126 (2018)
12. Gotze, M., Matic, S., Iordanou, C., Smaragdakis, G., Laoutaris, N.: Measuring web cookies in governmental websites. In: Proceedings of the ACM Web Science Conference, pp. 44–54 (2022)
13. Justdomains: DOMAIN-ONLY Filter Lists (2022). https://github.com/justdomains/blocklists. Accessed 10 Sept 2024
14. Lowe, P.: Blocklist for use with hosts files to block ads, trackers, and other nasty things (2001). https://pgl.yoyo.org/adservers/serverlist.php?hostformat=hosts&showintro=1&mimetype=plaintext. Accessed 10 Sept 2024
15. Mozilla: Public suffix list (2005). https://publicsuffix.org/. Accessed 10 Sept 2024
16. Network, M.D.: Cookies having independent partitioned state (chips) (2024). https://developer.mozilla.org/en-US/docs/Web/Privacy/State_Partitioning. Accessed 18 Sept 2024
17. Network, M.D.: Set-cookie (2024). https://developer.mozilla.org/en-US/docs/Web/HTTP/Headers/Set-Cookie#samesitesamesite-value. Accessed 18 Sept 2024
18. Rasaii, A., Singh, S., Gosain, D., Gasser, O.: Exploring the cookieverse: a multiperspective analysis of web cookies. In: Proceedings on the PAM, pp. 623–651. Springer, Cham (2023)
19. Solomos, K., Ilia, P., Ioannidis, S., Kourtellis, N.: Talon: an automated framework for cross-device tracking detection. In: Proceedings of RAID, pp. 227–241 (2019)
20. Starov, O., Nikiforakis, N.: Privacymeter: designing and developing a privacy-preserving browser extension. In: Proceedings on ESSoS, pp. 77–95. Springer, Cham (2018)

21. Wang, H., Lee, M.K., Wang, C.: Consumer privacy concerns about Internet marketing. Commun. ACM **41**(3), 63–70 (1998)
22. Zöllner, M., Feldmann, A., Dao, H.: Analysis scripts for Cookies Having Independent Partitioned State (CHIPS) measurement (2024). https://doi.org/10.17617/3. C9WI7C

Web Crawl Refusals: Insights From Common Crawl

Mostafa Ansar[1]([✉]), Anna Sperotto[1], and Ralph Holz[2]

[1] University of Twente, Enschede, The Netherlands
mostafa.ansar@ru.nl
[2] University of Münster, Münster, Germany

Abstract. Web crawlers are an indispensable tool for collecting research data. However, they may be blocked by servers for various reasons. This can reduce their coverage. In this early-stage work, we investigate server-side blocks encountered by Common Crawl (CC). We analyze page contents to cover a broader range of refusals than previous work. We construct fine-grained regular expressions to identify refusal pages with precision, finding that at least 1.68% of sites in a CC snapshot exhibit a form of explicit refusal. Significant contributors include large hosters. Our analysis categorizes the forms of refusal messages, from straight blocks to challenges and rate-limiting responses. We are able to extract the reasons for nearly half of the refusals we identify. We find an inconsistent and even incorrect use of HTTP status codes to indicate refusals. Examining the temporal dynamics of refusals, we find that most blocks resolve within one hour, but also that 80% of refusing domains block every request by CC. Our results show that website blocks deserve more attention as they have a relevant impact on crawling projects. We also conclude that standardization to signal refusals would be beneficial for both site operators and web crawlers.

Keywords: Web crawling · Common Crawl · Server-Side Blocking

1 Introduction

Web crawlers are essential tools for systematic data collection across various research fields. However, server-side blocking can significantly affect their coverage and accuracy. Understanding why crawlers are blocked, and the types of blocking behaviours they present, at scale is crucial for improving data collection methods. Previous studies on server-side blocking have primarily focused on geo-blocking or regulatory compliance by assessing website availability from different geographic locations [3,17,20]. These works often relied on analyzing HTTP status codes or errors generated by Content Distribution Network (CDNs) to identify blocks. While informative, such approaches do not capture the full range of blocking behaviors that affect web crawlers. To the best of our knowledge, no prior research has thoroughly examined the actual contents of pages

C. Testart et al. (Eds.): PAM 2025, LNCS 15567, pp. 197–214, 2025.
https://doi.org/10.1007/978-3-031-85960-1_9

to identify and categorize server-side blocks, leaving the nature of such blocks largely unknown. Our research addresses this gap by taking an initial step toward a more comprehensive understanding of server-side blocks by studying the blocks encountered by a well-known web crawling project. By analyzing data at web scale, we utilize a dataset significantly richer than those collected by previous small-scale crawling experiments. We define "refusals" as any content intentionally returned by a website to prevent a crawler from accessing the actual page content. In this early work, our contributions are as follows. *(i)* We devise a method based on regular expressions to identify refusals and categorize them by type, reason, and association with platforms or tools. *(ii)* We provide an in-depth analysis of refusals along these dimensions, identifying some platforms as particularly aggressive in blocking CC. We find great diversity in how refusals are communicated in HTTP responses, including a significant amount of misuse of HTTP status codes. *(iii)* We analyze how transient refusals are, finding that most persist indefinitely and some specifically target CC.

We highlight that further investigation into the impact of web site blocks is warranted, including comparisons for other crawling projects and longer-term studies. We conclude that the lack of a standard communication method between servers and crawlers makes it difficult for crawlers to know when to stop accessing a website or adjust their crawling behaviour. This could be rectified with an HTTP extension that communicates refusals and their reasons clearly to web crawlers, allowing them to honor refusals appropriately. We also provide recommendations for handling server-side blocks, offering general suggestions for all crawlers and specific considerations for CC.

2   Background and Related Work

Websites may block web crawlers for various reasons, *e.g.* to protect against malicious activity, enforce geo-blocking, prevent their content from being used for training ML models, or to avoid resource overload. The Robots Exclusion Protocol [15] allows website owners to specify the parts of their website that web crawlers may visit. RFC 9110 [10] specifies HTTP code *403* (Forbidden) to refuse access. Other codes, such as *406* (Not acceptable) are meant to be used for representation errors, despite their name. RFC 6585 [9] defines the very specific status code *429* (Too Many Requests) to indicate a server-side rate limit.

CC is a non-profit initiative. The crawler is designed [18] to be "polite" and comply with the Robots Exclusion Protocol, using *e.g.* five seconds wait between requests to the same host and employing an exponential back-off strategy on error. It identifies itself with a User-Agent header that is specific to CC. It does not process content that is dynamically generated on client-side, *e.g.* using JavaScript. According to CC's documentation, the fetching process happens over 14 days and is handled by 20 AWS EC2 spot nodes in N. Virginia. The documentation does not provide the public IP addresses.

The coverage of active measurements has long been recognized as a problem in literature. For instance, the authors of [16] already distributed their scans

Table 1. Status codes before and after pruning

Code	Description	All non200s	%	Pruned	%
301	Moved Permanently	235,772,654	41.97%	-	-
404	Not Found	175,006,242	31.16%	-	-
302	Found	114,777,210	20.44%	-	-
307	Temporary Redirect	6,003,819	1.07%	-	-
403	Forbidden	5,855,588	1.04%	5,855,588	26.87%
308	Permanent Redirect	4,905,497	0.87%	-	-
410	Gone	4,338,335	0.77%	4,338,335	19.91%
500	Internal Server Error	3,379,744	0.60%	3,379,744	15.51%
303	See Other	3,344,468	0.60%	-	-
406	Not Acceptable	1,676,200	0.30%	1,676,200	7.69%
400	Bad Request	1,528,691	0.27%	1,528,691	7.02%
401	Unauthorized	1,190,637	0.21%	1,190,637	5.46%
429	Too Many Requests	708,933	0.13%	708,933	3.25%
Other	-	3,143,206	0.56%	2,854,781	13.11%
Total	-	561,631,224	100.00%	21,790,009	100.00%

to improve coverage. The impact of the vantage point on coverage was studied in [22] for TCP scans and for HTTPS on sites in the Alexa Top 1 m list in [11]. In the context of web measurements, researchers have also compared crawling technologies and vantage points and found significant discrepancies in tracking and fingerprinting activities [14,23]. Web crawlers have also been classified based on their capability for circumventing anti-bot measures [4]. Some studies investigated the blocking of web crawlers, such as websites that block AI crawlers [13] or block access based on a browser fingerprint [21]. Other studies on website unavailability have focused mostly on censorship and server-side blocking related to geo-blocking [2,3,8,17,19]. The authors of [20] explored other reasons behind website unavailability by loading websites from various locations and identified three causes of server-side blocking: GDPR compliance, geo-blocking, and security reasons. In contrast, we use a web-scale dataset to perform manual content analysis to examine a wider range of refusals.

3   Methodology

Dataset. We use the CC-MAIN-2023-50 snapshot, which was compiled between 2023-11-28 and 2023-12-12 [7]. We use two parts of this snapshot: the general index file *Columnar URL index* and the archive *non-200 responses*. The *non-200 responses* archive contains all fetching attempts that did not receive a status code *200* ("200 OK") as a reply (see the end of this section for limitations of this approach). It consists of 3.43 TB of compressed data. We extract timestamps, server IPs, URIs, Fully Qualified Domain Name (FQDNs), registered domains, HTTP status codes and headers, and page textual contents. We use *pyasn* [5] to map IPs to AS numbers. We use the index to obtain records with status code 200 for FQDNs of interest.

Data Pruning. We obtain 561×10^6 records from the non-200 responses, summarized in Table 1. We prune all responses with status codes for redirections (*3xx*; these are rescheduled by CC for later crawls) as well as those where the content could not be found (*404*). This leaves us with 21.7×10^6 records.

Extracting Refusals. We extract refusal messages by building regular expression (REs) in an iterative process. To ensure accurate identification of refusals and to prevent false positives, we chose to construct REs manually. While we may consider using classifiers in future work, manual analysis of REs provided sufficient control and validation for our needs in this study. Our approach ascertains that we exclusively capture *explicit* refusals and not general errors.

In multiple iterations, we search our *page contents* for keywords that are common to (nearly) all refusals, such as "blocked", "banned", "restricted", etc. From there, and after manually selecting pages with explicit contents about access refusals, we build REs to cover these contents with very high specificity. We repeat this step until manual inspection gives us no further group of matches with more than 50 potential refusals. In total, we build 147 REs for refusals. Most messages that our REs are based on are in English, although we also include some from other languages that we could identify as refusals (e.g. Turkish, Russian, German, Portuguese, Slovak). In a similar process, and to validate how comprehensive our refusal REs are, we also build a set of 183 REs to capture content that is definitely *not* indicative of a refusal, *e.g.* internal server errors, and use them to remove also non-refusals from our data.

Outcome. In our pruned dataset, our REs identify 3.43×10^6 refusals, corresponding to 800,485 FQDNs, and 9.82×10^6 records as non-refusals (see Table 2). 4.2×10^6 records have no page content and hence our REs method is not applicable. A total of 4.3×10^6 records remain that we cannot further classify. Hence, our REs-based method allows us to cover 60.8% of our pruned dataset.

Checking the Coverage. We estimate how many refusals we may have missed in the 4.3×10^6 records we could not classify. We select a random sample of 385 records, a size determined to ensure a 95% confidence level with a 5% margin of error, and inspect them manually. We can identify only 9 records as explicit refusals. Extrapolating from this, our method should not have missed more than about 101×10^3 records, *i.e.* 3% more refusals. We hence believe that our RE-based method has good coverage for our chosen dataset.

Table 2. General statistics on refusals and assigned labels

Description	Count	Percentage (%)
Refusal	3,430,207	15.74
Non-refusal	9,817,878	45.06
Empty	4,222,824	19.38
No further classification	4,319,100	19.82
Total	21,790,009	100.00

Labelling. We manually associate each RE with labels based on the contents it captures. We define three kinds of labels to capture the characteristics of a refusal, shown in Table 3. Each refusal record has at least one label.

Type. The label *challenge* is used to indicate that site visitors must complete a challenge to access the content, such as a Captcha (which CC does not attempt to solve). *Checking* is intended for sites that ask visitors to wait for some check to be completed. *require_js* is used for pages that ask users to enable JavaScript or disable ad-blockers. The label *other429s* is special as it refers to records with status code *429* that cannot be described with other labels. Other forms of blocks are simply labelled *block*.

Reason. We use the label *security/malicious* for REs whose captured contents indicate that a security solution blocked the request or cited the prevention of harmful activities as the reason for the refusal. The label *excessive/suspicious* denotes content that cites "suspicious" activity as grounds for denying access, *e.g.* excessive access attempts, "spamming", "scraping", or other forms of information extraction. *Geo-blocking* refers to country-based or region-based refusals with respect to the requesting IP address. The label *IP/ASN reputation* is applied to content that attributes access denial to IP reputation, *e.g.* the presence of the IP address on a block list, the use of proxies or VPNs, or visiting from a cloud provider's IP address.

Tag. A good number of platforms or security providers reveal themselves in the page content or HTTP headers. We use this kind of label to indicate that a platform or security provider could be associated with a refusal. First, we analyze the page content that an RE captures and assign the tag where the provider is identifiable. Where it is not, we inspect the *Server* headers. If 99% of the records captured by an RE have a *Server* header specific to a platform (e.g. *Pepyaka*, a site building tool, or the hoster Wix [1]), and if there is a sufficient number of unique FQDNs (more than 1000) associated with those records, we assign the tag accordingly. See Table 12 for examples of the constructed REs and their labels. The full list is shared with the community online[1].

Transient Behavior. To analyze transient blocking behavior, we determine the rate at which refusals occur and the duration of refusals. We aggregate successes (responses with status code 200) with refusals by FQDN. Each FQDN is then

---

[1] https://github.com/mstfnsr/web_refusal_regex.

Table 3. Description and possible values for labels

Label	Description	Values
Type	The type of refusal content	block, challenge, checking, require_js, other429s, none
Reason	The reason for refusal provided in the contents	security/malicious, excessive/suspicious, geo-block, ip/asn reputation, none
Tag	A platform or security provider associated with the refusal	e.g., Cloudflare, Wix

assigned a distinct status code, type, reason, and tag, if available. Only 834 FQDNs have multiple associations (*e.g.* multiple tags or refusal reasons). We exclude these FQDNs from the later analysis of transient behavior to be able to attribute refusals to a single category. We obtain the refusal rate for each FQDN based on the set of successes and refusals. Finally, for each FQDN, we quantify the duration of refusals by measuring the minimum time between a refusal (after a success) and the next successful attempt.

A Note on Requester IPs. To measure the duration of a refusal, we record the time it takes for the refusal to resolve on its own. However, changes in the requester's IP address could also resolve blocks. To address this, we identify the AWS IPs used by CC and analyze how often they changed when accessing a single FQDN. We extract visitor IP addresses from our 561×10^6 non-200 records using regular expressions. After filtering out IPs not associated with Amazon (AS14618), we determine the most frequent ones by the number of reflecting FQDNs. Among 662 IPs within Amazon's AS, we found that 20 were frequently used—18 very frequently and 2 less often. This aligns with CC's documented use of 20 fetching nodes [18]. We then examine whether the IP that initially requested an FQDN changed in subsequent requests. In 99.4% of cases, the same IP accessed an FQDN within one hour. Therefore, we can measure refusal duration within this time frame.

Limitations. Being early work, our study naturally has limitations. *(i)* Our identification method relies on manual creation of REs, with our coverage of the pruned dataset being 60.8%. *(ii)* It is also limited to refusals that are explicit in the page content—refusals without any content or those ambiguous are not captured. While we find it plausible that refusals in the latter subset are not too common, further analysis is warranted. *(iii)* In this early work, the focus was on one snapshot of CC to demonstrate the potential for analyzing server-side blocks using large-scale web datasets. Generalizing the findings would require analyzing all records, including those with a status of 200, and considering the integration of other datasets and potentially conducting longitudinal analysis. *(iv)* We share any bias in CC's selection of domains, noting that CC prioritizes some domains [18] *(v)* We only analyze refusals at the level of FQDN in this paper. One could attempt to determine *path-specific* refusals as well. However,

CC does not necessarily visit enough pages per FQDN to allow strong conclusions, so additional, active scans would be necessary. Finally, *(vi)* Our research focuses on application-level reachability (CC does not log network failures).

4 Results

Breakdown of Refusals. We analyze the refusals by status code and labels.

By Status Code. Figure 1 shows the top status codes used for refusals by the number of records and FQDNs. We provide a reference for HTTP status codes in Table 9. Status code *403* (Forbidden) is the most frequently used code in terms of the number of records. However, by FQDNs, this is *406* (Not acceptable), which is also almost as prevalent in record count yet found for about 70% of all FQDNs with refusals. This is linked to the ModSecurity web application firewall; we analyze this later. Status code *429* (Too many requests) makes for the third-largest share. This code is special in that it already encodes a reason. Code *430* is unusual: according to IANA, it is unassigned. Refusals using the *500* series of codes (meant to indicate server-side problems) are very rare. The full status code distribution is shown in Table 11.

By Type. Table 4 displays the distribution of refusal types by the total number of records and the associated FQDNs. *Block* is the most common type of refusal, again with more than half related to ModSecurity.

By Reason. Table 5 categorizes the reasons for website refusals. About half of the records, and by far most FQDNs, do not provide information that we can map to a specific reason for a refusal. This is particularly common in the case of status code *406*. The most frequent identifiable reason is *excessive/suspicious*, which covers cases such as too many requests being made or bot-like behavior. The *security/malicious* category follows, covering refusals generated for security reasons or to fend off malicious behavior. We find that the reputation of the visitor's IP or AS is a much rarer reason, as is geographic origin (each <1%).

By Tag. Figure 2 shows the security providers (tools and services) we could associate with refusals. ModSecurity is the most common tag by both records and FQDNs. The second most common tag by number of records is Blogvault/Malcare, a WordPress plugin. In terms of FQDNs, Wix, Cloudflare, and Shopify are frequent blockers. Table 10 gives a full list.

The Case of ModSecurity. We can associate about 1.2×10^6 refusal records from 556×10^3 FQDNs (488×10^3 registered domains) with ModSecurity, a web application firewall. The status code is always *406*, which is *not* intended for refusals (see Sect. 2). The sites reside predominantly in just four ASes. The *Server* headers show that in 93% of cases, the web server is Apache. The remainder is Cloudflare's server. We identify the hosting providers using CAIDA's AS-to-organization dataset [6], the WHOIS, and with the public information the respectively identified companies publish. Table 6 shows that nearly 90% of the

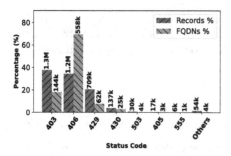

Fig. 1. Top status codes in refusals.   **Fig. 2.** Top tags in refusals.

Table 4. Frequency of type labels   **Table 5.** Frequency of reason labels

Type	Records		FQDNs	
	Count	%	Count	%
Block	2,717,399	79.22	739,602	92.48
Other 429 s	428,031	12.48	30,043	3.76
Checking	143,194	4.17	22,969	2.87
Challenge	78,678	2.29	4,996	0.62
Require JS	59,772	1.74	1,888	0.24
(None)	3,133	0.09	276	0.03
Total	3,430,207	100.00	799,774	100.00

Reason	Records		FQDNs	
	Count	%	Count	%
(None)	1,741,041	50.76	651,251	81.43
Excessive/suspic.	859,309	25.05	89,145	11.15
Security/malic.	803,538	23.43	56,180	7.02
Ip/asn reput.	19,047	0.56	2,248	0.28
Geo-block	7,272	0.21	917	0.11
Total	3,430,207	100.00	799,741	100.00

ModSecurity instances can be traced to a single hosting conglomerate that operates AS46606 and AS19871. Both ASes are associated with Newfold Digital Inc., previously known as Endurance International Group. AS46606 is Unified Layer, a web hosting company that was acquired by Endurance/Newfold. Newfold also operates many brands, including BlueHost, HostGator, HostMonster, ResellerClub, Domain.com, Network Solutions, and BigRock. AS394695 is Public Domain Registry, which seems unrelated at first sight. We briefly conduct a retroactive analysis of DNS records of a sample of FQDNs. As months had passed since the creation of our CC dataset, we only select FQDNs whose first *A record* still pointed to the respective AS. We collected 4096 samples from Unified Layer, 4028 from Network Solutions, and 3325 from PDR. If either the NS or PTR record contained the name of a company of interest, we mapped the FQDNs to that hoster. The respective column in Table 6 shows that the association to conglomerate holds. This suggests that the ModSecurity configuration has been centrally adopted over a *range* of providers.

Transiency of Refusals. Denoting the number of requests to an FQDN where the response is a refusal by r, and the number of successful requests (status *200*) to the same FQDN by s, we define the *refusal rate* as $\frac{r}{r+s}$. We use this metric to infer the transiency of refusals. We find that 635,358 (79.4%) of the FQDNs with refusals block CC *on every request*.

By Status Code. Table 7 provides the average refusal rate and standard deviation for common status codes for domains with refusals. We see a clear division: refusals with the status codes *406, 405, 444, 418, 510,* and *451* have refusal rates

Table 6. Mapping of ASes, ModSecurity-labeled FQDNs, and respective hosters

ASN/Name	Major Hosting Companies	FQDNs	%
46606/Unified Layer	55.78% Bluehost, 18.47% Hostgator, 6.13% Hostmonster, 4.27% ResellerClub, 3.88% Justhost, 1.63% Domain.com	351,390	63.11%
19871/Network Solutions	83.72% Hostgator	143,041	25.69%
13335/Cloudflare	-	40,681	7.31%
394695/PDR	55.02% ResellerClub, 12.05% HostGator, 11.12% BlueHost, 9.26% BigRock	16,815	3.02%
Others	-	4,096	0.88%
Total	-	556,833	100.00%

Table 7. Avg./Std. Dev. of refusal rate for top status codes in the refusal set

Code	Avg.%	Std.Dev.	FQDNs
406	99.76	4.22	557,618
403	39.89	41.70	144,347
429	53.16	43.16	62,418
430	24.38	38.83	24,697
503	70.02	39.86	3,919
405	95.18	20.48	2,558
444	99.24	7.47	1,562
555	33.58	32.31	1,071
401	87.57	27.32	342
500	34.58	44.12	198
418	97.83	13.07	173
510	98.45	9.66	141

Table 8. Avg./Std. Dev. of refusal rate by reason and tag

Reason/Tag	Avg.%	Std.Dev.	FQDNs
Excess./suspic.	45.65	44.10	89,643
Security/malic.	33.64	40.32	56,295
IP/ASN reput.	56.83	39.43	2,258
Geo-block	87.37	29.45	917
ModSecurity	99.76	4.19	556,751
Wix	34.10	38.26	56,176
Cloudflare	51.89	43.26	29,411
Shopify	24.38	38.83	24,696
Blogvault/M.	30.16	38.75	23,228
Cleantalk	74.92	33.12	3,951
Cloudfront	81.58	37.43	2,869
Wordfence	60.32	43.51	2,215

close to 100%, indicating a non-transient nature. The status codes *430, 555, 500,* and *403* have much lower average refusal rates and imply higher transiency.

Figure 3 presents an ECDF of the refusal rates. For clarity, we include only status codes with more than 1000 associated FQDNs and a refusal rate of less than 99%. Refusals with status code *430* have the most transient refusal behaviour. Nearly 80% of the FQDNs with this status code have a refusal rate lower than 30%. According to [12], this unofficial status code is specific to Shopify, which uses it to indicate that too many HTTP requests are being made. We can confirm this near-exclusive use as our REs also tag 99.8% of cases as Shopify. For the status code *429* (Too Many Requests), which is meant to signal rate limiting, we find that 40% of the FQDNs with refusals actually use it for *every* response, contradictory to its purpose.

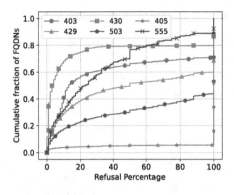
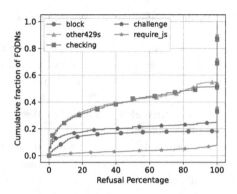

Fig. 3. ECDF of refusal rate per FQDN by status code

Fig. 4. ECDF of refusal rate per FQDN by type

By Type. Figure 4 shows an ECDF of refusal rates for different refusal types. *require_js* has the highest refusal rate. This is consistent with CC not processing JavaScript. The label *block*, which is our more general category, is largely associated with FQDNs using ModSecurity. Notably, *checking* and *other 429s* have a similar pattern but are more transient. It is plausible that they are also triggered by high request rates. The label *challenge* aligns more with *block*, indicating less transience.

By Reason. The first section of Table 8 shows the average refusal rate for each refusal reason for the FQDNs for which we identified a unique reason in the page content. This allows us to shed some more light on otherwise seemingly transient behavior. Geo-blocking has the highest average refusal rate but is actually rare. In fact, we find that some sites use geo-blocking messages only for specific URIs but not for others. The second highest average refusal rate is associated with the label *IP/ASN reputation*. Inspecting these cases more closely, we find that these instances sometimes resolve on visits that CC makes a few days later. Refusals with the label *security/malicious* are less persistent than those with the label *excessive/suspicious*. However, what constitutes "malicious" behavior can be expected to depend on each site's preferences, so we cannot draw strong conclusions from this. Figure 7 breaks the refusal rate down by reason.

By Tag. The second section of Table 8 shows the refusal rates for different tags. FQDNs associated with ModSecurity nearly always deny CC access. We access some of these FQDNs from the University of Twente's campus using different user agents: "CCBot" for CC, "curl/7.68.0" for *curl*, and one by Chrome 124 on Windows. We find that only "CCBot" is blocked, indicating a specific block. The ECDF of refusal rate by tags can be found in Fig. 8.

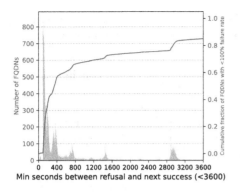

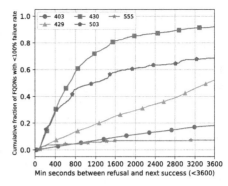

Fig. 5. Distribution of duration of transient refusals (<1h)

Fig. 6. Duration of transient refusals by status code (<1h)

Duration of Transient Refusals. Figure 5 illustrates the resolution of transient refusals over time by showing how many FQDNs unblock access within one hour. We identify spikes at specific intervals, *e.g.* around 100 and 2900 s. Given that CC's exact scheduling cannot be determined from the data, this suggests that sites may treat intervals around 1.5 and 45 min as potentially suitable for re-allowing access. We also find that about 85% of FQDNs unblock within 1 h.

By Status Code. Figure 6 shows an ECDF of the shortest duration between a first refusal and the next success, broken down by status code. For clarity, the figure only considers refusal rates of less than 90%. We see that refusals with status code *430*, which we know to be associated with Shopify, are the quickest to resolve (within 15 min for more than half the FQDNs). Unblocking happens more slowly for the other status codes. There is a notable difference to *403*.

5   Discussion and Conclusion

We found that about 1.68% of FQDNs display refusal behaviors, and some large hosters are significant contributors and use the same technology to achieve the effect. We also identified certain patterns such as the relationship between status codes and blocking persistence, the incorrect use of HTTP status codes, and the use of unofficial codes by large parties.

Further Research is Warranted. The first conclusion we offer is that our findings are not negligible artefacts. In this early work, we focused on only one data set from CC. Our results suggest that it is worthwhile to carry out similar studies over *(i)* longer periods of time and *(ii)* also for other web crawling projects. This is compounded by the current drive by AI companies to ingest web content without compensation, which may well lead to web site blocks becoming more frequent.

Lack of Standard Communication is an Issue. The second conclusion that we offer is that the current set of HTTP status codes is not sufficiently granular to enable crawlers to identify refusals with precision. There is even a misuse of the official status code *429*, which is often used for permanent blocks rather than to signal a request to slow down, or the semantically completely unrelated *406*. Such inconsistencies complicate the ability of crawlers to adapt their behaviour in response to server signals. This, in turn, may lead to them on missing web sites whose operators would not object to slower crawling by public-benefit projects.

Crawlers Can Make Adjustments. In the absence of clearer standards, crawlers should consider adopting flexible back-off strategies based on HTTP status codes. For instance, and for the time being, they should not carry out retries when they encounter status codes such as *406*. In the case of CC, ModSecurity accounts for 1.17% of all FQDNs (about 556×10^3), with a conglomerate of hosters adopting anti-bot measures, which we can also show to be specific to (at least) CC. As a first step, CC could improve their coverage by reaching out to these hosting providers to discuss the reasons for the restrictions on their user-agent. Additionally, rotating IP addresses between requests to the same FQDN would help bypass IP-based blocks, as would distributing the crawling activity over other cloud providers. It is possible that some blocks are simply due to the behavior of other cloud tenants and not CC. However, without further standardization, all these measures are stop-gaps, and new strategies would need to be developed as site operators adjust their own blocking behavior.

Acknowledgments. This work was partially supported by the research project 'CATRIN' (NWA. 1215.18.003) as part of the Dutch Research Council's (NWO) National Research Agenda (NWA).

Ethics. This work raises no ethical concerns. The CC dataset was ethically created [18]. We ran fewer than 70×10^3 DNS queries (about 12×10^3 FQDN samples) to identify their NS and PTR records, distributing them over time and sequentially to avoid network or nameserver load.

A   Additional Figures and Tables

Table 9. Freq. of status codes in pruned set. Asterisks refer to unofficial status codes

Status Code	Description	Record Count	Percentage (%)
403	Forbidden	5,855,588	26.87
410	Gone	4,338,335	19.91
500	Internal Server Error	3,379,744	15.51
503	Service Unavailable	1,812,300	8.32
406	Not Acceptable	1,676,200	7.69
400	Bad Request	1,528,691	7.02
401	Unauthorized	1,190,637	5.46
429	Too Many Requests	708,933	3.25
502	Bad Gateway	343,984	1.58
522	Connection Timed Out*	152,643	0.70
430	Request Header Fields Too Large*	137,609	0.63
504	Gateway Timeout	116,847	0.54
520	Unknown Error*	112,555	0.52
402	Payment Required	97,097	0.45
444	No Response*	41,874	0.19
405	Method Not Allowed	39,872	0.18
409	Conflict	30,404	0.14
202	Accepted	30,097	0.14
423	Locked	28,483	0.13
521	Web Server Is Down*	24,316	0.11
508	Loop Detected	14,296	0.07
204	No Content	12,850	0.06
412	Precondition Failed	12,168	0.06
418	I'm a teapot*	7,772	0.04
555	Custom status code*	7,506	0.03
Others	-	89,208	0.41
Total	-	21,790,009	100.00

Table 10. Frequency of tags in refusals

Type	Records		FQDNs	
	Count	Percentage (%)	Count	Percentage (%)
(None)	1,302,997	37.99	98,124	12.26
Modsecurity	1,177,945	34.34	556,751	69.58
Blogvault/malcare	342,060	9.97	23,228	2.90
Cloudflare	184,387	5.38	29,411	3.68
Wix	167,808	4.89	56,176	7.02
Shopify	137,389	4.01	24,696	3.09
Cloudfront	38,115	1.11	2,869	0.36
Cleantalk	30,089	0.88	3,951	0.49
Wordfence	16,955	0.49	2,215	0.28
Shieldpro	8,634	0.25	878	0.11
Deflect.ca	8,338	0.24	285	0.04
Google	4,550	0.13	76	0.01
Defender	2,932	0.09	320	0.04
Bitninja	2,482	0.07	583	0.07
Wexbo	2,440	0.07	184	0.02
Crowdsec	1,276	0.04	90	0.01
Tiger protect	944	0.03	105	0.01
Zb block	239	0.01	81	0.01
Virusdie	126	0.00	19	0.00
Cachewall	115	0.00	15	0.00
Ninjafirewall	98	0.00	25	0.00
Spamfirewall	89	0.00	25	0.00
Link11	42	0.00	4	0.00
Cidram	36	0.00	8	0.00
Zero spam	35	0.00	6	0.00
Blockscript	34	0.00	7	0.00
Security pro	27	0.00	3	0.00
Sysadminok	14	0.00	0	0.00
Aapenal	11	0.00	4	0.00
Total	3,430,207	100.00	800,139	100.00

Table 11. Frequency of status codes in refusals. The finer granularity (< 50 refusals) for the tail was obtained by manual investigation of refusals captured by the more generic regular expressions. Asterisks refer to unofficial status codes.

Code	Description	Records		FQDNs	
		Count	Percentage (%)	Count	Percentage (%)
403	Forbidden	1,296,614	37.80	144,247	18.03
406	Not Acceptable	1,181,016	34.43	557,610	69.72
429	Too Many Requests	708,933	20.67	61,911	7.74
430	Request Header Fields Too Large*	137,389	4.01	24,696	3.09
503	Service Unavailable	29,731	0.87	3,907	0.49
202	Accepted	23,721	0.69	964	0.12
405	Method Not Allowed	17,448	0.51	2,557	0.32
401	Unauthorized	10,131	0.30	342	0.04
410	Gone	6,433	0.19	67	0.01
400	Bad Request	5,858	0.17	125	0.02
555	Unknown Error*	5,544	0.16	1,070	0.13
444	No Response*	3,878	0.11	1,547	0.19
418	I'm a Teapot*	998	0.03	173	0.02
493	Request Header Too Large*	497	0.01	14	0.00
451	Unavailable For Legal Reasons	390	0.01	131	0.02
500	Internal Server Error	354	0.01	197	0.02
510	Not Extended	352	0.01	141	0.02
501	Not Implemented	294	0.01	3	0.00
201	Created	216	0.01	40	0.01
424	Failed Dependency	165	0.00	53	0.01
509	Bandwidth Limit Exceeded*	93	0.00	6	0.00
422	Unprocessable Entity	83	0.00	2	0.00
508	Loop Detected	21	0.00	16	0.00
484	Incomplete Request*	12	0.00	2	0.00
456	Ambiguous Error*	11	0.00	2	0.00
420	Enhance Your Calm*	8	0.00	2	0.00
455	Blocked by Windows Parental Controls*	7	0.00	2	0.00
409	Conflict	5	0.00	2	0.00
502	Bad Gateway	2	0.00	2	0.00
203	Non-Authoritative Information	2	0.00	1	0.00
522	Connection Timed Out*	1	0.00	1	0.00
Total		3,430,207	100.00	799,833	100.00

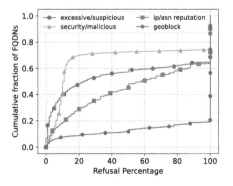

Fig. 7. Refusal rate per FQDN by reason.

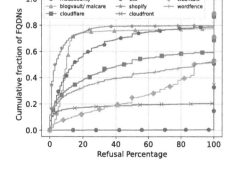

Fig. 8. Refusal rate per FQDN by tag.

Table 12. A subset of regular expressions with labels and full page textual contents

Field	Content
Text:	Cloudflare: Please enable cookies. Sorry, you have been blocked. You are unable to access [hidden]. Why have I been blocked? This website is using a security service to protect itself from online attacks. The action you just performed triggered the security solution. There are several actions that could trigger this block including submitting a certain word or phrase, a SQL command, or malformed data. What can I do to resolve this? You can email the site owner to let them know you were blocked. Please include what you were doing when this page came up and the Cloudflare Ray ID found at the bottom of this page. Cloudflare Ray ID: [hidden] • Your IP: click to reveal [hidden] • Performance & security by Cloudflare.
RegEx:	`^.{20,250}us(ing|es)a security service (to|for)protect(ion)? (itself from|against)online attacks`
Labels:	**Type:** block **Why:** security/malicious **Tag:** cloudflare
Text:	you have been blocked for 72 hours due to three (3) incorrect userid/password entries, or other suspicious activities. your ip address is: [hidden]
RegEx:	`^you have been blocked for \d+ hours due to .+ or other suspicious activities`
Labels:	**Type:** block **Why:** excessive/suspicious **Tag:** none
Text:	verifying if your connection is secure... please turn on javascript and reload the page. verifying if your connection is secure is protected by deflect.ca ddos protection for civil society
RegEx:	`^verifying if your connection is secure\.\.\.\s{5,15}please turn on javascript and reload the page`
Labels:	**Type:** checking **Why:** none **Tag:** none
Text:	human verification javascript is disabled in order to continue, you need to verify that you're not a robot by solving a captcha puzzle. the captcha puzzle requires javascript. enable javascript and then reload the page.
RegEx:	`^human verification\s{1,50}javascript is disabled`
Labels:	**Type:** challenge **Why:** none **Tag:** cloudfront
Text:	forbidden - visitors from your country are not permitted to browse this site.
RegEx:	`^.{0,70}visitors from your country are not permitted to`
Labels:	**Type:** block **Why:** geoblock **Tag:** none
Text:	kompass.complease enable js and disable any ad blocker
RegEx:	`^.{1,50}please enable js and disable any ad blocker`
Labels:	**Type:** require_js **Why:** none **Tag:** none
Text:	your ip address [hidden] has been blocked due to malicious activity reported to https://www.abuseipdb.com
RegEx:	`^your ip address .{6,39} has been blocked due to malicious activity reported to`
Labels:	**Type:** block **Why:** reputation **Tag:** none

References

1. Pepyaka webserver. https://webtechsurvey.com/technology/pepyaka. Accessed May 2024
2. Ablove, A., et al.: Digital discrimination of users in sanctioned states: the case of the cuba embargo. In: 33rd USENIX Security Symposium (USENIX Security 2024), Philadelphia, PA, pp. 3909–3926. USENIX Association (2024). https://www.usenix.org/conference/usenixsecurity24/presentation/ablove
3. Afroz, S., Tschantz, M.C., Sajid, S., Qazi, S.A., Javed, M., Paxson, V.: Exploring server-side blocking of regions. arXiv abs/1805.11606 (2018). https://api.semanticscholar.org/CorpusID:44131334
4. Ahmad, S.S., Dar, M.D., Zaffar, M.F., Vallina-Rodriguez, N., Nithyanand, R.: Apophanies or epiphanies? How crawlers impact our understanding of the web. In: Proceedings of The Web Conference 2020 (WWW 2020), pp. 271–280 (2020)
5. Asghari, H.: pyasn. https://github.com/hadiasghari/pyasn
6. Center for Applied Internet Data Analysis (CAIDA): AS Organizations Dataset (2024). https://catalog.caida.org/dataset/as_organizations. Accessed May 2024
7. Common Crawl: November/december 2023 crawl archive now available. https://www.commoncrawl.org/blog/november-december-2023-crawl-archive-now-available. Accessed May 2024
8. Darer, A., Farnan, O., Wright, J.: Automated discovery of internet censorship by web crawling. In: Proceedings of the 10th ACM Conference on Web Science (WebSci 2018), pp. 195–204 (2018)
9. Fielding, R.T., Nottingham, M.: Additional HTTP Status Codes. RFC 6585 (2012). https://doi.org/10.17487/RFC6585. https://www.rfc-editor.org/info/rfc6585
10. Fielding, R.T., Nottingham, M., Reschke, J.: HTTP Semantics. RFC 9110 (2022). https://doi.org/10.17487/RFC9110. https://www.rfc-editor.org/info/rfc9110
11. Holz, R., Braun, L., Kammenhuber, N., Carle, G.: The SSL landscape - a thorough analysis of the X.509 PKI using active and passive measurements. In: Proceedings of the ACM/USENIX 11th Annual Internet Measurement Conference (IMC), Berlin, Germany (2011)
12. http.dev: HTTP status codes. https://http.dev/status
13. Institute, R.: How many news websites block AI crawlers. Reuters Institute for the Study of Journalism (2023). https://reutersinstitute.politics.ox.ac.uk/how-many-news-websites-block-ai-crawlers#:~:text=Examining. Accessed May 2024
14. Invernizzi, L., Thomas, K., Kapravelos, A., Comanescu, O., Picod, J.M., Bursztein, E.: Cloak of visibility: detecting when machines browse a different web. In: 2016 IEEE Symposium on Security and Privacy (SP), pp. 743–758 (2016)
15. Koster, M., Illyes, G., Zeller, H., Sassman, L.: Robots Exclusion Protocol. RFC 9309 (2022). https://doi.org/10.17487/RFC9309. https://www.rfc-editor.org/info/rfc9309
16. Leonard, D., Loguinov, D.: Demystifying service discovery: implementing an internet-wide scanner. In: Proceedings of the ACM SIGCOMM Conference on Internet Measurement (IMC 2010), pp. 109–122 (2010)
17. McDonald, A., et al.: 403 forbidden: a global view of CDN geoblocking. In: Proceedings of the Internet Measurement Conference (IMC 2018), pp. 218–230 (2018)
18. Nagel, S.: Common crawl: data collection and use cases for NLP (2023). http://nlpl.eu/skeikampen23/nagel.230206.pdf. Accessed May 2024
19. Niaki, A.A., et al.: ICLab: a global, longitudinal internet censorship measurement platform. In: 2020 IEEE Symposium on Security and Privacy (SP), pp. 135–151 (2020)

20. Tschantz, M.C., Afroz, S., Sajid, S., Qazi, S.A., Javed, M., Paxson, V.: A bestiary of blocking: the motivations and modes behind website unavailability. In: 8th USENIX Workshop on Free and Open Communications on the Internet (FOCI 2018) (2018)
21. Vastel, A., Rudametkin, W., Rouvoy, R., Blanc, X.: FP-crawlers: studying the resilience of browser fingerprinting to block crawlers. In: NDSS Workshop on Measurements, Attacks, and Defenses for the Web, MADWeb 2020 (2020)
22. Wan, G., et al.: On the origin of scanning: the impact of location on Internet-wide scans. In: Proceedings of the ACM Internet Measurement Conference (IMC 2020), pp. 662–679 (2020)
23. Zeber, D., et al.: The representativeness of automated web crawls as a surrogate for human browsing. In: Proceedings of the Web Conference 2020 (WWW 2020), pp. 167–178 (2020)

Connectivity

To Adopt or Not to Adopt L4S-Compatible Congestion Control? Understanding Performance in a Partial L4S Deployment

Fatih Berkay Sarpkaya$^{(\boxtimes)}$ ⓘ, Fraida Fund ⓘ, and Shivendra Panwar ⓘ

NYU Tandon School of Engineering, Brooklyn, NY, USA
{fbs6417,ffund,panwar}@nyu.edu

Abstract. With few exceptions, the path to deployment for any Internet technology requires that there be some benefit to *unilateral* adoption of the new technology. In an Internet where the technology is not fully deployed, is an individual better off sticking to the status quo, or adopting the new technology? This question is especially relevant in the context of the Low Latency, Low Loss, Scalable Throughput (L4S) architecture, where the full benefit is realized only when compatible protocols (scalable congestion control, accurate ECN, and flow isolation at queues) are adopted at both endpoints of a connection and also at the bottleneck router. In this paper, we consider the perspective of the sender of an L4S flow using scalable congestion control, without knowing whether the bottleneck router uses an L4S queue, or whether other flows sharing the bottleneck queue are also using scalable congestion control. We show that whether the sender uses TCP Prague or BBRv2 as the scalable congestion control, it cannot be assured that it will not harm or be harmed by another flow sharing the bottleneck link. We further show that the harm is not necessarily mitigated when a scalable flow shares a bottleneck with multiple classic flows. Finally, we evaluate the approach of BBRv3, where scalable congestion control is used only when the path delay is small, with ECN feedback ignored otherwise, and show that it does not solve the coexistence problem.

Keywords: TCP · Congestion Control · Low Latency · L4S · AQM

1 Introduction

High-rate, latency-critical applications, such as online gaming, Virtual Reality (VR), and remote control, are increasingly prevalent on today's Internet. The Low Latency, Low Loss, Scalable Throughput (L4S) [1] architecture has attracted a great deal of attention from service providers and equipment vendors [2–9], including recent field trials by Comcast [3], inclusion in Low Latency DOCSIS [10] specifications, integration in Apple's operating systems [8], and

© The Author(s), under exclusive license to Springer Nature Switzerland AG 2025
C. Testart et al. (Eds.): PAM 2025, LNCS 15567, pp. 217–246, 2025.
https://doi.org/10.1007/978-3-031-85960-1_10

adoption in Nvidia's streaming service [11]. L4S is designed to enable both
high throughput and low latency while coexisting with classic (not necessarily latency sensitive) flows. It achieves this through scalable congestion control
algorithms (e.g., TCP Prague) [12,13], Accurate Explicit Congestion Notification
(AccECN) [14,15], and dual-queue Active Queue Management (AQM) [16–18].
Unlike other low-latency mechanisms, which may focus solely on specific components, L4S involves both endpoints and routers. When fully deployed, these
components enable L4S flows to achieve both high throughput and low latency.
However, as traffic traverses the Internet, it encounters network segments with
varying levels of L4S support. Some segments may fully implement all L4S components, while others may have partial or no support. As a result, L4S deployment will be incremental, and in the early stages, L4S flows will coexist with
other flow types at bottlenecks that may or may be L4S-compatible.

For an endpoint sending data across the Internet, the question of L4S adoption hinges on the decision of whether or not to use a scalable congestion control
algorithm (CCA) with AccECN, and a header setting that will classify it into L4S
queues at bottleneck routers. This sender must make the decision without full
knowledge of whether the bottleneck queue it encounters will be L4S-compatible,
or whether other flows sharing the bottleneck will also be scalable flows using
AccECN. In this work, we investigate two scalable CCAs, TCP Prague and
BBRv2 with AccECN, in partial L4S deployment scenarios including both L4S-
compatible and non-L4S bottlenecks, in order to better understand this decision.

Ultimately, we aim to answer four main research questions:

1. TCP Prague is a scalable congestion control prototype developed by the L4S
   team. Can senders be assured that TCP Prague will not cause harm to, or
   be harmed by, another flow at a shared bottleneck?
2. There is an implementation of BBRv2 that adopts some of the principles
   of scalable congestion control used by TCP Prague. Does L4S-compatible
   BBRv2 have more favorable properties for adoption than TCP Prague?
3. Is the harm caused by or to the L4S-compatible flow mitigated when the
   bottleneck is shared by a large number of flows?
4. In BBRv3, ECN is switched ON or OFF automatically, depending on whether
   or not a constant path delay threshold is exceeded. Is the BBRv3 approach
   more favorable for the deployment of L4S-compatible congestion control?

Since the sender does not know what type of queue it will encounter and
what type of flow will be sharing the bottleneck, if a TCP sender has some
reasonable expectation of encountering a pathological situation, then it probably should not adopt scalable congestion control. In our investigation of these
research questions, we seek to identify such situations.

This work builds on earlier evaluations of scalable congestion control, both
in the academic literature, in the IETF, and industry. The IETF Transport and
Services Working Group (TSVWG) is actively working on the development of
TCP Prague and the evaluation of L4S. However, beyond some early studies,
there has been limited research on L4S evaluation across different scenarios.

We will explore this in detail in Sect. 2. Our previous work [19] evaluates TCP Prague in specific scenarios and provides some initial findings and conclusions towards Research Question 1 (RQ1). In line with that earlier work and the likely initial deployment of L4S, we consider a residential home broadband scenario, but examine a wider range of CC protocols and bottleneck types that a scalable flow might encounter. This includes two key scalable CCAs, TCP Prague and BBRv2 with AccECN, as well as the most widely used non-scalable CCAs with which a scalable flow may coexist—CUBIC, BBRv1, v2, and v3—and a greater variety of queue types that might be present at the bottleneck router.

The rest of this paper is organized as follows: Sect. 2 provides a detailed discussion of the L4S architecture, briefly reviews early evaluation results from previous works, and discusses prior work on the deployment of new CCAs and expectations regarding fairness and harm. Section 3 outlines the experimental methodology, including the experiment topology, the CCAs used, and the different bottleneck types. Section 4 presents our findings along with a detailed discussion of the results. Finally, Sect. 5 concludes with a summary of the work and findings, and suggests directions for future research. Our experimental artifacts are available for use on the open-access testbed FABRIC [20], allowing others to build upon and validate our research[1]. A detailed artifact description is provided in Appendix A.

2   Background

In this paper, we will explore the broader question of whether or not L4S's scalable congestion control is ready for adoption, given that it may be used in a network where L4S is not fully deployed. In order to provide context for this investigation, we provide some background on the L4S architecture (Sect. 2.1) describe early evaluations of it (Sect. 2.2), and discuss more generally what it means for a new CCA to be "ready for adoption" (Sect. 2.3).

2.1   L4S Architecture

The L4S architecture [1] is designed to address the challenge of achieving both high throughput and ultra-low latency. L4S flows should be capable of maintaining very low queuing delay (i.e., less than 1 millisecond), low congestion loss, and high throughput. In order to achieve this, L4S uses three primary mechanisms: scalable congestion control, accurate ECN, and isolation of L4S and non-L4S flows at the bottleneck queue (ideally, with different ECN thresholds).

Scalable Congestion Control addresses a fundamental problem of classic congestion control, illustrated in Fig. 1. A sender using a classic loss-based CCA such as TCP CUBIC will increase its congestion window (CWND) until the bottleneck buffer fills, causing high queuing delay (first subplot). Alternatively, ECN marking may be used to signal congestion, potentially reducing the queuing delay

---

[1] Artifacts are available at: https://github.com/fatihsarpkaya/L4S-PAM2025.

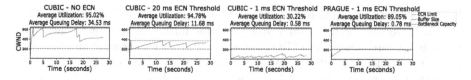

Fig. 1. Adapted from [13] and [19], we conduct a FABRIC experiment to illustrate the fundamental limitation of classic congestion control, using a line network with 100 Mbps bottleneck capacity, a base RTT of 25 ms, and a 2 BDP FIFO bottleneck with ECN. Artifacts to reproduce this are available at [21].

somewhat (second subplot). However, due to the sawtooth shape of its CWND - the result of using a fixed (large) multiplicative decrease when it receives a congestion signal - classic congestion control cannot fully utilize the bottleneck link when the ECN marking threshold is set very low, so it cannot achieve extremely low queuing delay (third subplot). Scalable congestion control addresses this by adjusting the CWND in much smaller increments, in proportion to the extent of the congestion, thereby achieving full link utilization with very low queuing delay (fourth subplot). It requires AccECN or DCTP-style ECN marking at the receiver, which we discuss next.

DCTCP-Style ECN and AccECN. TCP with classic ECN was designed to indicate at most one congestion event per round trip [22]. A classic ECN receiver persistently marks the ECE flag in the TCP header until the sender acknowledges it with a Congestion Window Reduced (CWR) flag. In DCTCP, the receiver provides more precise congestion feedback by ACKing every packet and setting the ECE flag only if the packet has a CE mark. It also accounts for delayed ACKs, using a simple state-machine mechanism to decide whether the ECN-Echo bit should be set or not based on the marking status of the last received packet [23]. Therefore, the behavior of the receiver is important for senders using the DCTCP-style scalable congestion control mechanism. If the receiver uses classic ECN marking, the sender may not accurately calculate the fraction of CE-marked packets. BBRv2 and BBRv3, under some settings, implement scalable congestion control with DCTCP-style ECN.

However, DCTCP-style ECN has some limitations. First, it lacks capability negotiation, assuming both sender and receiver use the same feedback mechanism without verifying compatibility. Second, its feedback becomes unreliable with packet loss, as it cannot effectively distinguish between loss and congestion, causing issues in interpreting feedback, especially with lost ACKs [15]. Due to these issues and the need for more precise feedback in scalable congestion controls within the L4S framework, DCTCP-style ECN is insufficient.

To address this, AccECN [24] uses a three-bit counter in the TCP header, utilizing the Accurate ECN (AE), CWR, and ECE flags to convey the exact number of packets marked with congestion. This counter, known as the ACE field, provides a precise measure of congestion levels, enabling senders to fine-tune their congestion window with greater precision. Notably, AccECN only governs the signaling of accurate ECN feedback between the TCP sender and receiver, and does not dictate how the sender responds to congestion [24].

Isolation of L4S and Non-L4S flows. Scalable CCAs achieve high throughput and low latency by using AccECN and adjusting their CWND in small increments in proportion to the extent of congestion. However, when these flows share a queue with classic CCAs, one flow type may capture much more of the link capacity than it should. To address this, the L4S architecture introduces the Dual-Queue Coupled AQM, with DualPI2 AQM as a prototype, which separates traffic into two queues: one for low latency flows and another for classic flows. Scalable flows negotiating AccECN should set the ECT(1) code point in the ECN header to be assigned to the low latency queue, while other flows are directed to the classic queue [18]. This design aims to maintain low latency for scalable flows while ensuring reasonable bandwidth sharing with classic flows.

In addition to isolating low latency and classic flows, the Dual-Queue Coupled AQM should also use different ECN marking thresholds for the two queues. As illustrated in Fig. 1, a classic flow cannot tolerate a very low ECN marking threshold, but a scalable flow can. A queue that provides only flow isolation, such as FQ or FQ-CoDel [25], can ensure that classic and low latency flows coexist without harm to one another. However, with a common ECN threshold for all queues (presumably, a higher threshold to accommodate the classic flows), the low-latency benefit of L4S cannot be fully realized by L4S flows. The Dual-Queue Coupled AQM and an L4S-aware FQ-CoDel implementation [26] assign a shallower ECN marking threshold for flows that set the ECT(1) code point.

What Scenarios is an L4S Flow Likely to Encounter? L4S architecture assumes ideal conditions—scalable congestion control and AccECN support on end hosts, along with flow isolation on routers. However, actual conditions on the Internet vary widely [27–29]. Some networks deploy ECN as part of AQMs like FQ-CoDel, but others do not. Issues like imperfect flow isolation due to hash collisions, VPN tunneling, or deliberate configurations can also arise. Additionally, misconfiguration, legacy behaviors, and policy decisions (like actively bleaching ECN bits) can unintentionally change or disable ECN functionality. Production traffic observations [30,31] reveal inconsistent congestion marking capabilities across environments, influenced by equipment age, geographic differences, and network configurations. These studies motivate our evaluations in the next section, considering various network scenarios L4S flows may encounter.

2.2   Early Evaluations of L4S Coexistence

A complete L4S deployment involves several mechanisms: scalable CC at the sender, AccECN or DCTCP-style ECN at the receiver, and flow isolation with different ECN thresholds at the bottleneck router. Incremental deployment of these mechanisms, ensuring L4S flows achieve low-latency and high-throughput performance without negatively impacting existing congestion control algorithms, is essential for successful Internet-wide adoption. Consequently, coexistence and deployment strategies have been key subjects of discussion and preliminary evaluation by the IETF TSVWG, industry, and academic literature.

One of the most challenging coexistence scenarios occurs when L4S and Classic CCAs share a single-queue Classic ECN bottleneck. Therefore, White [27] recommends prioritizing safe coexistence with Classic ECN traffic. It is suggested that the first phase of deployment should focus on enabling L4S-aware AQMs, such as DualQ or FQ-CoDel, at critical points like network edges and bottlenecks [1]. This incremental approach allows L4S flows to coexist with Classic flows, providing low-latency and low-loss benefits while minimizing the risks of unsafe coexistence. Deployment typically starts with upgrading AQMs at bottlenecks, followed by introducing L4S-compatible congestion control mechanisms, such as TCP Prague, on servers and end devices. When Classic ECN bottlenecks are detected, additional measures should be taken, like ECN fallback algorithm [32], to prevent issues like bandwidth starvation for Classic flows [27].

However, this deployment strategy has some pre-requisites. First, as discussed, the performance should be validated in various partial deployment scenarios to ensure that L4S can coexist with Classic ECN flows without causing performance degradation. This validation should encourage network operators to upgrade bottleneck routers and adopt scalable CCAs with AccECN feedback at network edges. Another challenge is upgrading bottlenecks, which may occur at locations like peering points or wireless access links, making it critical to focus on these locations [19]. Additionally, globally upgrading routers presents a significant challenge due to the extensive infrastructure involved. Thus, understanding the behavior of scalable CCAs in different partial L4S deployment scenarios is crucial and will likely remain critical for a long time.

Early evaluations and field trials of L4S have been discussed in IETF meetings [3,5]. [33] confirms that with a shared FQ-CoDel single queue or a single PIE queue using classic ECN signaling, TCP Prague flows dominate classic flows, whether or not the classic flows support ECN. [34–36] also confirm this issue with non-L4S-aware AQMs. Our previous work [19] had similar results for when TCP Prague shares a CoDel queue with CUBIC and non-L4S-compatible BBRv2.

Notably, [33] finds that DualPI2 gives Prague flows a throughput advantage over CUBIC, while in a FIFO queue, CUBIC dominates, with Prague behaving like NewReno. These observations are confirmed in [35]. However, our previous work [19] shows that CUBIC or non-L4S-compatible BBRv2 flows gain a slight advantage over Prague flows in DualPI2, and in a FIFO queue, Prague and CUBIC share bandwidth almost equally. This discrepancy is possibly due to differences in network setups, which can affect fairness as discussed in [34,37].

Most recently, we had observed [19] that across various bottleneck types and co-existence scenarios involving TCP Prague versus CUBIC or non-L4S-compatible BBRv2, only bottlenecks with per-flow isolation ensure a fair share of bandwidth, while only DualPI2 guarantees ultra-low latency for TCP Prague. However, this paper does not consider the full range of queue types or scalable CCAs that may be involved in an incremental L4S deployment.

2.3 "Ready for Adoption"

Beyond L4S specifically, there is a rich academic literature on what it means for a CCA to be ready for adoption, that provides important context for our study.

The classic metric used to assess CCA fairness is Jain's Fairness Index (JFI) [38]. However, several studies explore broader TCP fairness concepts and propose alternative metrics. In [39], fairness is evaluated using max-min fairness (MmF), focusing on how closely each flow achieves its MmF share during contention. This approach measures how much of the allocated bandwidth each flow gets relative to its fair share. In [40], fairness is calculated by normalizing the throughput difference between competing flows, with 0 representing perfect fairness, and deviations indicating one flow taking more bandwidth than the other. Similarly, [41] introduces a ratio-based fairness measure, which evaluates fairness by comparing the bytes transmitted between two flows. A value of 0 indicates perfect fairness, while negative or positive values indicate one flow dominates the other.

In [42], the authors argue that perfect flow rate fairness is not always necessary and that JFI alone does not capture positive or negative biases between flows. They propose that new CCAs should avoid causing harm to existing algorithms and introduce a harm-based threshold to measure a new CCA's negative impact on legacy algorithms. The goal is to ensure a new algorithm does no more harm than existing algorithms do to each other. This harm-based metric is used in [43], for example, to evaluate the fairness between BBR and BBRv2, showing how newer algorithms can be assessed through their impact on legacy flows. Furthermore, [44] confirms that the harm-based approach better evaluates CCA deployability in real-world networks compared to traditional fairness metrics.

Additionally, as discussed in [45], new CCAs should be evaluated against existing algorithms, ensuring that any new proposal does not introduce more harm than previous standards-track algorithms to flows sharing a common bottleneck. This approach ensures that newer CCAs do not unfairly dominate bandwidth at the expense of legacy flows, which is essential for incremental deployment.

From the discussion above it is clear that there are various methods to evaluate the extent to which a CCA achieves fairness, and no single approach is universally best. Therefore, our fairness evaluation reflects the principles discussed in [45] and [42], emphasizing harm-based fairness rather than strict 50-50 equality, which is not necessarily expected. Our evaluations aim to inform senders that "if you use scalable congestion control in this type of network, you may experience this behavior." The sender can then decide what best suits their application's needs and whether switching to scalable congestion control is worthwhile. For this reason, we will report throughput directly (instead of JFI) in Sect. 4. However, although we report results for all scenarios, in our discussion we focus especially on those where a flow gets less than 20% of bottleneck link bandwidth or more than 80% (when it should get 50%). This heuristic helps us identify the most problematic settings.

3 Experiment Methodology

To address the research questions in Sect. 1, we conduct systematic experiments and report the results. This section details our methodology.

Experiment Platform: We conduct experiments on FABRIC [20], a national scale experimental networking testbed. Each node in our experiment is a virtual machine running Ubuntu 22.04, with 4 cores and 32 GB RAM for single flow experiments and 8 cores and 64 GB RAM for multiple flow experiments.

Topology: Our network setup consists of two senders and two receivers, along with a delay node and a bottleneck router, as shown in Fig. 2. The delay node uses **netem** to emulate a base RTT, with half of the delay applied in each direction. At the router, we configure the bottleneck bandwidth and buffer size using the token bucket filter implemented in **tc-htb**.

Network Setting: We assume a bottleneck at the access link and emulate network conditions similar to those in a residential fixed broadband scenario, with a base RTT of 10 ms and a bottleneck link capacity of 100 Mbps. We choose to study the residential broadband setting in depth because of L4S's early momentum among cable providers [3,5,10].

Queue: In our experiments, we consider a wide variety of queue types that may be encountered at the bottleneck router.

First, we consider a variety of single queue types, including three that drop packets as a congestion signal and two that use ECN to mark packets:

- **FIFO:** a single drop tail queue without ECN support, realized with **tc-bfifo**.
- **Drop-based CoDel:** a single queue with CoDel AQM [46], which uses the local minimum queue size within a monitoring window as a measure of the standing queue, and drop packets if there is a standing queue exceeding a target value. We use **tc-codel** with a 5 ms target and ECN disabled.
- **Drop-based PIE:** a single queue with PIE [47] estimates the dequeue rate to calculate the current queue delay, adjusting the drop probability based on delay trends. We use **tc-pie** with a 5 ms target and ECN disabled.
- **FIFO + ECN:** a single drop tail queue with ECN support using a 5 ms marking threshold, realized with **tc-fq**. (Although **tc-fq** is multi-queue, we enforce it to operate as a single queue.) While such a bottleneck type is considered rare or non-existent in the Internet [27], it allows us to distinguish the effect of ECN from the effect of AQM, providing better insight into the mechanisms behind the results.
- **CoDel:** ECN enabled version of Drop-based CoDel AQM. We use **tc-codel** with a 5 ms target and the ECN option enabled, so that it marks packets for flows with ECN support and drops packets otherwise.

We also consider some queue types that implement multiple queues. All of these offer flow isolation, but the two queue types marked with a ⋆ also have separate ECN marking thresholds for realizing the full benefits of L4S.

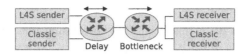

Fig. 2. Experiment Topology

- **FQ:** a fair queue with flow isolation and ECN (using a 5 ms marking threshold), realized with `tc-fq`.
- **FQ-CoDel:** combines fair queuing with the CoDel AQM. We realize this queue with `tc fq_codel`, with a 5 ms target and the ECN option enabled.
- ⋆ **L4S-aware FQ-CoDel:** extends the traditional FQ-CoDel algorithm to support L4S, allowing a shallow queueing threshold to be applied specifically to L4S packets. We realize this queue using `tc fq_codel`, with a 5 ms target and ECN enabled. Additionally, the `ce_threshold` is set to 1 ms, and `ce_threshold_selector` is configured as 0x01/0x01 to apply the low threshold exclusively to L4S flows.
- ⋆ **DualPI2:** a dual queue coupled AQM designed for L4S [18], realized using `tc-dualpi2` from the L4S repository [48] (commit `4579ffb`). We use the `target` parameter to set a 5 ms ECN threshold for the classic queue, while the L4S queue has a 1 ms ECN threshold.

For each queue type, we evaluate bottleneck buffer sizes that range from shallow to deep, considering the following multiples of the link's bandwidth-delay product (BDP): 0.5, 1, 2, 4, and 8.

Flow Generation: We generate TCP flow(s) from the L4S sender and from the classic sender using the `iperf3` tool, each for a duration of 60 s. For each flow, we record the average throughput and RTT values. The results presented are based on the averages from 10 trials.

L4S Flow CCA: There are widely available Linux implementations for two TCP CCAs - Prague and BBRv2 - that implement both scalable congestion control and ECT(1) code point setting (in order to be assigned to the low latency queue of an L4S bottleneck). Both of these use AccECN. We use the implementation from the L4S repository [48] (commit `4579ffb`). Notably, this L4S-compatible BBRv2 is not the "official" BBRv2 (that uses DCTCP-style ECN marking, and does not use the ECT(1) code point setting).

The Prague implementation includes an ECN Fallback heuristic [32], an optional feature to address fairness issues between TCP Prague and classic CCAs when they share a single queue with classic ECN. It allows Prague to fallback to classic behavior if it detects a classic ECN in use. While this feature is not enabled by default in the Linux implementation of Prague, it can be activated. We evaluate Prague both with the default setting, and with ECN Fallback activated.

Non-L4S Flow CCA: For the non-L4S flows, we focus on two CCAs that L4S flows are likely to encounter at a shared bottleneck.

TCP CUBIC [49] is the most widely used TCP variant on the Internet [50, 51]. We experiment with a classic CUBIC flow (using the Linux kernel 5.13.12 implementation), with and without ECN enabled at both endpoints.

TCP BBR [52] and its variants are widely deployed across the Internet [50], are used for all of Google's internal WAN traffic, and for public Internet traffic from services like Google.com and YouTube [53]. With respect to ECN, we consider a wide variety of ECN settings: Our experiments include BBRv1 (Linux kernel 5.13.12), which does not support ECN. The default BBRv2 implementation (from the v2alpha branch of the official BBR repository [54]) is used without ECN, with DCTCP-style ECN at the sender and classic ECN at the receiver (one-sided DCTCP-style ECN), or with DCTCP-style ECN at both endpoints (two-sided DCTCP-style ECN).

We also consider BBRv3 using the v3 branch of the official repository [54]. While BBRv3 has been recently released, the developers do not consider it ready for widespread deployment with its current coexistence and loss-handling properties [55]. Nevertheless, we are interested in exploring its potential. For BBRv3, even if ECN is enabled, it is not utilized when the path delay exceeds a fixed threshold. We explore this behavior in Sect. 4.4.

4   Experiment Results

In this section, we discuss the performance of L4S-compatible congestion controls—TCP Prague and L4S-compatible BBRv2—focusing on their throughput share and latency across various network scenarios, as previously described. We will also address our research questions throughout the discussion.

4.1   RQ1: Can Senders be Assured that TCP Prague will not Cause Harm to, or be Harmed by, Another Flow at a Shared Bottleneck?

To address our first research question, we evaluate the performance of TCP Prague and assess whether it is negatively impacted by other flows sharing the same bottleneck, or if it causes harm to those other flows.

First, we will evaluate the throughput and latency of a TCP Prague flow when it shares a bottleneck queue with a CUBIC flow. The throughput of the Prague flow (and the CUBIC flow, in parenthesis) is shown in Fig. 3 for single queue bottleneck scenarios, and in Fig. 4 for multi-queue bottleneck scenarios. The latency for each experiment is shown in Fig. 5 and Fig. 6.

Circumstances Where Prague is not Harmed by, nor Harmful to, a CUBIC Flow. These circumstances include drop-based bottlenecks, FQ bottlenecks, and DualPI2. Regarding the drop-based bottlenecks, as shown in Fig. 3, in FIFO queues without ECN support or AQM, TCP Prague achieves roughly its fair share, with slight advantages or disadvantages depending on the buffer size. Similarly, in drop-based bottleneck types that use AQMs such as PIE and CoDel, Prague shows slightly worse performance compared to CUBIC (Fig. 3). In these

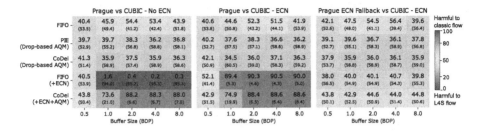

Fig. 3. Throughput of Prague (and CUBIC, in parentheses) in Mbps when sharing a bottleneck (Single Queue AQMs).

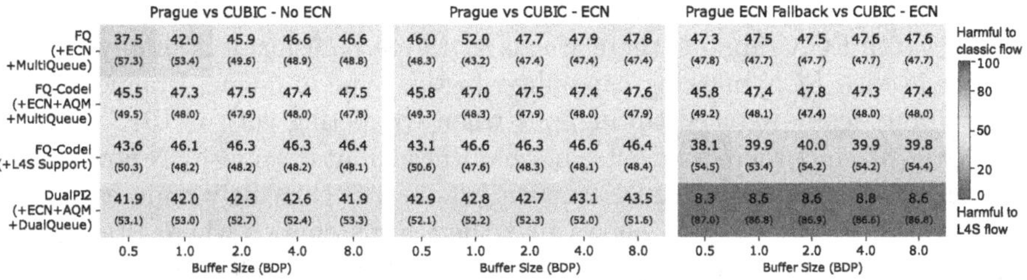

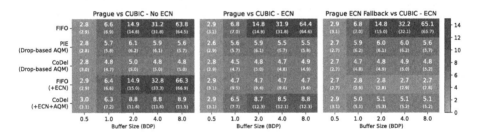

Fig. 4. Throughput of Prague (and CUBIC, in parentheses) in Mbps when sharing a bottleneck (multi/dual queue AQMs).

Fig. 5. Prague (CUBIC) queuing delay in ms when sharing bottleneck with a CUBIC flow. (single queue AQMs - ECN threshold is 5 ms, where applicable.)

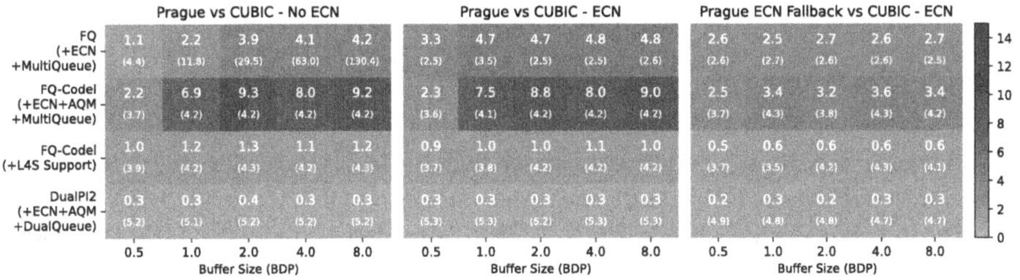

Fig. 6. Prague (and CUBIC, in parentheses) queuing delay (ms) when sharing a bottleneck (multi/dual queue AQMs).

cases, since ECN is inactive, the only congestion signal is the packet loss. When a loss is detected, Prague falls back to Reno behavior in the current Linux implementation [56]. It is well-established that CUBIC generally achieves higher throughput than Reno when sharing the same bottleneck [57]. Therefore, Prague, which effectively behaves like Reno, gets slightly lower throughput in most of the cases in our setting.

At FQ bottlenecks, as seen in Fig. 4, with or without ECN support of CUBIC flow, Prague gets almost its fair share in all scenarios. In L4S-aware FQ-CoDel, Prague flows also get very low queuing delay of around 1ms (Fig. 6). In DualPI2, Prague similarly gets almost its fair share with a slight disadvantage compared to CUBIC and its queueing delay is also lower than 0.5ms.

Circumstances Where Prague is Harmed Due to Coexistence with a CUBIC Flow. In FIFO with ECN support, there are no AQM mechanisms; it is simply a drop-tail queue with ECN marking capability. In this type of queue, Prague experiences dramatically reduced throughput when competing with CUBIC without ECN (Fig. 3), since there is no extra mechanism to limit the non-ECN flow. Moreover, in this bottleneck, Prague's queueing latency is extremely high, especially in deep buffers (Fig. 5). This shows that there are scenarios where Prague still experiences extremely high latency, even if it enables its ECN and goes through an ECN-enabled bottleneck. Prague with ECN fallback, which we discuss next, is also harmed by coexistence with CUBIC in a DualPI2 bottleneck.

Circumstances Where Prague Harms a CUBIC Flow. In single queue with ECN bottlenecks, Prague can be harmful. When competing with CUBIC that supports ECN, Prague harms the CUBIC flow due to their different reactions to ECN signals (Fig. 3). This is a well-known issue, as discussed in Sect. 2. In CoDel AQM with ECN support (Fig. 3), CoDel AQM drops non-ECN packets and marks ECN-capable packets, allowing Prague to maintain higher throughput.

This dominance of TCP Prague appears to be mitigated for this type of queue by Prague's ECN fallback algorithm. Prague detects the single-queue AQM with classic ECN support and falls back to classic ECN behavior. In this case, it achieves slightly lower throughput compared to its fair share, similar to what is observed in drop-based AQM scenarios (Fig. 3). However, it introduces other problems with DualPI2, as seen in Fig. 4, where Prague with ECN Fallback gets much less than its share of the link capacity. This is likely due to the heuristic incorrectly detecting that the queue is not using L4S AQM, as we suggested in [19].

Next, we evaluate TCP Prague against BBRv1/v2 flows. Since BBR is the second-most prevalent TCP variant among major websites [50], it is likely that TCP Prague flows may need to coexist with BBR on the Internet. For BBRv2, we consider two different ECN configurations: one-sided DCTCP-style ECN support (i.e. the receiver sends classic ECN ACKs), and two-sided DCTCP-style ECN support (i.e. the receiver sends DCTCP style ACKs). For coexistence scenarios with BBRv2, the throughput of the Prague flow (and the BBR flow, in parenthesis) is shown in Fig. 7 for single queue bottlenecks, and in Fig. 8 for multi-queue bottlenecks. The latency for each experiment is shown in Fig. 9 and Fig. 10. We

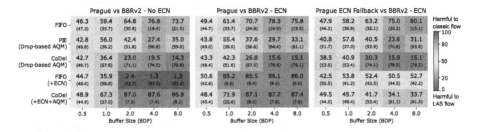

Fig. 7. Throughput of Prague (and BBRv2, in parentheses) in Mbps when sharing a bottleneck (single queue AQMs). (classic ECN marking on BBRv2 receiver)

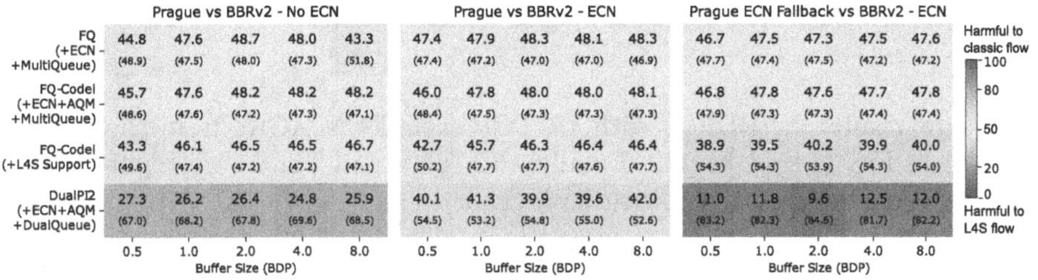

Fig. 8. Throughput of Prague (and BBRv2, in parentheses) in Mbps when sharing a bottleneck (multi/dual queue AQMs). (classic ECN marking on BBRv2 receiver)

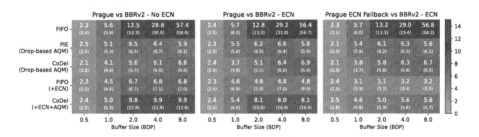

Fig. 9. Prague (and BBRv2, in parentheses) queuing delay (ms) when sharing a bottleneck (single queue AQMs). (classic ECN marking on BBRv2 receiver)

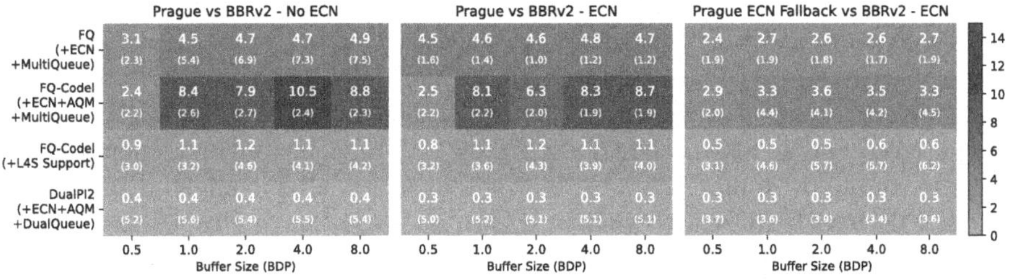

Fig. 10. Prague (and BBRv2, in parentheses) queuing delay (ms) when sharing a bottleneck (multi/dual queue AQMs). (classic ECN marking on BBRv2 receiver)

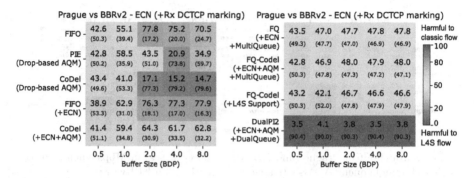

Prague vs BBRv2 - ECN (+Rx DCTCP marking)   Prague vs BBRv2 - ECN (+Rx DCTCP marking)

	0.5	1.0	2.0	4.0	8.0
FIFO	42.6 (50.3)	55.1 (39.4)	77.8 (17.2)	75.2 (20.0)	70.5 (24.7)
PIE (Drop-based AQM)	42.8 (50.2)	58.5 (35.9)	43.5 (51.0)	20.9 (73.8)	34.9 (59.7)
CoDel (Drop-based AQM)	43.4 (49.6)	41.0 (53.3)	17.1 (77.3)	15.2 (79.2)	14.7 (79.6)
FIFO (+ECN)	38.9 (53.3)	62.9 (31.0)	76.3 (18.1)	77.3 (17.0)	77.9 (16.3)
CoDel (+ECN+AQM)	41.4 (51.1)	59.4 (34.8)	64.3 (30.9)	61.7 (33.5)	62.8 (32.2)

Buffer Size (BDP)

	0.5	1.0	2.0	4.0	8.0
FQ (+ECN +MultiQueue)	43.5 (49.3)	47.0 (47.7)	47.7 (47.0)	47.8 (46.9)	47.8 (46.9)
FQ-Codel (+ECN+AQM +MultiQueue)	42.8 (50.3)	46.9 (47.8)	48.0 (47.3)	47.9 (47.2)	48.0 (47.1)
FQ-Codel (+L4S Support)	43.2 (50.3)	42.1 (52.0)	46.7 (47.8)	46.6 (47.9)	46.6 (47.9)
DualPI2 (+ECN+AQM +DualQueue)	3.5 (90.4)	4.1 (90.0)	3.8 (90.3)	3.5 (90.4)	3.8 (90.3)

Buffer Size (BDP)

Harmful to classic flow 100 — 80 — 50 — 20 — 0 Harmful to L4S flow

Fig. 11. Throughput of Prague (and BBRv2, in parentheses) in Mbps when sharing a bottleneck. (DCTCP-style ECN marking on BBRv2 receiver)

also show results vs. BBRv2 with DCTCP style ECN ACKs from the BBRv2 receiver in Fig. 11 and Fig. 12. Finally, in Fig. 13 and Fig. 14 we report results for TCP Prague coexistence with BBRv1.

Circumstances Where Prague is not Harmed by, nor Harmful to, a BBR Flow. FQ bottlenecks are mostly successful to provide fairness for both BBRv1 (Fig. 13) and BBRv2 (Fig. 8 and 11) when they share the bottleneck with TCP Prague flows. In shallow buffer single queue drop-based bottlenecks with BBRv2, Prague gets close to its fair share with a slight advantage or disadvantage (Fig. 7 and 11). In FIFO with large buffer sizes, Prague gets a slight advantage compared to BBRv1 (Fig. 13) and BBRv2 (Fig. 7 and 11). In DualPI2, Prague faces a slight disadvantage against BBRv2 as depicted in Fig. 8. The fallback algorithm for Prague works well and resolves co-existence issues with BBRv2 in single-queue ECN bottlenecks (Fig. 7). However, it introduces other problems with DualPI2 similar to CUBIC co-existence, which will be discussed later. In terms of latency, L4S-aware AQMs are successful in providing ultra-low latency for Prague competing with BBRv1 (Fig. 14) and BBRv2 (Fig. 10 and 12) flows. Moreover, Prague flows do not experience extremely high latency when passing through a single queue ECN-enabled bottleneck (Fig. 9), unlike what is observed in the Prague vs. CUBIC coexistence case (Fig. 5).

Circumstances Where Prague is Harmed Due to Coexistence with a BBR Flow. In single queue bottlenecks with shallow buffers, Prague's throughput is drastically reduced compared to BBRv1 (Fig. 13), as BBRv1 is not sensitive to packet loss, unlike Prague. This aligns with the well-known behavior of BBRv1 when compared to classic loss-based CCAs [58–60]. BBRv2, in contrast, shows better fairness in shallow buffers, due to its loss sensitivity, as documented in [59,60]. In the FIFO with ECN but without AQM, as also seen in Prague vs CUBIC, the non-ECN flow dominates the ECN flow (Fig. 7 and 13), consistent with our previous findings in [19]. For BBRv1, since it neither responds to ECN nor is sensitive to losses, it causes Prague's throughput to drastically decrease when no AQM is present in an ECN-supported bottleneck (Fig. 13). In FQ without AQM,

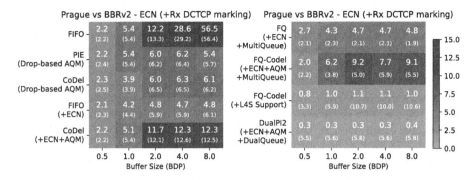

Fig. 12. Prague (and BBRv2, in parentheses) queuing delay (ms) when sharing a bottleneck. (DCTCP-style ECN marking on BBRv2 receiver)

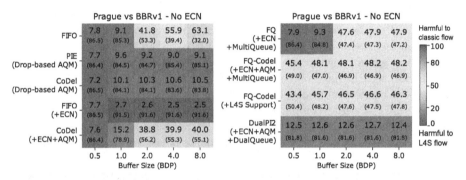

Fig. 13. Throughput of Prague (and BBRv1, in parentheses) in Mbps when sharing a bottleneck.

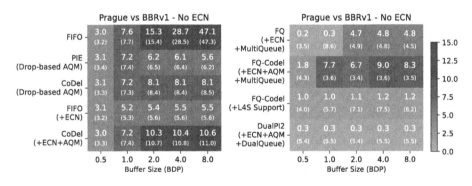

Fig. 14. Prague (and BBRv1, in parentheses) queuing delay (ms) when sharing a bottleneck.

in shallow buffers, the bottleneck fails to provide fairness and BBRv1 is harmful to Prague (Fig. 13). In drop-based AQMs, such as PIE and CoDel, BBRv1 consistently achieves significantly higher throughput compared to Prague across all buffer sizes (Fig. 13). This is due to Prague's loss sensitivity, in contrast to BBRv1. Even with larger buffer sizes, BBRv1 dominates because these AQMs use early-drop mechanisms based on target queueing latency, rather than tail-drop. In the case of BBRv2, for larger buffer sizes with drop-based AQMs, Prague is harmed (Fig. 7, and 11). This is because these AQMs use early-drop mechanisms, which increase the number of drops. Prague, effectively Reno in non-ECN bottlenecks, is more sensitive to drop events as a loss based CCA. This behaviour is observed also in [60]. In DualPI2, both two-sided DCTCP-style ECN BBRv2 (Fig. 11), and BBRv1 flows (Fig. 13), dominate Prague. This could be due to the inherent design of this AQM type, indicating that the coexistence of BBR flows in DualPI2 AQM requires further investigation. With this bottleneck, as also seen in Prague vs CUBIC case, the ECN fallback algorithm does not perform well (Fig. 8).

Circumstances Where Prague Harms a BBR Flow. In single queue bottlenecks with ECN, Prague operates as a scalable CCA and generally degrades BBRv2's performance especially for large buffer sizes (Fig. 7). In AQMs with ECN, the Prague flow gains a significant throughput advantage compared to the BBRv2 flow, as also seen in the Prague vs. CUBIC scenario (Fig. 3). This is due to the more precise congestion feedback provided by AccECN and the finer adjustments made by TCP Prague compared to BBRv2. (In this case, Prague's fallback algorithm appears to mitigate the harm.) BBRv2 with DCTCP-style marking on the receiver is similar (Fig. 11) but the harm is less severe due to the more refined CWND adjustments of the BBRv2 flow.

RQ1: Can senders be assured that TCP Prague will not cause harm to, or be harmed by, another flow at a shared bottleneck?

A Prague flow is likely to share a bottleneck with CUBIC or BBR.

In bottleneck queues that drop (rather than mark) packets, or those that enforce fairness, Prague and CUBIC appear to coexist without harm.

However, single queue ECN bottlenecks are more problematic. In particular, in a FIFO queue with ECN, either the Prague flow is harmed (when the CUBIC flow does not respond to ECN) or the CUBIC flow is harmed (if it does respond to ECN). The ECN fallback heuristic in Prague mitigates the problem in the single queue bottleneck, but has new problems in the L4S DualPI2 AQM setting.

The ultra-low latency benefits of TCP Prague are only realized with L4S-aware AQMs like FQ-CoDel and DualPI2.

In many single-queue bottleneck types, Prague does not coexist well with BBRv1/BBRv2, with either the Prague or the BBR flow capturing most of the link capacity. (This is partially, but not fully, mitigated if the BBRv2 flow uses DCTCP-style ECN marking with receiver support.)

Queues that enforce fairness are generally effective at preventing harm between Prague and BBR flows, but the DualPI2 AQM is not well tuned for BBR flows, and the Prague flow is disadvantaged as a result.

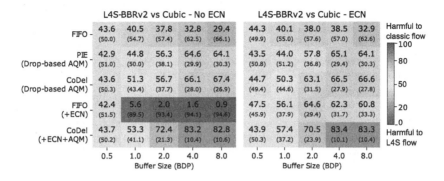

Fig. 15. Throughput of L4S-compatible BBRv2 (and CUBIC, in parentheses) in Mbps when sharing a bottleneck. (single queue AQMs)

4.2 RQ2: Does L4S-Compatible BBRv2 have More Favorable Properties for Adoption than TCP Prague?

In this section, we evaluate the throughput and latency of an L4S-compatible BBRv2 with AccECN when it shares a bottleneck queue with a CUBIC flow, a one-sided DCTCP-style ECN (only on the sender) BBRv2 flow, and a two-sided DCTCP-style ECN BBRv2 flow. We compare this to Prague coexistence with the same types of flows, to understand whether L4S-compatible BBRv2 has more favorable properties for adoption than TCP Prague.

The throughput of the L4S-compatible BBRv2 flow vs. the CUBIC flow (shown in parentheses) is in Fig. 15, and vs. the non-L4S-BBRv2 flow in Fig. 19 for single queue bottleneck scenarios. For multi-queue bottleneck scenarios, the throughput is shown in Fig. 16 and Fig. 20. The latency for each experiment is shown in Fig. 17 and Fig. 18 (vs. CUBIC, in parentheses), and in Fig. 21 and Fig. 22 (vs. non-L4S BBRv2, in parentheses).

Circumstances Where L4S-Compatible BBRv2 has More Favorable Properties for Adoption than Prague. L4S-compatible BBRv2 is less harmful than Prague when sharing a single ECN queue, especially a FIFO+ECN queue, with a CUBIC or BBRv2-DCTCP-style flow that is responsive to ECN (Fig. 15, and 19). In drop-based bottlenecks, such as FIFO, PIE, and CoDel, L4S-compatible BBRv2 provides stable performance and neither harms nor is harmed when sharing the bottleneck with another BBRv2 flow (Fig. 19). However, for Prague, sharing the bottleneck with BBRv2, particularly in single-queue bottlenecks, poses challenges, as explained in the previous section. When a DualPI2 AQM bottleneck is shared with a BBRv2 flow without ECN, Prague is slightly harmed (Fig. 8), while L4S-compatible BBRv2 achieves approximately a fair share (Fig. 20).

Circumstances Where L4S-Compatible BBRv2 is Similar to Prague. In most cases, the performance differences are minimal. For example, in drop-based AQMs, both L4S flows exhibit either a slight advantage or disadvantage compared to the CUBIC flow in the bottleneck (Fig. 15). In FQ bottlenecks, both

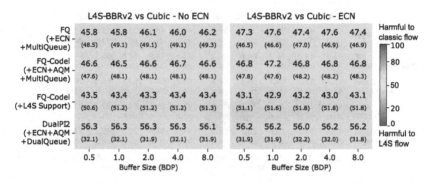

Fig. 16. Throughput of L4S-compatible BBRv2 (and CUBIC, in parentheses) in Mbps when sharing a bottleneck. (multi/dual queue AQMs)

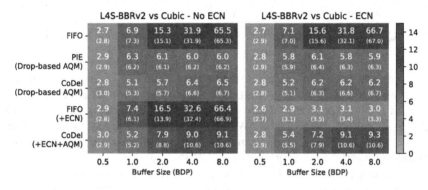

Fig. 17. L4S-compatible BBRv2 (and CUBIC, in parentheses) queuing delay (ms) when sharing a bottleneck. (single queue AQMs)

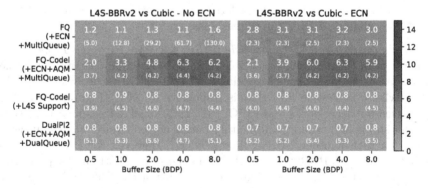

Fig. 18. L4S-compatible BBRv2 (and CUBIC, in parentheses) queuing delay (ms) when sharing a bottleneck. (multi/dual queue AQMs)

achieve roughly their fair share of throughput, and in L4S-aware bottlenecks, both maintain ultra-low latency (Fig. 16, 22). When the classic queue contains BBRv1 or two-sided DCTCP-style ECN-marking BBRv2, these flows dominate

	L4S-BBRv2 vs BBRv2 - No ECN					L4S-BBRv2 vs BBRv2 - ECN (classic marking on Receiver)					L4S-BBRv2 vs BBRv2 - ECN (DCTCP Style marking on Receiver)					
FIFO	46.5 (47.0)	52.0 (41.8)	48.0 (39.5)	54.2 (40.2)	53.7	47.1 (46.2)	50.2 (43.5)	47.6 (46.4)	56.5 (37.5)	55.0 (38.7)	50.6 (43.5)	52.1 (42.1)	60.9 (32.7)	54.5 (39.7)	57.9 (35.9)	Harmful to classic flow
PIE (Drop-based AQM)	49.8 (43.7)	50.3 (43.4)	48.8 (44.8)	54.3 (39.4)	49.8 (43.8)	49.2 (44.4)	51.9 (41.8)	53.3 (40.3)	45.8 (47.8)	48.5 (45.3)	49.1 (44.8)	55.4 (38.8)	48.7 (45.3)	46.4 (47.5)	49.9 (44.2)	
CoDel (Drop-based AQM)	49.0 (44.7)	54.7 (39.0)	48.2 (45.5)	46.9 (46.8)	50.5 (43.3)	48.3 (45.3)	52.4 (41.1)	56.4 (37.3)	47.5 (46.1)	47.7 (46.2)	48.3 (45.8)	55.3 (38.6)	40.3 (53.9)	47.4 (46.7)	48.9 (45.3)	
FIFO (+ECN)	44.9 (48.8)	39.6 (54.1)	8.3 (85.4)	3.5 (90.8)	3.4 (90.6)	51.8 (41.4)	61.4 (32.1)	53.2 (40.4)	55.3 (37.9)	54.1 (39.3)	50.4 (43.6)	56.9 (36.8)	48.3 (45.7)	51.0 (43.1)	49.5 (44.4)	
CoDel (+ECN+AQM)	49.2 (44.4)	50.4 (43.5)	70.5 (22.7)	79.9 (13.2)	83.6 (9.4)	49.7 (43.8)	54.7 (38.9)	66.4 (26.7)	83.7 (9.0)	84.1 (9.0)	50.6 (43.1)	47.5 (46.4)	40.8 (53.3)	55.6 (38.3)	57.5 (36.4)	Harmful to L4S flow
	0.5	1.0	2.0	4.0	8.0	0.5	1.0	2.0	4.0	8.0	0.5	1.0	2.0	4.0	8.0	
	Buffer Size (BDP)					Buffer Size (BDP)					Buffer Size (BDP)					

Fig. 19. Throughput of L4S-compatible BBRv2 (and non-L4S-compatible BBRv2, in parentheses) in Mbps when sharing a bottleneck (single queue AQMs)

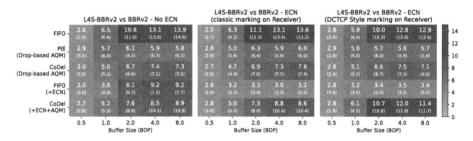

Fig. 20. Throughput of L4S-compatible BBRv2 (and non-L4S-compatible BBRv2, in parentheses) in Mbps when sharing a bottleneck. (multi/dual queue AQMs)

	L4S-BBRv2 vs BBRv2 - No ECN					L4S-BBRv2 vs BBRv2 - ECN (classic marking on Receiver)					L4S-BBRv2 vs BBRv2 - ECN (DCTCP Style marking on Receiver)					
FIFO	2.8 (2.9)	6.5 (6.4)	10.8 (11.0)	13.1 (13.0)	13.9 (14.0)	2.5 (2.7)	6.3 (6.4)	11.1 (11.3)	13.1 (13.4)	13.6 (13.2)	2.8 (2.9)	5.9 (6.4)	10.0 (10.3)	12.8 (12.6)	12.9 (12.6)	14
PIE (Drop-based AQM)	2.9 (3.0)	5.7 (6.0)	6.1 (6.3)	5.9 (6.3)	5.8 (6.1)	2.8 (2.9)	5.0 (5.4)	6.3 (6.4)	5.9 (5.9)	6.0 (6.0)	2.9 (2.9)	5.8 (6.0)	5.7 (6.0)	5.8 (5.9)	5.7 (5.6)	12
CoDel (Drop-based AQM)	3.0 (3.0)	5.0 (5.2)	6.7 (6.6)	7.4 (7.2)	7.3 (7.5)	2.7 (2.8)	4.7 (4.9)	6.9 (7.0)	7.3 (7.7)	7.6 (7.4)	2.8 (2.9)	5.1 (5.3)	6.6 (6.7)	7.5 (7.3)	7.1 (6.9)	8
FIFO (+ECN)	3.0 (3.0)	3.8 (4.0)	8.1 (6.7)	9.2 (7.2)	9.2 (7.7)	2.8 (2.9)	3.2 (3.3)	3.3 (3.4)	3.0 (3.3)	3.2 (3.5)	2.8 (2.8)	3.2 (3.4)	3.4 (3.5)	3.5 (3.5)	3.4 (3.5)	4
CoDel (+ECN+AQM)	2.7 (2.9)	5.2 (5.5)	7.6 (8.8)	8.5 (10.1)	8.9 (10.9)	2.8 (3.0)	5.0 (5.3)	7.3 (8.0)	8.8 (10.4)	8.6 (10.4)	2.8 (2.9)	6.1 (6.1)	10.7 (10.8)	12.0 (11.9)	11.4 (11.7)	2
	0.5	1.0	2.0	4.0	8.0	0.5	1.0	2.0	4.0	8.0	0.5	1.0	2.0	4.0	8.0	
	Buffer Size (BDP)					Buffer Size (BDP)					Buffer Size (BDP)					

Fig. 21. L4S-compatible BBRv2 (and non-L4S-compatible BBRv2, in parentheses) queuing delay (ms) when sharing a bottleneck. (single queue AQMs)

both L4S-compatible BBRv2 and Prague (Fig. 20, and Fig. 11). Although the performance of BBRv1 is not shown here, it is observed that when sharing a bottleneck with a BBRv1 flow, the performance of both L4S-compatible BBRv2 and Prague is similar across all bottleneck types (Fig. 13). In terms of latency, both Prague and L4S-compatible BBRv2 can experience extreme queuing latencies, even with ECN enabled, when competing with CUBIC on a FIFO+ECN bottleneck (Fig. 17), and both perform similarly in terms of latency when sharing the single queue bottleneck with BBRv2 (Fig. 21).

Circumstances Where L4S-Compatible BBRv2 has Less Favorable Properties for Adoption than Prague. In DualPI2, L4S-compatible BBRv2 experiences slightly

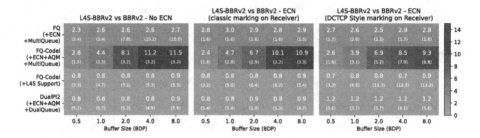

Fig. 22. L4S-compatible BBRv2 (and non-L4S-compatible BBRv2, in parentheses) queuing delay (ms) when sharing bottleneck with BBRv2 flow. (multi/dual queue AQMs)

higher queuing latency compared to Prague, though both maintain queuing latency under 1ms (Fig. 18, 22).

> **RQ2: Does L4S-compatible BBRv2 have more favorable properties for adoption than TCP Prague?**
>
> L4S-compatible BBRv2 is similar to Prague with respect to sharing single queue ECN-enabled bottlenecks with a CUBIC flow - neither is safe from harming, or being harmed, especially when the CUBIC flow ignores ECN. However, when sharing with a CUBIC flow that *does* respond to ECN, L4S-compatible BBRv2 is less harmful than Prague.
>
> When sharing a bottleneck with a non-L4S-compatible BBRv2 flow, L4S-compatible BBRv2 is generally less likely to harm or be harmed than Prague, especially in single queue and DualPI2 queues.

4.3   RQ3: Is the Harm Caused by or to the L4S-Compatible Flow Mitigated When the Bottleneck is Shared by a Large Number of Flows?

To address our third research question, we evaluate the performance of TCP Prague and L4S-compatible BBRv2 to understand the impact of the number of flows on the results previously discussed in RQ1 and RQ2 for the 1vs1 experiments. The average throughput of Prague flows is shown in Fig. 23 and L4S-compatible BBRv2 flows in Fig. 24.

Circumstances Where the Harm is not Mitigated. When a single Prague or L4S-compatible BBRv2 flow competes against multiple CUBIC flows, the L4S flow consistently achieves much higher throughput than its fair share - in the case of a single-queue ECN bottleneck, even against 25 CUBIC flows (Fig. 23, 24).

In DualPI2, a single BBRv2 flow maintains a significant throughput advantage over multiple CUBIC flows, even with up to 10 CUBIC flows (Fig. 24). However, when competing against 25 CUBIC flows, BBRv2 achieves a fair share

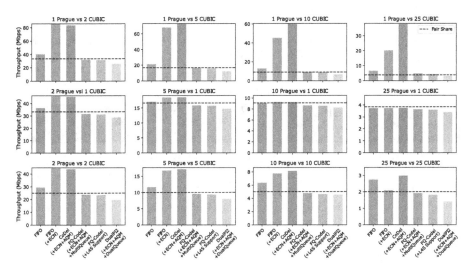

Fig. 23. 1 vs. many, many vs. many flow scenarios - Prague throughput (Mbps).

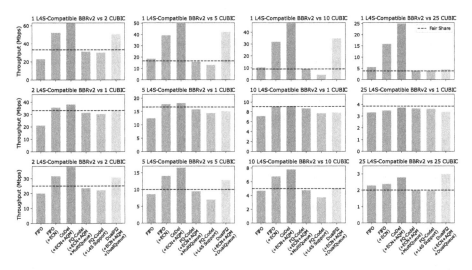

Fig. 24. 1 vs. many, many vs many flow scenarios - L4S-compatible BBRv2 throughput (Mbps).

of the throughput. This differs from Prague, where Prague flows generally achieve close to their fair share or slightly less across all settings with DualPI2.

Circumstances Where the Harm is Mitigated. Across all AQM types, the Prague flows tend to achieve their fair share in the 25 Prague vs. 25 CUBIC flows scenario, as illustrated in Fig. 23, showing they are not harmed by the CUBIC flows. On the other hand, with a high number of flows, such as 25 BBRv2 vs. 25 CUBIC, particularly with L4S-aware FQ-CoDel, BBRv2 flows experience around

10 ms of queuing latency, although not shown in the figure, which is significantly higher than their 1 ms target delay. This behavior could vary under different network configurations. However, this represents a possible scenario where the ultra-low latency benefit is not realized, demonstrating that even with an L4S-aware FQ-CoDel bottleneck, L4S flows can experience high queuing latency.

> RQ3: Is the harm caused by or to the L4S-compatible flow mitigated when the bottleneck is shared by a large number of flows?
>
> When *one* Prague or L4S-compatible BBRv2 flow shares a single-queue ECN bottleneck with *many* CUBIC flows, it captures $5 - 10\times$ its fair share of the link capacity, harming the CUBIC flows.
>
> However, when multiple Prague flows share a bottleneck with one CUBIC flow, or when multiple Prague and multiple CUBIC flows share a bottleneck, some of the issues described in Section 4.1 are mitigated.
>
> For BBRv2, aside from the issue noted above, as the number of flows increases—whether 1 BBRv2 vs. 25 CUBIC, 25 CUBIC vs. 1 BBRv2, or more flows—the harmful effects are mostly mitigated.
>
> When multiple L4S-compatible BBRv2 flows share an L4S-aware FQ bottleneck with multiple CUBIC flows, it is not guaranteed that the L4S flows will achieve ultra-low latency especially with high number of flows.

4.4   RQ4: Is the BBRv3 Approach More Favorable for the Deployment of L4S-Compatible Congestion Control?

In this section, we evaluate the coexistence of BBRv3 with Prague and L4S-compatible BBRv2. BBRv3's ECN behavior depends on the measured minimum RTT on the path. Even if the sender and receiver enable ECN, if the minRTT exceeds 5ms, the BBR sender does not respond to ECN. We evaluate this with a 10ms RTT, where ECN is not enabled effectively, and a 2 ms RTT, where ECN is enabled and the threshold is 1ms. We use a one-sided DCTCP-style ECN mechanism, with the receiver using classic ECN marking. Since the sender does not know the ECN marking types it will encounter, we consider arbitrary endpoints without specialized support, as would be the case in a real network scenario. The throughput of the Prague flow (and the BBRv3 flow, in parenthesis) is shown in Figs. 25 (single-queue), and Fig. 26 (multi-queue). Similarly, the throughput of the L4S-compatible BBRv2 flow (and the BBRv3 flow, in parenthesis) is shown in Figs. 27 (single-queue), and Fig. 28 (multi-queue).

Circumstances Where the BBRv3 Approach More Favorable. In FIFO+ECN, the harm caused by BBRv3 to Prague is less severe with short path delays (with ECN) compared to long path delays (without ECN) (Fig. 25). Beyond this, there is no significant performance advantage for BBRv3's approach in the coexistence of Prague and BBRv3. In multiple-queue bottlenecks, the performance is very similar in both cases (Fig. 26).

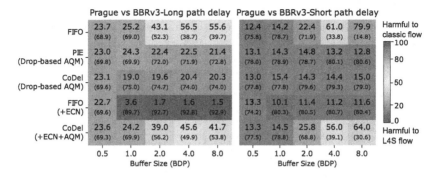

Fig. 25. Throughput of Prague (and BBRv3, in parentheses) in Mbps when sharing a bottleneck (single queue AQMs)

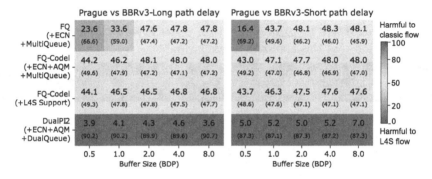

Fig. 26. Throughput of Prague (and BBRv3, in parentheses) in Mbps when sharing a bottleneck(multi/dual queue AQMs)

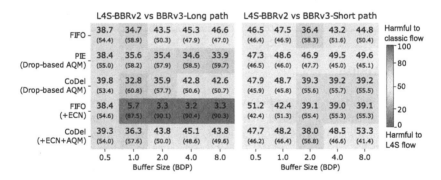

Fig. 27. Throughput of L4S-compatible BBRv2 (and BBRv3, in parentheses) in Mbps when sharing a bottleneck (single queue AQMs)

On the other hand, with L4S-compatible BBRv2 in short path delays, the harmful effects in FIFO+ECN are completely mitigated (Fig. 27). Furthermore, in DualPI2, the harm to BBR flows is less severe in short path delays with ECN compared to long path delays without ECN (Fig. 28).

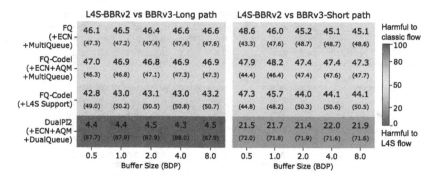

Fig. 28. Throughput of L4S-compatible BBRv2 (and BBRv3, in parentheses) in Mbps when sharing a bottleneck(multi/dual queue AQMs)

Circumstances Where the BBRv3 Approach is not Favorable. There is no significant indication that this approach is less favorable.

> **RQ4: Is the BBRv3 approach more favorable for the deployment of L4S-compatible congestion control?**
>
> For several types of single queue bottlenecks, and DualPI2, a Prague flow is harmed due to coexistence with a BBRv3 flow, whether the BBRv3 flow is responsive to ECN (short path delay) or not (long path delay).
>
> L4S-compatible BBRv2 generally coexists well with BBRv3 in either short or long path delay cases. The exceptions are FIFO+ECN with long path delays (no ECN), where BBRv3 harms the L4S-compatible BBRv2 flow — an issue mitigated with short path delays — and DualPI2 for both paths, where BBRv3 again harms the L4S-compatible BBRv2 flow.

5   Conclusion

In this work, we investigate the behavior that a sender may expect upon adopting an L4S-compatible congestion control, with a systematic evaluation in a setting based on a residential broadband network, considering a range of queue types and types of non-L4S flows at the shared bottleneck. We identify circumstances in which the L4S flow gets only a small fraction of the bottleneck link bandwidth, while the non-L4S flow dominates. We also identify circumstances in which the L4S flow is harmful to the non-L4S flow, capturing most of the bottleneck link bandwidth. Furthermore, we find that this effect is not always mitigated when more flows share the bottleneck link. Given that the sender of an L4S flow cannot be sure what type of queue is at the bottleneck or what other flows will share that queue, a range of outcomes for throughput and latency are possible.

Some key results are summarized in Table 1, and below:

- **In many settings with a single queue, the L4S flow harms or is harmed by the classic flow.** These outcomes depend on the behavior of the competing flow (e.g., whether it supports ECN or not, and whether it uses CUBIC or BBR). This effect is not necessarily mitigated when multiple flows are sharing the bottleneck link.
- **The DualPI2 AQM, which is designed specifically for L4S, is not well-tuned for sharing a link with BBR flows.** This finding is concerning because of the (increasing) prevalence of BBR on the Internet [50].
- **The low latency benefits of L4S are realized only when the bottle-neck queue isolates flows - with a fair queue or dual queue AQM.** This is by design, and is not a surprising result, but in combination with the other problems, further disincentivizes the adoption of L4S.

Table 1. Can a sender turn on L4S ($\checkmark$) or would it harm/be harmed if it did ($\times$)? ($\unicode{x26A1}$ indicates settings where ultra-low latency is achieved, otherwise it is not.)

AQM	CUBIC	BBRv1	BBRv2 (one-sided DCTCP ECN)	BBRv2 (two-sided DCTCP ECN)	BBRv3
SQ (Drop)	$\checkmark$ (Fig. 3, 15)	$\times$ (Fig. 13)	$\times$ Prague	$\checkmark$ L4S-BBRv2 (Fig. 7, 11, 19, 25, 27)	
SQ (ECN)	$\times$ (Fig. 3, 15)	$\times$ (Fig. 13)	$\times$ (Fig. 7, 19)	$\checkmark$ (Fig. 11, 19)	$\times$ (Fig. 25, 27)
DualPI2 ($\unicode{x26A1}$)	$\checkmark$ (Fig. 4, 16)	$\times$ (Fig. 13)	$\checkmark$ (Fig. 8, 20)	$\times$ (Fig. 11, 20)	$\times$ (Fig. 26, 28)
FQ ($\unicode{x26A1}$ if L4S-aware)	$\checkmark$ (Fig. 4, 13, 8, 26, 11, 16, 20, 28)				

This combination of factors - the possibility of being worse off with L4S than without, the possibility of causing harm to non-L4S flows, and that low-latency benefits are realized only in limited circumstances - may depress the adoption of L4S. As future work, we hope to investigate more directly the expected impact on L4S adoption, and strategies for mitigation.

In this study, we focused on a single network configuration with a base RTT of 10 ms and a bottleneck link capacity of 100 Mbps, to understand the residential broadband setting in depth. In real-world network paths, L4S flows will encounter a wide variety of network configurations, both in terms of the various ECN and AQM settings that were considered in this work, and different link capacities and delays not considered in this work. Some of these settings may be more favorable to L4S deployment than the one considered in our experiments. However, different results in other settings would not address the fundamental problem suggested by our results: **outside of a controlled environment, an L4S flow is reasonably likely to encounter a setting where it is harmed or causes harm.** Because an L4S flow cannot anticipate *which* setting it will encounter, the existence of some problematic behaviors in our "moderate" residential broadband network setting is concerning. As future work, we intend to extend our evaluation to include a broader range of network settings and more realistic traffic patterns. Additionally, our evaluation primarily focused on throughput and latency, while other metrics, such as jitter and flow completion time, could offer further insights. Future work will also explore these aspects.

Acknowledgements.. This research was supported by the New York State Center for Advanced Technology in Telecommunications and Distributed Systems (CATT), NYU WIRELESS, and the National Science Foundation (NSF) under Grant No. CNS-2148309 and OAC-2226408.

Disclosure of Interests. The authors have no competing interests to declare that are relevant to the content of this article.

Ethical Considerations. This paper does not raise any ethical issues.

A Artifact Description

We have made the artifacts used to run the FABRIC experiments and generate the figures in this paper publicly available [61].

To reproduce the results presented in this paper, shown in Figs. 3, 4, 5, 6, 7, 8, 9, 10, 11, 12, 13, 14, 15, 16, 17, 18, 19, 20, 21, 22, 23, 24, 25, 26, 27 and 28, please use the Jupyter notebooks `single_flow_experiments.ipynb` and `multiple_flow_experiments.ipynb`. These notebooks run the FABRIC experiments for single-flow and multiple-flow scenarios and generate the resulting data in JSON format.

The generated JSON files can then be used with the data analysis Jupyter notebooks to reproduce the figures in this paper. Detailed instructions for running the experiments and generating the figures are included in the notebooks.

References

1. Briscoe, B., Schepper, K.D., Bagnulo, M., White, G.: Low Latency, Low Loss, and Scalable Throughput (L4S) Internet Service: Architecture, RFC 9330 (2023). https://datatracker.ietf.org/doc/html/rfc9330
2. Willars, P., et al.: Enabling Time-Critical Applications Over 5G with Rate Adaptation. Ericsson and Deutsche Telekom, Technical repport. BNEW-21:025455 Uen, May 2021, White Paper
3. Comcast. Comcast Kicks Off Industry's First Low Latency DOCSIS Field Trials (2023). https://corporate.comcast.com/stories/comcast-kicks-off-industrys-first-low-latency-docsis-field-trials
4. Nokia Corporation. Nokia collaborates with Hololight to deliver reliable immersive XR experiences with latency-improving technology L4S (2023)
5. Livingood, J.: Dual Queue Low Latency Networking Update (2024). https://datatracker.ietf.org/meeting/121/materials/slides-121-tsvwg-sessb-41-deployment-experience-01.pdf

6. Schepper, K.D.: Understanding Prague for L4S. Presented at IETF 120 (2024). https://datatracker.ietf.org/meeting/120/materials/slides-120-iccrg-understanding-prague-for-l4s-00

7. Livingood, J.: ISP Dual Queue Networking Deployment Recommendations. Internet Engineering Task Force, Internet-Draft draft-livingood-low-latency-deployment-07 (2024). Work in Progress. https://datatracker.ietf.org/doc/draft-livingood-low-latency-deployment/07/

8. Apple Inc.: Reduce network delays with L4S. WWDC 2023, Apple Developer Videos (2023). https://developer.apple.com/videos/play/wwdc2023/10004

9. White, G.: L4S Interop Lays Groundwork for 10G Metaverse (2022). https://www.cablelabs.com/blog/l4s-interop-lays-groundwork-for-10g-metaverse

10. CableLabs. Low Latency DOCSIS. CableLabs Technologies (2024). https://www.cablelabs.com/technologies/low-latency-docsis

11. Corporation, N.: What is the L4S setting in the GeForce NOW streaming quality menu? https://nvidia.custhelp.com/app/answers/detail/a_id/5522

12. Schepper, K.D., Tilmans, O., Briscoe, B., Goel, V.: Prague Congestion Control. Internet Engineering Task Force, Internet-Draft draft-briscoe-iccrg-prague-congestion-control-03 (2023). Work in Progress https://datatracker.ietf.org/doc/draft-briscoe-iccrg-prague-congestion-control/03/

13. Briscoe, B., et al.: Implementing the "Prague Requirements" for Low Latency Low Loss Scalable Throughput (L4S). Netdev 0x13 (2019)

14. Briscoe, B., Kühlewind, M., Scheffenegger, R.: More Accurate Explicit Congestion Notification (ECN) Feedback in TCP. Internet Engineering Task Force, Internet-Draft draft-ietf-tcpm-accurate-ecn-28 (2023). Work in Progress. https://datatracker.ietf.org/doc/draft-ietf-tcpm-accurate-ecn/28/

15. Kühlewind, M., Scheffenegger, R., Briscoe, B.: Problem Statement and Requirements for Increased Accuracy in Explicit Congestion Notification (ECN) Feedback. RFC 7560 (2015). https://datatracker.ietf.org/doc/html/rfc7560

16. Albisser, O., De Schepper, K., Briscoe, B., Tilmans, O., Steen, H.: DUALPI2—Low Latency, Low Loss and Scalable (L4S) AQM. NetDev 0x13, Prague (2019)

17. Schepper, K.D., Albisser, O., Tilmans, O., Briscoe, B.: Dual Queue Coupled AQM: Deployable Very Low Queuing Delay for All (2022). https://arxiv.org/abs/2209.01078

18. Schepper, K.D., Briscoe, B., White, G.: Dual-Queue Coupled Active Queue Management (AQM) for Low Latency, Low Loss, and Scalable Throughput (L4S). RFC 9332 (2023). https://datatracker.ietf.org/doc/html/rfc9332

19. Sarpkaya, F.B., Srivastava, A., Fund, F., Panwar, S.: To switch or not to switch to TCP Prague? Incentives for adoption in a partial L4S deployment. In: Proceedings of the 2024 Applied Networking Research Workshop, ANRW 2024, pp. 45–52. Association for Computing Machinery, New York (2024). https://doi.org/10.1145/3673422.3674896

20. Baldin, I., et al.: FABRIC: a national-scale programmable experimental network infrastructure. IEEE Internet Comput. **23**(6), 38–47 (2019)

21. Fatih Berkay Sarpkaya, F.F.: Reproducing "Scalable Congestion Control Resolves the Delay Utilization Dilemma" (2024). https://github.com/fatihsarpkaya/TCP-ECN

22. Floyd, S., Ramakrishnan, D.K.K., Black, D.L.: The Addition of Explicit Congestion Notification (ECN) to IP. RFC 3168 (2001). https://datatracker.ietf.org/doc/html/rfc3168

23. Alizadeh, M., et al.: Data center TCP (DCTCP). SIGCOMM Comput. Commun. Rev. **40**(4), 63–74 (2010). https://doi.org/10.1145/1851275.1851192

24. Briscoe, B., Kühlewind, M., Scheffenegger, R.: More Accurate Explicit Congestion Notification (ECN) Feedback in TCP. Internet Engineering Task Force,
Internet-Draft draft-ietf-tcpm-accurate-ecn-30 (2024). Work in Progress. https://
datatracker.ietf.org/doc/draft-ietf-tcpm-accurate-ecn/30/
25. Hoeiland-Joergensen, T., McKenney, P., Taht, D., Gettys, J., Dumazet, E.: The
Flow Queue CoDel Packet Scheduler and Active Queue Management Algorithm.
RFC 8290 (2018)
26. Høiland-Jørgensen, T.: FQ_Codel: Generalise ce_threshold marking for subset of
traffic (2021). https://git.kernel.org/pub/scm/linux/kernel/git/netdev/net-next.
git/commit/?id=dfcb63ce1de6b10b. Accessed 01 Oct 2024
27. White, G.: Operational Guidance on Coexistence with Classic ECN during L4S
Deployment. Internet Engineering Task Force, Internet-Draft draft-ietf-tsvwg-
l4sops-06, Mar. 2024, work in Progress. https://datatracker.ietf.org/doc/draft-ietf-
tsvwg-l4sops/06/
28. Heist, P., Morton, J.: Explicit congestion notification (ECN) deployment observations. Work in Progress, Internet-Draft (2021). https://www.ietf.org/archive/id/
draft-heist-tsvwg-ecn-deployment-observations-02.html
29. Lim, H., et al.: A Fresh Look at ECN Traversal in the Wild (2022)
30. Holland, J.: CE-marking observations. IETF TSVWG Mailing List (2020). https://
mailarchive.ietf.org/arch/msg/tsvwg/2tbRHphJ8K_CE6is9n7iQy-VAZM/
31. Chen, C.-X., Nagaoka, K.: Analysis of the state of ECN on the Internet. IEICE
Trans. Inf. Syst. **E102-D**(5), 910–919 (2019)
32. Briscoe, B., Ahmed, A.S.: TCP Prague Fall-back on Detection of a Classic ECN
AQM (2021). https://arxiv.org/abs/1911.00710
33. Heist, P.: L4S Tests (2021). https://github.com/heistp/l4s-tests
34. Heist, P.: SCE-L4S Bakeoff (2019). https://github.com/heistp/sce-l4s-bakeoff
35. Henderson, T., Tilmans, O., White, G.: L4S Testing (2019). https://l4s.cablelabs.
com/l4s-testing/README.html. Accessed 12 June 2024
36. Henderson, T., Tilmans, O., White, G.: Testbed and Simulation Results for
TSVWG Scenarios (2019). https://l4s.cablelabs.com/l4s_issues.html. Accessed 12
June 2024
37. BoruOljira, D., Grinnemo, K.-J., Brunstrom, A., Taheri, J.: Validating the sharing
behavior and latency characteristics of the L4S architecture. ACM SIGCOMM
Comput. Commun. Rev. **50**(2), 37–44 (2020)
38. Jain, R., Chiu, D.M., Wr, H.: A quantitative measure of fairness and discrimination
for resource allocation in shared computer systems. CoRR, vol. cs.NI/9809099
(1998)
39. Philip, A.A., et al.: Prudentia: findings of an Internet fairness watchdog. In: Proceedings of the ACM SIGCOMM 2024 Conference, ACM SIGCOMM 2024, pp.
506–520. Association for Computing Machinery, New York (2024). https://doi.
org/10.1145/3651890.3672229
40. Xu, X., Claypool, M.: Measurement of cloud-based game streaming system
response to competing TCP cubic or TCP BBR flows. In: Proceedings of the
22nd ACM Internet Measurement Conference, IMC 2022, pp. 305–316. Association
for Computing Machinery, New York (2022). https://doi.org/10.1145/3517745.
3561464
41. Kunze, I., Rüth, J., Hohlfeld, O.: Congestion control in the wild–investigating content provider fairness. IEEE Trans. Netw. Serv. Manag. **17**(2), 1224–1238 (2020)
42. Ware, R., Mukerjee, M.K., Seshan, S., Sherry, J.: Beyond Jain's fairness index:
setting the bar for the deployment of congestion control algorithms. In: Proceedings

of the 18th ACM Workshop on Hot Topics in Networks, HotNets 2019, pp. 17–24. Association for Computing Machinery, New York (2019). https://doi.org/10.1145/3365609.3365855

43. Drucker, R., Baraskar, G., Balasubramanian, A., Gandhi, A.: BBR vs. BBRv2: a performance evaluation. In: 2024 16th International Conference on COMmunication Systems & NETworkS (COMSNETS), pp. 379–387 (2024)

44. Islam, S., Hiorth, K., Griwodz, C., Welzl, M.: Is it really necessary to go beyond a fairness metric for next-generation congestion control? In: Proceedings of the 2022 Applied Networking Research Workshop, ANRW 2022. Association for Computing Machinery, New York (2022). https://doi.org/10.1145/3547115.3547192

45. Duke, M., Fairhurst, G.: Specifying New Congestion Control Algorithms. Internet Engineering Task Force, Internet-Draft draft-ietf-ccwg-rfc5033bis-08 (2024). Work in Progress. https://datatracker.ietf.org/doc/draft-ietf-ccwg-rfc5033bis/08/

46. Nichols, K., Jacobson, V.: Controlling queue delay. Commun. ACM **55**(7), 42–50 (2012). https://doi.org/10.1145/2209249.2209264

47. Pan, R., Natarajan, P., Baker, F., White, G.: Proportional Integral Controller Enhanced (PIE): A Lightweight Control Scheme to Address the Bufferbloat Problem. RFC 8033 (2017). https://www.rfc-editor.org/info/rfc8033

48. L4S development hub. Linux kernel tree with L4S patches (2024). https://github.com/L4STeam/linux

49. Ha, S., Rhee, I., Xu, L.: CUBIC: a new TCP-friendly high-speed TCP variant. SIGOPS Oper. Syst. Rev. **42**(5), 64–74 (2008). https://doi.org/10.1145/1400097.1400105

50. Mishra, A., Sun, X., Jain, A., Pande, S., Joshi, R., Leong, B.: The great Internet TCP congestion control census. Proc. ACM Meas. Anal. Comput. Syst. **3**(3) (2019). https://doi.org/10.1145/3366693

51. Xu, L., Ha, S., Rhee, I., Goel, V., Eggert, L.: CUBIC for Fast and Long-Distance Networks. RFC 9438 (2023). https://www.rfc-editor.org/info/rfc9438

52. Cardwell, N., Cheng, Y., Gunn, C.S., Yeganeh, S.H., Jacobson, V.: BBR: Congestion-based congestion control: measuring bottleneck bandwidth and round-trip propagation time. Queue **14**(5), 20–53 (2016)

53. Cardwell, N., Cheng, Y., Gunn, C.S., et al.: BBRv3: CCWG Internet-Draft Update. Internet Engineering Task Force (IETF), Technical report (2024). Presented at IETF 120. https://datatracker.ietf.org/meeting/120/materials/slides-120-ccwg-bbrv3-ccwg-internet-draft-update-00

54. Google. BBR - Source code (2024). https://github.com/google/bbr

55. Group, B.D.: TCP BBR default in Ubuntu 24.04 (Linux 6.8) possibility? (2024). https://groups.google.com/g/bbr-dev/c/i-sZpfwPx-I/m/_u7A-IijAgAJ. Accessed 07 Oct 2024

56. Schepper, K.D., Tilmans, O., Briscoe, B., Goel, V.: Prague Congestion Control. Internet Engineering Task Force, Internet-Draft draft-briscoe-iccrg-prague-congestion-control-04 (2024). Work in Progress. https://datatracker.ietf.org/doc/draft-briscoe-iccrg-prague-congestion-control/04/

57. Chavan, S.: Should paced TCP Reno replace CUBIC in Linux? In: 2016 8th International Conference on Communication Systems and Networks (COMSNETS), pp. 1–8 (2016)

58. Ware, R., Mukerjee, M.K., Seshan, S., Sherry, J.: Modeling BBR's interactions with loss-based congestion control. In: Proceedings of the Internet Measurement Conference, IMC 2019, pp. 137–143. Association for Computing Machinery, New York (2019). https://doi.org/10.1145/3355369.3355604

59. Zeynali, D., Weyulu, E.N., Fathalli, S., Chandrasekaran, B., Feldmann, A.: Promises and potential of BBRv3. In: Passive and Active Measurement: 25th International Conference, PAM 2024, Virtual Event, 11–13 March 2024, Proceedings, Part II, pp. 249–272. Springer, Heidelberg (2024). https://doi.org/10.1007/978-3-031-56252-5_12

60. Scherrer, S., Legner, M., Perrig, A., Schmid, S.: Model-based insights on the performance, fairness, and stability of BBR. In: Proceedings of the 22nd ACM Internet Measurement Conference, IMC 2022, pp. 519–537. Association for Computing Machinery, New York (2022). https://doi.org/10.1145/3517745.3561420

61. Sarpkaya, F.B., Fund, F.: L4S-PAM2025 (2024). https://github.com/fatihsarpkaya/L4S-PAM2025

A Deep Dive into LEO Satellite Topology Design Parameters

Wenyi Morty Zhang[1]([✉]), Zihan Xu[2], and Sangeetha Abdu Jyothi[3,4]

[1] University of California, San Diego, USA
`wez049@ucsd.edu`
[2] Carnegie Mellon University, Pittsburgh, USA
[3] University of California, Irvine, USA
[4] VMware Research, Palo Alto, USA

Abstract. Low Earth Orbit (LEO) satellite networks are rapidly gaining traction today. Although several real-world deployments exist, our preliminary analysis of LEO topology performance with the soon-to-be operational Inter-Satellite Links (ISLs) reveals several interesting characteristics that are difficult to explain based on our current understanding of topologies. For example, a real-world satellite shell with a low density of satellites offers better latency performance than another shell with nearly double the number of satellites. In this work, we conduct an in-depth investigation of LEO satellite topology design parameters and their impact on network performance while using the ISLs. In particular, we focus on three design parameters: the number of orbits in a shell, the inclination of orbits, and the number of satellites per orbit. Through an extensive analysis of real-world and synthetic satellite configurations, we uncover several interesting properties of satellite topologies. Notably, there exist thresholds for the number of satellites per orbit and the number of orbits below which the latency performance degrades significantly. Moreover, network delay between a pair of traffic endpoints depends on the alignment of the satellite's orbit (Inclination) with the geographic locations of endpoints.

Keywords: Network Simulation · Measurement · Network Topology

1 Introduction

Low Earth Orbit (LEO) satellite networks are rapidly becoming a significant component of the backbone Internet infrastructure. They offer low latency and connectivity to remote areas not served by terrestrial fiber or wireless infrastructure. Today, several commercial providers are deploying massive LEO satellite constellations, including Starlink [44], Kuiper [21], OneWeb [36], and Telesat [46]. Unlike Geosynchronous Earth Orbit (GEO) and Medium Earth Orbit

---

W. M. Zhang and Z. Xu—Contributed equally to this work.

C. Testart et al. (Eds.): PAM 2025, LNCS 15567, pp. 247–275, 2025.
https://doi.org/10.1007/978-3-031-85960-1_11

(MEO) satellite networks, LEO networks require thousands of satellites to provide global coverage. The most prominent LEO provider today, Starlink, has launched approximately 6,426 satellites as of September 2024, with 6,371 currently operational [25]. Eventually, Starlink is slated to have over 12,000 satellites in its LEO constellation.

A distinguishing feature of LEO satellites, compared with GEO and MEO satellites, is the presence of Inter-Satellite Links (ISLs). These links allow LEO satellites to communicate with each other directly at the speed of light without relying on an intermediate ground station. Each Starlink satellite, for example, is equipped with four optical space laser generators and four laser signal receiver surfaces, supporting optical laser communication between neighboring satellites with a capacity of up to 80 Gbps [7, 14, 18, 20, 44, 47].

ISL-based communication is currently tested only in limited areas, and is currently used only in areas without ground stations [34, 41, 52]. However, it is expected that a network backbone entirely based on ISLs for end-to-end communication will be realized in the near future. In this context, the most studied topology is the +Grid topology [8, 15] in which each satellite has links to the two nearest satellites in its own orbit and to the two nearest satellites on adjacent orbits on either side. Communication using the +Grid inter-satellite topology is shown to reduce temporal variations in latency, offer greater resilience to weather variations typically encountered by ground stations, and achieve 3× the throughput compared to similar LEO networks without ISLs [8, 16, 19, 27].

Although there are several ongoing constellations deployments, our understanding of the impact of various design parameters on the performance of LEO topologies is limited, particularly in the presence of soon-to-be operational ISLs. Our preliminary analysis reveals several performance characteristics that cannot be explained based on the current understanding of LEO topology design. We analyze the latency characteristics of Starlink Shell 1 with +Grid topology and observe that using fewer than half the number of satellites of shell 1, we can achieve nearly 13.5% lower latency (detailed in Sect. 3) While past work has explored the topology design space in terms of various configurations of ISL links [8, 12, 13, 37, 49, 51, 54], the peculiarities discovered in our preliminary experiments underscore the need for systematic investigation of LEO topology characteristics.

In this work, we extend our preliminary work [53] and conduct an in-depth investigation of LEO satellite topology design parameters to help guide the design of future LEO topologies as well as routing and traffic engineering schemes. In particular, we analyze the impact of three design parameters—the number of orbits in a shell, the inclination of orbits, and the number of satellites per orbit—on the network performance. We also analyze how the relationship between the geographical distribution of traffic sources and the inclination of satellite orbits affects the performance of the constellation. While past work has analyzed the performance characteristics of a limited set of proposed commercial topologies [26, 27, 32, 39], our work presents the first comprehensive study across topology design parameters in a broad design space.

We analyze topologies of real-world LEO constellations: Starlink, Kuiper, Telesat, and a broad set of synthetic configurations. Since ISL usage is currently limited in real-world constellations, we rely on simulations to understand the performance of future ISL-enabled LEO backbone networks. We generate the synthetic topologies by varying the design parameters (number of orbits per shell, inclination of orbit, and number of satellites per orbit) over a wide range. We evaluate each configuration under a synthetic traffic matrix commonly used in prior work, a traffic matrix between the top 100 GDP city pairs [35, 40] spanning a significant fraction of Internet users. Our findings reveal several insights that are expected to hold across a broad range of traffic matrices.

Based on extensive experiments, we identify several important characteristics of LEO topology design. We highlight two key observations here. First, there exists a threshold for the number of satellites per orbit below which the performance degrades significantly. For example, when the number of satellites per orbit is below 28, there is a significant performance drop even when the total number of orbits is increased to a very high value of 59. Second, we show that the latency performance is better when the angle between the traffic endpoints is closely aligned with the satellite orbit inclination. In this case, most hops in the path follow intra-orbit links instead of inter-orbit links, thereby significantly improving the latency performance.

In summary, we make the following contributions:

- We conduct an in-depth investigation of the impact of three previously unexplored topology design parameters in LEO constellations: the number of orbits per shell, the number of satellites per orbit, and the inclination of orbits.
- We investigate three real-world constellations and a broad range of synthetic constellations to understand the impact of design parameters on several network performance metrics: RTT, number of path changes, hop count, etc.
- We identify the threshold for various design parameters below which the constellation performance degrades significantly. Using these observations, we are able to explain the better network performance of real-world constellations with fewer satellites.
- We examine the impact of the relationship between traffic distribution and the inclination of satellite orbits on network performance.
- We will open-source the code and data in this paper. This work does not raise any ethical concerns.

2   Background and Related Work

This section provides an overview of LEO satellite networks and the recent work on LEO topology design and LEO satellite network measurement.

LEO Constellation Structure. The Low Earth Orbit (LEO) satellite network relies on a group of satellites orbiting the Earth at low altitudes, ranging from 500 to 1500 km, much lower than traditional geostationary satellites at an altitude of 36,000 km. A large LEO satellite constellation may contain thousands of satellites

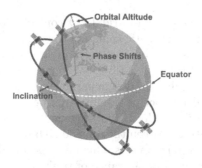

Fig. 1. Parameters of LEO constellation.

that are distributed across a number of orbits, where each orbit is a circular path around the globe.

In order to fully describe the LEO mega-constellation, several parameters are required, as shown in Fig. 1: (a) The *orbital altitude* of a satellite is its height above sea level, which, in turn, determines its velocity and coverage area; (b) The *number of orbits* in a shell determines the coverage. (c) The *number of satellites per orbit* in a constellation determines the density of the entire constellation. The density of the constellation affects the availability and redundancy of the network service; (d) The *inclination* of an orbital plane is the angle between the Equator and a satellite in that orbit traveling northward. The inclination of orbits determines the coverage region of the constellation. A lower inclination provides better coverage in equatorial regions while a higher inclination provides better coverage in polar regions; (e) *Phase shifts* of a satellite constellation determine the difference in position between one orbital plane and another. Existing constellations such as Starlink [44], Telesat [46], and Kuiper [21] apply uniform phase shift deployment, which evenly places the orbital planes in a full circle.

Inter-satellite Connectivity. Traditionally, satellite communication relied on Ground Station-Satellite Links (GSLs) using a bent-pipe space-ground architecture, where satellites only act as relays that transmit data to the next ground station [3,54]. However, this architecture's performance may be compromised by several factors. The signal transmission time between the satellite and the ground stations can result in significant latency. Also, GSLs are vulnerable to interference from other communication signals, weather conditions, and other sources [15,29,33]. In addition, the satellites in LEO constellations are highly dynamic, resulting in limited time windows to communicate with ground stations.

Today, satellites are equipped with lasers that enable Inter-Satellite Links (ISLs) to provide a promising improvement over GSLs. ISL-based communication architecture allows the satellites to communicate directly with each other and, in turn, reduces the reliance on ground stations. For example, each satellite in Starlink [44] has the hardware capabilities for four ISL links. The most studied topology is the +Grid topology [8,23,31,48], where each satellite connects to two adjacent satellites in the same orbit and the two nearest satellites on each of its neighboring orbits.

LEO Constellation Performance Analysis. Several past works measure the performance of existing satellite constellations. A recent study [39] investigates the performance of GEO satellite networks, highlighting the importance of ground station selection. Michel et al. [32] compare the performance of Starlink with GEO networks and show that the LEO constellation can achieve higher throughput and lower data transmission latency. Kassem et al. [26] examine the connectivity of Starlink, suggesting that the current bent-pipe connection results in high performance variability during bad weather conditions.

Real-world measurements can capture actual network performance but can only be performed with probes outside the LEO network since constellations such as Starlink are closed networks. This limitation prevents a comprehensive assessment of routing and throughput across the entire constellation. Additionally, real-world measurements cannot analyze undeployed or alternative constellation designs, such as inter-satellite links (ISLs), that differ from current real-world configurations (e.g., Starlink only partially utilizes ISLs). In contrast, simulation-based studies provide valuable insights into potential topologies and enable high-level investigations from the perspective of an LEO service provider.

Several works resorted to simulation-based performance analysis of LEO networks. Kassing et al. [27] developed a satellite network simulator and compared three prominent LEO satellite constellations (Starlink, Kuiper, and Telesat). Izhikevich et al. [24] introduced LEO HitchHiking to democratize LEO satellite measurements. Bhosale et al. [9] developed a model that captures the RTT variability exhibited in LEO networks.

Some recent works analyze the impact of satellite constellation parameter settings on performance, albeit under limited scope. Bhosale et al. [10] characterized route variability in LEO satellite networks, focusing on route churn and RTT variability. Basak et al. [5] focused on designing constellations under a specified budget for target markets. All prior work on simulation-based LEO constellation analysis [5,10,30,38] explores the performance of constellations over a limited range of parameter settings and provide a high-level overview of a small subset of satellite network characteristics. Moreover, certain performance characteristics of the constellation are inexplicable based on our current understanding. Therefore, a comprehensive investigation of the impact of parameter settings on constellation performance is currently needed. This work aims to fill this gap.

3   Motivation

To emphasize the importance of design parameter analysis, we compare the latency performance of two satellite constellations: Starlink shell 1 (S1) with 1584 satellites and our custom-designed example shell (E1) with 720 satellites. Both constellations share the same altitude but differ in orbit count (S1: 72, E1: 20), satellites per orbit (S1: 22, E1: 36), and inclination (S1: 53°, E1: 70°). Using these configurations in a +Grid topology, we evaluate latency between the top 100

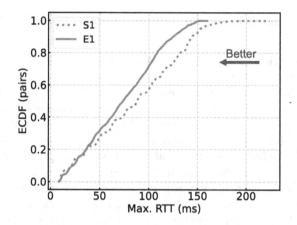

Fig. 2. Distribution of maximum RTT (ms) across top 100 city pairs using Starlink S1 and Custom-designed topology, Example E1.

most populous city pairs (details in Sect. 4). In Fig. 2, we present the ECDF of the maximum RTT for each constellation, revealing that E1 exhibits lower mean and tail latencies. This unexpected result challenges the assumption that higher satellite counts inherently improve performance, as S1, despite having nearly double the number of satellites, shows inferior latency. Given the disparities in all three design parameters between S1 and E1, identifying the specific factor contributing to S1's latency issues is challenging.

4   Experiment Design

In this section, we provide an overview of the evaluation metrics and experiment configurations that we use to understand the impact of various satellite topology design parameters.

4.1   Evaluation Metrics

The major factors that affect user experience of data transmission over a satellite network are latency and network stability. In order to quantify these factors, we organize the evaluation metrics into three categories: *(1) Round-trip time (RTT)*, *(2) Path changes*, and *(3) Hop count*.

Round-Trip Time (RTT). The round-trip time denotes the propagation latency, i.e., the time taken for a packet of data to travel from a sender to a receiver and back to the sender. The RTT depends on the total distance between sender and receiver, which includes (1) the line-of-sight distance from the sender to the first-hop satellite, (2) the sum of distances between satellites along the routing path, and (3) the distance from the last-hop satellite to the receiver. The RTT is computed as the total distance divided by the speed of light in vacuum ($3*10^8$ m/s). For satellite network evaluation, we consider the following characteristics of RTT:

(a) Max. (Min.) RTT, which denotes the maximum (minimum) RTT observed between the sender and the receiver during a specified period. RTT variations occur in satellite networks due to changes in topology caused by satellite motion.

(b) Max. RTT - Min. RTT, is the difference between the maximum RTT and minimum RTT observed between the sender and the receiver during a specified period. This metric reflects the fluctuations in RTT experienced by a connection.

Since RTT measurements are dependent on the distance between the sender and the receiver, we define two additional metrics that facilitate comparison of performance across different pairs of endpoints.

(c) Max. to Min. Slowdown captures the extent of variation in RTT observed between a pair of endpoints. It is defined as $S_m = \frac{max.RTT}{min.RTT}$, where *max. (min.) RTT* is the maximum (minimum) RTT during a period of time.

(d) Geodesic Slowdown is the slowdown with respect to the best possible path. It is defined as $S_g = \frac{max.RTT}{ideal.RTT}$, where *ideal.RTT* is the RTT obtained when directly transmitting data between two endpoints through the shortest Euclidean distance on the earth's surface at the speed of light.

Path Changes. The dynamic nature of LEO networks with constantly moving satellites results in changes in the routing paths over time. Frequent changes in these paths can lead to data transmission jitter, high computational overhead for updating routing tables, and loss of connectivity.

(e) The number of path changes between two endpoints over a period of time denotes the extent of network stability.

Hop Count. While using ISLs, data is transmitted between satellites over a series of hops. Each hop results in additional transmission delay as well as energy consumption. If the number of hops increases significantly, it may indicate high latency in transmitting data. Hence, we measure the following characteristics of hops between two endpoints:

(f) Average hop count denotes the average number of hops between a pair of endpoints during a specified period of time.

(g) Max. hop count - Min. hop count is the difference in the number of hops across paths during a specified period.

(h) Max. hop count/Min. hop count denotes the relative change in the number of hops between a pair of endpoints during a specific period of time.

4.2   Experiment Configurations

The end-to-end network performance over LEO constellations can vary widely based on a variety of configuration parameters. Under a given budget of the number of satellites, it is unclear what set of configurations would lead to optimal performance. Therefore, it is essential to understand the impact of each configuration parameter on network performance. What are the most important parameters affecting LEO mega-constellation network performance? In what ways and along what dimensions do they influence the performance of satellite networks? How do we design an optimal LEO mega-constellation? In order to scientifically and rigorously answer the above questions, we begin with the existing commercial LEO mega-constellations and expand to an in-depth analysis of synthetic LEO mega-constellations generated across a wide range of parameter settings. We design three key experiments to explore the impact of LEO mega-constellation parameter settings.

(i) Exploring Different Shells of the Existing LEO Mega-constellations. We first simulate three leading existing LEO mega-constellations and analyze the network performance of their shells: five shells for Starlink Phase I, three shells for Kuiper, and two shells for Telesat. Detailed parameter settings are given in Sect. 5.1.1. We focus on four of the most representative metrics—Max. RTT, Geodesic Slowdown, (Max. RTT - Min. RTT), Number (#) of Path Changes—to evaluate these shells, detailed experimental results are in Sect. 5.3.1.

(ii) Exploring Different Synthetic Configurations of LEO Mega-constellations. In order to explore the impact of parameters on network performance, we analyze different settings for three parameters—Orbit Number, Satellite Number per Orbit, and Inclination. We vary each parameter independently while fixing others and generate 20 synthetic LEO mega-constellations (the settings are shown in Sect. 5.1.2). We select the three most representative metrics: Max. RTT, Geodesic Slowdown, and Number (#) of Path Changes for evaluation, (detailed results in Sect. 5.3.2).

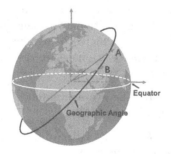

Fig. 3. Geographic Angle between City A and B.

(iii) Understanding the Impact of User Endpoints Location. Visualization of LEO paths reveals varying levels of zig-zag in paths between various user endpoint pairs [27]. We conjecture that the degree of alignment between the Inclination of the satellite orbit and the Geographic Angle [50] of the plane between source and destination endpoint locations could influence the latency performance. To verify this conjecture, we divide the traffic between user end-points into nine categories based on the Geographic Angle of the plane connecting them (shown in Fig. 3) and evaluate the network performance of these nine groups under different Inclination values of synthetic constellations. We choose the two most representative indicator: average hops and Geodesic Slowdown, for analysis. Max. RTT is not a suitable metric in this analysis since endpoint pairs in the nine groups have widely different distance distributions.

5   Evaluation

In this section, we provide an overview of the datasets used in our analysis, the implementation of our analysis framework, and our key observations while answering the following questions:

- What are the key parameters that influence the performance of an LEO network?
- Are there thresholds for each parameter above/below which the performance degrades significantly?
- Why does a shell with a low number of satellites outperform another shell with nearly double the number of satellites (Starlink S1 vs. custom-designed topology E1)?
- How does the difference between satellite orbit inclination and the geographical angle of the plane containing the source and destination location affect performance?

5.1   Datasets

5.1.1   Commercial LEO Mega-Constellations
In Table 1, we detail the configurations of the three leading commercial LEO mega-constellations used in our evaluation: Starlink [44], Kuiper [21], and Telesat [46].

5.1.2   Synthetic LEO Mega-Constellations
We generate multiple synthetic constellations to understand the impact of parameters better. We fix each parameter to a constant value and vary others. First, we fix the inclination angle to 53°, covering more than 90% of the cities on earth and almost all Internet user population, and synthesize satellite shells with different number of orbits (20, 33, 46, and 59) and number of satellites per orbit (20, 28, 36, and 44). These ranges reflect the median parameter settings in real-world constellations, ensuring relevance to practical deployment scenarios. The intervals are evenly distributed to capture a wide range of configurations without being overly sparse. We also avoid extreme values, as most ground stations are located within specific latitudinal ranges (neither too high nor too low), ensuring that the configurations are representative of realistic operational conditions. To understand the impact of inclination, we fix the number of orbits to 33 and the

Table 1. Shell configurations for Starlink's first phase (S1–S5), Kuiper (K1-K3), and Telesat (T1-T2).

Name	H (km)	Orb.	Sats/Orb	Total Sats	Incl.
S1	550	72	22	1584	53.0°
S2	570	36	20	720	70.0°
S3	560	6	58	348	97.6°
S4	540	72	22	1584	53.2°
S5	560	4	43	172	97.6°
K1	630	34	34	1156	51.9°
K2	610	36	36	1296	42°
K3	590	28	28	784	33°
T1	1015	27	13	351	98.98°
T2	1325	40	33	1320	50.88°

number of satellites per orbit to 28 and vary the inclination across four values (45°, 55°, 65°, and 75°). Thus, we have a total of 20 synthetic shells. We use a fixed orbital altitude of 570km for all synthetic shells. Note that we analyze the design parameter, the altitude of the satellite orbit, and find that variations in altitude had minimal impact on network performance in the altitude range of LEO satellites. Please refer to Appendix A for more details.

5.1.3 Traffic Matrix

To evaluate the performance of the LEO satellite-based networks, based on the known correlation between Internet penetration and GDP [2], we choose the Top 100 Gross Domestic Product (GDP) cities as a representative to generate the traffic matrices for Internet use requests, following the methodology of past work on satellite network performance [8]. The top 100 cities with the highest GDP encompass a significant portion of the global Internet population [2]. We collect the latitude and longitude of these Top 100 GDP cities and generate traffic matrices with one city as the source and another as the destination, with a total of 9,900 city pairs. We maintain constant traffic between the 9900 pairs of cities during the period of evaluation. For each time step in the simulation, we take into account the communication load between all pairs of cities and estimate their instantaneous network performance. Note that several observations in this paper hold independently of the traffic matrix.

5.2   Implementation

5.2.1   LEO Mega-Constellations Generation

Using an open-source LEO satellite network analysis platform, Hypatia [27], we generate the dynamic states of the LEO constellations under various configurations. Each experiment is conducted for a duration of 400 s. We snapshot the link pattern of LEO mega-constellations in 1-s increments and evaluate the network performance characteristics at each time step. Note that the topology patterns of constellations exhibit cyclical behavior with an approximate time period of 200 s. Hence, an evaluation period of 400 s is sufficient to cover the complete span of topology configurations and comprehensively reflect the performance patterns.

We use the NetworkX [17] library to generate a network graph of the LEO satellite-based network for each time interval, considering the satellite positions and link lengths between satellites and ground stations. We calculate the forwarding state for each node based on a range of routing strategies. Our implementation employs shortest-path routing, computed using the Floyd-Warshall algorithm [22]. The latest forwarding state is read into static routing table entries during each change event in the network. Based on the forwarding state in each snapshot, we estimate the various evaluation metrics using the city pairs-based traffic matrix. In order to simulate the dynamic states and compute the evaluation metrics, we rely on three files: the TLE file, the ISL file, and the TM file.

TLE File: The TLE format is a two-line element (TLE) standard format for representing the trajectory of an Earth-orbiting object [28]. It is essential for satellite mobility modeling. Using the configuration parameters of real-world and synthetic constellations, we calculate the movement of satellites in space and save their positions in the TLE file.

ISLs File: We connect each satellite using the +Grid topology and build the network for the LEO mega-constellations. We store these edges between satellites in an ISLs file, which contains the network graph.

TM File: To balance the coverage of users and computational overhead, we selected 100 cities with the highest Gross Domestic Product (GDP) as traffic endpoints. We consider all pairs of cities in this set and store the traffic endpoints in the Traffic Matrix file (TM file). This file contains the latitude, longitude, and city ID of all pairs of traffic endpoints.

5.2.2   Geographic Angle Between Traffic Endpoints Implementation

To investigate the impact of the alignment of the plane containing the source and destination of traffic with the satellite orbit inclination on network performance, we group the traffic endpoint pairs into nine categories based on their geographic angle (intervals of 10° ranging from 0°–10° to 80°–90°). The geographic angle is the angle between the plane connecting the endpoint pair and the equator.

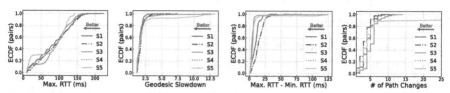

(a) Starlink shell 1-5 (b) Starlink shell 1-5 (c) Starlink shell 1-5 (d) Starlink shell 1-5

Fig. 4. The network performance of Starlink shells 1–5 (S1–S5) of Phase I. For all curves, lower values indicate better performance. Long tails indicate outliers with poor performance. The tail of S5 is truncated in (d) due to a very high number of path changes.

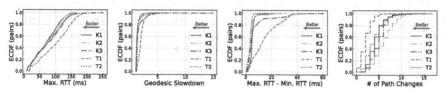

(a) Kuiper shell 1-3(b) Kuiper shell 1-3(c) Kuiper shell 1-3 &(d) Kuiper shell 1-3
& Telesat shell 1-2   & Telesat shell 1-2   Telesat shell 1-2   & Telesat shell 1-2

Fig. 5. The network performance of shells 1–3 (K1-K3) of Kuiper and shell 1 and 2 (T1, T2) of Telesat. For all curves, lower values indicate better performance. Long tails indicate outliers with poor performance.

5.3 Results

5.3.1 Real-World LEO Constellations' Performance

Max. RTT: We evaluate the maximum RTT observed between city pairs over a period of 400 s. In Fig. 4(a), we observe that different shells of Starlink have significant variations in maximum RTT. This behavior can be explained based on the shell configurations. Shells 1,2 and 4 have a large number of satellites and offer good coverage. However, shells 3 and 5 are sparse with many endpoints away from the poles unreachable during significant durations, causing large fluctuations in Max. RTT. In Fig. 5(a), we observe that both Kuiper and Telesat with shells that have large coverage also have an even distribution of Max. RTT.

Geodesic Slowdown: We investigate the geodesic slowdown of the three constellations and find that over 80% of the endpoint pairs have a maximum RTT less than 2.5× geodesic RTT, showing good latency reduction compared to today's terrestrial Internet networks (terrestrial fiber paths are often long-winded, and the speed of light in fiber is roughly two-thirds of the speed of light in air leading to poor latency performance on land [11]). However, some shells have a long tail for the geodesic slowdown. In Fig. 4(b), shells 2, 3, and 5 have longer tails than shells 1 and 4. Figure 5(b) also shows that when the total number of satellites decreases, the slowdown tends to have a longer tail. Prior work [27] indicated that a drastic increase in the ratio might be caused by short-distance data transmission—the latency overhead of ground station-satellite link resulting in significant inflation of geodesic slowdown. Besides the overhead, the sparsity of the satellite constellation also causes an increase in geodesic slowdown. Routing across a limited number of satellites results in a longer path than a fully covered satellite shell.

Max. RTT - Min. RTT: To examine the latency variation, we further explore the difference between maximum and minimum RTT over time. Figure 4(c) shows that for Starlink, over 90% of the endpoint pairs have latency variation less than 25 ms. Figure 5(c) shows that for Kuiper, over 90% of the endpoint pairs have latency variation less than 20 ms. We observe that shell 2 of Telesat has the lowest latency variation, with almost 100% of the endpoint pairs having less than 10 ms variation. Similar to the geodesic slowdown, the total number of satellites affects the tail of the latency variation.

Number of Path Changes: We investigate the number of path changes to understand the stability of LEO mega-constellations. Figure 5(d) shows that with fewer satellites, the shell has less number of path changes. However, in Fig. 4(d), we observe that with the smallest number of satellites, shells 3 and 5 have the greatest number of path changes. When the coverage of a satellite constellation is above a threshold, the number of path changes increases as the satellite density increases due to frequent shifts in the best available shortest path in a dense and dynamic network. However, below this threshold, the number of path changes is high due to poor coverage and loss of paths.

Real-World Constellation Analysis Key Takeaways:

- Very sparse shells can lead to a high variance in RTT.
- Path stability is affected by the number of satellites in the shell. The stability offered by a shell depends on its coverage. For shells with good coverage, the number of path changes increases as shell density increases.
- Typically, shells with a larger number of satellites and higher coverage offer a lower RTT, lower geodesic slowdown, and lower variance in RTT.

5.3.2   In-Depth Analysis of Synthetic Configurations

Number of Satellites Per Orbit: At an inclination angle of $53°$, we measure the network performance of synthetic LEO constellations by varying the number of satellites per orbit across (20, 28, 36, 44) and the number of orbits across (20, 33, 46, 59). The measurement results are shown in Fig. 6, Fig. 7, and Fig. 8. Note that the tails are very long in certain cases, and the ECDF is cropped in some plots for better visualization.

In Fig. 6 and Fig. 7, we observe that the distribution of Max. RTT and Geodesic Slowdown demonstrate similar behavior irrespective of the number of orbits. As the number of satellites per orbit (Sats/Orbit) increases, Max. RTT and Geodesic Slowdown decrease for a given orbit number. We also find that when the number of satellites per orbit is 20, the Max. RTT and Geodesic Slowdown are much higher than others (e.g., 2× higher than 28 Sats/Orbit in Fig. 6(a) and Fig. 7(a)). This effect is especially pronounced when the Orbit number is less than 33. The long tail effect is also more pronounced when Sats/Orbit

= 20 (tail at 250 ms+ vs. 150 ms when Sats/Orbit = 28). When Sats/Orbit increases beyond 28, the performance gains are marginal. For example, a 33% increase in satellite density from 36 to 48 results in a less than 2% reduction in Max. RTT and less than 1% reduction in Geodesic slowdown.

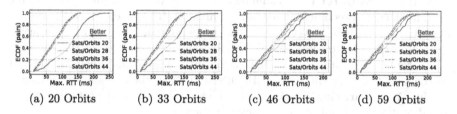

(a) 20 Orbits   (b) 33 Orbits   (c) 46 Orbits   (d) 59 Orbits

Fig. 6. The distribution of Maximum RTT(ms) while varying the number of satellites per orbit (Sats/Orbit). For all curves, lower values indicate better performance. Long tails indicate outliers with poor performance.

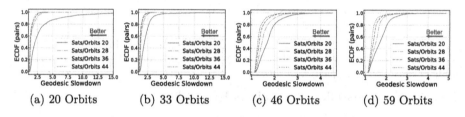

(a) 20 Orbits   (b) 33 Orbits   (c) 46 Orbits   (d) 59 Orbits

Fig. 7. The distribution of Geodesic Slowdown while varying the number of satellites per orbit (Sats/Orbit). For all curves, lower values indicate better performance. Long tails indicate outliers with poor performance. Sats/Orbit at 20 has a very long tail and is truncated in (a) and (b).

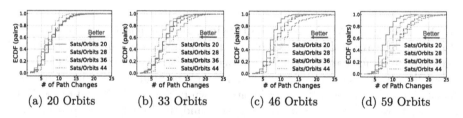

(a) 20 Orbits   (b) 33 Orbits   (c) 46 Orbits   (d) 59 Orbits

Fig. 8. The distribution of the number of Path Changes while varying the number of satellites per orbit (Sats/Orbit). For all curves, lower values indicate better performance. Long tails indicate outliers with poor performance. Long tails are truncated in all plots.

Note that while the differences between performance curves may be minimal in some experiments, we are interested in trends in performance changes as we vary each parameter. Hence, we highlight the performance trends by comparing plots across multiple parameter settings in our analysis.

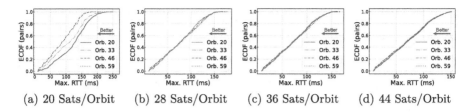

(a) 20 Sats/Orbit   (b) 28 Sats/Orbit   (c) 36 Sats/Orbit   (d) 44 Sats/Orbit

Fig. 9. The distribution of Maximum RTT(ms) while varying the number of orbits. For all curves, lower values indicate better performance. Long tails indicate outliers with poor performance.

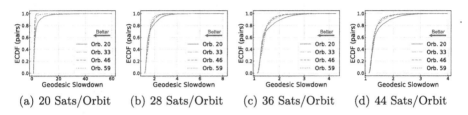

(a) 20 Sats/Orbit   (b) 28 Sats/Orbit   (c) 36 Sats/Orbit   (d) 44 Sats/Orbit

Fig. 10. The distribution of Geodesic Slowdown while varying the number of orbits. For all curves, lower values indicate better performance. Long tails indicate outliers with poor performance.

The variations in path change reflect a different behavior. When the number of orbits increases, the path stability of constellations with a lower number of satellites per orbit improves. For example, in Fig. 8(a), Sats/Orbits = 20 leads to the highest number of path changes (across over 80% of endpoint pairs); however, in Fig. 8(d), Sats/Orbits = 20 leads to the least number of path changes (across over 90% of endpoint pairs). Also, in Fig. 8(b), for a fixed number of Orbit = 33, the median number of path changes increases from 6 to 10 as the number of satellites per orbit increases.

These experiments reveal a strong correlation between the number of satellites per orbit (Sats/Orbit) and the network performance of the constellations. The Sats/Orbit will determine the distance between satellites in each orbit, with a lower distance between satellites as Sats/Orbit increases. With the gridded satellite network, a higher value of Sats/Orbit can lead to the routing path in the +Grid LEO constellation being more closer to the optimal geodesic transmission path. However, with the high level of dynamism under a high density of satellites, the optimal shortest paths will change at a faster rate. Therefore, the trade-off between latency and path stability needs to be considered during constellation design. 20 Sats/Orbit offers poor network performance, and hence, 28 or more Sats/Orbit are needed to achieve the combination of relatively low delay and a lower number of path changes.

Number of Orbits: With a constant inclination of 53° and constant satellites per orbit in the set (20, 28, 36, 44), we evaluate the variation in performance

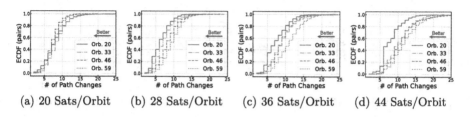

Fig. 11. The distribution of the number of Path Changes while varying the number of orbits. For all curves, lower values indicate better performance. Long tails indicate outliers with poor performance. Long tails are truncated in some plots.

by varying the number of orbits across 20, 33, 46, and 59. In Fig. 9(a), we see that when the Sats/Orbit = 20 (i.e., a large distance between satellites), the performance improves significantly as the number of orbits is increased from 20 to 59. Compared to 20 Orbits, a 65%, 120%, and 195% increase in orbits densities to 33, 44, and 59 Orbits leads to a 20%, 50%, and 50% decrease in the median value of Max. RTT. Similarly, significant improvement is observed in Geodesic Slowdown with Sats/Orbit = 20 in Fig. 10(a). Moreover, from Fig. 9 and Fig. 10, we observe marginal benefits when Sats/Orbit density increases beyond a threshold. Beyond 28 Sats/Orbit, an increase in the number of orbits has a minimal effect on the maximum RTT, reducing the maximum RTT from 175 ms to 150 ms.

In Fig. 10, we see that when Sats/Orbit is greater than 28, we achieve minimal improvement by increasing the number of orbits. Interestingly, most endpoint pairs have a Geodesic Slowdown in the range 1.4–2.5×. With the number of path changes, we observe similar behavior as previously noted, i.e., when the number of satellites per orbit increases, the path stability is higher with a lower number of orbits. For Sats/Orbits = 28, the median number of path changes increases from 6 to 9 when the number of orbits increases.

The above results align with our predictions for the LEO mega-constellation network. At a given number of satellites per orbit, as the number of orbits increases, the density of the satellite network also increases. This causes the inter-satellite routing route to be closer to the optimal geographical distance but leads to a higher number of shortest path changes. Also shown in Fig. 9 and Fig. 11, when the number of satellites per orbit is low, i.e., the satellite network has a low density, 20 Orbits cannot offer the ideal satellite network performance, and at least 33 Orbits are required to achieve relatively low delay and the number of path changes.

Inclination: With a fixed number of Sats/Orbits = 28 and a number of orbits of 33, we measure the variations in network performance with varying Inclinations (45°, 55°, 65°, and 75°) and show the results in Fig. 12. In Fig. 12(a), the variations in maximum RTT across inclinations are minimal, although Inclination = 75° has the largest Max. RTT. Moreover, the difference between maximum and minimum RTT, shown in Fig. 12(c), is below 16 ms for nearly 90% of endpoint

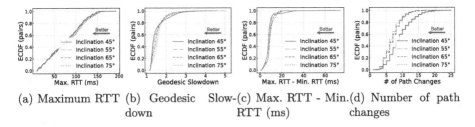

(a) Maximum RTT (b) Geodesic Slow-(c) Max. RTT - Min.(d) Number of path
                     down   RTT (ms)   changes

Fig. 12. The performance characteristics under varying values for Inclination. We use a constant number of orbits (33) and satellites per orbit (28) while varying the inclination.

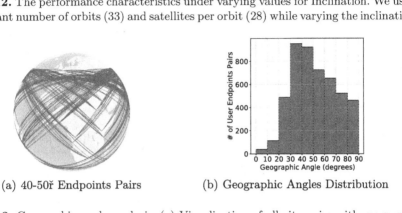

(a) 40-50° Endpoints Pairs   (b) Geographic Angles Distribution

Fig. 13. Geographic angle analysis: (a) Visualization of all city pairs with geographic angles in the range 40–50°. (b) The distribution of geographic angles of all 9900 city pairs used in our analysis.

pairs; however, at 45°, the tail can be as high as 60 ms. With Geodesic Slowdown in Fig. 12(b), the lower the inclination angle, the larger the fraction of endpoint pairs with a slowdown factor below 1.8×. In addition, as shown in Fig. 12(d), an inclination of 55° has the lowest median value of the number of path changes. The median value for inclinations 75° and 65° are similar, while the number of path changes at an inclination of 45° is the largest, with a median of 9. Overall, it is difficult to identify clear trends in network performance associated with variations in inclination. We conclude that the influence of Inclination on network performance is multi-dimensional and defer a detailed study at the intersection of patterns in the traffic matrix and inclination to Sect. 5.3.3.

Synthetic Constellation Analysis Key Takeaways:

- The number of satellites per orbit is a key determinant of network performance. As the number of satellites per orbit increases, the latency and geodesic slowdown in the network decreases (Fig. 6 & 7).
- We identify a threshold for the number of satellites per orbit, 28, below which the network performance degrades significantly (Fig. 6 & 7).
- Increasing the number of orbits is beneficial for performance only when the number of satellites per orbit is very low, i.e., below the identified threshold of 28 (Fig. 9 & 10).

- Inclination has a complex relationship with network performance and needs to be evaluated in conjunction with the traffic matrix for a better understanding (Fig. 12).

Why does Custom-Designed Topology, Example E1 Offer Better Performance Compared to Satrlink Shell 1? We circle back to the observation that led to our analysis: E1 offers better latency performance compared to S1 in spite of having only nearly half the number of satellites. Based on our synthetic constellation analysis, we identify that the poor performance of S1 is because its number of satellites per orbit (20) is lower than the minimum threshold required for good performance (28). When the number of satellites is below this threshold, it is difficult to compensate for the drop in performance, even with a much larger number of satellites. E1, on the other hand, has all its key design parameters above the performance threshold. Hence, E1 has better performance than S1.

5.3.3 Impact of Traffic Matrix

Traffic Distribution: We use the geographic angle of endpoint pairs to investigate the impact of traffic matrices (user distribution) on performance. The geographic angle is defined as the angle between the plane connecting the endpoint pair and the equator. We divide endpoint pairs into nine groups according to their geographic angle. For example, Fig. 13(a) shows endpoint pairs with geographic angles in the range 40–50°. Figure 13(b) shows the distribution of geographic angles of all city pairs. The majority of endpoint pairs are distributed within the range 20–90°, with the highest number of pairs in the range 30–40°.

Geodesic Slowdown Across Endpoint Pairs at Different Inclinations: Figure 14 shows the geodesic slowdown of endpoint pairs at various inclination angles of satellite constellations. The endpoints pairs are divided into nine groups, in intervals of 10° from 0° to 90°. We evaluate their performance under four values of orbit inclination (45°, 55°, 65°, and 75°). We observe that the performance of endpoint pairs varies based on their geographic angle and the alignment of their angle with respect to the satellite orbit inclination.

We observe that the latency performance is the best when the geographic angle of the endpoint pairs is aligned with the LEO constellation's orbital Inclination. Shown in Fig. 14(a)-(e), the shell with a 45° inclination offers the lowest slowdown for endpoint pairs with a geographic angle in the range 0–50°. While in Fig. 14(f): the shell with 55° has the best performance; in Fig. 14(g), the shell with 65° has the best performance; and in Fig. 14(h)–(i), the shell with 75° has the best performance.

We find that when the orbital inclination aligns with the geographic angle, the shortest path between endpoints follows more intra-orbital hops within the same orbit, leading to a better latency performance. In Fig. 15, the rule is clear, noticed the solid line in each subplot – the endpoint pairs aligned most with the inclination angle of LEO mega-constellations have the least value of Geodesic Slowdown. It is worth noting that the 0–10° range appears to perform better overall because the number of endpoint pairs in this range is limited, and

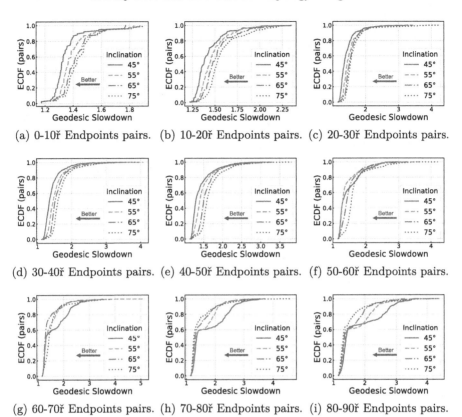

(a) 0-10ř Endpoints pairs. (b) 10-20ř Endpoints pairs. (c) 20-30ř Endpoints pairs.

(d) 30-40ř Endpoints pairs. (e) 40-50ř Endpoints pairs. (f) 50-60ř Endpoints pairs.

(g) 60-70ř Endpoints pairs. (h) 70-80ř Endpoints pairs. (i) 80-90ř Endpoints pairs.

Fig. 14. Evaluation of Geodesic Slowdown of nine groups of endpoint pairs with varying Inclination of orbits (1). For all curves, lower values indicate better performance. Long tails indicate outliers with poor performance.

the average distance between these endpoints is shorter. This results in lower geodesic slowdown values compared to other ranges. However, under the 0.6 ECDF, the 0–10° range exhibits relatively worse performance, indicating less consistency at lower percentiles despite its overall advantage. The performance degrades as the geographic angle of endpoints pairs diverges from this inclination in both directions. This shows that a LEO constellation aligned with the endpoint pairs' geographic angle offers better performance.

Average Hop Count for Different Endpoint Pairs Under Varying Inclination: We evaluate the average hop count for all nine groups of endpoint pairs under different inclinations and present the results in Fig. 16. Across all endpoint pairs, an inclination of 55° offers the best performance. Most commercial constellations today use an orbital angle very close to this value. Another interesting observation is that the inclination that offers the smallest average hop count is the one closest to the geographic angle of endpoint pairs. For example, for endpoint pairs with a geographic angle in the range of 40–50°, the constellation

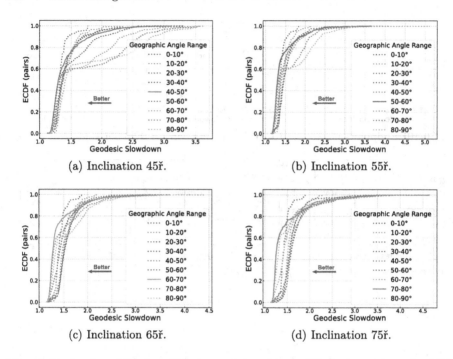

Fig. 15. Evaluation of Geodesic Slowdown of nine groups of Endpoints pairs under LEO mega-constellations with Inclination 45–75° (2). For all curves, lower values indicate better performance. Long tails indicate outliers with poor performance.

with an inclination of 45° offers the least average hop count. Similarly, 50–60° endpoint pairs fare best under an inclination of 55° and so on. When endpoint pairs have a geographic angle greater than 70°, the average hop count gradually decreases with an increase in inclination from 45° to 75°. Similarly, for endpoint pairs with a geographic angle of less than 40°, the average hop count gradually decreases as inclination decreases from 75° to 45°.

We present a more fine-grained analysis of the variation of average hop count across endpoint pairs based on both geographic angle and geographic distance. We choose four representative values of 50–60° endpoints pairs under different orbital inclination, 45°, 55°, 65° and 75°, in Fig. 17, respectively. Note that across both figures, the set of endpoint pairs that belong to each bin along the x-axis remains the same (since the distance between endpoint pairs is fixed). However, their average hop count (y-axis) can vary based on the inclination of the orbit.

By comparing the same column in Fig. 17(a)–(d), we observe that the number of average hops changes with the inclination. For example, consider endpoint pairs within the distance interval of 10000–12500 km and a geographic angle of 50–60° (i.e., the sixth column in each subplot of Fig. 17). Under the inclination of 45° (Fig. 17(a)), more than 120 endpoint pairs have an average hop count in the range 10–11, with only a tiny fraction with an average hop count of 9–10 or 11–12. However, under the inclination of 55° (Fig. 17(b)), most of the endpoint

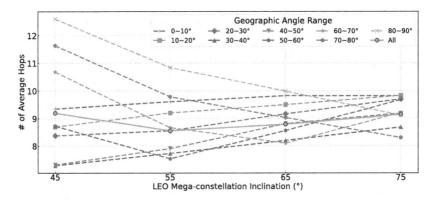

Fig. 16. Evaluation of Average Hop Count of nine groups of endpoint pairs under varying Inclination.

pairs have a smaller average hop count than in Fig. 17(a). Less than 40 endpoint pairs have an average hop count in the range of 10–11 and the remaining have an average hop count in the range of 8–9, thereby decreasing the overall average hop count. In contrast, for the sixth column's color block, as we increase the orbital angle (Fig. 17(b) vs. Figure 17(c) and Fig. 17(d)), the average hop count increases. This is because the orbital angle of 55° (Fig. 17(b)) is closer to the geographic angle for 50–60° endpoint pairs. The same pattern holds for all other groups of endpoint pairs and their more aligned inclinations.

From these two experiments, we confirm that alignment between the inclination or orbit and the geographic angle of endpoint pairs is positively correlated with a reduced average hop count and improved performance. When an orbit is more aligned with the geographic angle of endpoint pairs, the satellite path uses more intra-orbit hops and reduces inter-orbit zig-zag hops, which in turn reduces the hop count. Therefore, if endpoint traffic distributions can be known a priori, designing orbital angles that align closely with endpoint traffic distributions can improve performance.

Traffic Matrix Analysis Key Takeaways:

- The network delay is closest to optimal when the geographic angle of the traffic endpoints aligns closely with the orbital angle of the constellation.
- Average hop count is lower when the geographic angle of the traffic endpoints aligns closely with the orbital angle of the constellation.

5.4 Summary of Results

- The design of most commercial constellations (except S3 and S5) is well-suited to support communication between the top 100 cities. Considering both delay and link stability, S1, K2, and T2 offer the best performance in each of the three constellations, respectively.

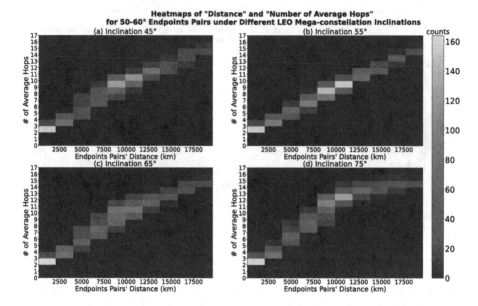

Fig. 17. Heatmap of "Distance" vs. "Number of Average Hops" for 50–60° Endpoints Pairs under different LEO mega-constellation inclinations (a) 45°, (b) 55° (c) 65° and (d) 75°. The 50–60° city pairs are further divided into bins based on their geodesic distance (along the x-axis). Comparing the same bin across (a) - (d) helps us understand the change in the number of average hops for the same city pairs under different inclinations. For example, 50°–60° city pairs have a lower average hop count in (b) when the inclination angle of the orbit is more closely aligned with their geographic angle.

- The two design parameters—the number of satellites per orbit and the number of orbits—strongly influence network performance. For high performance, the number of satellites per orbit should be above a threshold, which we empirically estimate as 28. Similarly, the performance is high when the number of orbits is at least 33.
- Network performance is not strongly correlated with the total number of satellites. Custom-designed E1 offers better latency performance than Starlink S1 in spite of much fewer satellites because both its key design parameters are above the performance threshold. The poor performance of Starlink S1 is due to its low number of satellites per orbit (20 vs. threshold of 28).
- The inclination of the LEO mega-constellation is important. The alignment between the inclination and the geographic angle of endpoint pairs is positively correlated with network performance. When the endpoint pairs are more aligned with the orbital angle, they experience lower delay and lower average hop count.

6   Discussion

In this section, we provide suggestions for the design of LEO mega-constellations and identify avenues for future work.

Suggestions for the Design of LEO Mega-constellations: We identify the thresholds for optimal performance as 33 for the number of orbits and 28 for the number of satellites per orbit. Also, future constellation design should aim for a reasonable satellite density. Moreover, network delay is minimized when the geographic angle between endpoint pairs is aligned with the orbital angle. Based on the known user distribution on Earth, the range from 45° to 55° is the ideal orbital inclination.

Impact of Topology Variations: The recommendations of this study are based on the assumption of LEO mega-constellations relying on ISL links and the +Grid topology. Although the +Grid topology is the most intuitive and popular structure, several recent papers investigate designs for better ISLs topologies [1, 4, 6, 42, 43, 45]. Our evaluation needs to be repeated for novel topologies.

Routing and Traffic Engineering: In this work, we assume a shortest path based routing scheme and ideal network conditions. In practice, the observed delay and hop count can vary based on the routing and traffic engineering schemes employed by the constellation operator. Moreover, the network load may not be uniformly distributed, with high congestion occurring closer to heavily populated areas. We do not make assumptions about any intelligent routing or TE schemes.

Multi-shell Analysis: Our analysis focuses on the network performance of a single shell. Currently deployed satellites do not support inter-shell communication even within the same LEO mega-constellation; their ISLs are designed to communicate only with satellites in the same shell. Understanding the aggregate network performance of multiple shells, each with different configuration settings, is an open problem.

Limitations: Our study relies solely on simulations and does not incorporate data from real-world constellations. We make several assumptions in our study—perfect satellite positioning, population-dependent user demand patterns, and ideal communication channels from the top 100 cities based on GDP. In practice, satellite network users are distributed globally, with users in remote locations being one of the target customer base. Considering a global user base will shift the distribution of RTT measurements. However, key findings such as improved latency performance when the geographic angle aligns with the orbit inclination are expected to hold true in all cases. Additionally, our evaluation does not consider routing, traffic engineering, and overheads arising from ISL reconfigurations.

Considering Real-World Network: Our work focuses on calculating shortest paths and routing packets without incorporating real-world network factors such as traffic throughput and congestion control algorithms. These factors can significantly impact network performance, especially under high traffic volumes or in scenarios involving cross-traffic. In future work, we aim to explore these aspects by simulating traffic matrices that include varying levels of congestion and implementing congestion control mechanisms. This will provide a more realistic evaluation of the network's performance and resilience under practical conditions.

7   Conclusion

We evaluate three key design parameters—the number of orbits per shell, the inclination of orbits, and the number of satellites per orbit—on real-world topologies of Starlink, Kuiper, Telesat, and a broad set of synthetic topologies. Our analysis reveals interesting insights and answers to previously inexplicable behavior patterns. We identify the parameter thresholds for optimal network performance, identify the causes of the poor performance of a high-density shell (S1) of Starlink compared to one with lower density (E1), and determine the impact of traffic endpoint locations on performance by analyzing their geographic angles. Our interesting observations underscore the need for a systematic analysis of the impact of design parameters in the context of the emerging domain of LEO mega-constellations. We highlight several avenues for future research in this space, including the impact of topology in relation to design parameters and multi-shell analysis.

Ethics. This work does not raise any ethical issues. All the code and data used in this work are available as open source. This work does not rely on any data that compromises the privacy of end users or the security of enterprises.

A   Altitude

Altitude is one of the potential parameters that could affect the network performance of the LEO mega-constellation. However, altitude may not be a factor affecting the absoluteness of the LEO mega-constellation. From the parameter setting of the LEO mega constellation, we can find that although different commercial satellites have different altitude Settings, the most extensive range ranges from 540 km for Starlink to 1325 km for Telesat. However, a change of a few hundred kilometers is only a hundredth of a change for an Earth over ten thousand kilometers across. It is reasonable to assume that the change in distance of several hundred kilometers may make altitude not a factor that can significantly affect the LEO mega-constellation. Our experiment confirms our hypothesis. We estimate the LEO mega-constellations with altitude = 540, 740, 940, and 1140 km, respectively. The other configurations are Orbits = 33, Sats/Orbits = 28, Inclination = 53°.

Altitude is not the Critical Parameter. The experiment result of a) Max. RTT, b) Min. RTT, c) Max. RTT - Min. RTT, d) Max. RTT/Min. RTT, e)

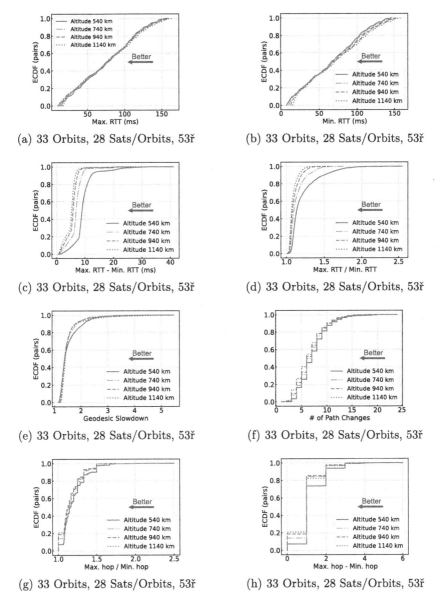

Fig. 18. The performance of changing LEO mega-constellations' Altitude.

Geodesic Slowdown, f) # of Path Change, g) Max. Hop/Min. Hop, h) Max. Hop - Min. Hop are shown in Fig. 18. From the result, we can see the difference in Max. RTT and Min, RTT between different altitude constellations are negligible. The Geodesic Slowdown, # of Path Change, Max. Hop/Min. Hop, Max. Hop - Min. Hop follows the same rules. Only the Max. RTT - Min. RTT,

Max. RTT/Min. RTT shows little difference between different altitude constellations: when the altitude increases, the fluctuation of RTT becomes less. However, the RTT fluctuation of most endpoints pairs is still within 10 ms. From what has been discussed above, we may conclude that altitude is not the critical parameter that could significantly determine the network performance of LEO mega-constellations.

References

1. Akyildiz, I.F., Ekici, E., Bender, M.D.: MLSR: a novel routing algorithm for multilayered satellite IP networks. IEEE/ACM Trans. Netw. **10**(3), 411–424 (2002)
2. Amiri, S., Reif, B.: Internet penetration and its correlation to gross domestic product: an analysis of the nordic countries. Int. J. Bus. Hum. Technol. **3**(2), 50–60 (2013)
3. Angeletti, P., De Gaudenzi, R., Lisi, M.: From "bent pipes" to "software defined payloads": evolution and trends of satellite communications systems. In: 26th International Communications Satellite Systems Conference (ICSSC) (2008)
4. Bai, J., Lu, X., Lu, Z., Peng, W.: A distributed hierarchical routing protocol for non-geo satellite networks. In: Workshops on Mobile and Wireless Networking/High Performance Scientific, Engineering Computing/Network Design and Architecture/Optical Networks Control and Management/Ad Hoc and Sensor Networks/Compil, pp. 148–154. IEEE (2004)
5. Basak, S., Pal, A., Bhattacherjee, D.: Exploring low-earth orbit network design. In: Proceedings of the 1st ACM Workshop on LEO Networking and Communication, pp. 1–6 (2023)
6. Beech, T.W., Cornara, S., Mora, M.B., Lecohier, G.: A study of three satellite constellation design algorithms. In: 14th International Symposium on Space Flight Dynamics (1999)
7. Bhattacherjee, D., Kassing, S., Licciardello, M., Singla, A.: In-orbit computing: an outlandish thought experiment? In: Proceedings of the 19th ACM Workshop on Hot Topics in Networks, pp. 197–204 (2020)
8. Bhattacherjee, D., Singla, A.: Network topology design at 27,000 km/hour. In: Proceedings of the 15th International Conference on Emerging Networking Experiments And Technologies, pp. 341–354 (2019)
9. Bhosale, V., Bhardwaj, K., Saeed, A.: Astrolabe: modeling RTT variability in Leo networks. In: Proceedings of the 1st ACM Workshop on LEO Networking and Communication, pp. 7–12 (2023)
10. Bhosale, V., Saeed, A., Bhardwaj, K., Gavrilovska, A.: A characterization of route variability in Leo satellite networks. In: International Conference on Passive and Active Network Measurement, pp. 313–342. Springer, Cham (2023)
11. Bozkurt, I.N., et al.: Why is the internet so slow?! In: Kaafar, M.A., Uhlig, S., Amann, J. (eds.) PAM 2017. LNCS, vol. 10176, pp. 173–187. Springer, Cham (2017). https://doi.org/10.1007/978-3-319-54328-4_13
12. Chang, H.S., et al.: Topological design and routing for low-earth orbit satellite networks. In: Proceedings of GLOBECOM 1995, vol. 1, pp. 529–535. IEEE (1995)

13. Chen, Q., Giambene, G., Yang, L., Fan, C., Chen, X.: Analysis of inter-satellite link paths for Leo mega-constellation networks. IEEE Trans. Veh. Technol. **70**(3), 2743–2755 (2021)
14. Defence, A., Space, S.: Towards the all optical satellite communications system (2018)
15. Del Portillo, I., Cameron, B.G., Crawley, E.F.: A technical comparison of three low earth orbit satellite constellation systems to provide global broadband. Acta Astronaut. **159**, 123–135 (2019)
16. Gavish, B., Kalvenes, J.: The impact of intersatellite communication links on Leos performance. Telecommun. Syst. **8**, 159–190 (1997)
17. Hagberg, A., Swart, P., S Chult, D.: Exploring network structure, dynamics, and function using networkx. Technical report, Los Alamos National Lab.(LANL), Los Alamos, NM (United States) (2008)
18. Handley, M.: Delay is not an option: low latency routing in space. In: Proceedings of the 17th ACM Workshop on Hot Topics in Networks, pp. 85–91 (2018)
19. Hauri, Y., Bhattacherjee, D., Grossmann, M., Singla, A.: " Internet from space" without inter-satellite links. In: Proceedings of the 19th ACM Workshop on Hot Topics in Networks, pp. 205–211 (2020)
20. Hecht, J.: Laser links will link small satellites to earth and each other. Laser Focus World, marec (2020)
21. Henry, C.: Amazon planning 3,236-satellite constellation for internet connectivity (2019). https://bit.ly/3qdAywU
22. Hougardy, S.: The Floyd-Warshall algorithm on graphs with negative cycles. Inf. Process. Lett. **110**(8–9), 279–281 (2010)
23. Hu, J., Cai, L., Zhao, C., Pan, J.: Directed percolation routing for ultra-reliable and low-latency services in low earth orbit (Leo) satellite networks. In: 2020 IEEE 92nd Vehicular Technology Conference (VTC2020-Fall), pp. 1–6. IEEE (2020)
24. Izhikevich, L., Tran, M., Izhikevich, K., Akiwate, G., Durumeric, Z.: Democratizing Leo satellite network measurement. arXiv preprint arXiv:2306.07469 (2023)
25. Jonathan: Jonathan's space pages starlink statistics (2024). https://planet4589.org/space/con/star/stats.html
26. Kassem, M.M., Raman, A., Perino, D., Sastry, N.: A browser-side view of starlink connectivity. In: Proceedings of the 22nd ACM Internet Measurement Conference, pp. 151–158 (2022)
27. Kassing, S., Bhattacherjee, D., Águas, A.B., Saethre, J.E., Singla, A.: Exploring the "internet from space" with hypatia. In: Proceedings of the ACM Internet Measurement Conference, pp. 214–229 (2020)
28. Kauderer, A., Dismukes, K.: Nasa HSF: definition of two-line element set coordinate system (2011). https://bit.ly/3TU2UIk
29. Leyva-Mayorga, I., et al.: Leo small-satellite constellations for 5G and beyond-5G communications. IEEE Access **8**, 184955–184964 (2020)
30. Li, Z., Zhang, W.M., Chen, W., Hu, Y., Lu, W.: Leo satellite network resilience analysis: a focus on critical satellites. In: Proceedings of the 2nd International Workshop on LEO Networking and Communication, LEO-NET 2024, pp. 13–18. Association for Computing Machinery, New York, (2024). https://doi.org/10.1145/3697253.3697267
31. Mclaughlin, J., Choi, J., Durairajan, R.: × grid: a location-oriented topology design for Leo satellites. In: Proceedings of the 1st ACM Workshop on LEO Networking and Communication, pp. 37–42 (2023)

32. Michel, F., Trevisan, M., Giordano, D., Bonaventure, O.: A first look at starlink performance. In: Proceedings of the 22nd ACM Internet Measurement Conference, pp. 130–136 (2022)
33. Motzigemba, M., Zech, H., Biller, P.: Optical inter satellite links for broadband networks. In: 2019 9th International Conference on Recent Advances in Space Technologies (RAST), pp. 509–512. IEEE (2019)
34. Müncheberg, S., Gal, C., Horwath, J., Kinter, H., Navajas, L.M., Soutullo, M.: Development status and breadboard results of a laser communication terminal for large Leo constellations. In: International Conference on Space Optics, ICSO 2018, vol. 11180, pp. 1180–1192. SPIE (2019)
35. Nordhaus, W., Chen, X.: Global gridded geographically based economic data (g-econ), version 4. NASA Socioeconomic Data and Applications Center (SEDAC) (2016)
36. OneWeb: Oneweb (2023). https://oneweb.net/
37. Pan, T., Huang, T., Li, X., Chen, Y., Xue, W., Liu, Y.: OPSPF: orbit prediction shortest path first routing for resilient Leo satellite networks. In: 2019 IEEE International Conference on Communications (ICC), ICC 2019, pp. 1–6. IEEE (2019)
38. Peluso, A.: Megaconstellations: is it possible to achieve the same performance using fewer satellites? Ph.D. thesis, Politecnico di Torino (2022)
39. Perdices, D., Perna, G., Trevisan, M., Giordano, D., Mellia, M.: When satellite is all you have: watching the internet from 550 ms. In: Proceedings of the 22nd ACM Internet Measurement Conference, pp. 137–150 (2022)
40. Perrig, A., Szalachowski, P., Reischuk, R.M., Chuat, L.: SCION: A Secure Internet Architecture. Springer, Cham (2017)
41. Smutny, B., et al.: 5.6 Gbps optical intersatellite communication link. In: Free-Space Laser Communication Technologies XXI, vol. 7199, pp. 38–45. SPIE (2009)
42. Song, G., Chao, M., Yang, B., Zheng, Y.: TLR: a traffic-light-based intelligent routing strategy for NGEO satellite IP networks. IEEE Trans. Wirel. Commun. **13**(6), 3380–3393 (2014)
43. Soret, B., Leyva-Mayorga, I., Popovski, P.: Inter-plane satellite matching in dense Leo constellations. In: 2019 IEEE Global Communications Conference (GLOBE-COM), pp. 1–6. IEEE (2019)
44. SpaceX: Starlink (2023). https://www.starlink.com
45. Taleb, T., Mashimo, D., Jamalipour, A., Kato, N., Nemoto, Y.: Explicit load balancing technique for NGEO satellite IP networks with on-board processing capabilities. IEEE/ACM Trans. Netw. **17**(1), 281–293 (2008)
46. Telesat: Telesat (2023). https://www.telesat.com
47. Wang, B.: Version 2 starlink with lasers and gen 2 spacex starlink bigger and faster (2021). https://bit.ly/42aJeRT
48. Wang, J., Xu, F., Sun, F.: Benchmarkinng of routing protocols for layered satellite networks. In: The Proceedings of the Multiconference on "Computational Engineering in Systems Applications", vol. 2, pp. 1087–1094. IEEE (2006)
49. Werner, M., Frings, J., Wauquiez, F., Maral, G.: Topological design, routing and capacity dimensioning for ISL networks in broadband Leo satellite systems. Int. J. Satell. Commun. **19**(6), 499–527 (2001)
50. Wikipedia: Bearing (angle). https://bit.ly/4etf1o9
51. Yang, H., et al.: Constellation structure design for Leo mega-constellation with optical intersatellite link. In: 2022 Asia Communications and Photonics Conference (ACP), pp. 1258–1261. IEEE (2022)
52. Zafar, R.: Starlink turns on laser satellites for region with four months long night (2018). https://bit.ly/436aFh7

53. Zhang, W., Xu, Z., Jyothi, S.A.: An in-depth investigation of Leo satellite topology design parameters. In: Proceedings of the 2nd International Workshop on LEO Networking and Communication, LEO-NET 2024, pp. 1–6. Association for Computing Machinery, New York (2024). https://doi.org/10.1145/3697253.3697263
54. Zhang, Y., Wu, Q., Lai, Z., Li, H.: Enabling low-latency-capable satellite-ground topology for emerging Leo satellite networks. In: IEEE Conference on Computer Communications, IEEE INFOCOM 2022, pp. 1329–1338. IEEE (2022)

Analyzing the Effect of an Extreme Weather Event on Telecommunications and Information Technology: Insights from 30 Days of Flooding

Leandro Marcio Bertholdo[1]($\boxtimes$)(iD), Renan Barreto Paredes[2](iD),
Gabriela de Lima Marin[3](iD), Cesar A. H. Loureiro[4](iD),
Milton Kaoru Kashiwakura[3], and Pedro de Botelho Marcos[2](iD)

[1] Federal University of Rio Grande do Sul, Porto Alegre, Brazil
`leandro.bertholdo@ufrgs.br`
[2] Federal University of Rio Grande, Porto Alegre, Brazil
`{renan.paredes,pbmarcos}@furg.br`
[3] Federal Institute of Rio Grande do Sul, Porto Alegre, Brazil
`{gmarin,mkaoruka}@nic.br`
[4] Brazilian Network Information Center (Nic.br), São Paulo, Brazil
`cesar.loureiro@ifrs.edu.br`

Abstract. In May 2024, weeks of severe rainfall in Rio Grande do Sul, Brazil caused widespread damage to infrastructure, impacting over 400 cities and 2.3 million people. This study presents the construction of comprehensive telecommunications datasets during this climatic event, encompassing Internet measurements, fiber cut reports, and Internet Exchange routing data. By correlating network disruptions with hydrological and operational factors, the dataset offers insights into the resilience of fiber networks, data centers, and Internet traffic during critical events. For each scenario, we investigate failures related to the Information and Communication Technology infrastructure and highlight the challenges faced when its resilience is critically tested. Preliminary findings reveal trends in connectivity restoration, infrastructure vulnerabilities, and user behavior changes. These datasets and pre-analysis aim to support future research on disaster recovery strategies and the development of robust telecommunications systems.

Keywords: Internet resilience · Climate event disruptions · Severe weather events · Infrastructure resilience · Brazilian telecommunications

1 Introduction

In May 2024, the state of Rio Grande do Sul, located in southern Brazil, experienced unprecedented severe weather events, resulting in damage to 84% of its cities [50]. This major climatic event caused various disruptions to the state's

C. Testart et al. (Eds.): PAM 2025, LNCS 15567, pp. 276–304, 2025.
https://doi.org/10.1007/978-3-031-85960-1_12

infrastructure, including harm to roads, bridges, electrical plants, data centers, communication systems, and houses, affecting the lives of millions of people. According to the state's Civil Defense Department, displaced individuals exceeded 300,000 and affected 2.3 million people [51]. Economic activity in the area was reduced by 94%, affecting commerce and industry [17].

In disaster scenarios such as this, communication systems play a critical role for several reasons. First, they facilitate coordination among rescue teams, enabling them to locate individuals needing assistance. Second, they allow individuals to communicate with family and friends, informing them of their safety and sharing crowd-sourced information, such as reports of blocked roads and damaged bridges. Finally, communication systems support the continuity of public services and economic activities, helping to maintain order and prevent looting in stores and supermarkets.

During this event, Rio Grande do Sul's communication systems and infrastructure were severely strained as some of its elements were partially or entirely disrupted by the consequences of the climate event. In this paper, we investigate how these events affected the resilience of the infrastructure and operations of the communications systems in Rio Grande do Sul. We analyze data from multiple sources and provide insight to improve ICT infrastructures.

We organize this paper as follows. Section 2 outlines the climate events and their impact on ICT infrastructures. Sections 3 through 5 examine disruptions to fiber networks, data centers, and long-distance circuits. Sections 6 and 7 analyze the impact on the regional Internet Exchange (IXP) and the perceived impact on Internet quality for end users, respectively. Section 8 assesses recovery efforts, while Sect. 9 compares this case with other weather-related events. Section 10 discusses lessons learned, and Sect. 11 highlights open challenges and future research directions.

2   Background and Sequence of Events

The unprecedented severe weather events of May 2024 caused catastrophic damage across 418 municipalities in Rio Grande do Sul, significantly impacting the state capital, Porto Alegre, and its metropolitan area. The civil defense classified the event as a Level III on a scale of four [50]. The most recent flooding event of similar magnitude occurred 83 years ago, in 1941, leading to the city constructing a flood protection system.

The disaster began with heavy rainfall on April 27 and intensified on April 29. The volume of rainfall surpassed 1,000 mm in the region (1 m of water height per square meter of land) [39], significantly impacting the valleys of the Taquari, Caí, Jacuí, Sinos, and Gravataí rivers. All these rivers are part of the so-called Guaíba Basin, flowing into the Guaíba River, which runs through the capital, Porto Alegre. The Guaíba River flows first into the Lagoa dos Patos and then to the ocean. The Lagoa dos Patos is the largest lagoon in South America, with a length of 265 km (map on Fig. 1).

In smaller cities, accumulated rainfall was the primary cause of flooding, while in the metropolitan area and the capital, natural and human factors contributed

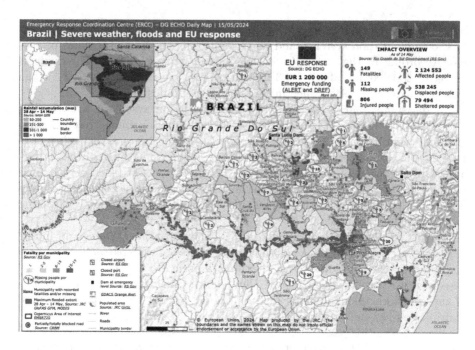

Fig. 1. Map of the areas affected by the 2024 floods in the state of Rio Grande do Sul. Source: ERCC GPM, Rio Grande do Sul Government, Copernicus EMSR.

to it. In addition to the high rainfall, strong winds prevented the water from Lagoa dos Patos from flowing into the ocean, creating a natural blockage and leading to excessive water accumulation in the Guaíba River, which caused prolonged flooding in the metropolitan area [24]. Furthermore, decades of neglected maintenance and updates to the Porto Alegre flood protection system increased the impacts of the disaster [28]. The flood protection system comprises 68 km of dikes, a protective wall, 23 pumping stations, and 14 floodgates [37].

The bad weather persisted for a month. During this time, forecast models from the Institute of Hydraulic Research at the Federal University of Rio Grande do Sul (IPH/UFRGS) accurately predicted the situation several days in advance. Using US (dashed blue) and EU (red) weather models, they projected a return to normal water levels by mid-June. Figure 2 illustrates the water level behavior during this period. The Guaíba River receded below the alert level on June 7th, but issues in the city's drainage system prolonged water retention in some areas.

This disaster underscores the severity of the climatic event and the extensive disruptions it caused to infrastructure and the lives of people in Rio Grande do Sul. The timeline of the disaster is presented in Table 1.

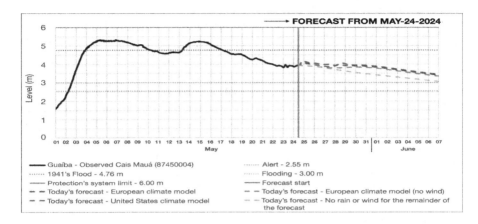

Fig. 2. Guaíba water level measurement and forecast [33].

Table 1. Significant events related to the flooding in Porto Alegre. Events affecting ICT infrastructure are marked.

Date	Event
April 27	The first storm impacts the Vale do Rio Pardo region [25]. Over 1,200 lightning strikes were recorded in Porto Alegre, making fiber cable maintenance unfeasible due to the risk of electrical discharge.
April 28	The National Institute of Meteorology (Inmet) issues an orange alert for storms across the state's southern half.
April 29	The energy grid is affected, and the shortage is a consequence of the heavy rain, wind, and hail recorded over the weekend. Several communities are isolated. Inmet has issued a red alert, indicating the onset of a major disaster.
April 30	The first deaths are reported, roads blocked, and bridges washed away. Guaíba River floods riverside areas and a state of emergency is declared.
May 1	Heavy rains cause landslides and widespread flooding, prompting evacuations in high-risk areas.
May 2	The last RNP fiber optics backbone redundancy failed, isolating the state's academic network. The Guaíba River reached a flood level of 3.60 meters for the first time.
May 3	Severe impacts in Porto Alegre include major transportation disruptions and infrastructure damage. Guaíba reaches 4.77 meters, breaking the 1941 record. Salgado Filho Airport closes, and communities in seven cities are evacuated.
May 4	The incumbent data center (ELEA-POA2) is shutdown [15].
May 5	The Guaíba River continues to rise, reaching a new historical peak of 5.35 meters. Main roads to Porto Alegre interrupted.
May 6	Mobile operators enabled free roaming on 3G, 4G, and 5G networks [8]. The PROCERGS data center was shut down [13], and the Scala data center ceased operations after three days on generators [53]. The government granted ISPs access to emergency roads, restricted to rescue operations, for cable repairs [14].
May 7	Long-distance circuit failures registered around 20% at PoP-RS/RNP, isolating several universities, hospitals, and research centers.
May 9	PROCERGS, PoP-RS/RNP, and CPFL-T share fiber and infrastructure in Porto Alegre to relocate the state government's crisis office.
May 20	Riots involving burning public transport buses caused new fiber cuts [29].
June 1	The Guaíba River level fell below the flooding level [22].
June 3	Guaíba River level rises again, surpassing the flood level [23].
June 7	The Guaíba River returns to its banks for the first time in a month [21].

3   Optical Fiber Networks

To investigate the impacts on optical fiber networks, we analyzed data from two backbone networks: an academic network (Metropoa) and an Internet Service Provider (ISP) backbone. The Metropoa network [44] is a 190 km optical fiber infrastructure in the Porto Alegre metropolitan area, connecting approximately 180,000 individuals across educational institutions, research centers, and university hospitals. Approximately 85% of its fiber paths are aerial, with the remaining 15% underground. The ISP operates a 500 km backbone network and an additional 2,000 km of last-mile infrastructure, serving 60,000 households, 20,000 of which were affected during the event.

In Brazil, most fiber is aerial, installed at a height of 4 m on utility poles, making it highly susceptible to climate events. During the incident, rescue teams intentionally cut many cables to allow the passage of high trucks and boats carrying rescued individuals, preventing accidents. Additionally, there was an increase in cable cuts for copper theft, often involving loose cables left hanging on power poles. Field technicians distinguish stolen cables, identified by straight cuts, from naturally broken cables, which typically show unevenly torn internal fibers. This information is documented in the Metrofiber datasets [3], which offer opportunities for further analysis and insights.

Here, we correlate a series of events affecting the Metropoa network over time and map the impact of climate-related events on this optical network in recent years. Both direct and indirect climate-related events are considered. Direct events include tree falls on cables during storms or cyclones, while indirect events involve cable breakages caused by fires triggered by damage to the electrical network during rainstorms.

In Fig. 3, we illustrate the impact of climate-related events on the number of cable damages in the aerial portion of the academic network between 2022 and 2024. These events include Cyclone Yakecan in May 2022 [20], thunderstorms in March 2023 [27], January 2024 [40], and March 2024 [9], as well as a significant flooding event in May 2024 [5] and the subsequent rebuilding process. Similar results for the ISP backbone are presented in Appendix.

The bad weather also increased the mean time to repair aerial cable cuts, as electrical storms made climbing poles to fix cables unsafe. This situation typically delayed repairs by one or two days. However, aerial networks made it possible to create new emergency paths or reconnect customers and servers by moving their ICT infrastructure to other locations, as the underground fiber was hard to access in these cases. On the other hand, no damage was recorded in the underground fiber network analyzed (two events in the last 12 years on 28 km of fiber). The reliability of the underground network proved advantageous, providing a secure path that enabled the network owner to offer fiber routes to institutions whose networks or data centers were damaged. By "reliable", we refer to a cable with all fiber routes intact, *i.e.*, all fibers fused in each splice box. Typically, providers only fuse active fibers, leaving unused fibers unfused in splice boxes to reduce repair costs.

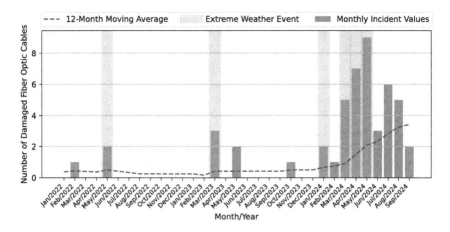

Fig. 3. Optical cable cuts and weather-related events in a fiber network backbone.

Following the 2022 cyclone, the municipality of Porto Alegre enacted a law requiring all energy and telecommunication cables to be installed underground within 15 years [6]. The new law was approved in May 2023, a year before the major flooding event. The Internet Providers Association estimates that underground installations are 50 times more expensive than aerial ones, with added challenges such as higher costs for fault detection and repairs [32]. Nationally, only 1% of energy and fiber cables are underground, compared to 10% in São Paulo and 9% in Porto Alegre, where underground installations are estimated to be 15 times more expensive than aerial alternatives [58].

Takeaway: Underground networks are more resilient to climate events than aerial ones. A resilient city should prioritize underground optical paths, ensuring all fibers, including unused ones, are pre-fused, and establish plans for alternative interconnections during emergencies.

4   Data Centers in the Region

In recent years, the municipality of Porto Alegre has incentivized businesses to establish operations in the 4th District, near the Guaíba River, by offering tax reductions [19]. This district, known for its proximity to the city center and airport, has become a hub for data centers, including ELEA-POA2, Scala Datacenter, and BRDigital Datacenter. Located along the banks of the Guaíba and Jacuí Rivers, these facilities were severely impacted by the flooding.

Starting on May 3, severe flooding in Porto Alegre caused the shutdown of several small and large data centers. A total of 21 out of the city's 35 known facilities went offline. Notable affected centers included the Court of Justice of Rio Grande do Sul (TJRS) [10], the Federal Court of Justice for the 4th Region (TRF4) [11], the Brazilian Micro and Small Business Support Service (SEBRAE-

RS) [54], ELEA-POA2, the incumbent[1] data center [15], and Scala Datacenter, a Tier-3 facility hosting an interconnection for the Rio Grande do Sul IXP [53].

The most significant incident occurred on May 6, 2024, involving the PRO-CERGS data center, a public facility responsible for data processing for the Rio Grande do Sul state government, located on reclaimed river land. Following a government decision to shut down a pumping station to mitigate the population's electric shock risk, the data center suffered extensive damage to its electrical systems and backup generators. Authorities shut down the facility to prevent further damage and potential data loss, leading to widespread outages that disrupted critical government services—such as online identity verification, tax processing, and social security payments. The main systems remained offline for over eleven days [48]. The incident underscored the vulnerability of critical infrastructure to extreme weather events.

In contrast, there were notable examples of resilience and adaptability. The BRDigital data center, located 600 m from the Guaíba River, continued to operate successfully by transporting fuel via boats into the building for its generators (details in [61]). The Bank of the State of Rio Grande do Sul (Banrisul) switched their operations to their second data center in the city, and the incumbent shifted 80% of their operations from ELEA-POA2 to ELEA-POA1, the last one located on higher ground. Data centers situated on high floors in flooded areas (e.g., the 25th floor), primarily used for radio and cellular network operations, faced unique challenges in maintaining fuel supplies. They relied on manual transport, boats, or external cranes to deliver fuel. After a week, these high-floor data centers were turned off.

Some other data centers near the flooded area were unaffected, such as the Federal University of Rio Grande do Sul and the municipality data processing center (PROCEMPA). In Fig. 4, we show a map of all known data centers in the city that were either shut down or continued operating during the flooding.

In the days following, various levels of government accelerated their migration to cloud solutions [59,64]. Meanwhile, smaller companies sought to rescue their servers and data to temporarily host them with any operational collocation provider in the region, aiming to resume at least part of their operations.

These responses highlight the importance of robust risk analysis in data center standards. The Brazilian NBR ISO/IEC 22237 series standards mention business risk analysis but do not specifically address flooding. The second part of this standard specifies minimum distances from specific locations such as airports, rivers, and gas stations. It is worth to mention some data centers are currently situated less than 100 m from the Guaíba River.

The ISO 27000 information security standard includes a specific table for environmental risks, including floods, where assets are located. This table classifies events as rare, frequent, and common, and these analyses are typically based on occurrences from the past 5 to 10 years to develop mitigation plans, not cov-

---

[1] The company managing the former government-owned telecom infrastructure under a concession agreement.

Fig. 4. Map showing data centers in Porto Alegre. Yellow pins indicate data centers shut down due to floods. Green pins represent those that remained active. The red area shows the water level on May 6th (5.35 m). (Color figure online)

ering the last flooding. This recent event will likely impact new risk analyses, discouraging the construction of new data centers in those flooded areas.

Takeaway: During a 30-day flood, keeping electrical generators operational and fueled is challenging. Ensure backup data centers are 30 km away, preferably at higher elevations. This event should influence future risk analysis in this area.

5   The National Research and Education Network (RNP) and Long-Distance (WAN) Circuits

The Point-of-Presence of the National Research and Education Network in Rio Grande do Sul (PoP-RS) provides high-bandwidth Internet access for the academic and research community, including several major university hospitals. PoP-RS/RNP is hosted in the Federal University of Rio Grande do Sul Data Center (CPD-UFRGS), which remained unaffected during this critical period. In this section, we analyze how the long-distance connections from PoP-RS behaved during this time.

Before the event, from April 20 to 26, no customer circuits were unavailable for more than 24 h. There were isolated issues from April 27 to 30, but still without a direct relation to the flood. However, starting on May 1, the number of problems increased significantly, reaching 19.7% unavailable circuits (see Fig. 5). After May 31, the number of circuits unavailable for more than 24 h had returned to normal. Upon deeper analysis, we found that these were institutions whose internal structures were affected by the flood. From May 1 to 31, 237 Internet circuit failures occurred in long-distance connections.

Fig. 5. Percentage of long-distance (WAN) circuits down for more than 24 h at PoP-RS/RNP.

A second fact is related to long-distance circuits connecting the PoP-RS to the National RNP backbone and, consequently, to the Internet. The PoP-RS has four circuits of 100Gbps to the RNP backbone: two paths using OPGW (Optical Ground Wire) fiber via Eletrosul power towers connecting to two other state capitals, PR (Paraná) and SC (Santa Catarina); one circuit via the BRDigital telecom operator, also to the PR capital; and one circuit via the Latin American Cooperation Network (RedClara) that connects PoP-RS to SP (São Paulo) but with a high RTT (Round-Trip Time) of around 100ms, due to the cable route passing through Uruguay, Argentina and Chile before SP.

During the climatic events on May 2, all backbone circuits were unavailable for 11 h due to landslides in the Serra Gaúcha region. Partial restoration occurred after maintenance on one of the power towers, which remained at risk of collapse for 3 days. Despite having four distinct circuits, it is crucial to consider the complete path of the circuits. In the observed situation, all cables were close to BR-116, which crosses the Serra Gaúcha (highlands in the state heavily affected at the event's beginning). Full operation was normalized only after the BrDigital operator rerouted its circuit along the coastal route via BR-101.

Maintaining the RNP connection to the countryside and national and international Internet access supported various activities, from assisting the civil defense in predicting flooding effects in the city by connecting research groups from the university, such as the hydrology department at UFRGS responsible for water level projections, to allowing those sheltering inside university facilities around the state to communicate with their families through free internet access.

Takeaway: The academic infrastructure for Internet connections, as well as for other ISPs, has only three routes out of the state: the main roads BR-101 and BR-116, and the high-tension (OPGW) network. Thus, to increase resilience, telecommunications companies should create new paths.

6   The Rio Grande do sul Internet Exchange Perspective

During these events, many ISPs and data centers had their infrastructures affected. They lost connectivity to their upstream and the Rio Grande do Sul Internet eXchange Point (IX.RS), leading to a 50% decrease in traffic volumes [55]. Figure 6 compares the traffic volumes during the first two weeks of the events. According to operators from IX.RS, the increasing traffic volume in the second-week results from (sixteen) ISPs recovering their connectivity to the IXP.

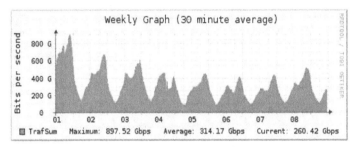

a IX.RS experienced a traffic loss from May 1 to May 7, 2024.

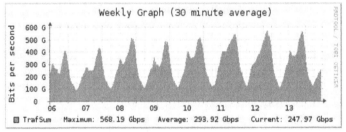

b Traffic recovery of IX.RS after its lowest point on May 6.

Fig. 6. The chart illustrates the IXP's traffic loss from May 1–6, followed by a recovery beginning on May 7. Traffic peaked at approximately 400 Gbit/s on May 6–7 and stabilized around 600 Gbit/s after May 13. As of November 2024, the IXP has not fully recovered to its typical level of around 1 Tbit/s, and the exact reasons for the traffic not fully recovering are still under investigation. X-axis represents days in May 2024.

In this section, we analyze routing data from IX-RS route servers (April 16 - May 24) to investigate the severe events' impact on connectivity and routes at the Porto Alegre IXP. A route server in an IXP is a critical component that simplifies and optimizes the exchange of routing information among participants [49]. These data are part of the SARA project, a Portuguese acronym for Routing Analysis System for Autonomous Systems [42].

We first analyze the connectivity impacts of connected members, reachable ASes, announced prefixes, and available routes on IX-RS. We show these results in Fig. 7, where we have the unfiltered results of the routing data from IX-RS. On April 27, considered the first storm of this event, the number of reachable ASes dropped around 10.1% to 5389 ASes compared to April 26. Although it did recover, as the storms progressed and the water level kept rising, we saw a similar drop on April 30.

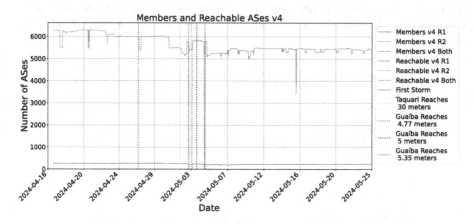

Fig. 7. RSIX customer reachability.

During the flooding of Porto Alegre and the Taquari River, surpassing 30 m, the number of reachable ASes and members significantly declined. On May 2, compared to April 26, reachable ASes dropped to 5,135 (a 14.4% decrease), and members fell to 245 (an 11.2% decrease). By May 5 at 05:51 AM UTC, these numbers declined to 5,093 reachable ASes (15.1%) and 185 members (33%). Notably, by May 24, the number of reachable ASes had not yet returned to regular levels. The drop in reachable ASes observed on May 15 is still under investigation. However, this drop did not involve ASes located in Rio Grande do Sul, as filtering the data for prefixes, members, or ASes in the state reveals no corresponding decline (Fig. 8).

By filtering to prefixes, members, or reachable ASes geolocated in the state of Rio Grande do Sul, we consider only instances where a member is located in the state or can reach a prefix, or AS, located in the state. With these criteria, we evaluate the connections provided by members in the state and the connections towards ASes in the state. When filtering the data, we observe that the first storm did not significantly impact the number of members or reachable ASes that meet the mentioned criteria. A decline can be seen, culminating in a sharp drop of members and reachable ASes on May 3rd, down 17% and 53%, respectively, together with Route Server 2 failing. The same happens again on May 4th, although in a shorter period, where we see a decline of 27.8% of members and 54.6% of reachable ASes. By May 24th, the number of ASes had not recovered, and they even suffered another drop on May 23rd due to another rainfall.

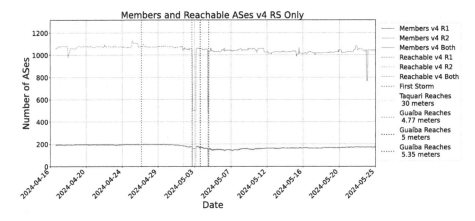

Fig. 8. RSIX customer reachability filtered by geolocation.

We also analyze the average path size of the routes announced at IX-RS of ASes from Rio Grande do Sul during the flooding period. We show these results in Fig. 9. We can notice that as the flooding propagates through the state, the path to each remaining network increases its average length (IPv4).

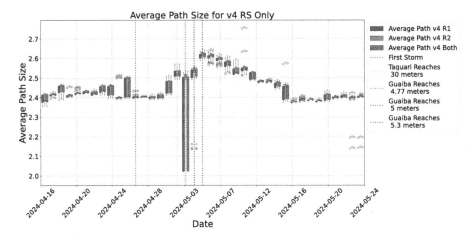

Fig. 9. Average path size on Rio Grande do Sul Internet Exchange during the most critical period.

Also, the first sharp decline in ASes, when the Guaíba River reached 4.77 m, reflected on the average path, especially in the 25th percentile, suggesting that the aforementioned decline affected routes with longer paths. The average path length started decreasing on the following days; by May 16, it had returned to similar levels before the floods began.

Despite the observable reduction in the number of connections and an increase in average path length, the IX-RS effectively maintained connectivity between ASes within Rio Grande do Sul and external ASes. This can be seen on May 7, when the number of members decreased by 25% while the number of reachable ASes only dropped 3%, taking into account both ASes (or prefixes) within the state and ASes connected through paths to those located in the state. It is important to note that the redundancy of route servers played a critical role in mitigating the impact of disruptions, particularly during critical moments such as May 3.

However, a thorough evaluation of how redundancy is implemented, along with the supporting infrastructure, is necessary to reduce the likelihood of route server failure. Such an evaluation would help ensure that potential failures do not propagate to other route servers, thereby preserving network stability. The Internet Exchange infrastructure comprises geographically diverse interconnection points (PIX) where customers connect. This structure is linked to a central node. Two route servers exist, one in the central node and one in another PIX.

Takeaway: The IX infrastructure was largely unaffected; however, having the central point redundancy in the exact physical location raises concerns. It is necessary to evaluate how redundancy is implemented and assess the supporting infrastructure to reduce the risk of failure in the Route Servers and the central structure.

7   SIMET Data: The End-User View

SIMET, a Portuguese acronym for Traffic Measurement System [7], has measured Internet quality in Brazil since 2005. Operated by NIC.br on behalf of the Brazilian Internet Steering Committee, the system enables quality tests through two methods: (1) on-demand tests used by end-users via a website or mobile application and (2) periodic tests conducted by software installed on personal computers, often in government-operated schools [56] and healthcare units [57]. This software is installed in 5,171 public schools across Rio Grande do Sul (vantage points), performing measurements every four hours. End-users within the state perform multiple on-demand measurements daily from over 100 different devices (vantage points).

In our first analysis, we compared the timeline of on-demand measurements from end users and schools to understand Internet activity in the region before, during, and after the event. During the analyzed period, we observed a notable increase in on-demand activity among end users. Specifically, 424 users conducted 1,085 tests between April 8 and April 12 (before the events), 567 users conducted 1,572 measurements between May 6 and May 10 (critical phase), and 474 users conducted 1,268 measurements between June 3 and June 7 (post-event) in Rio Grande do Sul.

Figure 10a illustrates the number of distinct end-user vantage points that performed measurements during this period. Historical data from the operator suggests that end users typically measure Internet quality when they experience or perceive poor connectivity. This behavior is evidenced by a 33% increase in users and a 45% increase in measurements during the critical phase. Notably, the number of users conducting measurements peaked on the day the Taquari River reached 30 m, representing a 63% increase compared to the highest measurement volume during the baseline period (April 8–26). Following this peak, the number of measurements gradually returned to typical levels.

It is important to note that this peak in activity was primarily observed in less affected cities. In contrast, the most affected areas experienced a decline in the number of users conducting measurements. This decline may indicate a broader reduction in users' ability to measure Internet quality during the most critical phases of the event. For additional details, refer to Appendix.

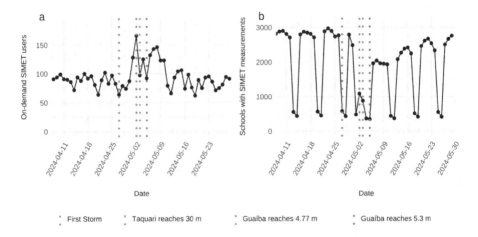

Fig. 10. Aggregate view of SIMET vantage points for (a) end-users and (b) schools in Rio Grande do Sul state, covering the baseline (April 8–26), the critical phase (May 1–10), and the following period (from May 23 onward). Weekend activity is consistently lower.

The observed increase in end-user activity on working days coincided with a decrease in school measurements during the event (Fig. 10b). Between April 8–12, 4,149 schools measured Internet quality at least once (around 3,000 per active day), compared to 3,182 schools from May 6–10. Recovery began on May 13, with 3,800 schools measuring Internet quality between May 27–31. This decline is attributed to school closures during the event, resulting in computers being turned off.

In our second analysis, we evaluate the spatial distribution of the end-users' and schools' measurements before and during the event. The overall increase in SIMET end-user measurements was not observed in the entire state. On-demand measurements increased in less affected cities but decreased in most affected ones (*i.e.*, Porto Alegre, Canoas, Eldorado Do Sul, Guaíba and Lajeado) during the event (Table 2).

Table 2. Number of on-demand measurements for the most and least affected cities, along with the percentage of measurements for each period (before, during, and after the weather events of May 2024). The most affected cities are Porto Alegre, Canoas, Eldorado do Sul, Guaíba, and Lajeado.

Time period	Most affected cities	Other cities
08 to 12-April-2024	230 (21.2%)	855 (78.8%)
06 to 10-May-2024	151 (9.6%)	1421 (90.4%)
03 to 07-June-2024	305 (24.1%)	963 (75.9%)

It is possible to observe a vacuum of measurements in the flooded area during the weeks following the flood (Fig. 12b). Although this decrease is not expected according to the idea that users measure the Internet quality when they are not satisfied, it can be explained by both a complete lack of Internet access, preventing users from being able to complete the measurement, or due to rearranging priorities (*i.e.*, people were using less the Internet because they were worried about other things). Further investigations should be able to determine which of these factors, if any, was the most important.

For the less affected cities, the expected increase indicates a perception of worsened Internet quality followed by a recovery after the event. In Table 3, we computed the quality measurements for end-users in the most affected cities. As mentioned, the median bandwidth for fixed and mobile Internet access diminished, but the mean round-trip-time (RTT) remained constant. A deeper investigation is needed to isolate areas inside each city. It is worth remembering that cities were divided between the flooding zones, where people lost their homes, and other parts, where life was close to normal.

Table 3. Statistics on SIMET measurements, median bandwidth, and RTT for fixed and mobile networks.

Time Period	Percentage of measurements from the total	Fixed Median bandwidth (Mbps)	Mobile Median bandwidth (Mbps)	Fixed Median RTT (ms)	Mobile Median RTT (ms)
08 to 12-April-2024	33.5%	94.4	119.5	31.9	28.6
06 to 10-May-2024	22.0%	92.7	101.2	31.3	23.7
03 to 07-June-2024	44.5%	92.0	69.5	33.4	36.7

As expected, the difference in the number of schools measuring Internet quality is not homogeneously distributed in space. The most affected cities, usually representing 6.1% of total measuring schools, suffered a greater decrease, representing 2.3% and 4.4% of measuring schools during and after the event. There was a decrease of 71% of schools measuring in the most affected cities between April and the beginning of May compared to only 23% in less affected cities. This decrease was observed in the flooded and immediate areas around it (Fig. 11). It is worth mentioning that among the six schools that sent measurements during the event and are located in a flooded area (Fig. 11b), five changed the ASN and IP addresses during the event. These schools' measurements went through 5, 4, 2, 1, and 1 IP addresses and 4, 2, 2, 1, and 1 different AS, respectively. This suggests that the computers with the software installed were relocated and subsequently activated in these new locations, enabling measurements during this period. We visited five schools in June, which remained inoperative after the event, and confirmed that some computers had been moved to another place.

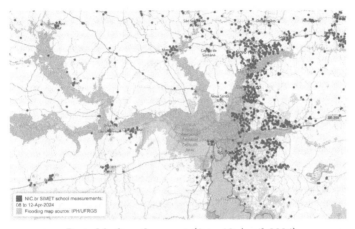

a Period before the event (8 to 12 April 2024).

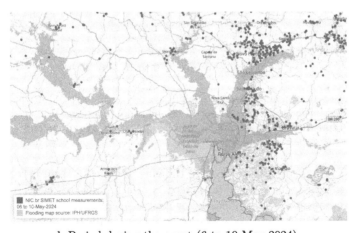

b Period during the event (6 to 10 May 2024).

Fig. 11. Measurements from public schools in 27 municipalities near the Porto Alegre metropolitan area with at least one Internet quality measurement recorded within a five-day period, before and during the events of May 2024.

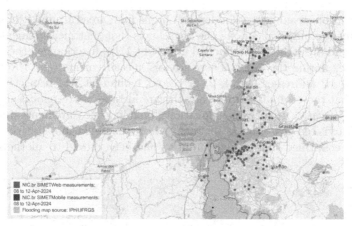

a Period before the event (08 to 12 April 2024).

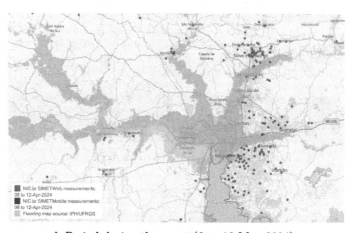

b Period during the event (6 to 10 May 2024).

Fig. 12. End-users on-demand measurements received from Porto Alegre metropolitan area before and during the events in May 2024. Blue dots represent web measurements; purple dots represent measurements via mobile app. (Color figure online)

Takeaway: It was possible to observe the effect of the flood on perceived end-user Internet experience along with its recovery for less affected cities considering both on-demand and school measurements. By combining these two types of measurements, it may be possible to detect critical failures in similar events.

8 Post-flooding Impact Assessment and Recovery Efforts

Five months after the event, numerous institutions are still recovering their networks and data centers. Internet connection prices have remained stable, and providers are actively replacing home equipment that was damaged or lost during the floods at no additional cost to customers. Since the onset of the disaster, the ISP Provider Association has been actively involved in collecting donations and redistributing resources to various small ISPs to mitigate their losses and support the rebuilding of their networks. Several key indicators have been provided to guide these efforts [31]. The provider association estimates a 36-month timeline to restore ISP operations to pre-event conditions, with total losses projected at R\$ 2 billion (US\$ 380 million).

Several institutions that previously operated their data centers have opted to migrate their operations to cloud-based solutions or relocate to unaffected data centers in other cities or states. The recent event has likely prompted one of the primary data center providers in the region to announce plans for constructing a new facility in an unaffected area. The proposed site is 34 km from the existing data center and is situated near significant power lines [52]. However, this presumed motivation has yet to be officially confirmed.

Of the 4,149 schools for which regular measurements were taken in April 2024, 181 (approximately 4.36%) remain non-operational since the event. Some of these schools reported total losses of ICT equipment, with recovery contingent upon government funding to replace the lost assets.

The local Internet Exchange Point (IXP) has not yet recovered to its pre-event traffic volume, remaining approximately 23% below prior levels. Despite this, all AS members have resumed active status. The number of ASes geolocated within the state[2] and reachable through the local IXP increased from 1,060 on April 16th to 1,141 on October 2nd, representing a 7% growth and continuing the trend observed before the event (Fig. 13).

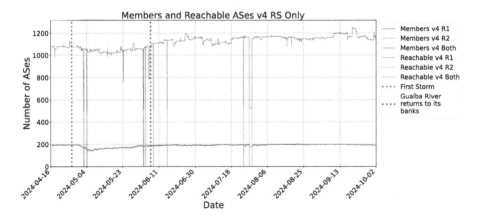

Fig. 13. Reachable ASes from the Rio Grande do Sul Internet Exchange Point.

---

[2] Those ASes with a registrant (owner) address in Rio Grande do Sul, based on an AS list provided by NIC.br.

IXP customers utilizing protected connectivity returned to normal parameters by June 2024 (take as reference Fig. 5). However, customers relying on unprotected fiber continued to experience a significant number of incidents for several months after May 2024, as issues involving fiber networks persisted due to city reconstruction efforts (refer to Fig. 3 and Appendix).

9 Related Work

Infrastructure resilience during extreme weather events, particularly within the telecommunications sector, has been extensively studied. These studies include analyses of the economic impacts [18,34], explorations of resilience metrics and methodologies [35,36,47,65], and investigations of the aftermath and recovery processes [12,16]. More recently, attention has shifted towards enhancing critical systems' resilience through machine learning approaches [1,35].

Most of these studies examine short-duration events like hurricanes, earthquakes, and storms. To the best of our knowledge, the most relevant comparisons to our research, based on documented events, are the flooding in New Orleans following Hurricane Katrina [38,41,43] and in Puerto Rico following Hurricanes Irma and Maria [12], which occurred in 2005 and 2017, respectively.

Hurricane Katrina severely impacted the Gulf Coast's telecommunications infrastructure, particularly in New Orleans, where extensive flooding and high winds caused widespread damage. The storm overwhelmed much of the region's communications infrastructure, including wireline networks and cellular systems. Over 70% of cellular sites were rendered inoperable, and widespread flooding damaged underground cables and key communication nodes [30]. In New Orleans, the failure of power supplies and fuel shortages for backup generators exacerbated the situation, leaving vast areas without communication for an extended period. Major failures were linked to three key issues: (1) flooding that damaged infrastructure, (2) insufficient power and fuel for backup generators, and (3) the failure of redundant pathways, which severely affected network resilience. Additionally, limited coordination between the communications industry and government agencies further delayed response efforts, compounded by inadequate security measures for infrastructure and personnel. A significant lesson learned from Katrina was the critical role of data accessibility in disaster response. The scarcity of publicly available data during the aftermath hindered recovery efforts, leading to initiatives such as the Climate Data Initiative to enhance open-data sharing [16]. This issue persisted even a decade after the disaster [63], prompting a governmental initiative to improve open-data access through efforts such as the Climate Data Initiative [62]. The experiences from Katrina have informed current disaster preparedness and emphasized the importance of ensuring reliable telecommunications during crises.

As discussed in [12], following two hurricanes, Puerto Rico's wireline, wireless, and cable networks were mainly rendered inoperable. The wireline telecommunications infrastructure was particularly affected, as it predominantly relied on aerial fiber-optic cables for cellular backhaul. By being exposed to environmental elements, these cables were highly vulnerable to storm damage, primarily because many were supported by poorly maintained poles owned by the Puerto Rico Electric Power Authority (PREPA). The hurricanes caused extensive damage, with over 90% of the private telecommunications infrastructure, including antennas and aerial cables, being affected. In the immediate aftermath, 95% of cellular sites were out of service, and 48 of 78 municipalities completely lost cellular connectivity. As a result, citizens were without Internet access or the ability to reach emergency services, such as 911, for weeks or even months. In response to the disaster, the Homeland Security Analysis Center proposed 33 courses of action (COAs) to improve the resilience of Puerto Rico's telecommunications infrastructure. These include enhancing network robustness and redundancy, strengthening emergency communications, implementing regulatory reforms, and establishing funding mechanisms. Some proposals are notably innovative, such as involving local communities in the planning and implementation processes to ensure the infrastructure meets their specific needs, and fostering Public-Private Partnerships (PPP) to fund and deploy more resilient broadband infrastructure.

The severe weather events in the Rio Grande do Sul, New Orleans, and Puerto Rico share several similarities regarding their impacts on telecommunications infrastructure. Both Puerto Rico and the Rio Grande do Sul heavily relied on aerial fiber-optic cables, which led to significant damage during hurricanes and floods. Similarly, New Orleans saw widespread damage to underground cables (Cooper) caused by flooding during Hurricane Katrina, and in Rio Grande do Sul, it was caused by landside and bridge collapse. Power and fuel shortages for generators were a common issue, and there were also reports of portable generators and other equipment being stolen. Rio Grande do Sul faced similar power-related challenges, with critical data centers shutting down due to floodwaters, further disrupting services. The loss of connectivity was also a significant outcome across all cases. The number of outages in cellular service was similar, with around 50% of cities being affected in Rio Grande do Sul [2].

Despite these similarities, there are notable differences between the three cases. In New Orleans, the damage primarily affected underground copper cables and communication nodes, whereas in Porto Alegre, although the underground fiber cables were inaccessible, no damage was reported, facilitating the recovery process for end-users broadband clients. The duration and extent of the impact also varied significantly. In Puerto Rico, connectivity losses persisted for months in some regions, reflecting a larger scale of infrastructure destruction. In contrast, in Rio Grande do Sul, the recovery process, though extensive, was already underway during the event. This rapid response may be attributed to the structure of the fiber and broadband market in Brazil. Large operators account for approximately 45% of broadband users and 35% of the optical fiber infrastructure, with the remaining market share distributed among thousands of smaller operators. These smaller operators collaborated by donating and sharing equipment, personnel, and fiber resources, which facilitated recovery efforts despite disruptions in transportation and supply chains.

Another key distinction is that when the New Orleans Central Exchange Office (CEO) was flooded, a major failure occurred in the phone system, whereas in Rio Grande do Sul, critical operations were shifted to a secondary data center located on higher ground, minimizing the impact of the disaster. Regarding Internet access, in the New Orleans region, connectivity to the rest of the country experienced minor interruptions, with less than 10% of ASes losing connectivity, while in Rio Grande do Sul, this figure exceeded 53% in one day.

The comparison of telecommunications infrastructure impacts in New Orleans, Puerto Rico, and Rio Grande do Sul highlights common challenges, such as widespread connectivity loss, infrastructure damage, and power shortages. However, significant differences emerged in the scale of damage and recovery timelines. While Puerto Rico experienced prolonged outages due to extensive destruction of aerial infrastructure, Rio Grande do Sul's recovery was more rapid, aided by market structure, collaborative efforts among smaller operators, and less damage in poles. Conversely, Rio Grande do Sul had a more significant impact on data centers in the area.

10   Lessons Learned

The extreme weather event that struck Rio Grande do Sul in May 2024 is a significant case study for understanding the resilience of telecommunications and information technology infrastructure. The extensive damage caused by severe rainfall and flooding highlighted some lessons for improving and enhancing ICT operations. We list the main ones here:

The Importance of Resilience in Fiber Infrastructure: Underground fiber networks have demonstrated greater resilience than aerial fibers during extreme weather events. However, their effectiveness depends on being *"consistent"* before incidents such as flooding. A resilient city should prioritize the placement of primary optical paths underground and establish contingency plans for alternative interconnection routes in emergencies.

Proactive Risk Management: Robust risk analysis in data center standards is essential. The NBR ISO/IEC data center standards should include comprehensive business risk analyses covering all known terrain situations, not just a recent window time of 5–10 years. This approach helps develop effective mitigation plans and ensures data centers are better prepared for such events.

Community and Collaborative Efforts: Community efforts and collaborations between ISPs, data centers, and government agencies were crucial in restoring services. Sharing equipment, cables, data center space, and resources greatly aided recovery efforts. Universities and academic infrastructure played a key role in supporting civil defense and other essential services, likely due to their tradition of collaboration with others.

Redundancy and Diversification: Redundant systems and diversified infrastructure routes are critical. The resilience demonstrated by the Rio Grande do

Sul IXP through its redundant route servers minimized the impact during critical moments. ISPs and data centers should diversify their physical locations and paths to prevent simultaneous failures during natural disasters.

Emergency Preparedness and Response: Immediate response measures, such as opening mobile networks for free-roaming and providing emergency access to roads for ISPs, were vital in maintaining communication. Planning for fuel transport and generator maintenance is crucial for data centers during prolonged power outages.

Impact of Natural and Human Factors: The flooding in the metropolitan area was intensified by natural factors (heavy rainfall and strong winds) and human factors (lack of maintenance and updates to flood protection systems). Addressing the human factors is essential to mitigate future risks.

Adaptation and Long-term Recovery: Long-term recovery should focus on strengthening infrastructure to withstand future climate events. Shifting to cloud solutions and relocating critical services to safer areas are key strategies. Reconstruction, potentially taking up to 36 months, should prioritize resilience.

Public Awareness and Communication: Effective communication systems are vital for coordinating rescues, informing the public, and maintaining order during disasters. Raising awareness about the importance of keeping telecommunications infrastructure can help mitigate future impacts.

These lessons highlight the long-term need for comprehensive planning, robust infrastructure, community collaboration, and proactive risk management to achieve resilience against extreme weather events and ensure the continuity of ICT services. Internet providers are rebuilding their infrastructure in the short term by exchanging equipment and fiber cables and seeking donations. Several companies have contributed thousands of dollars. Reestablishing customers' Internet access and equipment is expensive and time-consuming. The providers association estimates it will take three years to restore the ISPs' infrastructure in the area fully.

11   Open Challenges and Future Work

Despite significant progress in understanding, modeling, and addressing the resilience of ICT and power infrastructure during extreme weather events, several challenges still need to be discussed for further research.

Modeling Resilience at Scale: One key challenge is developing comprehensive models that quantify resilience across large-scale, dynamic, and dependent networks. These models must account for power, weather conditions, localized failures, and other variables. Several new research studies are trying to improve both the accuracy and scalability of these resilience models [35].

Data Availability and Analysis: Another critical challenge is obtaining detailed, large-scale data necessary for assessing resilience. Data on power distribution grids, ICT failures, and weather events are often fragmented and owned by various entities and private companies. Collaboration between these entities, policymakers, and researchers is essential to access this data and conduct the necessary analysis. The first step is to provide open or easily accessible data [62].

Developing Resilience Metrics: Existing reliability metrics, such as SAIFI (System Average Interruption Frequency Index) and SAIDI (System Average Interruption Duration Index) from the electrical power system, or MTTR (Mean Time to Repair) and MTBF (Mean Time Between Failures) from the ICT domain, are insufficient for characterizing resilience during severe weather events, as they were primarily designed for daily operations. There is a need to develop resilience metrics that incorporate external factors, such as weather variables and service restoration timelines. Such metrics require a multidisciplinary approach, integrating infrastructure, service management, and meteorology.

Leveraging Machine Learning and Data-Driven Methods: Integrating machine learning with spatiotemporal random processes to predict failures and optimize recovery is a promising yet challenging area. For example, using Phasor Measurement Units (PMUs) and ICT infrastructure data could improve failure detection and service restoration in smart cities. Still, these models account for complex, large-scale interdependencies.

Improving Measurement Infrastructure in the Region: Another avenue for exploration is the use of traceroutes passing through the affected area. The limited probing infrastructure in the region, such as RIPE Atlas [60], complicates comparisons with other events, such as those involving IXPs [4].

Deeper Analysis: Our initial analysis provides valuable insights into the local impact of the event, but several unanswered questions require deeper investigation and complementary data for a broader perspective. For instance, understanding why the IXP's traffic volume has not normalized six months after the event may involve analyzing the status of ASes before and after the event using additional datasets, such as from IODA (Internet Outage Detection and Analysis) [26] and Trinocular (ICMP probes to detect outages) [45,46].

Addressing these challenges will require interdisciplinary collaboration and the development of novel methodologies that integrate data-driven approaches, advanced modeling techniques, measurement infrastructure, and innovative resilience metrics. The results could significantly improve our ability to prepare for and respond to extreme weather events, ensuring more resilient infrastructure systems in the future.

12   Availability of Datasets and Additional Materials

In this study, we are cataloging data for future analyses and simulations. This data includes event timelines, hydrological causes, maps, data center conditions, and Internet measurements collected from end-users, public schools, and health units through the Simet system [7]. Additionally, we have gathered Internet routing and traffic data from the Porto Alegre Internet Exchange Point (IXP) (IX.br) and a mobile operator, documented fiber cuts and repairs across two metropolitan networks, and collected information on long-distance circuit outages. This dataset is supplemented with data from operator management systems, private sector contributions, and official reports.

We are progressively making intermediate datasets available to the community, as detailed in [3], subject to obtaining the necessary authorizations from all relevant stakeholders. All information used in this study is accurate and reflects the most recent data available as of September 2024.

13   Conclusion

In this paper, we have contributed by documenting the sequence of extreme weather events in May 2024 in Rio Grande do Sul, Brazil, specifically focusing on the resilience and recovery of Information and Communication Technology (ICT) infrastructure. The study assesses the impact of these events on various critical infrastructure components, including fiber optic networks, data centers, and the regional Internet Exchange Point (IXP), while also providing insights from an end-user perspective during the critical period. Our findings highlight the vulnerability of aerial fiber networks to climate-related disruptions and underscore the need for proactive measures to fully utilize the relative resilience of underground networks. They corroborate similar observations from events in Puerto Rico and New Orleans. Furthermore, we provide critical insights into the performance of affected data centers, which may inform discussions on risk analysis standards, such as ISO/IEC 22237. The study demonstrates a direct correlation between climate events in the region and increasingly frequent disruptions to aerial fiber infrastructure. We have compiled data from multiple sources with the aim of making it openly accessible for future research, particularly for machine learning studies on the resilience of critical infrastructure. Ultimately, our study reinforces the necessity of improved disaster preparedness, including enhancements in redundancy, risk management, and infrastructure planning, to mitigate the impact of future extreme weather events on ICT infrastructure.

Acknowledgments. We thank the anonymous reviewers and our shepherd for their valuable feedback on our paper. This work was supported in part by CNPq Grant 420934/2023-5. The views and conclusions contained herein are those of the authors and should not be interpreted as necessarily representing the official policies or endorsements, either expressed or implied, of the sponsors.

Ethical Considerations. This study utilizes anonymized and non-anonymized datasets from public sources and private entities, all of which have been published with the necessary consent. No personal or sensitive data were involved in the research. Data integrity is ensured through a collaborative effort between academic institutions and private operators, with transparency and interdisciplinary partnerships forming the foundation of trust. The primary objective of this study is to educate, assess, and facilitate learning through a neutral, non-judgmental approach.

A   Additional Information and Graphs

Fiber Damage: The Metro datasets in [3] provide detailed information on the dates, causes, and locations of incidents affecting two fiber backbones. Figure 14 presents data on incidents reported by a commercial (ISP) fiber backbone, showing trends consistent with those discussed in Sect. 3.

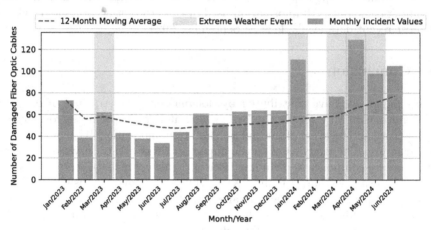

Fig. 14. Incidents affecting fiber paths in a 500 km ISP backbone in the region.

SIMET: The dataset provides comprehensive evaluations of Internet quality, measuring key performance metrics such as download and upload speeds, latency, jitter, and packet loss (via TWAMP). It also collects contextual data, including timestamps, IP protocol version (IPv4 or IPv6), IPv6 connectivity availability, NAT or CGNAT presence, and, with user consent, geolocation information. In Fig. 15, the time window is extended to enhance baseline identification and to present a breakdown by city groups within Rio Grande do Sul.

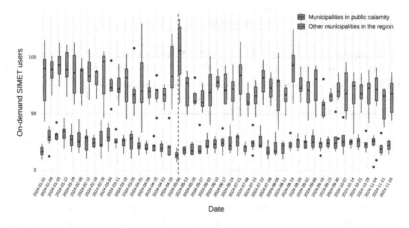

Fig. 15. Long-term weekly analysis of median and percentile metrics per unique end-user vantage point from January to November 2024. The dashed line indicates the worst week of the flooding in May 2024.

References

1. Alkhaleel, B.A.: Machine learning applications in the resilience of interdependent critical infrastructure systems - a systematic literature review. Int. J. Crit. Infrastruct. Prot. **44**, 100646 (2024)
2. Anatel: Anatel - recuperação das redes. https://informacoes.anatel.gov.br/paineis/utilidade-publica/recuperacao-das-redes. Accessed 10 Aug 2024
3. Bertholdo, L., Barreto, R.: Rsfloodsdatasets (2024). https://github.com/systemsfurg/RSFloodsDataset/
4. Bertholdo, L.M., Ceron, J.M., Granville, L.Z., van Rijswijk-Deij, R.: Forecasting the impact of IXP outages using anycast. In: TMA (2021)
5. Buschschlüter, V.: Brazil floods:hundreds of rio grande do sul towns under water (2024). https://www.bbc.com/news/world-latin-america-68968987
6. CamaraPOA: Camara de Vereadores de Porto Alegre Lei 13.402 (2023). https://camarapoa.rs.gov.br/draco/processos/137070/Lei_13402.pdf
7. CEPTRO: Medições - iniciativas para analisar e melhorar a qualidade e velocidade da internet no brasil (2024). https://medicoes.nic.br/
8. CNN: Operadoras de telefonia liberam sinal e oferecem internet no rs para facilitar comunicação (2024). https://www.cnnbrasil.com.br/economia/macroeconomia/operadoras-de-telefonia-liberam-sinal-e-oferecem-internet-no-rs-para-facilitar-comunicacao/
9. CNN: Temporal e ventos de 90 km/h causam estragos em porto alegre e deixam bairros sem energia (2024). https://www.cnnbrasil.com.br/nacional/temporal-causa-estragos-em-porto-alegre-e-deixa-bairros-sem-energia/
10. Conjur: TJ-RS suspende prazos processuais e só analisa medidas urgentes (2024). https://www.conjur.com.br/2024-mai-07/tj-rs-suspende-prazos-processuais-e-so-analisa-medidas-urgentes/
11. Convergencia Digital: Justiça desliga data center no Rio Grande do Sul (2024). https://convergenciadigital.com.br/mercado/justica-desliga-data-center-no-rio-grande-do-sul/
12. Cordova, A., Stanley, K., Kochhar, A., Consaul, R., Hodiak, J.: Building a resilient telecommunications sector in Puerto Rico in the aftermath of Hurricanes Irma and Maria. J. Critical Infrastruct. Policy **2**(1), 75–96 (2021)
13. CPovo: Com sede alagada, Procergs desliga datacenter e sites do governo do rs ficam fora do ar temporariamente (2024). https://www.correiodopovo.com.br/not
14. DNIT: Sei/dnit - 17714322 - ofício (2024). https://internetsul.com.br/files/Oficio_17714322
15. Elea: Em meio às enchentes de Porto Alegre, Elea continua operação na cidade. https://eleadatacenters.com/2024/05/07/em-meio-as-enchentes-de-porto-alegre-elea-digital-data-centers-continua-operacao-na-cidade/
16. FCC: Report and recommendations of the independent panel reviewing the impact of hurricane katrina on communications networks. https://transition.fcc.gov/pshs/docs/advisory/hkip/karrp.pdf (2006)
17. FIERGS: Indústria segue contabilizando perdas com as inundações no rio grande do sul (2024). https://www.fiergs.org.br/noticia/industria-segue-contabilizando-perdas-com-inundacoes-no-rio-grande-do-sul
18. Frame, D.J., et al.: Climate change attribution and the economic costs of extreme weather events: a study on damages from extreme rainfall and drought. Clim. Change **162**, 781–797 (2020)

19. G1RS: Câmara de porto alegre aprova incentivos ao 4ž distrito (2022). https:// g1.globo.com/rs/rio-grande-do-sul/noticia/2022/08/17/camara-de-porto-alegre-aprova-projeto-de-incentivos-ao-4o-distrito.ghtml
20. G1RS: Tempestade Yakecan deixa mais de 200 mil clientes sem energia elétrica no RS (2022). https://g1.globo.com/rs/rio-grande-do-sul/noticia/2022/05/18/tempestade-yakecan-deixa-familias-sem-energia-eletrica-no-rs-alerta-para-ventos-fortes-seguem-nesta-quarta.ghtml
21. G1RS: Guaíba fica abaixo da cota de alerta e registra menor marca em mais de um mês em porto alegre (2024). https://g1.globo.com/rs/rio-grande-do-sul/noticia/2024/06/07/nivel-guaiba-cota-de-alerta-porto-alegre.ghtml
22. G1RS: Nível do guaíba fica abaixo da cota de inundação pela primeira vez em um mês em porto alegre (2024). https://g1.globo.com/rs/rio-grande-do-sul/noticia/2024/06/01/nivel-do-guaiba-fica-abaixo-da-cota-de-inundacao-pela-primeira-vez-em-um-mes-em-porto-alegre.ghtml
23. G1RS: Nível no guaíba volta a subir, ultrapassa cota de inundação e porto alegre registra pontos de alagamento (2024). https://g1.globo.com/rs/rio-grande-do-sul/noticia/2024/06/03/nivel-no-guaiba-volta-a-subir-ultrapassa-cota-de-inundacao-e-porto-alegre-registra-pontos-de-alagamento.ghtml
24. G1RS: Temporais no RS: entenda como o relevo de porto alegre e as 'marés de tempestade' travam escoamento (2024). https://g1.globo.com/meio-ambiente/noticia/2024/05/07/temporais-no-rs-entenda-como-o-relevo-de-porto-alegre-e-as-mares-de-tempestade-travam-escoamento.ghtml
25. G1RS: Temporais no RS: veja cronologia de desastre que matou 75 pessoas (2024). https://g1.globo.com/rs/rio-grande-do-sul/noticia/2024/05/05/temporais-no-rs-veja-cronologia-de-desastre.ghtml
26. Gatech: Ioda | internet outage detection and analysis. https://ioda.live
27. GZH: Ao menos 52 mil pontos estão sem luz no RS em razão de temporais; Porto Alegre registra alagamentos em ruas (2023). https://gauchazh.clicrbs.com.br/geral/noticia/2023/03/ao-menos-52-mil-pontos-estao-sem-luz-no-rs-em-razao-de-temporais-porto-alegre-registra-alagamentos-em-ruas-clfudxn8b00250151yylijzxw.html
28. GZH: Falhas de manutenção e de projeto ampliaram nível da inundação em porto alegre (2024). https://gauchazh.clicrbs.com.br/porto-alegre/noticia/2024/05/falhas-de-manutencao-e-de-projeto-ampliaram-nivel-da-inundacao-em-porto-alegre-clw15ll0y00s6011hyc1p80ro.html
29. GZH: Morte de morador desaparecido motivou protesto com queima de ônibus em porto alegre (2024). https://gauchazh.clicrbs.com.br/seguranca/noticia/2024/05/morte-de-morador-desaparecido-motivou-protesto-com-queima-de-onibus-em-porto-alegre-clwf65q52004x014x9uqbg0aa.html
30. Herald, T.S.: Will your cell service work if a hurricane rolls through the coast, and will it be enough? (2018). https://www.govtech.com/em/disaster/will-your-cell-service-work-if-a-hurricane-rolls-through-the-coast-and-will-it-be-enough.html
31. InternetSul: Associação dos Provedores de Serviços e Informações da Internet. https://internetsul.com.br/ajuders
32. InternetSul: Reunião com a secretaria municipal para discutir os desafios e custos de dutos e cabos subterrâneos (2023). https://internetsul.com.br/noticias/internetsul-se-reuniu-com-a-secretaria-municipal-de-parcerias
33. IPH-UFRGS: Previsões atualizadas de níveis d'água no guaíba – terça-feira 04/06/24 (2024). https://www.ufrgs.br/iph/previsoes-atualizadas-de-niveis-dagua-no-guaiba-terca-feira-04-06-24-12h/

34. Jahn, M.: Economics of extreme weather events: terminology and regional impact models. Weather Clim. Extremes **10**, 29–39 (2015)
35. Ji, A., He, R., Chen, W., Zhang, L.: Computational methodologies for critical infrastructure resilience modeling: a review. Adv. Eng. Inform. **62**, 102663 (2024). https://doi.org/10.1016/j.aei.2024.102663
36. Ji, C., Wei, Y., Poor, H.V.: Resilience of energy infrastructure and services: modeling, data analytics, and metrics. IEEE **105**(7), 1354–1366 (2017)
37. Jornal da Universidade: O sistema de proteção contra inundações de porto alegre (2024). http://www.ufrgs.br/ufrgs/noticias/o-sistema-de-protecao-contra-inundacoes-de-porto-alegre
38. Kwasinski, A., Weaver, W.W., Chapman, P.L., Krein, P.T.: Telecommunications power plant damage assessment caused by hurricane katrina - site survey and follow-up results. In: Twenty-Eighth International Telecommunications Energy Conference, pp. 1–8 (2006). https://doi.org/10.1109/INTLEC.2006.251644
39. Metsul: Chuva que levou às enchentes no rio grande do sul superou 1000 mm (2024). https://metsul.com/chuva-que-levou-as-enchentes-no-rio-grande-do-sul-superou-1000-mm/
40. Metsul: Porto alegre tem noite de pavor com temporal violento e destrutivo (2024). https://metsul.com/2024-01-17-temporal-porto-alegre-vendaval/
41. NANOG: Hurricane Katrina Telecom Infrastructure Impacts, Solutions, and Opportunities (2006). https://www.youtube.com/watch?v=oel1jG9tOIM
42. NIC.br: Projeto sara (2024). https://sara.nic.br/
43. Parker, C.F., Stern, E.K., Paglia, E., Brown, C.: Preventable catastrophe? The hurricane Katrina disaster revisited. J. Contingencies Crisis Manag. **17**(4), 206–220 (2009)
44. PoP-RS/RNP: Rede metropoa (2024). https://metropoa.tche.br/sobre/
45. Pradkin, Y., Quan, K., Heidemann, J.: ANT Outage World Map (2024). https://outage.ant.isi.edu/
46. Quan, L., Heidemann, J., Pradkin, Y.: Trinocular: understanding internet reliability through adaptive probing. ACM SIGCOMM Comput. Commun. Rev. **43**(4), 255–266 (2013)
47. Reed, D.A., Kapur, K.C., Christie, R.D.: Methodology for assessing the resilience of networked infrastructure. IEEE Syst. J. **3**(2), 174–180 (2009)
48. Renner, M.: Procergs desliga data center (2024). https://www.baguete.com.br/noticias/07/05/2024/procergs-desliga-data-center
49. Richter, P., Smaragdakis, G., Feldmann, A., Chatzis, N., Boettger, J., Willinger, W.: Peering at peerings: On the role of IXP route servers. In: Proceedings of the 2014 Conference on Internet Measurement Conference, pp. 31–44 (2014)
50. RS, C.M.D.C.: Decreto amplia número de municípios em estado de calamidade e em situação de emergência - defesa civil do rio grande do sul (2024). https://www.defesacivil.rs.gov.br/decreto-amplia-numero-de-municipios-em-estado-de-calamidade-e-em-situacao-de-emergencia
51. RS, D.C.: Defesa civil atualiza balanço das enchentes no rs – 3/6, 9h - portal do estado do rio grande do sul (2024). https://estado.rs.gov.br/defesa-civil-atualiza-balanco-das-enchentes-no-rs-3-6-9h
52. RS-Gov: Com investimento de R$ 3 bilhões, Estado e Scala Data Centers assinam acordo para maior projeto de infraestrutura digital do RS - Portal do Estado do Rio Grande do Sul (2024). https://www.estado.rs.gov.br/com-investimento-inicial-de-r-3-bilhoes-governo-do-rs-e-scala-data-centers-assinam-acordo-para-o-maior-projeto-de-infraestrutu

53. Scala Datacenters: Press Release - Enchentes Rio Grande do Sul (2024). https://www.scaladatacenters.com/doc/Press_Release_Enchentes_Rio_Grande_do_Sul_Scala_Data_Centers.pdf
54. Sebrae: Devido a alagamento no Centro de POA, Sebrae RS desliga energia e Datacenter da Sede Metropolitana (2024). https://rs.agenciasebrae.com.br/dados/devido-a-alagamento-no-centro-de-poa-sebrae-rs-desliga-energia-e-datacenter-da-sede-metropolitana/
55. Silva, V.H.: Chuvas no rs: uso de internet em porto alegre cai pela metade com obstáculos para acesso (2024). https://g1.globo.com/tecnologia/noticia/2024/05/08/chuvas-no-rs-uso-de-internet-cai-pela-metade-com-obstaculos-para-acesso.ghtml
56. SIMET: Escolas (2024). https://conectividadenaeducacao.nic.br
57. SIMET: Saúde (2024). https://conectividadenasaude.nic.br
58. Simão, M.S., Ribeiro, E., Cardoso, B.B., Aurélio Izumida Martins, M., Lopes, M.F., Rodrigues, F.: Shared trench for burying cables in the conversion of overhead to underground networks. In: 2022 IEEE Conference on Technologies for Sustainability, pp. 120–124 (2022). https://doi.org/10.1109/SusTech53338.2022.9794206
59. Souza, P.: Exclusivo: Procergs migra dados para a nuvem em caráter de urgência por risco de inundação no rs - it forum (2024). https://itforum.com.br/noticias/procergs-migra-dados-nuvem-risco-inundacao/
60. Staff, RIPE NCC: RIPE atlas: a global internet measurement network. Internet Protocol J. **18**(3) (2015)
61. Teletime: No centro de Porto Alegre, a operação da BRDigital para manter dois datacenters funcionando (2024). https://teletime.com.br/08/05/2024/no-centro-de-porto-alegre-a-operacao-da-br-digital-para-manter-dois-datacenters-funcionando/
62. The Obama White House: The President's Climate Data Initiative: Empowering America's Communities to Prepare for Climate Change (2014). https://obamawhitehouse.archives.gov/the-press-office/2014/03/19/fact-sheet-presidents-climate-data-initiative-empowering-america-s-comm
63. The Obama White House: Ten Years After Katrina: New Orleans' Recovery, and What Data Had to Do with it (2015). https://medium.com/@ObamaWhiteHouse/ten-years-after-katrina-new-orleans-recovery-and-what-data-had-to-do-with-it-3df0bb2467e9
64. TJRS: Poder judiciário tribunal de justiça do estado do rio grande do sul (2024). https://www.tjrs.jus.br/novo/noticia/migracao-para-a-nuvem-proporcionara-nova-experiencia-a-usuarios/
65. Tornatore, M., et al.: A survey on network resiliency methodologies against weather-based disruptions. In: 8th International Workshop on Resilient Networks Design and Modeling, pp. 23–34. IEEE (2016)

Routing

Detecting Traffic Engineering from Public BGP Data

Omar Darwich[1($\boxtimes$)], Cristel Pelsser[2], and Kevin Vermeulen[1]

[1] LAAS-CNRS, Toulouse, France
Odarwich@laas.fr
[2] Université de Louvain, Ottignies-Louvain-la-Neuve, Belgium

Abstract. Routing is essential to the Internet functioning. However, more and more functions are added to BGP, the inter-AS routing protocol. In addition to providing connectivity for best effort service, it carries flow specification rules and blackholing signals to react to DDoS, routes for virtual private networks, IGP link-state database information among other uses. One such addition is the tweaking of BGP advertisements to engineer the traffic, to direct it on some preferred paths. In this paper we aim to estimate the impact of Traffic Engineering (TE) on the BGP ecosystem. We develop a method to detect the impact in space, that is, to find which traffic engineering technique impacts which prefix and which AS. We design a methodology to pinpoint TE events to quantify the impact on time. We find that on average, a BGP vantage point sees 35% of the announced prefixes impacted by TE. Quantifying the impact of TE on BGP stability, we find that TE events contribute to 39% of BGP updates and 44% of the BGP convergence time, and that prefixes belonging to hypergiants contribute the most to TE.

1 Introduction

The Internet is composed of a large number of independent networks that are interconnected, called Autonomous Systems (AS). They exchange routing information using the Border Gateway Protocol (BGP). This routing protocol enables Internet Service Providers (ISP) to configure routing policies meeting their economic relationships. While economical relationships take precedence and are implemented using the first attribute considered in the route selection, the local_pref, operators may wish finer control on their traffic. BGP provides a set of tools to engineer the incoming and outgoing traffic of operators.

Traffic Engineering (TE) can be practiced at different timescales. It is either done manually or using tools such as Noction [6], BGP-TE-TOOL [5] and Auto-Prepend [18]. Each change of routing configuration is an open door for potential miss-configuration [38] such as routing leaks, unintentional hijacks [19], routing loops, forwarding loops, and disconnections. Some popular outages are the result of routing configuration changes [2].

Despite the existence of TE mechanisms in BGP, their granularity is very coarse [25,43], especially for incoming traffic. Further, each service provider tries

C. Testart et al. (Eds.): PAM 2025, LNCS 15567, pp. 307–334, 2025.
https://doi.org/10.1007/978-3-031-85960-1_13

to achieve its own goals that may be in contradiction with other operators' needs. For instance, the TE systems from Google and Meta [45,51] aim to direct outgoing traffic to specific routers when the customer edge network may prefer a different provider for traffic from Google and Meta. Knowing the risk of performing changes in BGP and the little or sometimes inexistent results of performing TE [14], one can wonder whether it is worth the effort, and understand its impact on the BGP ecosystem.

In this paper, to bridge this gap, we perform the first large-scale study of the prevalence of the different TE techniques and how TE impacts BGP stability.

Our contributions are:

- New techniques to detect TE from BGP dumps and BGP updates, informed from operators and principled on BGP behavior.
- A longitudinal study on the impact of TE on affected prefixes and ASes, as well as the impact of TE on BGP stability.

Our main results include that our technique is highly accurate. Our technique has a precision of 0.996 precision and recall of 0.91 recall on our ground truth datasets. Using our technique to detect traffic engineering over the years, we find that TE has been and is widely used by operators. In 2024, a BGP vantage point sees an average number of prefixes affected by TE of 35%. We also find that TE has a significant impact on BGP stability finding that TE contributes to 39% of the BGP updates and 44% of the BGP convergence time of the BGP events[1].

2 Background and Related Work

First, we highlight the important elements of the Border Gateway Protocol (BGP) for our work. Then, we explain what is Traffic Engineering (TE), why it is used, and how it works from an interdomain point of view.

Networks or Autonomous Systems (ASes) exchange reachability information via BGP. The purpose of the protocol is for each AS to learn how to reach all the prefixes allocated on the Internet. A route to a prefix in BGP contains multiple attributes, including the sequence of AS numbers that need to be traveled. This sequence is called an AS Path. Interdomain TE is done by carefully crafting and manipulating BGP announcements to steer traffic as desired [42].

Quoitin *et al.* distinguish incoming and outgoing TE [42], where the goal is to influence how the traffic reaches an AS and how it leaves an AS, respectively. In this paper, we focus on incoming TE. The outgoing techniques are out of scope of this paper, but are presented in Appendix A for completeness.

2.1 Inbound TE

There are four classes of inbound traffic engineering techniques. We illustrate these techniques using Fig. 1.

---

[1] BGP events represent a subset of the total BGP updates, as we filter out continuous BGP updates that are likely to not be real BGP events (Sect. 3.2).

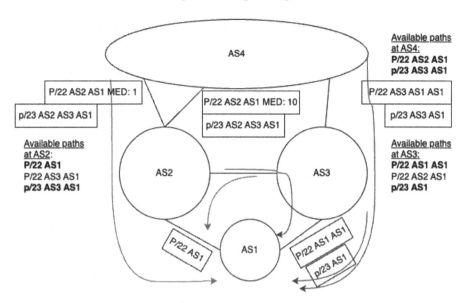

Fig. 1. Overview of incoming TE techniques: $p/23$ is a more specific prefix of $P/22$. $P/22AS1AS1$ is an advertisement of $P/22$ with AS path prepending. $AS2$ advertises a low MED on the left link and a higher MED on the right link.

Selective Advertisements: Routes for different prefixes are treated independently. The best announcement is selected for each prefix. ISPs may split their IP address space in sub-prefixes. The sub-prefixes are selectively advertised to some peers and not to others, where a peer can be a shared-cost peer, a customer or a provider. As our paper does not need to distinguish between peering types, we just use the term peers for the rest of the paper. To ensure reachability even in the case of connectivity failure to one peer, a superprefix covering the sub-prefixes is advertised to all peers. This route is only used when a sub-prefix route disappears. Because traffic is forwarded using the route for the most specific prefix, the selective advertisements of the sub-prefixes, when present, enable control of the incoming paths used for the different subprefixes.

In Fig. 1, $P/22$ is the super-prefix and $P/23$ one of its two sub-prefixes. $AS1$ advertises $P/22$ to both of its providers ($AS2$ and $AS3$). $p/23$ is solely advertised to $AS3$ to attract the traffic destined to the IP addresses in this prefix on link $AS3 - AS1$ instead via $AS2$. The paths selected for the sub-prefix $p/23$ by the different ASs are shown in blue. The paths to $P/22$ are in red. If link $AS3 - AS1$ fails. $p/23$ disappears from the routing tables in the different ASs. The IP addresses in $p/23$ are still reachable following the routes for $P/22$.

AS Path Prepending: The BGP decision process is composed of a set of rules that are applied in sequence [17]. One of these rules is to keep only the routes with the shortest AS paths. The intuition for this rule, not necessarily verified in practice, is that shorter paths have a lower delay. To indicate to a remote AS that a path is not preferred, an AS can add its AS number more than once to the path. This technique is called AS prepending. Since the path becomes longer, all things remaining equal, the path becomes less preferred than shorter paths.

In Fig. 1, $AS1$ prepends its AS path once when advertising $P/22$ to $AS3$. $AS3$ receives the path $AS1AS1$ from $AS1$ when it receives the path $AS2AS1$ from AS2. Since both have the same length, it chooses one of them based on the next rules. Here we assume it picks the path via $AS2$. Here all the traffic to $P/22$ except when destined to sub-prefix $p/23$ goes via $AS2$. The TE action enables to move all the traffic on link $AS2 - AS1$.

BGP Communities: BGP communities are a set of values attached to a BGP route. Each community value has semantics that is defined by each AS. A community value is attached to a BGP route by a router to be acted upon later by another router on the route. A community value may convey an action such as AS path prepending, not exporting the route to a peer, or to a set of peers, or setting the local-preference of a route to a value. A community value may be added to a route to instruct another AS to influence route advertisement and thus perform a TE action. These community values are called BGP action communities. Other BGP communities, which carry information such as where the route was learnt, are called information communities.

In Fig. 1, instead of prepending the AS path in $AS1$ toward $AS3$, $AS1$ could instruct $AS3$ to perform the prepending for $P/22$. In that case, we would most likely see the AS path $AS3AS3AS1$ instead of $AS3AS1AS1$. Alternatively, $AS1$ could attach the "no-export'' community toward $AS3$ for $P/22$. In both cases, we observe the same routes.

Multi-exit Discriminator: Multiply connected neighboring ASes may indicate which link they prefer the neighbor to send the traffic on using the Multi-Exit Discriminator (MED) attribute. A low MED value is inserted in the advertisements on the preferred links while a higher value is assigned on the less preferred ones. This attribute does not propagate further. It is rarely observed in public route collectors. We may remotely observe the local effect of the MED if location communities are also present in the announcements. It may also trigger some duplicate announcements [32]. Otherwise this TE technique will be invisible to publicly available route collectors.

In Fig. 1, a MED is attached by $AS2$ to the updates for prefix $P/22$ when advertised to $AS4$. The lowest MED route wins. Consequently, traffic uses the left link from $AS4$ to $AS2$ for the super-prefix.

Since TE with the MED attribute is invisible to public collectors, we focus on the 3 other techniques in the rest of the paper.

2.2   Related Work

Several works propose methods to help network operators engineer inbound TE. For instance, Chang *et al.* propose to automate AS path prepending [18], when

Sun *et al.* rely on more specific prefix advertisements to engineer inbound TE
for stub ASes [50]. Nakamura *et al.* show that outbound traffic can be influenced
using BGP EPE to pick the exit points and reach paths with shorter RTTs than
the delay experienced along the default best paths [40].

On the other hand, few works address the detection of TE, as a whole, and
rather focus on a specific question for a given TE technique. In [31], Gutierrez
proposes to detect AS path prepending from BGP updates with varying lengths
but constant nominal AS path (the AS path without duplicate ASes). This
technique misses the events that lead to a switch of path due to TE. Prior work
also looked at how path prepending was used by operators and the different
implications in terms of security and performance [39]. On BGP communities,
prior work proposed to classify them [36,37,48], as well as studying their impact
on security [35,49]. Our work is orthogonal to these works as it gives a landscape
of the usage of these different TE techniques, comparatively to each other.

Related to detecting TE events from BGP updates (Sect. 3.2), prior work has
analyzed BGP updates to detect typos [22], BGP sequences [13] or classify the
updates based on the attribute changes [33]. Our work proposes new principled
techniques to detect signals of TE from the BGP updates.

3   Detecting Traffic Engineering

Our goal is to capture the impact of TE in space and time on the BGP ecosystem. By space, we mean finding which prefixes and which ASes are impacted by
TE, and by which techniques. By time, we mean measuring the role of TE in
BGP instability. To find which prefixes are affected by TE, we translate the TE
techniques described in Sect. 2.1 into observable properties from BGP dumps
(Sect. 3.1). To measure the role of TE in BGP instability, we design a methodology to capture TE events from BGP updates based on insights on TE practices and how BGP should behave for TE and non TE events (Sect. 3.2).

3.1   Detecting TE from BGP Dumps

The BGP dumps from the BGP collectors contain, among other information, the
AS path and the BGP communities used to reach prefixes in the Internet, which we
use to reason about and find prefixes affected by TE. We refer to BGP collectors
as vantage points (VP) throughout the rest of this document. For each technique,
we explain how we derive whether a prefix is affected by this technique, and how
we derive if the origin AS is responsible for the TE, if we can.

Selective Advertisement. Our idea is that if we observe a prefix and a covering prefix with the same origin AS with different routes from the same vantage
point, it is likely that there is an AS on the path performing selective advertisement. Indeed, if the routes to the two prefixes were announced exactly in the

same way, then their path should be the same. However, in detail, it might be tricky to definitely identify selective advertisements. Indeed, suppose we have these two paths: A-B-C-O the path to the sub-prefix, A-B-E-O the path to the super-prefix, where O is the origin AS announcing the two prefixes. These paths could be the result of O performing selective advertisement, only announcing the sub-prefix to C, or B which sets a higher local preference to C for the sub-prefix, and a higher local preference to E for the super-prefix. To help differentiate, the view from multiple providers can help. Indeed, if from multiple providers, we see other paths like G-F-C-O and G-F-E-O, it is more likely to be selective advertisements than F and E applying exactly the same policies for the sub-prefix and the super-prefix. Therefore, if C and E have more than one common neighbor observed for the sub-prefix and the super-prefix (here B and F), we say there is selective advertisement on the sub-prefix and the super-prefix.

Notice that our technique allows us to differentiate between selective advertisement and an AS performing deaggregation of all its prefixes, for instance to prevent BGP hijacks. Indeed, in the case of deaggregation, the paths of the selective prefix and the super-prefix should be the same, whereas it is not the case in selective advertisement.

It can be tricky to identify the AS which wants to perform selective advertisement. In our previous example, the selective advertisement is performed by O as the AS paths of the sub-prefix and the super-prefix diverge directly after O. However, suppose that the paths to the sub-prefix and the super-prefix are now A-B-C-G-O and A-B-E-G-O. In that case, the selective advertisement could be performed by G, or by O. Indeed, O could use a community of G asking G to only announce the selective sub-prefix to B. Therefore, to be conservative, we only consider the cases where we can be definitive in saying that the selective advertisement is performed by the origin AS, *i.e.,* when the paths to the sub-prefix and the super-prefix directly diverge after the origin AS. These cases represent 81% of the prefixes with selective advertisement (Sect. 4.3).

AS Path Prepending. If we observe an AS path from a vantage point with an AS appearing multiple times subsequently, we say that the AS path contains prepending. We distinguish between origin prepending and intermediate prepending, depending on whether the origin AS is the prepended AS or not.

For origin AS prepending, the AS performing the TE must be the origin AS. For intermediate prepending, it might be harder to identify who is responsible, as it could be any AS between the prepended AS and the origin AS, so to not overestimate which ASes perform TE, we do not consider that intermediate prepending is made by the origin AS.

AS Path Poisoning. If we observe an AS path containing the pattern A-*-A, where the "star" is a sequence of ASes without A, we say that the AS path contains poisoning, and that A is the origin AS that performs the poisoning. When observing poisoning, the AS appearing multiple times in the AS-path did not receive the update a second time. Otherwise, it would have dropped the update, and we would not have seen it in the public data. It is also possible for a router to disable loop detection, which is typically used for ASes that lack a backbone and rely on another AS for internal connectivity [20]. These paths are often not seen at public collectors as the AS disabling the check is a stub. Third, these AS paths could also be due to BGP hijacks [47], and therefore the origin AS is not responsible for the TE action. In practice, we quantify the occurrences of AS path poisoning but we do not investigate their cause as they represent a negligible fraction of affected prefixes (<0.01%) (Sect. 5.2).

BGP Communities. To find communities, we use the methodology from prior work that classified the BGP communities between action and information [37], which obtained an accuracy of 96% on a dataset containing the BGP communities seen in a week of BGP data from May 2023. More specifically, we replicate prior work's technique [37], using the available code [34], on each week of our BGP updates (Sect. 5.1). Then, each prefix with a BGP community classified as action is said to be affected by TE. We conservatively do not consider prefix updates with the information community as being affected by TE. Moreover, we do not differentiate between the case where the action community was actually taken into account by the operator, and the case where the action community was ignored by the operator. For both, we say that the prefix was affected by TE, as we are interested in knowing how operators are performing TE, and not whether their operation is successful. This is similar to prepending being performed by an operator, but potentially ignored because BGP tie breakers with higher priority (*e.g.*, localpref) are used for path selection.

To identify whether the origin AS is responsible for the action community, we look for an action community of the form `penultimate_asn:xxx` where penultimate_asn is the AS just before the origin AS in the AS path. If such a community exists, then it is very likely that the action community has been set by the origin AS. However, this technique will give a lower bound on the set of origin ASes that performs traffic engineering, for the following reasons: (1) Prior work has shown that action communities might be off path, *i.e.*, the action community appear only on AS paths where the AS that has to perform the TE action is not on the AS path [37] (2) Some providers have action communities that do not start with their AS number. For instance, NTT has some communities starting with 65XXX [11], whereas their AS number is 2914 (3) An origin AS can try to influence the BGP announcement more than one hop away.

Finally, as communities are not verified on the path and can be set by anyone [49], our technique would not work if an AS (other than the origin AS) polluted an announcement with an action community of the form `penultimate_asn:xxx` (erroneously or maliciously).

We evaluate the limitations of our technique to detect the origin AS setting an action community in Sect. 4.3.

Other Techniques. The other techniques, namely setting different values of local preference, and the usage of the MED attribute are not visible at BGP vantage points. Their use can be inferred in the close vicinity of a VP only as shown by Cittadini et al. [21] for the local preference. Therefore, we do not try to find the prefixes affected by these TE techniques. Consequently, our study provides a lower bound of the quantity of traffic engineering performed on the internet.

3.2   Detecting TE Events from BGP Updates

Intuition: The methodology described in the previous section gives us a way to compute the set of prefixes on which TE techniques are applied, but does not give us a way to capture TE events, as BGP dumps only represent a single point in time. In this section, we design a methodology to capture TE events, based on two principled insights derived from time and space behavior of operators performing TE.

First, it is unlikely that operators perform TE on all their prefixes at the same time, and conversely, non TE events, such as link or device failures, are likely to affect all prefixes that are routed similarly at the same time. Tools like Traffic Manager [8] exemplify this approach by selectively applying TE to a subset of prefixes. We briefly give an overview of Traffic Manager later in this section. Indeed, there are multiple reasons for which operators would avoid performing TE on all their prefixes, among which we can cite: (1) Any configuration change represents a risk [52], and (2) Operators using TE to find potential alternate paths, either for load balancing or to mitigate congestion, will use only a fraction of prefixes to test the alternate paths [45].

Second, it is likely that if we observe multiple stable paths within a short period of time, an operator is performing TE, for instance for searching alternate paths, or testing failure scenarios [52]. Indeed, multiple stable paths are unlikely to be caused by outages, as most outages are short lived [41] and should not result in observing multiple stable paths, but rather either a very few stable paths corresponding to the state before the failure, the state during the failure, and the state after the restoration of the failure. Also, multiple stable paths are unlikely to happen from configuration errors preventing BGP to converge, as one would observe a lot of updates resulting in multiple unstable paths.

A TE system from a major CDN confirmed our intuitions [8]. This TE system is in charge of automatically shifting traffic from a datacenter to some others in case this datacenter was running hot. To achieve this goal, this TE system automatically drops some prefixes announced at a particular datacenter (but not all) to shift the desired amount of traffic. This mechanism confirms our first intuition that not all the prefixes experience TE at the same time. Then, another job of this TE system is to predict where the traffic would go in case of a failure of a peering session or even an entire datacenter. To achieve this prediction, the TE operation consists in withdrawing prefixes from the tested datacenter, waiting for convergence, and performing pings to the clients that were routed to that datacenter and observe to which other datacenter they are rerouted [23]. This operation is run continuously to keep the traffic prediction up to date, so it confirms our second intuition that some TE operations consist in testing failure scenarios that would translate into multiple stable paths.

We discussed with the CDN to confirm our understanding of their TE system, and the CDN also added that they could sometimes withdraw all the prefixes of one datacenter at once to simulate failures, which contradicts our first intuition. We further discuss this case in Sect. 6. As we design our technique to stick with our two intuitions (Sect. 3.2), it is likely that it would not be able to detect those events. However, even if one could consider these events as TE as these are not real failures and operator's operations, these simulated failure scenarios confirm our intuition of what would happen during a real failure.

We describe how we translate these two insights into concrete techniques in the next paragraphs.

Parsing BGP Events from BGP Updates. We say that a route to a prefix in BGP is stable if it lasts at least 15 min before receiving any other BGP update. This 15 min value is chosen for two reasons: (1) We want to ignore noisy prefixes with continuous updates [1,24]; (2) We are interested in BGP events corresponding to TE, not all the events, and operators should not announce their routes more frequently than every 15 min, as they could be penalized by route flap damping [30]. With this definition, a route change event is a sequence of BGP updates observed from a BGP vantage point for a prefix such that the routes before and after the updates are stable and different. We will use the term BGP event for this concept in the rest of the paper.

This definition of BGP events gives that over our dataset (Sect. 5.1), only 11% of the BGP updates are part of a BGP event. This is not surprising, as prior work has demonstrated that a significant fraction of the BGP updates were not due to real path change [13,32]. Some are due to the lack of adj-RIB-ins or presence of a partial adj-RIB-in in routers. Because the router does not store the routes it received, when a policy changes locally it needs to ask its neighbors to send their best route to compute its new best route. This is for example observed upon route validity change due to a ROA change. There is a current IETF draft that proposes a solution for the specific case of validity change [9].

Operators Should Rarely Perform TE on All Their Prefixes simultaneously. Our intuition, confirmed by a large CDN, is that a BGP event is likely due to TE only if a fraction in a group of prefixes that are routed similarly moves simultaneously. To translate this idea into a practical methodology, we use the notion of BGP atoms [12]. We use the same definition as in prior work, which defined a BGP atom as the set of prefixes that have the same AS path towards them, and so the BGP atoms are computed per vantage point.

To compute which BGP events are due to TE, for each BGP event, its associated prefix, called candidate TE prefix, and its vantage point, we compute the set of prefixes that were in the candidate TE prefix's BGP atom in a two-minute window before the starting time of the event, to account for BGP propagation

[28]. Then, we compute the fraction of prefixes in the atom that also experience an AS path change seen from the same vantage point during the BGP event. If this fraction is lower than a threshold α, we label the BGP event as TE. The threshold implements our first intuition that not all prefixes of an AS are affected in one TE event.

In addition, if we see a subsequent BGP event after the TE event where the AS path changes back to the path before the TE event, we also label the subsequent BGP event as TE: Let us suppose that an AS O announces a prefix p and our vantage point observes the path VP-A-O to reach p. Then, O performs TE on p so that we observe a BGP event where the path to reach p changes from VP-A-O to VP-B-O. To realize this change, O had to make the path VP-B-O more preferred than VP-A-O, using one of the techniques described in Sect. 2. If O uses selective advertisement or a community to not announce to A, or if O uses prepending, the AS path VP-A-O does not exist, so if we observe it back, it means that an additional TE action was performed to make it exist again. In theory, complex routing policies with multiple links between ASes and MED (Sect. 2.1) could invalidate our reasoning, but our heuristic works well in practice (Sect. 4.1).

To be clear, we only apply this technique when the first event is TE. Indeed, if the first event was not labeled as TE and was due, for instance, to a link failure, seeing the first AS path again could just indicate that it was restored.

Multiple Stable Paths are Likely Due to TE. Our second idea is based on how BGP should behave during an outage. Say we observe a path change for the prefix p announced by AS O. It is observed from the vantage point at AS VP, and the path changed from VP-A-O to VP-B-O, because of an outage. When the outage ends, assuming that there was no other BGP event during the outage (and most outages on the Internet are short lived [41], so this should be a reasonable assumption), BGP will typically converge back to the path before the outage, or to another one because the tie breaker used to select the path was the time when the router learnt the path.

In other words, in case of an outage, one should observe at most three stable AS paths, namely the path before the outage, the path during the outage, and the path after the outage, making a fourth one unlikely. Therefore, if we observe four stable AS paths during a short period of time, we label the BGP events corresponding to the different AS path changes as TE.

One challenge with this heuristic is to find the right time window where a sequence of stable paths can correspond to TE. Indeed, the longer the window, the higher the coverage will be, at the cost of precision. From discussion with operators, TE operations should not last more than a few hours in general. Indeed, operators can perform TE to react to timely events such as traffic peaks or proactively shift traffic [8], but they can also perform planned maintenance. For this last point, we obtained from the operators of the PEERING testbed [46] to forward the emails from their neighbors informing PEERING that there will be maintenance. Over the period of August-September 2024, PEER-

ING received three emails from two operators, where the maintenance time was between four and ten hours. We evaluate the tradeoff between precision and coverage in Sect. 4.1.

Summary. A BGP event is labeled as TE if it respects one of the two conditions described in the previous sections. Our methodology has three parameters: (1) the threshold α of the maximum fraction of prefixes in the same atom that can change path together during a TE event, (2) the number of stable paths that need to be observed over a short period of time for the events associated to be labeled as TE, and (3) the time window to use to find TE events based on the multiple stable paths. We evaluate our choice for these values in Sect. 4.1.

4   Evaluation

Overall, our technique has a precision of 0.996 with only 20 False Positives (FP) on our ground truth datasets, and a recall of 0.91 (Sect. 4.1). It also has a high "consistency" over events from multiple vantage points (Sect. 4.2). In addition, the parameters that we chose, namely the maximum fraction of prefixes in the same BGP atom simultaneously moving (0.5), the number of stable paths (4) and the duration to look for stable paths (4 h) to label TE events provide the best precision without sacrificing recall. Finally, our heuristics to capture prefixes with TE from BGP dumps correctly identify them on our ground truth (Sect. 4.3).

4.1   Precision and Recall

Datasets: To collect TE events, we use three different datasets: 1) a dataset from prior work using TE to mitigate DDoS attacks [44], called *DDoS TE dataset*, 2) a dataset from a project deployed on the PEERING testbed [46] using BGP action community to perform TE[2], called *PEERING action community TE dataset*, 3) and our own TE dataset, called *Own TE dataset*.

The DDoS TE is produced from a setup that primarily utilized two any-casted prefixes. One of these prefixes served as a control and remained unchanged throughout the experiments. For the second prefix, it was announced from five different sites with varying levels of prepending. Initially, no prepending was applied at any site. Gradually, one site at a time added prepending, ranging from 1 to 5 repetitions. The experiment also included a reverse prepending phase, where every site started with 5 repetitions of prepending on the prefix. One site at a time then reduced the prepending incrementally. This experimental design demonstrated how prepending could be employed in the context of an anycasted prefix to steer undesired traffic away from an affected anycast site during a DDoS event. We selected the data for the prepended prefix from the week of 2022/03/21.

---

[2] This work is ongoing work and an extension from prior work [52].

The PEERING action community TE dataset comes from an ongoing research work directly obtained from the authors, that performs TE in the context of failover. The authors announce a prefix from a main site and multiple backup sites using extensions of different BGP announcement strategies to influence how the clients are routed in case of the failure of the main site. In particular, for our context, they use BGP action communities from their backup sites to restrict the set of providers to which they announce their prefix. We obtained this dataset directly from the authors, which contain the logs of their announcement with the timestamp. The experiments were run on 28/3/2024.

Our own TE dataset contains four /24 prefixes belonging to a covering /22, that we announce from our AS during one week starting at 2023/07/10. Our AS has two upstream providers, and we perform selective advertisements for three of our /24 prefixes, changing the provider to which the prefix is announced every 3, 6, and 12 h respectively. The last /24 prefix and the /22 do not change their announcement.

To collect non TE events, we mimic prior work [16] to retrieve outages, which says that there is an outage if both the IODA platform [10] and the Cloudflare Radar [7] platform detect an outage. We retrieve two outages: one in AS 34700 from 2024/01/11 13:50 to 2024/01/12 00:30 UTC, and one in AS 27839 from 2023/01/12 20:10 to 2023/01/12 20:40 UTC. We call this dataset Outage dataset.

For the DDOS TE, Action community TE and the Own TE datasets, we have the precise timestamps of the announcements and withdrawals corresponding to TE events, so we can retrieve the corresponding updates in publicly available BGP data. We collect BGP updates from the RIPE RIS RRC00 full feed collector peers for the corresponding periods of time. We retrieve a total of 854 TE events for DDoS TE dataset, 216 events from the PEERING action community TE dataset, 4,850 TE events for the Own TE dataset, and 2,714 non TE events in the Outage dataset. For the non TE event, we only consider the events happening during the 15 min after the start of the outage as being part of the outage, and thus a non TE event.

Results: We label TE events with a positive label, and non TE events with a negative label. Table 1 shows the recall on the three datasets with TE events and the precision on the forth dataset with non TE events. Our technique has a high precision (>0.99) with only 20 false positives. The recall is also high (0.91), but not perfect, with only 2 false negatives for the DDoS TE dataset, 536 for the Own TE dataset and 0 for the PEERING action community TE dataset.

We investigate further the false negatives to understand why our technique failed to correctly classify them. For the Own TE dataset, 175 events are due to the overlapping periodicity of our announcements: As the three prefixes exactly changed their announcements every 3, 6, and 12 h, there are times where they all changed together while being in the same BGP atom, making our algorithm erroneously declare that these events were not due to TE. For the remaining 361 events, the prefix is alone in its atom and does not meet the criteria of the multiple paths, showing a limitation of our technique to detect TE.

Table 1. Performance of our TE detection technique on four different datasets.

Dataset	TP	TN	FP	FN
DDoS TE [44] (2022)	852	N/A	N/A	2
PEERING action community TE (2024)	216	N/A	N/A	0
Own TE (2023)	4314	N/A	N/A	536
Outage [16] (2023 and 2024)	N/A	2694	20	N/A

For the DDoS TE dataset, we observe that prefixes are alone in their atoms before changing paths. The high performance of our technique on this dataset is caused by the numerous stable paths observed during a short period of time.

Grid Search to Find the Right Parameters to Tune Our Technique: Table 2 shows the precision and recall when we vary the three parameters to label events as TE: (1) α, the threshold of the fraction of prefixes simultaneously moving in the same BGP atom, (2) the number of stable paths, and (3) the time period to observe those stable paths. We observe that values of $\alpha = 0.5$, 4 stable paths, and a time period of 4 h give the best tradeoff on our evaluation datasets, with a precision of 0.996 and a recall of 0.91, so we select these values for the rest of the paper. In Sect. 5.4, we evaluate how this choice affects our result.

Other Sources of Events and Negative Results: To be totally transparent, we also report on our unsuccessful attempts to gather additional ground truth datasets. First, we tried to gather TE events directly from operators. We sent a survey to NANOG, FRNOG, and SWINOG, asking the operators if they would like to help us evaluate our technique by giving pairs of (timestamp, prefix) corresponding to their TE operations. We got responses from two operators, one recommending to change a question in the survey, and another one specifying that this operator was actually performing TE with prepending, but could not provide more specific information as they were not keeping this kind of information, so it was not usable for us to collect TE events.

In addition, we directly contacted four operators in August and September 2024, our R&E network, one major transit provider, one Japanese provider and one major CDN, in which we had privileged contacts, but we did not obtain any response from the operational teams at the time of the submission.

4.2 Consistency

We evaluate the consistency of our technique over multiple vantage points, with the intuition that if a TE event is seen by a vantage point, other vantage points seeing an event at the same time should also label it as TE.

We define consistency as follows: assuming we have a set of events, containing at least one TE event, we define the consistency over a group as the number of events labeled as TE divided by the number of events of this set. The sets of events are computed by grouping events close in time to the *TE event* together.

Table 2. Precision and recall when performing a grid search on the three parameters: (1) α, the maximum fraction of prefixes that can move simultaneously in the same atom, (2) the number of stable paths observed, and (3) the time window duration where we observe those paths.

α	# of Stable paths	Time period for considering stable paths (hours)	Precision	Recall
0.3	3	4	0.98	0.87
0.3	3	6	0.72	0.91
0.3	3	8	0.72	0.92
0.3	4	4	0.998	0.82
0.3	4	6	0.87	0.85
0.3	4	8	0.86	0.87
0.3	5	4	0.999	0.81
0.3	5	6	0.98	0.82
0.3	5	8	0.96	0.82
0.5	3	4	0.98	0.94
0.5	3	6	0.73	0.96
0.5	3	8	0.73	0.97
0.5	4	4	0.996	0.91
0.5	4	6	0.88	0.93
0.5	4	8	0.86	0.94
0.5	5	4	0.998	0.9
0.5	5	6	0.98	0.91
0.5	5	8	0.96	0.91
0.7	3	4	0.98	0.94
0.7	3	6	0.73	0.96
0.7	3	8	0.73	0.97
0.7	4	4	0.99	0.91
0.7	4	6	0.88	0.93
0.7	4	8	0.86	0.94
0.7	5	4	0.99	0.9
0.7	5	6	0.98	0.91
0.7	5	8	0.96	0.91

For each TE event, we build a set of events from the detected events, from other vantage points, starting within a 2 min window of the TE event. As we want to count each event only once, we perform a disjoint set algorithm on these sets of events to obtain our final sets.

Datasets: We collect BGP updates from the RIPE RIS RRC00 full feed collector peers for the week of January 8th 2024 to January 15th 2024. Applying our methodology to detect TE events and grouping them to compute consistency, we obtain 14,547,990 groups of events containing at least one TE event.

Results: The average consistency over the different groups of events of 0.98, with 96% with a consistency of 1, showing that most of the vantage points agree that an event is TE when at least one vantage point says so. We also verify that there are indeed multiple vantage points that agree that there is a TE event when there is a TE event, and that we do not have a lot of cases where there is only one vantage point seeing the TE event, which could lead to a consistency of one. We find that 85% of the groups contain events from at least two vantage points, confirming that in most cases multiple vantage points qualify events as TE.

4.3   Prefixes Affected by TE and Origin ASes from BGP Dumps

Prefixes Affected by TE. Recall that there are four TE techniques that we measure from BGP dumps: Selective advertisement, AS path manipulation (prepending and poisoning), and BGP action community. Finding the prefixes affected by AS path manipulation is directly visible from the AS path attribute from the BGP dump. To infer the usage of BGP action communities, we use state of the art [37], and our inference will improve as this technique improves.

We are left with evaluating our heuristic to capture selective advertisement.

To do so, we use the first dataset described in Sect. 4.1, where we announce our own prefixes alternatively to each of our two providers. We verify that our set of prefixes inferred to be part of a selective advertisement contain our three prefixes, and find that it is indeed the case. This evaluation only checks that our heuristic is able to find prefixes with selective advertisement, but does not evaluate its precision. However, it is hard to evaluate the precision of the heuristic, as the cases where the heuristic could fail are hard to reproduce. Indeed, selective advertisements can be used for blackholing or scrubbing purposes for instance. We are unlikely to see successful blackholing as such a route is usually not exported beyond the AS dropping the traffic [3]. Some scrubbing may be categorized as more-specific advertisements. For example one can redirect traffic to an off-path scrubber by advertising a more specific prefix from the scrubber. This is the exact same purpose as TE where one tries to manipulate the path followed by the traffic. We can find signs of such scrubbing by investigating prefixes with multiple origin AS or prefixes with ROAs allowing multiple origin AS.

Origin ASes Performing TE. For all the TE techniques, to evaluate whether we are capable of identifying that the origin AS is responsible for the TE, we compute the fraction of the (VP, prefix) pairs where the origin AS is responsible. This gives an idea of the coverage of our simple heuristics. Figure 2 shows these fractions for the different techniques over the years. Obviously, for the origin

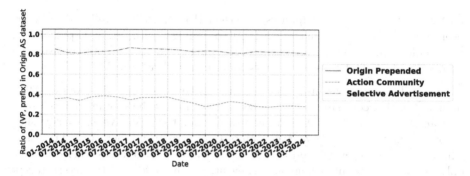

Fig. 2. Fraction of (prefix, VP) pairs with TE for which the origin AS performs the TE, over the years.

prepending technique (not shown on the graph), we are able to cover 100% of the (VP, prefix) pairs, while we are able to cover 33% of the (VP, prefix) pairs for action communities and 83% of the (VP, prefix) pairs for selective advertisement. The numbers are relatively stable over the years, varying from 29% to 39% for the action communities, and from 81% to 85% for the selective advertisement.

As a result, our study on which origin ASes perform TE (Sect. 5.3) only comprises the (VP, prefix) pairs for which we are able to infer that it is indeed the origin AS that performed TE, and therefore underestimate the number of origin ASes that are doing TE. However, these heuristics provide strong evidence that the origin AS is the one performing TE, and we choose to prioritize precision over coverage. Coverage for selective advertisement is acceptable, while we leave the design of more sophisticated heuristics to find the AS responsible for the TE in case of the presence of an action community for future work.

Finally, we perform an analysis of the peering relationships between the origin AS performing selective advertisement and the next AS on the AS-Path for the subprefix and superprefix. We used the IYP tool [26] to fetch the AS relationships provided by BGPKIT [15]. For all (prefix, VP) over the last 10 years of sampled data with selective advertisement, we compared the relationship of the origin AS to the next AS on the AS path for the subprefix, *i.e.,* the prefix selectively advertised, and the one of the superprefix. We found that the origin AS used two different providers for both prefixes in 8,284,827 instances. The origin AS preferred using a provider for the subprefix while using a peer for the superprefix 12,898,985 times. The origin AS used a peering relationship for the subprefix and a provider for the superprefix 10,157,301. Finally, The origin AS used two different peers in 16,458,100 instances. Note that in 824,656 instances the next AS in the AS path was reported to be a downstream from the origin AS either for the subprefix or the superprefix, and, in 33,783,811 instances, we did not have any known peering relationship between the origin AS and the next AS in the AS path for either the subprefix or the superprefix. These results show that all the possible different cases exist, with no strong domination of a particular AS relationship between the origin AS and the ASes it uses to perform selective advertisement.

5   Impact of Traffic Engineering

Overview: We find that TE techniques, since 2014, are widely used by operators, for each category of ASes. In 2024, a vantage point sees on average 11% of prefixes with origin prepending, 6% of prefixes with intermediate prepending, 10% of prefixes with an action community, and 13% of prefixes with selective advertisement (Sect. 5.2). Moreover, we find that hypergiants are the category of ASes that perform TE techniques on the most prefixes, relative to the number of prefixes that they own (Sect. 5.3). Using our methodology to analyze the impact of TE on BGP stability, we find that in 2024, 39% of the BGP updates and 44% of the BGP convergence time of the BGP events are caused by TE. Finally, exploring these numbers, we find that prefixes belonging to hypergiants contribute the most to BGP instability, relative to their small number of ASes (Sect. 5.4).

5.1   Datasets and Setup

We use our methodology to find TE prefixes from BGP dumps (Sect. 3.1) and from BGP updates (Sect. 3.2).

For the BGP dumps, we collect 21 snapshots over 10 years, from January 2014 to January 2024, one every six months, from all the full feed collector peers of RRC00, increasing from 18 in 2014 to 50 in 2024. For the BGP updates, we take the corresponding week of BGP updates starting at each of our BGP dumps. We discuss the sensitivity of collecting one week of updates in Sect. 5.4.

Then, we execute our different heuristics described in Sect. 3.1 on the BGP dumps to find prefixes with the different TE techniques. Finally, we run our algorithm to detect prefixes with TE events. This gives us two sets of prefixes with TE, which we call *TE prefix dumps* and *TE prefix events*.

Mapping Prefixes to Coarser Granularities. Throughout this section, we will present some results either per prefix, per AS and per AS type. To map a prefix to its AS, we simply look at the corresponding BGP dump. To map an AS to an AS type, we use the PeeringDB categorization [4], which contains 9 categories that are reported by the operators themselves. On our figures, we do not plot AS types with a very small number of ASes, such as Router Servers or Route collectors. Finally, we also remove the hypergiants from the content category to create their own category, to better emphasize some of our results about their participation in the TE. We retrieve the list of hypergiants from prior work [29]. For 2024, per category, we end up with 8,401 ASes for Cable/DSL/ISP, 3,219 ASes for Network Service Provider, 1,463 for Content, 940 from Enterprise, 138 from Hypergiant, 501 ASes for Educational/Research, 63 ASes for Government, and 294 ASes for Non-Profit. One might wonder the difference between the Cable/DSL/ISP and Network Service Provider categories. A manual look at dozens of ASes in these categories showed us that the frontier between the two

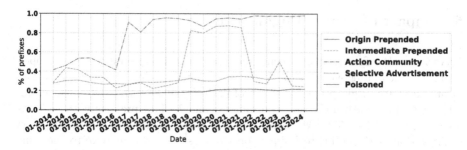

Fig. 3. Prevalence of the different TE techniques.

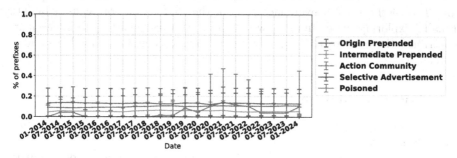

Fig. 4. Prevalence of TE techniques per VP, showing 25t, 50th, and 75th percentile.

categories was not clearly defined, as there are both transit providers and eyeball ASes in each category, although Network Service Provider seems to more correspond to transit while Cable/DSL/ISP to eyeball ASes. This distinction does not influence the takeaways of our results, so one can either consider it as a single or two separate categories.

5.2 Prefixes and ASes Impacted by TE

We use our TE prefix dumps dataset to find which prefixes and ASes are impacted by TE, and by which TE techniques.

Prevalence of TE Techniques: Figure 3 shows, over the years, the fraction of prefixes that have at least one collector peer seeing a TE technique among selective advertisement, AS path manipulation, and BGP action communities. We see that TE techniques are prevalent on the Internet, with BGP action communities being the most prevalent, with more than 99% of the prefixes affected since 2021. Path poisoning is the least prevalent, with less than 1% of the prefixes, while path prepending and selective advertisement are in between. Investigating the drop in path prepending between 2021 and 2022, we found that it was due in majority to AS 328474 and AS 174 which were prepended for 730,426 and 514,482 prefixes in 2021 and only 9 and 913 in 2022.

The 99% for action communities number is intriguing, so we complement our results per prefix with an analysis per vantage point. Figure 4 shows, over the

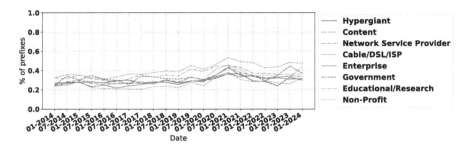

Fig. 5. Median number of prefixes affected by TE techniques per VP and per AS type. Prefixes from ASes in all AS types are affected by TE.

years, the 25, 50, and 75th percentiles across the vantage points of the fraction of prefixes that are affected by a TE technique. When looking at the median, selective advertisement is the most prevalent, with more than 12% of the prefixes affected since 2014. Path poisoning is still the least prevalent, with less than 0.01% of the prefixes. However, we see that the 75th for the BGP communities is higher than for the other techniques, showing greater variability across vantage points. Indeed, we find that 2 VPs contribute to 95% of the prefixes affected by action communities.

Prefixes and ASes Affected by TE: We study the type of origin ASes that are affected by TE. We map each prefix from our two datasets of TE prefixes to their AS type, and show on Fig. 5, for each AS type, the median fraction of prefixes affected by TE across the different vantage points. We observe that since 2014, all AS types are affected by TE, as the minimum fraction of prefixes over the years and across AS types is over 20%. However, there is only a small increase in the fraction of prefixes being affected across all AS types, with for instance, Hypergiants increasing from 27% to 30% between January 2014 and January 2024, and Cable/DSL/ISP increasing from 32% to 47% during the same dates.

5.3   Origin ASes Performing TE

After our analysis on which prefixes are affected by TE, we now investigate which origin ASes are performing TE, using the techniques described in Sect. 3.1. For each prefix affected by a TE technique and where the origin AS performs the TE, we compute the AS type of the origin AS. Figure 6 shows how each AS type contributes to the total number of prefixes with TE where the origin AS performs TE. We see that Network Service Provider and Cable/DSL/ISP networks are the most represented AS types, followed by Content and Hypergiants. A longitudinal analysis shows that there is a small increase of the fraction of prefixes taken by content and hypergiant, from 3% to 6% for content and from 6% to 10% for hypergiants between January 2014 to in January 2024 for content.

These results give a view of how different types of origin ASes perform TE on their prefixes. However, given that there are many more Network Service

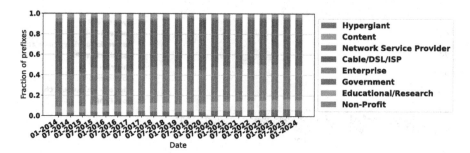

Fig. 6. Fraction of prefixes affected by TE where the origin AS is responsible for the TE, by origin AS type. Network Service Provider and Cable/DSL/ISP ASes are the ASes performing TE on the most prefixes.

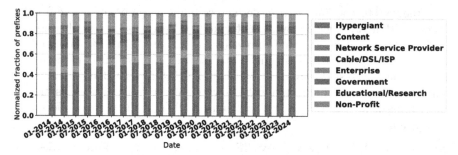

Fig. 7. Fraction of prefixes affected by TE where the origin AS is responsible for the TE, by origin AS type, normalized by the number of prefixes per origin AS type. Relatively to their small number of prefixes, Hypergiants ASes are the ASes performing TE on the most prefixes.

Provider and Cable/DSL/ISP ASes than in other categories, it is expected to see them practicing TE on more prefixes in absolute. To give another perspective, we normalize these results by the number of prefixes announced by each AS type. Figure 7 shows the normalized results, showing that relative to their number of prefixes, origin AS hypergiants perform more TE than other AS categories, and all over the years, varying from 42% in 2014 to 59% in 2024 of the normalized number of prefixes with TE, whereas the combination of Network Service Provider and Cable/DSL/ISP represent now 31% in 2014 and 21% in 2024 of the normalized number. For completeness, but not shown here, we mention that we computing the same plots as Fig. 6 and Fig. 7 per TE technique, obtaining similar results.

5.4   Impact of TE on BGP Instability

We look at three metrics: (1) The number of BGP events that are due to TE (2) The number of BGP updates that are due to TE; (3) The BGP convergence time taken by TE. This analysis is performed on the TE prefix events dataset.

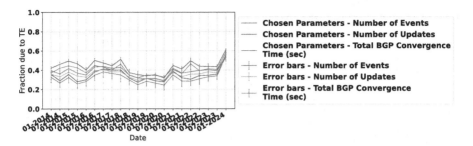

Fig. 8. Error bars of the fraction of the BGP events, BGP updates and BGP convergence time due to TE with 6 parameters set, plus the same metrics with the chosen values by our technique.

The number of BGP events due to TE is directly derived from our dataset. To compute the number of updates that are due to TE, we count, for each BGP event labeled as TE, the number of BGP updates between the path before and the path after the TE event. Similarly, to compute the convergence time taken by TE, we compute the difference between the two timestamps of the two BGP updates corresponding to the starting time and the ending time of the TE event.

Instead of computing our metrics on the whole dataset of BGP updates over 10 years, we sample them, taking one week of BGP updates every six months. We evaluate how our results are sensitive to this choice. We compute the error bars of the fraction of BGP updates and BGP convergence time that are due to TE over four consecutive weeks from January 2024. We find a mean of 52% and a standard deviation of 5% for TE events, a mean of 50% and a standard deviation of 5% for BGP updates, and a mean of 54% and a standard deviation of 6% for BGP convergence time. Moreover, over the month, the fractions are 50% for BGP updates and 54% for BGP convergence time. These numbers give an idea of the sensitivity of selecting an arbitrary week and how the results can slightly vary depending on the chosen week. We perform similar analysis on weeks in the different years, finding similar results.

Then, with these results in mind, we perform a longitudinal analysis of the impact of TE on our three metrics. Figure 8 shows the fraction of the BGP events, BGP updates and BGP convergence time due to TE over the last 10 years. We can definitely say that TE significantly contributes to BGP updates and BGP convergence time. On average, over the years, 35% of the BGP events, 39% of the BGP updates, and 44% of the BGP convergence time are due to TE. We can see that the impact of TE over the years varies between 32% to 55% for BGP updates and between 32% to 61% for BGP convergence time, with the maximum attained in January 2024. However, given the sensitivity of our results to the selection of the week, we conservatively say that we cannot conclude that TE takes a more important role to BGP instability in 2024 compared to 2014, but rather say that TE just has an important role in BGP instability, looking at the absolute values of our metrics.

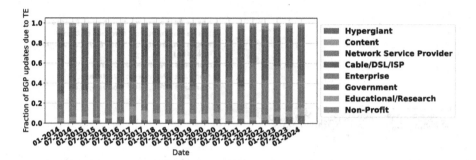

Fig. 9. Fraction of the BGP updates due to TE per origin AS type. Network Service Provider and Cable/DSL/ISP contribute the most.

Sensitivity to Parameters: We evaluate how the choice of the parameters alpha, the number of stable paths and the duration at which we look for those consecutive paths affect our longitudinal findings.

We ran our algorithm on the same one week sample of BGP updates over the last 10 years with 6 different parameter sets. We chose the parameters to be as conservative as possible in detecting TE. That is, we favor a high precision and choose the parameters which produce a precision of 0.99 or higher, from the sets listed in Table 2. It results the following parameter sets: (0.3, 4, 4), (0.3, 5, 4), (0.5, 4, 4), (0.5, 5, 4), (0.7, 4, 4) and (0.7, 5, 4) for alpha, the number of stable paths and the duration in hours which we look for those stable paths, respectively. Figure 8 shows error bars for the 3 metrics we study for the last 10 years. We can see that the values found using our chosen parameters (0.5, 4, 4) are similar to the average from the 6 runs with different parameters set. We found that BGP updates over the years moved from 35% to 32% when taking into account our parameters set with a 0.05 standard deviation on average. For the number of BGP updates it moved from 39% to 36% with a 0.06 standard deviation on average. Finally the average BGP convergence time due to TE moved for 44% to 40% with an average standard deviation of 0.06. To conclude, our results remain robust across a reasonable range of parameter values, suggesting our parameter selection is appropriate.

To Which ASes the Prefixes Contributing the Most to BGP Instability Belong to? After having shown global statistics about how TE affects BGP stability, we analyze to which ASes, and to which AS types the prefixes experiencing TE events belong to. To be very precise, we specifically do not phrase it as: "Which AS types contribute the most to BGP instability?" because for a prefix experiencing a TE event, we do not know whether the TE was performed by the origin AS or another AS. Therefore, our analysis shows which ASes and AS types contribute the most to BGP instability via TE because their prefixes do, but does not show which ASes actually perform the most TE operations.

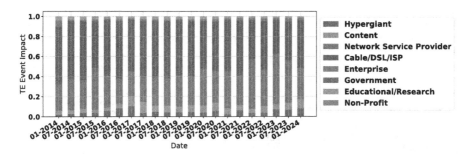

Fig. 10. Fraction of the BGP convergence time due to TE per origin AS type. Network Service Provider and Cable/DSL/ISP contribute the most.

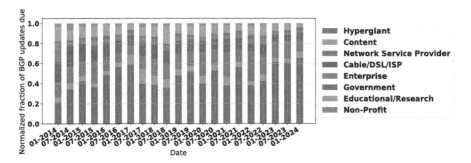

Fig. 11. Fraction of the BGP updates due to TE per origin AS type, normalized by the number of ASes per AS type. Hypergiants contribute the most.

For each TE event, we associate its AS and AS type as in Sect. 5.1. Figure 9 and Fig. 10 show the part taken by the different AS types in the number of BGP updates due to TE and the part in the BGP convergence time due to TE over the ten last years normalized by the total number of BGP updates due to TE and the total convergence time due to TE.

We can see that prefixes from Network Service Provider and Cable/DSL/ISP dominate for all years, with, for instance, in 2024, 32% and 48% of the BGP updates due to TE, versus 8% for the next most represented category, content ASes. Logically, we obtain similar results for BGP convergence time, with 34% and 48% of the convergence time due to TE that is taken by prefixes belonging to Network Service Provider and Cable/DSL/ISP.

However, to give another perspective, Fig. 11 and Fig. 12 show the same dataset, but normalized per the number of AS in each category. This gives an idea of the average participation of the prefixes of an AS in an AS category to BGP instability. Similarly to what we found in Sect. 5.3, this normalization shows that hypergiants, relatively to their small numbers of ASes, have the biggest fraction of prefixes participating to TE instability. Indeed, they are now the first AS type, representing 66% of the normalized number of BGP updates due to TE, and 60% of the total time of BGP convergence due to TE.

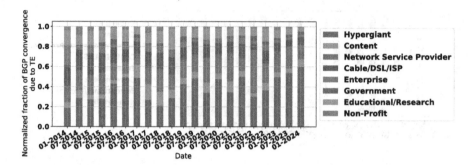

Fig. 12. Fraction of the BGP convergence time due to TE per origin AS type, normalized by the number of ASes per AS type. Hypergiants contribute the most.

Looking into more detail to which ASes belong the hypergiant prefixes, we find that the top 3 hypergiants ASes in 2024 are AS 16509 (Amazon), AS 396982 (Google), AS 13335 (Cloudflare). AS 16509 (Amazon) represents 45% of the BGP updates and 46% of the BGP convergence time of the 66% and 60% that are the contributions of hypergiants to the normalized numbers of BGP updates and BGP convergence time due to TE. AS 396982 (Google) represents 14% of the BGP updates and 20% of the BGP convergence time, while AS 13335 (Cloudflare) represents 8% of the BGP updates and 8% of the BGP convergence time.

6   Limitations

In this section we highlight potential limitations of our approach in capturing TE BGP events and in the validation of our methodology.

It is Possible for an Operator to Change Routes for all its Prefixes all at Once: As mentioned in Sect. 3.2, some operators can sometimes withdraw all the prefixes of one datacenter all at once to simulate failures. This action wouldn't be detected as TE by our algorithm.

Slow TE Actions Would not be Captured: Our algorithm looks for stable paths within a period of a few hours. If an operator performs their path changes over a longer period of time, our algorithm will fail to capture those events.

Conservative Parameter Selection: The two cases described above illustrate potential limitations in our TE detection methodology. Our conservative parameter selection prioritizes precision over recall, deliberately minimizing false positives at the expense of potentially missing some TE events. Consequently, our findings should be interpreted as a lower bound on the actual prevalence of Traffic Engineering in the Internet.

Validation Through Research Datasets: In Sect. 4.1, we evaluate our TE event detection algorithm using research-produced datasets. While operational

BGP data would provide additional validation perspectives, these datasets enable us to assess our methodology.

7 Conclusion

In this paper we presented a principled technique to capture interdomain TE from BGP dumps and BGP updates. Our technique achieves a high precision and a high recall on our ground truth datasets. With this technique, we perform a longitudinal study of the role of TE in BGP stability, both in terms of prefixes and ASes affected, and how it impacts BGP stability. On average, over our BGP collector peers, 35% of the prefixes are affected by at least one TE technique, while we find that TE contributes to 47% of the BGP updates and 54% of the BGP convergence time.

Ethics. Our work raises no ethical concerns.

A   Outbound TE

Outbound TE techniques rather rely on the local-pref attribute or changing IGP costs. The local-pref attribute is evaluated in the first rule of the decision process. Classically its role is to favor customer over peer-to-peer over provider routes [27]. An AS dedicates a range of non-overlapping values for each class of neighboring AS. It then sets a high local-pref value from the range to the preferred neighbor in a class. The local-pref is attached to the route and propagated only inside the AS. All routers in the AS then select the exits with the highest local-pref. The local-pref is not visible outside the AS.

BGP relies on the IGP cost to pick routes with the closest exit in the AS. This is the shortest IGP cost rule. A change in the shortest paths in an AS can lead to a change of routes followed by interdomain traffic. This modification can be solely internal to the AS (and eventually noticeable by a change of location community or the presence of BGP duplicate updates) or may translate in a modification of the AS-path.

References

1. BGP in 2020 - BGP update churn (2007). https://blog.apnic.net/2021/01/06/bgp-in-2020-bgp-update-churn/
2. Update about the October 4th outage (2012). https://engineering.fb.com/2021/10/04/networking-traffic/outage/
3. RFC 7999 (2016). https://www.rfc-editor.org/info/rfc7999
4. Peering DB (2019). https://www.peeringdb.com/
5. Automated Inter-AS Traffic Engineering: An open source approach and operational considerations (2022). https://ripe85.ripe.net/presentations/10-automated-interAS-TE.pdf, rIPE 85 meeting
6. Noction Intelligent Routing Platform (2023). https://www.noction.com

7. Cloudflare Radar (2024). https://developers.cloudflare.com/radar/
8. Cloudflare Traffic Manager (2024). https://blog.cloudflare.com/meet-traffic-manager/
9. IETF Draft (2024). https://www.ietf.org/archive/id/draft-ymbk-sidrops-rov-no-rr-02.html
10. IODA (2024). https://ioda.inetintel.cc.gatech.edu
11. NTT BGP communities (2024). https://www.gin.ntt.net/support-center/policies-procedures/routing/
12. Afek, Y., Ben-Shalom, O., Bremler-Barr, A.: On the structure and application of BGP policy atoms. In: Proceedings of the 2nd ACM SIGCOMM Workshop on Internet Measurement, pp. 209–214 (2002)
13. Ariemma, L., Liotta, S., Candela, M., Di Battista, G.: Long-lasting sequences of BGP updates. In: International Conference on Passive and Active Network Measurement, pp. 213–229. Springer, Cham (2021)
14. Arnold, T., et al.: Beating BGP is harder than we thought. In: Proceedings of the 18th ACM Workshop on Hot Topics in Networks, pp. 9–16 (2019)
15. bigkit: Fast, extensible, on-premise global BGP monitoring (2024). https://bgpkit.com/
16. Bischof, Z.S., et al.: Destination unreachable: characterizing internet outages and shutdowns. In: Proceedings of the ACM SIGCOMM 2023 Conference, pp. 608–621 (2023)
17. Caesar, M., Rexford, J.: BGP routing policies in ISP networks. IEEE Netw. **19**(6), 5–11 (2005)
18. Chang, R., Lo, M.: Inbound traffic engineering for multihomed ASS using as path prepending. IEEE Netw. **19**(2), 18–25 (2005). https://doi.org/10.1109/MNET.2005.1407694
19. Cho, S., Fontugne, R., Cho, K., Dainotti, A., Gill, P.: BGP hijacking classification. In: 2019 Network Traffic Measurement and Analysis Conference (TMA), pp. 25–32 (2019). https://doi.org/10.23919/TMA.2019.8784511
20. Cisco: Configure allows-in feature in BGP (2024). https://www.cisco.com/c/en/us/support/docs/ip/border-gateway-protocol-bgp/112236-allowas-in-bgp-config-example.html. Accessed 24 May 2024
21. Cittadini, L., Vissicchio, S., Donnet, B.: On the quality of BGP route collectors for iBGP policy inference. In: 2014 IFIP Networking Conference, pp. 1–9 (2014). https://doi.org/10.1109/IFIPNetworking.2014.6857091
22. David, L., Shavitt, Y.: BGP typo: a longitudinal study and remedies (2023)
23. De Vries, W.B., et al.: Broad and load-aware anycast mapping with verfploeter. In: Proceedings of the 2017 Internet Measurement Conference, pp. 477–488 (2017)
24. Elmokashfi, A., Kvalbein, A., Dovrolis, C.: BGP churn evolution: a perspective from the core. IEEE/ACM Trans. Netw. **20**(2), 571–584 (2011)
25. Feamster, N., Borkenhagen, J., Rexford, J.: Guidelines for interdomain traffic engineering. SIGCOMM Comput. Commun. Rev. **33**(5), 19–30 (2003). https://doi.org/10.1145/963985.963988
26. Fontugne, R., Tashiro, M., Sommese, R., Jonker, M., Bischof, Z.S., Aben, E.: The wisdom of the measurement crowd: Building the internet yellow pages a knowledge graph for the internet. In: Proceedings of the 2024 ACM on Internet Measurement Conference, pp. 183–198 (2024)
27. Gao, L., Rexford, J.: Stable Internet routing without global coordination. In: SIGMETRICS 2000 (2000)
28. Garcia-Martinez, A., Bagnulo, M.: Measuring BGP route propagation times. IEEE Commun. Lett. **23**(12), 2432–2436 (2019)

29. Gigis, P., et al.: Seven years in the life of hypergiants' off-nets. In: Proceedings of the 2021 ACM SIGCOMM 2021 Conference, pp. 516–533 (2021)
30. Gray, C., et al.: BGP beacons, network tomography, and Bayesian computation to locate route flap damping. In: Proceedings of the ACM IMC, pp. 492–505 (2020)
31. Gutiérrez, P.A.A.: Detection of trial and error traffic engineering with BGP-4. In: 2009 Fifth International Conference on Networking and Services, pp. 131–136 (2009). https://doi.org/10.1109/ICNS.2009.99
32. Hauweele, D., Quoitin, B., Pelsser, C., Bush, R.: What do parrots and BGP routers have in common? ACM SIGCOMM Comput. Commun. Rev. **46**(3), 1–6 (2018)
33. Kitabatake, T., Fontugne, R., Esaki, H.: BLT: a taxonomy and classification tool for mining BGP update messages. In: IEEE INFOCOM 2018 - IEEE Conference on Computer Communications Workshops (INFOCOM WKSHPS), pp. 409–414 (2018). https://doi.org/10.1109/INFCOMW.2018.8406955
34. Krenc, T.: BGP communities supplemental materials (2023). https://publicdata.caida.org/datasets/supplement/2023-imc-bgpcomms/
35. Krenc, T., Beverly, R., Smaragdakis, G.: Keep your communities clean: exploring the routing message impact of BGP communities. In: Proceedings of the 16th International Conference on Emerging Networking EXperiments and Technologies, pp. 443–450 (2020)
36. Krenc, T., Beverly, R., Smaragdakis, G.: As-level BGP community usage classification. In: Proceedings of the 21st ACM Internet Measurement Conference, pp. 577–592 (2021)
37. Krenc, T., Luckie, M., Marder, A., Claffy, K.: Coarse-grained inference of BGP community intent. In: Proceedings of the 2023 ACM on Internet Measurement Conference, IMC 2023, pp. 66–72. Association for Computing Machinery, New York (2023). https://doi.org/10.1145/3618257.3624838
38. Mahajan, R., Wetherall, D., Anderson, T.: Understanding BGP misconfiguration. In: Proceedings of the 2002 Conference on Applications, Technologies, Architectures, and Protocols for Computer Communications, SIGCOMM 2002, pp. 3–16. Association for Computing Machinery, New York (2002). https://doi.org/10.1145/633025.633027
39. Marcos, P., Prehn, L., Leal, L., Dainotti, A., Feldmann, A., Barcellos, M.: As-path prepending: there is no rose without a thorn. In: Proceedings of the ACM Internet Measurement Conference, pp. 506–520 (2020)
40. Nakamura, R., Shimizu, K., Kamata, T., Pelsser, C.: A first measurement with BGP egress peer engineering. In: Passive and Active Measurement - 23th International Conference, PAM 2022 (2022). https://pam2022.nl/accepted/
41. Quan, L., Heidemann, J., Pradkin, Y.: Trinocular: understanding internet reliability through adaptive probing. ACM SIGCOMM Comput. Commun. Rev. **43**(4), 255–266 (2013)
42. Quoitin, B., Pelsser, C., Swinnen, L., Bonaventure, O., Uhlig, S.: Interdomain traffic engineering with BGP. IEEE Commun. Mag. **41**(5), 122–128 (2003). https://doi.org/10.1109/MCOM.2003.1200112
43. Quoitin, B., Pelsser, C., Bonaventure, O., Uhlig, S.: A performance evaluation of BGP-based traffic engineering. Int. J. Netw. Manag. **15**(3), 177–191 (2005). https://doi.org/10.1002/nem.559. https://onlinelibrary.wiley.com/doi/abs/10.1002/nem.559
44. Rizvi, A.S.M., Bertholdo, L., Ceron, J., Heidemann, J.: Anycast agility: network playbooks to fight DDoS. In: 31st USENIX Security Symposium (USENIX Security 2022), pp. 4201–4218. USENIX Association, Boston (2022). https://www.usenix.org/conference/usenixsecurity22/presentation/rizvi

45. Schlinker, B., et al.: Engineering egress with edge fabric: steering oceans of content to the world. In: Proceedings of the ACM SIGCOMM (2017)
46. Schlinker, B., Arnold, T., Cunha, I., Katz-Bassett, E.: PEERING: virtualizing BGP at the edge for research. In: Proceedings of the ACM CoNEXT 2019 (2019)
47. Sermpezis, P., et al.: Artemis: neutralizing BGP hijacking within a minute. IEEE/ACM Trans. Netw. **26**(6), 2471–2486 (2018)
48. Silva, B.A., Jr., Mol, P., Fonseca, O., Cunha, I., Ferreira, R.A., Katz-Bassett, E.: Automatic inference of BGP location communities. Proc. ACM Measur. Anal. Comput. Syst. **6**(1), 1–23 (2022)
49. Streibelt, F., et al.: BGP communities: even more worms in the routing can. In: Proceedings of the Internet Measurement Conference 2018, pp. 279–292 (2018)
50. Sun, P., Vanbever, L., Rexford, J.: Scalable programmable inbound traffic engineering. In: Proceedings of the 1st ACM SIGCOMM Symposium on Software Defined Networking Research (2015)
51. Yap, K.K., et al.: Taking the edge off with espresso: scale, reliability and programmability for global Internet peering. In: Proceedings of the ACM SIGCOMM (2017)
52. Zhu, J., Vermeulen, K., Cunha, I., Katz-Bassett, E., Calder, M.: The best of both worlds: high availability CDN routing without compromising control. In: Proceedings of the 22nd ACM Internet Measurement Conference, pp. 655–663 (2022)

Global BGP Attacks that Evade Route Monitoring

Henry Birge-Lee[(✉)] ⓘ, Maria Apostolaki ⓘ, and Jennifer Rexford ⓘ

Princeton University, Princeton, NJ 08544, USA
birgelee@princeton.edu

Abstract. As the deployment of comprehensive Border Gateway Protocol (BGP) security measures is still in progress, BGP monitoring continues to play a critical role in protecting the Internet from routing attacks. Fundamentally, monitoring involves observing BGP feeds to detect suspicious announcements and taking defensive action. However, BGP monitoring relies on seeing the malicious BGP announcement in the first place. In this paper, we develop a novel attack that can hide itself from all BGP monitoring systems we tested while potentially affecting the majority of the Internet. The attack involves launching a sub-prefix hijack with the RFC-specified NO_EXPORT community attached to prevent networks with the malicious route installed from sending the route to BGP monitoring systems. While properly configured and deployed RPKI can prevent this attack and /24 prefixes are not viable targets of this attack, we examine the current route table and find that 38% of prefixes in the route table could still be targeted (see Sect. 4). We also ran experiments in four tier-1 networks and found all networks we studied could have a route installed that was hidden from global BGP monitoring. Finally, we propose a mitigation that significantly improves the robustness of the BGP monitoring ecosystem. Our paper aims to raise awareness of this issue and offer guidance to providers to protect against such attacks.

Keywords: Network Security · BGP · BGP Monitoring

1 Introduction

The Border Gateway Protocol (or BGP) allows for the exchange of routes between the independently-operated networks (known as Autonomous Systems or ASes) that comprise the Internet. BGP announcements contain reachability information for IP prefixes and are propagated from one network to the next to build the global IP routing table. However, BGP was designed with no form of message authentication, which allows adversaries to construct bogus BGP announcements for IP prefixes they do not control or legitimately route to. These incidents are known as BGP attacks or BGP hijacks. BGP attacks cause Internet traffic destined to a victim AS to be maliciously routed to the attacker's infrastructure. BGP attacks can cause significant damage, particularly as these

C. Testart et al. (Eds.): PAM 2025, LNCS 15567, pp. 335–357, 2025.
https://doi.org/10.1007/978-3-031-85960-1_14

routing attacks can be used to target higher-level applications run on top of the Internet [26,28,29,39,54,55].

While securing BGP is fundamental to the security of many critical applications that run on top of the Internet, robust BGP security is not practical today with available technologies. Relatively high-security proposals like BGPsec require updates to existing hardware and have not yet seen any production deployment [51]. Alternatives like Resource Public Key Infrastructure (RPKI) do have significant deployment but are still not ubiquitous and can suffer from misconfigurations [35,38].

A pragmatic and commonly used alternative to comprehensive BGP security is BGP monitoring. BGP monitoring involves observing BGP updates and flagging updates that appear suspicious. One advantage of BGP monitoring is that it leaves the BGP announcement syntax untouched. However, BGP monitoring has a core limitation: it cannot detect a route it cannot see [46]. Existing BGP monitoring systems have overcome this limitation by combining data from many vantage points spread across the Internet. With two of the most popular monitoring services (RIPE RIS and RouteViews) each having over 1000 different BGP peering sessions [2,3] with various top networks, this problem appears to be solved. Previous work on attacks that evade BGP monitoring only succeeded in affecting 2% of Internet hosts at best [31,46].

In this paper, we demonstrate that even with the vast number of peering sessions with monitoring services, if an adversary is capable of bypassing prefix filters and installing its route in the tables of tier-1 transit providers,[1] the adversary can launch a stealthy BGP attack (i.e., not seen by public BGP monitoring) that still succeeds. We introduce a novel attack on BGP monitoring that allows an adversary to stop networks peered with monitoring services from exporting the adversary's malicious announcements to monitoring services while still directing traffic via the adversary's route. Our attack involves the adversary tagging its BGP announcement with a specific value (the RFC-specified NO_EXPORT BGP community) so that networks using the adversary's route do *not* send it to BGP monitoring services. Even though this misuse of the NO_EXPORT community limits the spread of the adversary's route, the adversary can still install this route into networks commonly used to forward traffic to the victim using a *sub-prefix* BGP attack. This makes the effect of this attack substantial, sometimes even affecting the vast majority of the Internet.

We ethically demonstrate this attack in the wild (i.e., attacking an IP prefix we control) and found it can be highly effective, in our case capturing traffic from **all** of a sample of 1k random Internet hosts. Even while affecting nearly the entire Internet, this attack was invisible to all BGP monitoring services we studied (which included RouteViews, RIPE RIS, Cisco Crosswork Cloud, and ThousandEyes).

RPKI is an effective and deployed protection against this type of attack, and we studied the viability of the attack under the current RPKI deployment. We

---

[1] Several high-profile BGP attacks have involved adversaries directly installing routes into tier-1 transit networks [4–6].

found that 38% of prefixes in the route table are still vulnerable to this attack (as discussed in Sect. 4). We studied the behavior of the NO_EXPORT community at four tier-1 networks and found all networks we studied hid announcements from all monitoring services we studied when the community was attached. In fact, assuming an adversary only installed its malicious route at networks we confirmed were susceptible to this attack, the adversary could hijack traffic between 23% of random send/receiver AS pairs, according to our simulation. Finally, we conclude with recommendations that can significantly reduce the viability of this attack with simple configuration changes.

2   Threat Model

We assume an adversary capable of making a malicious BGP announcement with the aim of redirecting traffic. This traffic redirection can be used to attack several different critical applications that run atop the Internet [26,30,55]. The adversary also aims to avoid detection by BGP monitoring (i.e., launch a stealthy BGP attack) to prevent the victim from taking defensive action. We assume the adversary's announcement is not stopped by IP prefix filters (as is the case with observed real-world attacks [28,36,39]).

Furthermore, we assume the adversary will willingly seek new BGP transit or peer sessions to enable its attack. Internet eXchange Points (IXPs) have many networks colocated in a single location. This allows an adversary to cheaply establish many peer and transit sessions from a single Point of Presence. Furthermore, Virtual Machines (VMs) at IXPs can be rented quite cheaply (e.g., ~$30 a month [7]) and have ports on the IXP's peering LAN. Thus, these VMs can establish BGP sessions with other networks at the IXP [7–9].

Using an IXP VM, an adversary can approach colocated ISPs and request BGP sessions to propagate its malicious announcement. Social engineering or manipulation of Internet Routing Registry (IRR) data (as done in past attacks [36]) can persuade ISPs into white-listing a victim's IP prefixes on an adversary's BGP session. Many major BGP attacks have been launched by direct customers of tier-1 ISPs [4–6], and some adversaries have used multiple tier-1 ISPs to spread their attack [5].

3   Attack Details

Our attack relies on two key insights. First, the behavior of the RFC-defined NO_EXPORT community affects a network's sessions with BGP monitors. Second, because of longest-prefix-match forwarding, a network may be directing traffic over a route without hearing it or installing it into its RIB.

3.1   Hiding the Route: NO_EXPORT

At the core of our attack is the ability to hide a route from BGP monitoring systems even when that route is installed in routers that provide a feed to BGP

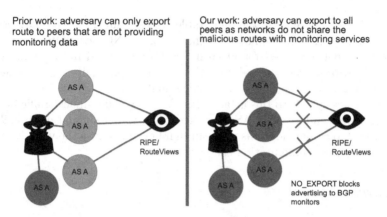

Fig. 1. Using our technique, an adversary can announce its malicious route to more peers while maintaining stealth. Even networks that directly provide data to monitoring services will not share the adversary's malicious route due to the behavior of the NO_EXPORT community on BGP monitoring sessions.

monitoring systems. We accomplish this using an RFC-defined "well-known" BGP community called NO_EXPORT.[2] BGP communities are 32-bit tags that can be attached to BGP announcements and can impact how routers hearing those announcements behave [33,40,53]. When attached to a BGP announcement, the NO_EXPORT community instructs routers not to export that BGP announcement beyond a confederation boundary. Most routing software honors this behavior by default [10,11], as support for the NO_EXPORT community is stipulated by the same RFC that defines BGP communities [33]. We utilize the key insight that **when the NO_EXPORT community is attached to a route, routers do not export that route on sessions with BGP monitoring systems**.

This is because most BGP monitoring systems use multi-hop External BGP (eBGP) sessions with participating peer networks to receive BGP updates [12–14]. To the routers that handle these sessions, they appear to be with an external neighboring network, and thus, the export restrictions of the NO_EXPORT community are applied. This creates the conditions that enable our attack: a router can have a route installed but not send it to monitoring systems. These conditions allow a malicious route to be announced directly to and used by networks that provide data to monitoring services while maintaining full stealth. This represents a significant improvement over previous work where a route would be detected if it was used by any AS sending data to BGP monitoring services [31,46]. These differences are highlighted in Fig. 1.

---

[2] The community NO_EXPORT_SUBCONFED has a similar behavior and can largely be used interchangeably with the NO_EXPORT community for this purpose.

3.2 Attracting Traffic: Sub-Prefix Hijacks

Hiding the route from BGP monitors does not, by itself, allow for a widespread attack. The use of the NO_EXPORT community means the adversary can only affect as many networks as it has direct BGP sessions. This is because all ASes use the same RFC-defined value for the NO_EXPORT community, so the first AS that sees an adversary's announcement will act upon the community and not export the adversary's route any further. This makes it difficult to scale to thousands of ASes.

However, the adversary can attract more traffic using a *sub-prefix* attack where it announces a longer, more-specific prefix than the victim (i.e., true prefix owner) it is targeting. Longest-prefix-match IP forwarding means that routers will always use the most-specific (longest) IP prefix possible that matches a particular packet. Thus, in any network with the adversary's sub-prefix attack installed, the adversary's route will take priority over the victim's. With this in mind, **the adversary can install its malicious sub-prefix route in large transit providers or upstream of the victim** that, due to their topological location, would naturally carry a large amount of the victim's Internet traffic. Even though the propagation of the adversary's announcement is limited by the NO_EXPORT community, the victim's benign BGP announcement attracts traffic to networks with the adversary's route installed. Longest-prefix-match forwarding then causes the traffic to detour to the adversary (see Fig. 2).[3]

3.3 Adversary Strategy

Combining these two techniques leads to the following attack strategy:

1. Select a victim prefix for the attack.
2. Use public BGP data to see which major transit providers carry traffic to that prefix (this can be trivially derived by seeing the most commonly used upstream ASes used for that prefix).
3. Rent a VM at an IXP where several of those transit providers colocate.
4. Approach these transit providers and request a BGP transit session.
5. Use social engineering and manipulation of routing data to trick these transit providers into whitelisting a sub-prefix of the victim's prefix.
6. Announce a malicious sub-prefix of the victim's prefix with the NO_EXPORT community.

This attack strategy is very effective as it affects traffic from a large portion of the Internet (potentially 100%, if an adversary installs the malicious route in all of a victim's neighbors) while being completely stealthy. Furthermore, although some steps, like the establishment of BGP transit sessions, bear a cost, this attack's stealth makes this infrastructure significantly more reusable. Presuming

---

[3] One potential countermeasure to protect against sub-prefix hijacks is RPKI. However, RPKI deployment is still not ubiquitous [15,43] and flaws in RPKI configurations still leave networks vulnerable to sub-prefix attacks [35].

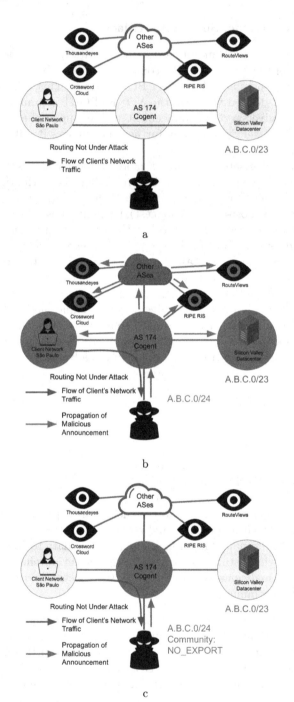

Fig. 2. Routing during benign operations (2a), a control non-stealthy attack (2b), and a stealthy attack (2c).

the attack goes undetected, the reputation cost of the attack is zero. This allows an adversary to potentially reuse its ASN, IXP VM, and transit links for many attacks. Stealthy attacks can avoid the negative reputation that often causes adversary infrastructure to get destroyed [5].

4   Viability of Launching a Sub-prefix Attack

This attack strategy relies on being able to launch a sub-prefix BGP attack against the victim. While many major ISPs filter customer BGP announcements with white-list filters based on IRR data, there are cases of adversaries using social engineering and/or malicious IRR data to circumvent such filters [28,36]. An adversary can also claim to be the upstream provider of a victim by adding the victim to its AS-SET in its IRR entry [36]. Being able to circumvent such filters and propagate its malicious BGP announcement is a requirement of any BGP attack and frequently occurs in the wild [5,28,36,39]. Barring strict prefix filters, two primary mechanisms remain to limit an adversary's ability to launch a sub-prefix attack: Resource Public Key Infrastructure (RPKI) and 24-bit prefix length filters.

RPKI is a cryptographic database of IP prefix ownership that can be used for filtering BGP announcements through a process known as Route Origin Validation or ROV [32]. ROV can be evaded by an adversary putting the ASN of the true prefix owner at the end of the AS path of its announcement. However, RPKI data also contains the required IP prefix length of any valid BGP announcement for a covered IP address. Route Origin Authorizations or ROAs are signed entries in RPKI databases that contain information regarding an allowed prefix, its length, and its appropriate origin ASN. ROAs have an optional max_length attribute which specifies the maximum IP prefix length for any BGP announcements of a sub-prefix covered by the ROA [35]. If the max_length is left empty, only the exact IP prefix length specified in the ROA is permitted. This system can be used to defend against sub-prefix attacks because ASes that perform ROV will reject announcements that are longer than a permitted prefix length. However, there are issues of network operators sometimes configuring overly permissive max lengths, which sometimes hinders RPKI's ability to prevent sub-prefix attacks [35]. If a max_length is specified, which is longer than the IP prefix seen in BGP, then an adversary can make a sub-prefix announcement for the victim's prefix, which is still RPKI valid and will not be filtered by ROV.

The other primary defense against sub-prefix attacks is 24-bit prefix length filters. In an effort to fight route table bloat, many network operators began capping the permitted maximum prefix length for default-free zone BGP announcements at 24 bits. Thus, BGP announcements for prefixes longer than 24 bits are often filtered [27]. While this often holds in general for global route propagation, there is a chance an ISP may choose to violate this rule for NO_EXPORT prefixes as these are not propagated beyond the receiving AS (thus reducing the impact of these smaller prefixes on the global route table).[4] While this may be true, /24 customer prefix filters are still a recommended best practice [56] and need to be considered when addressing the viability of sub-prefix attacks.

To better understand the viability of sub-prefix attacks, we downloaded the Routing Information Base (or RIBs) of all RIPE RIS collectors on August 16th, 2024. We filtered the RIBs to exclude any prefixes that had a private ASN as the origin AS, as these were likely internal-only announcements. Using these filtered RIBs, we collected a database of any IP prefixes seen in any RIS collector to find 1.3 million IP prefixes in total. We also ran the RPKI tool Routinator [48] to fetch the current RPKI database and condense it into a CSV output. Using this data, we performed a count of:

- How many IP prefixes are covered by RPKI?
- How many IP prefixes are covered by RPKI and have a maximum permissible length that is equal to the length observed in BGP?
- How many IP prefixes are 24 bits long?
- How many IP prefixes are 24 bits long or are covered by RPKI with a proper maximum length?

We found of the 1.3 million prefixes 711k (54%) were covered by an RPKI record. This result largely aligns with the NIST RPKI monitor, which currently reads 53% as of Sep 9 2024 [15]. However, this result changes dramatically when the appropriate max length is considered. Only 501k prefixes (38%) were in RPKI with a proper max length. This large threat surface introduced by max-length is also supported by past research on the max-length attribute [35].

We additionally found that 638k (49%) of prefixes had a length of 24 bits.[5] When we counted prefixes that had either a 24-bit length or were RPKI covered with a proper max length, we found that 811k (62%) prefixes had some protection against sub-prefix attacks. While this is substantial, it is a conservative estimate, assuming all ISPs perform ROV and filter /24 bit announcements. Several major ISPs are known not to do ROV [52], and prefixes longer than /24 are still propagated on occasion [27]. Regardless **at least 38% of the global route table is still vulnerable to sub-prefix attacks** making this stealthy attack still viable against a large number of victim prefixes.

5   Ethically Launching the Attack

We ethically launched this attack on the Internet using the cloud provider Vultr. Vultr allows customers with their own IP address space to make BGP announcements. Using space allocated by our affiliated institution Princeton University,

---

[4] This case is somewhat similar to the well-established allowing of prefixes longer than 24 bits for black-hole announcements [44].

[5] While this is a substantial percentage, it is worth noting that these are, by definition, some of the smallest prefixes in the route table so the fraction of IP addresses covered by 24-bit prefixes is likely significantly less than 49%.

we established BGP sessions with Vultr's routers from virtual machines at various Vultr data centers. We relied on the BIRD BGP daemon v1.6.8 running on Ubuntu 22.04 to handle the sessions with the Vultr routers and make BGP announcements. Our routers were configured as part of AS400065 which was the origin AS of our announcements (AS-VULTR AS20473 was the upstream). Also, note that Vultr operates several topologically disjoint data centers and does not use any private backbone for customer traffic. Because of this, these data centers can be thought of as distinct BGP-speaking nodes. With this real-world attack, we confirmed that the NO_EXPORT community offers stealth from monitoring services while allowing us to install a route into a major transit provider's network.

Our experimentation was completely ethical in that 1) all nodes making BGP announcements for these prefixes (including the ones being used as the adversary) had proper authorization to make these announcements, 2) the IP prefixes used were allocated specifically for research purposes and operated no real network services, 3) our experiment involved very few BGP announcements that did not pose any undue burden on production routers, and 4) we only used standard BGP attributes and community values that are commonly used in production routing configurations.

Normal Routing: We began by making a standard BGP announcement from Vultr's Silicon Valley data center for the prefix A.B.C.0/23 to the provider Cogent, which provides transit to that data center. This announcement provided routing for our webserver that was hosted in the Silicon Valley data center and served as the hypothetical victim's server. We confirmed this announcement had converged using various BGP looking glasses [16,17] (services provided by networks that allow operators to query routes used by those networks), and we confirmed data-plane connectivity to the webserver. At this point we configured four BGP monitoring services (Cisco Crosswork Cloud, ThousandEyes, RIPE RIS, and RouteViews) to monitor the victim's announcement and throw an alert if any sub-prefix announcements were noticed. We also configured a testing client in Vultr's São Paulo data center that had a BGP session with Vultr's upstream router that we used to 1) test connectivity to the victim's webserver and 2) use "show route" on our BGP router to observe this client's control-plane route to the victim's prefix. As expected, this client correctly routed to the victim's webserver and installed the proper control-plane route as announced by the victim.

Non-stealthy Attack: To verify our monitoring configuration, we made a non-stealthy control BGP hijack from the Vultr data center in New Jersey (which served as the adversary in our experiment) for a sub-prefix of the victim's prefix (A.B.C.0/24). This attack was effective in that traffic from our test client in São Paulo (as well as any other clients tested) was routed to the adversary. However, all control-plane monitors detected this attack. All four monitoring services generated notifications, and the Bird router at São Paulo had installed the adversary's prefix. Thus, while capable of hijacking the victim, this attack was highly noticeable.

Stealthy Attack: We withdrew this control announcement and updated our adversary's configurations to launch a stealthy attack, as discussed above. To do this, we attached BGP communities supported by Vultr to instruct it to only export our route to the provider Cogent. Cogent (AS 174) offers a Cogent-specific version (value 174:990) of the RFC 1997 NO_EXPORT community as specified in their routing guide for customers [18]. This was crucial for enabling our experiments as we were not a direct customer of Cogent but instead had to propagate our announcements through Vultr first.[6] Had we attached the RFC 1997 NO_EXPORT value to our BGP announcements, Vultr's border routers would interpret this community and apply export restrictions coming out of *Vultr's* network, preventing our announcement from ever reaching Cogent. On the other hand, the Cogent-specific NO_EXPORT value did not have any meaning to Vultr's routers and was transparently transited to Cogent, where the Cogent routers interpreted this community.

The adversary announcement for launching this attack was for the prefix A.B.C.0/24 and included a set of communities supported by Vultr that instructed Vultr only to export the adversary's route to Cogent and the 174:990 community supported by Cogent, preventing the exporting of the route beyond Cogent's network. In this manner, the stealthy attack was only in the route tables of Vultr's NJ data center and Cogent.

5.1 Attack Measurements

We confirmed this attack was both stealthy and effective via several measurements. We started by measuring the behavior of our São Paulo client, which routed traffic to the adversary instead of the victim. We used "show route" to examine the control plane route head by the client and found **the router still only showed the victim's announcement, meaning this client was affected by the adversary's attack while not hearing the malicious announcement in the control plane.** We expanded our measurements to look at the four BGP monitoring services we studied and found that none of them had thrown an alarm for the adversary's route. We further confirmed that Cogent was a peer of RIPE RIS (as specified in the RIS peer list [2]) and during our control announcement, Cogent's routers had exported the adversary route over this direct peering session. However, **when the NO_EXPORT community was applied, exporting of the route over the peering session with RIPE RIS was indeed suppressed.**[7] We further confirmed that the adver-

---

[6] This was because we did not want to invest in obtaining a tier-1 provider just for this experiment. However, the cost of a BGP transit session is minuscule compared to the gains offered by a BGP attack [28,39], making this a justifiable expense for the adversary.

[7] Cogent did not have a direct peering session with any of the other BGP monitoring services. Routes for the sub-prefix were suppressed in other monitoring services as well.

sary's route was installed in Cogent routers via the Cogent looking glass [17][8] demonstrating the ability to infect a network with a malicious route and suppress that network's reporting of the route to BGP monitoring services.

Having confirmed this announcement was fully stealthy to all the monitoring services we tested, we wanted to measure how much of the Internet was using the adversary's route unknowingly. To do this we took a sample of 4096 random IP addresses and ping scanned them with the command "nmap -sn -iR 4096". We are conscious of the ethical concerns with random scanning and ensured our technique was ethical by not performing any port scanning (preventing any behavior that could be seen as possibly probing for vulnerable services) and sending only a very small number ($\sim$3) of ICMP Echo requests to each host. We felt this scan was unlikely to raise any security alarms even on highly-monitored systems (as any public IP address is likely to be scanned several times as part of many projects) and imposed a negligible computational load even for under-provisioned systems. From this scan, we randomly selected 1000 responsive hosts to use in subsequent scans related to our attack.[9] This sample is representative of IPv4 addresses that respond to ICMP Echo.

With the adversary's attack active, we sent out ICMP Echo requests to each host in our sample from the victim's machine using a source IP address in the hijacked prefix. Thus, the host's ICMP Echo responses would be routed to the victim or the adversary, depending on whether that host's network was affected by the attack (see Fig. 3). When scanning the 1k sample, 739 hosts responded, all of which routed to the adversary (i.e., the victim was listening for responses but did not hear any while the adversary saw all 739 responses) **indicating that the attack had a global effect despite it being invisible to the route monitoring services we studied**. This was due to the victim exclusively using Cogent for transit and the adversary installing its malicious route into Cogent's route table.

6   Broader Viability of the Attack

At a high level, there are three elements that need to be present for this attack to be viable: 1) the major ISPs the adversary intends to poison with its malicious route need to honor the NO_EXPORT community and apply it to their BGP monitoring sessions 2) the adversary needs to be able to launch a sub-prefix BGP hijack against its victim (discussed in Sect. 4) and 3) traffic from enough source ASes need to be routed through the networks poisoned with the adversary's route for the attack to be effective. We analyze each of these aspects separately and find that each of these elements is viable in today's Internet ecosystem.

---

[8] The looking glass is not a BGP monitoring service as it is intended for manual debugging of routes and requires a high-latency query to be run for each route lookup command. Some looking glasses even explicitly prohibit automated queries [16]. Thus, we do not consider the presence of the sub-prefix route in the looking glass as attack detection by BGP monitoring.

[9] Not all hosts responded in subsequent scans, which reduced the effective sample size for each scan, but for consistency, we always sent to this same 1k host sample.

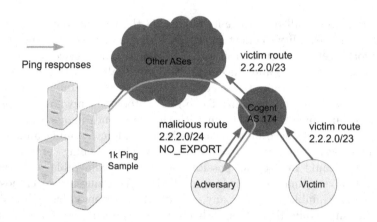

Fig. 3. The data plane during our real-world attack experiment. Because the victim exclusively used Cogent for transit and the adversary installed its malicious route into Cogent's network, all ICMP Echo (ping) packets from the 1k random host sample were routed to the adversary.

6.1   NO_EXPORT Behavior at Tier-1 ISPs

We studied the NO_EXPORT community behavior required to launch this attack at several tier-1 ISPs and confirmed the vulnerable behavior at all networks we studied. Even though RFC 1997 states that any BGP speaker that understands communities shall implement well-known communities, networks could conceivably strip these communities from BGP route announcements, or filter routes with these communities. Checking for these practices would require a direct connection to the associated network—not possible with our Vultr test environment. Instead, we reached out to the operators of several other tier-2 providers to assist us by making BGP announcements tagged with the NO_EXPORT community to their tier-1 providers. We were assisted by the operators of RGNet (AS3130 which used Sprintlink for transit) and NJEdge (AS21976 which used Telia and NTT for transit). These networks ran experiments using free IP blocks 192.83.230.0/24 and 130.156.183.0/24 respectively. Through this technique, we were able to confirm the behavior of the community at Arelion (AS 1299), NTT (AS 2914), and Sprintlink (AS 1239), in addition to Cogent (AS 174, which we tested through Vultr). At these networks, we confirmed the following behavior:

- These networks supported the NO_EXPORT community and installed routes with this community into their route tables (verified via looking glasses).
- These networks had a direct peering session with RIPE RIS [2] and RouteViews [3], except for Cogent, which only peered with RIPE RIS.
- These networks properly exported routes not tagged with the NO_EXPORT community to BGP monitoring but did not export our test announcements that contained the NO_EXPORT community.
- The announcements through these networks were *not* seen in Crosswork Cloud or ThousandEyes.

The networks we tested were all tier-1 ISPs that are on a significant number of paths. Even though it is difficult to scale these tests to large numbers of networks, our results strongly suggest the widespread viability of this attack. Based on the many networks known to support BGP communities [53], the language in RFC 1997 ("[these communities] operations shall be implemented in any community-attribute-aware BGP speaker"), and instructions for peering from BGP monitoring services [12–14], we believe the vast majority of networks are likely susceptible to this attack.

6.2 Impact of BMP and iBGP-Based Monitoring Systems

Our experiment focused on the two largest public BGP monitoring systems currently deployed: RouteViews and RIPE as well as two popular commercial offerings operated by Cisco: Cisco Crosswork Cloud and ThousandEyes. Based on customer configuration guides, all of these sources collect data primarily using eBGP peerings with participating networks [12–14, 19]. Other options do exist for providing BGP data to monitoring services, notably the BGP monitoring protocol (BMP) and iBGP. BMP is a protocol designed specifically for routers to send data to monitoring services [49] and can avoid the issues of the NO_EXPORT community. Additionally, some monitoring services use iBGP sessions to send BGP data, whereas peering routers still treat the monitoring service like another router but think the neighboring router is part of the same AS. This is achieved by the monitoring service establishing its BGP session using the same AS as the peer network. iBGP similarly avoids the export restrictions of the NO_EXPORT community, which is only applied at AS boundaries. The iBGP approach is currently used by the commercial network monitoring service Kentik [20].

Sadly, these methods lack adoption by the public BGP monitoring services, and data availability of commercial systems is significantly more limited. Many commercial systems only obtain BGP feeds from customers and provide data from those feeds for use by this individual customer. Even if commercial services do share feeds between customers, the viability of this approach relies on both the true prefix owner and the network with the malicious route in its table, both of which subscribe to the same commercial monitoring solution. Finally, as demonstrated by Cisco Crosswork Cloud and ThousandEyes, many commercial services are still dependent on data collected from eBGP sessions and some even have largely based their monitoring products off of RIPE and RouteViews data [21]. We believe that to have reliable detection of these stealthy attacks, changes must be made to the public monitoring infrastructure to make them detectable.

6.3 Simulating the Effective Spread of the Attack

We ran Internet topology simulations using the Gao-Rexford model of routing policies [34] to study the AS-level paths of Internet traffic between 150 randomly-chosen ASes. We measured the fraction of paths that contained an AS with the adversary's route installed under various different attack scenarios.

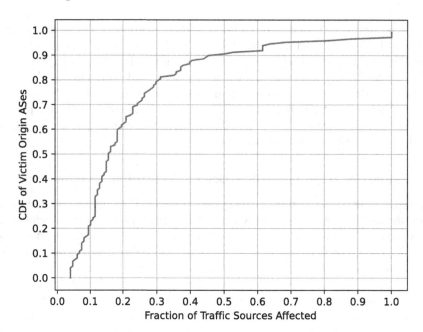

Fig. 4. A CDF of the fraction of traffic sources affected by a stealthy hijack launched by an adversary that installed malicious routes at the four ASes tested in this paper (that all are found to be vulnerable to the stealthy hijack).

We found that **by making its announcement to only five tier-1 ISPs, an adversary can on average hijack 37% of routes from random ASes to a victim destination.** Thus an adversary can still affect a large portion of the Internet even with the NO_EXPORT community limiting the spread of its announcement. Additionally, if the adversary announced to only the networks at which we confirmed the behavior of the NO_EXPORT community, the adversary could still, on average, hijack traffic from 23% of source ASes to an average destination AS. This vastly outperforms the capabilities of previous stealthy attacks (which often affected less than 2% of the Internet [46]).

We then ran Internet topology simulations using the Gao-Rexford model of routing policies [34] on the CAIDA AS-Relationships Data Set [1]. We simulated all routes between 150 randomly chosen ASes from the CAIDA topology. For each of the AS-level routes generated, we tested to see if one of the ASes the adversary could compromise with a stealthy attack was in the simulated path. If we so, we considered this path compromised as the source of the traffic would unknowingly send its traffic to an AS that had a stealthy attack installed in its route table (which would forward the traffic to the adversary). We grouped the data by origin AS, allowing us to obtain a percentage of traffic sources (i.e., source ASes) affected by the stealthy hijack for each origin AS.

We began by considering an adversary that only installed its route at the four networks we found vulnerable to the attack in Sect. 6.1: AS 1299, AS 2914, AS

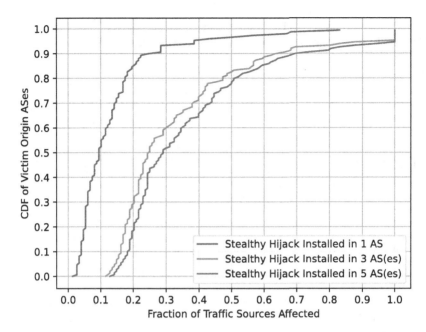

Fig. 5. A CDF of the fraction of traffic sources affected by a stealthy hijack launched by an adversary that installed malicious routes at the top 1, 3, and 5 networks by customer cone size.

1239, and AS 174. **Using only these networks, which we confirmed are vulnerable, an adversary could, on average, hijack traffic from 23% of the Internet.** The CDF of the percent of Internet traffic that can be hijacked by this adversary when targeting different victim destination ASes is shown in Fig. 4. Notably, some victim ASes (represented at the top right of the CDF) that used exclusively compromised providers for Internet connectivity have 100% of their traffic affected by the stealthy attack, representing the global effectiveness with 0% observability example we saw in our ethical real-world attack.

Given the behavior we exploit is stipulated in RFC 1997 (so all ASes capable of understanding communities should exhibit this behavior) and all ASes studied correctly conformed to this RFC, it is reasonable to assume the vast majority of major networks behave in this manner, particularly given the large amount of BGP community support [31,53]. Thus, we ran our simulation considering a strategic adversary that chooses ASes based on the size of their customer cones (i.e., the number of direct and indirect customers that AS has). Based on the CAIDA AS-rank customer cone counts [22], we modeled an adversary that compromised a varying number of the top ASes (in order of customer-cone size: AS 3356 lm, AS 1299 Arelion, AS 174 Cogent, AS 2914 NTT, AS 6762 Telecom Italia Sparkle). If an adversary only installs its stealthy hijack at the largest AS: 3356 (Lumen), it, on average, can affect routes to 0.13% of destinations. Using only the top 2 networks, an adversary can affect 18% of destinations on average.

This amount increases to 34%, 35% and 37% if the adversary installs its route in the top 3, 4, or 5 networks, respectively. A CDF of the effectiveness of these ¿ hijacks is shown in Fig. 5.

Overall, these simulations confirm that even if an adversary can only install its attack at a limited number of top networks, significant swaths of Internet traffic can be hijacked in a stealthy manner, making this hijack significantly more viable than previous techniques for launching stealthy BGP hijacks [46].

7 Defenses

7.1 Changes in BGP Configuration

At its core, this attack revolves around the fact that the well-known NO_EXPORT community restricts exporting to BGP monitoring sessions. The most immediate mitigation to this attack is to change that behavior. This behavior can be changed without even restricting the use of the NO_EXPORT community or changing the way BGP monitoring is configured. Instead, the RFC 1997 value for the NO_EXPORT community can be rewritten (via an ingress policy on eBGP sessions with external ASes) to a different AS-specific community. This community can then be matched on egress sessions with customers, peers, and providers to restrict exporting. However, this community would not have any effect on BGP sessions with monitoring services. We discuss additional configuration options to mitigate these attacks and show configuration examples in Appendix A.

7.2 Use of BGP Monitoring Protocol (BMP)

The BGP Monitoring Protocol (BMP) [49] is a protocol specifically designed for the monitoring of BGP updates and RIBs that can expose prefixes tagged with NO_EXPORT. BMP could potentially be run between peer networks and monitoring services in place of the standard eBGP multi-hop sessions thus allowing for full visibility of the RIBs of participating networks by monitoring services. BMP is supported in many leading BGP implementations [23,24] and has stand-alone implementations as well [25].

7.3 Increased Scope of BGP Monitoring

While the changes in BGP configurations and monitoring protocols proposed above vastly reduce the threat surface of this attack (as many major networks peer with BGP monitoring services), there is still a chance for an adversary to launch the attack at networks that do not peer with BGP monitoring services. Specifically, imagine the path between a traffic source and a victim AS pass through a transit provider T that does not peer with any BGP monitoring services. An adversary could still use the NO_EXPORT community to infect T with a malicious route and since T is not peering with a BGP monitoring service, the attack would remain stealthy. To this end, it is important that BGP monitoring services continue to expand the number of peers they use and attempt to peer with as many transit ASes as possible.

7.4 Use of RPKI

RPKI offers a cryptographic database of IP prefix ownership [42], which can be used to filter BGP announcements [32]. In addition to defining prefix ownership, RPKI defines the specific lengths of the IP prefixes that can be announced in BGP [35]. This can potentially prevent our stealthy BGP attack, which is based on a sub-prefix attack (although misuse of the max-length attribute can degrade RPKI's protection against sub-prefix attacks [35]). Limits on BGP prefix length hold even if an adversary bypasses traditional prefix ownership checks by prepending the victim's ASN to its announcement [38]. Thus, proper RPKI use is a strong mitigation for stealthy BGP attacks.

8 Related Work

8.1 Stealthy BGP Attacks

Milolidakis *et al.* studied smart BGP attacks that evaded public route collectors but used a vastly different mechanism to launch their attack (selective announcement to different BGP neighbors) and did not consider BGP communities or utilize any mechanism to prevent ASes that were peering with monitoring services from exporting the malicious route [45]. As these attacks must be limited only to ASes not peering with monitoring services, these attacks can only affect roughly 2% of the Internet in favorable circumstances.

Morillo *et al.* discuss hidden BGP hijacks that are not visible to networks affected by the hijacks because upstream networks perform ROV filtering on the malicious announcements [47]. Our attack similarly affects networks that do not have the malicious route installed, but in our attacks, the adversary intentionally limits the spread of the announcement via the NO_EXPORT community. Furthermore, while hidden hijacks are hidden from some ASes using the malicious route, there is no guarantee that they are hidden from monitoring services. Hidden hijacks involve the adversary announcing a standard, unrestricted, sub-prefix hijack (which usually has near-global visibility in BGP monitoring).

Heng discussed a BGP attack on a real network that evaded monitoring services by being localized to only a single source network (Yahoo mail) [37]. While this attack did affect a strategic target of interest to the adversary, it did not affect a significant portion of the Internet. Further, it can be seen as a real-world example of a smart BGP attack, as discussed by Milolidakis *et al.*. The malicious route used in the attack was not installed by any networks that were peering with monitoring services, and the adversary did not use any communities to control the propagation of its announcement. By use of the NO_EXPORT community, our attack has the potential to affect significantly more networks and remain stealthy.

Birge-Lee *et al.* discuss using BGP communities on equally-specific attacks to both enable BGP interception attacks and limit the spread of BGP attacks [31]. Our work has vastly different means and objectives than the previous work by Birge-Lee *et al.* The stealthy attacks presented by Birge-Lee *et al.* aimed to affect a single target of interest and **as few other hosts on the Internet as possible**, and this was realized by using BGP communities to shape equally-specific BGP attacks. Furthermore, the ability of these attacks to specifically evade BGP monitoring systems was not studied. Our work has a completely opposite objective (i.e., to affect as much of the Internet as possible, not just a single host) and achieves this using a sub-prefix BGP attack.

Miller *et al.* use the NO_EXPORT community in the context of BGP attacks that exploit traffic blackholing [44]. They do mention the community's ability to limit announcement spread and the use of the NO_EXPORT community on a sub-prefix BGP attack in conjunction with blackhole communities. However, they do not study the effect on BGP monitoring systems and, most crucially, do not come to the key insight that even ASes which provide data to BGP monitoring systems will inappropriately suppress information on the adversary's attack when the NO_EXPORT community is attached. Furthermore, using the NO_EXPORT community on blackhole announcements (where it is already a recommended best practice [44]) is significantly different than the use of the NO_EXPORT community on BGP hijacking announcements that actually maliciously deliver traffic to the adversary.

8.2   BGP Detection Systems

Given data from BGP monitoring, several works propose algorithms for detecting BGP attacks [38,41,50]. Our attacks' ability to achieve stealth is *independent* of what detection algorithm is used for processing BGP data as *none* of the adversary's malicious BGP announcements are seen by monitoring services. We do not exploit any specific BGP attack detection algorithm behavior but instead achieve stealth by preventing the adversary's malicious announcements from appearing in the BGP data fed into these algorithms in the first place.

9   Conclusion

This paper challenges the assumption that stealthy BGP hijacks are not globally effective and highlights the need to harden BGP monitoring based on our recommendations. Stealthy BGP attacks can be launched by using the well-known NO_EXPORT community on a sub-prefix BGP hijack. These attacks are highly effective at hijacking vast amounts of Internet traffic while remaining invisible to leading BGP monitoring services. These attacks are also not seen by affected ASes that are forwarding traffic to the adversary. While this is due to the RFC-specified behavior of the well-known NO_EXPORT community, simple changes to router configurations can mitigate this attack. These changes cause ASes peering with BGP monitoring services to still report routes tagged with the NO_EXPORT community. However, even with these changes, it is essential that BGP monitoring services peer with as many transit providers as possible. More broadly, the push for fundamentally more secure interdomain routing is essential as BGP monitoring will always be limited by the number of monitors available and what routes those monitors see. However, as we wait for robust solutions, securing ASes against stealthy BGP hijacks is essential.

10   Ethical Considerations

We took care to ensure that all of the research was ethical. All of our simulations and measurements used publicly-accessible data and did not derive any conclusions about individual users (that could be considered a privacy violation). Our ethical real-world attack was achieved by **attacking ourselves** and using only nodes (including the nodes we used for the adversary) that were authorized to announce our IP prefix. We obtained an IP prefix specifically set aside for network research from our affiliated institution Princeton University (that ran no real network services). Authorization for the use and BGP announcements of this prefix was given in a Letter of Authorization (LoA) signed by the relevant office at Princeton University. This LoA, as well as the Internet Routing Registry (IRR) entries for this prefix, contained all origin ASes used to originate the prefix in our 'experiments and, based on the LoA and the IRR entries, all of our upstream allowed our announcements. We only made announcements at a reasonable rate. Furthermore, given the well-known NO_EXPORT community is RFC standardized and SHOULD be supported by all BGP speakers that understand communities, we did not see any risk in sending out a BGP announcement with this community attached.

We also conducted random Internet scanning in this paper, but we made sure this scanning did not pose a volume, security, or privacy threat to the networks being scanned or the providers we used for the scanning. We scanned with a small sample (4096 hosts initially that was reduced to 1k hosts based on which hosts sent responses to our scans) using an extremely small number of packets (roughly 3 ICMP Echo packets) that were sent at a reasonable rate. This small frequency of packets does not pose an undue load, even on dated or under-provisioned equipment. We did not do any port scanning or scanning for support of protocols besides ICMP Echo, which prevented our scan from looking like an intrusion attempt. Finally, we did not record any information from the hosts that responded other than if they responded and whether their packets reached the victim or adversary during our attack.

Acknowledgments. We would like to thank Randy Bush at RGNet and the networking team at NJEdge for assisting with our experiments. We would also like to thank the Princeton Office of Information Technology for their support in this project. We thank the reviewers for their helpful feedback and Robert Beverly for shepherding our paper.

A Config Examples

This is an example of pseudocode for a router configuration that rewrites the
NO_EXPORT community at ingress to an AS-specific community that matches
the original NO_EXPORT behavior (except in the case of sessions with BGP
monitoring services).

```
filter neighbor_in {
    if NO_EXPORT in bgp_communities {
        bgp_communities.remove(NO_EXPORT);
        bgp_communities.add(ASN:123);
    }
    # Similar blocks need to also be include
    # for NO_ADVERTISE and NO_EXPORT_SUBCONFED
    ...
    accept;
}

filter neighbor_out {
    if ASN:123 in bgp_communities {
        reject;
    }
    accept;
}

protocol bgp neighbor {
    ...
    import filter neighbor_in;
    export filter neighbor_out;
}

protocol bgp  bgp_monitoring_service {
    ...
    import none;
    export all;
}
```

Another potential configuration change to mitigate this attack is to run BGP
sessions with monitoring services as Internal BGP (iBGP) sessions instead of
eBGP sessions. This way, routers would no longer consider BGP sessions with
monitoring services as crossing an AS boundary, and thus, the export restrictions of the NO_EXPORT community would not apply. There still may be some
attack surface left open by the RFC-standardized NO_ADVERTISE community [33] (which limits exporting to any other routers even in the same AS), but
these attacks are likely significantly less effective. If an adversary were to use the
NO_ADVERTISE community to launch an attack its malicious announcement
would be localized to only a single router.

References

1. The CAIDA AS relationships dataset (2023). https://www.caida.org/catalog/datasets/as-relationships/
2. (2024). https://www.ris.ripe.net/peerlist/all.shtml
3. (2024). https://www.routeviews.org/peers/peering-status.html
4. (2024). https://mailman.nanog.org/pipermail/nanog/2022-February/217602.html
5. (2024). https://mailman.nanog.org/pipermail/nanog/2018-June/096034.html
6. (2024). https://mailman.nanog.org/pipermail/nanog/2022-August/220320.html
7. (2024). https://ifog.ch/en/ip/ixp-access
8. (2024). https://www.bandwidth.co.uk/connectivity/reseller-ports/ams-ix
9. (2024). https://netactuate.com/remote-peering/ams-ix/
10. (2024). https://community.cisco.com/t5/networking-knowledge-base/bgp-communities-and-no-export-lab-scenario/ta-p/3154194
11. (2024). https://community.juniper.net/discussion/no-export-community-question
12. (2024). https://www.routeviews.org/routeviews/index.php/peering-request-form/
13. (2024). https://www.thousandeyes.com/blog/monitoring-bgp-routes-thousandeyes
14. (2024). https://www.ripe.net/analyse/internet-measurements/routing-information-service-ris/ris-peering-policy/
15. (2024). https://rpki-monitor.antd.nist.gov/
16. (2024). https://www.gin.ntt.net/looking-glass-landing/
17. (2024). https://www.cogentco.com/en/looking-glass
18. (2024). https://cogentco.com/files/docs/customer_service/guide/global_cogent_customer_user_guide.pdf
19. (2024). https://www.cisco.com/c/en/us/td/docs/cloud-systems-management/crosswork-network-automation/b_cisco-crosswork-cloud-user-guide/m_configure-peers-external-routing-analytics.html#Cisco_Concept.dita_abaecc2a-8423-40b3-808f-77b789e87c2d
20. (2024). https://kb.kentik.com/v0/Bd01.htm#Bd01-Router_BGP_Considerations
21. (2024). https://medium.com/thousandeyes-engineering/thousandeyes-bgp-monitors-fac4d272609c
22. (2024). https://asrank.caida.org/
23. (2024). https://www.cisco.com/c/en/us/td/docs/switches/lan/catalyst9600/software/release/17-6/configuration_guide/rtng/b_176_rtng_9600_cg/m9_176_rt_bgp_monitoring_protocol_cg.pdf
24. (2024). https://www.juniper.net/documentation/us/en/software/junos/cli-reference/topics/ref/statement/bmp-edit-routing-options.html
25. (2024). https://www.openbmp.org/
26. Apostolaki, M., Zohar, A., Vanbever, L.: Hijacking bitcoin: routing attacks on cryptocurrencies. In: IEEE Symposium on Security and Privacy (S&P) (2017)
27. Bayer, D.: Visibility of prefix lengths in IPv4 and IPv6 (2010). https://labs.ripe.net/author/dbayer/visibility-of-prefix-lengths-in-ipv4-and-ipv6/
28. Birge-Lee, H.: Attackers exploit fundamental flaw in the web's security to steal $2 million in cryptocurrency (2022). https://freedom-to-tinker.com/2022/03/09/attackers-exploit-fundamental-flaw-in-the-webs-security-to-steal-2-million-in-cryptocurrency/

29. Birge-Lee, H., Sun, Y., Edmundson, A., Rexford, J., Mittal, P.: Bamboozling certificate authorities with BGP. In: USENIX Security Symposium, pp. 833–849. USENIX Association, Baltimore (2018). https://www.usenix.org/conference/usenixsecurity18/presentation/birge-lee

30. Birge-Lee, H., Sun, Y., Edmundson, A., Rexford, J., Mittal, P.: Bamboozling certificate authorities with BGP. In: USENIX Security Symposium (2018)

31. Birge-Lee, H., Wang, L., Rexford, J., Mittal, P.: SICO: surgical interception attacks by manipulating BGP communities. In: ACM SIGSAC Conference on Computer and Communications Security (CCS) (2019). https://doi.org/10.1145/3319535.3363197

32. Bush, R.: Origin validation operation based on the resource public key infrastructure (RPKI). RFC 7115, RFC Editor (2014)

33. Chandra, R., Traina, P., Li, T.: BGP communities attribute. RFC 1997, RFC Editor (1996)

34. Gao, L., Rexford, J.: Stable internet routing without global coordination. IEEE/ACM Trans. Netw. **9**(6), 681–692 (2001)

35. Gilad, Y., Sagga, O., Goldberg, S.: MaxLength considered harmful to the RPKI. In: International Conference on Emerging Networking EXperiments and Technologies, p. 101–107. CoNEXT, Association for Computing Machinery, New York (2017). https://doi.org/10.1145/3143361.3143363

36. Goodin, D.: How 3ve's BGP hijackers eluded the internet – and made $29M (2018). https://arstechnica.com/information-technology/2018/12/how-3ves-bgp-hijackers-eluded-the-internet-and-made-29m/

37. Heng, L.: Invisible hijacking a case study of hijacking millions of IP address invisibly (2016). https://ripe72.ripe.net/presentations/45-Invisible_Hijacking.pdf

38. Holterbach, T., Alfroy, T., Phokeer, A.D., Dainotti, A., Pelsser, C.: A system to detect forged-origin hijacks. In: USENIX Symposium on Networked Systems Design and Implementation. USENIX Association (2024)

39. Kacherginsky, P.: Celer Bridge incident analysis (2022). https://www.coinbase.com/blog/celer-bridge-incident-analysis

40. Krenc, T., Luckie, M., Marder, A., Claffy, K.: Coarse-grained inference of BGP community intent. In: ACM Internet Measurement Conference, IMC, pp. 66–72. Association for Computing Machinery, New York (2023). https://doi.org/10.1145/3618257.3624838

41. Lad, M., Massey, D., Pei, D., Wu, Y., Zhang, B., Zhang, L.: PHAS: a prefix hijack alert system. In: USENIX Security Symposium. USENIX Association, Vancouver (2006). https://www.usenix.org/conference/15th-usenix-security-symposium/phas-prefix-hijack-alert-system

42. Lepinski, M., Kent, S.: An infrastructure to support secure internet routing. RFC 6480, RFC Editor (2012). http://www.rfc-editor.org/rfc/rfc6480.txt

43. Li, W., et al.: RoVista: measuring and understanding the route origin validation (ROV) in RPKI. In: ACM Internet Measurement Conference, Montreal, Canada (2023)

44. Miller, L., Pelsser, C.: A taxonomy of attacks using BGP blackholing. In: Sako, K., Schneider, S., Ryan, P.Y.A. (eds.) ESORICS 2019. LNCS, vol. 11735, pp. 107–127. Springer, Cham (2019). https://doi.org/10.1007/978-3-030-29959-0_6

45. Milolidakis, A., Bühler, T., Chiesa, M., Vanbever, L., Vissicchio, S.: Poster: smart BGP hijacks that evade public route collectors, p. 2 (2021)

46. Milolidakis, A., Bühler, T., Wang, K., Chiesa, M., Vanbever, L., Vissicchio, S.: On the effectiveness of BGP hijackers that evade public route collectors. IEEE Access **11**, 31092–31124 (2023). https://doi.org/10.1109/ACCESS.2023.3261128

47. Morillo, R., Furuness, J., Morris, C., Breslin, J., Herzberg, A., Wang, B.: ROV++: improved deployable defense against BGP hijacking. In: Network and Distributed System Security Symposium (NDSS) (2021)
48. NLnet Labs: Routinator 0.14.0 (2024). https://routinator.docs.nlnetlabs.nl/en/stable/
49. Scudder, J., Fernando, R., Stuart, S.: BGP monitoring protocol (BMP). RFC 7854, RFC Editor (2016)
50. Sermpezis, P., Kotronis, V., Gigis, P., Dimitropoulos, X., Cicalese, D., King, A., Dainotti, A.: ARTEMIS: neutralizing BGP Hijacking within a Minute. IEEE/ACM Trans. Netw. **26**(6), 2471–2486 (2018). https://doi.org/10.1109/TNET.2018.2869798
51. Siddiqui, A.: BGPSec – a reality now (2017). https://www.internetsociety.org/blog/2017/10/bgpsec-reality-now/
52. Snijders, J.: Cogent RPKI invalid filtering (2021). https://mailman.nanog.org/pipermail/nanog/2021-April/213346.html
53. Streibelt, F., et al.: BGP communities: even more worms in the routing can. In: ACM Internet Measurement Conference, IMC, pp. 279–292. Association for Computing Machinery, New York (2018). https://doi.org/10.1145/3278532.3278557
54. Sun, Y., et al.: Securing internet applications from routing attacks. Commun. ACM **64**(6), 86–96 (2021). https://doi.org/10.1145/3429775
55. Sun, Y., et al.: RAPTOR: routing attacks on privacy in tor. In: USENIX Security Symposium (2015)
56. Upadhaya, G.R.: BGP best practices for ISPs (2022). https://conference.apnic.net/22/docs/tut-routing-pres-bgp-bcp.pdf

Anycast

Characterizing Anycast Flipping: Prevalence and Impact

Xiao Zhang[1,2(✉)], Shihan Lin[1], Tingshan Huang[3], Bruce M. Maggs[1], Kyle Schomp[2], and Xiaowei Yang[1]

[1] Duke University, Durham, USA
xz234@alumni.duke.edu
[2] Cisco ThousandEyes, San Francisco, USA
[3] Akamai Technologies, Cambridge, USA

Abstract. A 2016 study by Wei and Heidemann showed that anycast routing of DNS queries to root name servers is fairly stable, with only 1% of RIPE Atlas vantage points "flipping" back and forth between different root name server sites. Continuing this study longitudinally, however, we observe that among the vantage points that collected data continuously from 2016 to 2024 the fraction that experience flipping has increased from 0.8% to 3.2%. Given this apparent increase, it is natural to ask how much anycast flipping impacts the performance of everyday tasks such as web browsing.

To measure this impact, we established a mock web page incorporating many embedded objects on an anycast-based CDN and downloaded the page from geographically distributed BrightData vantage points. We observed that packets within individual TCP flows almost always reach the same site, but different flows may flip to different sites. We found that 1,988 (10.9%) of 18,294 <vantage point, anycast IP> pairs suffer from frequent anycast flipping (i.e., a vantage point is directed to sites other than the most visited one of the anycast IP more than 50% of the time) and that 1,030 of these (5.6% of the total) suffer a median increase in round-trip time larger than 50 ms when directed to a site other than the most visited one.

We then used Mahimahi to emulate downloads of popular web sites, randomly applying the above-mentioned flipping probability (50%) and flipping latency penalty (50 ms) to CDN downloads. We found, for example, that there was a median increase in the First Contentful Paint metric ranging, across 3 vantage points and 20 web sites, from 20.7% to 52.6% for HTTP/1.1 browsers and from 18.3% to 46.6% for HTTP/2 browsers. These results suggest that for a small, but not negligible portion of clients, the impact of anycast flipping on web performance may be significant.

Xiao Zhang was with Duke University at the time this work was conducted. He is now with Cisco ThousandEyes.

C. Testart et al. (Eds.): PAM 2025, LNCS 15567, pp. 361–388, 2025.
https://doi.org/10.1007/978-3-031-85960-1_15

1   Introduction

IP anycast [31,35] is a routing paradigm that splits traffic among a set of physical sites. Operators advertise the same IP prefix – via the Border Gateway Protocol (BGP) [19] – from each site and traffic from clients to the prefix is routed to any one of the sites, distributing the traffic load across the sites. Further, IP anycast presents the opportunity to improve performance by routing clients to a proximal site [14,17,51]. For these reasons, IP anycast is widely adopted by large-scale network services, such as the Domain Name System (DNS) [30,43], content delivery networks (CDNs) [48] and DDoS mitigation services [32,45]. Thus, the efficient operation and performance of anycast networks is critical to today's Internet.

Clients of anycast services are commonly organized according to which sites they reach, and the set of clients reaching the same site is known as that site's "catchment". It is possible for a client to switch catchments. In the past, operators have raised concerns that such anycast "instability" could interrupt connection flows [28]. Because connection-oriented protocols typically store state at both ends of the connection, a change in site during a flow would break that flow. The existence of major services relying on anycast, however, belies the prevalence of broken flows. Indeed, previous work [49] demonstrates that changes in site occur rarely in measurements from RIPE Atlas [44] probes to the DNS root nameservers.

The same study, however, observes that 1% of the vantage points measured did "flip" frequently between catchments, sometimes changing with *each* measurement. In follow-up work [50], the authors show that flipping within TCP flows is rarer than flipping overall (impacting 0.15% of vantage points), and provide a plausible explanation that flipping occurs per-flow, rather than per-packet, so that all packets within a single flow reach the same site, preserving the connection. So, while flipping does occur, it is not observed to interrupt flows.

In our own measurements of anycast services, we observed high variability of round-trip-time (RTT). Intrigued, we set out to discover the source of the variability and found ourselves retreading the topic of flipping. While flipping is rare, using the same methodology as in [49] we found that for RIPE Atlas probes querying root name servers, flipping has more than quadrupled from 0.8% in 2016 to 3.2% in 2024, among the vantage points that collected data continuously over that time. In these experiments, a probe issues a query every four minutes, and a flip is said to occur if two consecutive queries by the same probe are routed to different root name server sites. Following the methodology in [49], a probe is said to be "flipping" if it averages at least one flip every ten minutes.

Investigating the cause of the increase through a longitudinal study, we find that increasing numbers of anycast sites – adding to the possibilities for flipping – contribute to the prevalence of flipping in 2024. With these changing network realities, we argue that anycast flipping is a more significant issue now, warranting further study of its impact on web performance.

Next, by downloading a mock web page with many embedded objects from a major anycast CDN through the BrightData residential proxy service [3], we confirm the finding that flipping rarely breaks connections and appears to occur per-flow. Furthermore, we find that the incidence of flipping from the BrightData vantage points to the CDN sites is perhaps even higher than from the RIPE Atlas probes to the root name servers. Because the CDN experiment differs from the DNS experiment (e.g., we didn't download the page every four minutes), we cannot adopt the same definition of flipping for both experiments. Instead we say that a vantage point is flipping if more than 10% of TCP connections are sent to a site other than the most common CDN site for that vantage point. With this definition, in the CDN experiment we found that 6,028 of 18,294 (33.0%) <BrightData vantage point, CDN anycast IP> pairs were flipping.

The CDN experiments also revealed that the round-trip time from a vantage point to the sites its requests are sent to can vary widely. Hence, we set out to measure the impact of flipping and the corresponding variations in latency on the time to download and render popular web sites.

In summary, this paper makes the following contributions:

1. We show that when querying DNS root name servers from RIPE Atlas probes, the prevalence of anycast flipping has increased from only 0.8% of probes in 2016 to 3.2% in 2024. We confirm the previous finding that flipping rarely breaks connections, and that flipping commonly occurs at the granularity of an entire flow. Further, using the modified 10% criteria for HTTP experiments, we find that flipping is also common when issuing requests from the BrightData residential proxy network [3] to a major anycast CDN, with 32.9% of <proxy, CDN anycast IP> pairs flipping.
2. We show that flipping can significantly deteriorate the RTT of a client to the website due to connecting to a further CDN site. For example, 20% of thße flipping vantage points have a median increase in RTT larger than 101.3 ms, and 10% have a median RTT increase larger than 167.7 ms.
3. We demonstrate that for clients that experience very frequent flipping and large latency penalties, the impact on web download performance can be significant. For example, we performed trace-driven emulations of 20 popular web sites with Mahimahi [33], extending it so that we could randomly apply a flipping probability of 50% to entire TCP flows and a flipping latency penalty of 50 ms. In this experiment, there was a median increase of more than 20.7%–52.6% in the First Contentful Paint metric for HTTP/1.1 browsers and 18.3%–46.6% for HTTP/2 browsers.

The current prevalence of anycast flipping, which is already significant and appears to be increasing, combined with the high latency penalties experienced by some clients when flipping occurs, calls for careful optimization of anycast deployments and perhaps even improved routing protocol design.

Ethical Considerations. Active measurements such as issuing DNS queries and downloading web pages cause load on the Internet infrastructure. As discussed later in the paper, we mitigated the impact of our experiments by issuing measurements at low rates or a small number of times. Our analysis of the frequency of DNS-query flipping is based on publicly available RIPE Atlas data,

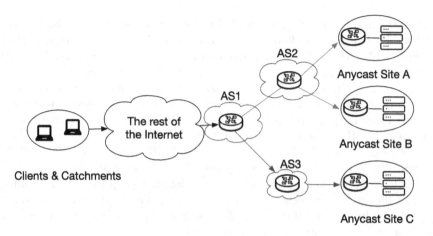

Fig. 1. An IP anycast deployment.

and did not require us to initiate any measurements. Our measurements of the anycast CDN were directed at a mock web site that was hosted using a free service provided by the CDN, the residential proxy is supported by Bright Initiative [7]. This work raises no other ethical issues.

Data and Code. Upon publication, the authors will make all data collected in this research and all code used to collect or process that data publicly available. The authors will also provide such data and code to the program committee upon request.

2   Background

In this section, we use network traces to illustrate several examples of anycast flipping in the Internet.

Figure 1 shows a simple anycast network with three sites, each one serviced by a single upstream autonomous system (AS). Routers at each of the sites peer with routers in the upstream AS and advertise a route to the same IP prefix. Upon receiving the advertisements, the upstream ASes propagate them further to other ASes. If a router receives multiple routes to the IP prefix (e.g., the router in AS1), it applies BGP best path selection [19] to choose a route to reach that prefix. Best path selection is a cascading comparison between metrics of the available routes, including – among others – the AS path length. Traffic from clients of the service to the IP prefix is then routed to different sites via the emergent properties of the different path selection choices made by routers in the Internet. The set of clients all reaching the same site is the *catchment* of the site.

Over time, catchments can change for a variety of reasons. One of the most straightforward is route updates. Upon each route advertisement/withdrawal, routers recompute the best path, which may be different from the previous one

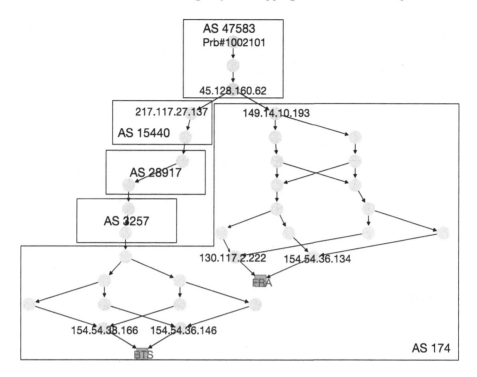

Fig. 2. Flipping at the border between two ASes

and originate at a different site. Wei and Heidemann [49] argue that updates are unlikely to cause frequent catchment changes due to BGP route flap damping (RFD) [47], although a sophisticated analysis by Gray et al. [22] provides a lower bound of only 9.1 on the percentage of ASes that implement RFD. But flipping can have other causes as well, including IGP Equal-Cost Multipath (ECMP), and BGP Multipath.

In this section we illustrate two examples that were collected from RIPE Atlas probes that we observed flipping. More details on our RIPE Atlas datasets are provided in Sect. 3.

In the first example, shown in Fig. 2, flipping takes place at the border of two ASes. The figure shows multiple traceroutes from RIPE Atlas probe #1002101 to the DNS C-root on Jan-02-2023. The traceroutes have been merged so that hops appearing in multiple traceroutes are represented by a single node in the graph. The probe flips between anycast sites in Frankfurt (FRA) and Bratislava (BTS). While the traceroutes produce numerous paths to the target anycast IP address, the third hop – the last in AS47583 – visually splits the paths among the two sites. Interestingly, the hops immediately after AS47583 are from two different ASes.

We are not sure what mechanism is responsible for flipping in this example. Originally, BGP Multipath required (among other things) the AS path of

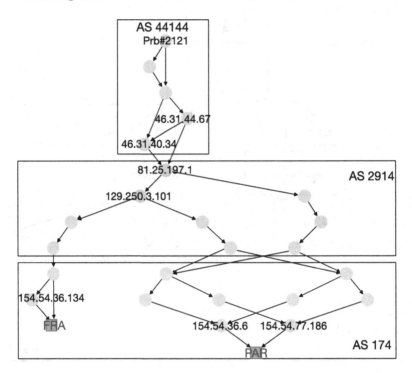

Fig. 3. Flipping internal to an AS

an alternate route to be strictly identical to the primary route in both the length and the sequence of AS numbers. As [26] notes, however, router configuration settings are often provided to relax the sequence requirement, e.g., Cisco's `multipath-relax` setting [1] and Juniper's `multiple-as` setting [2]. But in this example both the length and the sequence are different.

Figure 3 shows an example in which the flipping is internal to an AS. Probe #2121 flips between anycast sites of C-root in Frankfurt (FRA), and Paris (PAR) on Jan-02-2023. AS174 advertises routes to AS2914 in at least 3 places. Hop 81.25.197.1 forwards flows further within AS2914 that ultimately traverse different egress points to reach the different anycast sites. We speculate that AS174 applies ECMP internally to load balance traffic within the network, contributing to the flipping we observe.

3   Prevalence and Impact: Root DNS

In this section, we use RIPE Atlas's built-in measurements [39] to root DNS servers to characterize the prevalence of anycast flipping and its impact on the Atlas probe's RTT to each root DNS server. We first describe the measurement infrastructure and datasets we use. Then, we present how we infer anycast flipping from the datasets. Finally, we present the trend and degree of anycast flipping from RIPE Atlas probes to root DNS servers between 2016 and 2024.

3.1   RIPE Atlas's DNS CHAOS Queries

RIPE Atlas [44] is a global measurement infrastructure that has more than 11,000 active probes world-wide. It conducts several periodic measurements to all 13 root DNS servers and archives the measurement results for researchers to study the properties of the Internet. Specifically, we use the DNS CHAOS [16] measurement for this study. In this measurement, all probes send a DNS CHAOS query for the TXT field of the domain name `hostname.bind` to each root DNS server every four minutes. The probe records the response that it receives. A response to a CHAOS query from a root server includes a site identifier (ID), which we use to identify the catchment site of the query.

Datasets. To evaluate the trend of anycast flipping, we use the DNS CHAOS responses collected on the first Monday (24-h) of every half-year from the last half year of 2016 to the last half year of 2024, a total of 221 datasets. For comparison to [49], we similarly use all probes that RIPE reports active on the day of the dataset. For the first dataset collected on Jul, 04, 2016, there are 8,958 active probes; and for the most recent dataset collected on Jul, 01, 2024, the number of active probes increases to 12,724. The variability in active probes over the course of our longitudinal study could skew our findings on prevalence of anycast flipping, so separately we also study the 555 to 871 probes that are active across all datasets, per root DNS.

3.2   Root DNS Site Discovery

We parse the site ID out of the TXT record included in a server's response to determine the catchment site of a probe's CHAOS query and we use the change of the catchment site to detect anycast flipping (Sect. 3.4).

Each root DNS server uses a customized naming scheme to embed a site ID in the TXT record. For example, a site ID in a response from A-root can be 'nnn1-nlams-1a' or 'rootns-fra5', each consisting of several sections. The first section (e.g., 'nnn1' or 'rootns') indicates which DNS software is running on the responding server. The second section encodes the location of the site. In the first example, 'nlams' is the UN/LOCODE [20] for Amsterdam, Netherlands, while in the second example, 'fra' is the IATA [23] airport code for Frankfurt, Germany. The third section in the first example indicates the specific server/replica ID at the Amsterdam site. Similarly, the number '5' in the second section of the second example specifies the ID of the server located at the 'fra' site.

We manually examine the CHAOS responses from each root server and construct regular expressions to extract the site ID field from those responses. In addition, the site naming scheme of each root has also changed over the years. For example, L-root's scheme changed three times in the last eight years. Therefore, we use different regular expressions per root and per time period to extract the site ID from the TXT field of each CHAOS response. We note that some CHAOS replies do not follow any naming convention and appear to come from record injection attacks [38]. An example is a TXT record that includes the string `byaazbknliphsiiy.vla.yp-c.yandex.net`. The regular expressions we construct automatically filter such responses. For the datasets we use, we filter

2.0% − 2.2% of such responses. We include the regular expressions we construct in Appendix A.1. While there may be carefully crafted injections that also match the regular expressions, they would likely only impact our analysis to a very limited extent.

3.3   Geo-Locate a Catchment Site

In addition to identifying a catchment site, we also aim to geo-locate where the site is at the city level. This geo-location information enables us to measure the distance between catchment sites that a probe flips between. Since most root servers include geo hints such as UN/LOCODE or IATA codes in their site IDs, we first extract those geo-codes from the site IDs we obtain in the previous step. Second, we use a geo-location method to confirm that 1) the geo-code included in a site's identifier is accurate, and 2) resolve the locations of the sites that either contain erroneous geo-codes or do not contain valid geo hints. The second step is important because a site ID may include a wrong code. For example, a site used by A-root has 'tko' in its site identifier, which is the IATA code for the Tlokoeng airport in South Africa. However, using the geo-location method, we find that the site is actually located in Tokyo.

Our geo-location method works as follows. First, we pick the top three probes that have the lowest RTTs extracted from the same DNS request to a site. Because the RTT between two points at a distance of 100 km trip is approximately 1 ms at the speed of light in fiber, if the RTT of each probe to the site is less than 5 ms, and the geo-code in the site's identifier specifies a location that is within a radius of 500 km of one of the probes, we consider the site's geo-code accurate and use the geo-code as the site's location. For the remaining site IDs, we check whether the site identifiers contain any geo-hint that matches one of the three closest probes' locations. For example, a site of A-root contains the string 'elpek' in its ID. Although it complies with the format of a UN/LOCODE, it is not a valid UN/LOCODE. But the sub-string, 'pek' is the IATA airport code for Beijing, China, and the three probes within 5 ms of this site confirm that the site is in Beijing. Finally, for the remaining unresolved sites, we use IP-geo information [24] of the penultimate hop in a traceroute measurement from each of the three-closest probes that only targeting to this site to locate the site. For example, a site ID 's1.org' from I-root contains no valid geo-hint and is resolved in this final step. We verified that all of the site geo-locations developed using this method match the reported locations of root server sites from [6].

We use the dataset obtained on Jan 02, 2023 as an example to show how many sites we are able to resolve at each step. We extract a total of 1,014 site IDs. Among them, we confirm 808 of them as valid geo-codes in the first step. We are able to resolve 198 sites' locations in the second step. The final step (traceroute) resolves the remaining eight sites. Other datasets have similar results.

3.4   Estimating Anycast Flipping

After we obtain the site ID and the geo-location of each catchment site a probe reaches, we are able to quantify anycast flipping. We use the same anycast flip-

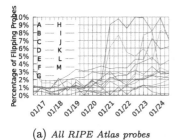

(a) *All RIPE Atlas probes*

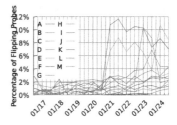

(b) *RIPE Atlas probes that are active throughout the past eight years*

Fig. 4. The percentage of RIPE Atlas probes that experience anycast flipping to root DNS servers over the past eight years. Left: All probes whose measurements are available. Right: the common subset of the probes that are active throughout the entire eight years.

ping detection and counting mechanism as in [49]. For each probe and for each dataset, we construct a time-series vector that consists of the catchment sites a probe reaches. If the catchment sites in two consecutive CHAOS responses are different, we count it as a flip. We then calculate the mean time between two flips across the whole day for each probe. Following the methodology in [49], if the mean flipping time is less than 10 min (1 flip per 2.5 rounds), then we consider this probe to experience anycast flipping. While we could devise other approaches to measuring anycast flipping, our goal is to revisit the findings in [49] and extend them to determine the relative prevalence of anycast flipping since 2016. To verify that we've reproduced the mechanism accurately, we compare the flipping results we obtain using the same dataset as used in [49] (Aug-01-2016) and confirm the results are almost identical. For example, on that day, C-root had a flipping fraction of 1.2% in our measurement, and it is the same value in [49], similar findings for the other roots. Therefore, we conclude that we are measuring the same phenomenon as in [49].

3.5   Longitudinal View of Anycast Flipping

Now, we describe our reproduction of the results from the 2016 study [49] and our longitudinal study of anycast flipping since then. Among all active probes, our longitudinal study finds that the percentage of RIPE Atlas probes that experience anycast flipping has increased from about 1.1% to 3.5% within the past eight years, when averaged across the DNS roots. Since the RIPE Atlas probe deployment has changed over those years, we also measure the increase in anycast flipping by holding the probes constant to only the subset of probes that are active for the entirety of the study, since this subset should be more likely to stay stable in the same network and geographical area than the other. This number varies per DNS root, between 555 for F-root and 871 for H-root. Again when averaged across the DNS roots, we find that anycast flipping has increased from 0.8% to 3.2% among the probes active throughout the entire study.

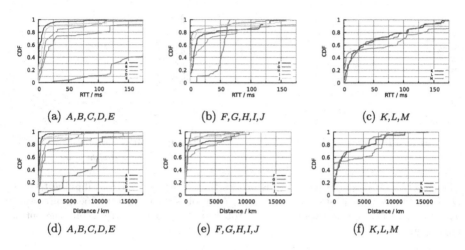

Fig. 5. Extra RTT and Extra Distance Caused by Anycast Flapping for Anycast Flipping Probes

We present the longitudinal percentage of anycast flipping probes in Fig. 4a and Fig. 4b, for all RIPE Atlas probes and the continuously active probes, respectively. As the trend is similar for both, we focus on describing the findings for all probes. For nine of the 13 roots, the probes have a significant increase in anycast flipping during our measurement period. The most noticeable changes occur with A-root and J-root. Eight years ago, anycast flipping with both roots was minimal, but now, A-root incurs one of the largest amounts of anycast flipping among RIPE Atlas probes, from 0.0% (only very few probes flipped at that time) to 7.1%. J-root sees a similar increase, although not as pronounced. Interestingly, both had a significant step between the second half year of 2020 and the first half year of 2021. We investigate A-root to better understand the causes.

A-root anycast flipping drastically increased from 2.0% to 9.8% between 2020 and 2021. On Jul-06-2020, RIPE Atlas probes received CHAOS TXT records that mapped to 21 sites, but half a year later the records mapped to two additional sites, 'mnz' and 'wie'. Further, 88.9% of the probes that started flipping in 2021 but were not in 2020 reached at least one of the two new sites. We suspect that A-root deployed the two new sites at this time and that the introduction of the new sites likely created new opportunities for BGP Multipath (see Sect. 2).

3.6   Does Flipping Break TCP Connections?

The prevalence of anycast CDNs suggests that anycast flipping does not tear down TCP connections, and the anycast flipping study [49] in 2016 found that very few RIPE Atlas probes consistently failed to build a TCP session with the J root name server and a small number of those probes also suffer from UDP anycast flipping.

We use the RIPE Atlas built-in measurement that sends TCP DNS queries to obtain the SOA field of route DNS servers to further confirm this phenomenon. Using a dataset obtained on Jan-02-2023, we find that 97.4%–98.0% of the probes can successfully establish TCP connections with a root DNS server. Only 220 probes cannot establish TCP connections to any root DNS server and among those probes, at most 8 of them experience anycast flipping to some root DNS servers. The very small overlap between probes that cannot establish a TCP connection and probes that experience anycast flipping suggests that anycast flipping is unlikely to break TCP connections for the majority of Internet paths.

3.7 Impact on RTTs

For each of the RIPE Atlas probes (154 - 1243 for different roots) that we observed flipping on Jan-02-2023 to a root DNS server, we compute the median RTT towards each of the anycast sites that they flip between. We then take the difference in the RTT to determine how much extra RTT flipping adds. Note that probes can flip between more than 2 sites – for A-root, 205 probes do. In that case, we take the difference between the minimum and maximum median RTTs to the sites, to determine the worst case extra RTT that flipping adds. Figure 5 shows the distribution per root of the extra RTT. In addition, we show the percentage of the probes whose difference in RTT exceeds 50ms and that flip among more than 2 sites in Table 1.

Table 1. Anycast flipping impact (>**50 ms difference**: Flipping that causes more than 50 ms round-trip-time difference between sites. >**2 sites**: Flipping that reaches more than 2 different anycast sites).

Root	Probes that flip	>50 ms difference	>2 sites
A	1243	38 (3.06%)	205 (16.49%)
B	162	156 (96.30%)	2 (1.23%)
C	154	40 (25.97%)	0 (0.00%)
D	573	84 (14.66%)	121 (21.12%)
E	309	24 (7.77%)	40 (12.94%)
F	249	45 (18.07%)	22 (8.84%)
G	164	106 (64.63%)	0 (0.00%)
H	965	114 (11.81%)	0 (0.00%)
I	334	83 (24.85%)	16 (4.79%)
J	746	71 (9.52%)	76 (10.19%)
K	265	92 (34.72%)	30 (11.32%)
L	542	177 (32.66%)	92 (16.97%)
M	288	130 (45.14%)	0 (0.00%)

For B-root and G-root, the difference in RTT is extreme: nearly 80% of the flipping RIPE Atlas probes experience extra RTT of over 120 ms/50 ms to B-root/G-root, respectively. More probes flip reaching A-root than any other root, but the extra RTT in A-root is minimal: the extra RTT for 90% (1118 out of 1243 probes) of the probes less than 12 ms, indicating that flipping in A-root occurs between nearby sites. For the other roots, the majority of probes experience modest extra RTT. Overall, though, 24 to 177 probes (0.2%–1.4% of all probes) experience more than $\geq$50 ms extra RTT to at least one root.

We measure the distance between a probe and its catchment site. In Fig. 5, we show the distribution of the extra distance corresponding to a probe's flipping sites with which we compute the extra RTT. As we can see, the long extra RTTs often correspond to long geographic distance between a probe's catchment sites. In G-root, however, the large extra RTT does not correspond to similarly large extra distance. We're uncertain why anycast flipping adds so much RTT in this case. In one extreme example, we highlight the case of RIPE Atlas probe #6506 which is reportedly located in Singapore. This probe flips between a C-root site located also in Singapore and another site in Los Angeles, USA.

4   Prevalence and Impact: Anycast CDN

We have observed anycast flipping in the root DNS IP anycast system. Does anycast flipping also impact anycast CDNs? To answer this question, we study anycast flipping in a major anycast CDN. In this section, we use BrightData [3], a proxy service provider, to explore the prevalence of anycast flipping using different vantage points than RIPE Atlas probes and with a new target: an anycast CDN.

4.1   Infrastructure

The RIPE-Atlas-based measurements can show us anycast flipping to the root name servers. To our knowledge, however, no existing measurements cover any-cast flipping to CDN servers. Therefore, we utilize a residential proxy service provider, BrightData [3], to measure anycast flipping to one of the largest any-cast CDNs. This residential proxy service has previously been used in other mea-surement studies, e.g. [15]. According to their website description, BrightData's infrastructure consists of more than 72 million proxy nodes. In our experiments, we uncover 9,568 unique vantage points (distinguished by IP address) that span 143 different countries and 1,912 different ASes.

4.2   Methodology

To measure anycast flipping, we build a mock webpage, consisting of one main page embedded with 50 one-pixel images. Next, we configure this webpage and all embedded images to be served by the anycast CDN and make them cacheable

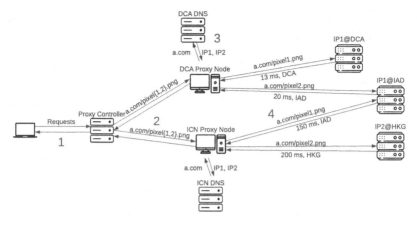

Fig. 6. This figure shows how we measure anycast flipping to an anycast CDN. The measurement machine connects to the proxy controller and selects the proxy nodes that send an HTTP request for the mock webpage we create. When a proxy node contacts its DNS server, it receives two IP addresses returned by the anycast CDN's DNS. A proxy node chooses either one or two IPs to send the HTTP requests. When anycast flipping happens, the DCA (Arlington, VA) proxy node reaches two CDN edge servers (DCA-Arlington, VA server and IAD-Dulles, VA server) when using the IP address IP1.

by the CDN. Therefore, a web client can retrieve them directly from the CDN's edge servers.

Figure 6 shows our experimental setup. Our measurement machine connects to BrightData's proxy controller and instructs the controller to select geographically distributed proxy nodes for experimentation. To simulate the webpage retrieval process from the anycast CDN server, we instrument `curl` to fetch the 50 pixel images through the proxy node.

The anycast CDN's DNS returns 2 IP anycast addresses in resolutions of our test hostname. Therefore, we aim to measure anycast flipping for each of these IP addresses, separately. With the help of BrightData's technical support, we append 'dns-remote-dns-peer-info'in the proxy's user name string in the HTTP request, which instructs the proxy nodes to return the target IP address in an HTTP header of the response.

When a proxy node receives the response from a CDN server, it records a performance timing profile that records the timing information including connect time of each request and attaches the profile to the response. We use this information to measure the RTT from the proxy node to each anycast site it reaches. We describe more detail in Sect. 4.4.

By default, BrightData may use a different proxy node per HTTP request. Since we wish to observe flipping per proxy node, this behavior is not desirable. Fortunately, we found a mechanism supported by BrightData to enforce a consistent session via the same proxy node for the current webpage we fetch [13]. To restrict all requests for fetching the mock webpage to use the same proxy node, we generate a random consistency token and concatenate it with our user-name registered with BrightData when we send the requests to the proxy service. With this mechanism, BrightData will use the same proxy node to send all the resource requests sharing the same consistency token. Further, BrightData allows a user to specify a geographic area to restrict the proxy selection. If an area is not provided, BrightData selects a proxy globally. Since we wish to study the impact of anycast flipping from as many vantage points as possible, we do not restrict proxy selection.

Although we use the consistency mechanism to ensure that BrightData does not switch proxy nodes in the middle of a mock page download session, we wish to validate that the mechanism is working as expected. We use the hashed IP field ('x-luminati-ip') in the responses to verify whether all 50 requests to the anycast CDN go through the same proxy node during the download session. We also made two additional requests to http://lumtest.com/myip.json with each download session to retrieve the proxy's public information (e.g., IP, AS number, geographical location). With this method, we found that among all 17,600 download sessions collected from May 31 to June 26 of 2024: 547 (3.1%) sessions did not succeed due to platform/proxy error; 713 (4.1%) sessions were issued from multiple proxy nodes (as many as 31 proxy nodes), even though we enforced the consistency token. For the remaining 16,340 download sessions, the same proxy node was used for all requests, but 186 (1.1%) sessions did not success-fully complete all 50 requests. As we mentioned above, we also used requests to http://lumtest.com/myip.json to enrich the proxy's information, when the hashed IP matches the hashed IP in all 50 requests of the download session. For 72 more download sessions, the hashed IP in the requests to http://lumtest.com/myip.json did not match the hashed IP in the download session, so we excluded them. In the end, we continue with 16,082 measurements (91% of all measurements) that have a complete resource download session, and valid IP information retrieved from the the same proxy node.

To study anycast flipping, we also need to detect which site responds to each HTTP request. Fortunately, the anycast CDN we use adds a header field in its responses that contains an IATA code to indicate which site responded to an HTTP request. Therefore, if we observe responses containing different IATA codes are received by the same proxy node in response to our 50 requests, then we consider that the proxy node experiences anycast flipping.

In total, we discover 9,445 unique proxy nodes from 1,902 different ASes that can measure the RTTs from proxy node to the anyast servers. In the following section, we use the measurements through these proxy nodes to measure the prevalence of anycast flipping with the anycast CDN.

4.3 Prevalence

We now present the results on how frequently we observe anycast flipping to the anycast CDN. Out of 9,445 unique proxy nodes with timing profile, we observe 18,294 unique <proxy, anycast IP> pairs, since a proxy node can select different anycast IPs in their download sessions of retrieving 50 different resources. Among

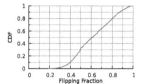 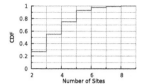 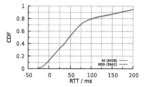

(a) *Fraction of requests reaching* (b) *# sites reached per proxy* (c) *ΔRTT of proxy nodes that*
the mode site   *node*   *flip between sites*

Fig. 7. Anycast flipping results to an anycast CDN measured using BrightData. The `All` line in the rightmost figure includes all proxy nodes that experience flipping, and the `90th` line includes the proxy nodes that reach their mode sites less than 90% the time.

the unique <proxy, anycast IP> pairs, 6,028 (33.0%) pairs reach multiple sites for their requests, *i.e.* experiencing anycast flipping.

Figure 7a shows a CDF of the fraction of the multiple requests that are responded to by the site that receives the largest number of requests (We define such a site as the "mode site"). A value close to 1 means that reaching a different site is very rare, which is not indicative of anycast flipping. So, we set a threshold ≤ 0.9 to focus on the proxy nodes that experience frequent anycast flipping. This threshold leaves out 386 rarely flipping <proxy, anycast IP> pairs.

We show the CDF of the number of sites the remaining 5,642 <proxy, anycast IP> pairs reach in Fig. 7b. As we can see, flipping between more than two sites is common, with 4,117 (68.3%) proxy nodes reaching three sites or more. In the extreme case, one proxy node flips between 9 different sites while downloading the 50 objects during our download session.

4.4   Impact on RTTs

Next, we investigate the impact of anycast flipping on the RTT from a client to an anycast CDN site. From the timing profile included in a BrightData HTTP response, we extract the connect time – from when a proxy node sends a TCP SYN packet to the anycast CDN to when the proxy node receives the SYN+ACK reply. This metric estimates the RTT from the proxy node to its catchment site of the CDN, independent of where we run our curl script. A similar method is also used in [15].

We calculate the difference in RTT for each <proxy, anycast IP> as follows. First, we calculate the median RTT, mRTT, per site. Next, we determine if the site that receives the largest number of requests, $site_x$, has the largest mRTT. If it does, then we find the minimum mRTT to any other site and subtract $site_x$ mRTT from it to determine the best case improvement in RTT that anycast flipping causes. If $site_x$ does not have the largest mRTT, then we find the maximum mRTT to any other site and subtract $site_x$ mRTT from it to determine the worst case additional RTT that anycast flipping causes. Figure 7c shows the CDF of these differences in RTT. Anycast flipping reduces RTT for less than 725

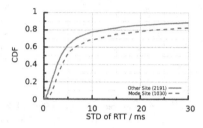

Fig. 8. CDF of standard deviation of RTT to individual sites for proxies that experience frequent flipping (> 50%) and a large increase in latency on flipping (> 50 ms). Minimum of 3 measurements per site.

(13.0%) <proxy, anycast IP> pairs, typically by small values. Similarly, other proxies see modest increases in median RTT due to flipping, but 2682 (47.5%) <proxy, anycast IP> pairs suffer from RTT differences that are larger than 50 ms, and 747 (13.3%) <proxy, anycast IP> pair suffer from RTT differences larger than 150 ms. Among those 5,642 **90th** flipping pairs, 1,988 pairs flip **frequently**, mode site fraction is ≤ 0.5. And combined with our observations on flipping rates, 1,030 (5.6% of all) <proxy, anycast IP> pairs which mode site fraction is ≤ 0.5 and have an RTT difference ≥50 ms. In the next section, we investigate what implications the RTT increase has on web performance.

5   Impact on Web Performance

The previous section demonstrates the impact that anycast flipping has on the RTTs between proxies and the anycast CDN. We now turn to how these RTT increases may impact web performance by emulating a client downloading an existing webpage and flipping between two servers, focusing on clients that experience high flipping rates and large increases in latency. In particular, in emulating web performance we set the flipping rate (i.e., the client's chance of downloading webpage resource from a closer/faster server.) for TCP connections to 50% and the increased latency when flipping to either 10ms or 50ms. These rates and latencies are experienced by 8.9% and 5.6% of the BrightData proxies, respectively. While these percentages are low, CDNs serve hundreds of millions of clients, so in absolute terms the number of affected clients may be quite large. Utilizing Mahimahi [33] measurements and emulations across 3 vantage points and 20 web sites, our experiments demonstrate that for a 50ms flipping latency penalty, the median increase in the First Contentful Paint metric ranges from 20.7% to 52.6% for HTTP/1.1 browsers and from 18.3% to 46.6% for HTTP/2 browsers. These results suggest for many clients the impact of flipping on web performance is significant.

We recognize that simply adding a fixed latency penalty whenever flipping occurs assumes that the latency to the most common anycast site would have remained the same had flipping not occurred. We do not have direct experimental evidence to support this assumption, as we did not conduct experiments in which anycast packets were sent by a single proxy to multiple anycast sites simultaneously. Nevertheless, there is reason to believe that the differences in latencies to anycast sites are primarily due to unvarying causes such as the latencies of the (uncongested) network links on the paths to the sites. In particular, the standard deviations of the latencies are small compared to the large latency increases seen by some proxies on flipping, suggesting that variable causes of delay, such as network congestion and server load, play a more minor role. For example, as Fig. 8 shows, among the <proxy, anycast IP> pairs that experience a mode site fraction ≤ than 0.5 and a median latency increase greater than 50 ms on flipping, 77.7% of the site landings' RTTs have a latency standard deviation under 10 ms when they flip to any particular site other than the most common. For the same group of <proxy, anycast IP> pairs, 68.7% of the site landings' RTTs have a standard deviation under 10 ms when they land on the mode site. In both cases, the statistics are quoted for sites with at least 3 measurements.

5.1 Infrastructure

To conduct our measurements we extend the web emulator Mahimahi. Mahimahi retrieves webpages, capturing all the resources – from different hosts – embedded in the webpage, and stores them locally. It enables replaying a webpage to a browser by serving the resources from Apache web servers, matching the resource and host associations collected during the capture. Optionally, Mahimahi can also add a synthetic delay during the replay. Thus, Mahimahi can emulate the web performance of a page load under varying network conditions. To study anycast flipping, we make several extensions to Mahimahi.

Per-Host Delay. While Mahimahi allows a configurable delay to be applied to fetching resources during webpage replay, it applies the same delay to all fetches. This simplification is not faithful to the original webpage retrieval (webpages typically include resources from diverse hosts), nor is it convenient for measuring the impact of anycast flipping. So, we add the ability to set different synthetic delays per Apache web server to Mahimahi.

Support for Anycast Flipping. The previous extension enables setting a delay per host, but with anycast flipping the delay to a specific host may vary depending upon the site reached. So we further extend Mahimahi to probabilistically apply additional delay per TCP flow to emulate flows reaching either a near site (i.e., no additional delay) or a far site (i.e., additional delay).

Support for HTTP/2. Mahimahi only supports HTTP/1.1 replay, yet HTTP/2 is frequently used today. Further, because anycast flipping operates on individual TCP flows and HTTP/2 handles multiplexing over the underlying transport differently than HTTP/1.1, we anticipate differences in the impact to each protocol. So, we update Mahimahi's Apache web server to support HTTP/2 by replacing the MPM prefork module ("mpm_prefork_module"), which does not support HTTP/2, with the MPM event module ("mpm_event_module"), and by adding HTTP/2 support with the "mod_http2" module.

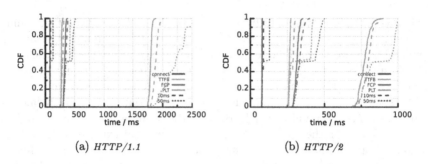

(a) *HTTP/1.1*   (b) *HTTP/2*

Fig. 9. Performance Impact of Anycast Flipping on the Mock Webpage

Revised Retrieval Step. Finally, we re-implement Mahimahi's retrieval mechanism This was necessary for two reasons. First, Mahimahi's retrieval does not support HTTP/2. Second, we need to collect the per-host delays used during emulation. To collect these delays we use 'tshark' to capture TCP packets on port 443. After retrieval, we extract the RTT to each host from the packet capture and apply the RTTs to Mahimahi's Apache web servers.

In emulation, our client is the headless Chrome browser in incognito mode, wrapped with Browsertime [4] to automate fetching webpages from Mahimahi and collect performance metrics.

5.2   Mock Webpage Results

To show the impact of anycast flipping, we emulate web browsing of our mock webpage using Mahimahi. First, we retrieve the mock webpage from our vantage point at Duke University using our revised retrieval step. Because all of the one-pixel images in our mock webpage are served by the CDN, a single host serves the entire webpage. During retrieval, we calculate the RTT to the CDN from our vantage point and match the delay in emulation to the RTT. We then use our instrumented browser to fetch the mock webpage from Mahimahi 100 times. Figure 9 in the solid lines shows the CDF across the 100 measurements of four key performance metrics: connect - the TCP connection time for the webpage root object, TTFB - time to first byte of the root object, FCP [5] - first contentful paint is visible on the screen, and PLT - the start of the JavaScript load event. Smaller values in these metrics mean that page loads more quickly and the web performance is better. We show the results for both HTTP/1.1 (Fig. 9a) and HTTP/2 (Fig. 9b).

Using the solid lines as our baseline, we next investigate the impact of two anycast flipping scenarios by selecting the single host serving our entire mock webpage to flip. To emulate anycast flipping observed in Sect. 4 that effects 6.3% of BrightData proxies, we set the probability of flipping to 50% and the additional RTT on a flip to 50ms—the dotted lines. We also run our emulations reducing the additional RTT to 10ms (which effects 9.7% of proxies) to see the impact of flipping when the RTT difference is less significant – the dashed lines.

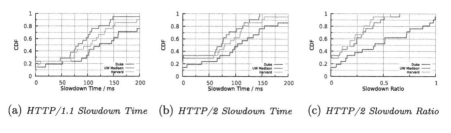

(a) *HTTP/1.1 Slowdown Time*   (b) *HTTP/2 Slowdown Time*   (c) *HTTP/2 Slowdown Ratio*

Fig. 10. Slowdown in Average First Contentful Paint on Top-20 webpages

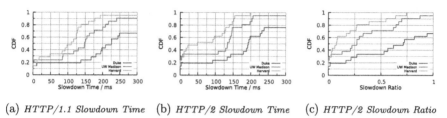

(a) *HTTP/1.1 Slowdown Time*   (b) *HTTP/2 Slowdown Time*   (c) *HTTP/2 Slowdown Ratio*

Fig. 11. Slowdown in 90th Percentile First Contentful Paint on Top-20 webpages

The metric values grow (become worse) as anycast flipping latency is added, regardless of protocol.

Consider the connected lines first. There is a noticeable step at roughly the middle of the distribution where flipping delay is added. Because flipping occurs per-flow and the flipping probability in our emulation is 50%, there is a 50% chance that the connection for the root object will reach the near site and the distributions in all three scenarios will be the same. However, if the connection for the root object is "unlucky", then the connect time is increased by 10/50 ms. This applies to both protocols.

Unlike HTTP/1.1, however, Chrome's implementation of HTTP/2 uses a single TCP connection per host and multiplexes all requests over the same connection. If the first connection for the root object is unlucky, then Chrome remains unlucky for the rest of the webpage fetch. This is evident in the steps visible in all other metrics. By comparison, Chrome's HTTP/1.1 implementation uses 6 TCP connections in total per host, giving it six opportunities to reach the near site. Moreover, we observe that Chrome dispatches HTTP requests on the first available connection, so the connections to the near site receive a disproportionate number of the 81 requests because each request completes faster than other requests on connections to the far site. As a result, HTTP/1.1 performance under anycast flipping degrades slower then HTTP/2. This is most visible in the PLT dotted lines where HTTP/2 performance becomes significantly worse when the single TCP connect flips to the far site, while HTTP/1.1 performance more gradually degrades in steps as each of the 6 TCP connections flips to the far site.

We note that HTTP/2 performance overall remains better than HTTP/1.1. Even though HTTP/1.1 establishes 6 TCP connections, the 80 HTTP requests

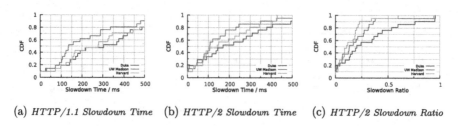

(a) *HTTP/1.1 Slowdown Time*   (b) *HTTP/2 Slowdown Time*   (c) *HTTP/2 Slowdown Ratio*

Fig. 12. Slowdown in Average Page Load Time on Top-20 webpages

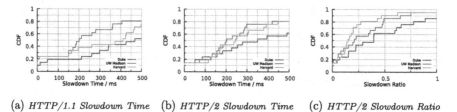

(a) *HTTP/1.1 Slowdown Time*   (b) *HTTP/2 Slowdown Time*   (c) *HTTP/2 Slowdown Ratio*

Fig. 13. Slowdown in 90th Percentile Page Load Time on Top-20 webpages

for one-pixel images are still transmitted serially across the connections. Meanwhile, because HTTP/2 removes head-of-line blocking, the 80 HTTP requests occur in parallel.

5.3 Popular Website Results

The mock webpage provides us with a synthetic view of the impact of anycast flipping, but real webpages typically aren't composed of 80 one-pixel images. So, next we explore the impact of anycast flipping on real webpages. In this analysis, we use the landing webpages of the top 20 most popular websites (Table 2 in Appendix A) from the Tranco list [37]. Also, in addition to our vantage point at Duke University, we use two vantage points (Harvard University and the University of Wisconsin-Madison) provided by CloudLab [18] to retrieve the 20 webpages, giving us three distinct environments to measure the impact of anycast flipping.

As with the mock website, we apply a 50% flipping probability and add 50ms on flips to the far site. However, unlike the mock website, real webpages aren't typically served by a single host. Indeed, we observe that the 20 webpages we retrieve are served by a variety of hosts, including several CDNs. To study the impact of anycast flipping, we take the approach of assuming each of the CDNs uses anycast and emulate flipping to their hosts.

For each webpage, we run the Mahimahi emulation 100 times without flipping and then 100 times with flipping. We then compute the average and 90th percentile for FCP and PLT (We do not present connect and TTFB here as the impact of these two metrics on web performance are also reflected on FCP and PLT). To ease visualization and comparison, we introduce two new metrics. Slowdown time is the difference between the same metric (e.g., average FCP) with anycast flipping and without anycast flipping. Slowdown ratio is slowdown time divided by the metric without anycast flipping. A slowdown ratio of 1.0 means that anycast flipping doubled the value of the underlying metric.

Figures 10a and 10b show the slowdown time for average FCP as a CDF across the 20 webpages for HTTP/1.1 and HTTP/2, respectively. For half of the webpages we study, the anycast flipping we emulate increases average FCP by 81–111ms for HTTP/1.1 and 77–108ms for HTTP/2, depending upon vantage point. Similarly, Figs. 11a and 11b show the equivalent results for the 90th percentile FCP and slowdown times over several hundred milliseconds are common. This logically follows from our results with the mock webpage, where we observe anycast flipping's impact is more significant in the tail of the distribution.

Interestingly, the results are similar regardless of protocol used, while on the mock webpage there was a notable difference. Not surprisingly, we find that hosting many objects on the same host is rare in real webpages. In fact, domain sharding – the process of splitting resources among many domain names to work around HTTP/1.1 head-of-line blocking by using additional parallel connections – is commonly used even with HTTP/2 [40]. Likely unintentionally, domain sharding currently mitigates that worst-case impact of anycast flipping on HTTP/2. Thus, website operators should consider the impact of anycast flipping on their websites before removing domain sharding.

Since there is no major difference in the results by protocol, we show the slowdown ratio of only HTTP/2 in Figs. 10c and 11c for average and 90th percentile FCP, respectively. The results vary by vantage point, which is to be expected as the RTTs to the hosts serving the webpages differ among the sites. Thus, the additional 50 ms from flipping will have more/less impact. For Harvard and University of Wisconsin-Madison, most sites have small slowdown ratios, indicating that anycast flipping from those vantage points often does not significantly degrade perceived performance. Duke University, on the other hand, has significantly larger slowdown ratios, showing the time added by anycast flipping is a larger portion of the overall FCP. However, turning to the 90th percentile for Harvard and University of Wisconsin-Madison, 8 webpages have slowdown ratios of about 0.5 or more, So, again, tail performance can be dramatically worse due to anycast flipping.

In Figs. 12 and 13, the results for PLT time are shown, and are similar. In summary, for several of the webpages studied, anycast flipping – at levels observed to impact 1.3% of BrightData residential proxies – can significantly impact web performance.

6   Related Work

Measuring IP Anycast Performance. IP anycast has long been used by
Internet services to provide automatic load balancing and latency reduction with
multiple anycast sites [11,14,34]. Many related works focus on measuring and
analyzing the performance of existing IP anycast systems, including DNS root
servers [21,25,27,29,30,32] and CDNs [14,25,48]. The main results from these
studies are consistent: Global IP anycast does not always route clients to the
sites that provide the lowest latency and does not always evenly distribute the
workload among the sites [41].

Many previous works assume that each client reaches only one anycast site,
which we observe is not true in practice. In our work, we show that, as many as
10% of the clients reach multiple different anycast sites due to anycast flipping.
Schomp and Al-Dalky [42] also observe that 17% of clients flip between sites in
proprietary DNS server logs, and speculate that one cause may be load balancers.

Load-Balancer Detection. From the examples in Sect. 2, load-balancing
within the network is one cause of anycast flipping. Load-balancers are a widely
deployed technique to utilize multiple links in order to support large traffic volumes. Paxson's measurement work on the diversity of routing behavior [36] is
the first work to show the impact on the performance due to the load balancing,
but only limited to unicast routing. Almeida et al. [8] proposed MCA (Multipath Classification Algorithm) to figure out the field in the packet used for load-
balancing along a path, which in the presence of anycast can cause different flows
– with different field values – to reach different sites. Paris traceroute [9] is a tool
to perform path traces in the presence of load balancers. By keeping the fields
load balancers might use constant, Paris traceroute tracks the complete path
along one branch of the load balancer at a time. None of these works, however,
consider the impact on anycast by load-balancers. Based on Paris traceroute,
Augustin et al. proposed a multipath detection algorithm to probe the multiple
paths of a load balancer [10]. Furthermore, Diamond-Miner [46] combines this
multipath detection algorithm [10] with high-speed randomized probing techniques [12] to construct the Internet-scale topology with multiple paths.

Lan and Heidemann's work [49] is the first work that quantifies anycast
flipping. In our work, we reproduced their results from 2016 with the same
method, and update their results with a longitudinal study from 2016 to 2023.
We find that anycast flipping is more common now, and extend our study to
measure the performance impact of anycast flipping.

7   Future Work

This paper leaves open a number of interesting directions for future work.

Limitations. The web browsing performance study reported in this paper has several limitations. Most prominently, it's likely that important applications other than web browsing are also impacted by anycast flipping, and should be evaluated. Putting aside other applications, the browsing analysis measures only the First Contentful Paint and Page Load Time metrics. Metrics such as Connect Time, Time to First Byte, and even customer conversion rate could also be considered. Perhaps more importantly, the clients from which the popular web sites were downloaded were not very diverse. For example, they did not include hosts on home networks or mobile hosts using cellular data connections. Finally, we only emulated two fixed flipping latency penalties (10 ms and 50 ms), both for the same flipping probability, 50%, which is a large flipping probability experienced by a relatively small fraction of clients. These values were selected based upon measurements of a single major anycast CDN. Yet, we know from our measurements of root DNS servers that anycast flipping impacts users of other anycast networks differently. Therefore, a more exhaustive study would evaluate a wider range of probabilities and penalties, selected from a larger set of anycast CDNs. Finally, our modeling of the flipping latency penalty assumes that an increase in the measured RTT is due to the change in routing to a different site, rather than the effect of a load balancing mechanism employed by the anycast CDN, which might apply to all sites. Whether such an assumption is warranted deserves more investigation.

Developing Techniques to Detect Anycast Flipping and Determine the Cause. In the cases of the root DNS servers and the anycast CDN studied in this paper the anycast site to which a client connects can be identified by techniques specific to these services, i.e., through the DNS CHAOS records provided by the root servers and the HTTP headers provided by the CDN. In general, however, it may be difficult for a client to determine even that the IP address that it connects to is an anycast address. Even more challenging is to determine why anycast flipping occurs when it does. There are a variety of possible reasons for flipping, including BGP and IGP route changes, IGP Equal-Cost Multipath (ECMP), and BGP Multipath. Anycast CDNs may even implement bespoke mechanisms to balance load among their anycast sites. While simple techniques like traceroute may identify route changes, the cause of the change is typically opaque to the client. Research on the prevalence and impact of anycast flipping would be enabled if there were more general techniques for detecting flipping and its causes.

Impact on Anycast CDN Cache Performance. If a browser requests the objects embedded on a web page from multiple anycast CDN sites chosen essentially at random, then in order to guarantee cache hits the CDN must store all of the objects at all of the sites. Alternatively, anycast flipping may reduce the cache hit rate. Our experiments with the anycast CDN were oblivious to this effect, as we measured only TCP connect time, and not object download time. But it would be interesting to further explore the effect of anycast flipping on caching.

Preventing Flipping. If it is deemed desirable to reduce the occurrence of anycast flipping, a number of potential approaches come to mind. First, at present Internet routers are generally oblivious to the notion of anycast addresses. If designated prefixes were reserved for anycast use, routers could disable load balancing for any datagrams or flows to those prefixes. Alternatively, perhaps datagrams could include "do-not-load-balance" tags. Second, anycast CDNs could employ a hybrid approach to delivering content, using an anycast address for the server delivering an HTML document, but then using a unicast address (for the same server site) for any embedded objects.

Mitigating Flipping. We observed that in the default Chrome implementation, in HTTP/1.1 multiple TCP connections are established to download the necessary content, and the connections that perform best are used to download more objects. This adaptive adjustment to anycast flipping mitigates the impact of anycast sites with poor performance.

8   Conclusions

In this paper, we revisited the anycast flipping problem and provided evidence that it is increasing in prevalence, and that for some clients it can significantly impact web-browsing performance.

First, in recreating the measurements from [49], we showed that anycast flipping, first observed in 2016, is still present in 2024 and has grown more prevalent. Next, to study the impact of anycast flipping on web browsing, we conducted a measurement study of a major anycast CDN, finding again that anycast flipping impacts a small but significant number of vantage points. Further, a quarter of the vantage points that suffer anycast flipping also experience a large increase of at least 50 ms when directed away from their most common site. Finally, we measure the impact that frequent flipping with a large latency penalty has on web-browsing performance through emulations using Mahimahi. We find that, for this small but non-negligible portion of clients, the impact of anycast flipping on web performance can be significant.

Acknowledgments. We thank the anonymous reviewers and our shepherd Marcel Flores for their helpful comments, and Ramesh K. Sitaraman for helpful suggestions. We sincerely thank the Bright Initiative [7] for supporting us with proxy access. This work was supported in part by the National Science Foundation under Award 2225448.

A Appendix

A.1 Geocodes Used by Different Roots

Table 2. Naming schemes used by different operators

Root	Operator	Naming Scheme	Regular Expression
A	Verisign	IATA, UN/LOCODE	`(rootns|nnn1)-((\w{3})\d|\w{2}(\w{3}).*)`
B	USC-ISI	IATA	`b\d-(\w{3})`
C	Cogent	IATA	`(\w{3})\d\w\.c\.root-servers\.org`
D	UMD	City/Country Code	`(\w{4})\d\.droot\.maxgigapop\.net`
E	NASA Ames	IATA	`\w\d{2}\.(\w*)\.eroot`
F	ISC	IATA	`\w{3}\.cf\.f\.root-servers\.org`
G	DoD NIC	Other	`groot-(\w{4})-\d`
H	ARL	IATA	`\d{3}\.(\w{3})\.h\.root-servers\.org`
I	Netnode	IATA, Other	`s\d\.(\w{3})`
J	Verisign	IATA, UN/LOCODE	`(rootns|nnn1)-((\w{3})\d|\w{2}(\w{3}).*)`
K	RIPE NCC	City/Country Code	`ns\d.(\w{2}-\w{3})\.k\.ripe\.net`
L	ICANN	City/Country Code	`(\w{2}-\w{3})-\w{2}`
M	WIDE	IATA	`M-(\w{3})-.*`

A.2 Top 20 Web Sites

www.amazon.com
www.apple.com
www.azure.com
www.baidu.com
www.bilibili.com
www.bing.com
www.facebook.com
www.google.com
www.instagram.com
www.linkedin.com
www.live.com
www.microsoft.com
www.netflix.com
www.pinterest.com
www.qq.com
www.twitter.com
www.wikipedia.org
www.wordpress.org
www.yahoo.com
www.youtube.com

References

1. BGP Bestpath AS-Path Multipath-Relax (2018). https://community.cisco.com/t5/routing/bgp-bestpath-as-path-multipath-relax/td-p/3709661
2. BGP User Guide: multipath (Protocols BGP) (2023). https://www.juniper.net/documentation/us/en/software/junos/bgp/topics/ref/statement/multipath-edit-protocols-bgp.html
3. Bright data, online proxy and web scraping platform (2023). https://brightdata.com/
4. Browsertime (2023). https://github.com/sitespeedio/browsertime
5. First contentful paint (FCP) (2023). https://web.dev/fcp
6. root-servers.org (2023). http://www.root-servers.org
7. Bright initiative, collaborative data solutions (2024). https://brightinitiative.com
8. Almeida, R., Cunha, I., Teixeira, R., Veitch, D., Diot, C.: Classification of load balancing in the internet. In: Proceedings of INFOCOM, pp. 1987–1996 (2020)
9. Augustin, B., et al.: Avoiding traceroute anomalies with Paris traceroute. In: Proceedings of IMC, pp. 153–158. ACM (2006)
10. Augustin, B., Friedman, T., Teixeira, R.: Multipath tracing with Paris traceroute. In: Workshop on End-to-End Monitoring Techniques and Services, pp. 1–8. IEEE (2007)
11. Ballani, H., Francis, P., Ratnasamy, S.: A measurement-based deployment proposal for IP anycast. In: Proceedings of IMC, pp. 231–244. ACM (2006)
12. Beverly, R.: Yarrp'ing the internet: randomized high-speed active topology discovery. In: Proceedings of the 2016 Internet Measurement Conference, pp. 413–420. ACM (2016)
13. BrightData: Session IP persistence (2023). https://help.brightdata.com/hc/en-us/articles/4413171447953-Session-IP-persistence
14. Calder, M., Flavel, A., Katz-Bassett, E., Mahajan, R., Padhye, J.: Analyzing the performance of an anycast CDN. In: Proceedings of IMC, pp. 531–537. ACM (2015)
15. Chhabra, R., Murley, P., Kumar, D., Bailey, M., Wang, G.: Measuring DNS-over-HTTPS performance around the world. In: Proceedings of IMC, pp. 351–365. ACM (2021)
16. Conrad, D.R., Woolf, S.: Requirements for a mechanism identifying a name server instance. RFC 4892 (2007). https://doi.org/10.17487/RFC4892, https://www.rfc-editor.org/info/rfc4892
17. De Vries, W.B., de O. Schmidt, R., Hardaker, W., Heidemann, J., de Boer, P.T., Pras, A.: Broad and load-aware anycast mapping with Verfploeter. In: Proceedings of IMC, pp. 477–488. ACM (2017)
18. Duplyakin, D., et al.: The design and operation of CloudLab. In: Proceedings of the USENIX Annual Technical Conference (ATC), pp. 1–14 (2019)
19. Rekhter, Y., Li, T., Hares, S.: A border gateway protocol 4 (BGP-4). RFC 4271, RFC Editor (2006)
20. United Nations Economic Commission for Europea: UN/LOCODE code list by country and territory | UNECE (2022). https://unece.org/trade/cefact/unlocode-code-list-country-and-territory
21. Giordano, D., et al.: A first characterization of anycast traffic from passive traces. In: Traffic Monitoring and Analysis workshop (TMA) (2016)
22. Gray, C., et al.: BGP beacons, network tomography, and Bayesian computation to locate route flap damping. In: Proceedings of IMC, pp. 492–505. ACM (2020)

23. (IATA), T.I.A.T.A.: IATA Airport Code (2022). https://www.iata.org/en/publications/directories/code-search/
24. ipinfo.io: IP Info (2023). https://ipinfo.io/
25. Koch, T., Li, K., Ardi, C., Katz-Bassett, E., Calder, M., Heidemann, J.: Anycast in context: a tale of two systems. In: Proceedings of SIGCOMM, pp. 398–417. ACM (2021)
26. Lapukhov, P., Tantsura, J.: Equal-cost multipath considerations for BGP. Internet Draft (2023)
27. Lentz, M., Levin, D., Castonguay, J., Spring, N., Bhattacharjee, B.: D-mystifying the D-root address change. In: Proceedings of IMC, pp. 57–62. ACM (2013)
28. Levine, M., Lyon, B., Underwood, T.: TCP anycast: don't believe the FUD - operational experience with TCP and Anycast. NANOG 37 (2006)
29. Liang, J., Jiang, J., Duan, H., Li, K., Wu, J.: Measuring query latency of top level DNS servers. In: Proceedings of PAM, pp. 145–154. Springer (2013)
30. Liu, Z., Huffaker, B., Fomenkov, M., Brownlee, N., et al.: Two days in the life of the DNS anycast root servers. In: Proceedings of PAM, pp. 125–134. Springer (2007)
31. Metz, C.: IP anycast point-to-(any) point communication. IEEE Internet Comput. **6**(2), 94–98 (2002)
32. Moura, G.C., et al.: Anycast vs. DDoS: evaluating the November 2015 root DNS event. In: Proceedings of IMC, pp. 255–270. ACM (2016)
33. Netravali, R., et al.: Mahimahi: accurate record-and-replay for HTTP. In: Proceedings of ATC, pp. 417–429. USENIX Association (2015)
34. de Oliveira Schmidt, R., Heidemann, J., Kuipers, J.H.: Anycast latency: how many sites are enough? In: Proceedings of PAM, pp. 188–200. Springer (2017)
35. Partridge, C., Mendez, T., Milliken, W.: Host anycasting service. RFC 1546, RFC Editor (1993)
36. Paxson, V.: End-to-end routing behavior in the internet. SIGCOMM Comput. Commun. Rev. **26**(4), 25–38 (1996)
37. Pochat, V.L., Van Goethem, T., Tajalizadehkhoob, S., Korczyński, M., Joosen, W.: Tranco: a research-oriented top sites ranking hardened against manipulation. In: Proceedings of NDSS. ISOC (2019)
38. Randall, A., et al.: Home is where the hijacking is: understanding DNS interception by residential routers. In: Proceedings of IMC, pp. 390–397. ACM (2021)
39. RIPE: RIPE Built-in Measurements (2023). https://atlas.ripe.net/docs/built-in-measurements/
40. Sander, C., Blöcher, L., Wehrle, K., Rüth, J.: Sharding and HTTP/2 connection reuse revisited: why are there still redundant connections? In: Proceedings of IMC, pp. 292–301 (2021)
41. Sarat, S., Pappas, V., Terzis, A.: On the use of anycast in DNS. In: Proceedings of 15th International Conference on Computer Communications and Networks, pp. 71–78. IEEE (2006)
42. Schomp, K., Al-Dalky, R.: Partitioning the internet using anycast catchments. SIGCOMM Comput. Commun. Rev. **50**(4), 3–9 (2020). https://doi.org/10.1145/3431832.3431834
43. Schomp, K., Bhardwaj, O., Kurdoglu, E., Muhaimen, M., Sitaraman, R.K.: Akamai DNS: providing authoritative answers to the world's queries. In: Proceedings of SIGCOMM, pp. 465–478. ACM (2020)
44. Staff, R.N.: Ripe atlas: a global internet measurement network. Internet Protocol J. **18**(3) (2015)
45. Technologies, A.: Prolexic routed (2020). https://www.akamai.com/us/en/multimedia/documents/product-brief/prolexic-routed-product-brief.pdf

46. Vermeulen, K., Rohrer, J.P., Beverly, R., Fourmaux, O., Friedman, T.: Diamond-miner: comprehensive discovery of the internet's topology diamonds. In: Proceedings of NSDI, pp. 479–493. USENIX Association (2020)

47. Villamizar, C., Chandra, R., Govindan, D.R.: BGP route flap damping. RFC 2439, RFC Editor (1998)

48. de Vries, W.B., Aljammāz, S., van Rijswijk-Deij, R.: Global-scale anycast network management with Verfploeter. In: Proceedings of Network Operations and Management Symposium (NOMS), pp. 1–9. IEEE (2020)

49. Wei, L., Heidemann, J.: Does anycast hang up on you? In: Proceedings of Network Traffic Measurement and Analysis Conference (TMA), pp. 1–9. IEEE (2017)

50. Wei, L., Heidemann, J.: Does anycast hang up on you (UDP and TCP)? IEEE Trans. Netw. Serv. Manage. (TNSM) **15**(2), 707–717 (2018)

51. Zhang, X., et al.: AnyOpt: predicting and optimizing IP anycast performance. In: Proceedings of SIGCOMM, pp. 447–462. ACM (2021)

An Empirical Evaluation of Longitudinal Anycast Catchment Stability

Remi Hendriks, Bernhard Degen, Bas Palinckx, Raffaele Sommese,
and Roland van Rijswijk-Deij(✉)

University of Twente, Enschede, The Netherlands
{remi.hendriks,b.j.degen,r.sommese,r.m.vanrijswijk}@utwente.nl

Abstract. Anycast is widely used to improve the availability and performance of, e.g., the DNS and content delivery. To use anycast one simply announces the same prefix from multiple points of presence (PoPs). BGP then takes care of routing clients to the "nearest" PoP. While seemingly simple, managing an anycast service is not without challenges. Factors outside operator control, such as remote peering and hidden MPLS tunnels, may route clients to suboptimal PoPs in terms of latency.

To successfully manage anycast, operators map catchments: the set of prefixes that reach each PoP of a service. Due to the dynamic nature of inter-domain routing, catchments change over time. While earlier work has looked at catchment stability in the short term and in a coarse-grained manner, we lack a detailed view on catchment stability over time. Understanding this is crucial for operators as it helps schedule catchment measurements and plan interventions using traffic engineering to redistribute traffic over PoPs.

In this work, we put long-term catchment stability on an empirical footing. Using an industry-grade anycast testbed with 32 globally distributed PoPs, we continuously map catchments for both IPv4 and IPv6 over a 6-month period and study catchment stability at different timescales, ranging from days to weeks and months. We show catchments are very stable in the short term, with 95% of prefixes routing to the same PoP on a one-week scale, and over 99% on a day-by-day basis. We also show, however, that sudden routing changes can have a major impact on catchments. Based on our longitudinal results, we make recommendations on the frequency with which to measure catchments.

1 Introduction

Anycast, a technique to use the same host address at multiple locations [10], is widely used to improve the resilience, availability and performance of services. For example, the DNS root system makes use of anycast to ensure that root server instances are highly available, close to end users [13]. Similarly, content delivery networks (CDNs) make use of anycast to steer clients to nearby replicas of popular content, enhancing the user experience by lowering latency and distributing the load of client populations over multiple replicas (e.g., [14]).

R. Hendriks and B. Degen—Shared first author.

C. Testart et al. (Eds.): PAM 2025, LNCS 15567, pp. 389–401, 2025.
https://doi.org/10.1007/978-3-031-85960-1_16

While the basic principle of anycast – using the same host address at multiple locations – is simple, managing an anycast service is challenging. Factors outside the control of an operator, ranging from remote peering, hidden tunnels and routing changes by upstreams, can adversely affect the performance of an anycast service, leading to clients ending up at a Point of Presence (PoP) that is suboptimal in terms of latency. To this end anycast operators make use of catchment mapping: determining which client prefixes end up at which PoP. Suboptimal mappings can then be addressed through traffic engineering, as discussed by, e.g., Koch et al. [8]. As we will discuss in Sect. 2, different methods exist for mapping anycast catchments. What all prior studies have in common, however, is that none study anycast catchment stability over significant periods of time. Understanding this is crucial for two reasons. First, operators need to make informed choices on how often to reassess anycast catchments, allowing them to plan when to update traffic engineering policies, or, e.g., to plan PoP maintenance windows. Second, work by De Vries et al. [17] has shown that accurate information about a PoP's catchment can help filter out spoofed denial-of-service traffic that ingresses at that PoP.

In this work, we therefore set out to put anycast catchment stability on an empirical footing. Using an industry-grade testbed consisting of 32 globally distributed nodes we perform daily catchment mappings for IPv4 and IPv6 using the state-of-the-art "Verfploeter" approach pioneered by De Vries [18]. We use the data we collect to study long-term anycast catchment stability. Our results show that in the short term, anycast catchments are very stable, and even in the long term, catchments remain relatively stable. We also show, however, that catchments may change abruptly when major routing events occur and that unannounced interventions by our commercial upstream can lead to drastic traffic shifts. We use our results to make recommendations for operators on how frequently to schedule catchment measurements.

2   Background and Related Work

Anycast – Anycast was first introduced in 1993 [10]. The goal of anycast is to distribute a service over multiple servers that share the same host address. Each site of an anycast service – usually referred to as a Point of Presence (PoP) – then announces the prefix that contains the host address(es) of the anycast service via BGP. The inter-domain routing system then routes clients to the "nearest" server in terms of topology and routing policy. Anycast is used extensively in the DNS (e.g., by the root servers) and by Content Delivery Networks (CDNs).

Catchment Mapping – as discussed, to manage an anycast service operators typically need to know which clients reach which PoP. In other words: clients from which parts of the address space are routed to which PoP. This information is useful for dimensioning PoPs in terms of resources, troubleshooting suboptimal routing, where clients get routed to remote PoPs with higher latency while a physically closer PoP is available, and understanding which PoPs clients switch to when a PoP is taken down for maintenance or hit by an outage.

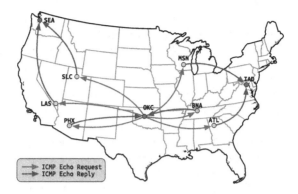

Fig. 1. The Verfploeter [18] method; an anycast site (red) sends ICMP probes to a hitlist, responses from clients (blue) end up at the "closest" anycast site. (Color figure online)

Earlier studies have introduced (combinations of) methods to map anycast catchments. A common method is to use external vantage points, either public vantage points, such as RIPE Atlas or PlanetLab [2–4,8,9,14], or openly available systems, such as open DNS resolvers [4]. A limitation of this approach is that these external vantage points typically represent only a fraction of the address space. An alternative is to analyze log data of anycast PoPs [2,6,8,14], but this only works if a service is already active and cannot be used for exploratory mapping to, e.g., optimise PoP placement before launching a service. Client-side measurements, e.g., injecting measurement code in served web pages [2], offer an attractive solution as they represent real users, but this approach is limited to the Web. Finally, Verfploeter – which we explain in detail below – uses active probing from an anycast address as source to map catchments based on probe responses from a hitlist of clients [18]. This approach has the advantage that it can be used independent of a running anycast service, and can target a wide range of clients. A limitation is that clients need to be responsive to probes.

Verfploeter – In this paper we make use of the Verfploeter anycast catchment mapping technique, as it is easy to deploy and does not require us to run an active anycast service. Figure 1 provides a bird's eye overview of how the technique works. The intuition is as follows: the anycast service (red circles in the figure) sends out ICMP Echo Request probes to a hitlist of IP addresses (e.g., the USC ISI hitlist [16]) and uses an anycasted host address as source address (red arrows). Responsive hosts (blue circles) on the hitlist will then respond to this anycast address, and will automatically be routed to the "closest" PoP of the anycast services (blue arrows). This allows the anycast operator to map the catchment of each PoP.

Catchment Stability – so far, we have discussed methods to measure anycast catchment. What we are interested in for this paper is the longitudinal stability of these catchments, in other words: how often and to what extent do catchments of PoPs change over shorter or longer periods of time? Previous works [2,17,18] have looked at catchment stability but only in the short term, ranging from a single day to a maximum of two weeks. In this paper, we bridge this gap based on an in-depth study of stability using day-to-day measurements spanning 6 months.

3 Methodology and Dataset

Methodology – Our measurement setup consists of an anycast testbed comprising 32 nodes, geographically distributed across 20 countries on six continents [1]. The nodes are hosted on Vultr, one of the few cloud providers that supports BGP announcements for smaller customers. We argue that our testbed is representative of small to medium sized industry-grade anycast deployments, as Vultr is widely used for anycast services. Based on a recent measurement of anycast services we obtained from the MAnycast2 team [15], we see 130 ASNs using Vultr to anycast prefixes, of which 33 exclusively use Vultr. Users include, e.g., top-level domain operators, such as SIDN for .nl and TWNIC for .tw. We note that the effectiveness of our method may require further investigation for larger-scale networks such as Cloudflare with hundreds of nodes.

We have been actively announcing a /24 IPv4 prefix and a /40 IPv6 prefix at all sites since March 21, 2024. While there have been occasional instances of site inactivity due to Vultr outages or technical issues, such occurrences are rare, and the deployment has remained largely consistent over time.

Each day at 00:00h UTC, we perform a catchment mapping using the Verfploeter methodology. To determine the catchment targets (i.e., the clients for which we wish to establish their corresponding anycast node catchment), we utilize several hitlists. For IPv4, we employ the hitlist provided by USC/ISI as part of their IPv4 Internet census [16]. For IPv6, we use a combination of sources: the TU Munich IPv6 hitlist [5] and a list of IPv6 addresses taken from AAAA DNS records collected by the OpenINTEL project [12]. These sources tend to fluctuate over time as we update them; therefore, in our analyses we only consider prefixes that are present throughout the entire period of our study.

We perform our measurements using ICMP. To ensure that our findings hold for transport-layer protocols, we conducted a scan using TCP. We find 1.1 M prefixes responsive to both TCP and ICMP, of these 97.7% have a consistent catchment. We suspect that the remaining 2.3% route differently due to *e.g.* route flips and load-balancing. Overall, these results show that our catchment mappings with ICMP hold for transport-layer protocols. Furthermore, analysis shows that we do not significantly increase coverage by considering both which is why we only consider catchment mappings using ICMP.

We also augment the original Verfploeter concept by extending sending of probes from a single PoP to distributed sending from all PoPs. This improves our ability to run faster back-to-back scans, with less packet loss. We verified that this changed approach produces accurate mappings that match mappings where probes are sent from a single anycast node. Our daily measurements generate approximately 1,000 packets per second from all sites, with a completion time of 95 min. To investigate sub-daily variations in catchment behavior, we scheduled

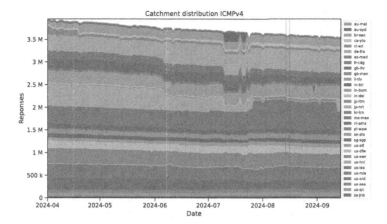

Fig. 2. Distribution of /24 prefixes over catchments. At the start there are about 4 M responsive /24 prefixes. The hitlist was updated on March 23 (before the start of our analyses), and August 14 and 16 (indicated by vertical lines). Catchments size across different nodes highly varies due to geographical interconnections. The responsiveness decline is mostly attributable to the hitlist aging.

an hourly measurement from a single node in Frankfurt from September 17, 2024, at a higher rate of 5,000 packets per second to ensure full hitlist scanning completes within one hour.

Ethics – in our measurement traffic, we encode the sending site, receiving site, transmission time, and reception time in the ICMP payload, along with an opt-out URL and a description of the measurements. As part of our responsible scanning practices, we have updated the rDNS records and marked the abuse contacts in the RIR data associated with our testbed prefixes to facilitate easy opt-out for operators.

Dataset – in total, we collected an average of 3.7 M responsive IPv4 /24 prefixes and 0.7 M responsive IPv6 /40 prefixes over 178 days between March 21, 2024, and September 14, 2024. Of these, 3.5 M IPv4 /24 prefixes and 0.5 M IPv6 /40 prefixes were consistently responsive throughout the entire analysis period.

4   Results

In this section, we present the results of our analyses, focusing first on the stability of catchments over time, and then investigating catchment changes in more detail by presenting a case study on a specific anycast node that experienced a significant shift in its catchment.

4.1   Catchment Stability over Time

As a first step in our analysis, we evaluated the catchment size over time starting from April 1st, 2024 for each node. We chose to begin our analysis on April

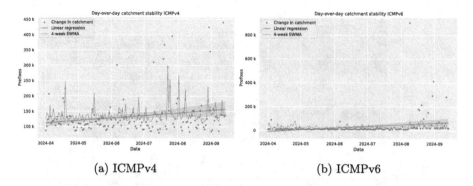

Fig. 3. Stability of catchments day-over-day. The points are the number of prefixes falling in different catchments as compared to the previous day. The blue line is a linear regression model fit to the stability data. The translucent bands depict the corresponding confidence interval at level $\gamma = 95\%$. The orange line is the exponentially-weighted average over the last 28 days. (Color figure online)

1st, rather than March 21st, to avoid the instabilities observed during the initial days following the announcement. Figure 2 shows the catchment distribution over time for all 32 nodes in our testbed. The first notable observation is the significant variance in catchment size across different nodes for IPv4 addresses. This variation is largely attributable to the diverse geographical distribution of the nodes in our testbed, the size of the regions they serve in terms of IP addresses, and the networks to which the nodes are interconnected. Another point of interest is that at the beginning of our measurements, we observe approximately 4 million responses; however, as the hitlist ages, we lose approximately 0.5 million responses. This result is unsurprising, and is mostly attributable to the hitlists aging as the authors of the ISI hitlist also observed this behavior in their original study [11]. Figure 2 also highlights several notable events. On March 27, kr-icn's catchment more than triples in size, while us-sea and jp-nrt experience a reduction. On July 10, jp-nrt loses the majority of its traffic, while au-syd's catchment expands by nearly five times. Between July 27 and September 12, kr-icn observes approximately 200 k more prefixes than usual, while jp-nrt's catchment shrinks. Additionally, on August 30, in-blr experiences a short-lived growth in catchment. Later in the paper (Sect. 4.2), we will investigate some of these events to understand the reasons behind these catchment shifts.

The catchment sizes illustrated above provide insight into the degree of hegemony a particular node exhibits over time across a series of clients. However, they do not offer a clear picture of how many prefixes shift from one catchment to another. To address this, we examined the day-to-day churn in anycast catchments by plotting the number of prefixes that shift between catchments. In Fig. 3, we observe that while most daily catchment shifts for all nodes range between 100 k and 150 k prefixes, there are occasional spikes, likely caused by rerouting events, that lead to significant changes in catchment size. This behavior is clearly visible in both IPv4 (Fig. 3a) and IPv6 (Fig. 3b), with spikes reaching up to 400 k

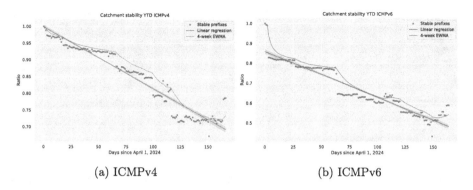

(a) ICMPv4　　　　　　　　　　　　　　　(b) ICMPv6

Fig. 4. Stability of catchments since the first measurement. The ratio of stable prefixes at time t_x is calculated as the number of prefixes in the same catchment at times t_0 and t_x divided by the number of prefixes responsive at times t_0 and t_x. The blue line is a linear regression model fit to the stability data. The translucent bands depict the corresponding confidence interval at level $\gamma = 95\%$. The orange line is the exponentially-weighted average of the last 28 days. (Color figure online)

prefixes shifting catchments in a single day. For IPv6, we also observed a shift of 900 k prefixes in August. After deeper investigation, we attributed this anomaly to a significant inflation of the IPv6 hitlist we use on that day. We also investigated sub-daily changes, by mapping the catchment hourly. In this case, we saw $\sim$78 k ($<$2% of the total) prefixes shifting catchment every hour compared to 4 M that remain stable. Overall, the results indicate that anycast catchments remain relatively stable in day-to-day operations.

While catchments remain stable on a day-to-day basis, we want to understand whether this stability holds over a more extended period. In other words, *to what extent does the catchment measured at a specific point reflect the future state of an anycast deployment's catchment?* To explore this aspect, we evaluated the stability of catchments over time by focusing only on the responsive prefixes throughout the entire analysis period. We considered the catchment on the first day of our analysis, April 1st, as the representative catchment and calculated how much each subsequent day's catchment differed from that of the first day. This was done by computing the ratio between the number of prefixes remaining in the same catchment on a given day and the number of prefixes in that catchment on the first day. A ratio of 1 indicates that all prefixes remain in their original catchment, while, for example, a ratio of 0.5 indicates that half of the prefixes have moved to the catchment of other anycast nodes.

For IPv4 (Fig. 4a), we observe that the original mapping remains valid for up to 2 months if operators accept an error rate (i.e., % of prefixes wrongly mapped) of 10% of the original catchment. We also notice that the decline is fairly gradual on average (based on a 4-week moving average), though there are days where this accelerates, likely due to re-routing events. For IPv6 (Fig. 4b), we observe a more turbulent behavior. In this case, after just 4 days, the original

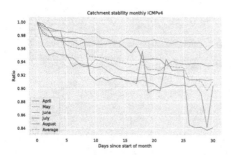
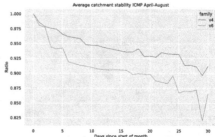

(a) Monthly stability with respect to the beginning of the month.

(b) Average monthly stability of ICMPv4 and ICMPv6 compared. We observe that IPv4 routing appears more stable on average and exhibits less variability.

Fig. 5. Stability of catchments over time. The ratio of stable prefixes at time t_x is calculated as the number of prefixes in the same catchment at times t_0 and t_x divided by the number of prefixes responsive at both times t_0 and t_x.

catchment mapping no longer reflects the current status, with nearly 20% of the clients shifting to a different node. Upon deeper investigation, we attribute this behavior to two primary factors: the smaller size of the IPv6 catchment, which is 7-fold smaller than the respective IPv4 catchment, leading to an amplification of shifting trends in our analysis, and the extreme variability of the IPv6 hitlist we use to map catchments, as also noted by its creators [5].

The previous analysis heavily depends on the representativeness of the selected starting day. To verify whether the previous assumptions hold true when selecting different starting days as the representative catchment, we computed the same catchment stability for different months, using the first day of each month as the representative day. As seen in Fig. 5a, while catchments remain stable on average until the end of the month, in two of the worst-case scenarios (July and August), the representativeness of the original catchment deteriorates rapidly after the 3rd week. We therefore suggest that a scan every 2–3 weeks is the minimum requirement for a reasonable indication of the catchment for IPv4.

In contrast, for IPv6, we observe a faster decline on average across all the months analyzed. This decline, in addition to the fast turnover of the IPv6 hitlist, suggests that more frequent scans of the catchment are necessary to obtain a good representation of the IPv6 space – ideally on a daily basis. The big difference between IPv4 and IPv6 is also illustrated when we compare both in Fig. 5b, which shows the average intra-month catchment stability over all months analyzed.

4.2   Diving Into Catchment Changes

In the previous section, we investigated the churn of prefixes in terms of percentages and observed that after 2 months, the original catchment was no longer representative of the current state of the deployment. The obvious follow-up question is: *between which nodes do prefixes shift the most?*

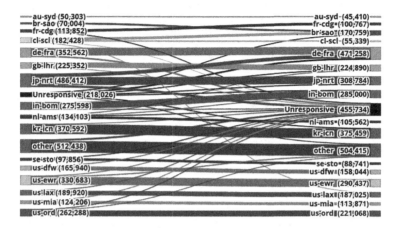

Fig. 6. Catchment shifts between April 1 (left) and July 1 (right), filtering on changes of >10,000 prefixes for the 16 largest sites.

We compared the catchment of April 1st with that of July 1st and analyzed the shift of client prefixes among different catchments over this time interval. Figure 6 shows the catchment changes for the 16 largest Vultr sites in terms of catchment, with the remaining 16 grouped into 'other'. Only shifts with more than 10,000 prefix changes are shown in the graph. The left side of the graph represents the catchment on April 1st, while the right side represents July 1st.

The majority (72%) of prefixes did not change sites over the analysis period. However, a significant portion (28%) did switch, with many of these (18%) moving between different continents over large geographic distances.

For some sites, we noticed a substantial number of catchment changes (e.g., br-sao, cl-scl, jp-nrt, de-fra, us-ewr), indicating possible major re-routing events leading to significant flows of clients shifting between catchments.

To assess whether such catchment shifts are caused by instances of geographical transfer of IP addresses, we compared IP2Location data [7] for April 1st and July 1st that shows a negligible number (0.8%) of prefixes moved location.

A deeper analysis of these large flows shows that they originate from a few ASes, suggesting that while catchment changes are considerable and lead to inter-continental routing, they are confined to a few ASes. This implies that the situation could be easily addressed by the anycast operator using BGP path manipulation (*e.g.* path prepending). We leave this to future work.

We argue that this risk of inter-continental routing is a fundamental reason for frequent active catchment analysis for anycast services. This would help network operators avoid severe performance degradation due to traffic being rerouted halfway across the globe instead of being directed to the nearest topological and geographical PoP.

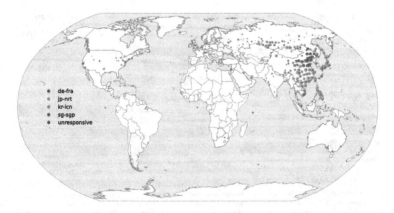

Fig. 7. Visualization of the geolocation of prefixes in the catchment of jp-nrt on April 1st, and where they re-routed to on July 1st indicated with pie charts.

4.3   Zooming in Further: a Case Study of jp-nrt

Among our major sites, in terms of catchment, we observe the largest change in catchment for jp-nrt (our anycast site in Tokyo, Japan). For this site we observe a catchment of 486 k /24 IPv4 prefixes on April 1st, and a catchment of 308 k prefixes on July 1st (a change of −36%). The change in catchment can be seen in Fig. 6, where we see most traffic went either to de-fra or became unresponsive.

Figure 7 zooms in on this case. We display the locations of the addresses that route to jp-nrt on April 1st, using *ip2location*. The map shows that the majority of prefixes originate from east Asia, as expected. Furthermore, we observe many prefixes in Russia route to Tokyo. Additionally, we find prefixes located in distant regions (e.g., USA, and Western Europe) routing to Tokyo. However, for these distant prefixes we measure low latency responses that would violate the speed-of-light, indicating *ip2location* likely reports incorrect locations for these instances. Next, using the colors of the circles we show where these prefixes routed to on July 1st (after the 36% reduction in catchment), the mapping of color to anycast site is displayed in the legend. We observe that most changes in catchment are regional, e.g., prefixes in Thailand change to Seoul, prefixes in north eastern China switch to Frankfurt. For those that remained in Tokyo's catchment we observe many are located in Russia and Eastern Asia. Investigating prefixes that switched catchment, we observe the large changes of Chinese prefixes originate from China Unicom (AS4837, AS4808).

Finally, we show the difference in RTT in Table 1 grouped by catchment change. We find that the Chinese prefixes that switched to de-fra more than tripled in RTT, whilst those that remained in Tokyo's catchment had a slight reduction in mean RTT. Furthermore, prefixes that switched to kr-icn see a slight increase in mean RTT, whereas those that switched to sg-sgp had a substantial decrease in RTT. Evaluating the *total* change in catchment for these groups, we find the overall mean RTT to nearly double.

Table 1. Differences in RTT for the largest catchment changes observed at jp-nrt between April 1st and July 1st.

New site in July	Number of prefixes	Mean RTT to JP-NRT	Mean RTT to new site
de-fra	125,418	73.0 ms	255.3 ms (+250%)
jp-nrt*	296,304	89.5 ms	83.4 ms (-7%)
kr-icn	9,291	92.7 ms	99.4 ms (+7%)
sg-sgp	1,134	59.5 ms	43.5 ms (-27%)
Total	432,147	84.0 ms	141.1 ms (+68%)
unresponsive	78,153	81.7 ms	*n/a*

Following July 1st, our commercial upstream provider withdrew our announcement at Tokyo, without notice, leaving the site inactive for several weeks. For this reason, we did not evaluate behavior of this catchment after this date.

This case study shows catchment changes that can largely be grouped into regional changes caused by few ASes. Furthermore, we find catchment changes can both improve and worsen mean latency, leading in some cases to ruinous cross-continental changes in catchment. This case study underscores the need to regularly map catchments to detect such changes promptly allowing operators to take steps to implement traffic engineering measures to address latency inflation (a problem also discussed by, *e.g.* Calder et al. [2]).

5   Conclusions

In this work, we put long-term catchment stability on an empirical footing to help network operators establish a baseline for their catchment scanning intervals. Our analysis showed that catchments are stable for both IPv4 and IPv6 in the short term (day-to-day operations). In the long term, IPv4 catchments are more stable than their IPv6 counterparts, with stability lasting over 3 weeks, assuming an error rate of 10%. In contrast, the representativeness of the IPv6 catchment decreases after just 2 days, mostly due to a lack of stable hitlists for IPv6. To maintain a good representation of the status of their anycast catchment, we recommend that network operators repeat catchment measurements on a weekly basis for IPv4 and a daily basis for IPv6. These measurements will help them to promptly identify and mitigate cases of suboptimal routing. Next steps are understanding what causes shifts in catchment by *e.g.* looking at BGP route changes and path changes using traceroute. Furthermore, zooming out, understanding catchment stability is a key ingredient to studying the use of catchment data to detect spoofing and off-site traffic detection, as first suggested by De Vries *et al.* [17]. We plan to use the lessons we learned about catchment stability to study spoofing and off-site traffic detection in depth in future work.

References

1. Vultr data center worldwide locations (2024). https://www.vultr.com/features/datacenter-locations/
2. Calder, M., Flavel, A., Katz-Bassett, E., Mahajan, R., Padhye, J.: Analyzing the performance of an anycast CDN. In: Proceedings of the 2015 Internet Measurement Conference, IMC 2015, pp. 531–537. Association for Computing Machinery, New York (2015)
3. Cicalese, D., Augé, J., Joumblatt, D., Friedman, T., Rossi, D.: Characterizing IPv4 anycast adoption and deployment. In: Proceedings of the 11th ACM Conference on Emerging Networking Experiments and Technologies, CoNEXT 2015. Association for Computing Machinery, New York (2015). https://doi.org/10.1145/2716281.2836101
4. Fan, X., Heidemann, J., Govindan, R.: Evaluating anycast in the domain name system. In: 2013 Proceedings IEEE INFOCOM, pp. 1681–1689 (2013). https://doi.org/10.1109/INFCOM.2013.6566965
5. Gasser, O., et al.: Clusters in the expanse: understanding and unbiasing IPv6 hitlists. In: Proceedings of the Internet Measurement Conference 2018, IMC 2018, pp. 364–378. Association for Computing Machinery, New York (2018)
6. Giordano, D., et al.: A first characterization of anycast traffic from passive traces. In: Botta, A., Sadre, R., Bustamante, F.E. (eds.) Traffic Monitoring and Analysis - 8th International Workshop, TMA 2016, Louvain la Neuve, Belgium, 7–8 April 2016. IFIP (2016). http://dl.ifip.org/db/conf/tma/tma2016/tma2016-final30.pdf
7. IP2Location: IP Address to IP Location and Proxy Information. https://www.ip2location.com/. Accessed 12 July 2024
8. Koch, T., Katz-Bassett, E., Heidemann, J., Calder, M., Ardi, C., Li, K.: Anycast in context: a tale of two systems. In: Proceedings of the 2021 ACM SIGCOMM 2021 Conference, SIGCOMM 2021, pp. 398–417. Association for Computing Machinery, New York (2021)
9. Moura, G.C., et al.: Anycast vs. DDoS: evaluating the November 2015 root DNS event. In: Proceedings of the 2016 Internet Measurement Conference, IMC 2016, pp. 255–270. Association for Computing Machinery, New York (2016)
10. Partridge, C., Mendez, T., Milliken, W.: Host anycasting service. RFC 1546, IETF (1993). http://tools.ietf.org/rfc/rfc1546.txt
11. Quan, L., Heidemann, J., Pradkin, Y.: Trinocular: understanding internet reliability through adaptive probing. In: Proceedings of the ACM SIGCOMM 2013 Conference, SIGCOMM 2013, pp. 255–266. Association for Computing Machinery, New York (2013)
12. van Rijswijk-Deij, R., Jonker, M., Sperotto, A., Pras, A.: A high-performance, scalable infrastructure for large-scale active DNS measurements. IEEE J. Sel. Areas Commun. **34**(6), 1877–1888 (2016). https://doi.org/10.1109/JSAC.2016.2558918
13. RSSAC: Root Server Technical Operations Association (2024). https://root-servers.org
14. Schomp, K., Bhardwaj, O., Kurdoglu, E., Muhaimen, M., Sitaraman, R.K.: Akamai DNS: providing authoritative answers to the world's queries, SIGCOMM 2020, pp. 465–478. Association for Computing Machinery, New York (2020)
15. Sommese, R., et al.: MAnycast2: using anycast to measure anycast. In: Proceedings of the ACM Internet Measurement Conference, IMC 2020, pp. 456–463. Association for Computing Machinery, New York (2020)

16. USC/LANDER project: Internet Addresses Survey Dataset (2024). http://www.isi.edu/ant/lander. PREDICT ID: USC-LANDER/internet_address_hitlist_it108w-20240711

17. de Vries, W.B., Aljammāz, S., Rijswijk-Deij, R.v.: Global-scale anycast network management with verfploeter. In: NOMS 2020 - 2020 IEEE/IFIP Network Operations and Management Symposium, pp. 1–9 (2020)

18. de Vries, W.B., de O. Schmidt, R., Hardaker, W., Heidemann, J., de Boer, P.T., Pras, A.: Broad and load-aware anycast mapping with verfploeter. In: Proceedings of the 2017 Internet Measurement Conference, IMC 2017, pp. 477–488. Association for Computing Machinery, New York (2017)

Phishing and Fraud

Partnërka in Crime: Characterizing Deceptive Affiliate Marketing Offers

Victor Le Pochat[1]([✉]) [iD], Cameron Ballard[2], Lieven Desmet[1] [iD],
Wouter Joosen[1] [iD], Damon McCoy[2] [iD], and Tobias Lauinger[2] [iD]

[1] DistriNet, KU Leuven, Leuven, Belgium
victorlepochat.work@gmail.com
[2] New York University, New York, USA

Abstract. The deceptive affiliate marketing ecosystem enables a variety of online scams causing consumers to lose money or personal data. In this model, affiliates promote deceptive products and services on behalf of merchants in exchange for a commission, mediated by affiliate networks. We monitor the ecosystem holistically by taking the vantage point of affiliates and collecting ground truth from 23 aggregators that list deceptive products and services available for promotion across scam types and affiliate networks. Using our novel longitudinal data set, we characterize the ecosystem by taxonomizing the 9 main categories of deceptive products and services composing the ecosystem, and describing the main tactics used to mislead consumers. We quantify the extent of the nearly 450,000 offers in the ecosystem and the differences in the value that is attached to different types of scams, monetization models, and countries. Finally, we identify core affiliate networks and analyze longitudinal trends to track the dynamics of the ecosystem over time. The more complete coverage provided by our novel data set enables not only a broader understanding of the ecosystem, but also adds insights and metadata for developing earlier, data-driven interventions to protect consumers.

1 Introduction

Internet users are regularly exposed to deceptive products and services online [85, 105]. Scammers seek to defraud users through low-quality products and services, such as questionable dietary supplements [11] or cryptocurrency investment platforms [93], or seek to trick users into installing potentially unwanted software [64,85,97,102] or into disclosing personal data, such as through fake contests [18]. Simultaneously, these products and services are promoted using misleading advertisements, employing tactics such as fake celebrity endorsements [11,23,28,114], manipulative "clickbait" headlines [121], and other "dark patterns" [76]. Despite long-term awareness of these harms (since at least the late 2000s [91,99]), numerous regulatory interventions [29–31,33–41], and media investigations [14,24,61,65,80,81,94,106,119], this wide range of deceptive operations continues to defraud consumers worldwide at a massive scale. Individual operations reach revenues of hundreds of millions of U.S. dollars [24,28,40,78],

C. Testart et al. (Eds.): PAM 2025, LNCS 15567, pp. 405–436, 2025.
https://doi.org/10.1007/978-3-031-85960-1_17

and total spend on deceptive ads through one large tracker was estimated at $1.7 billion a year [28].

While the different scams may seemingly be unconnected, we observe that many are embedded in the **deceptive affiliate marketing** ecosystem [11, 30, 101, 114].[1] In this model, *merchants* outsource the marketing of their low-quality products and services ('offers') to independent *affiliates*, who exploit advertising channels to run deceptive ads that promote these offers, in return for a commission on each successful conversion. While legitimate affiliate marketing programs are common, prior work documented how this advertising model is also central to many cybercriminal activities [91, 101], for example illegal pharmaceuticals [58, 72, 78, 91], counterfeit luxury goods [59, 107], and ransomware [53]. We reveal how it is also used in promoting and propagating other online scams.

In this paper, we comprehensively measure *how* and by *whom* the deceptive affiliate marketing ecosystem is operated. We use a novel ground-truth vantage point on the ecosystem to create a large-scale longitudinal data set that enables us to identify the relations between merchants and affiliates. We take the point of view of affiliates themselves, discovering deceptive products and services on so-called *aggregators*, which the affiliates use to search offers across many merchants at once. The advantage of this novel data set is that it provides us with complete 'insider' data on the breadth of deceptive products on offer, across all verticals (categories), countries, device configurations, and targeted populations, making our work global and longitudinal. Moreover, these aggregators publish metadata that is unavailable in traffic-based measurements, including the commission paid out to affiliates, which enables us to quantify the monetary dynamics of the ecosystem and how the different scams within it compare, which was previously impossible to achieve.

Our novel vantage point allows us to overcome inherent limitations in coverage from prior research that measures online scams from a user's perspective through the collection of traffic on deceptive ads or websites [43, 72, 90, 98, 105], which leads to only observing a subset of traffic sources, ads and scams. Instead, we provide a broad view on the connection between these scams and the deceptive affiliate marketing ecosystem that supports them. In addition, in contrast to prior work on affiliate models in cybercrime, we identify how a third, intermediary actor emerges. *Affiliate networks* serve as the primary point of contact for both merchants and their affiliates, and mediate their interactions by supporting them in attracting affiliates or discovering merchants respectively, and subsequently tracking sales and paying commissions. We describe how these affiliate networks run as large operations that have a central role in the ecosystem [19], which makes them a valuable target to prioritize and maximize the impact of technical, financial, and legal interventions [62].

To characterize the current state of the deceptive affiliate marketing ecosystem, we collect an extensive data set from 23 aggregators over more than 4 years. We analyze nearly 450,000 deceptive offers (i.e., products and services available for promotion) across 1,165 affiliate networks, which we derive after normaliz-

---

[1] Affiliate programs are also known as "partnërka" in Russian [91].

ing offers across aggregators and filtering out legitimate offers. We develop a new taxonomy with 9 verticals (i.e., categories) of products and services that constitute the deceptive affiliate marketing ecosystem. We observe that merchants use a wide variety of deceptive tactics to mislead consumers across these verticals: making exaggerated claims, misrepresenting endorsements, using dark patterns [76] to pressure users, and tricking unsuspecting customers into authorizing (recurring) payments. In general, products and services are of low quality and overpriced. Using our taxonomy, we then quantify how the payouts to affiliates depend on the type of product and what a customer has to do or pay to "complete" the offer, to compare the monetary incentives from the affiliate's point of view across the range of scams in the ecosystem. The most lucrative offers relate to investment scams, capitalizing on trends such as cryptocurrency, with payouts in the hundreds of U.S. dollars once customers make a deposit to a fraudulent trading platform. Physical goods (e.g., useless health and beauty products) and subscription services (e.g., fake dating sites) also command relatively higher payouts, while virtual goods, app installs, or providing personal data pay single-digit figures, or less. At the country level, offer selections and payouts differ based on income levels, monetization methods, and regulations. Our data also allows us to identify the largest affiliate networks that mediate the ecosystem, and quantify their scale. Finally, we observe longitudinal trends in the emergence of offers, verticals, and networks, showing the dynamism of the ecosystem.

In summary, our contributions are:

- We study the deceptive affiliate marketing ecosystem from the previously unexplored vantage point of the affiliates themselves, and present our ongoing data collection of a novel data source: 23 'aggregators' that allow us to discover offers across all verticals and countries, allowing for early intervention (Sect. 3).
- We develop a taxonomy of 9 verticals (Sect. 4), and label offers to establish their deceptive nature. We find a broad spectrum of tactics designed to mislead users and coax them into handing over money or personal data.
- We collect 449,891 offers across 1,165 affiliate networks to quantify the breadth of the ecosystem (Sect. 5). We find different valuations across verticals, monetization models (e.g., physical vs. virtual goods), and countries.
- We discuss how specialization drives access to the ecosystem, contributing to its growth, and how intervention strategies can prevent users from being harmed by deceptive affiliate marketing offers (Sect. 6).

2   Key Concepts

We introduce key concepts and terms, as they are used in the ecosystem itself, based on ecosystem guides and resources [7, 8, 22, 52]. Figure 1 summarizes the main ecosystem players, and the flow of payments and traffic between them.

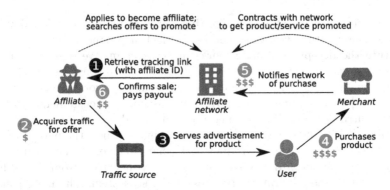

Fig. 1. A typical flow for a cost-per-sale offer shows how the three main types of ecosystem players engage to promote an offer and collect payment.

Ecosystem Players. There are three main types of players in the affiliate marketing ecosystem. **Merchants** (advertisers) have a product or service that they want to promote and sell. They seek **affiliates** (publishers, marketers, partners) who will promote the merchant's product. Merchants and affiliates find each other through **affiliate networks** (advertiser network) that act as intermediaries. These networks also provide the technical and financial infrastructure that ultimately pays the affiliate when they successfully promoted the merchant's product. There is a many-to-many-to-many relation in the ecosystem: affiliates can promote offers of any number of merchants, a merchant's offers can be promoted by any number of affiliates. A network can accept any number of affiliates and merchants, and affiliates and merchants can join any number of networks. Next to these three players, third parties provide supporting services, such as ad tracking tools, landing page builders, forums, or the offer aggregators that we use (Sect. 3).

Monetization. Merchants post **offers** to affiliate networks, who in turn make these offers available to affiliates for promotion. An offer is usually for one specific product, belonging to a certain **vertical** (niche, category). An offer will also include restrictions on who the product may be advertised to. Offers are usually targeted at specific **countries**, which are divided into **tiers** to reflect their perceived wealth, and therefore attractiveness. Certain advertising channels may also be (dis)allowed. Additionally, an offer stipulates the conditions and payment amounts for a successful **conversion**, i.e., the action that a customer has to take for the affiliate to be paid out (e.g., a payment or submission of an email address). Usually, the affiliate receives a one-time fixed-amount **payout** (commission) upon conversion. Alternatively, an affiliate can be paid through revenue sharing (RevShare), where they receive a percentage of all sales made to the customer over some period of time. The merchant will pay these payouts plus a service fee to the affiliate network, who passes the payout onto the affiliate. Two models prevail for awarding a payout: **cost per sale** (CPS, pay per sale, PPS) where a customer must pay for the product or service, and **cost per**

Table 1. An example of metadata available for an offer, upon which we base our analysis. Fields in *italics* are computed during data postprocessing. Note that not all metadata is always available, as quantified in Subsect. 5.1.

Field	Value	Field	Value
Name	QuantumAi (AU) (CPS)	Payout	560 USD
Normalized name	*quantumai*	Conversion type	CPS (cost-per-sale)
Affiliate network	AdsMain	Countries	{Australia}
Verticals	{Crypto offers, Finance}	Aggregators	{Affplus, Affscanner, OfferVault}
Normalized vertical	*Finance*	Observed on	{2020-05-06, 2020-05-07, ...}

lead (CPL, pay per lead, PPL) where a customer only needs to provide their contact information or personal data ('lead generation'). Within the ecosystem, the term **CPA marketing** (cost per action, cost per acquisition) is often used as a synonym for affiliate marketing. In the CPA model, a consumer action is required for the merchant to pay the affiliate, distinguishing it from advertising models where the merchant pays per ad click or impression.

Redirect Chain. The affiliate receives a **tracking link** (affiliate link) from the affiliate network, which contains a unique affiliate ID. The affiliate then selects a **traffic source** through which they promote the offer: e.g., their own website, email, or advertisements on platforms such as search engines or social networks. The customer is then redirected from the affiliate link to the **landing page** (offer page, lander) maintained by the merchant, where the customer can complete the offer. The merchant reports the affiliate ID that triggered the conversion to the network, which will pay the offer's payout to the affiliate.

3   Data Collection and Processing

We scrape offer data from *"offer aggregators"* that operate as search engines, who collect offers from multiple affiliate networks (and therefore across multiple merchants) and publish them in one interface where affiliates can search and filter them. Affiliates can find interesting offers and the affiliate networks that manage them through the aggregator, but will still need to separately join those networks. Aggregators provide broader coverage than individual affiliate networks, and unlike the latter, make their data public without requiring registration with an affiliate network, which may entail a vetting procedure. In contrast to traffic-based measurements, aggregators index current and past offers, and provide key metadata such as the network, vertical, countries, and conversion terms. Table 1 shows an example of the offer metadata that aggregators make available.

3.1   Aggregator Discovery

We employ a multi-tiered approach to discover the most common aggregators. We use the Google search engine with generic keywords (such as "affiliate offers",

Table 2. Overview of the offer aggregators for which we collected data. We list the number of records retrieved (including duplicates of the same network offer retrieved every day), the number of network offers observed (merged on normalized offer name), and the number of networks observed.

Aggregator	# networks	# network offers	# records
English-language aggregators of deceptive offers (16)			
AdNetworksHub	2	386	85,273
Affbank	144	257,464	62,041,167
Affhomes	49	14,542	11,413,418
affNext	9	3,097	2,494,100
Affplus	229	338,132	41,053,017
Affpub	75	20,945	3,306,317
Affscanner	62	69,769	14,826,290
BestAffiliatePrograms	56	50,444	13,757,137
BigFishOffers	7	56,869	39,504,203
Click4ads	147	72,164	7,706,208
Horje	–	24,662	43,523,554
oDigger	71	46,938	8,068,918
OfferLibrary	24	44,020	16,947,738
OfferVault	240	190,609	25,357,080
WOW TRK	33	47,638	10,146,934
XOffers	126	6,083	15,183

Aggregator	# networks	# network offers	# records
Russian-language aggregators of deceptive offers (7)			
ActualTraffic	74	22,334	4,341,738
Admakler	8	2,656	2,721,448
atlasio	36	8,569	3,678,416
AVF	32	3,044	984,910
CPA Daily	116	82,882	5,592,100
CPA Inform	38	34,684	17,541,949
Partnerkin	90	114,023	16,784,124
English-language aggregators of reputable offers (4)			
Affi.io	125	200,634	5,673,271
FMTC	45	52,993	3,216,827
LinkPizza	11	13,927	2,689,686
Publisher Rest	59	19,403	8,988,989

"CPA offers") and with the names of major networks listed on previously discovered aggregators (such as AdCombo, MaxBounty). We also consult specialized forums (AffiliateFix, affLift, BlackHatWorld) and sponsor lists for major affiliate conferences (Affiliate Summit, Affiliate World) to find additional aggregators. We continue searching aggregators until we reach saturation. Overall, we cover 16 English- and 7 Russian-language aggregators of deceptive offers (Table 2). In addition, we collect data from 4 aggregators for reputable mainstream brands, in order to filter reputable offers from our data set (Subsect. 3.4).

3.2   Retrieval

We extract available offers through web page scrapers custom-built for every aggregator. Unless a better parsable format is available (e.g., JSON), we retrieve raw HTML through simple HTTP requests and then extract offer data from relevant elements. Most aggregators present a paginated overview listing all offers, which we retrieve and store on a daily basis. Where necessary, we implement additional logic that addresses frequently occurring limits on the number of offers that the pagination supports, e.g., by collecting offers network by network through additional filters. Afterwards, for each offer, we request more detailed data by visiting and scraping the individual offer page that is linked from the overview. We retrieve and store detailed data for newly seen offers once a day, but recollect detailed data for all offers once a week. We believe this scraping frequency strikes a good balance between timeliness of the data and consumption of scraping resources. Moreover, we optimize scraping wherever possible, e.g., using internal APIs and maximizing the number of offers per page, which also reduces strain on the aggregators.

3.3   Normalization

The records in our offer data contain duplicates of four kinds: identical offers of the same network on one aggregator that we retrieve on multiple days; identical offers of the same network that are published on multiple aggregators; slightly differing offers of the same network (e.g., a different targeted country but the same product/service); and offers published by multiple networks. Not all aggregators merge offers across all these dimensions, so we must first discover and merge duplicate offers ourselves. Since not all aggregators provide the same metadata, merging offers also improves data completeness.

We opt to merge offers if they share their (normalized) name. Our intuition is that the offer name lists the product or service name, and that this name is relatively unique. Given the variation in available metadata across aggregators, other fields, including an aggregator's internal identifier, are unreliable for ensuring that similar offers will be merged. Our name normalization algorithm extracts and removes common keywords that are unrelated to the product or service but rather describe the offer's terms (e.g., 'CPL'). This ensures that we merge offers for the same product/service across countries or conversion requirements. In addition, we strip punctuation and convert to lowercase. We use 449,891 *offers* to refer to distinctly named products and services, which derive from *network offers*, which are distinct pairs of product/service name and affiliate network.

Aggregators may use different labels for the same offer verticals. We relabel them according to our taxonomy of verticals (Sect. 4), manually mapping original vertical labels used at least 1,000 times. Based on this labeling, we map 412,519 offers (91.7%) to one of our nine verticals. 11.3% of offers mapped to multiple verticals, for which we applied majority voting to select the most common vertical, after stripping more generic verticals (i.e., e-commerce and software). We opt to use only the categorization provided by the aggregators instead of classifying offers through, e.g., a machine learning model, as the metadata does not necessarily allow a reliable automated classification. The offer's name, for instance, may reference a unique product or service name without a clear indication of its vertical. A description may not always be available, or contain generic keywords related to an offer's terms that are not indicative of the vertical.

3.4   Filtering Reputable Offers

The affiliate marketing model is not inherently malicious or deceptive. Many reputable businesses use affiliate marketing, with larger brands often operating their own program,[2] and smaller brands joining reputable affiliate networks.[3] Even the aggregators of deceptive offers list some reputable offers. As we aim to study deceptive offers, we identify and remove as many reputable offers as possible from our data set. For this purpose, we collect offers from 4 additional aggregators, also discovered through an online search, for which we confirm through manual

---

[2] For example Amazon (https://affiliate-program.amazon.com/) or eBay (https://partnernetwork.ebay.com/).

[3] For example Awin https://www.awin.com/ or CJ (https://www.cj.com/.

inspection of an offer sample that they list reputable offers from mainstream brands.[4] We manually identify and remove 97 affiliate networks that appear on both types of aggregators and that promote reputable products and services. We further remove offers if their landing page URL has the same domain as an affiliate program listed on an aggregator of reputable offers under a 'bare' root domain (i.e., with an empty path). These measures resulted in the removal of 298,947 legitimate offers from our data set. Our approach errs on the side of retaining reputable offers rather than removing deceptive offers, to ensure we capture deception in the ecosystem as broadly as possible.

4   Analysis of Offer Verticals and Deceptive Tactics

In the first part of our analysis, we study the different scams that are all prevalent in the deceptive affiliate marketing ecosystem. While prior work has studied individual scam categories, it did not situate them within the broader ecosystem, thus to date we lack a holistic overview of the ecosystem. To establish this holistic overview and show how the ecosystem underlies a variety of deceptive practices on the web, we build a common taxonomy covering the nine main verticals (categories) of deceptive products and services provided by merchants and promoted by affiliates. We develop this taxonomy starting from guides from major affiliate marketing ecosystem players [1–3, 22, 44, 67, 84, 103] as well as the categories listed in the offer aggregators, and further refine it through a manual review of a sample of 750 offers by four authors as well as an analysis of common phrases present in the offer names. For each of the nine verticals in our taxonomy, we qualitatively describe the primary tactics used to mislead consumers, also referencing prior observations of these tactics, to understand in more depth how they are shared or differ across verticals.

1. **Dating/adult** Dating services promoted through affiliate marketing usually operate on a subscription basis, often through short-term trials and recurring billing that may be hard to cancel [13, 61]. Sites further deceive users by listing fake profiles that sites themselves admit (in their terms) to be only for "entertainment" purposes [13]. These profiles are meant to elicit chat messages, for which customers have to pay [65]. These sites also make unsubstantiated claims about the speed and ease of finding a match on the site, supported by fake testimonials. Separately, some sites show adult content, which may be undesirable or inappropriate for users to see, especially if it is shown in a non-adult context or to minors.
2. **Entertainment** Entertainment offers largely cover two types: content distribution platforms, such as for videos or music (also visible in offer names), and mobile content portals, with offer names referencing mobile carriers (e.g., Claro, Movistar, Vodafone). As we did not sign up for these sites, we are unaware whether they (legally) host any (interesting) content. Both are prone to hidden subscriptions, and also collect personal data such as email addresses or phone numbers, potentially for abuse through resale.

---

[4] Note that 'reputable' or 'mainstream' does not imply that the brand is large.

3. **Finance** Trading platforms for cryptocurrencies (with Bitcoin being the most common phrase in offer names), binary options, foreign exchange, or commodities (e.g., oil) make exaggerated 'get-rich-quick' claims that users can earn vast amounts of money in a short time, supported by fake user testimonials and fake celebrity endorsements. However, users may instead lose their investment or are unable to withdraw funds, after having been pushed to make large deposits [14,106]. These trading platforms have been linked to fraud in the past and are therefore often heavily regulated or even prohibited [110]. Some offers concern 'business opportunities' ('BizOpp') for building one's own business, often in the form of self-help guides. Finally, some sites collect personal data for lead generation on credit, skewed towards payday loans with excessive interest rates; insurance, often with low coverage [80]; or banks, e.g., account sign-ups. Some offers claimed to help obtain Social Security disability benefits, possibly targeting vulnerable populations.

4. **Gambling** Online gambling sites provide e.g., casino games (the most common offer name phrase) or sports betting. These sites claim large potential earnings for users, and offer large "welcome bonuses" that may actually be difficult to earn. The sites often operate with valid licenses from permissive countries, e.g., Curaçao and Malta [75], but may be illegal to visit or advertise in some countries [116].

5. **Games** Games or game guides on mobile (with carrier references in offer names) often entail hidden recurring subscriptions, to an extent that Chrome has introduced warnings for them [92]. For browser and other mobile games, developers may simply require that users install their game, and monetize users separately, e.g., using microtransactions.

6. **Health/beauty** Health/beauty offers cover products for, a.o., weight loss (e.g., keto diet), 'nutraceuticals' (foods and supplements with claimed health benefits), CBD, male enhancement, or skincare, as are visible in offer names. Affiliates were also found to promote price-gouged masks [95], and go so far as promoting quack cures for diseases such as diabetes. These physical goods may actually be shipped to consumers [72], but they may unknowingly start a subscription for regular deliveries [11,41]. Products may have no actual utility, in particular compared to the claims made, and users consider these supplements particularly "scammy" [121]. Likely fake testimonials from doctors, regular consumers, and celebrities [11,23,28,114] further acclaim the products. The low value of these products may also be apparent from a need to add disclaimers such as "not FDA approved".

7. **Software** Promoted software applications are often 'utilities': software that purports to protect or improve devices, visible in offer names through common phrases such as antivirus software, VPNs, media but also (fake) Flash players, WhatsApp add-ons, ad-blocking browser extensions, or "phone cleanup" tools, both on desktop and mobile [102]. On the one hand, these may be mainstream apps whose affiliate programs are 'arbitraged', i.e., deceptive affiliate networks 'repackage' affiliate programs from reputable merchants [27], a.o., to make them more accessible to affiliates [6]. On the other hand, these may be low-quality apps that are monetized directly through recurring mobile

subscriptions or intrusive advertisements. Users find ads for these software downloads deceptive [121]. Common offer name keywords show these offers are often targeted at specific platforms, e.g., Chrome or iPhones. Outright malware is also sometimes spread, such as the Shlayer trojan through fake Flash Player software [56]. Next to utilities, offers may concern purchased incentivized app installs, where users are rewarded for installing the app [27,115]. As the practice artificially boosts app installs, the practice is discouraged or prohibited by major app stores [27].

8. **Sweepstakes** Free products (with iPhone and Samsung Galaxy being common in offer names) or vouchers/gift cards (Amazon being common) are given away in exchange for a user action [18,20]. A user may need to leave contact details, to be sold to third parties ('lead generation'). A user may alternatively be required to submit their credit card details, (unknowingly) starting subscriptions [28], for e.g., low-quality streaming sites, recipe catalogues, discount shops, or website builders. These giveaways often suggest affiliation with major brands who have warned users not to participate [46,57]. Users may also be prematurely congratulated, addressed as a 'winner' or told they can claim the prize even though they might not win the contest. The giveaways may actually happen, although a product may be substituted for a gift card of the same value, and their terms are often very limited with only a handful items being given away per year [28]. Instead of contests, products/gift cards may also be given as a reward for completing other offers.

9. **E-commerce** This vertical includes a variety of deceptive products and services for sale that do not fit the other categories. These can be physical goods, ranging from electronics ("electricity saving boxes") to lucky charms (money amulets), with exaggerated claims about their utility and likely fake testimonials from customers. Arbitrage of existing affiliate programs for online shops, travel sites, etc. also exists, as does lead generation for, e.g., home improvement (solar panel incentive programs).

In general, deception lies in a mismatch between price and value, with products and services being of dubious quality or egregiously priced. In addition, merchants deceive consumers by persuading them with exaggerated claims, hiding important terms and conditions in small print, or hiding the implications of the offers, such as recurring payments or the sale of personal data to third parties. Abuse of "dark patterns" to pressure users [76], such as timers and indicators that the offer will expire soon or fake user activity notifications ("X has just bought Y"), as well as fake endorsements by experts, celebrities, purported previous buyers, or unaffiliated brands to gain trust are all common. In the US, the Federal Trade Commission has alleged that these practices violate various consumer protection laws, such as the FTC Act [30,32,40]. In the European Union, the unfair commercial practices directive is similarly interpreted to ban such practices [21]. Outside actors also recognize the deception within the ecosystem and the harms that stem from it. Many verticals within the deceptive affiliate marketing ecosystem concern industries that are considered high-risk by financial institutions, with "more operational, regulatory, and reputational risk" [26] including higher levels of fraud [48], forcing merchants into transacting with a small set of banks who are willing to take the risk [77]. The ecosystem appears to be diverse and ever-evolving in the scams that are perpetrated, warranting the broad and continuous monitoring provided by our data collection.

5 Quantitative Analysis of Offers

In the second part of our analysis, we quantitatively characterize the dynamics and differentiation within the deceptive affiliate marketing ecosystem. Using the metadata unique to our data set, we seek to understand how the monetary incentives for affiliates depend on the type of scam and how it is monetized. This provides context for the strategies that ecosystem players might use and the risks they might be willing to take to propagate scams. In particular, we want to leverage our more comprehensive coverage to see whether users will see different abuse, e.g., depending on where they live, as this insight is necessary to develop comprehensive interventions that globally protect users. Finally, we also want to observe whether there is concentration in the ecosystem, as identifying the large-scale ecosystem players that enable a large number and variety of scams is useful to prioritize interventions. Note that our view on the ecosystem only allows us to analyze how many offers merchants publish and make available to affiliates. We cannot know which offers affiliates promote more or less, more successfully convert, and therefore cause the most harm to consumers.

5.1 Summary Statistics

For our analysis, we use data collected between March 24, 2020 and September 1, 2024, providing us longitudinal coverage[5]. We collect 449,891 *offers*, i.e., distinctly named products and services. These derive from 625,106 *network offers* across 1,165 affiliate networks, i.e., distinct pairs of product/service name and affiliate network. Between aggregators, 70.8% of networks and 62.1% of offers are only listed on 1 aggregator, showing that collecting data from many aggregators increases our coverage. We specifically find 150 networks that are only listed on the Russian-language aggregators, supporting our decision to include them. Orthogonally, combining metadata across aggregators improves data completeness: for 36.3% of offers, one aggregator had metadata that was missing at another aggregator. Through the aggregators, we capture data on a broad set of affiliate networks, thus we observe a larger share of the ecosystem than if we were to focus on specific affiliate networks.

5.2 Payouts and Conversion Criteria

The merchant who makes an offer available will pay the affiliate an agreed payout if the affiliate achieve that, after advertising the offer to a consumer, that

---

[5] Gaps in coverage do occur: aggregators became unavailable while others were added later on; aggregators blocked our scrapers or changed their site layout which broke our scrapers, or our scraping infrastructure was down.

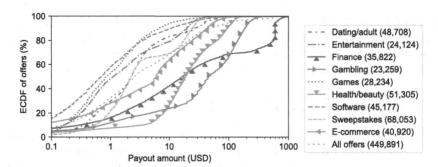

Fig. 2. The cumulative distribution of median payouts for offers per vertical shows that scam types significantly differ in their valuation within the ecosystem. (Legend lists number of offers).

consumer takes the required action to 'convert' the offer, i.e., fulfill the offer's condition. The payouts to affiliates reflect how much the ecosystem values offers across certain dimensions, such as the vertical or conversion criteria, which we analyze in this section. Throughout this section, we compute a median payout across all observed payouts for offers, i.e., over countries, affiliate networks, time, and aggregators, and convert all payouts to U.S. dollars using exchange rates on September 1, 2024. 444,745 (98.9%) offers have payout metadata.

We first plot the cumulative distribution of payouts per normalized vertical (Subsect. 3.3) in Fig. 2, giving us insight into how much merchants are willing to pay affiliates depending on the type of product or service and therefore the type of scam. *Finance*, *Gambling*, and *Health/beauty* command the highest payouts, with over half of offers having a median payout of more than $10. Conversely, over 60% of offers in the remaining verticals (other than *E-commerce*) have a payout of less than $5. Across all offers, the median payout is $2.60. In order to better understand how much different types of deceptive offers and the associated conversion types are worth to affiliates, we extract common phrases from offer titles and compute the median payout for the respective offers.

In general, high payouts reflect that a consumer needs to make a (higher) payment to the merchant. We see payouts of over $100 for 31.4% of *Finance* offers, specifically trading and investment platforms, with 'Bitcoin' and 'crypto' offers having a median payout of $582.5 and $550.0, respectively. A successful conversion requires affiliates to convince consumers to make a minimum deposit, usually $250. (Interestingly, the payouts to affiliates sometimes exceed this deposit). This suggests that the merchants of these platforms believe that users will invest large amounts of money over time, and are therefore willing to incentivize affiliates to promote the platforms through the promise of large rewards [50]. On a similar note, *Gambling* offers command higher payouts when they require players make a deposit to a gambling website, with 'casino' offers having a median payout of $87.5. For *Health/beauty* and *E-commerce* offers, the delivery of physical goods inherently solicits larger payments and thus higher affiliate payouts. For example, the median payout for 'keto' diet offers is $80.0, and is $41.7 for 'gadgets.' However, physical goods have a higher cost to produce and ship than for virtual trading or gambling platforms, so payouts are not as high as they are for the latter platforms. For *Dating/adult* and *Sweepstakes* offers, around 15% and 35% of offers respectively have around 10 times higher payouts than the rest of the vertical, which usually coincides with the offer converting on a consumer paying for a (trial/premium) subscription. *Entertainment*, *Games*, and *Software* offers have the lowest payouts, even when they require consumers to make a payment. *Games* 'subscription' offers, for example, have a median payout of $4.2. Presumably, this is due to the typically lower sales prices of the respective digital goods.

When offers convert on a consumer action other than a payment, affiliate payouts tend to be lower. In these cases, merchants need to monetize their offers indirectly, such as by leveraging the consumer's personal data. Lead generation offers in the *Finance* vertical, for instance, yield relatively high median payouts (e.g., $11.0 per consumer submitting their personal data in 'loans' offers) compared to lead generation offers in other verticals, but they are an order of magnitude smaller than for investment platform offers requiring a deposit. Other common types of offer conversion are registration on a website, which exists in all verticals but is most prevalent for *Dating/adult*, *Entertainment*, and *Gambling*, or the installation of an app (*Games* and *Software*).

The distribution of payouts per conversion type [22] across all verticals (Fig. 3) confirms this relationship. The lowest payouts are a median of $0.5 for app installs (CPI, cost per install). This is followed by two forms of lead generation. Median payouts are slightly higher at $2.95 when a consumer confirms the validity of their contact details (DOI, double opt-in – clicking a confirmation link in an email, for instance) as opposed to $2.0 for only providing the data (SOI, single opt-in). Once consumers make payments, payouts increase around tenfold compared to the value of personal data for leads. The payout depends on the payment method: at $15.35, the median is slightly lower for cash-on-delivery (COD – payment upon receipt of the item) than the $21.2 for 'credit card submit' (CCSubmit). This may cover the risk of non-payment on delivery for a product that is already shipped, compared to a credit card that can be charged ahead of shipment, but could also reflect the popularity of COD in emerging markets [47], where offer payouts are lower overall (Subsect. 5.3). Finally, at $165.7, median payouts are the highest for offers where the consumer makes a deposit, which correlates with offers where no goods need to be shipped.

Different conversion types and payouts likely drive affiliates to pursue different strategies to attract audiences that might result in a successful conversion. Knowledge of what an affiliate needs to achieve for a conversion, and how much they can afford to spend on promotional efforts to acquire conversions, can help researchers devise more targeted measurements or interventions.

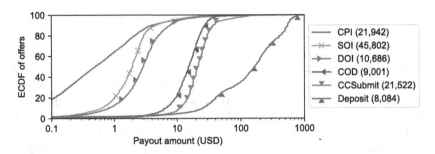

Fig. 3. The cumulative distribution of median payouts for offers per conversion type shows that higher payments or sharing more personal data by consumers correlates with the valuation of an offer. (Legend lists number of offers).

5.3 Targeted Countries

Another interesting aspect of affiliate offers is how merchants target their deceptive products or services at specific countries. The ecosystem usually separates countries into three tiers, depending on purchasing power, language skills, and regulatory frameworks. We describe these tiers based on the definitions from major ecosystem players [51,70,79,104,111–113]. *Tier-1* countries comprise English-speaking Western countries, and usually also the rest of Western Europe and wealthy Asian countries. They are considered the most desirable, as consumers have high incomes. This means that many traffic sources and offers with high payouts are available to affiliates. However, competition between affiliates might be higher and markets tend to be more regulated, restricting which (deceptive) products, services, and promotional tactics are allowed. *Tier-2* countries tend to comprise Latin America, the Middle East, Eastern Europe and Russia, and some Southeast Asian countries. Consumers in these countries have moderate incomes. The tier is seen as a starting point for affiliates, with fewer legal restrictions and cheaper traffic, but also lower payouts and conversions. *Tier-3* countries comprise most African countries, and the remaining countries in South America and Asia. Consumers in this tier have the lowest purchasing power, and are less attractive to affiliates as payouts are low. Local languages and customs may make consumers less accessible, but this also means there is less competition for cheaper traffic in a less regulated market.

Out of the 406,705 offers with associated country data (90.4% of all offers), 77,069 (18.9%) target a worldwide audience.[6] Conversely, 229,272 (56.4%) of offers with country data are targeted at only one country. In absolute numbers, the United States has the most offers, at 87,550 offers (Fig. 4). Germany comes a distant second at 35,587 offers. Overall, more offers are targeted to countries in North America, Europe, Russia, Australia, South Africa, and to a lesser extent

---

[6] They list (an equivalent of) 'Worldwide' as their country or in their name, or cover over 100 countries. For reference, the United Nations has 193 member states, and 249 territories have been assigned an ISO 3166-1 alpha-2 code.

Fig. 4. There is an uneven distribution in the number of offers per country where merchants target that country. This distribution correlates with the 'tiers' in which the ecosystem separates countries, which itself depends on purchasing power, language skills, and regulatory frameworks.

Brazil and India. This correlates with the higher 'tiers' assigned to these countries, suggesting merchants prefer selling products and services to higher-income audiences.

In terms of verticals, a country tends to have a higher or lower share of its targeted offers in higher or lower-paying verticals in accordance with the country's tier. Due to space constraints, we report on the most significant findings from our analysis of each vertical's share of a country's total targeted offers. *Dating/adult* offers have a relatively high share of offers in most countries, no matter the tier; it is also the most common vertical overall. *Finance* offers tend to be more frequent in tier-2 locations, such as Latin America (e.g., 32.4% in Bolivia), the Middle East (e.g., 27.2% in Oman), and the Baltics (e.g., 24.3% in Latvia). *Gambling* offers are more frequent in CIS countries, led by Turkmenistan at 45.5%. *Health/beauty* offers are more frequent in Eastern Europe, e.g., 65.8% in Bosnia and Herzegovina and 50.6% in Montenegro. while other *E-commerce* product offers are particularly frequent in Russia (28.3%) and CIS countries (e.g., 24.0% in Kazakhstan). *Sweepstakes* are common mostly in tier 1: Europe (e.g., 32.1% in France, 27.0% in Germany), the United States (22.0%), and Australia (22.0%), but also Indonesia (23.8%) and Singapore (23.2%). Digital goods in the *Entertainment*, *Games*, and *Software* verticals are most common in tier-2 and 3 countries, i.e., Latin America, Africa, the Middle East, and parts of Asia. These offers are mostly mobile-based, and may therefore reflect the wider availability of mobile payments compared to other payment methods in these countries. The above analysis shows that specialization also occurs on the country axis. Differing offer market shares of verticals in countries primarily depends on the willingness and ability of merchants to do business in a country, which in turn relates to the (perceived) profitability, as gauged by intrinsic consumer interest but also factors such as income, but may also depend on external factors such as the availability of payment methods, ease of fulfillment, legal restrictions, etc.

Table 3. The top 5 affiliate networks specialize in the countries they target, as shown by their top 5 countries in terms of percentage of offers. (Offers can target multiple countries, so percentages per network do not sum to 100%).

Network	Country 1		Country 2		Country 3		Country 4		Country 5	
mobusi	ZA	9.05%	TH	7.77%	IT	6.61%	BR	6.18%	IN	5.84%
goldengoose	SA	7.27%	CH	4.73%	ZA	4.49%	RO	4.32%	TR	4.27%
algoaffiliates	US	96.24%	FR	93.79%	DE	93.75%	CH	93.74%	CA	93.74%
mylead	PL	24.68%	DE	22.16%	US	17.27%	AU	17.10%	CA	14.94%
trafficlight	RU	50.21%	KZ	15.20%	BY	8.87%	UA	8.34%	IT	8.13%

5.4 Affiliate Networks

The offers in our data set originate from 1,165 affiliate networks. We see a concentration of offers with large networks: 50% of all offers stem from only 47 networks. Between networks, 17.6% of offers with the same name are listed on more than 1 network, suggesting that certain merchants seek to increase their reach of potential affiliates through multiple networks. Our analysis confirms the tendency for specialization in this cybercriminal ecosystem [101,109], as affiliate networks tend to specialize in one or a handful of verticals. 50.4% of networks have only one vertical with at least 5% of their offers. Similar to the distribution for offers, *Dating/adult* is the most common vertical, with 403 networks having more than 5% of their offers in this vertical (Table 4). Figure 6 shows the top 20 affiliate networks according to the number of offers, with the three largest affiliate networks in our data, Mobusi, Golden Goose and Algo Affiliates, listing over 27,000 products and services each. Of note is that some of these networks have previously been linked to scams: ClickDealer was linked to Bitcoin investment scams [14,106] Adscend Media was sued for spreading spam [108], and CPALead was linked to survey scams [18]. The latter two accusations date from 2012 and 2013, respectively, highlighting the longevity of these affiliate networks and their deceptive tactics.

Among the top 3, we again see a different focus in terms of targeted verticals. Mobusi and Golden Goose target mobile devices with *Dating/adult, Entertainment, Games,* and *Software* offers, while Algo Affiliates has a strong focus on *Finance* offers. According to their websites, these three networks have over 20,000, 10,000 and 100,000 affiliates, respectively, reinforcing the vast scale of the deceptive ecosystem. In the same spirit, specialization happens at a country level: among the 5 affiliate networks with the most offers, offers target a very varied set of countries (Table 3). For example, the countries that Mobusi targets most are mostly tier-2 countries, while Golden Goose, Algo Affiliates and MyLead target mostly tier-1 countries, and Traffic Light targets CIS countries.

Finally, the longitudinal aspect of our data set gives us a view on affiliate networks entering or leaving the market. Omitting the start and end of our measurement period (to account for left/right censoring), we saw 639 networks

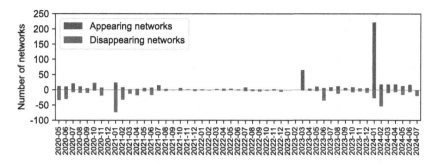

Fig. 5. Affiliate networks (dis)appear over our 4-year measurement of aggregators.

Table 4. Networks differ in the verticals they specialize in, as shown by the number of networks for whom the vertical covers at least a given percentage (1, 5, or 10%) of their offers.

Vertical	# networks			Vertical	# networks		
	1%	5%	10%		1%	5%	10%
Dating/adult	519	403	321	Gambling	327	205	170
Finance	520	376	291	Software	320	177	122
E-commerce	499	360	278	Other	172	105	87
Sweepstakes	361	280	218	Games	208	97	65
Health/beauty	432	271	206	Entertainment	217	74	46

appear and 544 networks disappear over our 4 years measuring offer aggregators (Fig. 5), which may reflect networks being created or disbanded as well as networks deciding to start or stop advertising their offers on aggregators. This shows the dynamism of the ecosystem, and highlights the need to monitor it longitudinally to discover and target new deceptive actors.

5.5 Longitudinal Popularity

Through the longitudinal view that our data set provides on the ecosystem, we can observe the emergence of new topics in deceptive offers. After the initialization of our data set in March 2020, the count of newly observed offers has been fairly stable over time (Fig. 7), at an average rate of around 4,000 offers per week. Compared to this global trend, we see that the release of new and popular products coincides with merchants creating new offers that mention them. As one case study (Fig. 7), we see that *Sweepstakes* offers where different iPhone models are promised as a prize start appearing on or slightly before the products' release dates. This suggests that ecosystem players are capitalizing on the novelty of these products to make their offers more attractive, and that aggregator data can be useful for discovering new offers referencing these products early on. On

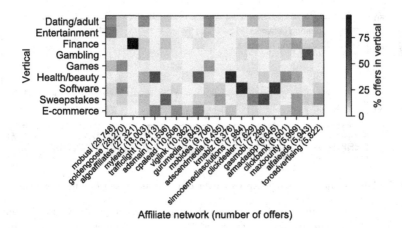

Fig. 6. For the 20 networks with the most offers, the proportion of offers per vertical shows that networks specialize in the scam types they manage.

the level of verticals, we also measure the longitudinal trends within the relative share of new offers for each vertical (Fig. 8). Among the most significant trends, *Dating/adult* offers were more common in 2020 and 2021, perhaps owing to the COVID-19 pandemic and lockdowns making virtual dating sites more attractive. *Finance* offers spiked mid-2022, before receding to a much lower level, although these offers seem to resurge in 2024. *Software* offers see an increase over time, achieving a peak share of offers in 2024 that was four times higher than the lowest shares in 2020 or 2021. Ecosystem players are therefore also adapting to long-term trends, causing certain scams to fall out of favor or in contrast are published by merchants more often, which reinforces the need to monitor the ecosystem and its evolution over time.

5.6   Summary

The deceptive affiliate marketing ecosystem enables a broad variety of online scams – even though they might seem unconnected at first – with both more well-known scams such as unwanted software, and previously less studied scams such as finance or entertainment scams. Through the payout metadata unique to our data set, we see that some offers yield very high rewards, up to hundreds of dollars for investment scams. Payouts correlate with what the consumer provides in terms of money or personal data. This can inform which affiliates are attracted to the offers and the tactics they are willing to use to achieve a certain revenue. The deceptive affiliate marketing ecosystem operates on a global scale, but the selection of scams is adapted to the country, reflecting, a.o., incomes. In general, offers can be targeted at very specific audiences. Through the longitudinal view that our data set provides, we also discover that affiliate marketers capitalize on new trends. Our data set can be used to achieve broad coverage of the ecosystem to develop more comprehensive interventions that protect consumers across

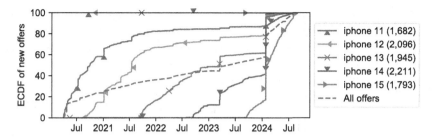

Fig. 7. The longitudinal cumulative distribution of newly observed offers overall shows that the ecosystem grows steadily. The distribution of offers containing keywords for iPhone product launches is related to the release dates (shown by markers along the top), which shows that merchants capitalize on new trends.

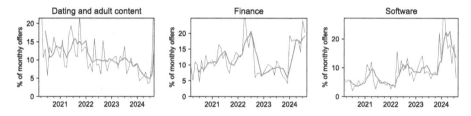

Fig. 8. The longitudinal share of new offers (i.e., observed for the first time in our data set) per month for three selected categories shows that the publication of offers from different scam types is affected by long-term trends. The thick orange line is a four-month moving average, the thin blue line is the monthly share. (Color figure online)

countries, verticals, and time. In addition, we can use it to identify the large affiliate networks, against which interventions may be the most effective.

6 Discussion

Specialization. The deceptive affiliate marketing ecosystem embeds specialization across multiple dimensions, a trend that has been observed in other cyber-criminal ecosystems [54,87,88,101,109] and that we observe as well. Affiliate marketing is itself a form of specialization, where merchants no longer need to manage advertising themselves and can focus on fulfillment, and instead contract promotion out to individual affiliates. These affiliates can focus on marketing the offers to specific audiences that they believe to be the most susceptible to the deceptive scams, through the most effective advertising channels. We find that our third main actor, the affiliate network, extends this division of labor, managing affiliate recruitment, offer tracking, and commission transfers. These affiliate networks also introduce centralization through their 'marketplace' for online scams, where affiliates can easily discover a large offer inventory and merchants can easily access a large pool of affiliates, increasing the ease with which ecosystem players can encounter each other and trade services.

With the affiliate network acting as a central party to all transactions, affiliates become disconnected from the concrete merchants whose products they promote, and see offers as a commodity; the same holds for merchants towards the affiliates promoting their products. This ties in with risk distribution: merchants only need to pay affiliates when the product or service actually is sold, while affiliates can be agile in switching merchants if the product or service does not perform well. Similarly, these distributed responsibilities could be seen as liability distribution: affiliates, affiliate networks, and merchants could claim they are unaware of the deceptive practices of the other parties, or at least not responsible for them. Nevertheless, we see that some ecosystem players openly acknowledge, discuss, or even encourage deceptive tactics [4,12,28,66,73], suggesting complicity in the scams. This relates to our broader observation that the deceptive affiliate marketing ecosystem is "hiding in plain sight" [88]: the offer aggregators from which we obtain our data operate in the open, as do most of the actors and supporting services, who seem to consider their individual participation in the ecosystem above board. In this light, we also consider that the listing of reputable products and services on deceptive offer aggregators (Sect. 3.4) can still attract abuse. Reputable and deceptive offers are intertwined on these aggregators, so affiliates browsing the aggregators may not (be able to) distinguish between these two kinds of offers. Reputable brands may then be harmed when affiliates use abusive tactics to promote their products [27].

Throughout our analysis in Sects. 4 and 5, we also observe specialization within the set of offers that merchants make available to affiliates. We taxonomized offers into nine verticals for which we see greatly varying payouts, which correlate with the varying valuation for the countries where the offer is available. This means that merchants and affiliates can select their level of expertise but also comfort and exposure to intervention with regards to the scams they want to engage in. Indeed, new affiliates are recommended to promote lower payout offers [15,22], i.e., those from specific verticals and (tiers of) countries, in part as they are said to more easily convert, have less competition, and are less regulated. These new affiliates (and merchants) may start off with 'small-scale' scams, which nevertheless deceive users into losing money or personal data. Then, through the experience they gain, affiliates and merchants may eventually "graduate" to more high-profile, high-payout scams, such as harmful scams for nutraceuticals, gambling sites, or financial products, increasing the harm to online consumers. All these elements of specialization combined – distribution of tasks, risk and liability; networks centralizing offers; and diversification of offers – therefore increase the ease of joining the deceptive affiliate marketing ecosystem, and contribute to its scale and growth, as we observed in our longitudinal analysis (Sect. 5.5). Having our ground-truth vantage point helps in understanding this specialization and maintaining wide coverage of the ecosystem despite it, which is crucial for broadly effective interventions.

Intervention. Ultimately, consumers should be prevented from viewing deceptive offers, while merchants, affiliate networks, and affiliates should face consequences for publishing deceptive offers. The division of responsibilities between the deceptive affiliate marketing ecosystem players can both help and hinder such interventions. It provides more venues for intervention: as long as one of the links in the chain from traffic source to landing page is broken, a consumer is no longer able to complete the offer. Conversely, any one intervention will only address a small part of the ecosystem, as all other players can remain active. However, any intervention introduces an additional burden for ecosystem players, and may prevent or deter them from participating in the ecosystem.

On a technical level, interventions can start on the consumer's side: through client-side blocks of deceptive offers, e.g., through (DNS-based) blocklists, browser interstitials or extensions blocking affiliate marketing-related URLs or detecting deceptive affiliate marketing content. These interventions have relatively low overhead and can therefore be deployed quickly, but only protect the users who install them. The early look provided by our data set, tracking new offers as they emerge on aggregators, can lead to faster ingestion of offers and landing pages into blocklists, potentially even preventing users from ever seeing the offer. Next, the traffic source could detect and take down ads for or links to known deceptive offers, preventing all users of that traffic source from being redirected to those offers. Finally, along the redirect chain from the traffic source to the landing page, the supporting infrastructure, such as servers or domain names, can be taken down [107]. Such a takedown may be requested by law enforcement or by affected brands [10,55,69] and implemented by registries, registrars and/or hosting providers. This process protects any Internet user from seeing the deceptive offer, as (in the end) the landing page becomes unreachable. However, takedowns involve more stakeholders and have more overhead [55], and may therefore be slower to take effect. To maximize their impact and effectiveness, they should target the "bottleneck" infrastructure resources in the redirect chain [71,100], such as affiliate network tracking domains. These can be identified by combining our data set with end-to-end measurements starting from the traffic source.

Beyond technical interventions, while deceptive affiliate marketing operates in a 'grey zone,' consumer protection regulators can take action against unfair or misleading commercial practices [25], including novel techniques that users may perceive as deceptive [121]. For example, in the United States, the Federal Trade Commission has the authority to regulate on practices such as deceptive advertising [31,42], and has previously targeted deceptive affiliate marketing ecosystem players [29–31,33–41]. Interventions against financial services may also be effective in disincentivizing ecosystem players by disrupting their revenue streams [60,77,101]. Our data set can expand the discovery by regulators of new types of scams or deceptive techniques, and help in identifying the major ecosystem players and attributing infrastructure to them, in order to further enable comprehensive interventions.

Limitations. While we saw that the 23 deceptive offer aggregators covered a wide variety of verticals and affiliate networks, they may not cover all types of online abuse that uses the affiliate marketing model. Notably missing from our data set are offers related to two trades of physical goods where researchers have previously observed the affiliate marketing model, pharmaceuticals [58,78] and counterfeit goods [59], as well as online crimes such as bulletproof hosting providers [86] and ransomware [17,86]. The more obvious illegality of these crimes may make it too risky to publish these offers openly on aggregators. However, the prior studies suggest that the relation between affiliates and merchants is more direct, without affiliate networks as intermediaries. The merchants may therefore rely more on word-of-mouth marketing, as to inherently select for affiliates who are more deeply involved in the ecosystem and may more likely convert offers, and therefore would not need aggregators to list their offers. In addition, affiliate networks that do publish offers on aggregators might have private offers that are only available to those affiliates who are registered with the network, or with a proven track record [22]. Again, the deceptive offers that we discover and study may serve as a stepping stone towards these even more harmful ecosystems, which confirms the need to also target the deceptive affiliate marketing ecosystem.

While we cannot independently confirm the origin and reliability of the offer data that aggregators provide, we have good reason to believe that aggregators obtain it directly from affiliate networks. Metadata from some aggregators refers to the offer management platforms of affiliate networks as data sources, suggesting that they are directly integrated. Aggregators also advertise their platform for networks to list their offers (usually for a fee) [5,45,83,122], suggesting they actively collaborate to publish offer data. In addition, we argue that networks and aggregators have an incentive to provide correct data to affiliates. Next to the commercial benefits of accurately representing the available offers, underground activities operate on a reputation system, where breaches of trust result in negative feedback on e.g., underground forums [49]. Similarly, we expect dishonest aggregators or networks to be called out. If inaccuracies in the data are present, we expect them to be due to parsing errors or data staleness rather than malicious intent. We therefore consider the aggregator data reliable for our purpose.

Since we focus on gaining insights into the dynamics of the deceptive affiliate marketing offers that merchants make available, we cannot use our data set on its own to measure the ecosystem from the sides of consumers and affiliates. Future work can leverage the global overview from our data set to support end-to-end measurements with broad coverage, therefore improving the validity of future insights into the ecosystem. Such comprehensive end-to-end data can be used to determine how often consumers see and complete deceptive affiliate marketing offers. With data from traffic sources, it becomes possible to study how the advertising material created by affiliates is deceptive [120,121], as well as which traffic sources are more commonly (ab)used for deceptive advertising [105,120]. End-to-end traffic can also allow to identify the most active affiliates, affiliate networks, and merchants. In addition, while we quantify the monetary value of a successful conversion to the merchant, we cannot estimate the cost to the affiliate for obtaining a successful conversion, in particular the differences across offers, verticals, and countries. This also means we cannot reliably calculate total earnings across the ecosystem. Finally, in-depth investigation of the corporate entities behind main ecosystem players [24,119] can further support interventions.

Ethical Considerations. Given the often malicious nature of the players in the ecosystem, we must carefully consider how we conduct our study and treat our findings. We believe that the goals of our study will bring about significant benefits to understanding and even combating the malicious practices within the affiliate marketing ecosystems, which therefore also justifies certain experimental techniques to obtain data on and insights into the ecosystem. Ethical evaluations conducted in previous studies have lead to a consensus that given appropriate measures, the use of scraping is ethically justified especially when studying malicious ecosystems [74,89,96]. To the best of our knowledge, the scraped offer data does not contain personally identifiable information, and our research was not considered eligible for ethical review from our university, due to it not being on human subjects. We will share both the data set used for this study and the data that is still continuously being collected with other researchers and parties of interest, including law enforcement when applicable.

By scraping offer aggregators, we avoid the need to register for individual affiliate networks. We observe that this registration process ranges from basic username/password registration, over providing contact details (email address, phone number, instant messaging accounts), to more extensive vetting including interviews with those managing the affiliate network. Next to reducing the effort in collecting data, we do not expose ourselves to the players in the ecosystem, nor do we have to resort to deception when describing our goals or contact details.

7   Related Work

Prior work discussed how certain types of cybercrime use the affiliate marketing model. Samosseiko [91] first outlined the role of affiliate networks in spam-advertised pharmacies and counterfeit software, focusing on Russian 'partnerka' networks. Kanich *et al.* [58] and McCoy *et al.* [78] studied the purchases and revenues on major pharmaceutical and counterfeit software affiliate networks, using leaked ground truth of the networks. Levchenko *et al.* [72] linked products advertised in spam to their respective affiliate networks, and studied to what extent they relied on shared network and payment infrastructure. As part of their systematization of the underground economy, Thomas *et al.* [101] describe how the affiliate marketing model is central to many organized cybercrime operations. For example, certain bulletproof hosting providers [86] or ransomware-as-a-service providers [17,118] operate through affiliate programs.

Further work identified affiliate marketing in detailed studies of specific malicious ecosystems. Caballero *et al.* [16] analyzed the affiliate structure behind 'pay-per-install' malware. Kotzias *et al.* [64] and Thomas *et al.* [102] analyzed popular 'pay-per-install' affiliate programs. Stone-Gross *et al.* [97] studied the major actors and economics of fake antivirus software. Karami *et al.* [59] analyzed 'Tower of Power,' an affiliate program for herbal supplements and replica luxury goods. Clark and McCoy [18] analyzed the affiliate networks behind survey scams distributed through Facebook ads. White [114] describes the identification and subsequent takedown of one affiliate marketing campaign abusing celebrity endorsements to advertise nutraceuticals. Vadrevu and Perdisci [105], Koide *et al.* [63], and Yang *et al.* [117] describe detection and blocking techniques for "social engineering ads" which cover a subset of the scams that we observe, without connecting them to the deceptive affiliate marketing ecosystem. Compared to these prior works, which were done from the vantage point of a user and limited to a few verticals or traffic sources each, our vantage point and study provides a broader view on the ecosystem.

Finally, leveraging ground-truth data has proven valuable to studying cybercriminal ecosystems holistically, having been used for, a.o., online anonymous markets [68], stolen payment card marketplaces [9], and Bitcoin mixing services [82]. We are the first to use ground-truth offer metadata to study the deceptive affiliate marketing ecosystem, using it to discover deceptive products and services across all major verticals, countries, and potential traffic sources, which allows us to find new scams such as cryptocurrency investment platforms that were not yet studied in prior work, and to quantify and compare the monetary value that the ecosystem attaches to specific verticals and conversion types.

8   Conclusion

We provide an overview of the deceptive affiliate marketing ecosystem and the offers (products/services) that are promoted through it, using our longitudinal and ongoing data collection from 23 offer aggregators. We show how this ecosystem brings together a variety of scams observed on the web today. Ecosystem players deploy a wide range of tactics to mislead users, meant to suggest high quality, reputation, or demand, even though the products and services on offer tend to actually be of very low value. Depending on parameters such as the offer vertical and country, the products and services that are promoted, the affiliate networks that make them available, and the value that is assigned to them differs, highlighting the added value of the comprehensive coverage provided by our vantage points. This specialization makes the deceptive affiliate marketing ecosystem attractive and accessible to new players, resulting in its continued growth over time.

A crucial step towards combating the deceptive affiliate marketing scams is holistically understanding the inner workings and dynamics of this ecosystem. Our study provides a first global overview of this ecosystem, which becomes especially important given the specialization that is embedded in the cybercriminal deceptive affiliate marketing ecosystem, with its diverse actors and scam types. When combined with our data set, measurements on a variety of traffic sources can provide a comprehensive end-to-end view of the ecosystem, the interactions between the players, and the dynamics that steer them. Our continuous data collection pipeline provides crucial metadata that enables near real-time monitoring of newly emerging scams, which can lead to more extensive, effective and impactful interventions, to ultimately protect consumers from being scammed on the web. To support this, we will share our data with researchers and stakeholders to enrich other measurements and deploy powerful, effective and targeted defenses to prevent users from being exposed to deceptive affiliate marketing and losing their money or personal data.[7]

Acknowledgments. We thank the anonymous reviewers for their valuable feedback. We thank the participants of the SecWeb 2021 workshop and IEEE S&P 2022 poster session for their feedback on an early version of this research. This research is partially funded by the Research Fund KU Leuven, the Cybersecurity Research Programme Flanders, and the National Science Foundation under grant 2039693. This research was supported by the Research Foundation - Flanders (FWO) through a PhD fellowship (11A3419N, 11A3421N), junior postdoctoral fellowship (1298825N) and a research visit grant (V426920N) held by Victor Le Pochat. Victor Le Pochat is currently employed by the European Commission. The views and opinions of the author expressed herein are personal and do not necessarily reflect those of the European Commission or other EU institutions.

References

1. A Complete Overview of the Health & Beauty (Nutra) Vertical. Advidi (2017). https://advidi.com/overview-health-beauty-nutra-vertical/
2. A Complete Overview of the Mainstream Vertical. Advidi (2017). https://advidi.com/complete-overview-mainstream-vertical/
3. A Guide to the Finance Vertical. Advidi (2020). https://advidi.com/a-guide-to-the-finance-vertical/
4. Ad Creatives Review. Pushground Blog (2021). https://www.pushground.com/blog/ad-creatives-review
5. Add Your Network/Program. Affplus. https://www.affplus.com/add-network
6. Affiliate Marketer's Guide to Antivirus and VPNs. Pushground Blog (2021). https://www.pushground.com/blog/antivirus-advertising-guide
7. affilinc Ltd. AffiliateFix (2021). https://www.affiliatefix.com/
8. affLIFT, LLC. affLIFT (2021). https://afflift.com
9. Aliapoulios, M., Ballard, C., Bhalerao, R., Lauinger, T., McCoy, D.: Swiped: analyzing ground-truth data of a marketplace for stolen debit and credit cards. In: USENIX Security, pp. 4151–4168 (2021). https://www.usenix.org/conference/usenixsecurity21/presentation/aliapoulios
10. Alowaisheq, E., et al.: Cracking the wall of confinement: understanding and analyzing malicious domain take-downs. In: NDSS (2019). https://doi.org/10.14722/ndss.2019.23243.
11. Steven Baker, C.: Subscription traps and deceptive free trials scam millions with misleading ads and fake celebrity endorsements. Better Business Bureau (2018). https://www.bbb.org/article/investigations/18929-subscription-traps-and-deceptive-free-trials-scam-millions-with-misleading-ads-and-fake-celebrity-endorsements
12. Ban Your Stereotypes about FB. AdCombo (2018). https://blog.adcombo.com/ban-your-stereotypes-about-fb/

---

[7] See https://deceptive-affiliate-marketing.distrinet-research.be/.

13. BBB Scam Alert: Looking for Love? Don't Fall for a Fake Dating Website. Better Business Bureau (2021). https://www.bbb.org/article/news-releases/24477-bbb-scam-alert-looking-love-dont-fall-for-a-fake-dating-service

14. Eric van den Berg. De verborgen industrie die Bitcoinadvertenties op Facebook zet: 'Ze weten niet eens dat we bestaan!'. In: Brandpunt+ (2019). https://www.npo3.nl/brandpuntplus/de-verborgen-industrie-die-bitcoinadvertenties-op-facebook-zet-ze-weten-niet-eens-dat-we-bestaan

15. Magdalena Bober. The Ultimate Guide to Finding Profitable CPA Offers in Affiliate Marketing. Zeropark (2020). https://zeropark.com/blog/ultimate-guide-to-finding-profitable-cpa-offers/

16. Caballero, J., Grier, C., Kreibich, C., Paxson, V.: Measuring pay-per-install: the commoditization of malware distribution. In: USENIX Security (2011)

17. Cable, J., Gray, I.W., McCoy , D.:Showing the receipts: understanding the modern ransomware ecosystem. In: eCrime (2024)

18. Clark, J.W., McCoy, D.: There are no free iPads: an analysis of survey scams as a business. In: 6th USENIX Workshop on Large-Scale Exploits and Emergent Threats (2013)

19. Clayton, R., Moore, T., Christin, N.: Concentrating Correctly on Cybercrime Concentration. In: 14th Annual Workshop on Economics and Information Security (2015)

20. Cluley, G.: Beware! Free apple products used as lure in text scams. Naked Security (2012). https://nakedsecurity.sophos.com/2012/08/08/free-apple-products-text-scam/

21. Commission Notice – Guidance on the Interpretation and Application of Directive 2005/29/EC of the European Parliament and of the Council concerning unfair business-to-consumer commercial practices in the internal market. In: Official Journal of the European Union C 526.2021/C 526/01, pp. 1–129 (2021). https://eur-lex.europa.eu/legal-content/EN/TXT/?uri=CELEX:52021XC1229(05)

22. Patrick, D.: How to find CPA offers: choosing the best CPA offer to promote. Adsterra (2021). https://adsterra.com/blog/how-to-find-the-best-cpa-offers/

23. Dangu, J.: Fake Celebrity-Endorsed Bitcoin Scam Abuses Ad Tech to Net $1M in 1 Day. Confiant (2020). https://blog.confiant.com/fake-celebrity-endorsed-scam-abuses-ad-tech-to-net-1m-in-one-day-ffe330258e3c

24. De Rosa, N., Yates, J., Noël, B.: Un empire montr é alais de l'arnaque en ligne. Radio-Canada.ca (2021). https://ici.radio-canada.ca/recit-numerique/2140/adcenter-hyuna-philip-keezer-streaming-concours

25. Micklitz, H.W., Durovic, M.: International law on (un)fair commercial practices. In: Internationalization of Consumer Law. SPS, pp. 25–48. Springer, Cham (2017). https://doi.org/10.1007/978-3-319-45312-5_3

26. Everything You Need To Know About High-Risk Industries. LegitScript (2023). https://www.legitscript.com/fraud-risk-and-prevention/high-risk-industries/

27. Farooqi, S., Feal, Á., Lauinger, T., McCoy, D., Shafiq, Z., Vallina-Rodriguez, N.: Understanding incentivized mobile app installs on google play store. In: IMC, pp. 696–709 (2020). https://doi.org/10.1145/3419394.3423662

28. Faux, Z.: They go out and find the morons for me. In: Bloomberg Businessweek, vol. 4564, pp. 56–61 (2018). ISSN 0007-7135

29. Federal Trade Commission. Affiliate Marketers to Pay More Than $4 Million to Settle Charges That They Promoted a Fraudulent Business Coaching and Investment Scheme (2020). https://www.ftc.gov/news-events/press-releases/2020/03/affiliate-marketers-pay-more-4-million-settle-charges-they

30. Federal Trade Commission. Another Group of Marketers Behind Phony 'Gift Card' Text Spam Settles FTC Complaint (2014). https://www.ftc.gov/news-events/press-releases/2014/02/another-group-marketers-behind-phony-gift-card-text-spam-settles

31. Federal Trade Commission. Enforcement Policy Statement on Deceptively Formatted Advertisements. Federal Register **81**(74), 22596–22601 (2016). https://www.ftc.gov/system/files/documents/public_statements/896923/151222deceptiveenforcement.pdf

32. Federal Trade Commission. Fauxmats, False Claims, Phony Celebrity Endorsements, and Unauthorized Charges (2017). https://www.ftc.gov/business-guidance/blog/2017/11/fauxmats-false-claims-phony-celebrity-endorsements-and-unauthorized-charges

33. Federal Trade Commission. Federal Court Rules Affiliate Marketing Network and Its Parent Company Must Turn Over $11.9 Million They Received From Deceptive Marketing Scheme (2015). https://www.ftc.gov/news-events/press-releases/2015/04/federal-court-rules-affiliate-marketing-network-its-parent

34. Federal Trade Commission. FTC Announces Crackdown on Deceptively Marketed CBD Products (2020). https://www.ftc.gov/news-events/press-releases/2020/12/ftc-announces-crackdown-deceptively-marketed-cbd-products

35. Federal Trade Commission. FTC Charges Marketers Used Massive Spam Campaign To Pitch Bogus Weight-Loss Products (2016). https://www.ftc.gov/news-events/press-releases/2016/06/ftc-charges-marketers-used-massive-spam-campaign-pitch-bogus

36. Federal Trade Commission. FTC Charges Online Marketing Scheme with Deceiving Shoppers (2017). https://www.ftc.gov/news-events/press-releases/2017/08/ftc-charges-online-marketing-scheme-deceiving-shoppers

37. Federal Trade Commission. FTC Seeks to Halt 10 Operators of Fake News Sites from Making Deceptive Claims About Acai Berry Weight Loss Products (2011). https://www.ftc.gov/news-events/press-releases/2011/04/ftc-seeks-halt-10-operators-fake-news-sites-making-deceptive

38. Federal Trade Commission. FTC Settlement Bars Spam Email Marketing, Baseless Weight-Loss Claims by Diet-Pill Operation (2017). https://www.ftc.gov/news-events/press-releases/2017/03/ftc-settlement-bars-spam-email-marketing-baseless-weight-loss

39. Federal Trade Commission. Geniux Dietary Supplement Sellers Barred from Unsupported Cognitive Improvement Claims (2019). https://www.ftc.gov/news-events/press-releases/2019/04/geniux-dietary-supplement-sellers-barred-unsupported-cognitive

40. Federal Trade Commission. Internet Marketers of Dietary Supplement and Skincare Products Banned from Deceptive Advertising and Billing Practices (2017). https://www.ftc.gov/news-events/press-releases/2017/11/internet-marketers-dietary-supplement-skincare-products-banned

41. Federal Trade Commission. Marketers Behind Fake News Sites Settle FTC Charges of Deceptive Advertising (2012). https://www.ftc.gov/news-events/press-releases/2012/11/marketers-behind-fake-news-sites-settle-ftc-charges-deceptive

42. FTC Policy Statement on Deception (1984). https://www.ftc.gov/system/files/documents/public_statements/410531/831014deceptionstmt.pdf

43. Gao, H., Hu, J., Wilson, C.: Detecting and characterizing social spam campaigns. In: 10th Internet Measurement Conference (2010)

44. Gawron, K.: Ranking of the Best Affiliate Marketing Niches for 2021. Zeropark Blog (2021). https://zeropark.com/blog/affiliate-marketing-best-niches-2021/
45. Get Your Offers Listed on the Offer Engine. WOW TRK. https://www.wowtrk.com/list-offers/
46. Gray, S.: Lidl shoppers urged to watch out for £500 gift card scam - 'don't share personal details'. Express.co.uk (2021). https://www.express.co.uk/life-style/life/1438930/lidl-uk-scam-warning-gift-cards-email-latest-news
47. Hamed, S., El-Deeb, S.: Cash on delivery as a determinant of E-commerce growth in emerging markets. J. Glob. Mark. **33**(4), 242–265 (2020). https://doi.org/10.1080/08911762.2020.1738002
48. High-risk merchant accounts explained. Stripe (2024). https://stripe.com/resources/more/high-risk-merchant-accounts-explained
49. Holt, T.J., Lampke, E.: Exploring stolen data markets online: products and market forces. Crim. Just. Stud. **23**(1), 33–50 (2010). https://doi.org/10.1080/14786011003634415
50. Hooker, T.: Fact Check: Are Crypto Payouts Real?- PropellerAds Blog. PropellerAds Blog (2020). https://propellerads.com/blog/adv-fact-check-are-crypto-payouts-real/
51. Hooker, T.: GEO master: understanding the different country tiers. ActiveRevenue (2020). https://activerevenue.com/blog/2020/03/26/geo-master-understanding-the-different-country-tiers/
52. How to Promote Affiliate Offers. Affise (2022). https://affise.com/blog/how-to-promote-affiliate-offers/
53. Huang, D.Y., et al.: Tracking ransomware end-to-end. In: IEEE S&P, pp. 618–631 (2018). https://doi.org/10.1109/SP.2018.00047
54. Huang, K., Siegel, M., Madnick, S.: Systematically understanding the cyber attack business: a survey. ACM Comput. Surv. **51**(4) (2018). https://doi.org/10.1145/3199674
55. Hutchings, A., Clayton, R., Anderson, R.: Taking down websites to prevent crime. eCrime, pp. 1–10 (2016). https://doi.org/10.1109/ECRIME.2016.7487947
56. Ivanov, A.V., Kuzin, M., Mogilin, I.: Shlayer Trojan Attacks One in Ten macOS Users. Securelist (2020). https://securelist.com/shlayer-for-macos/95724/
57. Johnson, J.: Aldi Scam: Supermarket Shares Warning over £250 Voucher Scam Message. Express.co.uk (2020). https://www.express.co.uk/life-style/food/1278219/aldi-scam-message-voucher-coupon
58. Kanich, C., et al.: Show me the money: characterizing spam-advertised revenue. In: USENIX Security (2011)
59. Karami, M., Ghaemi, S., McCoy, D.: Folex: an analysis of an herbal and counterfeit luxury goods affiliate program. In: eCrime, pp. 1–9 (2013). https://doi.org/10.1109/eCRS.2013.6805782
60. Karami, M., Park, Y., McCoy, D.: Stress testing the booters: understanding and undermining the business of DDoS services. In: 25th International Conference on World Wide Web, pp. 1033–1043 (2016). https://doi.org/10.1145/2872427.2883004
61. Kasprak, A.: Savage memes and lunar dreams: deceptive dating sites' intimate ties to firefly aerospace. In: Snopes.com (2020). https://www.snopes.com/news/2020/02/12/savage-memes-lunar-dreams/
62. Kesari, A., Hoofnagle, C., McCoy, D.: Deterring cybercrime: focus on intermediaries. Berkeley Technol. Law J. **32**(3), 1093–1134 (2017). https://heinonline.org/HOL/P?h=hein.journals/berktech32%5C&i=1137

63. Koide, T., Chiba, D., Akiyama, M.: To get lost is to learn the way: automatically collecting multi-step social engineering attacks on the web. In: ASIACCS, pp. 394–408 (2020). https://doi.org/10.1145/3320269.3384714
64. Kotzias, P., Bilge, L., Antipolis, S., Caballero, J.: Measuring PUP prevalence and PUP distribution through pay-per-install services. In: USENIX Security (2016)
65. Krona, S.: Därför fåring;r du mystiska vänförfrågningar på sociala medier. In: SVT Nyheter (2020). https://www.svt.se/nyheter/darfor-far-du-mystiska-vanforfragningar-pa-sociala-medier
66. Kukułka, M.:How to run affiliate marketing antivirus campaigns with push traffic? Zeropark Blog (2021). https://zeropark.com/blog/affiliate-marketing-antivirus-campaigns-push-traffic/
67. Kukułka, M.: Top Affiliate Offers in 2021. Zeropark Blog (2021). https://zeropark.com/blog/top-affiliate-offers-in-2021/
68. van de Laarschot, J., van Wegberg, R.: Risky business? Investigating the security practices of vendors on an online anonymous market using ground-truth data. In: USENIX Security, pp. 4079–4095 (2021). https://www.usenix.org/conference/usenixsecurity21/presentation/van-de-laarschot
69. Le Pochat, V., et al.: A practical approach for taking down avalanche botnets under real-world constraints. In: NDSS (2020). https://doi.org/10.14722/ndss.2020.24161
70. Lenihan, N.: Complete List of Country Tiers for Affiliate Marketing. affLIFT (2020). https://afflift.com/f/threads/complete-list-of-country-tiers.3444/
71. Leontiadis, N., Moore, T., Christin, N.: Measuring and analyzing search-redirection attacks in the illicit online prescription drug trade. In: USENIX Security (2011)
72. Levchenko, K., et al.: Click trajectories: end-to-end analysis of the spam value chain. In: S&P, pp. 431–446 (2011). https://doi.org/10.1109/SP.2011.24
73. Leveraging Facebook for Affiliate Marketing in 2020. Everad (2020). https://blog.everad.com/en/leveraging-facebook-for-affiliate-marketing-in-2020/
74. Martin, J., Christin, N.: Ethics in cryptomarket research. Int. J. Drug Policy **35**, 84–91 (2016). https://doi.org/10.1016/j.drugpo.2016.05.006
75. Marx, W.: A sunny place for a shady business. In: Bloomberg Businessweek, vol. 4724, pp. 42–47 (2021). ISSN 0007-7135
76. Mathur, A., et al.: Dark patterns at scale: findings from a crawl of 11K shopping websites. In: Proceedings of the ACM on Human-Computer Interaction, vol. 3, no. CSCW, pp. 81:1–81:32 (2019). https://doi.org/10.1145/3359183
77. McCoy, D., Dharmdasani, H., Kreibich, C., Voelker, G.M., Savage, S.: Priceless: the role of payments in abuse-advertised goods. In: CCS, pp. 845–856 (2012). https://doi.org/10.1145/2382196.2382285
78. McCoy, D., et al.: PharmaLeaks: understanding the business of online pharmaceutical affiliate programs. In: 21st USENIX Security Symposium (2012)
79. Media Buying Campaign: How to Choose GEO? Udonis (2018). https://www.blog.udonis.co/digital-marketing/media-buying-campaign-geos
80. Merrill, J.B., Allen, M.: "Trumpcare" does not exist. Nevertheless Facebook and Google cash in on misleading ads for "Garbage" health insurance. In: ProPublica (2020). https://www.propublica.org/article/trumpcare-does-not-exist-nevertheless-facebook-and-google-cash-in-on-misleading-ads-for-garbage-health-insurance
81. Merrill, J.B., Kozlowska, H.: How Facebook fueled a precious-metal scheme targeting older conservatives. In: Quartz (2019). https://qz.com/1751030/facebook-ads-lured-seniors-into-giving-savings-to-metals-com/

82. Miedema, F., Lubbertsen, K., Schrama, V., van Wegberg, R.: Mixed signals: analyzing ground-truth data on the users and economics of a bitcoin mixing service. In: USENIX Security, pp. 751–768 (2023). https://www.usenix.org/conference/usenixsecurity23/presentation/miedema

83. Moreva, U.: CPA aggregators. Cheating or the best solution for marketers? Affbank (2018). https://affbank.com/blog/https%5C%3A%5C%2F%5C%2Faffbank.com%5C%2Fblog%5C%2Fcpa_aggregators

84. Nazarova, D., Bystrova, I.: Supreme guide to affiliate marketing verticals. RedTrack (2020). https://redtrackmarketing.s3.eu-central-1.amazonaws.com/Affiliate+Marketing+Verticals+Guide.pdf

85. Nelms, T., Perdisci, R., Antonakakis, M., Ahamad, M.: Towards measuring and mitigating social engineering software download attacks. In: USENIX Security, pp. 773–789 (2016)

86. Noroozian, A., et al.: Platforms in everything: analyzing ground-truth data on the anatomy and economics of bullet-proof hosting. In: USENIX Security, pp. 1341–1356 (2019)

87. Paquet-Clouston, M., García, S.: On the motivations and challenges of affiliates involved in cybercrime. In: Trends in Organized Crime (2022). https://doi.org/10.1007/s12117-022-09474-x

88. Paquet-Clouston, M., Paquette, S.-O., Garcia, S., Erquiaga, M.J.: Entanglement: cybercrime connections of a public forum population. In: J. Cybersecur. **8**(1) (2022). https://doi.org/10.1093/cybsec/tyac010

89. Pastrana, S., Thomas, D.R., Hutchings, A., Clayton, R.: CrimeBB: enabling cybercrime research on underground forums at scale. In: 2018 World Wide Web Conference, pp. 1845–1854 (2018). https://doi.org/10.1145/3178876.3186178

90. Redmiles, E.M., Chachra, N., Waismeyer, B.: Examining the demand for spam: who clicks? In: 2018 CHI Conference on Human Factors in Computing Systems, pp. 1–10 (2018). https://doi.org/10.1145/3173574.3173786

91. Samosseiko, D.: The partnerka - what is it, and why should you care?. In: 19th Virus Bulletin International Conference, pp. 115–120 (2009). https://www.sophos.com/en-us/medialibrary/PDFs/technical%20papers/samosseikovb2009paper.pdf

92. Schechter, E., Ruscone, G.G., El Idrissi, B.S.: Notifying Users of Unclear Subscription Pages. Chromium Blog (2018). https://blog.chromium.org/2018/11/notifying-users-of-unclear-subscription.html

93. Silverman, C.: Ads Inc. Shut down, but the tools it used to trick people on Facebook have lived on. In: BuzzFeed News (2020). https://www.buzzfeednews.com/article/craigsilverman/ads-inc-crypto-scams-facebook

94. Silverman, C.: How a massive facebook scam siphoned millions of dollars from unsuspecting boomers. In: BuzzFeed News (2019). https://www.buzzfeednews.com/article/craigsilverman/facebook-subscription-trap-free-trial-scam-ads-inc

95. Silverman, C., Davis, T.: Coronavirus mask ads were emailed to millions of americans with unsafe claims and inflated prices. In: BuzzFeed News (2020). https://www.buzzfeednews.com/article/craigsilverman/coronavirus-mask-ads-were-emailed-to-millions-of-americans

96. Soska, K., Christin, N.: Measuring the longitudinal evolution of the online anonymous marketplace ecosystem. In: USENIX Security, pp. 33–48 (2015)

97. Stone-Gross, B., Abman, R., Kemmerer, R.A., Kruegel, C., Steigerwald, D.G., Vigna, G.: The Underground economy of fake antivirus software. In: Economics of Information Security and Privacy III, pp. 55–78 (2013)

98. Subramani, K., Yuan, X., Setayeshfar, O., Vadrevu, P., Lee, K.H., Perdisci, R.: When push comes to ads: measuring the rise of (malicious) push advertising. In: IMC, pp. 724–737 (2020). https://doi.org/10.1145/3419394.3423631

99. Sullivan, S.: I May never text again: more Facebook spam. News from the Lab - F-Secure Labs (2010). https://archive.f-secure.com/weblog/archives/00002016.html

100. Szurdi, J., Luo, M., Kondracki, B., Nikiforakis, N., Christin, N.: Where are you taking me? Understanding abusive traffic distribution systems. In: Web Conference, pp. 3613–3624 (2021). https://doi.org/10.1145/3442381.3450071

101. Thomas, K., et al.: Framing dependencies introduced by underground commoditization. In: 14th Annual Workshop on the Economics of Information Security (2015)

102. Thomas, K., et al.: Investigating commercial pay-per-install and the distribution of unwanted software. In: USENIX Security, pp. 721–738 (2016)

103. Top Affiliate Marketing Verticals of 2021. Pushground Blog (2021). https://www.pushground.com/blog/top-affiliate-marketing-verticals

104. Types of Inventory Available. Zeropark (2020). https://web.archive.org/web/20200926093930/https://doc.zeropark.com/en/inventory_types.html

105. Vadrevu, P., Perdisci, R.: What you see is NOT what you get: discovering and tracking social engineering attack campaigns. In: IMC, pp. 308–321 (2019). https://doi.org/10.1145/3355369.3355600

106. Verheyden, T., Meijer, F., Dorjbayar, A.: Wij klikten op een valse advertentie met Philippe Geubels zodat u het niet hoeft te doen. In: VRT NWS (2019). https://www.vrt.be/vrtnws/nl/2019/09/04/wij-klikten-op-de-nepadvertenties-met-philippe-geubbels-en-kwame/

107. Wang, D.Y., et al.: Search + seizure: the effectiveness of interventions on SEO campaigns. In: 2014 Internet Measurement Conference, pp. 359–372 (2014). https://doi.org/10.1145/2663716.2663738

108. Washington State AG and Facebook Target "Clickjackers" | Washington State. Washington State Office of the Attorney General (2012). https://www.atg.wa.gov/news/news-releases/washington-state-ag-and-facebook-target-clickjackers

109. van Wegberg, R., et al.: Plug and prey? Measuring the commoditization of cybercrime via online anonymous markets. In: USENIX Security, pp. 1009–1026 (2018)

110. Weinglass, S.: Israel bans binary options industry, finally closing vast, 10-year fraud. In: The Times of Israel (2017). https://www.timesofisrael.com/israel-bans-entire-binary-options-industry-finally-closing-vast-10-year-fraud/

111. Wewe Media. Complete List of TIERS & Countries. AffiliateFix (2018). https://www.affiliatefix.com/threads/complete-list-of-tiers-countries.147158/

112. What Is a Tier of Traffic and What Tier Should You Choose? PropellerAds Blog (2018). https://propellerads.com/blog/what-is-a-tier-of-traffic-and-what-tier-should-you-choose/

113. What Tier to Choose for Ads Campaign. RichAds Blog (2020). https://richads.com/blog/what-tier-to-choose-profitable-geos-for-advertising-campaigns-in-tier-1-2-or-3/

114. White, J.: Takedowns and Adventures in Deceptive Affiliate Marketing. Unit42 (2019). https://unit42.paloaltonetworks.com/takedowns-and-adventures-in-deceptive-affiliate-marketing/

115. Xu, X., et al.: Dissecting mobile offerwall advertisements: an explorative study. In: 2020 IEEE 20th International Conference on Software Quality, Reliability and Security, pp. 518–526 (2020). https://doi.org/10.1109/QRS51102.2020.00072

116. Yang, H., et al.: Casino royale: a deep exploration of illegal online gambling. In: 2019 Annual Computer Security Applications Conference, pp. 500–513 (2019). https://doi.org/10.1145/3359789.3359817

117. Yang, Z., Allen, J., Landen, M., Perdisci, R., Lee, W.: TRIDENT: towards detecting and mitigating web-based social engineering attacks. In: USENIX Security, pp. 6701–6718 (2023). https://www.usenix.org/conference/usenixsecurity23/presentation/yang-zheng

118. Yuste, J., Pastrana, S.: Avaddon ransomware: an in-depth analysis and decryption of infected systems. Comput. Secur. **109**, 102388 (2021). https://doi.org/10.1016/j.cose.2021.102388

119. Zellweger, C., Kohler, F.: How scam networks use fake celebrity ads to lure online investors. SWI swissinfo.ch (2024). https://www.swissinfo.ch/eng/life-aging/how-scam-networks-use-fake-celebrity-ads-to-lure-investors/82568794

120. Zeng, E., Kohno, T., Roesner, F.: Bad news: clickbait and deceptive ads on news and misinformation websites. In: *ConPro* (2020)

121. E., Kohno, T., Roesner, F.: What makes a "bad" ad? User perceptions of problematic online advertising. In: CHI, vol. 361 (2021). https://doi.org/10.1145/3411764.3445459

122. Zulma Corporation Limited. Add Your Network. OfferVault. https://offervault.com/add-your-network

Characterizing the Networks Sending Enterprise Phishing Emails

Elisa Luo[1,2,3(✉)], Liane Young[1], Grant Ho[3,4], M. H. Afifi[2],
Marco Schweighauser[2], Ethan Katz-Bassett[1], and Asaf Cidon[1,2]

[1] Columbia University, New York, USA
[2] Barracuda Networks, Campbell, USA
[3] UC San Diego,San Diego, USA
e4luo@ucsd.edu
[4] University of Chicago, Chicago, USA

Abstract. Phishing attacks on enterprise employees present one of the most costly and potent threats to organizations. We explore an understudied facet of enterprise phishing attacks: the email relay infrastructure behind successfully delivered phishing emails. We draw on a dataset spanning one year across thousands of enterprises, billions of emails, and over 800,000 delivered phishing attacks. Our work sheds light on the network origins of phishing emails received by real-world enterprises, differences in email traffic we observe from networks sending phishing emails, and how these characteristics change over time.

Surprisingly, we find that over one-third of the phishing email in our dataset originates from highly reputable networks, including Amazon and Microsoft. Their total volume of phishing email is consistently high across multiple months in our dataset, even though the overwhelming majority of email sent by these networks is benign. In contrast, we observe that a large portion of phishing emails originate from networks where the vast majority of emails they send are phishing, but their email traffic is not consistent over time. Taken together, our results explain why no singular defense strategy, such as static blocklists (which are commonly used in email security filters deployed by organizations in our dataset), is effective at blocking enterprise phishing. Based on our offline analysis, we partnered with a large email security company to deploy a classifier that uses dynamically updated network-based features. In a production environment over a period of 4.5 months, our new detector was able to identify 3–5% more enterprise email attacks that were previously undetected by the company's existing classifiers.

1 Introduction

Phishing attacks remain one of the most costly threats to enterprises, resulting in billions of dollars in losses [11], disrupting critical infrastructure [5], and imperiling national security [35,51]. Although a substantial body of research has proposed various countermeasures [1,21,28,44,46,49], the continued and widespread success of phishing illustrates the need for better defenses.

© The Author(s), under exclusive license to Springer Nature Switzerland AG 2025
C. Testart et al. (Eds.): PAM 2025, LNCS 15567, pp. 437–466, 2025.
https://doi.org/10.1007/978-3-031-85960-1_18

Prior work on spam and mass phishing campaigns have proposed simple blocklists as a defense [17,38,46], with an implicit premise that phishing emails will emanate from stable and predominantly malicious servers. In practice, many organizations do use IP address-based blocklists, including many of the ones in our email dataset (Sect. 3.3). However, these methods have limited efficacy against enterprise phishing; in our dataset alone, they fail to block hundreds of thousands of phishing emails. This limitation arises because blocklists often grow stale and can suffer from slow updating delays as they tend to rely on user reports [48]. Given the evolving web and cloud landscape – where IP addresses and servers frequently change ownership, host multiple independent tenants in parallel, and/or host legitimate services that have been compromised by attackers – the efficacy of such methods against modern enterprise phishing remains unclear.

Our work seeks to better understand the network characteristics of modern enterprise phishing attacks, with the aim of identifying more nuanced and effective defenses that go beyond static blocklisting. Performing this analysis, which explores and characterizes the email infrastructure responsible for routing phishing emails, requires a large-scale dataset of both phishing and clean emails from many enterprises. Although some studies have involved large corpora of phishing emails [7,18,49], they focus on the content in email messages, the infrastructure used to host phishing *websites*, or involve attacks targeted primarily at *consumers* (as opposed to enterprise organizations), leaving questions about the email delivery infrastructure unexplored.

To this end, we present the first large-scale study of the email delivery infrastructure used for enterprise phishing emails. This paper involves a collaboration between academic researchers and Barracuda Networks, a large email security provider. We analyze the email delivery path information (from the email headers) across emails received by thousands of organizations. Our dataset consists of over 800,000 successfully delivered phishing emails and 4 billion non-phishing emails, across three different months (Jan 2020, Oct 2020, and Jan 2021). Importantly, the emails captured in our dataset have *not been already blocked* by any pre-filtering services (e.g., Mimecast, Proofpoint) that organizations may employ, providing a representative view of real-world enterprise inboxes.

Using this data, our paper investigates the following questions:

1. What networks do enterprise phishing emails originate from?
2. How does the email delivery infrastructure used in enterprise phishing attacks evolve over time?
3. Can we use the delivery origin of an email to improve phishing detection?

Our analysis reveals several insights relevant to designing defenses. First, networks can be categorized by how much email sent from their servers is benign vs. phishing (Sect. 4.1). On one end of the spectrum, the infrastructure of several prominent hosting companies (including Microsoft Azure and Amazon AWS) send a large volume of phishing emails, even though the vast majority of their outbound email is benign. These "low-phishing-concentration" networks remain stable throughout the three months in our data. On the other hand, a small number of IP addresses and networks send a large amount of phishing emails and only a small volume of benign emails. In contrast, this set of "high-phishing-concentration" networks is not stable over time (Sect. 4.3), suggesting that some subset of attackers actively switch to different networks to evade detection.

We apply the results of our empirical analysis in Barracuda's production environment, where we monitor the rate and proportion of phishing emails coming from each network in an online fashion and demonstrate that we can use these dynamically updated features to detect previously undetected phishing attacks with a low false positive rate (Sect. 6). Ultimately, the analysis and experiment results from our work suggest that we can better combat modern enterprise phishing by targeting the email delivery infrastructure they abuse through a diverse set of technical and policy-based defenses.

2 Background

Our paper studies the network characteristics of phishing emails received by enterprises. We focus on emails sent from outside the recipient's organization, and make no assumptions about the kind of infrastructure or tools used by the attacker (*e.g.* the emails might come from a compromised external account or reflect spoofing from an attacker-controlled server). Below, we review the key networking-related information contained within email headers and provide an overview of related work.

Fig. 1. Example of email delivery with multiple mail servers. Barracuda collects and analyzes emails from the recipient's mail servers.

2.1 Email Headers

In addition to their message content, emails contain a set of headers specified by the Simple Mail Transfer Protocol (SMTP). When Alice sends an email, her mail client attaches *envelope* headers that specify the recipients' email addresses (*RCPT TO*) and a return address for the sender (*MAIL FROM*). The email also contains human-readable headers that a recipient's email client will display as the email's sender and recipient (*FROM* and *TO* headers respectively).

For each recipient, a copy of Alice's email will get routed through a series of mail servers (relays) until they arrive at the recipient's (Bob's) mail server. Each relay will append a *RECEIVED* Header to the email message that records information about the prior hop of the delivery path: the IP address (and/or hostname) of the prior relay server and IP address (and/or hostname) of the current mail server receiving the email. In the simplest case, Alice's mail server will transmit her email directly to Bob's mail server, without traversing any intermediate mail relays, resulting in a single *RECEIVED* header. However, in more complex scenarios, Alice's email might route through a series of mail servers, producing a set *RECEIVED* headers. For example, Alice or Bob might use a large email provider that routes emails through a series of internal mail servers for scalability and load balancing purposes. Figure 1 illustrates an example of email delivery that involves multiple mail servers, where the *RECEIVED* headers might be: [Received, from 3.3.3.3 by 4.4.4.4], [Received, from 2.2.2.2 by 3.3.3.3], [Received, from 1.1.1.1 by 2.2.2.2].

The set of *RECEIVED* headers describes the email *relay path*, the underlying delivery infrastructure that an email traverses from sender to recipient. We refer to the first (earliest) server in *RECEIVED* header as the *originating server* and its IP address as the *originating IP address* (*e.g.* 1.1.1.1 in Fig. 1). Since Barracuda collects and analyzes emails from the recipients' mail servers, our data contains the full set of headers after email delivery.

2.2 Related Work

Below, we discuss several areas of research that are most relevant to this work.

Phishing Websites and URLs: Prior research proposes many methods to detect phishing websites and URLs [13,26,37,42,50,52,56] and analzyed the infrastructure used to host phishing websites [4,31]. To detect malicious URLs, detectors can extract lexical features [13,37], or features based on a URL's domain [26]. Prior work has also proposed machine learning detectors that use features relating to a website's content, such as text from the rendered HTML DOM and images embedded in web pages [33,50,52,56]. Unfortunately, phishing attacks have become increasingly sophisticated and employ various evasion strategies [16,32,49,50,55]. For example, recent studies indicate that attackers increasingly rely on compromised, legitimate websites or carefully craft their domain names to thwart URL-based detectors [33,43].

Phishing Email Detection: Prior work on detecting email attacks has predominantly used suspicious signals in the email's content [3,7,10,14,18,19,47]. These approaches train machine learning models with features related to the email's text, URLs or attachments, and metadata such as the timing of the email and the consistency of its sender and recipient headers. However, the continued success of phishing illustrates that existing defenses still have significant room to improve.

Email Authentication Protocols: Several authentication protocols aim to combat spoofed emails. The Sender Policy Framework (SPF) allows a domain to add an allowlist to its DNS record that specifies the set of IP addresses allowed to send email on its behalf. In DKIM (DomainKeys Identified Email), domains add a public verification key to their DNS record and then append a private-key signature to emails they send. DMARC (Domain-based Message Authentica-tion, Reporting, and Conformance) allows domains to specify a policy for how recipients should treat emails that fail to authenticate under either of the above protocols. While protocols can provide insight into the validity of a sender of an email, they cannot defend against other forms of deception, such as attacks that use compromised accounts or employ visually deceptive names. Furthermore, recent work shows it is very common for these authentication methods to break or be misconfigured [9,40].

Malicious Email Delivery Infrastructure: Closer to our work, several studies have examined the email delivery infrastructure used in spam emails, a different and less deceptive email-based attack [17,20,25,38,39,42,53,54]. Ramachandran et al. [39] found that a small number of autonomous systems (ASes) send the majority of spam and benign emails. Building upon these results, prior work has found that using network-level information about an email's origin such as IP address and AS can improve spam detection both in machine learning models [17] and blocklists [38,46]. Furthermore, Fukushi et al. [12] found that thousands of IP addresses from popular cloud hosting services get blocked as a result of sending spam. They note that these IP addresses remain on blocklists for an average of 20–30 days, and due to the transient nature of cloud service IP addresses (e.g., machines shifting between users) this can create issues for benign users if such IP addresses remain on blocklists for too long.

Efficacy of Modern Blocklists: Recognizing the limitations of static blocklists and allowlists, some spam filters, such as SpamAssassin, assign a "reputation" score to received emails based on how many spam or benign emails were received in the past from their IP and email addresses [45]. Although several modern block-lists (such as SURBL and Spamhause) receive frequent updates, they either do not include network-based features (in the case of SURBL) or focus primarily on spam (in the case of Spamhause), which is a different threat than the more tar-geted and deceptive emails used for enterprise phishing. Furthermore, blocklists present several practical limitations: recent prior work [23] shows that the data sources of such blocklists are opaque and of questionable quality, and the ven-dors providing these lists rarely explain their data collection and classification methodology. Finally, blocklists fundamentally require someone to first report the attack, which not only introduces a delay [48], but also means they cannot protect against unreported or previously unseen sources of attacks.

Although the prior work shows using network-level characteristics of an email's origin can help thwart spam, it remains an open question whether modern phishing campaigns targeting enterprises rely on similarly positioned infrastruc-ture and whether phishing exhibits other interesting network-level behaviors.

3   Data

Our dataset provides a unique view of enterprise phishing emails at scale, con-sisting of over 800,000 phishing emails and 4 billion clean emails received by enterprise users from external senders. The data spans 3 one-month periods: January 2020, October 2020, and January 2021, and contains the SMTP headers of emails received by enterprises who use Barracuda's services and have opted in to using their data for research purposes. All the enterprises in our dataset use Microsoft Office 365 (O365) as their email provider. Our dataset consists of emails that have been *successfully* delivered to enterprise O365 accounts, so it does not contain emails that get blocked before delivery (e.g., by an organization's spam filter). Thus, our data reflects the typical phishing and clean emails that enterprise users actually encounter on a daily basis.

We analyze the effects of these email filtering services in Sect. 3.3 and show that organizations that deploy such filters do not encounter different phishing attacks as a result. Then, in Sect. 3.4 we analyze the accuracy of the network origin of emails (*e.g.* if attackers are forging *RECEIVED* headers). In Sect. 3.5, we compare the rates of email authentication protocols between clean and phishing emails. Finally, in Sect. 3.6, we discuss potential limitations with our dataset. While we focus on analyzing the network characteristics of the phishing emails in our dataset, such a large-scale enterprise dataset could also be used to develop a phishing attack taxonomy or discover clusters of related attacks.

3.1 Email Classification

We label emails as "phishing" or "not-phishing" via a set of Barracuda's commercial detectors that detect phishing emails with embedded URLs. The detectors use text-based signals extracted from an email's body as well as features extracted from the embedded URL (*e.g.* features from its DNS entry). These classifiers do not incorporate features related to the network characteristics of an email and have an estimated precision of over 99% for phishing emails that contain a link. The precision was calculated by a team of analysts at Barracuda who manually analyze samples of emails labeled as attacks by the classifiers. We also manually validated that a random sample of approximately 500 emails (from distinct campaigns) labeled as phishing within our dataset were indeed phishing emails by inspecting the subject line, email body, and sender information. Given the scale of our dataset (which prohibits manual labeling) and low false positive rate of these classifiers, we treat Barracuda's classifiers' labels as ground truth. Because our work focuses on the characteristics of enterprise phishing emails, we refer to non-phishing emails as benign or "clean", although a small subset of these emails might correspond to phishing or other forms of abusive emails (such as extortion and scams). As we show in Sect. 6, despite the existence of false negatives in our dataset, we identify a set of useful features related to the network origins of emails that helps uncover new, previously unclassified phishing emails.

3.2 General Statistics

Table 1 summarizes the size of our data set. Each month in our dataset contains 200,000 - 300,000 phishing emails and over 1 billion clean emails. Phishing emails

Table 1. Aggregate statistics of dataset.

Statistic	Jan 2020	Oct 2020	Jan 2021
Phishing emails	218,079	307,279	282,689
Phishing campaigns	67,176	80,703	73,925
Unique IP addresses (phishing)	16,027	20,596	12,743
Unique ASes (phishing)	2,808	3,317	2,075
Clean emails	~2B	~1B	~1.3B

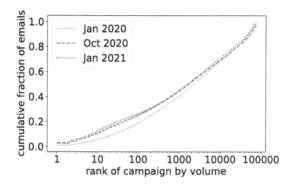

Fig. 2. Cumulative fraction of phishing emails per campaign.

originate from over 12,000 distinct IP addresses across each month of data (row 3). For our analysis, we also mapped IP addresses to the autonomous system (AS) they belong to using the Cymru IP address to ASN mapping API [8].

Campaign Analysis: We computed the number of distinct campaigns in our dataset to understand whether the phishing emails in our data reflect a range of different attacks. Following prior work [18], we define a phishing campaign as a set of phishing emails that contain the same *FROM* address and normalized subject line (lower-cased with spaces and symbols removed). Figure 2 shows the cumulative fraction of phishing emails, as a function of each campaign, ranked by phishing volume. Although the top-sending campaigns contribute significant volume, (*e.g.* the top-1000 campaigns account for over 40% of the email volume in all three periods), we find that the distribution is heavy-tailed and conclude that no single campaign is skewing our dataset. While our work mainly focuses on high-volume phishers, future work could explore smaller campaigns to reveal patterns and threats in more targeted attacks.

Data Cleaning: We first removed all *RECEIVED* headers whose IP address fell within a reserved or private address range. Then, we extracted the origin IP address (as defined in Sect. 2.1) from the remaining set of headers (*i.e.* from the first header without a private or reserved IP address).

3.3   Effect of Email Filtering Services

Some organizations employ additional email filters (*e.g.* spam filters or blocklists) that prevent some emails from reaching their users' inboxes (and thus are not captured by our dataset). In this section, we measure the prevalence and effect of these "pre-filtering" services on our dataset. We find that 75% of organizations use some pre-filtering services (e.g., a spam filter from Mimecast or Barracuda). To determine whether an organization uses a pre-filtering service, we analyzed their MX record: If their MX record points directly to Microsoft Office 365's IP addresses, then the organization likely does not use an external filtering service, and all email will be delivered to users' O365 accounts.[1] To understand the impact of pre-filtering on our dataset, we examined whether organizations that do not pre-filter their emails encounter uniquely different phishing attacks as a result (as opposed to natural variations in phishing attacks received by different enterprises).

Using the data from Jan 2020, we compared the phishing attacks received only by organizations without pre-filtering (55,515 emails) to attacks at organizations that do apply pre-filters (162,564 emails). Across organizations with no filtering, 41,474 emails originated from an IP address that also sent phishing emails to organizations with filters, while 14,041 emails originated from IP addresses that were only seen in phishing emails at organizations without filtering. We checked the inverse relationship by comparing the phishing attacks received only by organizations without pre-filtering to attacks received only by an equally-sized random sample of organizations that do apply pre-filters (54,871 emails). Interestingly, we found the number of phishing emails received only by organizations with pre-filtering was similar at 14,823. These numbers did not significantly change when comparing at the AS granularity, or when we grouped the emails by phishing campaign.

Thus, we find that the majority of phishing emails in our dataset originate from IP addresses observed in the inboxes of both organizations that use pre-filtering services and organizations that do not. While both sets of organizations receive some phishing emails from distinct sets of origin IP addresses, the volume of phishing emails from the distinct origin IP addresses is comparable. These results suggest that 1) a significant number of phishing attacks still bypass traditional email filters; and 2) our dataset provides a representative view of phishing emails received by real-world enterprises despite the use of email pre-filtering.

3.4   Accuracy of Network Origin

In this section, we analyze the fidelity of the *RECEIVED* headers in phishing emails. In particular, an attacker could obfuscate their origins by adding additional arbitrary *RECEIVED* headers to the start of an email's delivery path. However, the recipient's mail server generates the last set of *RECEIVED* headers, including the IP address of the server that delivered the email directly to the

---

[1] Email classified as spam by Microsoft will still appear in a user's account, but within a spam folder (which our dataset includes).

Table 2. Proportion of emails that pass authentication in Jan'20.

Protocol: Pass Rate	Clean	Phishing
SPF or DKIM	39.6%	23.3%
SPF and DKIM	10.0%	10.1%
DMARC	30.0%	10.4%

recipient's server. Thus, we can reliably determine the email relay immediately preceding the recipient's mail server.

We extract the *RECEIVED* header that contains reliable sender information as follows: We first find the header that contains the IP address of the recipient's mail server based on the recipient's DNS MX record.[2] From this header, we then know that the previous *RECEIVED* header was generated by the recipient's mail server. As a result, this header reliably reports the IP address of the server from which it received the email.

Based on a series of tests comparing reliable email relay information and potentially forged information, we find that at least 90.6% of phishing emails in our dataset do *not* spoof the origin IP address in their *RECEIVED* headers (at least not in ways that impact our analysis). For additional information on the tests, see Appendix B, which suggests that for the vast majority of phishing emails, we do not see strong evidence of email delivery path forgery.

3.5   Email Authentication

Given the low implementation and high misconfiguration rates of email authentication protocols found by prior work (such as [9]) we investigated whether email authentication rates differed between clean and phishing emails within our dataset. Table 2 compares the proportion of phishing and clean emails that pass various authentication checks in our data in January 2020; these statistics remain consistent in October 2020 and January 2021. Although clean emails pass at a higher rate than phishing emails, less than half of clean emails pass DMARC validation, and 10.4% of phishing emails pass DMARC checks. Thus, while we find that email authentication rates differ slightly between phishing and clean emails, they fail to provide a reliable signal for detecting phishing. We confirm this finding in Sect. 6, where we find that email authentication protocols are the least important features when distinguishing between clean and phishing emails.

3.6   Limitations

Although we empirically determine that the usage of pre-filtering does not significantly bias our dataset (Sect. 3.3), we acknowledge that using MX records

---

[2] To avoid additional evasion, if multiple headers claim to involve recipient server, our analysis only uses the last of these to ensure it reflects the true recipient server's information. We also ensured that we used the historical DNS MX record from the corresponding time period the email was delivered.

to infer the usage of pre-filtering may be imperfect. Specifically, some organizations may use multiple filtering layers not detectable through solely inspecting their MX records (e.g., if they route email through security apps within O365). Other biases may arise from the fact that our dataset consists predominantly of organizations based in the U.S. and Europe (so it may not be reflective of phishing emails targeting other parts of the globe). Our dataset only captures data up to 2021 and may not reflect any changes in the landscape of email phishing since then. Additionally, although our dataset consists of billions of emails, it contains only a small number of phishing emails that come from major email service providers, such as Gmail or Outlook[3]. A potential explanation is that major email providers have tight security controls on the outbound emails from accounts they manage, which limits the type (e.g., emails with a spoofed FROM address) and volume (i.e., rate limits on outbound emails [15]) of emails that can be sent by attackers that use accounts on these services.

3.7   Ethics

The characterization was conducted on an existing dataset of email headers from organizations who are active customers of Barracuda Networks. Per Barracuda's policies, all fetched emails were stored encrypted. Only the researchers working on this project and authorized employees at Barracuda were allowed to access the data, under a data-sharing agreement with the researchers' institution and via standard, strict access control policies. The academic researchers analyzing this data submitted this study and received approval from their institution's IRB. See Appendix A for further discussion on our ethical considerations.

4   Delivery Infrastructure Characterization

In this section, we investigate the ASes and IP addresses of the email delivery infrastructure the emails in our dataset. First, we examine the distribution of phishing emails sent per IP and AS (Sect. 4.1). We find that a small set of IP addresses accounts for a substantial portion of phishing emails. We then characterize AS behaviors from two perspectives: the fraction of emails sent from an AS that are phishing (Sect. 4.2) and the stability of the set of ASes utilized for phishing attacks (Sect. 4.3). We conclude with an analysis of the geographical distribution of the email delivery infrastructure (Sect. 4.4).

4.1   Network Origin Distribution of Phishing Emails

In this section, we find a significant volumes of phishing comes from a handful of ASes and IP addresses that do not send large amounts of clean emails, suggesting that network origin reputation features, extracted from the email delivery path, can be a useful signal for detecting phishing emails.

---

[3] In total, ~8 million emails originate from Google's address space, and fewer than 50 phishing emails originate from published Gmail or Outlook IP address ranges.

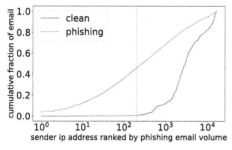 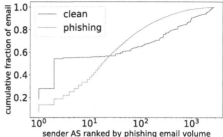

Fig. 3. Cumulative fraction of phishing emails by originating IP address. The 200 highest-volume sending IP addresses account for around 50% phishing emails.

Fig. 4. Cumulative fraction of phishing emails sent across the ASes of an email's originating IP address.

Sender IP Address Distribution: Figure 3 shows the cumulative fraction of clean and phishing emails sent per source IP address, sorted by the number of phishing emails each sent. Although our dataset includes phishing emails successfully delivered from over 10,000 unique IP addresses, the distribution is very skewed, with around 50% of the phishing emails in our data coming from the top 200 IP addresses alone. These IP addresses account for less than 1% of the clean emails. This result is in contrast to prior work on spam [39], which found that, while a small set of IP addresses accounted for a significant amount of spam, the majority of clean emails also originated from this same address set.

AS Distribution: We illustrate the distribution of phishing emails per AS in Fig. 4 (where the x-axis is sorted by the volume of phishing emails that originated from each AS). We find that approximately 80% of the phishing emails in our dataset come from just 100 ASes, which represent fewer than 1% of all ASes. This same set of 100 ASes accounts for nearly 70% of the clean emails in our dataset. Nearly 60% of clean emails in this set originate from the top three ASes (2 belonging to Amazon and 1 belonging to Microsoft). Excluding Amazon and Microsoft, the top-100 ASes still account for the majority of phishing emails in our data, but less than 10% of the clean emails.

Takeaways: These findings suggest that network-based reputation features can help detect previously undetected phishing attacks from some networks (e.g., not Amazon or Microsoft). In subsequent sections, we explore additional aspects about the networks sending phishing emails that can bolster the performance of such features.

4.2   Phishing Concentration Across Networks

To characterize variations in behavior of the networks sending phishing emails, we divided the ASes in our dataset into three categories, low, medium, and high phishing concentration, using the following metrics: (1) the volume of delivered

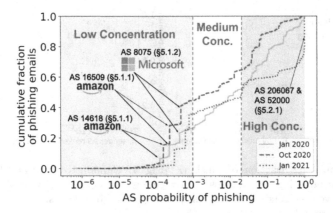

Fig. 5. Cumulative fraction of phishing emails as a function of phishing probability of an AS, including AS phishing concentration categories. In January 2021, AS 206067 and AS 52000 had probabilities of phishing of 99.8% (with 6550 delivered phishing emails) and 100% (with 1673 delivered phishing emails), respectively.

phishing email originating from each network; and (2) the AS's *probability of phishing*, defined as the fraction of delivered phishing emails originating from a network divided by the total number of emails (clean and phishing) from that network. The heuristics for each category are as follows:

- **Low phishing concentration network:** an AS where less than 0.1% of its sent emails are phishing.
- **Medium phishing concentration network:** an AS where more than or equal to 0.1% and less than 2% of its sent emails are phishing.
- **High phishing concentration network:** an AS with more than or equal to 2% of its sent emails labeled as phishing and has sent more than 150 phishing emails in one month. This 150-email threshold removes any ASes that sent very few total emails, which could lead to skewed probability values.[4]

We chose to focus on the AS-granularity to reveal coarser-grain patterns (e.g., large volumes of phishing emails from reputable ASes). We further explore more fine-grained patterns (i.e., at the IP address level) in our case studies (Sect. 5.1).

Table 3 summarizes the proportion and size of each phishing concentration category, and Fig. 5 shows the distributions of phishing emails across networks' probability of phishing. This distribution is similar for each of the three time periods, with a few low phishing concentration (but high phishing volume) networks contributing to nearly one-third of all phishing email.

Low Phishing Concentration Networks: Three networks belonging to Amazon (AS 16509 and AS 14618) and Microsoft (AS 8075) are responsible for over 85%

---

[4] ASes that sent less than 150 emails collectively account for 5.5% of all phishing emails in January 2020, 2.7% in October 2020, and 5% in January 2021.

Table 3. Number of ASes for which a low (<0.1%), medium (0.1%-2%), or high (≥2%) proportion of their emails are phishing, and percent of phishing emails originating from each category.

Category	Jan 2020		Oct 2020		Jan 2021		Overall
	# of ASes	% Phishing Emails Sent	# of ASes	% Phishing Emails Sent	# of ASes	% Phishing Emails Sent	% Phishing Emails Sent
Low Concentration	608	26.58	537	44.64	311	35.66	35.63
Medium Concentration	1031	25.39	502	19.94	397	13.82	19.73
High Concentration	62	42.5	44	32.76	61	43.72	39.66

Table 4. Email volume over time of the top 3 low phishing concentration networks.

ASN	Date	# Phishing	# Clean
14618 (Amazon)	Jan 2020	6,144	49,655,611
	Oct 2020	10,574	68,629,830
	Jan 2021	12,518	40,778,516
16509 (Amazon)	Jan 2020	7,845	35,086,658
	Oct 2020	10,902	46,979,360
	Jan 2021	14,465	23,541,485
8075 (Microsoft)	Jan 2020	7,507	17,481,559
	Oct 2020	10,727	22,886,922
	Jan 2021	11,839	15,272,305

of all phishing emails from networks in this category, and 31% of all phishing email in our dataset. Despite the large amount of phishing emails originating from their address space, these ASes are classified as low phishing concentration as they are also the source of tens of millions of legitimate emails (Table 4), accounting for 60% of all legitimate email (as seen in the three large jumps in Fig. 4).

Medium Phishing Concentration Networks: This category accounts for the lowest share of phishing emails (19.7%) and includes some smaller Internet hosting companies. These networks are largely used to send benign email, but still originate an higher than average proportion of phishing.

High Phishing Concentration Networks: ASes in this category typically send a relatively small number of emails overall but a high proportion of phishing emails. This category contains the networks responsible for the largest amount of phishing email in our dataset: over 39.7%. We find that many high phishing concentration networks are legitimate hosting companies. To classify the networks, we visited the companies' webpages and validated our classifications by comparing them to CAIDA's inferences [6] and to ASes' self-classifications on PeeringDB [34] (when available). In most cases, our classification of an AS as a

Table 5. The 9 persistent high phishing concentration networks and their phishing email volume over our three datasets. Networks that provide hosting services are bolded.

| ASN | Owner | Phishing Email Volume | | |
		Jan 2020	Oct 2020	Jan 2021
4808	CHINA169-BJ	2143	2405	2163
9009	**M247 Ltd**	955	3207	2135
31863	**Centrilogic**	557	605	1141
40676	**Psychz Networks**	1974	210	618
54290	**Hostwinds**	2422	1340	401
60068	**CDN77**	414	459	373
64236	**Unreal Servers**	2014	353	372
135905	VNPT-AS-VN	581	274	355
197226	**SPRINT S.A.**	636	332	288

hosting provider was validated by PeeringDB and/or CAIDA classifying it as a CONTENT provider. Most cases of disagreement were due to the AS offering *both* hosting and consumer Internet services.

We found that on average, 67.6% of networks we classified as high-concentration provide hosting services. Aside from Internet hosting companies, the vast majority of the remaining ASes are Internet service providers, with only 1–2% belonging to other AS types, such as ENTERPRISE or EDUCATIONAL/RE-SEARCH. We suspect many of these networks are unwitting hosts of attackers, who quickly send a large amount of phishing email before moving on to new network infrastructure (e.g., after getting caught), although some could be bullet-proof hosting providers that use resources from legitimate upstream providers [31]. We examine some of these "transient" malicious networks in more detail in our case studies (Sect. 5).

Takeaways: Using network-based reputation features may be more useful for thwarting phishing emails originating from high phishing concentration networks. On the other hand, since low phishing concentration networks originate a large amount of legitimate email traffic, such reputation features will be unlikely to accurately capture all phishing activity (e.g., Amazon/Microsoft IP addresses are unlikely to show up on fraud-activity-based blocklists).

4.3   How Does Phishing Delivery Infrastructure Change Over Time?

In this section, we characterize the stability the email delivery infrastructure used to send enterprise phishing emails. In particular, we examine the stability of high phishing concentration networks and the top-100 ASes by phishing volume rank over a period of one year.

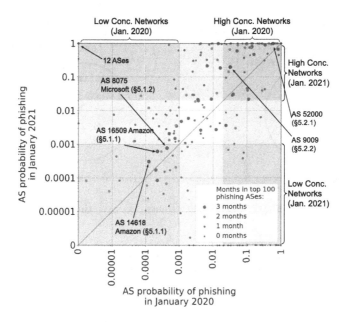

Fig. 6. AS probability of phishing in Jan '20 and '21. Each point is AS that sent 100 or more phishing emails in *either* Jan '20 or Jan '21. Purple regions correspond to high phishing concentration ASes.

Year-to-Year Comparison of Phishing Probability: Comparing the fraction of an AS's emails to Barracuda customers that are phishing in January 2020 (X axis) to the fraction that are phishing in January 2021 (Y axis) (for ASes that sent at least 100 phishing emails), we find that most ASes fall fairly close to the line $X = Y$, meaning they maintain a consistent probability of phishing across the two time periods (Fig. 6). The ASes in the top-right corner of Fig. 6 have a consistently high probability of phishing, although many transition from being very likely to send phishing emails in 2020 (compared to the global fraction of email that is phishing) to sending exclusively phishing emails in 2021. We find that all ASes with a probability of phishing of 0 in either time frame did not send emails during that month, meaning they were actively used by attackers in one year and did not send any emails during the other month to organizations in our dataset.

Stability of High Phishing Concentration Networks: Of the 132 ASes we classify as high phishing concentration during at least one of the months in our dataset, the majority are only high-concentration for one month (Fig. 7a). Only 26 ASes (19.6%) are classified as high phishing concentration in at least two out of three months of our data, and 9 ASes (6.8%) are high-concentration across all three months. When combined, over 25,000 phishing emails originate from the 9 persistent high phishing concentration networks across the three months in our data (Table 5).

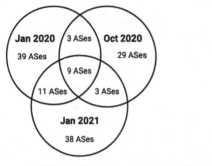 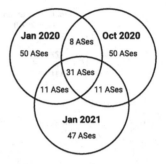

(a) High phishing concentration ASes.   (b) Top-100 ASes by phishing volume.

Fig. 7. Persistence of networks over time.

Stability of Top-100 ASes by Phishing Email Count: Out of the top-100 networks by phishing volume, many consistently rank among the top-100 over time: 31 remain across all three months in our data, and 61 ASes appear in the top-100 phishing networks across at least two months (Fig. 7b). Overall, the top-100 ASes by phishing volume account for 83% of the total volume of delivered phishing emails. The 31 ASes that are consistently in the top-100 account for 44%-51% of the total phishing email, and the 61 ASes account for 49%-65%. Of the 31 persistent networks, 26 provide hosting services, while the remaining 5 ASes are Internet service providers.

Takeaways: While some networks are consistently reused to send phishing emails, a larger proportion of phishing email delivery infrastructure is comparatively transient. These nuances suggest that incorporating temporal aspects of network behavior may help improve phishing detection while maintaining a low false positive rate. In Sect. 5, we investigate these nuances in more detail and discuss defensive ideas that leverage our insights. We empirically confirm this idea in a real-world, production environment in Sect. 6.

4.4   Geographical Routes of Phishing Emails

In this section, we examine the geographical distribution of the email delivery infrastructure used to send phishing emails. We matched the IP addresses across our dataset's RECEIVED headers to their country using the MaxMind Geolite2 database [27]. We matched addresses that MaxMind did not geolocate by using WhoIS to identify the country that the IP address was registered under.

There are some caveats with this analysis due to the inaccuracy of geolocating IP addresses. For example, prior work notes that, while geolocation databases obtain good accuracy (85%, and MaxMind reports a coverage of 80%), they are not perfect, with the two leading factors behind errors in geolocation are IP addresses that belong to ASes with a global presence and IP addresses that change ownership through merger and acquisition [24]. Our analysis attempts to

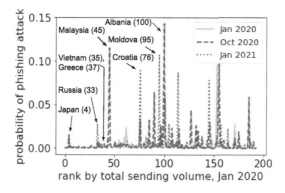

Fig. 8. Probability of sending phishing for countries that sent over 1,000 emails across 3 months, ranked by volume in Jan '20.

address some of these limitations by studying location at the country granularity, which MaxMind claims are 99.8% correct [27]   and which prior work shows to be reasonably accurate [36], but we acknowledge that imperfect data might inherently lead to some inaccuracies. Furthermore, results can vary based on a company's location and the location of those who send it legitimate email. Our results are specific to the Barracuda customers in our dataset, which are largely based in the US.

Probability of Phishing by Origin Country: For countries with more than 1000 emails in our dataset, Fig. 8 shows the probability of emails from each country that were phishing. Similar to the distribution by AS, the countries with the highest email volume (by originating IP address) also have a low probability of phishing. However, several countries have a significant amount of outbound email that contains a high proportion of phishing emails. For example, in at least one month of our dataset, five countries rank in the top-100 countries by sending volume where over 5% of these emails are phishing.

Geographic Routes of Phishing Emails: Widening our geographic analysis from just the origin IP address to the full email relay path, we found that phishing emails tend to route through more countries than clean emails (Fig. 9). In terms of exact paths, most emails, clean and phishing, route through a small number of distinct country sequences. Figure 10 shows that after mapping the IP addresses in an email's delivery path to their country, the top-25 country routes account for over 60% of phishing traffic in our dataset. The most common path taken by both clean and phishing emails traversed servers that resided solely within the US, reflecting the large proportion of US-based organizations in our data. However, we find that this country route accounts for over 70% of traffic for all clean emails across all time periods in our data, while less than half of all phishing attacks were routed only through the United States. The second-most-common route was traffic routed from US-based servers to UK-based servers,

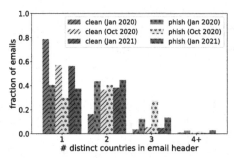 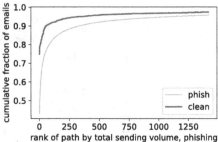

Fig. 9. The distribution of countries in an email's relay path across our datasets for clean and phishing emails.

Fig. 10. Cumulative fraction of emails that traverse specific country-routes ranked by phishing volume per country-route.

while the third-most-common route was from Germany to the US. Both of these paths routed a slightly higher fraction of the overall phishing emails than their fraction of clean emails, but these routes each carried 5% or less of the total emails each month.

Takeaways: Our analysis shows that the number of countries in the email delivery path and the countries themselves within the path could provide a useful feature to improve phishing detection, as long as a defender accounts for limitations of geolocation and dataset biases.

5   Case Studies

In this section, we investigate several nuances in network behavior by examining some illustrative examples of ASes (and the IP addresses contained within them) in both the low and high-phishing concentration categories. First, we take a deeper dive into the two prominent low-concentration networks, Amazon and Microsoft (Sect. 5.1). Next, we explore two contrasting examples of high-phishing-concentration networks: one that remains high concentration across the three months (Sect. 5.2), and one that is comparatively transient, sending phishing emails in short bursts in a single month (Sect. 5.2). In particular, we find that many networks are quite unstable (over even a period of one month) with respect to their phishing email traffic, motivating the need for more dynamic solutions than static blocklists.

5.1   Low Phishing Concentration Networks

We examine specific IP addresses in ranges owned by Amazon and Microsoft to better understand why a significant fraction (31%) of all phishing email in our dataset originate from ASes owned by these two companies (however, phishing still constitutes less than 0.01% of the total email sent from these networks). In

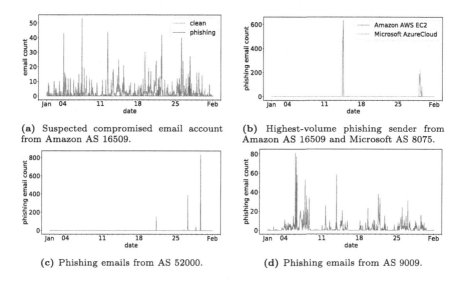

(a) Suspected compromised email account from Amazon AS 16509.

(b) Highest-volume phishing sender from Amazon AS 16509 and Microsoft AS 8075.

(c) Phishing emails from AS 52000.

(d) Phishing emails from AS 9009.

Fig. 11. Phishing over time for particular IP addresses and ASes during January 2021.

some cases, we find that attackers use hosting services provided by Amazon and Microsoft (i.e., AWS and Azure) to send phishing email (whether it be through compromising or deploying a mail server on these platforms). Additionally, we detect a potential case of account hijacking.

Amazon: AS 14618 & AS 16509. Based on the aggregate email traffic from the Amazon IP address responsible for the largest number of phishing email (1,324 emails in January 2021) and additional information from the email headers, we identify this IP address, which belongs to a published EC2 IP address range[5], to correspond to a "dedicated" phishing email server. The emails originating from this IP address contained 388 unique FROM_EMAIL values where the email address was *noreply@domain.com* across different domains. This information suggests that the attackers were spoofing the FROM_EMAIL value in their attacks. Furthermore, all the phishing emails from this IP address were sent within a short period of time (as shown in the blue curve in Fig. 11b). We captured 458 emails that were not classified as phishing from this IP address, and did not see any phishing emails in other time snapshots. This large burst of seemingly spoofed emails suggest the attackers either set up their own email server on AWS or compromised a legitimate server to send a large amount of phishing emails.

---

[5] On aggregate, 39.36% (7,623 emails) of all phishing email originating from Amazon's ASes come from a published EC2 IP address range (based on Amazon's published IP address ranges, we were unable to determine the other Amazon services for the remaining phishing emails) [2].

Table 6. Phishing sending lifespan and email volume for the top-10 phishing senders by IP within AS 9009 in January 2021.

Phishing Lifespan	# Phishing	# Clean
15 days 11:59:34	245	10
1 days 16:32:37	127	19
0 days 09:10:08	96	2
10 days 12:38:23	81	0
9 days 08:24:46	71	2
1 days 17:15:40	71	0
7 days 23:46:46	67	88
21 days 03:07:51	64	4
0 days 05:47:59	60	3
0 days 01:03:14	53	0

Table 7. Clean and phishing email volume over time of AS 9009.

Time Period	# Phishing	# Clean
Jan 2020	955	29099
Oct 2020	3207	47560
Jan 2021	2135	8685

We were also able to identify a phishing attack potentially enabled by account hijacking. We found a smaller volume of phishing email originating from a single Amazon IP address, where the FROM_EMAIL address contained a legitimate corporate domain and a human-looking user name (*e.g. jane.smith@company.com*). The account sent 115 phishing emails to Barracuda customers in January 2021, but did not send any phishing emails in January 2020 or October 2020. Moreover, we found about 1,500–2,000 clean emails originating from this IP address in our dataset. Given the low proportion of phishing email and longer duration of approximately 1 week (as shown in Fig. 11a), which matches the findings of prior work on compromised email accounts that shows that compromise incidents can last for days and even weeks [18,41]), we find it likely that this is a case of email account compromise. This case may benefit from a separate defense, such as looking for unusual patterns in account activity [41].

Microsoft: AS 8075. Similar to the first case we studied in Amazon's ASes, we observe that the IP address in Microsoft's AS that sent the most phishing emails behaves most like an attacker-controlled server. In total, this IP address, which falls within an Azure Cloud range[6], sent 2,465 phishing emails and 20 clean emails in January 2021, with 578 unique FROM_EMAIL values, where the FROM_EMAIL values for all the phishing emails are in the form of NOREPLY@DOMAIN with different domains. Given the high number of emails, the wide-range of unique domains, and the generic NOREPLY@ addresses, this scenario is most consistent with an attacker using email spoofing to forge sender

---

[6] Among the phishing emails from Microsoft's networks, we determined that 99.6% came from Azure Cloud IP address ranges, with the rest from Exchange Online and Sharepoint [29,30].

names. This IP address also exhibited a "bursty" email sending behavior (as shown in the orange curve in Fig. 11b), similar to the first Amazon case study (the blue curve), and we did not find any phishing email from this IP address in the 2020 datasets.

The fact that the highest volume servers send their attacks in such short bursts (Fig. 11b) suggests that they may be shut down after a short time *and* that the pattern may be exploited as part of detection. Cloud providers could use these patterns as a signal to identify VMs abused for sending malicious email. Similarly, enterprise email defenses can potentially quarantine large email bursts from a previously-unseen sending server. This attack strategy also illustrates the limitations of using purely network-reputation-based defenses against phishing.

5.2   High Phishing Concentration Networks

In Sect. 4.3 we found that some high phishing concentration networks remain consistently classified as such over our three time periods, while others are transient. Here, we examine each of the two cases: one that sends phishing emails during only one month in our dataset (and displayed similar patterns to our Amazon and Microsoft case studies), and one that consistently sends many phishing emails over the three time periods. In particular, we highlight the instability ("burstiness") of the IP addresses within these ASes responsible for sending phishing email.

Bursty High Phishing Concentration Network: AS 52000. Attackers used the IP addresses from AS 52000 (a Russian hosting company with data centers in the Netherlands, Russia, and the U.S.) to send phishing email for very short lifetimes: across the entire month, we see phishing email from these addresses for less than 24 h total, and the highest volume phishing email senders among these IP addresses sent all of their attacks within short 30-minute windows. We saw two large bursts of phishing email in January 2021 (Fig. 11c) comprising a total of 1,673 phishing emails from AS 52000; no other emails in our dataset originate from this network during that month. We found phishing emails from 20 unique IP addresses within this AS, and the emails span 533 campaigns (as defined in Sect. 3.2). No phishing emails originated from this AS outside of these two bursts in Jan 2021.

This behavior suggests an attacker who abuses cloud-hosted servers to send large bursts of phishing emails before switching to new infrastructure (*e.g.* because a provider terminates their services). While on aggregate AS 52000 (and the IP addresses within it) have a poor reputation (in terms of the proportion of fraudulent activity detected), the burstiness of the phishing email traffic means that these IP addresses would be unlikely to end up on established blocklists. Instead, a time-series-based anomaly detector that analyzes the volume of a particular network's email traffic could potentially flag periods of higher phishing risk, which smaller hosting companies could employ to flag suspect servers.

Persistent High Phishing Concentration Network: AS 9009. We observed a consistently high volume and proportion of phishing email originating from AS 9009 (which belongs to a UK-based hosting company). This AS was one of the 9 networks we classified as high phishing concentration for all three time periods (Table 7). In contrast to the bursty behavior observed in the prior case studies, as shown in Fig. 11d, we find that phishing attacks regularly originated from this network throughout the month of January 2021 (the other months in our data had similar distributions). The phishing emails from AS 9009 span 1,031 unique phishing campaigns and come from 151 unique IP addresses, where 32 of these IP addresses send over 20 phishing emails each. One reason for the high number of unique phishing IP addresses and campaigns might be that multiple attackers use this AS to send phishing emails.

To shed light on the volatility of the phishing IP addresses within AS 9009, we calculated the phishing email sending lifespan of each IP address, *i.e.* the time between the first phishing email we saw from the IP address to the last phishing email (because we compute this duration over 1 month windows, the maximum lifespan is 31 days). In January 2021, the average lifespan of a phishing IP address from this AS is 41.5 h. However, as shown in Table 6, many of the IP addresses with the highest phishing volumes continuously send phishing emails for extended periods (weeks) of time. In this case, IP-based reputation features would be useful for blocking phishing email. Furthermore, this longer-lived malicious behavior suggests the need to adopt additional technical or policy-based defenses to help curtail attacks coming from such networks.

6   Experiences In Production

In Sects. 4.3 and 5.1, we showed that the set of networks sending phishing emails is not stable over time. Many networks only send high volumes of phishing emails for a limited time (4.3), potentially reflecting the behavior of account takeover (5.1.1) or compromised Azure or EC2 instances (5.1.2). Because this analysis suggests that phishing detection rates can be improved by accounting for these temporal conditions, we worked with Barracuda Networks to deploy a classifier that better adapts to changing attacker behavior. We found that our approach enables Barracuda to identify phishing attacks that were not identified by their existing email classifiers or by pre-filters that customers already deployed, without incurring additional false positives.

Feature Importance for Phishing Detection: First, as a proof of concept and to better understand which features are more important for phishing detection, we trained a Random Forest model on 12 features based on our analysis in Sect. 4 to differentiate clean and phishing emails in our dataset. Figure 12 depicts the relative importance of these features based on Gini importance [22]. The proof of concept classifier confirmed our understanding that probability and volume of phishing by origin IP address were indeed the most important for phishing detection. Because of the complexities and real-world impact of modifying

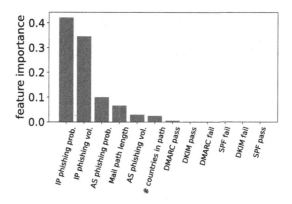

Fig. 12. Relative importance of features.

production classifiers, we chose to use only these two features (which were not already incorporated in any of Barracuda's existing classifiers).

Production Classifier Design: Our classifier aims to better adapt to networks that only send high volumes of enterprise phishing emails for a relatively short period of time, while still capturing persistently malicious senders. To this end, we designed our classifier to dynamically recalculate, on a daily basis, the features it uses to make a decision about whether an email is phishing or not. To do this, for each IP address from which Barracuda sees emails, it counts the number of phishing emails and the number of clean emails (according to Barracuda's existing classifiers) seen in a sliding window of the last n days. While some high-phishing-concentration IP addresses are only active for 30 min (e.g., Sect. 5.2), we found through testing different time windows that the day-granularity best captured phishing email while minimizing false positives. Then, our detector uses the number of phishing emails and the ratio of phishing to clean emails to calculate a "phishing-risk" score. This score is used to make an independent, binary decision about whether an email that has previously been classified as benign by any of Barracuda's production classifiers is phishing. We first conducted offline experiments with historical phishing detection data, testing the performance of window sizes n from 0–90 days and different thresholds for the "phishing-risk" score. Then, to determine their optimal values in Barracuda's production environment, we conducted smaller-scale online experiments with some promising values derived from the offline experiments. Importantly, any attacks our classifier finds were *previously undetected* by Barracuda's existing classifiers.

Classification Results: Over a span of nearly 5 months, the new detector increased the number of emails flagged as phishing by 3–5% per day (beyond those detected by Barracuda's existing detectors), with no false positives based on manual inspection. For one day per week during the first month of deployment, members of Barracuda's security team manually examined all emails that were classified as attacks by the new detector, or reported by their users. Interestingly, manual inspection found that this detector detected phishing and also other types of email attacks (e.g., business email compromise, scams, and spam).

Takeaways: In a real-world deployment, we demonstrated that capturing the changes of networks' email sending behavior over time can lead to an improved phishing detection rate, without an increase in false positives. In particular, our classifier demonstrates a strict improvement over static sender-reputation features - we are able to reliably find additional attacks even though some spam filters used by organizations in our dataset already employ sender reputation scoring heuristics [45]. We note that an attacker could evade this defense by sending a low volume of phishing emails from a large number of IP addresses, but such a strategy would incur additional operational costs and could still be (partially) blocked by existing methods.

7   Conclusions and Key Lessons

We presented a large-scale analysis of the characteristics of the network delivery infrastructure behind phishing emails targeting enterprises. Our findings provide a useful avenue for improving phishing defenses, which we demonstrate apply in a real-world production environment with the classifier we deployed at Barracuda that was able to block an additional 3–5% of previously undetected phishing emails. We distill takeaways for how the community can apply both technical and policy-based defenses based on our results.

Features Targeting the Network Origins of an Email are Promising: Our analysis revealed that most phishing emails in our dataset came from a few hundred IP addresses and ASes. Additionally, excluding Amazon and Microsoft, the top-100 ASes by phishing volume account for fewer than 5% of clean emails in our dataset, and many phishing emails come from what we termed *high-concentration networks*, those with more than 2% of their emails labeled as phishing (Sect. 4.2). Given that these networks are both the origins of a substantial volume of phishing emails and have a relatively large ratio of phishing to clean emails, reputation features about an email's originating network have the potential to provide high-impact signals of phishing. However, since a non-negligible volume of clean email originates from these same networks, strict blocklists may yield a higher-than-acceptable false positive rate. Instead, our results suggest that combining these features with others will improve phishing email detection while maintaining a low false positive rate.

Network Phishing Behavior Over Time is an Important Consideration for Detection: Our results showed that some networks have highly variable amounts and/or proportions of phishing emails that they send over time (Sect. 4.3). This phenomenon provides a possible explanation for why static lists of suspicious sender IP addresses or ASes, such as those used by many organizations in our dataset, prove insufficient at defending against enterprise phishing attacks. Our findings suggest that defenders need more agile and flexible methods of incorporating network-based characteristics, rather than static approaches like blocklists, to successfully defend against phishing attacks. To illustrate this, we showed that, in a production environment, incorporating dynamically updated features can help uncover a significant number of previously-undetected phishing emails (Sect. 6).

Internet Hosting Services are a Major Source of Phishing: The rise of Infrastructure-as-a-Service (IaaS) has provided an easy path for attackers to acquire infrastructure (Sect. 4.2 and Sect. 5), with servers on prominent and reputable cloud hosting providers, such as Amazon AWS and Microsoft Azure, being responsible for nearly one-third of all phishing emails in our dataset. An additional quarter of the phishing emails come from smaller cloud hosting companies that are among the *high-concentration networks* we identified. These results suggests that Internet hosting companies are well-positioned to significantly curtail the volume of phishing emails. Future work should investigate whether networks operators can take steps to detect and stop *outbound* emails sent from their infrastructure, or whether adopting stricter security policies around email originating for cloud hosting services can decrease their phishing volume.

Attackers Face Insufficient Defensive Pressure on their Delivery Infrastructure: Many networks consistently send a high volume or concentration of phishing emails across multiple months in our datasets (Sect. 4.3), suggesting that attackers do not face significant pressure to change servers and that information about an email's delivery origin remains an underutilized avenue for mitigating phishing attacks. We hope our results provide impetus for changing this.

Acknowledgements. We thank our anonymous reviewers and shepherd for their insightful and constructive feedback. This work was supported in part by the NSF CNS-2106530, CNS-2143868 and CNS-2403431 awards, and the UCSD CSE Postdoctoral Fellows program. This work was supported in part by the NSF CNS-2106530 and CNS-2143868 awards, and the UCSD CSE Postdoctoral Fellows program.

A   Ethical Considerations

In addition to consulting with and obtaining approval from our institution's IRB (AAAT8774 (Y01M00)), we carefully considered the ethics of our research along three key dimensions discussed in the Menlo Report: (1) does our research present minimal risk to the well-being and rights of participants? (2) does our work take appropriate measures to minimize such risks? (3) do the benefits of our research outweigh the risks?

In terms of benefits from the research, improving the community's defenses and understanding of phishing attacks has clear benefits both to the organizations in our study and to society at-large, given the widespread threat posed by enterprise phishing attacks. Soundly and accurately studying the problem of enterprise phishing fundamentally requires analysis of large-scale, real-world email data, which makes accessing and using our study's data inherently necessary. To minimize the harms of using such data, the clean emails that we have access to in our dataset (i.e., emails from legitimate, non-attacker users), do not include sensitive attributes such as the email message body, subject line, or sender name and email address. The data in our study comes from enterprise email accounts, whose organizations have consented to using their data for research purposes such as ours. Given the scale and nature our dataset, obtaining individual consent from each user is clearly infeasible. Furthermore, the email accounts involved in our dataset are owned and provided by each enterprise, and it is commonplace and reasonable for enterprises to monitor and scan their employees' work account emails for malicious activity. As such, our work's use of this data does not increase the risks or jeopardize the well-being of these users, particularly given that our analysis involves a strictly less sensitive version of this already-collected data. Weighing this collection of factors, such as the minimal risk to participants' welfare posed by our study, against the benefits of our research, we believe our work properly aligns with the ethical norms and principles of our field.

B   Email Network Origin Validation

We identify cases that are not forged based on the following four tests using the IP address of an email's MX-identified sender and purported origin IP address (the first public and non-reserved IP listed in the RECEIVED headers). Combining tests, we find at least 90.6% of phishing emails in our dataset do *not* spoof the origin IP addresses in their RECEIVED headers, at least in ways that impact our analysis.

First, for 66% of phishing emails, the IP address of the MX-identified sender and the origin IP address belong to the same AS. Since most of our analysis focuses on the AS-granularity, this criteria ensures that any spoofing for this set of phishing emails will not distort or bias our results. To calibrate expectations, we ran the same analysis on the benign emails in our dataset, for which the sender has no reason to forge their headers; 73% of these emails had the same AS for both their purported origin IP address and the IP address of the MX-identified sender (a similar proportion to the phishing emails). Second, if a phishing email's pair of MX-identified sender IP address and origin IP address exactly matches a pair seen for benign emails, then we also label these as instances where the RECEIVED headers were not modified. In total, an additional 16.2% of the total phishing emails matched this criteria. Third, an additional 2% of the total phishing emails satisfied an even stronger property, where their entire relay path (all IP addresses in their RECEIVED header) had an exact match with a path seen in our benign email dataset. Finally, for an additional 6.4% of phishing emails, the IP address listed in the recipient's MX record only appeared once in the RECEIVED headers, and it matched the purported origin IP address in the email exactly (5.9%) or belonged to the same AS (0.5%). These appear to be internal emails that were flagged by O365 as emails sent from an external source. Such cases can occur when emails are sent between different domains that belong to the same O365 account. Such single AS paths are not the focus of our paper's analysis, which investigates the AS or country-level characteristics of the delivery path before the recipient's servers.

The set of heuristics above cover 90.6% of all of the phishing emails in our dataset. For the remaining 9.4%, we investigate the distribution of path lengths (total number of RECEIVED headers) and compare to the path lengths of the clean emails in our dataset. The remaining 9.4% includes only emails with at least three headers, since empirically, our tests above established that all shorter paths were not forged. So, we compare the distribution of path lengths of these remaining emails to clean and phishing emails with at least three headers. As seen in Fig. 13, the path length distribution between the remaining phishing emails (green) is very similar to the clean emails (and to the overall set of phishing emails) in our dataset.

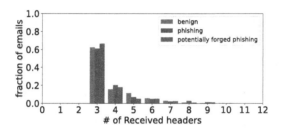

Fig. 13. Distribution of path lengths for emails with ≥ 3 headers. The green bars show the distribution for the 10% phishing emails that do not match one of our validation criteria (Sect. 3.4). (Color figure online)

This similarity suggests that attacker manipulation did not have a significant impact on the paths we observe, since such tampering would lead to a longer path length (assuming that the attacker is positioned at the beginning of the email delivery path).

References

1. Allodi, L., Chotza, T., Panina, E., Zannone, N.: The need for new antiphishing measures against spear-phishing attacks. IEEE Secu. Priv. **18**(2), 23–34 (2019)
2. AWS IP address ranges (2021). https://docs.amazon.com/general/latest/gr/aws-ip-ranges.html
3. Bergholz, A., Chang, J.H., Paass, G., Reichartz, F., Strobel, S.: Improved phishing detection using model-based features. In: CEAS (2008)
4. Bitaab, M., et al.: Scam pandemic: how attackers exploit public fear through phishing. In: Symposium on Electronic Crime Research (eCrime) (2020)

5. Browne, R.: Hackers behind Colonial Pipeline attack reportedly received $90 million in bitcoin before shutting down (2021). https://www.cnbc.com/2021/05/18/colonial-pipeline-hackers-darkside-received-90-million-in-bitcoin.html

6. CAIDA AS classification (2020) https://www.caida.org/catalog/datasets/as-classification/. Accessed 9 Dec 2020

7. Cidon, A., Gavish, L., Bleier, I., Korshun, N., Schweighauser, M., Tsitkin, A.: High precision detection of business email compromise. In: USENIX Security Symposium (2019)

8. Cymru, T.: IP to ASN Mapping Service. https://team-cymru.com/community-services/ip-asn-mapping/

9. Czybik, S., Horlboge, M., Rieck, K.: Lazy gatekeepers: a large-scale study on SPF configuration in the wild. In: ACM Internet Measurement Conference (IMC) (2023)

10. Duman, S., Kalkan-Cakmakci, K., Egele, M., Robertson, W., Kirda, E.: Email-Profiler: spearphishing filtering with header and stylometric features of emails. In: COMPSAC (2016)

11. FBI: Business Email Compromise The $26 Billion Scam (2019). https://www.ic3.gov/Media/Y2019/PSA190910

12. Fukushi, N., Chiba, D., Akiyama, M., Uchida, M.: A comprehensive measurement of cloud service abuse. J. Inf. Process. **29** (2021)

13. Garera, S., Provos, N., Chew, M., Rubin, A.D.: A framework for detection and measurement of phishing attacks. In: ACM Workshop on Recurring Malcode (2007)

14. Gascon, H., Ullrich, S., Stritter, B., Rieck, K.: Reading between the lines: content-agnostic detection of spear-phishing emails. In: Bailey, M., Holz, T., Stamatogiannakis, M., Ioannidis, S. (eds.) Research in Attacks, Intrusions, and Defenses (2018)

15. Google: Gmail sending limits in Google Workspace. https://support.google.com/a/answer/166852/gmail-sending-limits-in-google-workspace?hl=en

16. Han, X., Kheir, N., Balzarotti, D.: PhishEye: live monitoring of sandboxed phishing kits. In: ACM CCS (2016)

17. Hao, S., Syed, N.A., Feamster, N., Gray, A.G., Krasser, S.: Detecting spammers with snare: Spatio-temporal network-level automatic reputation engine. In: USENIX Security Symposium, vol. 9 (2009)

18. Ho, G., et al.: Detecting and characterizing lateral phishing at scale. In: USENIX Security Symposium (2019)

19. Ho, G., Sharma, A., Javed, M., Paxson, V., Wagner, D.: Detecting credential spearphishing in enterprise settings. In: USENIX Security Symposium (2017)

20. John, J.P., Moshchuk, A., Gribble, S.D., Krishnamurthy, A.: Studying spamming botnets using botlab. In: NSDI, vol. 9 (2009)

21. Khonji, M., Iraqi, Y., Jones, A.: Phishing detection: a literature survey. IEEE Commun. Surv. Tutorials **15**(4), 2091–2121 (2013)

22. Learn, S.: Decision Trees: Mathematical Formulation. https://scikit-learn.org/stable/modules/tree.html#tree-mathematical-formulation

23. Li, V.G., Dunn, M., Pearce, P., McCoy, D., Voelker, G.M., Savage, S.: Reading the tea leaves: a comparative analysis of threat intelligence. In: USENIX Security Symposium (2019)

24. Livadariu, I., et al.: On the accuracy of country-level IP geolocation. In: ANRW 2020: Proceedings of the Applied Networking Research Workshop, pp. 67–73 (2020)

25. Lumezanu, C., Feamster, N.: Observing common spam in twitter and email. In: Proceedings of the 2012 Internet Measurement Conference, pp. 461–466 (2012)

26. Ma, J., Saul, L.K., Savage, S., Voelker, G.M.: Beyond blacklists: learning to detect malicious web sites from suspicious URLs. In: ACM Conference on Knowledge Discovery and Data Mining (KDD) (2009)

27. Maxmind database (2021). queried the geolite2 database. https://dev.maxmind.com/geoip/geolite2-free-geolocation-data

28. Medvet, E., Kirda, E., Kruegel, C.: Visual-similarity-based phishing detection. In: Proceedings of the 4th International Conference on Security and Privacy in Communication Networks, pp. 1–6 (2008)

29. Microsoft: Azure public IP prefixes (2021). https://docs.microsoft.com/en-us/azure/virtual-network/public-ip-address-prefix

30. Microsoft: Office 365 URLs and IP address ranges (2021). https://docs.microsoft.com/en-us/microsoft-365/enterprise/urls-and-ip-address-ranges?view=o365-worldwide

31. Noroozian, A., et al.: Platforms in everything: analyzing ground-truth data on the anatomy and economics of bullet-proof hosting. In: USENIX Security Symposium, pp. 1341–1356 (2019)

32. Oest, A., et al.: PhishTime: continuous longitudinal measurement of the effectiveness of anti-phishing blacklists. In: USENIX Security Symposium (USENIX) (2020)

33. Oest, A., et al.: Sunrise to sunset: analyzing the end-to-end life cycle and effectiveness of phishing attacks at scale. In: USENIX Security Symposium (USENIX) (2020)

34. Peering DB (2021). https://www.peeringdb.com/

35. Perlroth, N.: Hackers are targeting nuclear facilities, homeland security dept. and F.B.I. say (2017). https://www.nytimes.com/2017/07/06/technology/nuclear-plant-hack-report.html

36. Poese, I., Uhlig, S., Ali Kaafar, M., Donnet, B., Gueye, B.: IP geolocation databases: unreliable? In: SIGCOMM CCR, vol. 41 (2011)

37. Prakash, P., Kumar, M., Kompella, R.R., Gupta, M.: Phishnet: predictive blacklisting to detect phishing attacks. In: IEEE INFOCOM (2010)

38. Qian, Z., Mao, Z.M., Xie, Y., Yu, F.: On network-level clusters for spam detection. In: NDSS (2010)

39. Ramachandran, A., Feamster, N.: Understanding the network-level behavior of spammers. In: Proceedings of the 2006 Conference on Applications, Technologies, Architectures, and Protocols for Computer Communications, pp. 291–302 (2006)

40. Security, H.N.: Only 14% of domains worldwide truly protected from spoofing with DMARC enforcement. https://www.helpnetsecurity.com/2021/03/23/domains-protected-dmarc/

41. Shah, N., Ho, G., Schweighauser, M., Afifi, M.H., Cidon, A., Wagner, D.A.: A large-scale analysis of attacker activity in compromised enterprise accounts. CoRR **abs/2007.14030** (2020). https://arxiv.org/abs/2007.14030

42. Sheng, S., Wardman, B., Warner, G., Cranor, L., Hong, J., Zhang, C.: An empirical analysis of phishing blacklists (2009)

43. Silva, R.D., Nabeel, M., Elvitigala, C., Khalil, I., Yu, T., Keppitiyagama, C.: Compromised or attacker-owned: a large scale classification and study of hosting domains of malicious URLs. In: USENIX Security Symposium (USENIX) (2021)

44. Simoiu, C., Zand, A., Thomas, K., Bursztein, E.: Who is targeted by email-based phishing and malware? Measuring factors that differentiate risk. In: Proceedings of the ACM Internet Measurement Conference, pp. 567–576 (2020)

45. SpamAssasin AutoWhitelist. https://cwiki.apache.org/confluence/display/SPAMASSASSIN/AutoWhitelist

46. Stone-Gross, B., Kruegel, C., Almeroth, K., Moser, A., Kirda, E.: Fire: finding rogue networks. In: Annual Computer Security Applications Conference (2009)

47. Stringhini, G., Thonnard, O.: That ain't you: blocking spearphishing through behavioral modelling. In: DIMVA (2015)
48. Sun, Z., et al.: From victims to defenders: an exploration of the phishing attack reporting ecosystem. In: International Symposium on Research in Attacks, Intrusions, and Defenses (RAID) (2024)
49. Thomas, K., et al.: Data breaches, phishing, or malware? Understanding the risks of stolen credentials. In: ACM CCS (2017)
50. Tian, K., Jan, S.T., Hu, H., Yao, D., Wang, G.: Needle in a haystack: tracking down elite phishing domains in the wild. In: ACM Internet Measurement Conference (IMC) (2018)
51. Vaas, L.: How hackers broke into John Podesta, DNC Gmail accounts (2016). https://nakedsecurity.sophos.com/2016/10/25/how-hackers-broke-into-john-podesta-dnc-gmail-accounts/
52. Whittaker, C., Ryner, B., Nazif, M.: Large-scale automatic classification of phishing pages. In: NDSS (2010)
53. Xie, Y., Yu, F., Achan, K., Panigrahy, R., Hulten, G., Osipkov, I.: Spamming botnets: signatures and characteristics. ACM SIGCOMM Comput. Commun. Rev. **38**(4), 171–182 (2008)
54. Yardi, S., Romero, D., Schoenebeck, G., Boyd, D.: Detecting spam in a Twitter network. First Monday (2010)
55. Zhang, P., et al.: CrawlPhish: large-scale analysis of client-side cloaking techniques in phishing. In: IEEE Symposium on Security and Privacy (S&P) (2021)
56. Zhang, Y., Hong, J.I., Cranor, L.F.: Cantina: a content-based approach to detecting phishing web sites. In: International Conference on World Wide Web (WWW) (2007)

5G

A Large-Scale Study of the Potential of Multi-carrier Access in the 5G Era

Fukun Chen[1], Moinak Ghoshal[1(✉)], Enfu Nan[1], Phuc Dinh[1], Imran Khan[1], Z. Jonny Kong[2], Y. Charlie Hu[2], and Dimitrios Koutsonikolas[1]

[1] Northeastern University, Boston, USA
{chen.fuk,ghoshal.m,nan.e,dinh.p,khan.i,d.koutsonikolas}@northeastern.edu
[2] Purdue University, West Lafayette, USA
{kong102,ychu}@purdue.edu

Abstract. Despite much promise, numerous recent studies have shown that 5G coverage remains sporadic and its performance is often suboptimal, leading to degraded QoE for high-throughput, low-latency applications. While two alternative approaches to multi-carrier access, link selection and link aggregation, have been proposed and shown to potentially enhance performance, their actual performance benefit in real-world 5G deployments remains unclear. In this paper, we conduct an extensive measurement campaign involving multiple cross-country driving trips spread out over 12 months and covering a total of 8k+ Km, while simultaneously measuring the performance of the three major US mobile operators, and explore the potential of multi-carrier access to improve throughput and latency. Our measurements show that there exists a substantial amount of diversity in cellular network performance across different operators at a given time and location in terms of both throughput and RTT. Our trace-driven analysis shows that multi-carrier access techniques have the potential to provide significant performance gains over the single-path throughput/RTT of the worst-performing operator.

1 Introduction

In recent years, an emerging class of mobile applications, including Augmented Reality (AR), Virtual Reality (VR), Mixed Reality (MR), Connected Autonomous Vehicles (CAVs), and the Metaverse, has gained significant traction. These applications demand exceptionally high bandwidth and low latency from underlying wireless networks. 5G NR, rolled out in 2019, holds the promise to meet these demands unlike its predecessor (LTE), through advancements such as higher-order modulation, beamforming, massive MIMO, and wider channels.

However, recent measurement studies [11,14,15,29,39] have shown that 5G coverage remains sporadic and performance often falls short of expectations, resulting in a degraded Quality of Experience (QoE) for these demanding applications. A promising solution to enhance performance is leveraging multi-carrier

---

F. Chen and M. Ghoshal—Are co-primary authors.

© The Author(s), under exclusive license to Springer Nature Switzerland AG 2025
C. Testart et al. (Eds.): PAM 2025, LNCS 15567, pp. 469–484, 2025.
https://doi.org/10.1007/978-3-031-85960-1_19

access in mobile networks. Broadly, this can be approached in one of two ways: (a) selecting the optimal link based on real-time performance [5,20,35], or (b) aggregating multiple links (e.g., via a multipath transport protocol such as MPTCP [24] or MPQUIC [23]) to achieve higher overall throughput. Either approach comes with its own trade-offs. For example, while link aggregation can boost throughput, it may underperform compared to the single-path performance, especially in cases of very heterogeneous links [8,19]. Conversely, selecting a single best link offers potential performance gains in such scenarios but introduces overhead related to frequent link switching in dynamic network conditions [20,35], which may impact application performance, while its maximum possible gain is theoretically lower than that of a multipath solution. Which approach achieves higher performance depends on the diversity and dynamics of the per-link performance in real-world deployments.

Previous research efforts [9,20,31,35,41,42] have primarily focused on designing systems that leverage link aggregation or link selection to improve application performance. However, these approaches have been evaluated in limited settings only. To date, there has been no large-scale real-world study measuring the performance of different carriers, quantifying their diversity in coverage and performance, and analyzing the potential of multi-carrier access approaches in real-world cellular deployments.

To bridge this gap, in this paper, we conduct an extensive measurement campaign involving three cross-country driving trips (Los Angeles to Boston, Boston to Chicago, and Boston to Atlanta) covering a total of 8k+ Km spread out over a 12-month period (August 2022 to August 2023), while *simultaneously measuring the performance of the three major US mobile operators*. The goal of our study is twofold: (a) to analyze the operator diversity in cellular network performance at a given location and time and (b) to gain critical insights into the potential gains of the two multi-carrier access approaches – link selection and link aggregation – in real-world environments. *Our dataset is publicly available at* [1]. The main findings of our study are as follows:

- Our dataset shows a substantial amount of diversity in cellular network performance across different operators at a given time and location in terms of both throughput and RTT, suggesting that the overall network performance can significantly benefit from multi-carrier access solutions.
- Our trace-driven analysis of the theoretical gains of the two multi-carrier access techniques – link selection and link aggregation – assuming optimal link selection/multipath scheduling algorithms, shows that the multi-carrier access schemes provide a median relative throughput gain of 15–309% (DL: 15–111 Mbps, UL: 1–9 Mbps) and a median RTT improvement of 8–20% (5–12 ms) compared to the single-path throughput/RTT of the worst-performing operator.
- The best-operator coherence time – the time during which one operator continuously outperforms another operator – is in the order of several tens of s in the median case, suggesting that link selection techniques can be effective in real-world scenarios without suffering from high switching overhead.

- The probability of handovers to happen at the same time for an operator pair is nearly 0, suggesting that link aggregation can effectively mask handover-induced communication disruptions in real-world cellular network deployments.

2 Related Work

5G Measurements. Since the rollout of 5G in 2019, a large number of studies [7, 10–15, 17, 22, 25–28, 33, 36, 37, 39, 40] have measured various aspects of 5G performance including coverage, network performance, carrier aggregation, resource allocation, handovers, beamforming, and application QoE. To the best of our knowledge, there is no other large-scale measurement work studying the performance diversity among different cellular operators and evaluating the benefits and trade-offs of multi-carrier access in 5G networks.

Multi-carrier Access in Cellular Networks. Most works with respect to multi-carrier access in cellular networks focus on systems apsects [9, 18, 20, 30, 31, 35, 41, 42]. These works propose protocols for link selection [20, 35] or multipath schedulers [9, 18, 30, 31, 41, 42] for MPTCP or MPQUIC to improve throughput [30], latency [18], or application QoE [9, 21, 30, 31, 41, 42], and most of them have performed evaluation in limited settings. These works are orthogonal to ours, which focuses on quantifying the diversity in cellular network performance and the potential benefits of multi-carrier access techniques over cellular networks in the 5G era. The work in [38] evaluates the performance of several MPTCP schedulers over one 5G and one LTE or WiFi link using simulations while the work in [19] evaluates the performance of MPTCP over LTE networks in high-speed trains. The works closest to ours are [2, 3, 34], which similar to this work, evaluate the potential gains of multi-carrier access, but *in the pre-5G era*. Additionally, these works focus on critical intelligent transportation services (ITS), evaluating network availability and transfer time of critical ITS messages, while our work evaluates throughput and RTT, two metrics that are applicable to a variety of applications. To our best knowledge, our work is the first to empirically evaluate the potential of both multi-carrier access techniques over real-world 5G deployments, featuring a mix of 5G and LTE links, via a large-scale measurement campaign comprising multiple cross-country drives.

3 Methodology

We conducted experiments over the three major U.S. mobile operators: Verizon, T-Mobile, and AT&T. We used Samsung Galaxy S21 Ultra smartphones as User Equipment (UE) and utilized AWS EC2 to measure downlink/uplink (DL/UL) throughput and ICMP-based PING to measure round-trip time (RTT). All our experiments were conducted with 3 UEs, each connected to a different operator, to *concurrently* measure the performance over the three operators. More details about the methodology can be found in Appendix A.

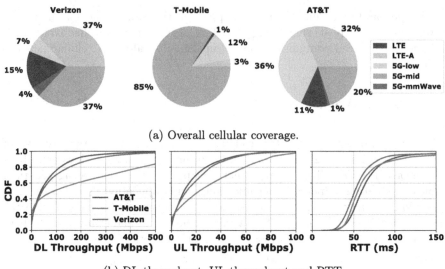

(a) Overall cellular coverage.

(b) DL throughput, UL throughput and RTT.

Fig. 1. Operator-wise coverage and performance comparison.

4   Results

4.1   Coverage and Single-Operator Performance

We begin by taking a look at the overall cellular technology coverage and the corresponding network performance for all three operators. Figure 1a shows the cellular technology coverage for all three operators. 5 years after 5G rollout, we observe a variagated distribution of different cellular technologies among the three operators. While T-Mobile exhibits an impressive 5G coverage ($\geq 97\%$), for Verizon and AT&T, the overall 5G coverage is much lower, 48% and 57%, respectively. Further breakdown of the 5G bands into low-speed 5G (5G-low) and high-speed 5G (5G-mid, and 5G-mmWave), shows that for T-Mobile and Verizon, the majority of the 5G coverage is contributed by high-speed 5G: 85% and 41%. On the other hand, for AT&T, 5G-low dominates the overall 5G coverage (36%).

Consequently, in Fig. 1b, we observe that T-Mobile provides the best performance in terms of DL and UL throughput in the median and the 75-th percentile. On the other hand, Verizon provides the lowest RTT among the three operators. One reason for this is the use of the Amazon Wavelength edge servers, which are accessible only via the Verizon network, in select cities. Additionally, operators are often times known to not elevate the cellular technology from LTE to 5G in the absence of heavy traffic [14], which is a possible reason for the T-Mobile to not achieve the best RTT even though it has the highest 5G coverage.

Overall, *we observe large disparities among the three operators in terms of both coverage and performance (throughput and RTT). These observations motivate the need for multi-carrier solutions to enhance mobile network performance.*

In subsequent sections, we take a deeper look in quantifying the disparity in performance across operators at a given time and location, and theoretically analyze the efficacy of multi-carrier solutions.

4.2 Operator Diversity in Cellular Network Performance

In this section, we take a deeper look at the diversity in cellular network performance at a given location and time. We consider only the throughput (RTT) samples collected concurrently for any pair of operators, and calculate the throughput (RTT) difference for each operator pair.

Throughput Diversity. Figure 2a shows the CDF of the throughput difference at a given location and time for each pair of operators. We observe substantial diversity at a given location and time across operators in both traffic directions. The throughput difference between any pair of operators is often higher than 200 (25) Mbps and sometimes exceeds 400 (50) Mbps in the DL (UL) direction.

Recall from Fig. 1a that there exists a large variability in terms of cellular technology coverage across the three operators and the disparity in performance among different operators could be because of different operators using different cellular technology. To understand the impact of different cellular technologies on such diverse performance among different operators, we break down the throughput samples pairs for each pair of operators into four bins based on technology used by the two operators: HT-HT, HT-LT, LT-HT, LT-LT, where HT represents high-speed 5G (5G-mmWave and 5G-mid band), and LT represents LTE, LTE-A, and 5G-low. We classify 5G-mid band and 5G-mmWave as HT, because these are the two 5G technologies that can achieve Gbps throughput, in contrast to 5G low and LTE. This classification is also followed by the three major cellular providers in the US, which classify their 5G high throughput technology as a mix of 5G-mid band and 5G-mmwave, for example, 5G Ultra-Wideband for Verizon, 5G Ultra-Capacity for T-Mobile, and 5G+ for AT&T.

Figure 2b plots the distribution of the 4 bins for each operator pair in the DL and UL direction. We observe no single bin dominating for all operator pairs and traffic directions. For Verizon-T-Mobile, a significant portion of the samples consist of HT-HT and LT-HT combinations in the DL direction, while LT-HT dominates in the UL direction, thanks to the significantly higher T-Mobile coverage in the 5G midband (Fig. 1a). Due to the same reason, in the case of T-Mobile-AT&T, the majority of samples belong to the HT-LT bin. On the other hand, for AT&T-Verizon, we see a different trend, with LT-HT and LT-LT being the most prevalent combinations in the DL direction and LT-LT dominating in the UL direction.

Figures 2c, 2d plot the CDFs of throughput difference for each bin. For the HT-HT bin, T-Mobile outperforms Verizon and AT&T in both traffic directions most of the time. Additionally, Verizon HT performs slightly better in contrast to AT&T's HT, especially in the DL direction, probably because of better 5G-mmWave coverage (Fig. 1a). In contrast, for the LT-LT bin, for all operator pairs in the DL direction and AT&T-Verizon in the UL direction, the throughput

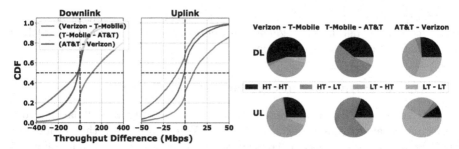

(a) CDF of throughput difference for differ-   (b) Technology-breakdown for different
ent operator pairs.   operator pairs.

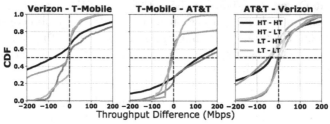

(c) CDFs of DL throughput difference for each operator pair broken down by technology.

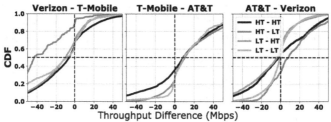

(d) CDFs of UL throughput difference for each operator pair broken down by technology.

Fig. 2. Operator-wise throughput diversity for concurrent tests.

difference curve is symmetric around 0, indicating roughly equal probability
for one operator to outperform the other one. On the other hand, T-Mobile
outperforms the other two operators in the UL direction. Overall, *the throughput
difference between any pair of operators can be very large (more than 200 Mbps
for HT-HT in the DL direction, and several tens of Mbps for HT-HT in the UL
direction and for LT-LT in both directions), indicating substantial performance
diversity across operators even for the same technology.*

Regarding the two heterogeneous bins (LT-HT, and HT-LT), one would
expect the operator using an HT technology to always outperform the operator with an LT technology. However, our results, aligned with the findings of
two previous works [14,17], show that this is not always the case. For example,

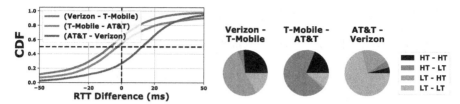

(a) CDF of RTT difference for different operator pairs. (b) Technology breakdown for different operator pairs.

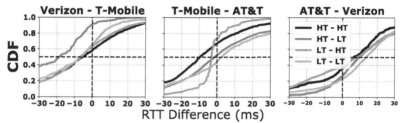

(c) CDFs of RTT difference for each operator pair broken down by technology.

Fig. 3. Operator-wise RTT diversity for concurrent tests.

in the case of T-Mobile-AT&T, where more than 50% of the samples are HT-LT in both directions, 20–30% of the time the HT throughput of T-Mobile is lower than the LT throughput of AT&T. Similarly, for Verizon-T-Mobile, where around 40% and 70% of the DL and UL samples respectively are LT-HT, Verizon's DL and UL LT throughput is higher than T-Mobile's HT throughput around 30% of the time. Overall, *our results show that connecting to an HT technology does not always guarantee better throughput compared to an LT technology, which further contributes to the diversity across operators in terms of performance. Consequently, a simple link selection scheme that always prefers an HT network over an LT one does not always work in practice.*

RTT Diversity. Next, we look at the performance diversity in terms of RTT in Fig. 3a. Similar to throughput, we observe significant diversity in terms of RTT across operators at a given time and location. Figure 3b, which breaks down the RTT difference samples into the 4 bins (HT-HT, HT-LT, LT-LT, LT-HT), shows that the dominant bin is LT-HT for Verizon-T-Mobile, HT-LT for T-Mobile-AT&T, and LT-LT for AT&T-Verizon, suggesting that two operators (Verizon, AT&T) often do not upgrade the UE to 5G midband/mmWave for low-rate ICMP traffic. Further, Fig. 3c shows that at least 55–60% of the time (90% in some cases like Verizon-T-Mobile HT-LT) Verizon outperforms the other two operators across all bins. For T-Mobile-AT&T, T-Mobile performs better than AT&T 60% of the time in the HT-HT case, whereas for LT-LT and for HT-LT, the RTT difference curves are symmetric around 0 in the LT-LT and HT-LT cases. Interestingly for the LT-HT bin, T-Mobile outperforms AT&T 75% of the time. Overall, *our results show large RTT disparities, often more than 20 ms for all three operator pairs, which can significantly affect the QoE of latency-critical applications (AR, VR, CAVs). For example, an edge/cloud-assisted AR app that offloads frames to a server to perform object detection, requires an and-to-end latency of 33 ms. Additionally, similar to the throughput results, selecting an HT network does not always guarantee lower RTT.*

4.3   Potential Benefits of Multi-carrier Cellular Access

Our results in the previous section showed very large diversity in terms of network performance across different operators at a given location and time, suggesting that applications can benefit significantly from multi-carrier access techniques. In this section, we use our dataset to explore the theoretical (upper bound) benefits and trade-offs of the two multi-carrier access techniques – link selection and link aggregation.

We assume dual-sim smartphones capable of simultaneously using two different cellular networks.[1] Since our goal is to investigate the maximum possible gain of the two aggregation techniques over the performance of a single network, we assume that the link selection or link aggregation is performed by two oracles. In the case of link selection, the oracle (*Max*) always chooses the best network in terms of performance at a given time, and we ignore the network switching overhead; hence, the *Max* throughput is always equal to the single-path throughput over the best network. In the case of link aggregation, the oracle (*Sum*) performs optimal packet scheduling over the two links and we ignore the impact of congestion control; hence the *Sum* throughput is always equal to the sum of the single-path throughputs over the two networks.

Figure 4 compares the relative and absolute throughput gain of *Max* and *Sum* over single-path throughput for all operator pairs. We plot both the absolute and relative throughput gains, because the relative gain can sometimes be misleading. For example, improving throughput from 1 Mbps to 2 Mbps and from 100 Mbps to 200 Mbps both correspond to a 100% relative gain, but the latter is much more important in practice.

First, in Figs. 4a, 4c, 4e, we observe significant relative throughput gains ((red or black solid lines)) of *Max* over the worst-performing operator, ranging from 51–208% and 15–91% in the median case and from 538–868% and 169–330% at the 75-th percentile, in the DL and UL direction, respectively. These relative gains translate to an absolute throughput gain of 15–111 Mbps (1–9 Mbps) in the median case, and up to 339 Mbps (33 Mbps) at the 75-th percentile, for the DL (UL) direction (Figs. 4b, 4d, 4f), highlighting the efficacy of link selection as a multi-carrier access scheme, especially in the DL direction. In general, the benefit of *Max* is higher in cases where there is a high degree of heterogeneity in the performance of the two operators. For example, in Figs. 4a and 4c, where T-Mobile is one of the operators, the gain of *Max* over the worst performing

---

[1] Using two sim cards on smartphones is more practical than using three sims.

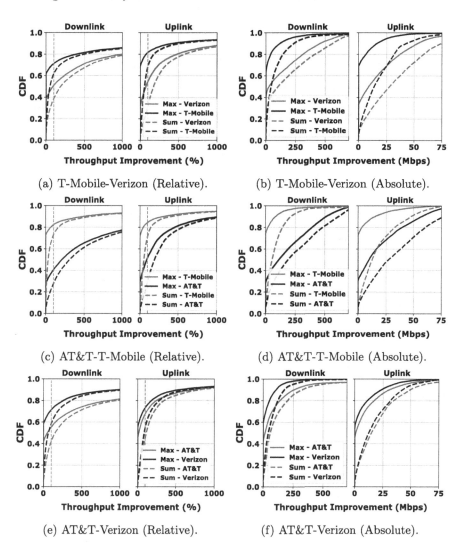

Fig. 4. CDFs of throughput improvement of *Max* and *Sum* over a single operator for all operator pairs. The grey dashed line shows the 100% mark. (Color figure online)

operator (Verizon or AT&T) is higher compared to the more homogeneous operator pair (Verizon and AT&T) in Fig. 4e.

Next, we study the benefits of *Sum* (red and black dashed lines in Fig. 4). We observe that there is an additional gain in using *Sum* over *Max* in all cases. For example, in Fig. 4b the median DL throughput improvement of *Max* over Verizon is 26 Mbps (red solid line) while aggregating Verizon and T-Mobile links provides a throughput improvement of 102 Mbps. Overall, the relative gain of *Sum* over a single operator ranges from 31–309% in the median case and 113–

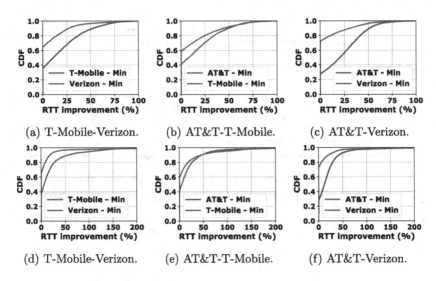

Fig. 5. CDFs of relative ((a), (b), (c)) and absolute ((d), (e), (f)) RTT improvement of *Min* over a single operator for all operator pairs.

967% at the 75-th percentile for DL and from 52–191% in the median case and 113–433% at the 75-th percentile for UL. Additionally, *Sum* offers significant gains over both operators, while *Max* mainly improves the performance over the worst of the two operators. For example, *Max* improves the performance over the best-performing operator (T-Mobile in Figs. 4a and 4c, Verizon in Fig. 4e) in the DL direction only 25–49% of the time, while *Sum* improves the performance over the same operator 75–90% of the time.

We also quantify the performance gain of multi-carrier access with respect to the RTT. Here we consider an `oracle` *Min* that chooses the link with the minimum RTT.[2] Figure 5 plots the CDF of absolute and relative improvement of *Min* over a single operator for all operator pairs. The median relative RTT improvement over the worst-performing operator ranges from 8–20% translating to an actual improvement of 5–12 ms. Further, the absolute gain over the worst-performing operator at the 75-th percentile is higher than 15 ms for all three operator pairs. As we noted in §4.2, this is a significant improvement for latency-critical applications such as AR, VR, and CAVs, which require end-to-end latencies in the order of a few tens of ms.

Although our analysis assumes an `oracle` and disregards link switching overhead and the impact of congestion control, the results in this section clearly indicate that both multi-carrier access techniques have the potential to provide substantial performance benefits over cellular networks in the 5G era.

---

[2] In practice, this can be achieved by sending every packet over both networks.

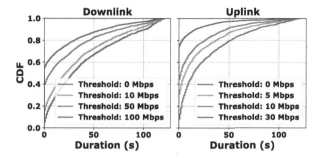

Fig. 6. Best-operator coherence time.

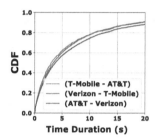

Fig. 7. Inter-operator handover intervals.

4.4 Practical Considerations

To further understand the potential of the two `oracle` systems, Sum and Max, in real world scenarios, in this section, we investigate two practical issues: (a) **Best-operator coherence time**: the time during which one operator continuously outperforms another operator, and (b) **Handover distribution for each pair of operators**: the handover occurrence times for two operators.

(a) **Best-operator coherence time.** For Max to be effective in practice, one operator should consistently offer better performance than the other operator for a substantial amount of time, as rapid switching between the two operators could incur high switching overhead and negate the potential gains. In Fig. 6, we plot the CDF of the duration during which the throughput of one operator is consistently higher than the throughput of the other operator by a threshold Θ for all three operator pairs and different values of Θ. We observe that, for $\Theta = 0$, the coherence time of the best operator is very high – 12/37/76 s in the DL direction and 6/19/47 in the UL direction at the 25-th/50-th/75-th percentile. With higher thresholds, the coherence time naturally decreases, however, we still observe high coherence time at the 75-th percentile. For example, in the DL direction, 20% of the time the throughput of a given operator remains higher than the throughput of the other operator by at least 100 Mbps for durations longer than 30 s. These results suggest that link selection as a multi-carrier access technique is likely to perform well in practice.

(b) Handover distribution. Handovers in cellular networks are viewed as temporary disruptions in the communication as the phone's connection transfers from the old base station to the new one. Previous work [16] has shown that handovers in 5G networks can significantly affect the application QoE. Link aggregation techniques have the potential to mask such disruptions, by sending all the packets over one link when the other operator's link is temporarily disrupted due to a handover, if handovers for the two operators occur at different times, but offer no protection if handovers occur simultaneously (or very close to each other). In Fig. 7, we plot the CDF of the *inter-operator handover interval* for a given operator pair, defined as the time span between a handover in one operator's network and the nearest handover in the other carrier network. We observe that the probability of handovers to happen at the same time for an operator pair is nearly 0 and the median inter-operator handover interval is about 3 s. This finding is in line with the findings in [19], which studied the potential of MPTCP over multiple LTE networks in the case of high-speed rails. Given that the handover duration is typically shorter than 200 ms [14,16], *link aggregation shows high promise to mask handover-induced disruptions in real-world cellular network deployments.*

5   Conclusion

We performed the first large-scale empirical study of the potential gains of the two multi-carrier access approaches – link selection and link aggregation – in real-world environments in the 5G era via an extensive measurement campaign involving three cross-country driving trips covering a total of 8k+ Km spread out over a 12-month period, while simultaneously measuring the performance of the three major US mobile operators. Our measurements show that there exists a substantial amount of diversity in cellular network performance across different operators at a given time and location in terms of both throughput and RTT. Our trace-driven analysis of the theoretical gains of the two multi-carrier access techniques shows that they can provide significant gains over the single-path throughput/RTT of the worst-performing operator, especially in the DL direction. Additionally, our results show that the best-operator coherence time is in the order of several tens of s in the median case and the probability of handovers to happen at the same time for an operator pair is nearly 0. Although our analysis assumed optimal link selection/multipath scheduling algorithms and ignored link switching overheads and the impact of congestion control, a number of recent works [9,18,20,30,31,35,41,42] have proposed practical link selection/aggregation schemes that have been shown to work well under limited evaluation settings. Our work suggests that such schemes have a great potential and should be further explored to improve performance and QoE of bandwidth intensive and latency-critical 5G "killer" apps.

Appendix

A   Methodology

5G Carriers, User Equipment (UE), and Servers. We obtained multiple unlimited data plans from the three major U.S. service providers, Verizon, T-Mobile, and AT&T, to conduct our experiments. All three carriers have deployed 5G low-band, mid-band, and high-band (mmWave) services across the country, predominantly co-existing with LTE via the Non-Stand Alone (NSA) architecture. T-Mobile is the only U.S. carrier currently offering both NSA and Standalone (SA) 5G services. We used Samsung Galaxy S21 Ultra smartphones as our UEs, which support most of the 5G frequency bands available in the U.S. Since commercial off-the-shelf smartphones do not provide access to low-level KPIs such as handover details or 5G frequency bands, we used Accuver XCAL Solo [4] devices, which tap into the Qualcomm diagnostic (diag) interface to capture signaling messages exchanged between the UE and the base station. For server-side infrastructure, we utilized AWS EC2 cloud instances for tests with all three operators, as well as AWS Wavelength [6] edge servers for specific Verizon tests conducted in selected cities along our driving routes.

Fig. 8. Measurement routes.

Measurement Routes. We conducted three measurement campaigns spread out over a 12-month (August 2022 to August 2023) and covering over 8,000 km of driving across the US. The routes of these measurement campaigns are shown in Fig. 8. In August 2022, we performed a cross-country drive from Los Angeles to Boston, crossing Las Vegas, Salt Lake City, Denver, Omaha, Des Moines, Chicago, Indianapolis, Columbus, Cleveland, and Buffalo. In May 2023 (05/13/2023–05/16/2023), we conducted a driving trip from Boston to Chicago, covering the same major cities of the 2022 trip along the route. In August 2023 (08/05/2023–08/08/2023), we conducted a second driving trip from Boston to Atlanta, passing through Providence, New Haven, New York City, Baltimore, Washington, Richmond, Durham, and Charlotte. All measurement data reported in this study were collected on interstate highways, in suburban areas, and within city limits. Additional measurements were conducted within several major cities encountered along the routes. The vehicle speed ranged from 5 miles per hour in cities to 100 miles per hour in inter-state highways.

Experimental Methodology. We conducted three types of tests: backlogged downlink and uplink throughput tests, both using nuttcp [32], and round-trip time (RTT) tests using ICMP-based ping, in a round robin fashion throughout the driving trips. The nuttcp tests lasted for 30–180 seconds each while the RTT tests ran for 20–30 seconds each. The throughput and RTT samples were logged at intervals of 500 ms and 200 ms, respectively.

References

1. Dataset: A Large-Scale Study of the Potential of Multi-Carrier Access in the 5G Era (2025). https://github.com/NUWiNS/pam2025-multi-carrier-dataset
2. Abdesslem, F.B., Abrahamsson, H., Ahlgren, B.: Measuring mobile network multi-access for time-critical C-ITS applications. In: 2018 Network Traffic Measurement and Analysis Conference (TMA) (2018)
3. Abrahamsson, H., Abdesslem, F.B., Ahlgren, B., Brunstrom, A., Marsh, I., Björkman, M.: Connected vehicles in cellular networks: multi-access versus single-access performance. In: 2018 Network Traffic Measurement and Analysis Conference (TMA) (2018)
4. XCAL Solo. https://accuver.com/sub/products/view.php?idx=11;
5. Ahuja, K., Singh, B., Khanna, R.: Network selection algorithm based on link quality parameters for heterogeneous wireless networks. Optik **125**(14), 3657–3662 (2014)
6. What is AWS Wavelength?. https://docs.aws.amazon.com/wavelength/latest/developerguide/what-is-wavelength.html
7. Caso, G., et al.: An initial look into the performance evolution of 5G non-standalone networks. In: Proceedings of IFIP/IEEE TMA (2023)
8. Deng, S., Netravali, R., Sivaraman, A., Balakrishnan, H.: WiFi, LTE, or both? Measuring multi-homed wireless internet performance. In: Proceedings of ACM IMC (2014)
9. Dhawaskar Sathyanarayana, S., Lee, K., Grunwald, D., Ha, S.: Converge: QoE-driven multipath video conferencing over WebRTC. In: Proceedings of ACM SIGCOMM (2023)
10. Dinh, P., Ghoshal, M., Koutsonikolas, D., Widmer, J.: Demystifying resource allocation policies in operational 5G mmWave networks. In: Proceedings of IEEE WoWMoM (2022)
11. Fezeu, R.A.K., et al.: Mid-Band 5G: a measurement study in Europe and US. In: Proceedings of ACM SIGCOMM (2024)
12. Fezeu, R.A.K., et al.: Roaming across the European Union in the 5G era: performance, challenges, and opportunities. In: Proceedings of IEEE INFOCOM (2023)
13. Fiandrino, C., Juárez Martínez-Villanueva, D., Widmer, J.: Uncovering 5G performance on public transit systems with an app-based measurement study. In: Proceedings of ACM MSWiM (2022)
14. Ghoshal, M., Khan, I., Kong, Z.J., Dinh, P., Meng, J., Hu, Y.C., Koutsonikolas, D.: Performance of cellular networks on the wheels. In: Proceedings of ACM IMC 2023 (2023)

15. Ghoshal, M., et al.: An in-depth study of uplink performance of 5G MmWave networks. In: Proceedings of the ACM SIGCOMM 5G-MeMU Workshop (2022)
16. Hassan, A., et al.: Vivisecting mobility management in 5G cellular networks. In: Proceedings of ACM SIGCOMM (2022)
17. Kousias, K., et al.: Coverage and performance analysis of 5G non-standalone deployments. In: Proceedings of ACM WiNTECH (2022)
18. Lee, H., Flinn, J., Tonshal, B.: RAVEN: improving interactive latency for the connected car. In: Proceedings of ACM MobiCom (2018)
19. Li, L., et al.: A measurement study on multi-path TCP with multiple cellular carriers on high speed rails. In: Proceedings of ACM SIGCOMM (2018)
20. Li, Y., et al.: iCellular: device-customized cellular network access on commodity smartphones. In: Proceedings of USENIX NSDI) (2016)
21. Lv, G., et al.: Chorus: coordinating mobile multipath scheduling and adaptive video streaming. In: Proceedings of ACM MobiCom (2024)
22. Moreno, J., Contini, M., Aguiar, A.: 5G NSA performance: a measurement study. In: Proceedings of IFIP WONS (2024)
23. Multipath QUIC. https://multipath-quic.org
24. MultiPath TCP. https://www.multipath-tcp.org
25. Narayanan, A., et al.: A first look at commercial 5G performance on smartphones. In: Proceedings of ACM WWW (2020)
26. Narayanan, A., et al.: Lumos5G: mapping and predicting commercial mmWave 5G throughput. In: Proceedings of ACM IMC (2020)
27. Narayanan, A., et al.: A comparative measurement study of commercial 5G mmWave deployments. In: In Proceedings of IEEE INFOCOM (2022)
28. Narayanan, A., et al.: A variegated look at 5G in the wild: performance, power, and QoE implications. In: Proceedings of ACM SIGCOMM (2021)
29. Narayanan, A., et al.: A variegated look at 5G in the wild: performance, power, and QoE implications. In: Proceedings of ACM SIGCOMM (2021)
30. Ni, Y., et al.: POLYCORN: data-driven cross-layer multipath networking for high-speed railway through composable schedulerlets. In: Proceedings of USENIX NSDI (2023)
31. Ni, Y., et al.: Cellfusion: multipath vehicle-to-cloud video streaming with network coding in the wild. In: Proceedings of ACM SIGCOMM (2023)
32. nuttcp - Network Performance Measurement Tool. https://www.nuttcp.net
33. Parastar, P., Alay, A.L.O.O., Caso, G., Perino, D.: Spotlight on 5G: performance, device evolution and challenges from a mobile operator perspective. In: Proceedings of IEEE INFOCOM (2023)
34. Rabitsch, A., et al.: Utilizing multi-connectivity to reduce latency and enhance availability for vehicle to infrastructure communication. IEEE Trans. Mob. Comput. **21**(5), 1874–1891 (2022)
35. Ramadan, E., Narayanan, A., Dayalan, U.K., Fezeu, R.A.K., Qian, F., Zhang, Z.L.: Case for 5G-aware video streaming applications. In: Proceedings of ACM SIGCOMM 5G-MeMu (2021)
36. Rochman, M.I., et al.: A comprehensive analysis of the coverage and performance of 4G and 5G deployments. Comput. Netw. **237** (2023)
37. Rochman, M.I., Ye, W., Zhang, Z.L., Ghosh, M.: A comprehensive real-world evaluation of 5G improvements over 4G in low- and mid-bands. Technical report 2312.00957[cs.NI] (2023)
38. Wu, H., Caso, G., Ferlin, S., Alay, O., Brunstrom, A.: Multipath scheduling for 5G networks: evaluation and outlook. IEEE Commun. Mag. **59**(4), 44–50 (2021)

39. Xu, D., et al.: Understanding operational 5G: a first measurement study on its coverage, performance and energy consumption. In: Proceedings of ACM SIGCOMM (2020)
40. Yang, X., et al.: Mobile access bandwidth in practice: measurement, analysis, and implications. In: Proceedings of ACM SIGCOMM (2022)
41. Zheng, Z., et al.: XLINK: QoE-driven multi-path QUIC transport in large-scale video services. In: Proceedings of SIGCOMM (2021)
42. Zhou, Y., et al.: AUGUR: practical mobile multipath transport service for low tail latency in real-time streaming. In: Proceedings of USENIX NSDI (2024)

5G Performance: A Multidimensional Variability Analysis

Varshika Srinivasavaradhan$^{(\boxtimes)}$, Jiayi Liu, and Elizabeth M. Belding

University of California, Santa Barbara, USA
`{varshika,jiayi979,ebelding}@ucsb.edu`

Abstract. 5G networks have been broadly touted as a revolution in cellular performance. However, these networks have significant architectural, spectrum and physical layer options, such that the delivered performance can be variable. The disparity in smartphone hardware and software platforms adds another layer of performance uncertainty. Our goal in this work is to characterize the impact of these features on 5G performance. To do so, we analyze a dataset of nearly 1.75 million crowd-sourced Ookla® Speedtest Intelligence® cellular network measurements over three years and eight U.S. cities. We employ a novel approach by grouping Speedtest results based on both performance metrics and their deviation, while also accounting for spatial distribution and frequency band characteristics. By using statistical distance measures, we quantify the impact of multiple PHY layer and device-specific features across these multidimensional groups. We complement our in-the-wild analysis with a controlled study to validate our findings. We observe that PHY layer parameters, such as channel quality index and signal strength are the primary drivers of performance variability within each frequency range. However, between frequency ranges, user equipment hardware emerges as the dominant factor, highlighting that the equipments themselves play a critical role in determining whether users can fully utilize 5G capabilities. This underscores the importance of advancing device hardware to keep pace with the rapid evolution of network technologies.

1 Introduction

5G technology has promised be a connectivity panacea, a dense grid of intelligent wireless devices that deliver "multi-Gbps peak rates, ultra-low latency, massive capacity, and more uniform user experience" [52]. The last four years have seen an explosion of 5G network deployment across the U.S. and worldwide [4,5,14]. Consistent with other advanced wireless technologies, there exists a plethora of 5G architectural and physical (PHY) layer options. There is also a wide range of 5G-capable devices and chipsets, from "5G-ready" cell phones developed in the late 2010s, to modern devices that support advanced 5G features like mmWave technology and carrier aggregation for enhanced connectivity [9,12].

This array of deployment and usage options brings into question whether all configurations receive the multi-Gbps, high-performance experience touted

© The Author(s), under exclusive license to Springer Nature Switzerland AG 2025
C. Testart et al. (Eds.): PAM 2025, LNCS 15567, pp. 485–501, 2025.
https://doi.org/10.1007/978-3-031-85960-1_20

by marketing campaigns. Prior work has noted wide variability in 5G performance [40,49,60]. We build on these findings to contextualize 5G network performance based on PHY layer and device features and quantify the impact of these features on measured performance. Specifically, we ask the question: *how variable is 5G performance, and which specific network and device features have the most significant impact on measured performance?*

To answer this question, we utilize a novel dataset of 1.75M individual crowdsourced Ookla® Speedtest® measurements from eight U.S. cities across three years. Although past work has shown that crowdsourced speed measurements may contain biases due to their uncontrolled collection [27,33,51], they nevertheless are a critical, rich source of "in-the-wild" network performance data [44,50,53,55]. Hence, we analyze the features in this dataset and apply statistical measures to quantify their impact on 5G performance. However, because of potential biases in the crowdsourced data, we supplement this dataset through experimentation and generate an additional 3.7k Speedtest measurements on three commonly-used cellular device types and cellular carriers. We confirm our analytical findings in this more controlled setting.

We begin by analyzing three years, from 2021 to 2023, of 5G crowdsourced performance trends from three independent carriers. We find wide divergence in measured download speeds, both for individual carriers and between carriers. Notably, *the bottom 30% of 5G tests perform <u>worse</u> than the top 25% of 4G tests, even in 2023.* Motivated by this wide variability and poor performance, we employ statistical distance measures to quantify the impact of the PHY layer, device and other features on 5G download speed and latency. For each carrier in our study, we first group tests based on frequency to account for differences in wave propagation characteristics. Within each frequency range, we further categorize tests by H3 resolution 9 hexagons [22][1] to control for location-specific parameters. We then analyze each group based on both average performance (speed and latency) and variability. Our novel methodological contribution is in applying Kullback-Leibler divergence to quantify the divergence between performance distributions, allowing us to systematically identify the features that most significantly impact 5G variability. By computing the statistical distance between the consistently high-performing group and each of the other groups, we identify key features that have the most significant impact on 5G performance variability. This approach allows us to identify features that affect 5G performance both within each frequency range and across the different frequency ranges. *We find that within each frequency range, cell density and PHY layer parameters, such as channel quality index (CQI), signal strength (RSRP) and signal quality (RSRQ), unsurprisingly, are the primary contributors to performance variability. However, across frequency bands, user equipment, specifically the chipset models and software, show high divergence values for all carriers in our study.* Our results demonstrate that 5G deployment alone does not guarantee high performance. Rather, careful attention to PHY configurations, modern devices, and sufficient cell tower densities are needed to reap the benefits that 5G promises.

---

[1] An H3 geospatial index has an average area of $0.73\,\mathrm{km}^2$ [24].

2   Data and Experiment Setup

To quantify 5G performance variability and identify key influencing factors, we analyze multiple complementary datasets. In the following section, we describe each of our data sources, including crowdsourced and controlled measurements, along with our methodologies. We also discuss the limitations of our approach.

Speedtest Intelligence Data. The Ookla® Speedtest® platform offers users the ability to measure Internet connection quality through either a web-based portal or a dedicated mobile application [18] using a network of over 16k measurement servers world-wide [11]. Over the past decade, Speedtest has garnered extensive usage among both consumers and policymakers [1,3,10]. For each Speedtest, a geographically close test server with the lowest latency is automatically selected [16] and TCP connections are used to saturate the link between the client and the test server to measure network speed and latency. We utilize the Speedtest Intelligence dataset with crowdsourced measurements collected between January 1, 2021 and December 31, 2023, which we obtained through a Data Use Agreement[2] (DUA). In contrast to the publicly available aggregated Ookla data, the DUA dataset contains additional Speedtest data points, each with multiple features, such as upload/download throughput, latency, cellular carrier, user equipment (UE) and software details, chipset, and other relevant geospatial information. Because our study analyzes cellular network performance, we focus on cellular Speedtest measurements from iOS and Android smartphone applications. Tests report additional metadata, including PHY metrics (RSRP, signal-to-noise ratio (SNR), RSRQ, CQI); type of cellular radio frequency (RF) technology (2G, 3G, 4G LTE, 5G NR); RF band frequency; channel width; and available kernel memory(for Android measurements) and 5G deployment mode (non-standalone (NSA) 5G vs standalone (SA) 5G) for iOS measurements. Our dataset contains a total of 1.75 million measurements (700k 4G and 1.04M 5G measurements) collected from eight U.S. cities from three major U.S. cellular carriers. For interested readers, we enumerate the number of data points per city and carrier in Table 2 of the Appendix. Each of the cities has a population between 400k and 700k and covers an area of 90–350 sq. miles.

Tower Maps Data. We utilize Tower Maps [20], a proprietary dataset of cell tower locations in the U.S. that includes details such as accurate location information, tower height, and construction date, to augment our analysis. While the data does not specify the radio type for each tower, it allows us to estimate the density of cellular infrastructure around Speedtest takers. By integrating this information with our data, we can analyze how the presence and concentration of nearby towers correlates with measured 5G performance, offering insight into the relationship between infrastructure density and user experience.

Controlled Experiments. To verify our results from the crowdsourced dataset, we conduct controlled Speedtest measurements for 15 days in April 2024, a dura-

---

[2] Due to our data use agreement, we are unable to disclose carrier names, specific locations, or chipset details.

tion that captures both hourly and weekly usage patterns while controlling for device and location variables. We use three popular Android phone models, which were also common models in our crowdsourced dataset: Samsung Galaxy S20+ and S23, and Google Pixel 7, each with a different chipset. We utilize three phones of each model, for a total of nine experiment phones. For consistency, we purchase nine SIM cards with identical cell plans for each of the same three cellular carriers analyzed in the crowdsourced data. We conduct Speedtests at regular intervals using nine SIM cards per carrier; Speedtests are run sequentially on each phone, and the cell carrier is rotated after each test set. We conduct our experiments in eight locations identified to have 5G coverage, as indicated by the National Broadband Map [17] and the carrier official websites. In many cases, multiple test sets are conducted per location, per carrier. To analyze PHY layer and cell tower information, we utilize Accuver XCAL-M [21], a professional tool that can extract information from the Qualcomm diag [2]. Since the Google Pixel 7 chipset is not compatible with XCAL-M, we run open source Android applications CellMapper and NetMonster [7,15] on these phones during Speedtest measurements to obtain the same granular information.

Limitations. Prior research [27,33,51] has recognized potential shortcomings of crowdsourced network performance metrics. Crowdsourced tests are uncontrolled and hence can introduce biases related to the test-taker, geographic location, network conditions (congestion or poor service), device type and characteristics, and the lack of cellular data plan details (e.g., speed caps or throttling limits). Additionally, our dataset lacks information on features such as beam management strategies and resource blocks available, which can impact measured performance. However, our objective is to study 5G network performance as measured by Ookla Speedtest; to identify the network and device features that contribute to 5G performance variability; and to quantify the impact of these features on measured performance. We believe the impact of inherent dataset biases on our analysis is limited. Nevertheless, *we confirm all findings derived from the crowdsourced data with the data generated by our controlled experiments.*

3   Dissecting 5G Performance

We begin with a longitudinal analysis of 4G and 5G to characterize their evolving usage and performance in our time window, during which 5G deployment increased significantly [13,19]. While the focus of our study is 5G, we include some initial data on 4G to contextualize the transition period from 4G to 5G. Then, we dig deeper and analyse the key factors that affect in-the-wild 5G performance and quantify the variability using statistical distance measures. We validate our results through controlled experiments. While we also analyze upload speed, we focus our presented analysis on download speed and latency. Download speed is often a key determinant of user experience [8] and the variability in download speeds is much greater than that of upload speeds. Latency also plays a crucial role, particularly for interactive applications and overall responsiveness. We confirm that the trends represented by download speeds are consistent with those in upload speeds.

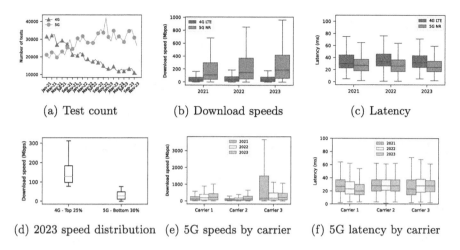

(a) Test count   (b) Download speeds   (c) Latency

(d) 2023 speed distribution   (e) 5G speeds by carrier   (f) 5G latency by carrier

Fig. 1. Longitudinal evolution of test taking and measured download speeds.

3.1 Longitudinal Trends

We begin by characterizing Speedtest usage and measured performance over time to study changes that correlate with growing 5G deployment. Figure 1(a) illustrates these temporal trends, aggregated monthly over the three cellular carriers and eight cities. It indicates a general upward trajectory in the number of 5G Speedtests, while 4G Speedtests decrease by 61% during the same period.

Corresponding with the 5G test-taking trend is an increase in median 5G download speed, more than doubling over the three year period, as shown in Fig. 1(b), which illustrates the range of measured download speeds annually for each cellular technology. Unlike 5G, 4G speed remains stable. A similar trend is observed in 5G latency, shown in Fig. 1(c), with the median value decreasing by about 10ms from 2021 to 2023. These trends are a likely indication of increasingly widespread 5G deployment and availability, coupled with an increase in 5G-capable UEs and a movement away from 4G. Interesting, however, is the wide range in 5G download speed performance, which grows annually: in 2021, the difference between the 25th and 75th percentiles was 245 Mbps, while in 2023 it was nearly 400 Mbps. This wide, and growing, range of speeds is our first indication of the wide variability in 5G performance. Further, Fig. 1(b) indicates some overlap in 4G and 5G performance, even as late as 2023. When we take a closer look, we find that, even in 2023, the bottom 30% of 5G download speeds are **worse** than the top 25% of 4G tests (Fig. 1(d)). *Given this highly variable 5G performance, we ask: what key network and device features most significantly impact 5G performance?* As described earlier, the range of 5G network features, PHY layer options, and devices is wide. Our goal is to discover which of these features contribute most substantially to measured performance.

We conclude our longitudinal analysis by examining the 5G download speed and latency of each carrier individually in Figs. 1(e) and 1(f), respectively. We observe a growth of over 200% in the 75th percentile download speeds for car-

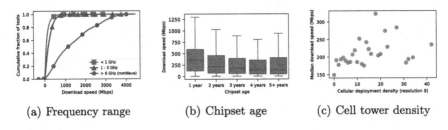

(a) Frequency range   (b) Chipset age   (c) Cell tower density

Fig. 2. Effect of key features in our dataset on measured downloads speeds.

riers 1 and 2. While the latency of carrier 2 does not show huge improvements, carrier 1 exhibits a 50% decline in median latency. On the other hand, carrier 3's performance decreases significantly after 2021. While this is interesting, it is orthogonal to our analysis. We include a deeper exploration of this anomaly in the Appendix for interested readers.

3.2 Feature Analysis

In this section, we analyze measured Speedtest download speed and latency, disaggregating by test metadata to quantify performance differentials due to each feature. The test metadata we primarily focus on includes 5G RF technology, 5G PHY parameters such as RSRP, RSRQ and CQI[3]; UE features, such as device model and chipset; and cell tower density. For each feature category, we use the Speedtest datapoints that have the corresponding metadata. For brevity, we present only the findings for download speed here; we confirm our findings are consistent for latency.

Radio Frequency (RF) Technology. 5G networks operate in a variety of frequency ranges: low-band (<1 GHz), mid-band (1–6 GHz), and mmWave (> 6 GHz). The characteristics of wave propagation in these bands naturally lend themselves to widely varying performance. To study the impact of these RF features, we utilize the 100k 5G tests from Android devices that contain frequency information. We have included details of the count of Speedtests across frequency bands for each year in Tables 3 and 4 of the Appendix. Figure 2(a) illustrates the significant impact radio frequency has on performance: mmWave 5G achieves median download speeds of over 1200 Mbps, a 1400% increase from the medians of sub-6 GHz speeds. On the other hand, there is minimal difference between low-band and mid-band 5G. Finally, our dataset lacked labelled measurements for NSA and SA 5G deployment modes in Android measurements. Hence, our analysis does not include these specific architectural configurations.

Device Hardware. Next, we analyze the distribution of 5G download speed by chipset age[4] in Fig. 2(b). We observe that the median value improves significantly

---

[3] RSRP is the average power received from a 5G reference signal. RSRQ indicates how clearly the signal can be heard over interference. CQI is a mechanism by which the UE informs the base station about channel quality.

[4] We define chipset age as the number of years since a chipset was introduced.

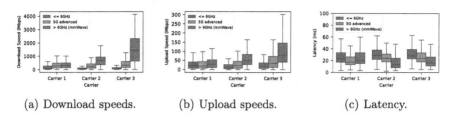

(a) Download speeds.   (b) Upload speeds.   (c) Latency.

Fig. 3. Effect of frequency on measured network performance metrics.

with newer chipsets, with the latest models achieving speeds twice as fast as those of chipsets that are 5 years old.

Cell Tower Density. 726k Speedtest measurements have GPS-level location information in our dataset. We use this subset to study the relationship between cellular deployment density and measured download speeds, presented in Fig. 2(c). We utilize cell tower data obtained from Tower Maps and compute the number of cell towers within the H3 resolution 9 hexagon of each Speedtest measurement; we call this cell tower density. We find that cell tower density and median download speeds have a moderate correlation (0.38). While this suggests a positive relationship, other important factors that could impact speeds, like cellular load, are not available in our metadata, limiting further analysis.

3.3 Quantifying 5G Variability In-the-Wild

Our analysis reveals significant variability of in-the-wild 5G performance. Based on this trend, our goal in this section is to analyze this variability by estimating the impact of each feature on the measured download speed and latency to better characterize the factors that influence 5G performance. To do so, we use a subset of 370k Android measurements labelled with both PHY layer and device chipset information. Additionally, we compute cell tower density at the location of these measurements. While machine learning approaches can be valuable in analyzing large datasets such as ours, any biases in the crowdsourced Speedtest data, as well as the limited information about signal propagation and antenna beamforming characteristics, pose challenges for these methods in this context. Hence, we instead apply a statistical approach that quantifies the (dis)similarity between two distributions. This method allows us to directly compare features across performance groups and identify the ones that differ most between them.

Statistical Distance. Statistical distance quantifies the distance between two statistical objects, such as two probability distributions or samples [28], and is typically used in machine learning for anomaly detection, classification, and model evaluation [31,34,57,59]. We apply *Kullback-Leibler (KL) divergence* to this new context; KL divergence quantifies the dissimilarity between two probability distributions, ranges from 0 (identical) to infinity (highly dissimilar),

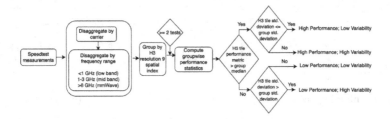

Fig. 4. Classification of tests for distance calculation.

Table 1. Feature descriptions for network performance analysis.

Group	< 1 GHz (1)	1–6 GHz (2)	> 6 GHz (3)
High Performance – Low Variability **(A)**	A1	A2	A3
High Performance – High Variability **(B)**	B1	B2	B3
Low Performance – High Variability **(C)**	C1	C2	C3
Low Performance – Low Variability **(D)**	D1	D2	D3

and can be applied to both categorical and continuous features. We describe KL divergence in more detail in the Appendix. To apply the divergence model, we need more than one distribution for comparison. We utilize two key observations from our preliminary analysis. First, different carriers adopt distinct deployment strategies, leading to significant performance variations. Second, 5G operates across different frequency ranges, each with its own signal propagation characteristics, which directly influences performance; we show in Fig. 3 the impact of frequency bands on network performance metrics for each carrier in our study. Based on these observations, we employ a novel methodology to group the crowdsourced dataset in a way that isolates specific test variables and controls for inherent data variations. Figure 4 gives an overview of our methodology, which we describe in detail next.

Methodology. We begin by disaggregating the Speedtests by cellular carriers to account for differences in their deployment strategies. We then group the tests by frequency range. This allows us to isolate the effect of frequency while controlling for carrier-specific variations. In this analysis, we include only the 100k Speedtest measurements that are labelled with frequency range information. Within each frequency range, we group the tests by H3 resolution 9 hexagons. This spatial grouping serves two key purposes: it allows us to control for location-specific factors, and it aligns with the FCC's method of computing mobile broadband coverage in the U.S. [17]. To assess whether neighboring H3 hexagons exhibit similar 5G performance and thereby validate the relevance of this grouping, we leverage the Moran's I [23] statistic.[5] Our analysis reveals that all three

---

[5] Moran's I statistic has been widely used in past research [32,41,64] to analyze the spatial distribution of a variable of interest within a specific geographic area. It is described in more detail in the Appendix.

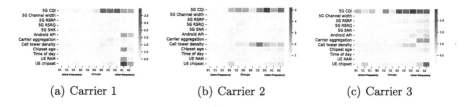

(a) Carrier 1   (b) Carrier 2   (c) Carrier 3

Fig. 5. KL divergence metrics - download speed.

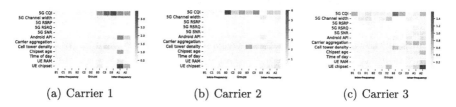

(a) Carrier 1   (b) Carrier 2   (c) Carrier 3

Fig. 6. KL divergence metrics - latency.

carriers show a positive spatial autocorrelation across all eight cities for both download speed and latency. We present the average Moran's I statistic across all eight cities in Table 6 of the Appendix. This justifies our use of H3-based spatial grouping to control for location-specific factors.

For each H3 hexagon, we compute the average and standard deviation of 5G download speed and latency to assess performance and its variability by carrier and frequency range. Using the distribution of means and standard deviations, we define the performance and variance thresholds, listed on the right side of Fig. 4. This results in four categories (A-D) per frequency range (1–3) and per carrier, as outlined in Table 1. Our approach allows us to isolate the effect of frequency while examining the performance variation within each frequency range. We then compute the divergence between these groups to quantify the impact of features on 5G performance both within and between frequency ranges.

To analyze performance within each frequency range, we designate its respective "High Performance – Low Variability" group as the reference group; these are groups A1, A2, A3, as labeled in the table. This allows us to identify which features diverge from optimal features within each frequency range. To analyze performance differences between frequency ranges, we also need an overall reference point. For this, we select the "High Performance – Low Variability" group in the highest frequency range (mmWave) as our overall reference group (Group A3). This enables us to identify the features that diverge when comparing optimal performance at lower frequencies to the theoretical best-case scenario of 5G technology. By using these reference groups, we can systematically analyze performance variations both within and across frequency ranges, revealing factors that influence 5G network performance. For every other group, we calculate the pairwise KL divergence for each individual feature between that group and the reference group. We include a variety of PHY layer, performance, device,

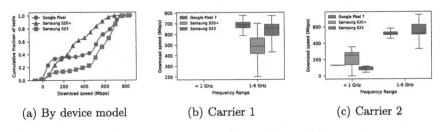

(a) By device model	(b) Carrier 1	(c) Carrier 2

Fig. 7. Download speeds by frequency and device model (each with a different chipset).

time and cell tower density features; we list each feature we study in Table 6 in the Appendix. We perform Laplace smoothing [6] for any zero probability event we encounter in our reference distribution. These distance measures allow us to quantify, for each group, the dissimilarity between the distributions of individual features between itself and the reference group.

Results. We show detailed results for KL divergence from our statistical distance computation for download speed and latency in Figs. 5 and 6, respectively. Our analysis reveals consistent patterns across all carriers, despite their different deployment strategies. Within each frequency range, PHY layer parameters, such as CQI (Row 1 on the y-axis), show the highest divergence, confirming that difference in signal quality leads to difference in network performance, as one would expect. As frequency increases, cell tower density becomes increasingly influential, likely due to shorter wavelengths and therefore smaller coverage areas. For inter-frequency comparisons (e.g. A1 and A2 on the x-axis), while PHY layer parameters remain important, device-related factors, particularly hardware features such as chipset model and age, and software features such as Android API, demonstrate significant divergence for all carriers. For instance, chipset model has a KL divergence of approximately 3, 1 and 2 for carriers 1, 2 and 3, respectively. This suggests that device capabilities play a crucial role in determining 5G performance across different frequency bands. Finally, we note that time of day shows low divergence, implying minimal impact on performance variability.

3.4 Experimental Validation

Our analysis in Sect. 3.3 yielded multiple findings about key features that affect 5G performance as measured by crowdsourced Speedtests. In this section, we confirm these findings in a controlled environment through the use of additional experiments, described in Sect. 2. Specifically, we analyze 3,750 5G Speedtest measurements that we collect over 15 days on nine phones. Each phone model supports the full range of frequency bands available in our measurement locations [17]. Figure 7(a) illustrates the download speeds by phone model. The Samsung S23 and Google Pixel 7 models perform well, with median download speeds reaching approximately 600 Mbps; tests on the Samsung S20+, an older phone, measure lower download speeds, with a median of 400 Mbps. On the other hand, measured latency (not shown) on all phone models is nearly identical. In the remaining analysis, we use only 5G tests from carriers 1 and 2; carrier 3, despite claims of 5G service, never connected to a 5G cell in our test locations. We leave deeper exploration of this occurrence for future work.

Measuring Variability. Our goal is to ensure the findings from our crowd-sourced data analysis are replicable in a controlled setup where data biases are minimized. To this end, we perform a detailed analysis of our controlled Speedtest measurements disaggregated by UE model, frequency band, and carrier. For carrier 1, measurements in the same frequency range yield similar median download speeds for the S23 and the Pixel 7 models (650 Mbps), while the S20+ shows slightly lower speeds (450 Mbps), as shown in Fig. 7(b). However, for carrier 2 (Fig. 7(c)), the Samsung S20+ phones consistently connect to cells operating in lower frequency bands, while the Samsung S23 and Google Pixel 7 phones connect to cells in higher frequency bands, even when running tests from the same physical location as the S20+. This suggests that while older device chipsets support higher frequency bands, newer chipsets are likely optimized to utilize these higher bands. This could explain why these newer models tend to connect to cells operating in higher frequency bands, and highlights the importance of chipset optimization for utilizing higher frequency bands effectively. We confim that our findings for latency are similar, and present them in Fig. 8 of the Appendix, for completeness.

4 Related Work

Prior work has utilized speed test data to study broadband performance [44, 50,53,55,56] and characterize the utility and usability of the speed tests themselves [27,29,54]. Other work has studied the nuances of speed test design, showing how different measurement strategies contribute to varying results [25,33,37,42,43,51,65]. In [42,51], the authors highlight the importance of including metadata to improve the accuracy of performance conclusions.

In the context of mobile broadband, the authors of [26] highlight the challenges in measuring performance. Mobile access bandwidth for over 3.5 million users is analyzed in [61], highlighting the interdependence of different cellular technologies. The influence of device and PHY layer parameters on cellular performance was investigated in [30,58]. Finally, a variety of measurement studies have focused on the identification of features that affect 5G speeds, latency, application quality of experience and power consumption, both in localized settings as well as in-the-wild through drive tests; 5G speeds are predicted using these features as well [35,36,38,39,45–49,62,63]. Recently, the authors of [40] conducted an in-depth analysis of 5G performance across three U.S. operators in two cities, revealing under-utilization of 5G's capabilities.

In comparison to similar studies, our research uses fine-grained, individual crowdsourced Speedtest measurements, complemented by controlled experiment data, to comprehensively assess the impact of diverse factors on cellular network performance and identify key factors that explain 5G performance variability.

5 Conclusion

Our analysis of 5G network performance variability using statistical divergence measures reveals that PHY layer parameters, particularly CQI and RSRP, show higher divergence within frequency bands, especially in mmWave frequencies. This pattern aligns with known RF signal propagation characteristics, where higher frequencies have shorter coverage ranges and are more sensitive to environmental factors. Across frequency bands, device hardware, notably chipsets, exhibit significant divergence, highlighting the need for advancements in device hardware to support the rapid evolution of network technologies. We observe that crowdsourced data with comprehensive metadata can effectively capture these nuanced performance variations, underscoring the need for speed test platforms to include such data to facilitate more accurate interpretation of mobile broadband performance. Such comprehensive data will support more informed decision-making by regulatory bodies and network operators in planning 5G infrastructure investments and also addressing potential disparities in user experience across different devices and locations.

Acknowledgements. This work was funded in part by National Science Foundation (NSF) Internet Measurement Research award #2220388. We also thank Ookla for sharing their data with us.

A Appendix – Supplemental Material

Table 2. Summary of Speedtest measurements from Ookla (City 1–8) and our own experiments. Carrier 1, 2 and 3 data are for 5G.

City	Total 4G	Total 5G	Carrier 1	Carrier 2	Carrier 3
City 1	147,443	191,274	80,464	40,994	69,816
City 2	116,738	154,498	76,960	21,468	56,070
City 3	96,904	180,672	101,727	31,737	47,208
City 4	110,766	147,512	94,496	28,451	24,565
City 5	71,530	90,759	60,765	2,108	27,886
City 6	56,321	107,078	33,932	31,701	41,445
City 7	52,233	80,362	37,390	17,552	25,420
City 8	47,555	86,572	33,950	24,037	28,585
Experiment		3,746	1,639	1,780	327
Total	699,490	1,042,473	521,323	198,828	322,322

Table 3. Annual Speedtest counts by frequency range.

Year	≤6 GHz	>6 GHz (mmWave)
2021	58,908	12,404
2022	76,662	11,844
2023	57,771	4,639

Table 4. Annual Speedtest counts by frequency range for the data analyzed.

Year	<1 GHz	1–6 GHz	>6 GHz (mmWave)
2021	20,125	14,054	12,020
2022	7,531	7,163	11,160
2023	6,637	10,457	4,565

Table 5. Moran's I statistic by carrier and frequency band.

Carrier	Frequency	Download		Latency	
		Moran's I	p-value	Moran's I	p-value
Carrier 1	< 1 GHz	0.326237	0.001	0.063199	0.002
	1–6 GHz	0.251701	0.001	0.111560	0.001
	> 6 GHz (mmWave)	0.398084	0.001	0.320770	0.001
Carrier 2	< 1 GHz	0.344306	0.001	0.108204	0.005
	1–6 GHz	0.352893	0.001	0.134938	0.018
	> 6 GHz (mmWave)	0.580837	0.001	0.288536	0.002
Carrier 3	< 1 GHz	0.329644	0.001	0.299311	0.001
	1–6 GHz	0.215944	0.001	0.282385	0.001
	> 6 GHz (mmWave)	0.391790	0.001	0.505062	0.001

Ethics Statement. Our study does not include human subjects research. Ookla's data sharing under the DUA is fully anonymized and does not reveal full IP addresses, safeguarding the identities of individual users. Moreover, for the subset of measurements with GPS geolocation, Ookla only shares truncated coordinates, ensuring they cannot be associated with any user or residence (Table 5).

Kullback-Leibler Divergence. *Kullback-Leibler (KL) divergence* is a measure of how one probability distribution diverges from a second, expected probability distribution. The KL divergence can take on values in the range of $[0, \infty)$. A KL divergence of 0 indicates that the two distributions are identical. As the divergence increases, it signifies that the two distributions are increasingly dissimilar. It is important to note that KL divergence is not symmetric, and for distributions which do not have the same support, KL divergence is not bounded. The KL divergence between two discrete probability distributions P and Q in the same sample space, $\mathcal{X}$, is given by:

$$KL(P \parallel Q) = \sum_{x \in \mathcal{X}} P(x) \log \left(\frac{P(x)}{Q(x)} \right) \tag{1}$$

Moran's I Statistic. Moran's I statistic is a measure of spatial autocorrelation that quantifies the degree to which similar values of a variable are clustered in

Table 6. Feature descriptions for network performance analysis.

Feature	Description
Download speed	Rate of data transfer from server to client in Mbps
Upload speed	Rate of data transfer from client to server in Mbps
Latency	Time delay in network communication
Frequency range	Spectrum band used for transmission
Signal strength (SS-RSRP)	Measured power of 5G reference signals
Signal quality (SS-RSRQ)	Quality of 5G reference signals
Signal strength (RSRP)	Measured power of 4G reference signals
Signal quality (RSRQ)	Quality of 4G reference signals
Signal-to-noise ratio (SS-SINR)	Ratio of signal power to noise power for 5G
Channel quality Index (CQI)	Indicator of downlink channel quality
Channel width	Width of frequency band for data transmission
Carrier aggregation	Use of multiple carriers to increase performance
Device chipset	Processor type in the mobile device
Device RAM	Memory storage of the device
Chipset age	Age of chipset
Android API version	Level of Android operating system
Hour of day	Time of measurement (0–23)
Cell tower density (resolution 9)	Cell tower density at resolution 9 H3 hexagons

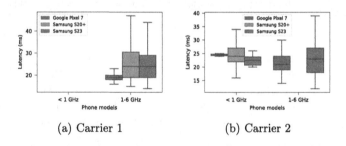

(a) Carrier 1   (b) Carrier 2

Fig. 8. Impact of frequency band and device chipset on latency.

a geographical area. This statistic is commonly employed to assess the spatial distribution of variables. A positive Moran's I value indicates that similar values tend to be located near one another, while a negative value implies that dissimilar values are found close together. A value of zero signifies no spatial association.

Analysis of Carrier 3's Performance Drop. As noted in Fig. 1(e), carrier 3's performance actually decreases significantly after 2021. To analyze this trend more carefully, we examine the longitudinal performance of the three carriers for illustrative cities in Fig. 9. We find that performance for carrier 3 was much better in 2021 than in subsequent years in some cities (e.g. city 2), while in other cities (e.g. cities 1 and 3) it generally improves over time. This differs from the performance of carriers 1 and 2, which show either general upward

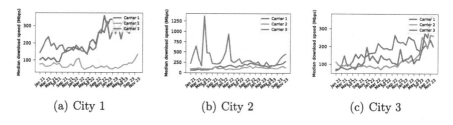

(a) City 1   (b) City 2   (c) City 3

Fig. 9. Longitudinal performance of all three carriers in selected representative cities.

trends or fairly stable performance. More analysis on carrier 3 tests shows that the majority of tests in 2021 are labelled as mmWave, while in 2022 and 2023 combined, only 1.3k of 71k tests are labelled mmWave. We hypothesize that this could be because of major mmWave deployments in 2021, followed by increased sub 6 GHz 5G deployments in subsequent years by carrier 3 that offer a better coverage radius than mmWave; however, with the available data we are unable to validate our hypothesis.

References

1. How Fast Is Your Internet? (2016). https://tinyurl.com/2yrn99z4
2. Qualcomm Linux Modems by Quectel & Co (2019). https://tinyurl.com/dtywzznh
3. The Importance Of An Internet Speed Test (2019). https://tinyurl.com/2wxaxrvc
4. U.S. Policy on 5G Technology (2019). https://tinyurl.com/4vbszdzu
5. When was 5G introduced? (2019). https://tinyurl.com/yck2yd58
6. Laplace smoothing (2020). https://tinyurl.com/nhc3p4d3
7. NetMonster: Android network monitoring app (2020). https://netmonster.app
8. What are good download and upload speeds for home internet? (2020). https://tinyurl.com/2w96rjew
9. MediaTek Launches First mmWave Chipset for Seamless 5G Smartphone Connectivity (2022). https://tinyurl.com/52d37k53
10. Speedtest is the world's #1 internet utility (2022). https://www.ookla.com/
11. The Speedtest Server Network^{TM} (2022). https://www.ookla.com/network
12. Use your device to its greatest potential (2022). https://tinyurl.com/a5sn4hjb
13. When did 5G come out? (2022). https://tinyurl.com/bdhurmpw
14. 5G network coverage outlook (2023). https://tinyurl.com/vzujbku9
15. CellMapper (2023). https://www.cellmapper.net/
16. How does Speedtest select a server? (2023) https://tinyurl.com/5n7cj6dc
17. National Broadband Map (2023). https://broadbandmap.fcc.gov/home
18. Ookla's Speedtest.net (2023). https://www.speedtest.net
19. T-Mobile US builds a commanding lead over rivals AT&T and Verizon (2023). https://tinyurl.com/5n8z5397
20. Tower Maps (2023). https://www.towermaps.com/
21. XCAL: World's Leading Drive Test Tool (2023). https://tinyurl.com/nkh8mu5c
22. H3 Spatial Index (2024). https://h3geo.org/
23. Moran's I (2024). https://www.statisticshowto.com/morans-i/
24. Tables of Cell Statistics Across Resolutions (2024). https://tinyurl.com/448w9kzf

25. Bauer, S., Clark, D.D., Lehr, W.: Understanding broadband speed measurements. In: *TPRC* (2010)
26. Bauer, S., Lehr, W.: Measuring mobile broadband performance. TPRC (2018)
27. Canadi, I., Barford, P., Sommers, J.: Revisiting broadband performance. In: IMC (2012)
28. Chung, J., Kannappan, P., Ng, C., Sahoo, P.: Measures of distance between probability distributions. J. Math. Anal. Appl. (1989)
29. Clark, D.D., Wedeman, S.: Measurement, meaning and purpose: exploring the M-Lab NDT dataset. In: TPRC (2021)
30. Dasari, M., Vargas, S., Bhattacharya, A., Balasubramanian, A., Das, S.R., Ferdman, M.: Impact of device performance on mobile internet QoE. In: IMC (2018)
31. Deasy, J., Simidjievski, N., Lió, P.: Constraining variational inference with geometric Jensen-Shannon divergence. In: NeurIPS (2020)
32. Fan, A., Lei, F., Mancenido, M., Maceachren, A.M., Maciejewski, R.: Understanding reader takeaways in thematic maps under varying text, detail, and spatial autocorrelation. In: ACM CHI (2024)
33. Feamster, N., Livingood, J.: Measuring internet speed: current challenges and future recommendations. Commun. ACM (2020)
34. Feng, L., Wang, H., Jin, B., Li, H., Xue, M., Wang, L.: Learning a distance metric by balancing KL-divergence for imbalanced datasets. IEEE Trans. Syst. Man, Cybern. Syst. (2019)
35. Fezeu, R.A., et al.: An in-depth measurement analysis of 5G mmwave PHY latency and its impact on End-to-End delay. In: PAM (2023)
36. Ghoshal, M., et al.: Performance of cellular networks on the wheels. In: IMC (2023)
37. Han, J., Lyu, M., Sivaraman, V.: On the validity of internet speed test tools and broadband measurement programs. In: AINTEC (2022)
38. Hassan, A., et al.: Vivisecting mobility management in 5G cellular networks. In: SIGCOMM (2022)
39. K. Fezeu, R.A., et al.: Unveiling the 5G mid-band landscape: from network deployment to performance and application QoE. In: SIGCOMM (2024)
40. Liu, Y., Peng, C.: A close look at 5G in the wild: unrealized potentials and implications. In: IEEE INFOCOM (2023)
41. Locke, D.H., Ossola, A., Minor, E., Lin, B.B.: Spatial contagion structures urban vegetation from parcel to landscape. People Nat. (2021)
42. MacMillan, K., Mangla, T., Richardson, M., Feamster, N.: Best practices for collecting speed test data. In: TPRC (2022)
43. MacMillan, K., Mangla, T., Saxon, J., Marwell, N.P., Feamster, N.: A comparative analysis of Ookla speedtest and measurement labs network diagnostic test (NDT7). In: ACM SIGMETRICS (2023)
44. Mangla, T., Paul, U., Gupta, A., Marwell, N.P., Feamster, N.: Internet inequity in chicago: adoption, affordability, and availability. In: TPRC (2022)
45. Minovski, D., Ögren, N., Mitra, K., Åhlund, C.: Throughput prediction using machine learning in LTE and 5G networks. IEEE Trans. Mob. Comput. (2023)
46. Narayanan, A., et al.: A first look at commercial 5G performance on smartphones. In: WWW (2020)
47. Narayanan, A., et al.: Lumos5G: mapping and predicting commercial MmWave 5G throughput. In: IMC (2020)
48. Narayanan, A., et al.: A comparative measurement study of commercial 5G mmWave deployments. In: IEEE INFOCOM (2022)
49. Narayanan, A., et al.: A variegated look at 5G in the wild: performance, power, and QoE implications. In: SIGCOMM (2021)

50. Paul, U., Liu, J., Adarsh, V., Gu, M., Gupta, A., Belding, E.: Characterizing performance inequity across U.S. Ookla Speedtest Users (2021). https://arxiv.org/abs/2110.12038
51. Paul, U., Liu, J., Gu, M., Gupta, A., Belding, E.: The importance of contextualization of crowdsourced active speed test measurements. In: IMC (2022)
52. Qualcomm: Everything you need to know about 5G. https://www.qualcomm.com/invention/5g/what-is-5g
53. Sanchez-Arias, R., Jaimes, L.G., Taj, S., Habib, M.S.: Understanding the state of broadband connectivity: an analysis of speedtests and emerging technologies. IEEE Access (2023)
54. Sharma, T., Schmitt, P., Bronzino, F., Feamster, N., Marwell, N.: From point data to geographic boundaries: regionalizing crowdsourced latency measurements (2024). https://arxiv.org/abs/2405.11138
55. Sommers, J., Barford, P.: Cell vs. WiFi: on the performance of metro area mobile connections. In: IMC (2012)
56. Srinivasavaradhan, V., Park, O., Belding, E.: Mapping cellular network evolution and infrastructure criticality: a nationwide analysis. In: TPRC (2024)
57. Stoecklin, M.: Anomaly detection by finding feature distribution outliers. In: ACM CoNEXT (2006)
58. Sui, K., et al.: Characterizing and improving WiFi latency in large-scale operational networks. In: MobiSys (2016)
59. Sutter, T., Daunhawer, I., Vogt, J.: Multimodal generative learning utilizing Jensen-Shannon-divergence. NeurIPS (2020)
60. Xu, D., et al.: Understanding operational 5G: a first measurement study on its coverage performance and energy consumption. In: SIGCOMM (2020)
61. Yang, X., et al.: Mobile access bandwidth in practice: measurement, analysis, and implications. In: SIGCOMM (2022)
62. Ye, W., et al.: Dissecting carrier aggregation in 5G networks: measurement. QoE implications and prediction. In: SIGCOMM (2024)
63. Yuan, X., et al.: Understanding 5G performance for real-world services: a content provider's perspective. In: SIGCOMM (2022)
64. Zahnd, W., Bell, N., Larson, A.: Geographic, racial/ethnic, and socioeconomic inequities in broadband access. J. Rural Health (2021)
65. Zhang, Z., Shen, J., Mok, R.K.P.: Empirical characterization of Ookla's speed test platform: analyzing server deployment, policy impact, and user coverage. In: CCWC (2024)

Author Index

Printed in the United States
by Baker & Taylor Publisher Services